# Airline e-Commerce

From the few tickets that were sold by Alaska Airlines and former British Midland in December 1995 via the industry's first airline booking engine websites, global online travel has grown to generate today more than half a trillion dollars in annual revenue. This development has brought significant changes to the airline business, travel markets, and consumers. Today, airlines worldwide not only use e-commerce for online marketing and selling but also as a platform to offer unique services and capabilities that have no counterpart in the physical world.

This book is an in-depth introduction to airline e-commerce. It covers a broad scope of areas that are essential to an airline's ongoing digital transformation:

- digital properties and features
- e-marketing
- e-sales and distribution
- web customer service
- e-commerce organization
- e-commerce strategy.

Written by an airline e-commerce expert and illustrated with numerous examples of leading airlines in this area, Dr Hanke provides for comprehensive "behind-the-scenes" details of how airline e-commerce works. This book is a crucial companion for students and practitioners alike because it allows the reader to acquire a thorough foundation of airline e-commerce. Furthermore, the book enables the reader to appreciate the ramifications of airline e-commerce in certain corporate areas and to take effective action for a successful e-commerce strategy.

**Michael Hanke**, formerly with United Airlines, leading the carrier's worldwide e-commerce activities for united.com, is founder and managing director of SkaiBlu, an airline e-commerce consultancy based in the US. He received his doctorate in Air Transportation from Cranfield University, UK; his graduate studies were completed at the London School of Economics with an MSc in International Strategy and Diplomacy, and at Embry-Riddle Aeronautical University with an MBA. Michael earned his undergraduate degree in Business Administration at the University of Hamburg, Germany. He holds an FAA private pilot license.

# Airline e-Commerce

Log on. Take off.

Michael Hanke

Routledge
Taylor & Francis Group

LONDON AND NEW YORK

First published 2016
by Routledge
2 Park Square, Milton Park, Abingdon, Oxon OX14 4RN

and by Routledge
711 Third Avenue, New York, NY 10017

*Routledge is an imprint of the Taylor and Francis Group, an informa business*

© 2016 Michael Hanke

*British Library Cataloguing in Publication Data*
A catalogue record for this book is available from the British Library

*Library of Congress Cataloging in Publication Data*
Hanke, Michael, 1963–
Airline e-Commerce / Michael Hanke. – 1 Edition.
pages cm
1. Airlines–Rates. 2. Airlines–Customer services. 3. Aeronautics, Commercial–Passenger traffic. 4. Electronic commerce. I. Title.
HE9783.5.H36 2015
387.7'420688–dc23
2015023564

ISBN: 978-0-415-77579-3 (hbk)
ISBN: 978-0-415-77580-9 (pbk)
ISBN: 978-1-315-66040-0 (ebk)

Typeset in Bembo
by Cenveo Publisher Services

# Dedications

To my son Mattias and his future

and

To Marcio Montarroyos, jazz musician and friend

# Contents

# Figures

# Tables

# Preface

The year 2015 marked the 20th anniversary of airline e-commerce. From the first few tickets that were sold by Alaska Airlines and former British Midland in December 1995 via the industry's first airline booking engine websites, global online travel has grown to generate today more than half a trillion dollars in annual revenue. This development has brought significant changes to the airline business, travel markets, and consumers. At the same time, e-commerce itself has been transformed in to something much broader. From being a venue for online marketing and online selling, it has become a platform for airlines to offer unique services and capabilities that have no counterpart in the physical world. Facebook, Google, and Twitter are a few examples of this new airline e-commerce.

Airline e-commerce in all its forms is still projected to grow. Arguably, its rise is *the* big story in today's airline business and it will define airlines and travelers in the 21st century. Participating in the movement toward airline e-commerce are not only low-cost carriers like easyJet and JetBlue that introduced e-commerce early and aggressively as an integral part of their business models. There are also traditional airlines including American Airlines and KLM that have fully embraced it and have become e-commerce leaders.

Considering the continued growth and diffusion of e-commerce, students and practitioners involved in the airline industry need to have a thorough foundation in this area. This book is written for tomorrow's managers. They face the challenge of managing the dual story of e-commerce: the "e" story which is about the continuing evolution of internet-based technology and the ever-growing proliferation of new devices and applications that also find their way into the airline business or even originate there. Then there is the "commerce" story marked by ongoing debates. They include "airlines vs online travel agencies," "GDS distribution vs direct connect," "digital data privacy vs security," "self-service vs assisted customer service," and "mobile sales vs desktop sales," just to name a few topics. An airline that navigates through these issues successfully stands a good chance to become one of the leading e-commerce carriers.

There is no lack of commentators and books that touch on airline e-commerce. However, they typically focus on a small slice of the story with popular topics such as online advertising and promotion, mobile shopping, and social media. Furthermore, it appears they approach the subject from the outside because they may have not been in the airline e-commerce trenches.

This book addresses these gaps. It takes an integrative approach and covers the broad scope of airline e-commerce by drawing on the many different areas where it effects the airline business. The areas of product management, marketing, sales and distribution, customer service, organizational structures/human resource management, and strategy are all part of this. Only when dealing with e-commerce in its totality can an airline be successful in cyberspace.

Equally important is that this book is in many ways an insider account. I have been fortunate to be professionally involved in airline management for over 25 years. In the year 2000, after holding several sales and marketing roles with the company, United Airlines offered me the opportunity to lead the launch of united.com in the company's 25 international markets around the world. For six years, I was responsible for United's e-commerce strategy, online sales and marketing, and web customer service in the international arena. This experience not only gave me a profound insight into the interwoven relationship between business and technology, but also made it very clear how much e-commerce was on the verge of permeating the entire airline business.

At the same time, it taught me how non-US centric e-commerce was about to become. This is not an insignificant detail considering that Chinese is the number two language used on the internet today.

In 2006, I founded SkaiBlu, an airline e-commerce consultancy based in New York and Los Angeles. One of our first clients was Air China. They wanted to build a global web presence for airchina.com before the Beijing Summer Olympics in 2008 and faced challenges similar to those of United Airlines just a few years earlier. Since then, SkaiBlu's client portfolio has grown to over 20 companies including Air Mauritius, China Airlines, EgyptAir, and LAM Mozambique Airlines.

SkaiBlu also offers corporate seminars on airline e-commerce. I have conducted them for a variety of companies including Airbus Training Academy, Arab Air Carrier Organization, Avianca, Croatia Airlines, EVA Air, Royal Jordanian, Saudia, and Turkish Airlines. The participants tabled many e-commerce challenges their companies were facing and I am grateful for the insight I have learned as a result of the open—and sometimes difficult—discussions we had. My gratitude also extends to the students that have attended my e-commerce guest lectures and courses, notably at Depaul University in Chicago, International University Bad Honnef in Germany, and Toulouse Business School. More than once, they questioned any conventional wisdoms and thereby brought a different perspective to airline e-commerce.

All this experience helps bring out a certain "frontline" perspective that I have tried to maintain throughout this book. If nothing else, it adds a dose of realism and hopefully makes the e-commerce story shared in this book even a bit entertaining.

Addressed in this book are those e-commerce areas that are critically required by an airline to compete successfully in cyberspace.

Chapter 1 (Introduction) provides a brief history of airline e-commerce, outlines the factors driving and enabling it, and presents the various internet business models airlines apply today. These include: web content model, advertising model, e-commerce model, and broker model. The broker model also touches on data brokerage. There are high-level reviews of the differences between legacy airlines and dotcom airlines and what it means for managing airline e-commerce. Also discussed is the importance of the attention economy and its impact on the management of the travel lifecycle.

Chapter 2 (Airline digital properties and features) presents the major platforms used for airline e-commerce. These include desktop/laptop, mobile (mobile site and mobile app), social media, airport kiosk, and inflight. Wearable computing, virtual applications, and the Internet of Things (IoT) as emerging platforms are also covered. For each platform, the main features are discussed including web content, web service, and web booking features where applicable. Furthermore, this chapter shows how personalization, globalization, and web accessibility impact airline e-commerce. It also outlines how an airline website booking engine works.

Chapter 3 (Airline e-marketing) presents the rising importance of online advertising and promotion in airline marketing. Details on airline spending in this area are shared. The importance of digital consumer profiling techniques is highlighted and the role of traditional media formats such as TV, print, and radio in airline online marketing is discussed. Additionally, key online media formats including search marketing, online display marketing, email marketing, and social media marketing are introduced. Numerous e-marketing metrics to measure the effectiveness of online media formats are presented.

Also discussed is the meaning of airline digital brand management. The role of ICANN, the history of domain names in the airline industry, and today's importance of web domain names in airline digital brand management are highlighted. Managing a digital airline brand means paying attention to website design. Best practices related to an airline website's digital look and feel and its ergonomics are introduced. The significance of an airline website style guide is also discussed. Finally, the relationship between airlines and digital media agencies is featured. Profiles of the main types of digital media agencies airlines work with, what services they specifically offer, and how they work are also included.

Chapter 4 (Airline e-sales and distribution) opens with a brief history of airline sales and distribution. It details the size of the global online travel market and introduces key online travel regions. It shows how airlines have designed their relationship with the target audience via dis-intermediation, re-intermediation, and counter-mediation. Key segments in the leisure and corporate travel market are introduced. The chapter features the main sales and distribution stakeholders in airline e-commerce including global distribution systems (GDSs), online travel agencies (OTAs), and meta-search engines. The rising importance of fare merchandising and airlines becoming retailers are also reviewed.

As part of a discussion on sales and distribution costs, various cost categories in today's travel eco system are introduced. IATA's NDC distribution concept and the importance of "direct connect" are discussed. The area of airline web pricing is also featured. The chapter showcases numerous types of web fare products including web fare discounts, promo-code fares, personalized fares, and low fare guarantee. Finally, the emergence of new players in the online travel space such as Apple, Facebook, and

Google is assessed and how they could disrupt the current online sales and distribution system.

Chapter 5 (Airline web customer service) defines what "good" customer service means and profiles today's preferences of travelers for certain web-based customer service options. It reviews the differences between customer self-service and assisted customer service and presents the full range of customer service options airlines offer as part of an omni-channel web customer service. Included in this review are fairly new service options such as chat, virtual assistants or avatars, social customer care offered via Twitter, Facebook, and travel forums.

The chapter also compares the cost by customer service channel and the benefits an airline realizes when the web traveler exercises self-service. Organizational responsibilities for customer service at airlines are presented, along with metrics on how to measure the effectiveness of customer service. This issue of fractured customer service experiences and how to overcome them with the deployment of an integrated, multi-service channel strategy is discussed.

Chapter 6 (The airline e-commerce organization) starts with the introduction of the five major change periods that have impacted the evolution of airline e-commerce organizations over time. The role of resources, values, and processes in an airline e-commerce organization are discussed and the main types of organizational structures that airlines apply are introduced. The focus is on the "dedicated" e-commerce organization as a popular organization model.

Also, in the context of the four organizational levels of leadership, management, line, and third parties, there is a discussion of the key roles and areas in an airline e-commerce organization. The ideal leadership and what an airline should look out for when appointing an e-commerce leader are also topics. The chapter addresses the challenges in the airline e-commerce organization including staffing, channel dis-/ re-intermediation, and evolving vendor relationships. Finally, the future of airline e-commerce organizations is covered. The rise of work place diversity, the emergence of hyperarchies, the role of tiger teams, and the synchronized airline e-commerce organization are discussed.

Chapter 7 (Airline e-commerce strategy) opens with a definition of and reasons for an airline e-commerce strategy. It discusses the four levels of airline e-commerce (experimentation, absorption, integration, transformation) and introduces the drivers of them. The drivers include mission, goals, strategic analysis, and supporting organizational arrangements. The development of an airline e-commerce strategy is discussed with specific steps from initiation to implementation including dealing with the "people factor" and change management.

To determine how suited an airline is to manage the next frontiers in cyberspace, a digital assessment tool called DAS (Digital Airline Score) is introduced. It allows the evaluation of an airline's level of e-commerce advancement. DAS focuses on the adoption and use of e-commerce measured across seven attributes: four are fundamental for operating a digital brand and include data privacy, digital performance, digital property, and digital brand appearance and protection. Three are differentiators in the airline e-commerce value chain accounting for online advertising and promotion, e-sales and distribution, and web customer service. Thirty-five carriers based on DAS were analyzed, and they fell into one of the four categories of constrained, emerging, transitional, or advanced e-commerce carrier. Various recommendations are offered for airlines to move to the level of an advanced e-commerce carrier.

Now, allow me to share with you what is going on behind the scenes. I hope you will enjoy this tour through the airline industry's cyberspace.

# Acknowledgments

No book is written in a vacuum and this one is no exception. Numerous people and places have contributed to making this project a reality. Above all, I am indebted to my parents, Traute and Heinz–Kurt Hanke. Although they are not around anymore, I have been thinking about them a great deal throughout the years of writing this book. They have always led by action—and much less by words—to focus and stay the course. This credo has been helpful in moments of doubts—and there were many.

I also thank my fiancée, Karen for her enormous patience and support to push forward. This was especially the case during the final months when it looked like this book would never be completed as new challenges kept on popping up.

During my 15 years at United Airlines, I had the opportunity to work with many colleagues from around the world who are fun, talented, and enthusiastic. They are an integral part of this book. For the rest: well, you know who you are. My gratitude extends to Scott Praven, United's former chief marketing officer and head of united. com. He looked at a draft of this book and provided helpful feedback.

I would like to thank Rigas Doganis. His inputs on the early version of this book were simply unmeasurable and to receive critical advice from him was an honor. His book *Flying Off Course* planted a seed with me many years ago when I was student to embark on a book project myself one day. Furthermore, my thanks go to Stephen Shaw. He took time to review my early work and his recommendations on how to improve some sections were invaluable.

Another person I would like to mention here is Rod Temperton. To the best of my knowledge, he has no affiliation with the airline industry or airline e-commerce in particular. However, he is one the best songwriters the music scene has ever seen. More than once during my late-night writing sessions, I listened to the many songs he had contributed to the group Heatwave and other performers including George Benson, Herbie Hancock, Michael Jackson and Quincy Jones. In a way, his music is part of this book. Speaking about music, I also would like to thank Los Angeles-based jazz radio station 88.1 FM. Especially DJ Bob Parlocha who always hosted a great program that more than once accompanied me when I was researching, reviewing, and writing.

# Chapter 1

# Introduction to e-commerce in the airline industry

The internet was invented for travel.

Scott Praven, former United Airlines chief marketing officer
and head of united.com

## 1.1 THE OPPORTUNITY

Few innovations in the history of mankind offer as many actual and potential benefits as e-commerce does. Today, for any business, it is therefore no longer a question of *if* but *how* to deal with e-commerce. The opportunity to leverage it to enhance one's competitiveness in the marketplace is simply too big and no airline in the world can afford to ignore it—unless it wants to drive itself out of business.

So how big is this opportunity? Let us start with some basic statistics on consumer adoption. From humble beginnings in the mid-1990s to today, the commercial internet has come a long and fast way. In 1995, less than 0.5% of the world's population

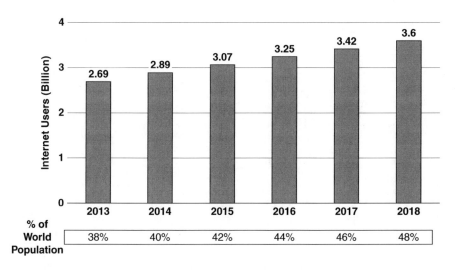

**Figure 1.1** *Worldwide internet users and penetration: Growing and growing*

*Source:* FT.com (2014)[1]

or 16 million people were internet users[2]. This is an incredibly small number compared with the 42% or over three billion people in 2015 (Figure 1.1). To put these numbers into perspective: Facebook in 2015 with 1.5 billion active users is almost 94 times larger than the entire global internet population from 1995.

The internet has also become more pervasive due to the ongoing proliferation of connected devices. Desktops, smart phones, and tablets have been joined by smart TVs and cars, computing wearables, and connected everyday objects (also referred to as the Internet of Things or IoT). In total, we are talking about an estimated 10 billion devices in 2015. This number is predicted to jump to almost 35 billion by 2019.[3] Clearly, tomorrow's travelers will be connected like no other generation before.

Online shopping by consumers (the so-called Business-to-Consumer or B2C trade) has turned into big business. In 2012 for the first time, global B2C sales topped $1 trillion. This is expected to more than double to $2.3 trillion in 2017.[4] Airline tickets contribute significantly to this online sales story. After books and clothing/accessories/shoes, they are the third most popular item bought on the internet.[5]

Total global travel generates more than a trillion dollars every year. In 2015, sales exceeded $1.2 trillion and there is more growth ahead. By the same token, online travel not only accounts for a significant share of this but it also grows at a faster rate.[6] In 2015, online travel worldwide accounted for more than $533 billion and the forecast is a steady increase through 2019 with $762 billion. The online travel penetration rate has grown in all travel regions (Figure 1.2). The bulk of global online travel sales comes from the air sector. Depending on the data source used, it ranges somewhere between 30% and 40%. Other popular online travel products include travel accommodation and car rental.

A powerful combination of factors fuels this impressive development. Among them are inexpensive access to an ever more ubiquitous internet, online travel's mass market

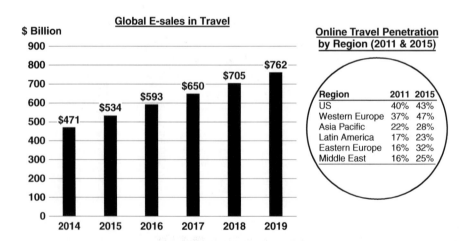

*Figure 1.2* Global online sales in travel (2015–19) and regional online travel penetration rates (2011–15) (rounded figures)

*Source:* eMarketer (2015)[7] Phocuswright[8]

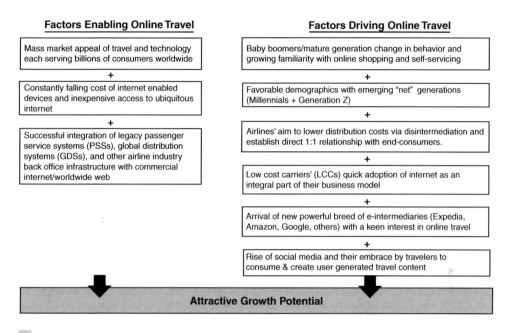

**Factors Enabling Online Travel**

Mass market appeal of travel and technology each serving billions of consumers worldwide

+

Constantly falling cost of internet enabled devices and inexpensive access to ubiquitous internet

+

Successful integration of legacy passenger service systems (PSSs), global distribution systems (GDSs), and other airline industry back office infrastructure with commercial internet/worldwide web

**Factors Driving Online Travel**

Baby boomers/mature generation change in behavior and growing familiarity with online shopping and self-servicing

+

Favorable demographics with emerging "net" generations (Millennials + Generation Z)

+

Airlines' aim to lower distribution costs via disintermediation and establish direct 1:1 relationship with end-consumers.

+

Low cost carriers' (LCCs) quick adoption of internet as an integral part of their business model

+

Arrival of new powerful breed of e-intermediaries (Expedia, Amazon, Google, others) with a keen interest in online travel

+

Rise of social media and their embrace by travelers to consume & create user generated travel content

**Attractive Growth Potential**

*Figure 1.3* *Why is online travel growing?*

appeal, changing shopper behavior, favorable demographics, and the arrival of large marketing and technology savvy companies in the travel space (Figure 1.3). In essence, an airline that aims to capture its share of this growth story needs to go digital.

## 1.2 AIRLINE E-COMMERCE: WHAT IS IT REALLY?

Although the engagement varies widely from company to company, all commercial carriers in the world today are participants in cyberspace in some shape or form. Even Haiti's Tortug Air with www.tortugair.com or Congolese airline Compagnie Africaine d'Aviation with www.caacongo.com, based in countries that are among the poorest on earth, have a web presence.

E-commerce is not just on or off. There are "fifty shades of e-commerce" and the different forms depend on the degree of digitization of the three dimensions involved in any commercial activity:

- the product dimension
- the agent dimension
- the process dimension.

Any of these three dimensions could be physical or digital. Accordingly, e-commerce, could be "pure," "partial," or "non-existent" (Figure 1.4). For example, a customer checks with an airline's airport ticket office to buy a paper ticket from an airline representative and pays cash for it. There are no digital but only physical aspects in this transaction. Hence, one would speak of "traditional commerce." However, imagine the same customer engages an airline's digital property such as the company's

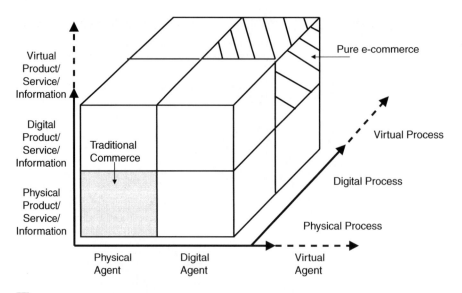

**Figure 1.4** *The dimensions of e-commerce*

*Source:* Whinston et al. (1997)[9]

website—we refer to such a person as a "web traveler"—and uses a credit card to complete the online purchase of an e-ticket. This scenario involves digital aspects such as the digital agent (the airline website) and the digital process (customer using an online form of payment and receiving an e-ticket).

To be clear about the digitization of the airline product: Unlike companies in media, music, and film industries that have been faced with the challenge of commercializing digital versions of their physical core products, airlines do not have this issue. The inflight product, the customer service infrastructure in the airport, and the destinations in a route network are all examples of an airline's core physical product that cannot be digitized. Therefore, airline e-commerce should always be partial and never pure.

"Should" is the appropriate word because there is a dimension beyond digitization. It is called virtualization and it already impacts the physical aspect of air travel. With the introduction of virtual worlds such as Second Life in 2003, traveling in a computer-based simulated interactive 3D environment via avatars has become an option for some people who want to "fly" or teleport on an airline's route network anywhere in the virtual world. Brazilian airline TAM was the first real-world airline to launch its presence on Second Life in 2007.[10]

In recent years, several airlines have become engaged in virtualization via the introduction of website avatars, holograms, and augmented reality applications. A new twist to virtualization recently emerged with Qantas. In January 2015, the Australian carrier announced the test of virtual reality headsets on selected long-haul flights in first class. Passenger can use them for inflight entertainment and to learn more information about the carrier's services and destinations. Similarly, in summer of 2015, Dutch LCC Transavia launched a trial on several European routes from Amsterdam and deployed virtual reality headsets as part of its inflight entertainment. This new combination of physical, digital, and virtual aspects in managing the airline business is likely to grow in the future.

The overall trend points to a "purer" e-commerce environment in the airline industry. Since its beginnings in the early 1990s, airlines have gradually increased the digitization of their value chain. The digital properties of airlines have significantly evolved from being basic agents that provide limited static information about an airline's products and services. Today, they are sophisticated one-stop platforms offering a wide spectrum of dynamic informational content and interactive applications for shopping and self-servicing. E-ticketing, online shopping carts handling web bookings and payments, and self-service features for web check-in, flight status queries, or frequent flyer program (FFP) account management are all examples of this digitization.

Moving forward throughout this book, there will not be any semantic difference between "pure" and "partial" airline e-commerce. We will just refer to airline-commerce as long as we keep in the back of our mind that it involves different degrees of digitization and that it actually exists the moment any single one of the three dimensions involved in a commercial transaction is digital.

One comment on e-commerce versus e-business. The mainstream media uses both terms interchangeably while academia has relatively little agreement on what term stands for what. This book adopts the view that e-business involves electronic transactions within a company and those with other suppliers while e-commerce focuses on the interaction with individuals and companies that consume and/or mediate. The main theme of this book is e-commerce. If e-business is indeed encountered in the context of a particular example, it will be called out as such.

On a related note, the internet and World Wide Web are so intertwined with each other that it is not uncommon to assume that they are synonymous. They are not. The World Wide Web is part of the internet and did not come onto the scene until 1991, 30 years after the internet was born. The web is a collection of multimedia services and information accessible via the internet. The internet is the interconnection (network) of computers all over the world. Therefore, when referring to airlines on the web, technically it would be correct to state "on the internet" instead. Throughout this book, we frequently use the term "cyberspace" in order to capture the world of computer networks including the web and also to account for augmented realities/virtual realities.

Airlines adopt and use e-commerce essentially with a tri-fold purpose:

- For marketing and selling travel products
- For customer service
- For information sharing and exchange.

Accordingly, a definition of airline e-commerce is:

**The adoption and use of the internet and digital applications to market and sell airline products, deliver customer service, and share/exchange information.**

5

## 1.3 HOW DID IT GET STARTED? A BRIEF OVERVIEW OF THE BEGINNING OF AIRLINE E-COMMERCE

The trade of travel has been around since the early days of civilization with leisure tourism going as far back as the Babylonian and Egyptian empires 600 BC. The electronic era in travel did not begin until the 20th century. Like so many times in history before, there is a general progressive pattern whereby technology develops first, is then commercially applied and becomes more widespread as it is adopted by mainstream business and consumers. In the wake of this development, several issues of societal, cultural, and even political nature arise.

The emergence of airline e-commerce is embedded in the evolution of the internet whose roots go back to the heydays of the Cold War in the early 1960s. It is beyond the focus of this book to elaborate in greater detail on the many specific internet developments and events that occurred since then. However, we showcase a few milestones based on a framework proposed by Laudon and Traver.[11] They have identified three evolutionary key stages: Innovation Stage, Institutionalization Stage, and Commercialization Stage (Table 1.1).

*Table 1.1* Development of internet timelines

*The innovation stage from 1961 to 1974*

| | |
|---|---|
| 1961 | The Massachusetts Institute of Technology (MIT) comes up with the concept of data transmission in the form of so-called "packet switching." |
| 1962 | MIT manifests a vision of a global computer network. |
| 1963 | The US Department of Defense (DoD) becomes the largest funder of early internet efforts. |
| 1966 | The DoD support leads to the creation of ARPANET (Advance Research Project Agency Network), the world's first operational packet switching network and the core component of what would become today's internet. |
| 1969 | The first successful sending of a packet switched message from UCLA to Stanford. |
| 1972 | The first internet killer application is introduced: Email. |
| 1973 | The Ethernet and local are networks, client/server computing is born. |
| 1974 | The internet communications protocol TCP/IP is invented. |

*The institutionalization stage from 1975 to 1995*

| | |
|---|---|
| 1980 | The personal computer (PC) is invented with Altair, Apple, and IBM introducing their products. |
| 1983 | The "civilian" internet is born as ARPA separates the military and civilian network traffic. |
| 1984 | Introduction of hyperlinked documents allowing users to jump from one page to another. Also, the domain name system (DNS) is introduced. First ever domain name registered: Symbolics.com. |
| 1986 | The National Science Foundation (NSF) adopts the internet as an inter-university network. |
| 1988 | CERN in Switzerland proposes the use of worldwide network of hyperlinked documents based on a common language called HTML (Hyper Text Markup Language), thus giving birth to the internet supported World Wide Web service (www). |

*Table 1.1* continued

*The innovation stage from 1961 to 1974*

| | |
|---|---|
| 1991 | The World Wide Web is released by CERN. |
| 1993 | The first graphical internet browser called "Mosaic" is invented allowing ordinary web users to connect to HTML pages on the web via a point and click device. |
| 1994 | Netscape Corporation is formed and offers the first commercial web browser. The first banner advertisement appears on Hotwired.com, the commercial era of the internet begins. |

*The commercialization stage from 1995 to today*

| | |
|---|---|
| 1995 | The NSF privatizes the internet backbone and commercial telecom carriers take it over. The internet is now a fully civilian version. Amazon and eBay are founded. |
| 1998 | The Internet Corporation for Assigned Names and Numbers (ICANN) is founded. |
| 1999 | The internet becomes accessible by mobile phone. |
| 2002 | Social media take off with Friendster as the first modern social website. Facebook launches in 2004. |
| 2008 | Cloud computing becomes a billion-dollar industry. |
| 2009 | Internet-enabled smartphones become a major new web access platform. |
| 2011 | ICANN expands domain name system. |
| 2012 | A new fiber optic technology is devised that promises to increase bandwidth dramatically and could ease congestion. |
| 2013 | Google introduces Google Glass, one of the first possible wearable computers for the mainstream. |
| 2014 | Scientists create image recognition software capable of recognizing and describing the content of photographs and videos with far greater accuracy than ever before, sometimes even mimicking human levels of understanding. |
| 2015 | Apple launches its smart watch product line, possibly opening the mass market for wearables. |

*Source:* Laudon and Traver (2013)[12] and author

Airline e-commerce emerged in 1995 during the internet's commercial phase (Figure 1.5). This is correct in so far as the release of the World Wide Web (or simply web) as a service on the internet in 1991 and specifically the launch of the first commercial browser MOSAIC in 1994 ushered in the launch of the first official airline websites: www.southwest.com and www.cathaypacific.com went live in March 1995 and December 1995, respectively. Note that the denotation of "official" is important here in order to distinguish them from unofficial websites that had already been launched by industry outsiders like airline enthusiasts who simply wanted a web presence with basic information on their favorite airline. These first sites were used for basic e-marketing activities and featured information about an airline's products and services. Most carriers started their cyberspace journey with this type of "brochureware" site, a term used to indicate that the website and its content were a direct extension of existing printed promotional material.

However, missing was a booking engine that could handle online transactions for ticket purchases. This changed in 1995 when Alaska Airlines and then British

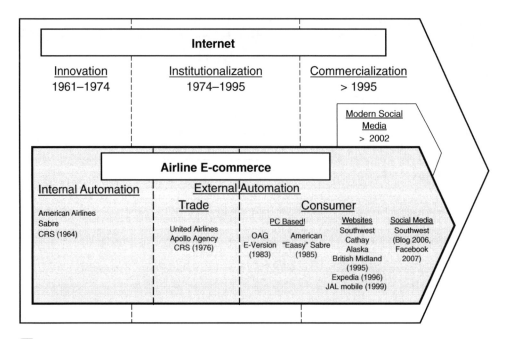

**Figure 1.5** *Stages in the development of the internet and airline e-commerce*

Midland Airways (BMI) launched the airline industry's first booking engine websites in December that year. Incidentally, in October 1996, Expedia.com, the world's first online travel agency (OTA) went live as Microsoft Expedia Travel Services, a division within the Microsoft Corporation. Expedia was followed in December the same year by another new and major OTA called Travelocity, a subsidiary of Sabre Holdings, itself a subsidiary of American Airlines.

The launch of these two OTAs by companies known for their savviness in technology undoubtedly put more airlines on notice and that the time might have come to include travelers in the digital marketplace and enable online ticket shopping features for them. Outside the travel space, equally important players were emerging that popularized online shopping for end-consumers. Mentioned should be US-based Dell Computers that was one of the first most successful online retailers. It was also the first website in the world generating one million dollars in online sales on a single day in 1996. Another company that has become a household name is Amazon. Founded in 1994 and starting as an online bookstore, it quickly diversified to sell, among other things, CDs, DVDs, apparel, toys, and even furniture and jewelry. Apparently, shoppers were ready to buy online and travelers even started benchmarking airlines against these new online retailers.

The term "e-commerce" was coined during the Commercial Phase and ever since then has been associated with doing business over the internet. However, the e-commercialization of air travel actually predates the commercial phase of the internet from the mid-1990s by three decades. The airline industry's era of e-commerce truly began with the roll-out of the first computer reservation system (CRS) Sabre in 1964 by American Airlines that in many ways laid the seeds for today's e-commerce principles. In the following years, other airlines around the world introduced CRSs as well. This allowed them to manage electronically the growing volume and complexity of seat inventory and pricing data internally more efficiently and effectively.

In 1976, airline e-commerce assumed another dimension. It was the year when United Airlines as the first carrier opened its Apollo CRS to an outside audience and furnished access to its long-time distribution partners, the travel agencies. By externalizing CRSs via special terminals that were installed in their offices by airlines, travel agencies could now research and book tickets for their respective clients. Thus, the industry's first "Business-to-Business" (B2B) information exchange and industry-wide electronic marketplace were born. Through a CRS, travel agents could easily retrieve the information needed about many airlines and they had greater information-searching and booking capabilities. The only audience missing now from being able to search and book airline tickets were the end-consumers themselves.

This situation changed with the emergence of the personal computer (PC) in 1980. First to offer a PC technology-based tool was the *Official Airline Guide* (OAG) in 1983. Their product featured airline timetables, fares, and fare rule search and was essentially an electronic version of its then existing paper copy. In 1985, American Airlines (AA) introduced "Eaasy Sabre," a PC-based online connection for travelers to its CRS that was also enabled to do airline ticket bookings. Other airlines followed with their respective PC-based products such as PARS Travelshopper by Northwest, United with UA Connection, and Lufthansa with the Lufthansa Info Flyaway disk. The door for end-consumers who could now book airline tickets directly themselves with a computer via the internet was officially opened and would not be closed again. Within a decade, this form of airline e-commerce had actually become widespread among travelers.

However, the playing field of how end-consumers would use e-commerce changed again, this time due to the invention of the previously mentioned browser. With this tool, users could connect to a website, point and click on the web pages, and receive an immediate response. In other words, travelers were now empowered to explore and purchase a variety of product and service options on their own. By taking control of the travel planning and online purchase process, the stage was set for web travelers. By the end of the 1990s, airlines' disk-based products such as Eaasy Sabre had all disappeared as more and more airlines decided to upgrade their websites with booking tools or so-called internet booking engines (IBEs).

Unbeknownst to Western travel markets at the time, Japan had already started its journey into the mobile online travel space. In 1999, Japan Airlines (JAL) was one of the first to offer online ticket booking and self-servicing features on a smart phone released by NTT DoCoMo. However, it was the introduction of the popular Apple iPhone in 2007 that led to the mass adoption of smart phones in many countries. Since then, airlines around the world have been busy with expanding their mobile presence via mobile sites and mobile apps. Following the evolutionary footsteps of their desktop websites, carriers started to offer product information and basic self-service features first. Over time, they also made available booking tools and introduced mobile apps. A new "social" dimension was added to the marketplace when social media entered the mainstream in 2002. The first airline to use social media in the industry was Southwest Airlines when they launched their company blog "Nuts About Southwest" in 2006. In 2007, Southwest was also the world's first airline to release a Facebook website.

The launch of the first generation websites that were essentially basic platforms for e-marketing and e-sales led to a deeper and wider involvement by airlines in e-commerce. Websites were re-designed for an improved digital look and feel, and to accommodate a growing number of features to not only support the shift to more e-marketing and e-sales activities, but also to enable customer self-servicing—online check-in and flight status are illustrative examples. At the same time, many airlines also expanded their web presence beyond home markets and launched their first local websites in other countries. This kind of web presence is part of an evolutionary development that one may refer to as Airline e-Commerce 1.0. This nomenclature is in analogy to the Web 1.0, Web 2.0, and Web 3.0 whereby one refers to different development stages of the web. These stages do not indicate a particular technical specification but reflect cumulative changes of how the web is used – in our context of how airlines and web travelers use it.

Airlines also realized that in order to compete effectively in cyberspace, dedicated resources, new processes, and know-how were needed. In other words, as e-commerce became more of a mainstream field, the priority of airlines shifted to operational aspects. This step is one of the few, arguably the only one left, to realize a competitive advantage and differentiate oneself in cyberspace when facing rivals that essentially apply the same technology—until something new arrives on the scene. E-Commerce developed a larger inward focus with airlines re-engineering their internal systems and structures. During this period, the first e-commerce organizations with full-time staff and budgetary resources emerged, accompanied by new governance rules of the game that would help manage this new area of the airline business better than in the past.

With the advent of social media and airlines making it a priority of their e-commerce activities starting in 2007–2008, the stage for airline e-commerce 2.0 was set. This stage is characterized by an new unprecedented participatory interaction between airlines and web travelers. Some carriers introduced corporate blogs while many launched their presence on numerous third party platforms. These included Facebook, Twitter, and YouTube that would be used now for a more informal and impromptu dialogue with web travelers that takes place in real-time and in public. Importantly, web travelers were allowed for the first time to interact and collaborate with each other and with airlines via social media platforms as creators of user-generated content. All this is a marked departure from airline e-commerce 1.0 where web travelers had been limited to passive viewing of airline website content and conducting online sales and service transactions. In a way, by contributing content and increasing participation in their interaction with airlines, web travelers have taken some control of carriers' digital brands.

So where are we heading now? It appears that we are entering the stage of airline e-commerce 3.0. It deals with e-customer relationship management (CRM) and personalization. (Figure 1.6). Supported by big data and proprietary computer, a growing number of airlines are looking into utilizing digital insights on web

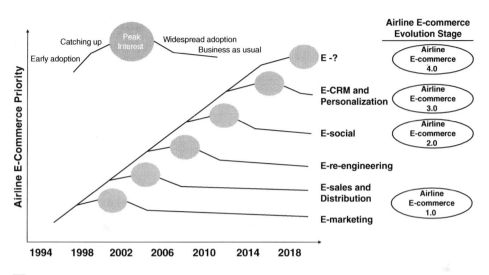

**Figure 1.6** *Airline e-commerce priorities and airline e-commerce evolution stage*

travelers' behaviors and preferences (by the way, almost anybody deals in big data these days, the question is whether they are put to effective use. This is where proprietary algorithms enter the picture – think of Google's search engine algorithm). This allows them to understand web travelers' needs better and to provide for uniquely tailored, personalized offerings to web travelers. Areas such as fares, products, and customer service would therefore become de-commoditized.

This development reflects a new level of intelligence applied to airline e-commerce and is often referred to as the "semantic" aspect of the web. Transforming relationships with web travelers and making them more meaningful based on internet ubiquity, database connectivity, and algorithm applications is a key element for an airline's future success in cyberspace.

It is unclear at this stage what airline e-commerce 4.0 and the priority in airline e-commerce will be about. For some industry observers, it is associated with the rise of ultra-intelligent electronic agents that may assist future web travelers in all aspects of their trips. For others, it has less to do with a particular technology but more with lines between devices and humans becoming increasingly blurred if not disappearing altogether (think of implanted computer chips). Whatever the next frontier is in cyberspace, an airline needs to stay tuned-in and well connected to macro and micro developments in order to preserve its competitiveness in the online travel marketplace.

## 1.4 FUNDAMENTAL AIRLINE E-COMMERCE CONCEPTS

### 1.4.1 Introduction of airline internet business models

In the world of cyberspace, an airline can tap into several revenue generative activities. Selling airline tickets and, increasingly, associated ancillaries via cross- and up-selling, is a key area. However, there are other notable activities. They include selling advertising space to third parties and earning commissions from other travel partners such as hotels and car rental companies.

One way of describing how an airline generates revenue is through its business model. In essence, a business model describes the rationale of how a company creates, delivers, and captures value. This could be economic, social, or in some other form of value so as to sustain the business. The value proposition of the business model enters typically in the form of increased revenue, reduced costs, and/or higher customer satisfaction.

Airlines have adopted a few principal internet business models (Table 1.2). They include:

- the content model
- the advertising model
- the e-commerce model
- the brokerage model.

The sequence by which these models are presented is not accidental but reflects largely their evolution and when they appeared in the online market place. These internet business models are not mutually exclusive. Many airlines apply a mix of them, although e-commerce has clearly emerged as the primary driver of generating online revenue. More details on each of them are shared below.

**Table 1.2** *Major internet business models of airlines*

| Internet business model | Source of value | Additional information |
|---|---|---|
| Content model | Cost savings from reduced manpower because of self-serving web traveler | Airline site used by web traveler for consumption and self-servicing including information on fares, schedule, frequent flyer program (FFP), FAQ, and others |
| | Insight in web traveler behavior from web analytics | Tracking and measurement technology such as page e-tags and cookies to follow web traveler's digital footprint |
| | Repeat site traffic from satisfied web traveler | Relevant, engaging, and well-designed content generating repeat site visitors |
| Advertising model | Fee from third party advertising on airline e-media assets | Mainly text and display advertising on airline digital properties |
| E-commerce model | Selling of airline products, services, and web traveler data | Ranges from the sales of base fares to merchandised fares and in a few cases even web traveler data |
| Brokerage model | Commission from facilitating purchases of ancillary travel products and service providers | Involves traditional hotels, car rentals, cruise companies, and travel insurance providers and new sharing economy providers |

*Content model*

The content model, the first generation internet business model that arrived in the marketplace, generally works on a subscription basis and charges web users for accessing content. Most airlines feature plenty of information on their digital properties. This is available at no extra cost to anyone who wishes to access it. Democratizing web content and providing information on their products and services free of charge means that airlines do not derive any revenue streams from the content model. Nevertheless, site content represents a source of value to an airline although it might not be as clear and direct as in some of the other internet business models.

First, site content can lead to cost savings from reduced manpower, particularly in the traditional customer contact areas like call centers. Let us remember that a web traveler exercises what is called self-service. When looking for information on a specific topic (e.g. fare specials or ticket refund handling), a web traveler may consult the airline's digital properties such as a website or mobile site. They surf through various content sections and retrieve information themselves for consumption or self-help.

Second, airlines can collect data from web travelers accessing content on their digital properties. With web analytics applications using tracking and measurement technology such as web page tagging and various types of cookies, an airline can obtain unprecedented insight into the behavior of its target audience. In the era of big data, this constitutes enormous value and it also enables airlines to personalize its interaction with web travelers much better. Certainly, airlines have collected data on travelers before the internet turned commercial. However, the speed, scale, and frequency of data collection were smaller, data analytics tools were less sophisticated, and data results were not available instantly. Nowadays, airlines operate in a different environment.

Third, content represents a source of value to an airline because of the repeat traffic it can generate as a result of a web traveler's satisfaction. Content that is irrelevant, not engaging, out of date, and even poorly edited creates the impression of a weak digital brand. If there is also a lack of intuitive content presentation that translates into user-unfriendly site navigation, web travelers (and potentially their peers if the word gets out via social media) are unlikely to return after their initial visit. In essence, digital content matters and the higher its quality, the more benefits an airline can derive from its existence.

Could airline website content be monetized? Theoretically yes. This can be done by charging web users in return for being able to access content that features privileged information like fare promotions for example. Most carriers reject this approach. After all, it is already challenging enough to attract people to a website. The next step then is to persuade a web user to complete a purchase. Therefore, charging an access fee is not conducive to generating business.

However, there is always an exception and it involves ultra-low cost carriers (ULCCs). As part of their strategy to generate ancillary revenue streams, some of them sell annual membership programs to web travelers. Examples include the V-Club of Mexican ULCC Volaris, the Wizz Club of Hungary-based Wizz Air, and

*Figure 1.7* Spirit Airlines' $9 Fare Club

*Source:* spirit.com (2015)[13] with kind permission of Spirit Airlines

the $9 Fare Club Spirit Airlines, an ULCC in the United States. Among the privileges a web traveler receives when buying a membership is also exclusive access to promotional fare content on the carriers' websites (Figure 1.7). Volaris generated more than $3.5 million from selling memberships to its V-Club in 2014.[14]

On a relevant side note, access to content on airline digital properties is governed by the principle of net neutrality. Accordingly, the internet used for access today is an open and unbiased network that, among other things, does not discriminate against type of legal content, web user, digital platform, and website. This should not be taken for granted. There are a number of powerful players—AT&T in the United States is one of them—that advocate a "two-tier" system with tolls and preferential treatment of selected internet traffic. If such a set-up was ever implemented, one most likely would see the creation of new business and revenue models. In this scenario, maybe web travelers would have to pay a premium for fast access to an airline website or to secure access to a wide range of airline websites. Airlines and web travelers should stay tuned on this topic.

*Advertising model*

Advertising from third parties has been a source of revenue for airlines for several decades. The ad model started very likely with print brochureware. In return for paying the airline a fee, advertisers placed ads in order to promote their products and services. An early example is the inflight magazine, started by Pan Am in the early 1940s. A 1965 "Clipper" inflight copy of that carrier owned by the author shows that out of the 39 pages, 16 are used by advertisers such as tobacco companies and watch makers.

Over time, other media assets were added. Inflight videos, napkins, headrest covers, amenity kits, and even occasionally the fuselage of an aircraft are some examples. Many airlines have increased their engagement in this area and some even work through a dedicated group of employees or outside firms to manage these media assets and generate incremental revenue for themselves.

With the advent of the commercial internet, it was only natural for airlines to check out how advertising revenue could be generated with this new medium. Examples of popular online media assets that airlines offer to third parties for advertising placements include website banners, email newsletters, mobile boarding pass, and inflight wi-fi time session sponsorships. Until 2014, Delta Airlines operated a dedicated website for interested advertisers. On www.deltaskymedia.com, the carrier offered a wide range of media assets available for advertising (the site has been folded into delta.com where advertisers can find contact information). Some carriers stay away from cyberspace advertising altogether. This is because of their concern over diluting their brand or lack of expertise on how to manage this type of activity. Those airlines pursuing it typically seek advertisers that have some degree of affiliation to travel such as hotels or telecom companies.

Occasionally, airlines barter with advertising partners. In this case, as opposed to collecting a fee for the ad placements, the airline agrees to an exchange whereby in return for accepting e-media placements from an advertiser, it places e-media with the third party at the same time. Such arrangement is sometimes in place between airlines and car rental companies or hotels.

*E-Commerce model*

With the emergence of shopping cart technology in the 1990s, the e-commerce model arrived on the scene. It was now possible for merchants including airlines to handle purchase transactions online. Since then, selling tickets has become the principal pursuit of an airline's commercial activity in cyberspace.

Besides selling tickets for their own flights, some carriers also offer on their digital properties flights that are operated by other airlines. The choice is typically limited to codeshare and alliance partners. For example, a web traveler does not find a Lufthansa-operated flight on emirates.com. Why this limitation? After all, in the offline world, airlines (at least those that are International Air Transport Association (IATA) members) can and do issue tickets for itineraries involving non–partner airlines. The reason for this practice is not technology related because booking engine platforms and interline e-ticketing agreements can theoretically handle any multi-carrier itinerary. The answer has to do with policy reasons. Economic interest to keep the online revenue with the company or within an airline alliance is the main driver for this approach. Furthermore, airlines do not want to incur additional cost by handling web travelers who may have been disserved by another non–codeshare/non–alliance airline.

At many airlines, the e-commerce model is no longer only about offering standard fare products. It increasingly deals with fare merchandising, a retailer approach that involves à la carte fare add-ons, branded fares, and fare families with pre-specified products/services.

Examples of this new approach are plenty. Depending on the carrier involved, items such as luggage check-in, seat reservation, a day pass for an airline's airport lounge, priority boarding, and inflight wi-fi may be part of an à la carte fare menu or part of a branded fare/fare family. Considering the significant incremental revenue streams that airlines can generate in this area, it is unlikely that they will ever return to the pre-fare merchandising days.

In regards to the e-commerce model, one issue that comes up more and more is the sale of consumer data. There is growing acknowledgment that *the* currency of today's digital economy is data. Related businesses have sprung up in recent years that exclusively deal with the management of consumer data. The airline industry is a rich source when it comes to consumer data and many airlines are engaged in data collection on a large scale. The main reason for this activity is a legal requirement and it is done on behalf of government agencies for security and law enforcement reasons. Additionally, airlines also collect data for the purpose of digitally profiling web travelers. Some carriers monetize on this activity and sell the data to third parties.

LCC Ryanair is one example. In 2013, although emphasizing that the data involved are anonymized, the carrier signed an agreement to sell website user data of ryanair.com to a US company called Adara. Adara assists advertisers, including those that want to target web travelers in running data-based marketing campaigns.[15] Qantas is another example of an airline that has become involved full-time in data handling. In September 2014, they launched a Business-to-Business (B2B) company called Red Planet. Red Planet operates a data- and digital media-buying platform that collects and overlays loyalty data from frequent flyer programs (FFPs), credit cards, and employee reward programs, and sells them to marketers and advertisers for data-driven online marketing. Other data-related services offered include analytics and research.[16]

It should be noted that the data management practices by airlines, from collection and storage to protection and sharing with third parties are generally not very transparent. Publicly available information through airline website privacy policies is often cryptic and to what extent, if at all, airlines are actually involved in selling data is currently unknown. Because of growing public concern in the United States, for example, a legislative initiative to gain better insight in this matter was launched in August 2014 by US senator John Rockefeller. Among other issues, this inquiry looks at whether US carriers sell passenger data to third parties.[17] However, assuming that an adequate legal/regulatory framework can be established that addresses these concerns, it is reasonable to assume that data will gain more importance also with airlines in the future as a revenue source.

In addition to selling air fares and traveler data, some airlines may also sell actual merchandise on their websites. For example, web travelers on airnewzealand.co.nz found items including airplane models, special ceramic cups, and retro bags for sale as part of the carrier's 75th anniversary celebration in 2015.

*Brokerage model*

The brokerage model involves "market-makers" by bringing buyers and sellers together. Airlines engage in this model by featuring ancillary travel partners such as hotel, car rental, cruise, and travel insurance companies on their digital properties. For each facilitated transaction between these partners and web travelers, an airline earns a commission fee. The ancillary partners' products are offered on a stand-alone basis (hotels and cars are most common) and in combination with the airline flight as part of a travel package. This is often presented on airline website homepages as "Flight+Hotel," "Flight+Car," and "Travel Package." The commission is generally a percentage or a fixed monetary amount of the total value of the ancillary purchase.

This brokerage model has been in place for a long time in the airline industry. It has been adopted from the offline world when customers booking a ticket via an airline's call center or city ticket office also bought products from other travel partners at the same time. An airline generally works with multiple hotel and car suppliers, although not all of them are viewed as equals. It is rather common for an airline to strike preferred agreements with selected ancillary travel partners. These partners receive more prominent exposure on the airline's digital properties and in return reward the airline with a higher compensation in the event of a web traveler's purchase.

Besides cooperating with traditional hotel and car rental partners, airlines have also begun to enter deals with major peer-to-peer hospitality and ride-sharing transport providers. This is not surprising considering the growing role of the sharing economy in the travel space. Companies such as Airbnb and Uber have become key players and their popularity with travelers is huge. They command enormous supply inventories—in 2015, Airbnb had access to over one million properties in 34,000 cities and 190 countries while Uber operates in 300 cities in 58 countries—and therefore do not pale in significance when compared with what some people may refer to as old-fashioned hotel, car rental/taxicab companies.

In December 2014, KLM announced a partnership with Airbnb. It allows web travelers using KLM's digital properties to search for accommodations on Airbnb when booking flights. At the same time, the airline has also developed a travel guide featuring details of Airbnb's lodgings in more than 600 destinations. In the fall of 2014, United Airlines became the first carrier to join forces with Uber. Accordingly, by way of United's mobile app, web travelers can find Uber taxi information including the types of vehicles available, estimated wait times, and prices. The web traveler then may connect to the Uber service by using the airline's mobile app to select a ride.

It is only a question of time when more airlines will (have to) enter partnerships as described above. The idea of using sharing services skews to younger generations of web travelers, notably Generation Y or the so-called Millennials aged between 18 and 34. They are the up-and-coming source of travel demand for airlines and are attracted to sharing services more than older generations. At the same time, companies such as Airbnb are also in the process of expanding business travel programs which will make them appealing beyond price-sensitive leisure travelers. In other words, not offering sharing services as part of its online ancillary travel product/service portfolio may make an airline website less attractive to potential customers and the airline would also lose out on additional potential commission payments.

### 1.4.2 The different types of e-activities by airlines in cyberspace

Airlines are engaged in a wide variety of e-activities in cyberspace. Some are done for purely commercial reasons, others have a social or charity motive. It has become common practice to differentiate these activities based on the transacting parties involved. Figure 1.8 provides for an overview of how networked an airline today can be.

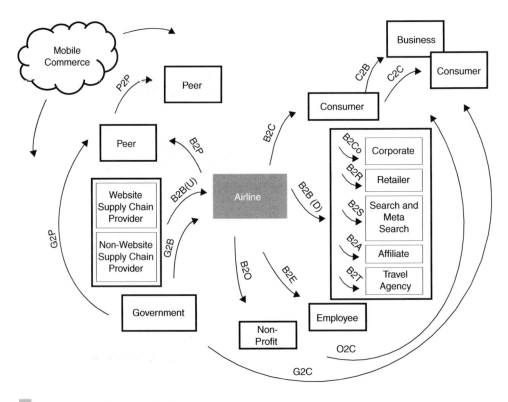

**Figure 1.8** *The networked airline*

Table 1.3 elaborates on each of these different types of e-activities in further detail.

**Table 1.3** *Common types of e-activities involving airlines*

| Type of e-activity | Description | Example |
|---|---|---|
| **1. B2C** (Business-to-Consumer) | General airline retail website selling travel products and services online to the travelling public. | www.virgin-atlantic.com |
| **2. B2B (D)** (Business-to-Business, Downstream) | Online relationship between airlines and business corporations that consume, distribute, or market web products and services supplied by airlines. | |
| **2a. B2Co** (Business-to-Corporate) | A microsite within the general airline retail website dedicated to managing small and medium-sized corporate accounts that enroll and handle their business travel via the airline website and often receive special incentives such as mileage bonuses and fare discounts. | Lufthansa (www.lufthansa.com/de/en/For-corporate-customers.com) |
| **2b. B2R** (Business-to-Retail) | Online distribution of airline products and services through mass retailers known for high brand recognition. These retailers can have their origins in the offline world and now have an online presence also but included as well are pure online players. | www.searsvacation.com & www.amazon.com |
| **2c. B2S** (Business-to-Search) | Online distribution and marketing via search and meta-travel search engines. For search marketing, airlines typically engage in both natural (or organic) search and paid (or sponsored) search with a variety of (meta-) search engine providers. | www.google.com/flights |
| **2d. B2A** (Business-to-Affiliate) | Online marketing of airline products and services via affiliate network programs. Companies joining such program market the airlines on their respective website and earn a special commission if a sale is referred to the airline website. | Austrian Airlines (http://affiliate.austrian.com/partner.html) |
| **2e. B2T** (Business-to-Travel Agency) | Online relationship between airlines and their travel agency partners. This includes online sales and distribution via OTAs and traditional agency websites and the management of travel agency programs on the airline's website. | www.opodo.com and Qantas.com (www.qantas.com.au/agents/dyn/qf/intro/home) |
| **3. C2B** (Consumer-to-Business) | This approach is also referred to as a reverse auction since it is the web traveler who initiates the business by inviting bids from airlines to offer a product or service at a price the web traveler is willing to pay. | www.priceline.com |
| **4. C2C** (Consumer-to-Consumer) | Through third party website platforms, web traveler interacts directly with other web travelers for the sale or purchase of travel products and services. | ebay.com |

**Table 1.3** *continued*

| Type of e-activity | Description | Example |
|---|---|---|
| **5. B2E** (Business-to-Employee) | Also referred to as an intranet, B2E deals with the business within an organization and is closed to people who are not employees of the company. | JetBlue (www.hellojetblue.com) |
| | The focus is on the sharing of an airline's information on business intelligence, corporate communication, and employee benefits. Intranets can also feature internal blogs allowing for informal communication among employees and even replacing to some extent e-mails and/or meetings, especially when employees from disperse geographic locations are involved. Airlines occasionally pitch promotions to employees of other third party companies via their respective intranets on designated B2E website pages. | |
| **6. B2P** (Business-to-Peer) | Involves social media such as blogs and social networks. Most airlines participate in third party platforms like Facebook, Twitter, and YouTube while some even operate their own blog websites. Used by employees from various organizational levels, the engagement in social media is primarily for marketing and customer service purposes. | South African Airways (www.facebook.com/FlySAA) and Delta Airlines (takingoff.delta.com) |
| **7. B2O** (Business-to-Other) | Airline using its website to promote charity and community causes and to provide for (non)-financial support. | Alaska Air (www.alaskaair.com/content/about-us/social-responsibility/alaska-airlines-foundation.aspx) |
| **8. P2P** (Peer-to-Peer) | Web travelers engage directly with other web travelers via third party and their own social media. Popular are blogs, chatrooms, and web forums. Reasons for engagement include collaboration, sharing of reviews and opinions, and seeking support from/offering advice to fellow travelers. | www.Tripadvisor.com, www.airlinequality.com, www.flyertalk.com |
| **9. B2B (U)** (Business-to-Business, Upstream) | Online relationships between airlines and businesses suppliers whose inputs become part of the airline's website offerings in the marketplace. Differentiation between website and non-website supplier with the former providing input to the airline in the form of site content and technology applications and web services. The latter type of a B2B upstream provider includes companies furnishing for the airline's non-web supply needs ranging from office supplies to aircraft spare parts. | www.lonelyplanet.biz www.aeroxchange.com |

**Table 1.3** *continued*

| Type of e-activity | Description | Example |
|---|---|---|
| **10. G2P** (Government-to-Peer) | Informal communication via blog by governmental offices/agencies with the traveling public for issues such as travel advisories, security guidelines, and government policies. | US Transport Security Administration (http://blog.tsa.gov) |
| **11. G2B** (Government-to-Business) | Governmental agencies/offices engaging with airlines via special websites to conduct business. Examples include online applications for landing permits or the license to carry hazardous cargo aboard an aircraft. | UAE Government (www.dcaa.gov.ae/ UserLogin/MasterPage. aspx?pg=NCO) |
| **12. G2C** (Government-to-Consumer) | Governmental agencies/offices providing via their websites information on air travel-related topics, ranging from on-time performance by airlines to general travel tips. | US Government (www.usa.gov/Citizen/ Topics/Travel/Air.shtml) |
| **13. O2C** (Other-to-Consumer) | Non-profit organizations interacting online with web travelers and seeking their support for charitable causes—for example via mile donations. | Make-A-Wish Foundation (www.wish.org/help/ donate_airline_miles) |
| **14. M-commerce** (Mobile Commerce) | Airlines to engage with web travelers via mobile presence (mobile site and/or mobile app). | American Airlines (http://mobile.aa.com), British Airways (www. britishairways.com/ travel/iphone-app/ public/en_gb) |

### 1.4.3 The interdisciplinary nature of airline e-commerce

Airline e-commerce has not evolved in a vacuum. It is based on several disciplines that generally exist at an airline and they all contribute to varying degrees to make it what it is: An interdisciplinary area that can only be as good as its individual pieces. Figure 1.9 shows the many different areas with some samples of particular topics where e-commerce plays a role today at an airline. From marketing, sales and distribution, and customer service to corporate communication, IT, and inflight, e-commerce has become essential in these corporate disciplines. At the same time, as much as they are impacted by e-commerce, they also exert their influence on it. In other words, this is not a one-way street. Other areas include an airline's frequent flyer program, the legal department, and human resources. Finance and accounting, emergency response planning, corporate education and training should be also mentioned. The fact that multiple stakeholders each own a piece of e-commerce does not make its management easy. For airline e-commerce as a whole to be successful, the individual pieces must be managed well. Leading e-commerce carriers understand this and they approach the management of e-commerce in an all-inclusive way.

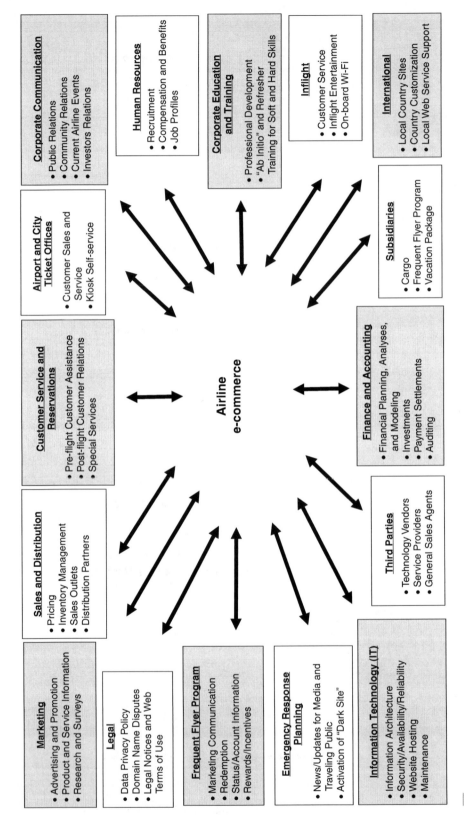

**Figure 1.9** *Major disciplines of airline e-commerce*

## 1.5 THE VALUE PROPOSITION OF AIRLINE E-COMMERCE

A value proposition of airline e-commerce is essentially a statement of the superior benefits resulting from a carrier's engagement in cyberspace versus an offline situation.

From an airline perspective, the benefits of e-commerce are as follows:

- The (re)-establishment of a relationship directly with end consumers. This "direct-to-consumer" approach offers the best value only directly, it drives loyalty, supports new pricing and revenue models and the consumer comes to the airline first.
- The taking of new control of its destiny by re-engineering business processes including those related to sales, marketing, and customer service and having transactions done cost efficiently, electronically, and simply.

From a web traveler point of view, e-commerce's greatest advantage has been the transformation in the relationship with airlines and the shift from a supplier-centered to a customer-centered focus (Table 1.4).

Some people also refer to the so-called 3 Cs in this regard:

- *Convenience.* The web traveler can do business with the airline in cyberspace any time and from anywhere.
- *Control.* The web traveler is in charge of the interactions with the airline and determines themselves how much time to spend on the airline's digital properties and what decisions to take.
- *Choice.* The web traveler selects from a variety of options to fulfill their requirements for the interaction with the airline website.

## 1.6 NEW RULES OF THE GAME: THE ATTENTION ECONOMY

The economies of many countries have been significantly transformed in the sense that they are managing or dealing with information in some shape or form. We clearly live in an environment marked by a growing abundance of information and there is no end in sight to this trend. "Information overload" is one of the terms

**Table 1.4** *The transformation of the customer relationship*

| Airline centered | Web traveler centered |
|---|---|
| • Airline chooses hours of operation | • Airline is always available and the web traveler determines the hours |
| • Airline chooses location of service | • The service is delivered at the web traveler's location |
| • Airline delivers services | • Web traveler serves him/herself |
| • Airline focuses on its sales and distribution chain | • Focus of airline on web traveler needs |
| • Airline manages a one-to-many relationships | • One-to-one relationship |

popularly used to describe what is going on. In 2015, the world boasted approximately one billion websites.[18] Although less than 0.1% accounted for 50% of the internet's total traffic, this still leaves over one million websites to deal with. This tables an important issue that airlines are also affected by and need to manage: How to attract and keep a web traveler's attention?

Figure 1.10 shows the kind of visitor volumes selected airline websites and other travel players attract: ryanair.com and southwest.com are the most popular digital properties among airlines while Expedia and AirBnB are the top performers for online travel in a wider context. At the same time, what Figure 1.10 also illustrates is that airlines are just one of many in the universe of websites that compete for the attention of web users. The next best website is only one mouse click away. Unlike traditional economics that is concerned with managing the scarcity of resources against unlimited demand by people who always want more of whatever it is— goods, services, money, power, love, etc.—there is a different "dilemma" in the world of web economics. Information as a resource is actually unlimited while attention (or demand) is limited. Nobel laureate Herman Simon is considered one the first people to have articulated that information consumes the attention of its recipients and that "a wealth of information creates a poverty of attention and a need to allocate that attention efficiently among the overabundance of information sources that might consume it."[19]

With attention by consumers including those of web travelers being scarce and desirable, airlines need to be aware that attention services in cyberspace are important. Postings on social media websites, email alerts, search engine marketing, last-minute pitches for upgrades, and post-flight travel tips and feedback sharing are all examples to create attention. An airline that aims at "sticking out" needs to offer these attention services throughout the entire travel life cycle. This is not an easy

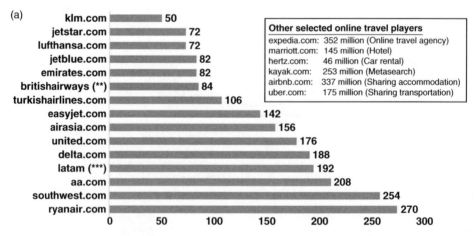

** = includes britishairways.com and ba.com
*** = combines lan.com and tam.com.br

*Figure 1.10a Estimated yearly website visits (million, desktops and .com domain name only)*

(b)

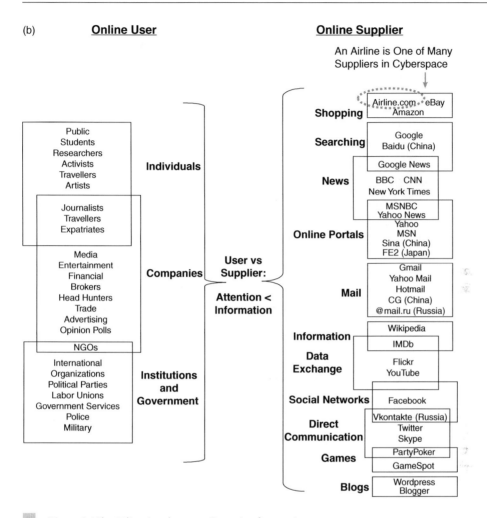

**Figure 1.10b** *Airlines in cyberspace: Competing for attention*

*Source:* Based on data by similarweb.com[20] and International Herald Tribune's State of the World Atlas[21]

undertaking considering the multiple devices and channels web travelers use today. However, focusing merely on the customer's travel research and booking activities, as airlines have done traditionally in the past, is not sufficient anymore (Figure 1.11). Additionally, knowing that web travelers have a choice where their attention is spent, an airline must also focus on delivering relevant information. Doing so allows airlines to pass through the web travelers' information filter that they apply to separate substance from noise. What makes an airline's attention services relevant? In essence, when they are provided at the appropriate stage and time during the travel life cycle. Increasingly crucial in this regard is also personalization. The more an airline is able to uniquely tailor its offerings to an individual's needs and wants based on their prefer- ence profile, the more likely a web traveler sees the relevancy—and this ultimately creates opportunities for an airline to sell. We will touch on personalization

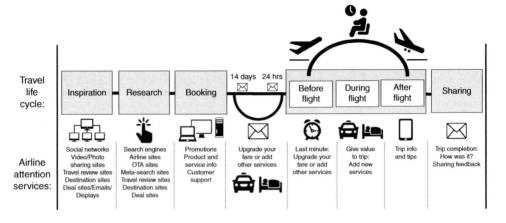

**Figure 1.11** *The travel life cycle in the attention marketplace*

throughout our airline e-commerce discussion. This is because it can be a crucial differentiator for airlines that have tried for a long time to de-commoditize their products and services.

### 1.7 LEGACY AIRLINES VS "DOTCOM" AIRLINES

In the world of airline e-commerce, there are essentially two generations of airlines. Those with origins before the emergence of the commercial internet in the second half of the 1990s and those after. The former, often referred to as legacy airlines ("incumbent" or "traditional" airlines are also popular labels), deal with the internet principally as a facilitator to manage their business activities. The latter, the so-called "dotcom" or "born-on-the-net" airlines have always viewed the internet as a core of future commerce and have made it a key foundation of their business model. Low cost carriers (LCCs) and ultra-low cost carriers (ULCCs) typically fall into this category.

This generational issue matters because it positions airlines to some extent differently in the marketplace because of their historical background. Some of today's legacy airlines still face a variety of challenges to undo traditional business practices (Figure 1.12). Thus their engagement in cyberspace adds a separate, complex dimension to their e-commerce agenda that dotcom airlines do not have to deal with.

For instance, as a result of their initiatives to shift business online, legacy airlines often encounter challenges in the sales and distribution area. "Channel conflict" is a common term used to describe this situation. In the early days of e-commerce, airlines had plenty of channel conflict with traditional airline business partners such as offline travel agencies. In key travel markets such as North America and Europe, this particular issue is settled now—at least in the leisure travel segment. This is because airlines and OTAs have largely captured this former offline business. However, it is still alive in other parts of the world and undoubtedly weighs on an airline's sales and distribution activities. By the same token, channel conflict between airlines and corporate travel agencies is still

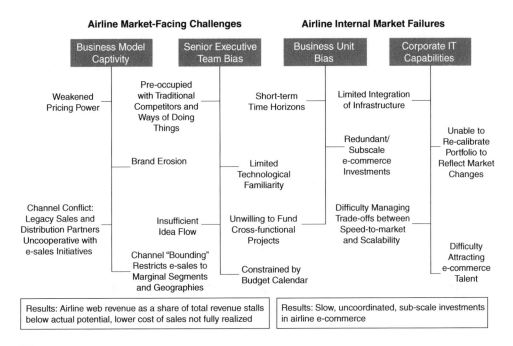

**Figure 1.12** *The challenge for traditional airlines*

*Source:* Based on "Working Council for CIOs" (1999)[22]

very much a current issue. The same can also be said for the situation where some airlines have been running into conflicts with global distribution systems (GDSs) because of their so-called direct connect strategy. This strategy assumes that an airline bypasses a GDS and establishes a direct link between its internal systems and third party retail outlets such as travel agencies for distribution in the marketplace.

Dotcom airlines have never had to cut relationships with traditional partners such as travel agencies and GDSs. For them, concern how to manage the shift to an online world has not existed. Early on, their website was positioned as the primary sales outlet and within a few years dotcom airlines like JetBlue and easyJet generated the large majority of their total revenue online. Only a few major airlines with an established history in the offline world have managed to transform themselves ahead of their traditional rivals and adopt significant elements of dotcom airlines. Among them are North American carriers including Air Canada, Alaska Airlines, American Airlines, and Delta Airlines. From Europe, they include Aer Lingus, British Airways, and KLM, while Air New Zealand and Qantas from Asia Pacific are also good examples. Southwest Airlines is another example although they have always been a successful direct-to-customer airline and therefore could morph swiftly into a dotcom airline.

Being "born late" is not an automatic guarantee for a successful presence in cyberspace. However, from an airline e-commerce point of view, it definitely helps to have little legacy in the offline world. Nevertheless, an airline that wants to compete effectively online has to establish and constantly grow certain e-core competencies. These apply irrespective of airline type.

## 1.8 MANAGERIAL ISSUES IN AIRLINE E-COMMERCE

It is clear that e-commerce is here to stay and this means that every airline needs to go digital. With this outset, it is important to recognize the following:

- *The acknowledgement that every airline requires an ongoing digital transformation.* The market environment changes at an ever-increasing pace and competition from both established and new players intensifies at a growing rate. For an airline to successfully compete in the online travel market space, it needs to be more agile in its overall strategy approach than in the past. Furthermore, the different pieces of the strategy—be it the objectives, the strategic analysis, the value chain competencies and organizations—all require some degree of adaption and improvement to work in the digital world. This is and will remain particularly challenging for traditional carriers.
- *The necessity to continuously increase the digital equity within an airline.* Regularly taking an inventory of the company's e-competencies is crucial for any airline. The goal is to understand what the digital assets and liabilities are with the ultimate aim of strengthening the digital balance sheet. Frequent liabilities such as an inadequate e-commerce strategy and organizational structures, IT systems, and corporate processes all designed for an analog world must be minimized if not eliminated. At the same time, several key activities must be strengthened. They include the development of a comprehensive website product and service suite and the improvement of value chain competencies in marketing, sales and distribution, and customer service. Additionally, the performance of analytics on customers/competitors/suppliers, the hiring of qualified people, and the ongoing support are also crucial.

Understanding airline e-commerce in its totality is not an easy task since there are so many different aspects involved. However, it is useful to think of it as involving seven interrelated key areas that are crucial to understand and strengthen if an airline wants to be successful with it. The seven key e-commerce areas are: Organization, resources, schedule, portfolio, value chain, technology, and governance (Figure 1.13). Each of them has its unique set of questions and considerations that need to be addressed for effective airline e-commerce but not one is more important than another.

### 1.8.1 Some managerial key questions

1. What do we expect to accomplish?
2. How does e-commerce affect our sales and distribution channels, business partners and suppliers?
3. What is the impact of e-commerce on the way we conduct business today and tomorrow?

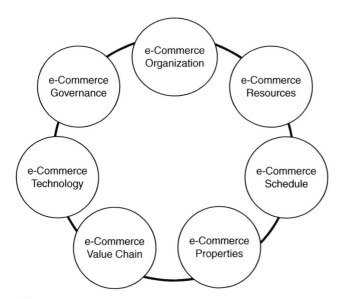

**Figure 1.13** *The seven success factors in airline e-commerce: what core competencies are crucial?*

4. How will we measure success (and failure)?
5. What is the competitive situation?
6. How much does it cost?
7. Do we expect a return on investment in the short term or is this a long-term deal?
8. How can one evaluate the magnitude of the business pressures?
9. What should our corporate strategy be towards e-commerce?

Throughout the next chapters, we will address the seven success factors in airline e-commerce and the answers to the above questions will become clearer.

## NOTES

1 FT.com (2014) "Internet to hit 3bn users in 2015 - emarketer", http://www.ft.com/intl/fastft/239702/internet-hit-3bn-users-2015-emarketer (accessed December 3, 2015).

2 InternetWorldStats.com (2015) "Internet Growth Statistics," www.internetworldstats.com/emarketing.htm (accessed April 7, 2015).

3 BI Intelligence (2014) "The Internet of Everything 2015," www.slideshare.net/bi_intelligence/bii-the-internet-of-everything-2015 (accessed April 7, 2015).

4 RetailCustomerExperience.com (2014) "Global e-commerce sales to hit $1.5 trillion, driven by growth in emerging markets," www.retailcustomerexperience.com/articles/global-e-commerce-sales-to-hit-15-trillion-driven-by-growth-in-emerging-markets/ (accessed April 7, 2015).

5 Nielsen (2010) "Global online shopping report," www.nielsen.com/us/en/insights/news/2010/global-online-shopping-report.html (accessed April 7, 2015).

6  Phocuswright (2015) "The year ahead in digital travel," www.phocuswright.com/Free-Travel-Research/The-Year-Ahead-in-Digital-Travel#.VVD4yGd0zIU (accessed February 12, 2015).

7  eMarketer (2015) "Digital Travel Sales Will Total More than $533 million," http://www.emarketer.com/Article/Worldwide-Digital-Travel-Sales-Will-Total-More-than-533-Billion-2015/1013392, (accessed on December 30, 2015).

8  Phocuswright (2015) "Phocuswright ATM Middle East," PhocuswrightATMMiddleEastTravel Presentation.pdf (accessed December 30, 2015).

9  Whinston, A.B., Stahl, D.O., and Choi, S. (1997) *The Economics of Electronic Commerce*, Indianapolis, IN: Macmillan Technical Publishing.

10 Khalip, A. (2007) "Brazil TAM airline takes off to Second Life skies," www.reuters.com/article/2007/04/13/us-secondlife-airline-brazil-idUSN1240331620070413 (accessed April 7, 2015).

11 Laudon, K.C. and Traver, C.G. (2013) *E-Commerce: Business, Technology, Society*, Harlow, UK: Pearson Education, pp. 104–107.

12 Ibid.

13 Spirit Airlines (2015) "Spirit," www.spirit.com/Default.aspx (accessed February 5, 2015).

14 Sorenson, J. (2015) "The cartrawler yearbook of ancillary revenue," www.ideaworkscompany.com/wp-content/uploads/2015/09/2015-Ancillary-Revenue-Yearbook.pdf (accessed September 26, 2015).

15 Schaal, D. (2013) "Ryanair signs advertising contract to sell user data," http://skift.com/2013/04/25/ryanair-signs-advertising-contract-to-sell-passenger-data/ (accessed April 7, 2015).

16 Jones, S. and Ward, M. (2014) "Qantas loyalty launches marketing services red planet," http://mumbrella.com.au/qantas-loyalty-launches-marketing-services-business-red-planet-250624 (accessed March 13, 2015).

17 Elliot, C. (2014) "Are domestic airlines making money by fleecing consumers?" www.washingtonpost.com/lifestyle/travel/are-domestic-airlines-making-money-by-fleecing-consumers/2014/08/28/5d2c7c08-2a19-11e4-958c-268a320a60ce_story.html (accessed April 7, 2015).

18 LaFrance, A. (2015) "How Many Websites Are There?" http://www.theatlantic.com/technology/archive/2015/09/how-many-websites-are-there/408151/ (accessed October 3, 2015).

19 Simon, H.A. (1971) "Designing organizations for an information-rich world," in Greenberger, M. (ed.) *Computers, Communication, and the Public Interest*, Baltimore, MD: Johns Hopkins Press, pp. 40–41.

20 Similarweb.com (2015) "Website traffic & mobile app analytics", www.similarweb.com (accessed January 3, 2016).

21 Smith, D. (2012) *State of the World Atlas*, 8th edition, International Herald Tribune Atlas, Oxford: New Internationalist.

22 Working Council for CIOs (1999) *The Great Leap Forward, Principled Roles of the Corporate Center in Steering E-Business*, Corporate Executive Board, Washington, DC: 1999 Presentation Materials, pp. 12–13.

# Chapter 2

# Airline digital properties and features

Users do not care about what is inside the box, as long as the box does what they need done.

Jeff Raskin, Scientist

## 2.1 AIRLINE DIGITAL PROPERTIES AND FEATURES: AN OVERVIEW

Airlines around the world conduct e-commerce via a range of digital properties. The key platform used for a carrier's online marketing, sales, and service activities is still the desktop/laptop. However, mobile is on its way to quickly catching up. Other common e-commerce venues airlines use include social media, inflight, and the airport kiosk. At the same time, new digital properties, while still in their infancy, are emerging and are likely to play a larger role in the future. These emerging digital properties are computing wearables, virtual reality, and the Internet of Things (IoT) (Figure 2.1).

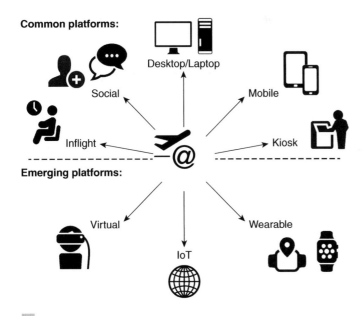

**Figure 2.1** *Digital properties in airline e-commerce*

For a desktop presence, an airline at a minimum operates what may be also referred to as a core website. This website is geared to the main target audience, typically addressing web travelers from leisure and corporate market segments. The core website of an airline is the focus in this book's discussion.

At the same time, the larger the size of a company's operation and the more diverse its product/service portfolio, the more likely it is that an airline manages a number of website properties besides the core site. One may also speak of a website family in this respect. These additional "member" sites are similarly branded as the core site but are otherwise stand-alone because they are managed separately by corporate entities dedicated to that respective line of business. Popular examples are an airline's frequent flyer website or air cargo website (Table 2.1). These websites are typically linked to the core website.

## 2.2 FEATURES ON AIRLINE E-COMMERCE PROPERTIES: A QUICK TOUR

The features available on the many digital properties are constantly growing in terms of numbers and sophistication. Figure 2.2 provides for an overview of what an airline may offer to web travelers in 2015.

**Table 2.1** *Different types of non-core airline websites*

| Types of website | Description/Example |
| --- | --- |
| 1. Tour/holiday package website | Operates the tour/holiday package arm of an airline in cyberspace. American Airlines' aavacations.com and Virgin Atlantic's virginholidays.co.uk are examples. |
| 2. Cargo business website | Handles a carrier's online cargo business. Examples include Singapore Airlines' siacargo.com and Japan Airlines' jalcargo.com. |
| 3. Frequent flyer program website | Air China's PhoenixMiles website is featured at phoenixmiles.com, Lufthansa operates milesandmore.com as an FFP website. |
| 4. A parent/holding company website | Used specifically for media queries and investor relations purposes. Scandinavian Airlines System (SAS) features such a website at sasgroup.net. |
| 5. Media advertising website | Offers various off/online media assets to third parties for advertising and promotion placements. Delta's deltaskymedia.com is an example. |
| 6. Career website | Posts any vacancies and where applicants can submit their résumé. Aer Linges operates this type of website at careers.aerlingus.com. |
| 7. Co-branded marketing site | Temporary in nature and deployed to support a particular online marketing campaign. It features an airline and its marketing partner(s). |

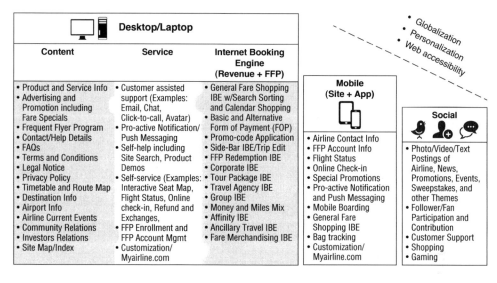

| <br>Desktop/Laptop | | |
|---|---|---|
| **Content** | **Service** | **Internet Booking Engine (Revenue + FFP)** |
| • Product and Service Info<br>• Advertising and Promotion including Fare Specials<br>• Frequent Flyer Program<br>• Contact/Help Details<br>• FAQs<br>• Terms and Conditions<br>• Legal Notice<br>• Privacy Policy<br>• Timetable and Route Map<br>• Destination Info<br>• Airport Info<br>• Airline Current Events<br>• Community Relations<br>• Investors Relations<br>• Site Map/Index | • Customer assisted support (Examples: Email, Chat, Click-to-call, Avatar)<br>• Pro-active Notification/ Push Messaging<br>• Self-help including Site Search, Product Demos<br>• Self-service (Examples: Interactive Seat Map, Flight Status, Online check-in, Refund and Exchanges,<br>• FFP Enrollment and FFP Account Mgmt<br>• Customization/ Myairline.com | • General Fare Shopping IBE w/Search Sorting and Calendar Shopping<br>• Basic and Alternative Form of Payment (FOP)<br>• Promo-code Application<br>• Side-Bar IBE/Trip Edit<br>• FFP Redemption IBE<br>• Corporate IBE<br>• Tour Package IBE<br>• Travel Agency IBE<br>• Group IBE<br>• Money and Miles Mix<br>• Affinity IBE<br>• Ancillary Travel IBE<br>• Fare Merchandising IBE |

- • Globalization
- • Personalization
- • Web accessibility

**Mobile (Site + App)**

- • Airline Contact Info
- • FFP Account Info
- • Flight Status
- • Online Check-in
- • Special Promotions
- • Pro-active Notification and Push Messaging
- • Mobile Boarding
- • General Fare Shopping IBE
- • Bag tracking
- • Customization/ Myairline.com

**Social**

- • Photo/Video/Text Postings of Airline, News, Promotions, Events, Sweepstakes, and other Themes
- • Follower/Fan Participation and Contribution
- • Customer Support
- • Shopping
- • Gaming

**Inflight**

- • Inflight Wi-fi Options:
  - -Internet on Passenger Device
  - -Multi-media on Passenger Device
  - -Mobile Services (SMS, voice, other)
- • Inflight Duty-free Shopping
- • Booking of Destination Services
- • Chat system (passenger-to-crew and passenger-to-passenger)

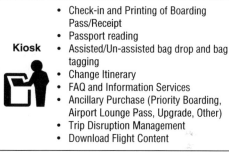

**Kiosk**

- • Check-in and Printing of Boarding Pass/Receipt
- • Passport reading
- • Assisted/Un-assisted bag drop and bag tagging
- • Change Itinerary
- • FAQ and Information Services
- • Ancillary Purchase (Priority Boarding, Airport Lounge Pass, Upgrade, Other)
- • Trip Disruption Management
- • Download Flight Content

**Wearable**

- • Boarding Pass
- • Flight Status
- • Contact Information
- • Promotions
- • Pro-active Notification

**Virtual**

- • Product and Service Information
- • Travel Logistics Support
- • Entertainment

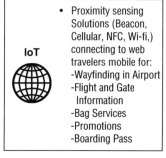

**IoT**

- • Proximity sensing Solutions (Beacon, Cellular, NFC, Wi-fi,) connecting to web travelers mobile for:
  - -Wayfinding in Airport
  - -Flight and Gate Information
  - -Bag Services
  - -Promotions
  - -Boarding Pass

*Figure 2.2* *Common features on airline e-commerce properties*

## 2.2.1 Features of airline website on desktop/laptop platforms

An airline's core website is made up of multiple pieces that are designed to appear integrated to the web traveler. These pieces include site content, customer service applications, and internet booking engine functionalities. Each of them has a variety of features that have more or less become common on many airline websites. Our discussion below shares more detail on each of them.

*Website content features*

Website content occupies by far the largest real estate on a website. It is not uncommon for even a smaller carrier to manage a few hundred web pages while a larger airline's site can easily involve several thousand. Content keeps growing as airlines continuously add more information to their sites. For airlines concerned with providing a good web traveler's user experience, this issue poses an ongoing challenge. This can only be managed effectively with smart website design—we will come back to this topic in more detail in Chapter 3.

Some content has a legal/regulatory purpose and is a "must-have." An airline risks running into legal issues if this is missing, incomplete, or out of date. At a minimum, a carrier should be concerned with:

■ a comprehensive purchase terms and condition section outlining the contractual details relevant for managing online ticket purchases on the carrier's website
■ a legal notice that spells out intellectual property rights, provides for protection in case of featuring inaccurate/incomplete content, and states a disclaimer regarding certain third party websites
■ a data privacy policy section that explains in detail the carrier's data management practices and how a web traveler's data are protected.

Depending on financial disclosure regulations for publicly traded companies, some airlines may also be required to share certain information in an "Investor's Relations" section.

Besides legally relevant information, carriers feature contact details of their company. They are relevant for web travelers who want to engage with the carrier to do business or to seek assisted customer service because they have an issue that requires resolution. Phone/fax numbers and postal/office addresses are common examples. In this regard, we should mention frequently asked question (FAQ) sections as well. They contain valuable information about an airline's products/services and are typically offered as part of a website's help page. A site map/index is also often featured and serves as the website's navigation directory to quickly locate certain content.

There is a lot of content dedicated to a variety of commercial topics. Advertising and promotion, particularly fare promotions, as well as product and service information are some examples. Information on frequent flyer programs (FFP), destinations, and airports are part of this. Airlines have deep roots in this kind of online content. This is because most of them started their journey into cyberspace with brochureware sites that had literally copied and pasted information from print material into web pages.

Several airlines have begun to feature social content on their web pages. Some incorporate live feeds from social media platforms such as Twitter and showcase them in a dedicated section on the website. Figure 2.3 is an example of Qantas sharing tweets on its website homepage. Other carriers have created special social media pages where they seek a two-way dialogue with web travelers. For instance, Scandinavian carrier SAS uses a "My SAS Idea" section where it invites web travelers to share thoughts and inputs for travel products/services.

Content of this nature is likely to grow in the future as carriers look for ways to engage their target audience more and make their website more appealing (or "stickier" in e-commerce vernacular). At the same time, today's consumers expect to be heard. Carriers need to show that they are good listeners. This involves relinquishing some control over the brand but this is an effective approach to turn a web traveler into a brand advocate for the airline.

## Website service features

Airline websites offer tools that allow web travelers to receive help. Email is an example. It is the internet-based service tool most universally available as part of an airline's options for customer support. Selected carriers also offer other live support options including chat and click-to-call.

Additionally, artificial means of customer support may be provided. One example are avatars. Alaska Airlines and Virgin Australia have been offering avatars for some years now. We elaborate on them in Chapter 5. For now, it should suffice to state that one of the key drivers for deploying avatars is to realize the benefits of assisted

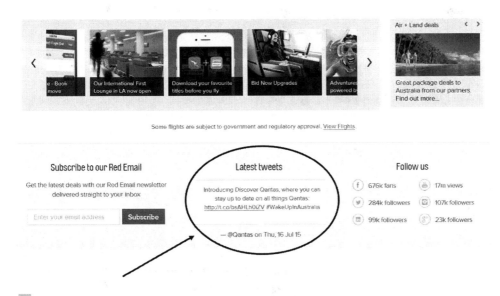

*Figure 2.3a* *"Socializing" airline website content: Qantas Tweets*

Source: qantas.com.au (2015)[1] with kind permission of Qantas

**Figure 2.3b** *"Socializing" airline website content: My SAS Idea*

*Source:* flysas.com (2015)[2] with kind permission of SAS

service—visual appearance and real-time one-on-one interaction—and offer them at the low cost of self-service. Avatars fulfill this objective to an extent. A growing number of carriers are introducing intelligent personal assistants (IPAs). Although mostly geared toward mobile devices, they are also available on desktop/laptop platforms in selected cases. Take for instance Microsoft's "XiaoIce," an IPA specifically developed for China Southern Airlines. Travel and itinerary notifications are particularly popular service features on IPAs.

Besides those customer support options that involve assistance from a carrier's staff, web travelers also finds a range of self-help features on today's airline websites. Common examples are site product demos and site search that are helpful for resolving an issue. Furthermore, standard self-service tools are offered as well. Web travelers use them as part of their online ticket purchase and trip management. Examples include seat selection on an interactive aircraft seat map, flight status, check-in, and online refunds and exchanges. In regards to an airline's frequent flyer program (FFP), enrollment and account access/management are typical features.

By featuring a variety of self-help/self-service tools on their websites, an airline can realize significant cost savings. This is because it is the web travelers who do the work and an airline therefore needs less manpower to provide for customer support. E-Commerce savvy airlines design their websites in such a way that web travelers can easily find and use service options that allow them to self-support.

Customization as a service feature has emerged on several airline websites in the form of "myairline.com." This feature is not to be confused with personalization.

With customization, it is the web traveler who has explicit control to configure a particular setting on a website to what they want to see and experience online. An example of this application is "Create My Profile" on brusselsairlines.com (Figure 2.4). A web traveler can indicate in a profile section their preferences for areas such as communication of flight irregularities (e.g. phone vs SMS text vs email), flight seating (aisle vs window) or favorite departure airports. Also, this information enables the airline to tailor its products and services to a certain degree to the web traveler's preferences. The customization of an airline website in the fashion of what Yahoo offers with "MyYahoo" is generally not available to web travelers. With MyYahoo, web users can apply their own themes, re-arrange the site layout, and add their favorite content pieces to the homepage.

*Website internet booking engine features*

As far as sales applications are concerned, airlines at a minimum offer an internet booking engine (IBE). An IBE is a piece of software between an airline's website and the company's supply system. It allows a web traveler to manage their general fare shopping process. In essence, this includes the search, selection, and payment of a specified itinerary with origin/destination, travel dates, and class of service. It also covers the booking of services such as seats and meals.

Most airlines are now in their second or third generation of booking engines that have become quite sophisticated when compared with their predecessors from the 1990s/early 2000s. Among the typical IBE features found on airline websites today are:

- booking capability for one-way/round trip/multi-city itinerary, codeshare partner flights, and frequent flyer redemptions

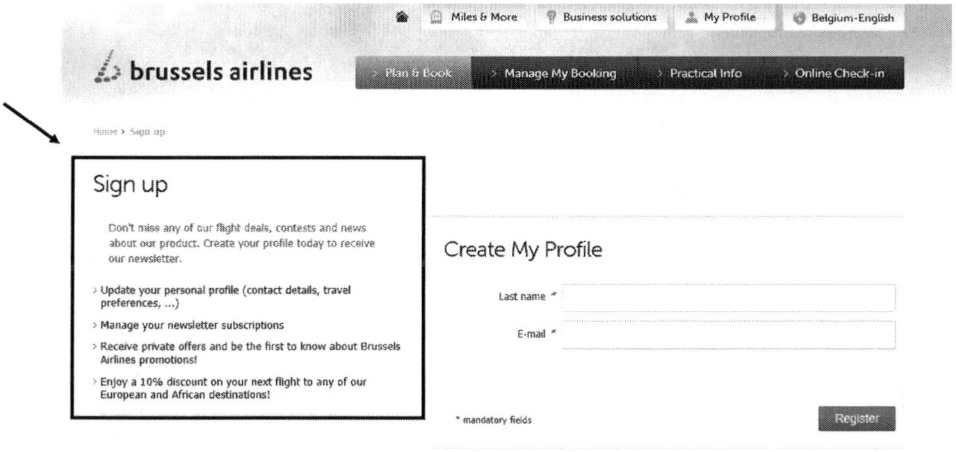

**Figure 2.4** *Customization with "Create My Profile" on brusselsairlines.com*

*Source:* brusselsairlines.com (2015)[3]

- flight sorting by price and number of stops
- Standalone cross-sell ancillaries (travel insurance, car rental, hotel)
- flexible and alternative date search (popularly referred to as calendar shopping)
- dynamic packaging with cross-sell travel partners (e.g. flight+hotel)
- fare merchandising
- multiple languages.

Depending on the competitive dynamics, web traveler demand, and budgetary resources, a carrier may also offer a number of specially configured IBEs such as for the corporate, group travel, and travel agency market.

For today's web travelers, the process of buying a ticket on an airline's digital property is a rather commoditized experience. In other words, there is little

## SNAPSHOT: HOW DOES AN IBE WORK?

An IBE supports multiple business processes including the shopping and purchasing of travel products (e.g. air, hotel, car, and dynamic packages), payment, data storage, and others. It operates as an intermediary between the web traveler who accesses the airline's website and the supply system of a travel provider (Figure 2.5). It is also possible that the IBE taps into a GDS in order to access travel supply. The supply of an airline is a product made up of its fares, schedules, and seat inventory.

The key features of an IBE are its business rules and processes that take the travel provider's supply and provide for the capability to shop and purchase. This includes:

- pricing rules
- the management of static content such as imagery and amenities
- the management of dynamic content including fares, schedules, and seat inventory
- specially configured displays for different customers
- real-time connectivity for the handling of online payment
- the aggregation of multiple travel products if packaging is involved
- possibly even the management of a web traveler's records including history, preferences, and current trip plans.

An IBE's business processes are instrumental in determining its value and differentiation versus other IBEs. The link between an IBE and a supply system requires some level of customization in the area of communications protocols and data formatting.

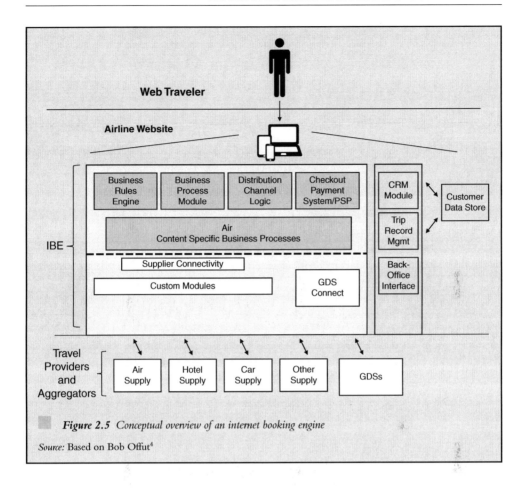

**Figure 2.5** *Conceptual overview of an internet booking engine*

*Source:* Based on Bob Offut[4]

differentiation—putting an airline's fare specials aside for a moment—when looking across multiple airline websites. To a degree, this is the result of several factors:

- The generic website platforms that a handful of technology suppliers including Amadeus, Sabre, and SITA offer in the marketplace and many airlines subscribe to.
- The inherently linear website booking path from selecting travel parameters in the beginning to receiving an email confirmation in the end.
- The fact that website IBE features, no matter how edgy today and only available from a few airlines, can be copied quickly and be offered by many competitors tomorrow.

However, there are some noteworthy developments that point to more differentiation in the future. Some carriers have decided to offer additional booking tools, sometimes labelled affinity IBEs, that borrow elements from social media. Take for instance the "Inspire Me" feature on emirates.com. Here, web travelers do not have to enter a specific destination but just indicate their general interest like "beach" or "safari." The booking engine then provides suggestions where to go. Figure 2.6

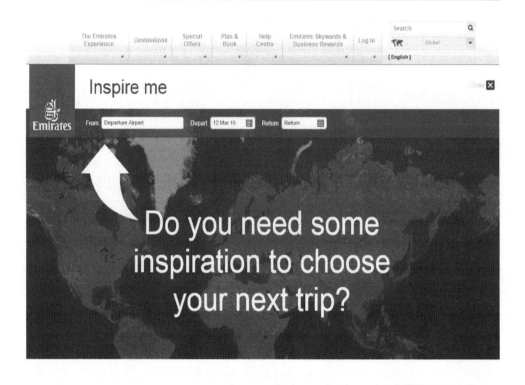

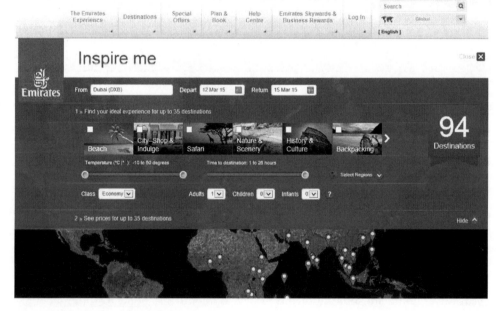

*Figure 2.6* Emirates' "Inspire me" booking tool

*Source:* emirates.com (2015)[5]

shows an example of a query for a four-day trip originating in Dubai. A total of 94 destinations are recommended. This then could be further filtered depending on the type of trip considered.

Another and much more significant game changer in terms of differentiation comes from fare merchandising. A growing number of carriers configure their IBEs to handle à la carte fares, branded fares, and fare families. This allows an airline to offer a booking experience to web travelers that is more distinguished from that on rival websites.

In this regard, our discussion on IBEs is incomplete without mentioning online forms of payment (FOPs). Since the early days of e-commerce, they have expanded vastly beyond standard credit cards. Today, many airlines offer a greater variety to make online ticket purchases for web travelers more convenient (and also lower cost for themselves because the processing fees of credit card companies are not small). Typically, the alternative FOPs vary by country and carrier. Among them, we find the cash payment option (available for "book now, pay later schemes" when the customer shops online and reserves the ticket for a later pick-up and payment at a carrier's office), cheques, debit cards, e-wallets like PayPal, gift cards/eVouchers, and the Universal Air Travel Plan (UATP) for corporate clients. More unusual FOPs involve ticket purchases by mobile payment—Kenya Airways has been offering this option since 2009 in Kenya via a company called M-Pesa that uses short messaging service (SMS)—and even wire services like Western Union.

Some of the recent additions to alternative FOPs by airlines include:

- *Bitcoin*, a software-based payment system. In 2014, Air Baltic became the first airline to accept this digital currency.
- *Social payment* via Twitter and Facebook. Since 2014, KLM has been offering this feature whereby web travelers are sent a hyperlink on these social media platforms to a secure payment environment.
- *Smart card payments*. In Spring 2015, LCC Hong Kong Express partnered with smart card operator Octopus Cards to launch an in-flight Octopus-based payment service. Passengers on all HK Express flights may use their regular Octopus card to purchase in-flight items including onboard upgrades. Smart cards are prepaid rechargeable contactless payment cards and common in many Asian cities. All Nippon Airways has had a similar smart card partnership in Japan since 2013.
- *Apple Pay*, Apple's new mobile payment system. JetBlue announced in February 2015 that passenger could use it for inflight purchases.

In order to handle the online financial transaction related to a web traveler's purchases, IBEs often interface with so-called payment service providers (PSPs). PSPs work behind the scenes and handle the payment logistics including the authorization and settlements of financial transaction in multiple currencies. They are an indispensable partner for airlines in their e-commerce activities.

Before moving on in our discussion and addressing the features available on mobile platforms in the next section, it is important to emphasize that the desktop/

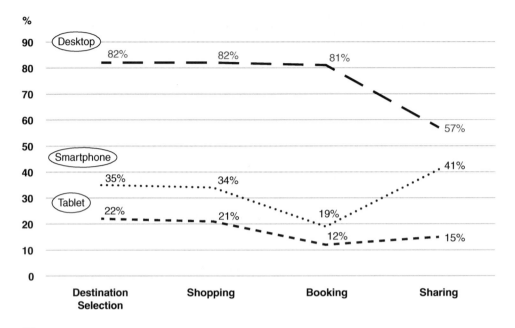

**Figure 2.7** *Devices used by web travelers during the travel life cycle*

*Source:* Phocuswright (2014)[6]

laptop still plays the dominate role in all phases of the travel life cycle (Figure 2.7). Therefore, despite all the hype surrounding mobiles, an airline should not lose focus on this platform type when it comes to maintaining a competitive presence in cyberspace.

### 2.2.2 Features on mobile platforms

Ever since the first iPhone came out in 2007 and ushered in the mainstream era of the smartphone, the rise of this platform in the last several years has been phenomenal. Currently, two billion people have a smart phone and this number is expected to double by 2020. No technology in human history has been adopted faster than the mobile phone. There are now more than one billion tablet users and the forecast is 1.5 billion by the end of the decade. In key travel markets such as the US and Europe, smartphone ownership among travelers now exceeds 75%. In Asia, 30% of the population is expected to have a smart phone by 2016.[7] In the online travel space, mobile platforms have already become an integral part in many web travelers' activities, although their focus is generally on non–booking activities (Figure 2.8).

Airlines will keep on introducing more mobile-optimized features for content, sales and service. In particular service features appear to be pushed by carriers and are becoming a universal standard. For example, in 2014, more than 50% of carriers worldwide boasted service features such as flight status, online check-in, and mobile boarding passes.[8] This share is likely to be well over 90% by 2018. This is the result

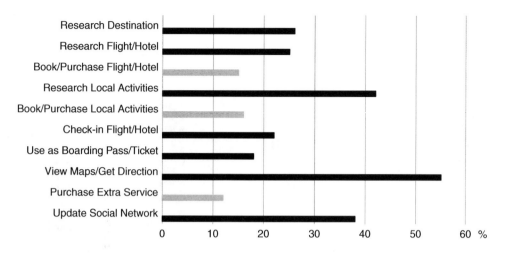

**Figure 2.8** *What are web travelers' main activities on mobile devices?*

Source: Phocuswright (2014)[9]

of major investments/R&D in mobile services between 2015 and 2018: 92% of airlines are committed to do this for smart phones and 85% for tablets.[10]

Focusing on self-service check-in for a moment, it is estimated that it will account for 24% of all customer check-ins by 2018, up from 9% in 2015. This makes it the second largest category after the airport check-in with 29% and ahead of desktop/laptop check-ins with 20%.[11]

This change in web traveler behavior is largely driven by LCCs. Already in 2015, they managed 23% of all check-ins via mobile platforms, something that the industry as a whole is not expected to achieve until 2018. How well this mobile self-service feature appears to resonate with travelers is exemplified by Southwest Airlines. In their case, over one million travelers use the mobile self-check-in feature every month.[12]

Besides service features, launching/expanding mobile booking functionalities is a clearly identified ambition by airlines. Many of them want to make shopping on mobile as widely available as on their websites. Some 75% of carriers believe that they will have achieved this by 2017.[13]

What can web travelers expect to see on their mobile devices? If it is as wide ranging as what is offered on airline websites, mobile shopping would cover fare merchandising features such as the purchase of priority boarding privileges, seat reservation, and inflight wi-fi pass. Even personalization, for instance via specifically targeted sales offers to mobile users, is a possibility. Additionally, non-flight ancillaries including hotel and car and even duty-free shopping would be part of the mix as well. Figure 2.9 shows how mature mobile shopping is expected to become in a few years.

Our discussion of mobiles should also touch on airline mobile apps. Following the general release of apps in the marketplace in 2008, Southwest was the first carrier to offer one on the iPhone in 2009. Today, next to a mobile site, many airlines also offer a mobile app. Table 2.2 is a snapshot of standard features available on selected carriers' apps.

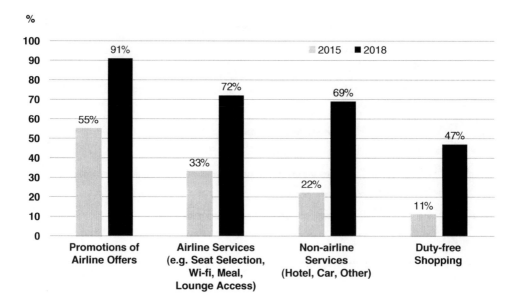

**Figure 2.9** *More shopping on mobile*

*Source:* SITA (2015)[14]

One trademark of leading e-commerce carriers is that they generally look for early adoption of new technology applications. Moreover, they also attempt to break the mold of standard features and offer something unusual to web travelers. Besides earning bragging rights from a public relations perspective, this approach can generate tangible benefits in terms of increased web traveler engagement, enhanced customer

**Table 2.2** *Mobile app features: Who offers what (March 2015)?*

| Carrier | Review Reservation | Booking | Award Booking | Seat Map & Assignment | Check-in & Mobile Boarding Pass |
|---|---|---|---|---|---|
| Air Canada | ☑ | ☑ | No | ☑ | ☑ |
| Alaska | ☑ | ☑ | ☑ | ☑ | ☑ |
| American | ☑ | Links to Mobile Site | No | No | ☑ |
| British Airways | ☑ | ☑ | ☑ | ☑ | ☑ |
| Delta | ☑ | ☑ | ☑ | ☑ | ☑ |
| JetBlue | ☑ | ☑ | ☑ | ☑ | ☑ |
| KLM | ☑ | ☑ | No | ☑ | ☑ |
| Southwest | ☑ | ☑ | ☑ | No | ☑ |
| United | ☑ | ☑ | ☑ | ☑ | ☑ |

*Source:* Kerr (2015)[15]

service, and revenue uptakes. A few airlines have launched some interesting mobile apps features:

- *Delta.* Offers a wide range of features including taking a picture of the web traveler's parking spot and storing it (so that they find their car upon return from their trip), selecting which Sky Club one has access to depending on the web traveler's credentials, storing destination's weather forecast, and forms of payment and receipts.
- *JetBlue.* The carrier's app allows the generation of a single boarding pass for multiple people on the same flight. Moreover, it lists current movies showing, the DirecTV channel lineup, and the onboard snack and drink menus. For fun, web travelers can create a postcard by taking a picture, personalizing it, and sending it to friends and family.
- *KLM.* It offers a "Trip Shake" app that helps travelers find new places to go by shaking their mobile phone. The app enables users to choose a continent or travel date and be presented by more than 100 options. Users are shown a ticket price and can then either click through to book or shake the phone for another option until they find something they like. Destinations and prices can also be shared via social media. A separate app called "Aviation Empire" is a fun game that allows users to learn about KLM's history and run their own airline.
- *Turkish Airlines.* Its app allows users fast booking and completion of ticket purchase in less than one minute rather than the usual six to eight minutes. Personal details are stored and cargo customers can even check on the status of their shipments with the airline.
- *United.* The carrier features a booking tool for ground transport provider Uber and allows the scanning of passports as part of checking in for an international flight.

Several closing observations on mobiles should be made. The enthusiastic embrace of this technology platform by both consumers and organizations is amazing and in many ways is reminiscent of the internet boom years from the mid-1990s to the early 2000s. With the shift to mobile adoption continuing and largely spurred by today's "mobile-first" millennial generation, airlines will undoubtedly continue investing in mobiles.

However, as recent as in 2014, a SITA survey indicated that only around 40% of carriers think that mobile performs "at least as expected."[16] Conversely, this means that approximately 60% view this technology platform as an underperformer, or worse, the performance of mobile services is not even actively tracked by some carriers (Figure 2.10). The latter point is particularly worrying. Competing successfully in the mobile travel space requires the use of performance indicators. The number of mobile app downloads, mobile self-service usage data, cost savings, efficiency gains, and new revenue streams are only a few examples of items that should be tracked. Rushing into the adoption of new technology platforms, be it mobiles, social media, wearable computing or something else, for fear of being left behind is not a sound approach and should be avoided.

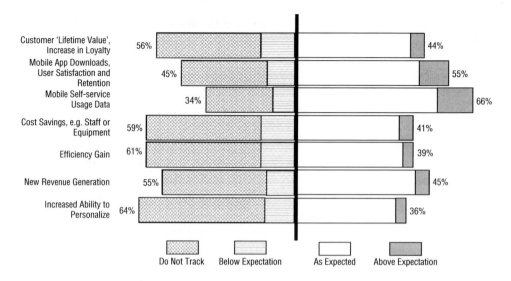

**Figure 2.10** *Performance indicators for mobile investments*

*Source:* SITA (2014)[17]

Another question that should be raised is how effective airlines have been in their efforts to accommodate mobile in all aspects of the travel life cycle. Probably not too well considering that today's web travelers' frustration level with mobile is not insignificant. Too small screens, less useful than desktops, and too slow connections are some of the reasons cited (Figure 2.11). Fact is that many airlines have repurposed whatever content and functionalities already existed for websites on desktops for a "lite" version on a mobile platform. In order to improve mobile uptake rates among web travelers, it might be better to approach the introduction of features from a genuine mobile perspective.

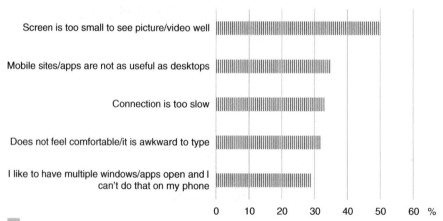

**Figure 2.11** *Web traveler mobile frustrations*

*Source:* Rose (2012)[18]

In this respect, user-friendly design is paramount above all factors considering the smaller screen of mobile devices. At the same time, we should mention the growing role of speech recognition applications. They allow web travelers to talk to their mobile device and search for travel information without typing. It has already been proven in the early 1990s that travel lends itself well to a speech recognition application because it involves a very finite set of commands (origin/destination, dates, and travel brands).[19] More sophisticated speech recognition applications are available today with the increasingly popular intelligent personal assistants (IPAs) that we have already mentioned earlier. An IPA is essentially a software program that completes certain tasks for the user, provides for answers to a user's questions, and also makes recommendations. Google Now, Apple Siri, and Microsoft Cortana are IPA examples that have been around for several years now and and they also use voice recognition applications. Facebook just launched its own digital helper called "M" in fall 2015. With IPAs driven by voice commands, web travelers are already a significant step closer to a more useful way of interacting with mobile devices for travel purposes, particularly when it comes to service-related issues. Figure 2.12 shows where voice recognition may be useful in the travel life cycle.

### 2.2.3 Features on social media platforms

Prominent digital properties used by airlines in e-commerce are their social media sites. These include sites owned and operated by an airline. Examples are corporate blogs such as JetBlue's "Blue Tale" and gaming sites as offered by KLM with "Aviation Empire." There are also those social media sites that are airline managed but owned by a third party. An example is Facebook, the world's largest and most popular social media company in terms of followers. For third party social media websites, a carrier has to match their form and function and cannot apply its own branding—unlike for other platforms.

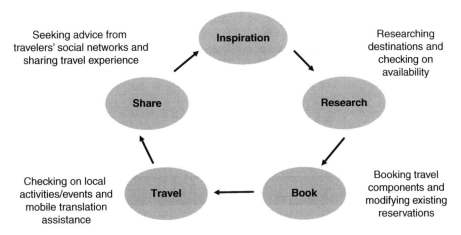

**Figure 2.12** *Adding voice to mobile travel applications*

*Source:* Rose (2014)[20]

Airlines using social media websites have been and still are largely concerned with building their company's digital brand and reputation. The top third party social media players used for this purpose include Facebook, Twitter, LinkedIn, and You-Tube. Postings are a main social site feature. They generally cover airline news, events, and promotional messages and come in the form of static/interactive text, images, and videos. The goal of these postings is increasing the two-way engagement with the market place and attracting more followers/fans.

Several carriers including American, JetBlue, and KLM have gone beyond the focus on merely building large followings with sales and brand related postings. They have launched a number of service features that allow the handling of customer support for web travelers. Examples include web traveler forums where web travelers can obtain support from other web travelers as well as airline Twitter and accounts that are exclusively dedicated to managing customer service issues.

When it comes to social media site features that enable online ticket purchases, the picture is not too exciting. The majority of airlines simply link web travelers back to their core site. There were earlier efforts by some carriers to allow web travelers to complete bookings within a social network environment. However, initial euphoria around 2010/11 that the launch of social media specific IBEs could generate new revenue streams quickly dissipated. For instance, Delta Airlines, one of the world's first carriers to launch an IBE on Facebook in 2010 was also the first two years later to disable this feature because of lack of demand by web travelers. What did not help was the fact that the booking features on Facebook were just a fraction of those offered on Delta's core site. It seems that the industry has yet to find more suitable tools/approach if it wants web travelers to conduct purchase transactions on carriers' social media sites.

KLM is an example of an airline that has moved successfully in this direction. In February 2014, it introduced social pay. Web travelers who use Facebook or Twitter to purchase a ticket, rebook a flight, or arrange for extras such as an upgrade or additional baggage can pay through these channels as well. How does this work? Web travelers send the airline a payment request via Facebook or Twitter and KLM in return replies with a private message that includes a payment link. The web traveler's payment details then are transmitted through a specially secure link and they receive a confirmation from KLM upon completion of the transaction. A similar feature has emerged in the hotel sector with US-based hotel chain Loews. In their case, a web traveler uses the hashtag of #bookloews to initiate the booking of a room via Twitter. A Loews customer service representative (CSR) then responds with a special link that takes a web traveler to a private chat room where the booking process is completed.[21]

### 2.2.4 Features on inflight platforms

Inflight has also evolved to become an area for airlines' online activities. We should not only think of inflight wi-fi but also of aircraft intranets and inflight portals that a growing number of carriers offer. Inflight duty-free shopping, the booking of destination services, and even chat systems have become more common. In this regard, Air New Zealand is an illustrative example. In 2014, it launched a new inflight entertainment system that goes significantly beyond offering standard content like music and movies. Among the new features is a chat system that allows passengers to communicate with the crew as well as a TripAdvisor app that provides for destination information.[22]

Interestingly, the days where these inflight chat systems are tied into a carrier-owned hard/software set-up may be numbered. For instance, Arke, a Dutch leisure carrier and a member airline of the TUI group, in August 2015 became the world's first airline to let passengers order food, snacks, and duty free items with their own devices for delivery to their seats.

How seismic the shift with inflight platforms has become is also clear when looking at new approaches that some carriers have adopted in terms of inflight entertainment content and delivery. For example, in May 2015, JetBlue announced a tie-up with Amazon Prime allowing members of the online streaming service to stream movies and television shows using the carrier's onboard wi-fi service. In October 2015, Virgin America entered a similar partnership with Netflix whereby travelers can stream content from their Netflix account while flying, exactly as they would at home.

Singapore Airlines offer its own twist on letting travelers use their own digital devices. In their case, they launched the industry's first companion mobile application, which will help to enhance the end-to-end passenger experience. Specifically, passengers can start their inflight entertainment experience while they are on the ground. Passengers will be able to enter their flight details and browse the entertainment choices that will be available on their flight. Once onboard, the passenger's mobile device can be synchronized with the seatback screen which will then call up their selected entertainment choices. The app is integrated with the airline's existing app and it also offers access to the inflight magazine and destination information. The companion app may also be be operated as a second screen. Passengers thus can use their own device to browse the inflight entertainment library, read the inflight magazine or view the flight moving map without interrupting what they are watching on the seatback screen.

E-Commerce is not only for an airline's web travelers but also increasingly deployed to empower customer-facing airline staff. Particularly airline cabin crews and customer service representatives on the ground should be mentioned. Take for example KLM. They have equipped their flight attendants with iPads to show any social media queries from passengers on their flight. The carrier's social care team may ask the flight attendant to take the query offline, resolve any issue, and report back. In one case, a customer's complaint about a cold inflight meal was reported through this system. On the return flight, the cabin crew made sure that this passenger would be one of the first to receive their meal and an apology for earlier problems.[23]

## 2.2.5 Features on kiosk platforms

Airline e-commerce is also increasingly conducted via airport kiosks. These include common use and dedicated airline kiosks. Both the number of airport kiosks and the availability beyond self-service check-in are forecasted to increase. By 2017, for example, check-in kiosks will be almost universal with 92% of airports providing for them.[24] Furthermore, in order to encourage more use of kiosks by travelers, airports and airlines have been looking into offering a variety of new features. These include additional self-service features such as passport readers and bag drop/tagging, general FAQ and information services, airline ancillary purchases, and trip disruption management.

### 2.2.6 Features on wearable computing platforms

Features associated with wearable computing are still small in numbers as this platform has not entered the mainstream yet. For now, it seems that existing features found today on mobile platforms are extended to wearables such as a smartwatch. Due to their small interface, booking features—at least as we currently apply them—are unlikely on wearables. Nevertheless, added value for on-the-go and in-destination applications are feasible. An example is the pro-active customer notification of a flight or boarding passes.

Since Apple rolled out its smart watch in March 2015, a flurry of airline announcements on their launch of a smart watch app has taken place. In Europe, easyJet and Iberia were among the first movers. They have been joined already by airBerlin, British Airways, KLM, and Virgin Atlantic. In the US, American, Delta, and JetBlue were among the early adopters. Dubai-based Emirates' smart watch app is the first of its kind in the Middle East. Launched in April 2015, it allows web travelers to review their upcoming trips, access real-time flight and journey information, receive timely notifications of gate or baggage belt changes, and access their boarding passes (Figure 2.13).

Another wearable that has caught the interest of airlines involves Google Glass. Several carriers participated in pilot programs in 2014 including Virgin Atlantic and LCC Spring Airlines from China. Virgin issued staff at Heathrow airport Google Glass in order to keep first-class passengers up to date on flight information, weather,

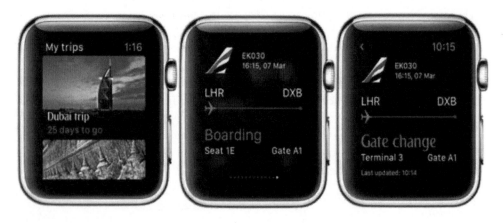

**Figure 2.13** *Emirates' Apple smart watch*

*Source:* Future Travel Experience (2015)[25]

and local events at their destination. Spring Airlines was the first airline to equip flight attendants with Google Glass to help improve onboard customer service. Cabin crew used it to help identify specific passengers who had requested food and beverages. Despite the initial benefits identified by companies participating in the pilot program, Google decided to discontinue the sale of Google Glass in early 2015. The high price tag (around $1,200), the nerdy look of its users, inadequacy for staff under working conditions (too fragile, battery overheating), and privacy concerns were among the reasons. Nevertheless, it is expected that Google will follow up with another version in the future.

Another interesting application of a wearable is Air New Zealand's digital wristband for unaccompanied minors (UMs). The airline carries 28,000 UMs every year and the high-tech bracelet replaces the current paper system. A chip implanted in the bracelet and connected to a mobile application provides parents with real-time information on where exactly their child is during the trip.[26]

The outlook for wearables is certainly positive. In 2015, the number of units expected to be shipped globally was approximately 100 million, a volume that may to grow to approximately 230 million in 2020. The bulk of these are smart watches[27] but the world of wearables is quite diverse. It also includes earbuds/headphones, items embedded in clothing, and contact lenses (Figure 2.14).

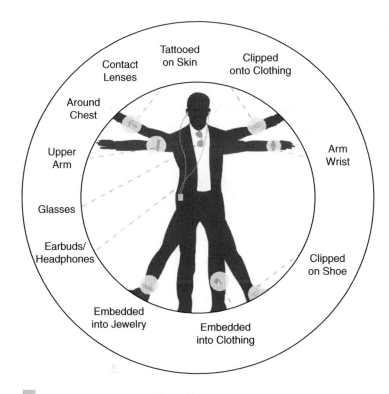

*Figure 2.14* *The world of wearables*

*Source:* Based on Dr4Ward (2014)[28]

There is no end in sight to what airlines may offer next, or, to be more precise, what travelers may demand next in the world of wearable computing. Airlines will find a way to participate in this growth story. However, despite the headline-catching announcements by some carriers on their new Apple smart watch applications, the majority of airlines are still cautious when it comes to wearable computing. Apparently, only 7% of airlines have looked at this technology more closely at this stage. Uncertainties surrounding consumer adoption and product qualities are the main reasons for many carriers to hold back with their engagement on a larger scale.[29]

### 2.2.7 Features on virtual reality platforms

Virtual reality has taken on many different forms. In the online travel marketplace, virtual worlds, website avatars, holograms, and augmented reality are common areas of application. As far as virtual worlds are concerned, airlines may be attracted to them because of the opportunity to promote their brands and also sell their products/services (albeit in virtual form).

However, the heydays of popular virtual worlds such as Second Life that managed to attract major corporate entities and even made it on to the cover of *Business Week* in 2006 are gone. The presence of airlines including those of TAM and KLM that had opened operations there in 2007 and 2008, respectively, quickly faded once it became evident that it would not be the new future of marketing. Furthermore, the emerging popularity of social media showed that people were more interested in interacting with other people in the real world. There is some speculation that Second Life might be reincarnated because it is working on integrating the virtual reality headset by Oculus Rift, a company that was acquired by Facebook in 2014. If and when that occurs and virtual worlds again might attract mainstream consumer interest, some carriers possibly may revisit the idea of a virtual world presence. In the foreseeable future, however, virtual worlds are not an area for airline e-commerce in any significant way.

A more common virtual application with airlines are avatars. An avatar is a computer representation of a person. Alaska Airlines pioneered its use on alaskaair.com in 2008. Airlines use this technology on their websites for customer servicing and to assist web travelers with information about the carrier's products/services.

Holograms and augmented reality also apply virtual elements. Since 2011, several airports in Europe and the United States have introduced holograms of real-life customer service staff to speed up security queues. The holograms are typically projected on life-size surfaces, modeled after real airport staff, and assist departing passengers in the security zones. Augmented reality has also become increasingly common with airlines in recent years. In essence, it is technology that superimposes computer-generated images on a person's real view, thus creating a composite view of real and virtual scenes. The area of digital marketing is especially popular for them and a more in-depth discussion on this subject is presented in Chapter 3.

New areas of virtual application emerge all the time. As briefly mentioned in Chapter 1, Qantas initiated a three-month virtual headset trial program in spring

2015 on selected long-haul flights from Sydney to Los Angeles for passengers in first class. The product features special programming content including destination and service information. Virtual tours of the company's Airbus A380 aircraft, LAX Airport lounge, and virtual visits to national parks in Australia are some of the examples.[30] Since November 2015, Virgin Atlantic has also started offering a virtual reality application. Built in partnership with Microsoft for Windows smart phones and tablets, it sells the airline's Upper-Class experience to people who have not purchased a ticket yet. Corporate client offices, roadshows, and corporate lobby locations are some of the "ground" venues for experiencing the VIP check-in at London Heathrow, a relaxation in the carrier's airport lounge "Club House", and the aircraft cabin of Upper-Class. The airline wanted to provide for an engaging experience to business travelers where they are during the day. These developments are an indication that VR could expand beyond games and 3D movies which are its key domains of application so far. More airlines will begin to test virtual reality technology inflight and on the ground. It is therefore no longer a question of when but how to adopt this technology.

However, fully immersive virtual reality where the technology delivers believable experiences of sight, sound, touch, and smell is probably another 40 to 50 years away and even then it may only happen if it is directly connected to a human being's nervous system (who knows: this may also be the ultimate substitute for travel...).

### 2.2.8 Features on IoT platforms

The Internet of Things (IoT) is about everyday objects being connected to the internet. This enables unprecedented tracking, data collection, analysis, and control. In the context of the online travel marketplace, this means that more things than ever will be connected to web travelers, be it in an airport or elsewhere. One key device part of the IoT revolution can be a web traveler's smartphone.

This everyday object connectivity requires significant infrastructure in smart devices, location technology, and intelligent software that can deal with massive amounts of data and find a relevant solution for an individual web traveler in a specific context.

For example, the use of beacons, which will allow airlines to reap the benefits of sensors and the ability to match location with other information, is predicted to rise from currently 9% to 44% by 2018.[31] Beacons are part of the proximity-sensing infrastructure that also includes cellular, near-frequency communication (NFC), and wi-fi at airports that airlines have been busy deploying in recent years. Many more related projects are in the works and pave the way for the IoT. Some 76% of airlines understand the concept of IoT and 86% assume that its benefits will become clear within the next three years.[32]

The goal of IoT is to improve the travel experience of web travelers and minimize/eliminate "pain points" as much as possible. Even elements of surprise if not delight are supposed to be part of it. Top areas airlines are focused on include:

- *Way-finding*. As more beacons are installed throughout airport terminals, a web traveler's smartphone device and airline/airport apps will be active way-finding maps. For instance, information will be available where the web traveler has to go to catch a connecting flight and how much time it takes to get there. Tailoring this information to an individual means that possible mobility limitations or disabilities are accounted for.
- *Bag services*. IoT is supposed to increase a web traveler's control of their luggage. One of the most common uses of beacons will be for bag services with many airlines deploying them in bag drop and bag claim areas. Web travelers will know at all times where their bags are and how long it takes to receive them.
- *Booking and shopping are transformed with "smart" retail*. IoT can be used to offer individualized promotions by airport retailers as the web traveler walks by certain stores. It could point to the nearest restaurant based on a web traveler's dining preferences (with access to reviews by other web travelers) and advise how much time could be spent in duty-free shopping before heading to the gate and not delaying a flight departure.

Airlines are working on "beaconizing" their apps, and once implemented, web travelers will start to enjoy some of the benefits described above.

## 2.3 THE IMPACT OF GLOBALIZATION, PERSONALIZATION, AND WEB ACCESSIBILITY ON DIGITAL AIRLINE E-COMMERCE PROPERTIES

### 2.3.1 Globalization features

An airline that operates an international route network often maintains country specific websites. The old adage that all politics are local also has some validity for a carrier's global web presence. Localization of website content, customer service, and IBEs via native languages and locally relevant information is key for an airline's e-commerce activities to be successful in specific markets.

Unfortunately for web travelers, the globalization with some carriers has not matured enough to provide a positive user experience. Operating in multiple countries and delivering a locally adjusted web presence while maintaining a globally unified digital brand is a challenge. In order to manage this effectively, an airline should address several key issues. These include the balancing of organizational needs for central control by the head office versus local autonomy by staff in the field. Accounting for differences in e-commerce operating conditions is also key. We just need to think about consumers' affinity/culture/readiness to shop online, the state of the overall internet infrastructure, and the legal/regulatory framework. These are all factors that differ—in some cases significantly—from country to country.

In order to support localized websites, a carrier should follow several globalization best practices that have emerged over the last 10–15 years:

- Support of local web traveler's language. This is essential to connect to people. For example, Oman Air, that serves multiple destinations in Europe, probably misses out on business opportunities because of not offering local languages like French, German, and Italian on their website omanair.com.

  Geolocation and language negotiation applications on the backend can help present the right language to local web travelers. However, translations should be handled by professionals (and not by a statistical machine translation service such as Google Translate), otherwise the risk of improper language handling is too great. Some carriers even mix multiple languages on a single web page. This hurts the brand image significantly and should be avoided.

  Importantly, a carrier should maintain language parity among different digital properties. If an airline's web presence comprises a website, a mobile site, mobile app, and social media, there should be no "second class" property whereby the mobile site, for example, is only presented in English to the traveling public.

- Registration of local domain names because it helps extend a brand subtly into local markets. For example, when serving Brazil or Australia, an airline should use domain name extensions with .br for Brazil or .com.au. Local web travelers often default to these first and not to .com. We cover this topic in detail in Chapter 3 under the topic of domain name management.

- Improvement of discoverability of local sites with visual/navigational clues in the website header ("country/region" are common links) or even feature a universal gateway page. Figure 2.15 shows Japan Airlines' jal.com as an example of such a page that has become the standard with many airlines. In the case of Japan

**Figure 2.15** *Gateway page of Japan Airlines*

*Source:* jal.com (2015)[33] with kind permission of Japan Airlines

Airlines, when selecting France as a home country, the web traveler is offered three languages (English, French, Japanese). Once these selections are completed, a web traveler then can proceed to the respective localized web version for France.

- Country flags should be avoided because they do not scale well visually and they often carry cultural and political issues that may cause problems. Some of the most globally successful sites including Google or Facebook do not use flags at all.
- Extension of participation in digital properties beyond mega brands like Facebook. Tapping into local players—in social media this would include Weibo in China and VKontakte in Russia—generally translates into a highly engaged audience despite the smaller fan/follower base that exists locally.
- Deployment of global website design templates allows for more with less resources. Moreover, it also enables a common use of tools and processes by airline staff around the world. At the same time, the end-consumer is presented with a unified global brand. "Renegade" sites built and managed locally are detrimental because they are not connected to the carrier's global digital brand (other than the company's logo maybe) and therefore may invoke trust issues and confusion with web travelers. Mid-/long-term, they are not helpful for building the airline's online business because local staff lack adequate resources and comprehensive e-commerce know-how. Unless there are strong business reasons to maintain them, they should be folded and repurposed for a global presence.

Global design templates still allow the accommodation of web content, service, and IBE features that are localized. Examples include price quotations in local currency, local address/date formats, local customer service phone numbers, local imagery, local news, and local online payment options.

Airlines that excel in e-commerce globalization are those that do not differentiate the world in terms of domestic and international markets. They strive to be global players serving local web travelers. This view ensures that online users around the world are treated equally.

### 2.3.2 Personalization features

Personalization is a feature and a capability. It co-exists with "targeting," "one-to-one marketing," "big data," and "merchandising." It involves behind-the-scenes applications and processes that take into account all the insight an airline has established about a web traveler. It is primarily based on observations/tracking of a web traveler's behavior, characteristics, preferences, and to some extent also on information that the web traveler has shared with the airline. In essence, the key enabler of personalization is big data generated with e-tracking technology applications. With this insight, an airline can deliver uniquely tailored offerings such as fares, products, and customer service options.

Online retailers like Amazon are well known for excelling in the digital profiling of shoppers and offering them individualized purchase recommendations. One might even argue that they "had" to personalize their shopping experience because their catalog is so huge that people barely scratch the surface. In other words, personalization drives discovery and allows online users to find products and services that they never knew existed. As an airline's "catalog" will undeniably grow due to merchandising (Ryanair has gone on record for stating that they want to become the "Amazon in the airline industry"), personalization will help shorten the distance between a web traveler and what they want. Airlines should take notice that an estimated one third of Amazon's sales comes from its recommendation and personalization systems.[34] One-to-one targeting can benefit customers in the form of a more efficient and effective purchase process, while companies can boast their brand equity, strengthen brand loyalty, and improve their revenue.

The concept of segmentation has existed along political, religious, and lifestyle lines for a long time. Its application in a business context is fairly recent and is fundamentally rooted in the idea that individual shoppers expect their suppliers to know who they are and want they want. The "cult of the individual" gained momentum in the mid-2000s: *Time* magazine voted in 2006 "You" as the person of the year as a result of the growing prominence of user-generated information created by individuals for a larger audience. Around the same time, the iPhone was introduced and social media including Facebook and Twitter expanded on a global scale—all this generated new valuable data streams.

In terms of airline e-commerce, personalization has evolved from early forms such as addressing travelers by their name in email marketing communications to today's delivery of individualized marketing and sales messages based on an individual's behavior. Over 80% of airlines are focused on personalization, yet for many the ability to make it happen is non-existent or weak.[35] Common is the engagement in mass merchandising that segments based on factors such as origin/destination and macro segmentation that accounts for lifestyle factors. Fewer airlines can target micro segments—travelers with very similar behavior—and even less offer truly unique products/services to individuals (Figure 2.16). This is a bit surprising considering that

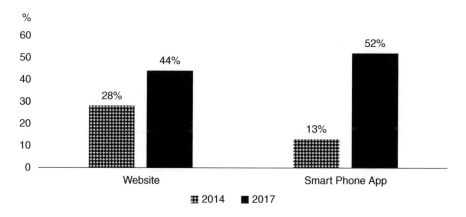

**Figure 2.16** *Airlines offering truly targeted/personalized service experience based on real-time passenger data*

*Source:* SITA (2014)[36]

airlines have been collecting massive amounts of data about their target audience for some time now.

Reasons include multiple and disconnected customer databases at airlines, organizational silos that prevent critical data sharing, lack of proper IT infrastructure within airlines and, on an industry-wide basis, an inadequate inhouse know-how for managing analytics. Furthermore, concerns on the consumer side about data privacy and possible discrimination still need a resolution as well. Nevertheless, personalization has compelling advantages: Airlines can sell more by selling differently and they can service better. From the web traveler perspective, they are offered more relevant products/services. Considering these factors and the fact that online travel is on a growth trajectory for years to come, there will be a strong push to overcome challenges of organizational, infrastructural, and legal/regulatory nature. This means that airlines will mature in their sophistication level. In other words, we will see more airlines implementing personalization features across the entire travel life cycle for all digital touchpoints with travelers.

For instance, personalized air fares would not any longer be based on impersonal factors such as travel times and destinations but on who the web traveler is. Lufthansa's February 2015 announcement as the first airline in the world to implement an Amadeus booking tool that allows the tailoring of offers to corporate travelers points already in this direction.[37] Also, personalized customer service would be possible because customer service representatives on the ground and in the air have prior knowledge of the web traveler's history and preferences. Some airlines might even go as far as the Brazilian carrier TAM did in summer 2015. As part of its Sao Paulo–Milan route anniversary celebration, it provided each passenger with a personalized copy of its inflight magazine. This was made possible by accessing people's Facebook accounts and creating articles with photos and information that they like to read based on their interests. A photo of the passenger was also on the cover.

The era of personalization in travel is about to begin thanks to the availability of smart technology and the many digital footprints web travelers leave behind in whatever they do online.

### 2.3.3 Website accessibility

A growing number of countries are involved in a process to establish a legislative framework in order to provide disabled web users with equal access to airline websites. With website accessibility, airlines around the world have to upgrade all features to allow web users that suffer from some defined form of disability to have equal access. The US Department of Transport, for instance, ruled in 2013 that all commercial carriers' websites serving the US market would need to be compliant with effect from December 2015 (this was eventually extended to June 2016 since many carriers would not have been ready). Other countries are expected to embark on similar legislative action soon. The initial focus is on desktop/laptop platforms, but mobiles will be addressed in a second compliance wave. Social media sites like

Facebook have already been pro-active on the subject of accessibility for some time and unlike airlines are in the forefront of this area.

## 2.4 WHAT PLATFORMS AND FEATURES TO IMPLEMENT AND HOW?

Aside from mandated features because of legal/regulatory reasons, the answer to this question is largely driven by the constantly evolving market place. This means taking into account what web travelers want and what competitors offer. Additionally, the online travel marketplace is influenced by non-airline industry players. E-Commerce savvy airlines often look for guidance and inspiration from leaders in the field including Amazon, Apple, and Netflix. This is also important because web travelers often benchmark their expectations and experience against those leading brands outside the travel space.

It is imperative that two key questions drive the decision-making process to adopt new ways of doing business: Will the new platform/feature save a company money? Will it offer a competitive advantage? Both these questions need to be looked at in detail and addressed as part of a larger strategic assessment as to where an airline currently stands and where it wants to be. If specific advantages can be identified—for example, in the form of increased revenue, enhanced customer satisfaction, and/or cost reduction—the next step would be to establish an e-commerce development road map with a timeline of two to four years into the future.

It is beyond the scope of this chapter to elaborate in detail on how to go about prioritizing the introduction of new platforms/features. However, it should suffice to say that this process has to be thorough, rigorous, and cross-departmental. In this respect, cash-flow analyses and the identification of resource requirements are crucial. Also important is an impact assessment in terms of cost savings, efficiency improvements, revenue/web traveler satisfaction gains, and staff working procedures. Likewise, from drawing up the initial feature specifications all the way to testing the prototype, web traveler involvement is crucial. This can be accomplished via focus groups and other feedback mechanisms.

The quality of an airline's digital brand is determined by a number of fundamental factors. Digital properties (number and type of platforms and website features) undoubtedly play a role. A large range of platforms, website types, and website features indicates a solid presence in cyber presence. The more diversified this presence is, the higher is a carrier's chance to monopolize a web traveler's attention. This also means that a web traveler spends less time and attention on the digital properties of rivals.

At the same time, the most diverse website types and most advanced features on an airline's website are worthless if they are not properly maintained. Out-of-date and missing content, especially with legal/regulatory relevance, irregular content updates, improper editing procedures, and a fragmented global web presence hurt an airline's digital brand appearance. Likewise, a poor performance of digital platforms in terms of web page download speed (ideally in less than 4 seconds) and uptime availability (ideally 99.5% and higher) are equally detrimental to the competitiveness of an airline's presence in cyberspace. If all these fundamental e-commerce factors are not in proper shape, it will be difficult for an airline to differentiate itself in areas such as online advertising and promotion, e-sales and distribution, and web customer service.

## NOTES

1 Qantas (2015) "Qantas," qantas.com.au (accessed July17, 2015).

2 SAS (2015) "SAS," https://mysasidea.flysas.net/ (accessed July 3, 2015).

3 Brussels Airlines (2015) "Create My Profile," www.brusselsairlines.com/ (accessed March 5, 2015).

4 Offutt, Bob, "Internet Booking Engines," *Phocuswright's Data Point*, 2008, p. 4.

5 Emirates (2015) "Inspire Me: Find inspiration for your next journey," www.emirates.com/us/english/plan_book/inspire-me/inspire-me.aspx (accessed March 3, 2015).

6 PhocusWright (2014) "Mobile End-to-End: The Impact of Mobile across Search, Shop, Buy, Share," www.phocuswright.com/Free-Travel-Research/Mobile-End-to-End-The-Impact-of-Mobile-Across-Search-Shop-Buy-Share#.VgpUjLRN38s (accessed February 18, 2015).

7 Tnooz (2015) "Asia Online Travel Infographics," www.tnooz.com/article/erevmax-asia-online-travel/ (accessed July 19, 2015).

8 Ibid.

9 PhocusWright, "Mobile End-to-End".

10 Ibid.

11 SITA (2015) "Airline IT Trends Survey 2015," https://secure.sita.aero/globalassets/docs/surveys--reports/airline-it-trends-survey-2015.pdf (accessed June 29, 2015).

12 Finley, T. (2013) "You're app-solutely going to love this news!" www.blogsouthwest.com/youre-app-solutely-going-to-love-this-news/ (accessed March 28, 2015).

13 SITA (2014) "2014 SITA Airline IT Trends Survey," www.sita.aero/globalassets/docs/surveys--reports/airline-it-trends-survey-2014.pdf (accessed January 4, 2015).

14 SITA, "Airline IT Trends Survey 2015."

15 Kerr, R. (2015) "10 airline mobile apps that make travel easier," http://thepointsguy.com/2015/03/10-airline-mobile-apps-that-make-travel-easier/ (accessed March 28, 2015).

16 SITA, "2014 SITA Airline IT Trends Survey."

17 Ibid.

18 Rose, N. (2014) "API management: the key to improving the consumer travel experience," www.phocuswright.com/Free-Travel-Research/API-Management-The-Key-to-Improving-The-Consumer-Travel-Experience#.VVJEXmd0zIU (accessed February 12, 2015).

19 Alford Strategic Development (2010) "Appendix – Travel planning ideal for speech recognition" www.slideshare.net/fullscreen/JonathanAlford/jonathan-alford-googleita-software-voice-search-overview-v-public10nov10/11 (accessed March 28, 2015).

20 Rose, N. (2012) "Why voice interaction will change mobile travel", www.traveltechnology.com/2012/01/why-voice-interaction-will-change-mobile-travel/ (accessed March 28, 2015).

21 Prabu, K. (2014) "KLM to (kind of) allow flight payments via Twitter and Facebook," www.tnooz.com/article/klm-flight-payment-twitter-facebook/#sthash.QmxiaQDk.dpuf (accessed May 14, 2015).

22 Flynn, D. (2014) "Air New Zealand's new Boeing 787-9 inflight entertainment system," www.ausbt.com.au/air-new-zealand-s-new-boeing-787-9-inflight-entertainment-system (accessed December 13, 2015).

23 Econsultancy.com (2014) "How KLM nails social customer care," https://econsultancy.com/blog/64779-how-klm-nails-social-customer-care (accessed November 13, 2014)·

24 SITA (2014) "Airport IT Trends 2014," https://secure.sita.aero/globalassets/docs/surveys--reports/airport-it-trends-survey-2014.pdf (accessed June 2, 2015).

25 FutureTravelExperience.com (2015) "Emirates is latest carrier to unveil Apple Watch app," www.futuretravelexperience.com/2015/03/emirates-latest-carrier-unveil-apple-watch-app/ (accessed March 28, 2015).

26 Raymond Kollau (September 2015) "Air New Zealand to track unaccompanied minors via digital bracelet and mobile app," www.airlinetrends.com/category/airline-crew (accessed on October 1, 2015).

27 Small Business Labs (2015) "Smartwatches forecast to drive wearable computing market," www.smallbizlabs.com/2015/02/smartwatches-forecast-to-drive-wearable-computing-market.html (accessed March 28, 2015).

28 Dr4ward (2014) "What is the modern vitruvian man for all wearable technology?" http://www.dr4ward.com/dr4ward/2014/03/what-is-the-modern-vitruvian-man-for-all-wearable-technology-infographic.html (accessed April 2, 2015).

29 SITA (2015) "2015 SITA Airline IT Trends Survey."

30 Graser, M. (2015) "Qantas first airline to offer virtual reality headsets to passengers," http://variety.com/2015/digital/news/qantas-first-airline-to-offer-virtual-reality-headsets-to-passengers-120141836 (accessed March 28, 2015).

31 SITA, "2015 SITA Airline IT Trends Survey."

32 Ibid.

33 Japan Airlines (2015) "Japan Airlines," www.jal.com/ (accessed May 3, 2015).

34 Mayer-Schoönberger, V., and Cukier, K. (2013) *Big Data*. London: John Murray, p. 52.

35 SITA (2015), "2015 SITA Airline IT Trends Survey."

36 SITA (2014), "2014 SITA Airline IT Trends Survey".

37 Amadeus (2015) "New Amadeus technology helps Lufthansa to personalize travel experience of corporate customers" http://www.amadeus.com/web/amadeus/en_US-US/Amadeus-Home/News-and-events/News/02172015_New-Amadeus-tech-helps-Lufthansa-to-personalize-travel/1259071352352-Page-AMAD_DetailPpal?assetid=1319621166438&assettype=PressRelease_C (accessed March 28, 2015).

# Chapter 3

# Airline e-marketing

Half the money I spend on advertising is wasted; the trouble is I don't know which half.

John Wanamaker

## 3.1 INTRODUCTION

Communication lies at the core of interaction between an airline and its target audience. The communication can be verbal or non-verbal, frequent or sporadic, one-to-one or one-to-many, and its message can be brand or sales focused. Whatever the combination, communication is *the* crucial basis if an airline wants to be successful in cyberspace. This is where marketing or its internet based cousin—e-marketing—enters the picture. Marketing is generally concerned with the:

■ creation of new customers and the retention of existing customers
■ stimulation of revenue
■ development and maintenance of brand awareness.

The advent of the internet does not alter these principles but it adds a new, technology-based dimension. It allows an airline to be more customer-centric and efficient while travelers are given new and more power, influence, and choice. In our discussion of e-marketing, we focus on online advertising, promotion, and public relations as the principal communication venues. Their use aims at supporting an airline's corporate objectives such as satisfying web travelers' wants and needs and generating a reasonable profit.

## 3.2 THE RISE OF AIRLINE E-MARKETING

Using digital formats for communication in the market place is not any longer in an infant stage. When looking at online advertising specifically, it is over a decade old and the actual spending on it is impressive. For the first time in 2012, online advertising topped $100 billion worldwide. For 2015, estimates put this share at about $160 billion or almost 28% of total global media spending. This makes digital the second largest advertising format after TV.[1,2] Looking further ahead, online advertising in

2018 is expected to be $218 billion or 32% of total ad spending. This highlights the continuous shift from offline, in particular print, to online media.[3]

We can get a glimpse of the relative significance of online advertising in the travel industry when taking a look at the United States as the world's top spender on digital advertising and the single largest travel market. In 2015, the US travel industry estimated spending $4.8 billion on digital advertising, a figure expected to grow to $6.4 billion in 2018 (Figure 3.1).[4] The travel industry's share of total digital ad spending is approximately 8% throughout this timeframe. This puts travel as an industry category among the Top 10 spenders.

All of this is a remarkable development since it highlights the rising importance of online marketing. However, let us remind ourselves that there is significant variation among individual carriers. Some are known to spend 50% of their advertising budget on online media formats. LCCs generally allocate even more than that to online. Equally important to point out in this ongoing hype about e-marketing is that offline marketing is not dead. As we will learn soon, it actually plays a significant role for airline e-commerce.

With the arrival of the commercial internet, the airline industry also started to use digital media. Some of them have been around for over ten years now. Banners appeared first in 1994 and Google's Adwords for search engine marketing was launched in 2000. Of more recent origin are social advertising launched by Facebook in 2006 and mobile advertising going live in 2007 (see Figure 3.2).

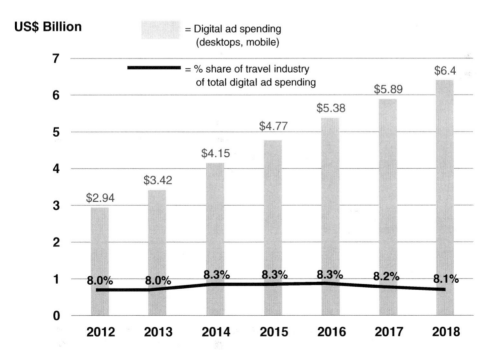

**Figure 3.1** *US travel industry digital ad spending, 2011–2017 ($billion, % share of travel industry)*

Source: eMarketer.com (2014)[5]

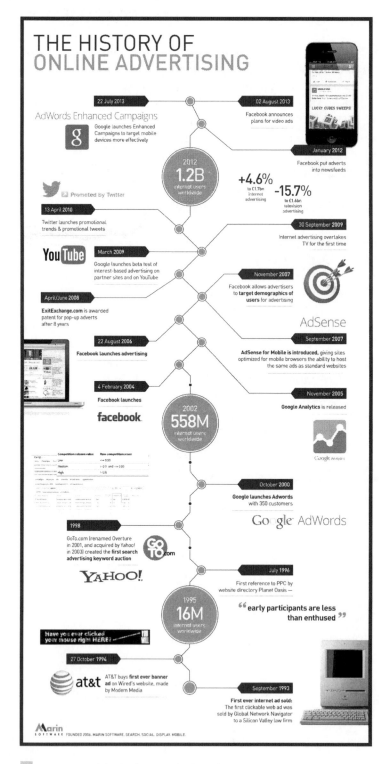

**Figure 3.2** *The development of online advertising: 1993–2013*

Source: marketingmag.com.au (2013)[6]

The bulk of the travel industry's digital advertising spending goes toward direct response advertising. This type of advertising is geared to trigger an immediate reaction by web travelers like purchasing a ticket as a result of a carrier's fare promotion. In 2014 in the United States, $3.1 billion or 74% of the total digital travel spending was allocated to it. Brand advertising is the other focus and accounted for $1.1 billion or 26%.[7]

## 3.3 WHY IS E-MARKETING SO ATTRACTIVE?

An obvious reason why airlines have adopted e-marketing is to be in sync with the digital uptake of their target audience. Travelers are known to be connected to internet devices more than the average consumer. Airlines need to be present where their customers are. Equally important is the fact that e-marketing has several inherent and powerful advantages over traditional marketing. They include:

- lower cost
- more accurate targeting
- multi-media possibilities and interactivity
- instant measurability of campaign results.

### 3.3.1 Lower cost

Digital media are significantly less expensive than their counterparts in the offline world. A common metric for comparing cost across different media formats is cpm (cost per mille or cost per thousand). Used for both traditional and digital advertising, it relates to the cost incurred for reaching a potential thousand customers who have been exposed to an ad. Depending on the data source, the answer differs but it is generally acknowledged that cpms for online media formats are substantially lower than for offline formats. Table 3.1 gives us some idea for selected media formats.

*Table 3.1* Advertising cost by media format (median values)

| Media format | Median cost per thousand (USD) |
|---|---|
| Newspapers | $32.5 |
| TV Spot (Prime Time) | $24.8 |
| Magazine | $14.0 |
| Radio | $13.5 |
| Digital Mobile Display | $3.0 |
| Digital Display | $1.9 |

*Source:* oaaa.org (2014)[8]

**65**

### 3.3.2 More accurate targeting

A key in making a marketing campaign successful is to narrow down the target audience so that only the segment receiving the marketing message ideally consists of strong buyers. Reaching out to customers based on their geographical location, demographics, and other behavioral variables including purchase history is nothing new. However, digital media allow for a high degree of targeting that is unprecedented.

Contextual advertising and 1:1 advertising are examples. Contextual advertising is involved when an ad is served to a specific individual visiting a website. A so-called contextual ad system scans the text of a website for certain keywords and sentences. It then returns ads to the web page based on what the user is viewing either through banner ads or ad words placed on the page. For example, if a web traveler is viewing a website about South Africa and the site uses contextual advertising, they may see an ad placement by South African Airways for relevant fares.

In regards to 1:1 advertising, in the past, an airline was faced with a trade-off dilemma between the number of people it could engage with (the so-called reach) and the amount of information it could tailor to a specific audience (the richness). When an airline wanted to communicate to a large audience, it usually chose print, TV, or radio. Doing so allowed for large reach but it sacrificed the degree of personalization of the message. However, if a tailor-made "rich" message was delivered to a specific customer, airlines could only communicate with a limited number of people because of the physical constraints of message delivery systems (branch offices and sales account executives) and costs.

With the commercial internet, however, such restrictions became history. Now, an airline is able to collect a variety of user data, craft 1:1 messages, and deliver them at little cost to a worldwide audience. Gone are the days of trading off between reach and richness (Figure 3.3).

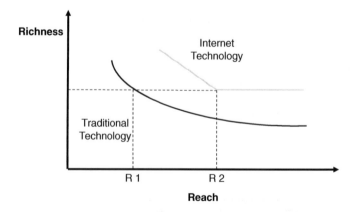

**Figure 3.3** *The changing trade-off between reach and richness*

*Source:* Evans and Wurster (1997)[9]

### 3.3.3 Multimedia possibilities

Unlike many offline media formats, online marketing can—and often does—combine different forms of content. The content may include text, audio, imagery, video, and also interactive elements. It is not uncommon to have all of them featured at the same time and this makes online marketing formats truly unique. Moreover, we should also highlight the ease of interaction with digital media. It allows web travelers to interact with the ad wherever and whenever they want it and spend as much time with it as they want.

### 3.3.4 Measurability

The value of traditional marketing is often unclear and reliable numbers are a challenge to obtain. In pre-internet days, an airline had a good idea about its total revenue production and total marketing expenditures. However, establishing a specific causality between certain revenue streams coming from particular market segments and certain offline media formats has always been difficult. One key reason has been the lack of appropriate tools. Customer surveys, market research, and brand studies could only provide for limited insight.

Enter the internet and the era of big data. E-tag-driven technology in online marketing lifts the cap on this limitation and provides new insights. For example, information on the audience's origin is now available. This is because of data that capture traffic sources—examples are third party websites, queries on search engines, social networks, e-mails, advertising campaigns—and geography by locating users through their IP address, mobile, and wearable device.

Additionally, we should mention the tracking of conversion data which allows the source of e-commerce revenue to be identified. It is possible now to establish a link between the cost of a particular marketing activity and the revenue it generates. Thus, an airline can distinguish low- from high-performing marketing campaigns. Figure 3.4 shows common marketing metrics used.

However, the insight is far from being perfect. Users are known to switch devices and browsers while e-tags such as cookies can be deleted or expire. The biggest obstacle in achieving a better understanding has to do with the controversial so-called last-click attribution. Accordingly, only the last online media format used by an individual is credited with the conversion to a sale. This view obviously ignores the whole journey of a web traveler that can involve several subsequent interactions—even offline—until a sale is scored (Figure 3.5).

Importantly, these journeys vary by travelers in different countries. For example, in Brazil, travelers generally take notice first of display ads, followed by social media, generic paid search, and brand paid search as further interactions. The last direct interaction before the purchase is often email. In Japan, the situation is different. There, travelers often interact first with a company's email while brand paid search is typically the last interaction before a booking. An airline that aims at effective marketing in cyberspace is required to not only acknowledge

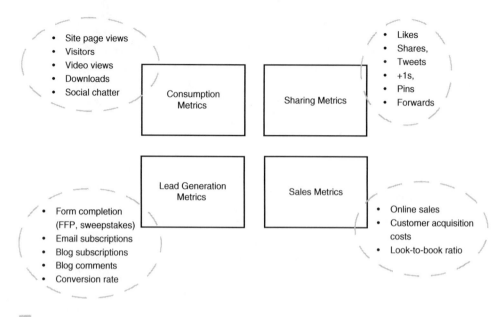

**Figure 3.4** *Popular metrics in e-marketing*

*Source:* Roberts and Zahay (2014)[10]

that various media influence a web traveler's purchase decision, but also to realize that the sequence by which these media are best deployed varies by travel market.

Unfortunately, it seems that many companies in the travel space do not work with this information. For example, in the United States, a whopping 35% of travel advertisers use the last-click model while other models that provide far more insight are not widespread. For instance the multi-device model tracking touch-points across multiple devices or the cross-channel model which measures the influence of both off- and online advertising are only used by 17% and 15%, respectively.[11] Given the lack of better insight, it is no surprise that 46% of travel advertisers struggle to decide in which online media formats to invest.[12] Unless travel companies including airlines improve their capabilities in this area, a proper assessment of an ad campaign's performance and its finetuning is still elusive. It seems that John Wanamaker's introductory quotation for this chapter still carries some weight today.

## 3.4 FIRST MARKETING PRINCIPLE: "KNOW YOUR CUSTOMER"

An airline that wants to be successful with its e-marketing efforts must acquire com-prehensive insight about web travelers. The better the insight, the more effective the targeting. Approaches based on geography and demographics have always been use-ful for airlines to understand their target audience better and craft marketing com-munication accordingly. Also popular is the segmentation of travelers by trip purpose (leisure, business, visiting friends and relatives) (Figure 3.6).

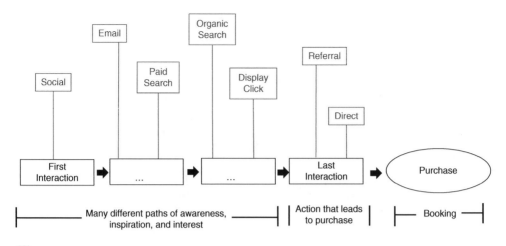

**Figure 3.5** *How do travelers get to travel decision-making?*

*Source:* Weps (2014)[13]

However, these standard ways of traveler segmentation fall short. They do not explicitly recognize the enormous role internet-based technology plays in today's marketplace. Therefore, what is required is the introduction of a digital dimension when dissecting and assessing the target audience. By digitally profiling travelers, an airline gains important insight and can address crucial questions:

■ What are the online access devices used by travelers: Desktop/laptop, mobile, wearable, virtual, Internet of Things?
■ What are the technology attitudes and behaviors travelers demonstrate?
■ What is the online media consumption in terms of where it takes place, its scope, frequency, and other factors?

A segmentation technique that captures this spectrum of digital aspects is referred to as "technographics." The technology and research company Forrester Research adopted it as a concept and introduced ten specific categories to describe certain types of digital consumers including web travelers (Figure 3.7).

For instance, one category of consumer is labelled "Hand Shakers." These are professionals with a somewhat negative attitude toward technology and who prefer face-to-face interactions with colleagues and clients. "Fast Forwards," however, are technology optimists and early adopters who try to use internet-based devices wherever they can in their workplace. Forrester expanded this concept later to mobile and social technographics. Digital consumer profiling with a technique such as technographics can make an airline's e-marketing initiatives more effective. Not doing so means sub-optimal campaign results and the waste of precious budgetary resources.

One area where many airlines still underperform has to do with e-marketing campaigns involving mobile devices. The issue specifically is the lack

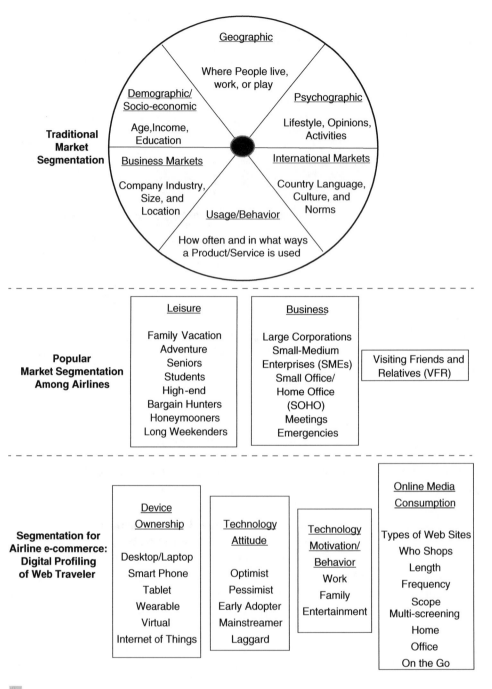

**Figure 3.6** *How to segment travelers?*

of communication optimized for mobile devices. Mobile web travelers accessing a carrier's email newsletter, Facebook account, or sponsored search ad are often directed to a desktop web page that is very difficult to use on a mobile device. Also,

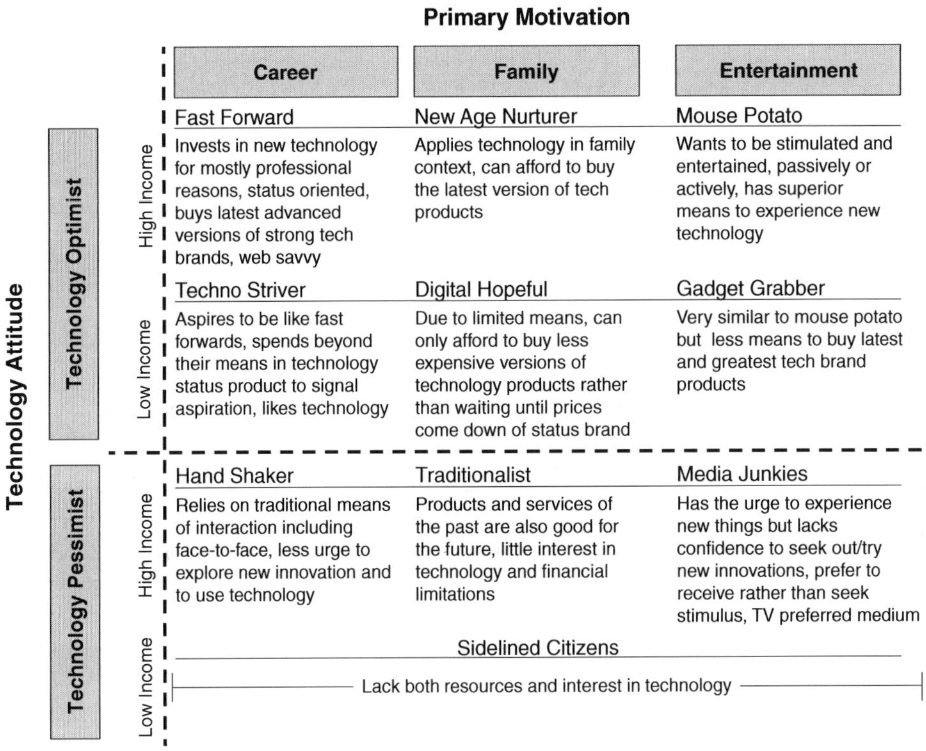

**Primary Motivation**

| | | Career | Family | Entertainment |
|---|---|---|---|---|
| Technology Optimist | High Income | **Fast Forward**<br>Invests in new technology for mostly professional reasons, status oriented, buys latest advanced versions of strong tech brands, web savvy | **New Age Nurturer**<br>Applies technology in family context, can afford to buy the latest version of tech products | **Mouse Potato**<br>Wants to be stimulated and entertained, passively or actively, has superior means to experience new technology |
| Technology Optimist | Low Income | **Techno Striver**<br>Aspires to be like fast forwards, spends beyond their means in technology status product to signal aspiration, likes technology | **Digital Hopeful**<br>Due to limited means, can only afford to buy less expensive versions of technology products rather than waiting until prices come down of status brand | **Gadget Grabber**<br>Very similar to mouse potato but less means to buy latest and greatest tech brand products |
| Technology Pessimist | High Income | **Hand Shaker**<br>Relies on traditional means of interaction including face-to-face, less urge to explore new innovation and to use technology | **Traditionalist**<br>Products and services of the past are also good for the future, little interest in technology and financial limitations | **Media Junkies**<br>Has the urge to experience new things but lacks confidence to seek out/try new innovations, prefer to receive rather than seek stimulus, TV preferred medium |
| Technology Pessimist | Low Income | **Sidelined Citizens** | | |
| | | — Lack both resources and interest in technology — | | |

*Technology Attitude* (left vertical axis)

**Figure 3.7** *Segmentation concepts for the digital world: Technographics*

Source: CatapultRPM (2012)[14]

many airlines still lump smart phones and tablets into a single category. This approach ignores that web travelers have actually a different information consumption on each.

Another area where airlines need to apply a more differentiated approach deals with the type of social media users. For instance, in Forrester social technographics terms, there are "Spectators" that consume social media content. They watch, listen, and read what is going. "Critics," however, are those that post ratings/reviews and contribute to blogs and forums while "Creators" produce their own content by uploading videos and publishing blogs. In particular the latter two categories often have significant influence in the social media sphere because of their popularity and large fan base. An airline that aims at effective social media marketing must find ways to leverage these types of users.

Digital profiling can be overlaid with other more traditional ways of market segmentation. An example of how this looks like is provided in Figure 3.8. It shows a demographics-based consumer segmentation with digital profiling highlights for each consumer generation.

Age and technology adoption are closely intertwined. As an individual gets older and settles in certain ways of doing things in life, their affinity to embrace

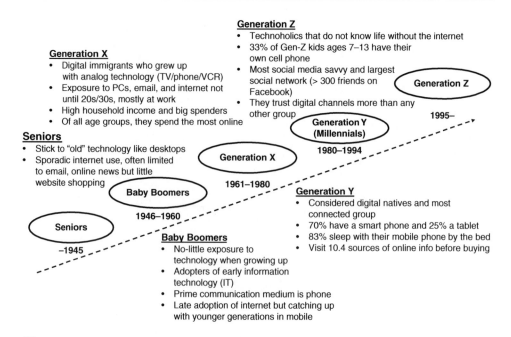

**Generation Z**
- Technoholics that do not know life without the internet
- 33% of Gen-Z kids ages 7–13 have their own cell phone
- Most social media savvy and largest social network (> 300 friends on Facebook)
- They trust digital channels more than any other group

**Generation X**
- Digital immigrants who grew up with analog technology (TV/phone/VCR)
- Exposure to PCs, email, and internet not until 20s/30s, mostly at work
- High household income and big spenders
- Of all age groups, they spend the most online

**Seniors**
- Stick to "old" technology like desktops
- Sporadic internet use, often limited to email, online news but little website shopping

**Baby Boomers**
- No-little exposure to technology when growing up
- Adopters of early information technology (IT)
- Prime communication medium is phone
- Late adoption of internet but catching up with younger generations in mobile

**Generation Y**
- Considered digital natives and most connected group
- 70% have a smart phone and 25% a tablet
- 83% sleep with their mobile phone by the bed
- Visit 10.4 sources of online info before buying

Generation Z — 1995–
Generation Y (Millennials) — 1980–1994
Generation X — 1961–1980
Baby Boomers — 1946–1960
Seniors — –1945

**Figure 3.8** *Changing demographics and the emergence of the "net" generation*

*Source:* news.yahoo.com (2013),[15] tommytoy.typepad.com (2013),[16] tourismintelligence.ca (2014),[17] bcgperspectives.com (2014),[18] Sverdlov (2012)[19]

new technology becomes less natural. Key reasons why people from their mid–late twenties onwards still adopt new tech devices are largely related to pressure at the workplace and from peers. An airline that targets consumers from multiple generations needs to take into consideration their overall digital profile. For example, persuading a pre-internet baby boomer to migrate from offline sales channels to one of the many digital platforms an airline operates requires a different approach than interacting with internet savvy web travelers from younger generations.

It is no accident that leading e-commerce airlines often feature "how to" tutorial content on their websites. This is generally geared toward pre-internet generations of travelers that appreciate demos of online products. They explain how to handle an online booking, a web check-in, or a mobile boarding pass. We cover this area in greater detail in Chapter 5.

## 3.5 THE RISE OF THE MILLENNIAL TRAVELER

If an airline wants to prioritize a single consumer generation, it should be Generation Y. The millennial generation is the future in the online travel space. The airline industry is currently driven by baby boomers' travel needs but this will change in the next five to ten years. This is the result of the millennial generation that will enter their peak earning, spending, and traveling years. Millennials personify the digital traveler like no other generation.

Relevant to appreciating this generation's behavior in the travel life cycle are the following:[20, 21]

- There are 80% who say travel reviews are important in their travel decisions.
- A total of 75% report having travel apps on their smartphones including those of traditional carriers such as American and Delta.
- Some 57% update social media every day while traveling.
- There are 32% who use smart phones for travel bookings while 20% use tablets for the same purpose.
- On business trips, once onboard, millennials are four times more likely than non-millennials to pay for wi-fi, twice as likely to watch downloads on their mobile devices, and 60% more likely to watch in-flight entertainment.
- Millennials are twice as likely as non-millennials to use their mobile phones to show travel pictures to friends, share travel photos on social media, blog or recount travel experiences online, and post travel reviews.
- Millennials also report doing more travel research and comparisons over the internet and making greater use of search engines for travel purposes.
- Millennials are more likely to broadcast negative experiences than positive ones.
- Millennials are less cautious than non-millennials about sharing personal information online, such as brand preferences, where they live, household composition, loyalty status and numbers, age and general personal information, frequent destinations, preferred airports, and personal hobbies.
- Gaming is highly popular among millennials and their desire to achieve and share achievement badges is more prominent that with non-millennial travelers.

An interesting phenomenon associated with millennials is the rise of the do-it-yourself (DIY) traveler. They are sometimes also referred to as the silent traveler. Due to the omni-presence of mobile devices and social media, DIY travelers can research and book online, check-in via mobile, self-check-in their luggage and fly without interacting with anyone. If issues arise, they turn to their mobile devices and social media first.

Take for instance the passenger on Turkish Airlines who while inflight complained about the cabin temperature. As opposed to talking to a flight attendant directly, the individual accessed Facebook through the airplane's wi-fi system and shared his issue with the airline and other social media users. Turkish Airlines replied in real-time and informed the captain of the flight to change the temperature. The flight attendant provided this update to the traveler who in turn left an enthusiastic review on Facebook.[22] A traveler from the baby boomer generation probably would have simply used the flight attendant call button, but many millennials are different. Appealing to this generation of travelers via mobile and social media is absolutely crucial.

Before entering our next section that introduces various media formats airlines deploy to communicate with web travelers, let us remember one aspect in closing. The essential factors that make a traveler choose to buy a ticket on one particular airline or not have not really changed. An airline that keeps on attracting business is the one that consistently delivers on its brand promise. However, the playing field has changed. From researching and booking a ticket online to checking in for a flight to using a mobile phone to tweeting about the inflight experience, the interfaces between a traveler and airline have become substantially digitized. For a four-day leisure trip, the average consumer spends 42 hours online—the equivalent of a full workweek—by dreaming about, researching, planning, and making reservations, and then sharing their experiences while they travel or when they get back home.[23] Therefore knowing the web traveler's digital environment and how the web traveler "ticks" digitally can translate into an enormous competitive advantage for an airline.

## 3.6 AIRLINE MARKETING COMMUNICATION WITH WEB TRAVELERS

### 3.6.1 Media channels

Airlines conduct marketing communication via owned, paid, and earned media channels:

- *Owned media.* These communication channels belong to the carrier. They are developed, updated, and optimized by the airline. In cyberspace, beyond their own website, airlines have constantly expanded their owned media. Mobile platforms and social media accounts are examples of recent additions. The more owned media channels an airline operates and the more attractive they are, the more opportunities exist to engage in direct communication with travelers.
- *Paid media.* The airline purchases the content (the "what"), space (the "where"), and timing (the "when") on third party properties. Adword placements with search engine providers are a digital example, a TV ad or radio broadcast are offline examples. For their planning and execution, paid media communication generally involves the support of digital media agencies. Paid media is not obsolescent but under increasing pressure due to high cost and declining response rates by customers. However, paid media generally works as an important accelerant for marketing communication through owned and earned media. Without it, communication with and by web travelers would be rather silent.
- *Earned media.* Earned media is the result of behavior by the airline. Earned media is not owned or paid for. The web traveler is the channel and the airline has no control over the communication. Social media are a key venue in this. Earned media essentially involve word-of-mouth marketing and web travelers play a huge role in spreading communication further. An airline should focus a significant part of its time and energy on this area because communication through earned media is more authentic and more amplified than via owned or paid media.

Each of these media channels has a number of benefits and challenges that an airline must be aware of (Figure 3.9). At the same time, it is important to recognize the interconnectedness among them. They all influence each other and arguably

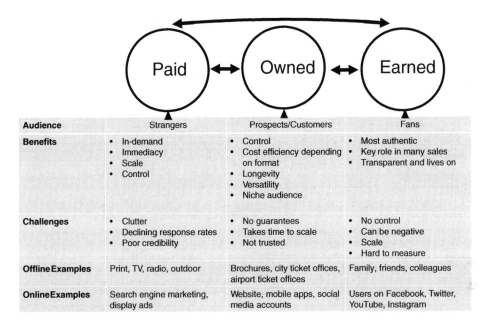

| Audience | Strangers | Prospects/Customers | Fans |
|---|---|---|---|
| **Benefits** | • In-demand<br>• Immediacy<br>• Scale<br>• Control | • Control<br>• Cost efficiency depending on format<br>• Longevity<br>• Versatility<br>• Niche audience | • Most authentic<br>• Key role in many sales<br>• Transparent and lives on |
| **Challenges** | • Clutter<br>• Declining response rates<br>• Poor credibility | • No guarantees<br>• Takes time to scale<br>• Not trusted | • No control<br>• Can be negative<br>• Scale<br>• Hard to measure |
| **Offline Examples** | Print, TV, radio, outdoor | Brochures, city ticket offices, airport ticket offices | Family, friends, colleagues |
| **Online Examples** | Search engine marketing, display ads | Website, mobile apps, social media accounts | Users on Facebook, Twitter, YouTube, Instagram |

***Figure 3.9*** *Types of marketing channels used by airlines*

*Source:* Based on Corcoran (2009)[24]

need each other. Therefore it should not come as a surprise that the differences between paid, earned, and owned media have become increasingly blurred in recent years.

For instance, an airline could distribute a special fare promotion on owned media such as its Twitter account. JetBlue is well known as a social media savvy airline that frequently uses this type of media format. However, what happens when web travelers re-tweet this promotion to other people? In this case, owned media transforms into earned media. Likewise, a growing number of carriers place paid content on social media platforms that are traditionally more associated with earned media.

### 3.6.2 Media formats

The spectrum of media formats airlines commonly use today for marketing communication is wide and fragmented. We find numerous traditional offline and new online formats. Print and radio have been around since the early days of air transportation. Others including mobile and social are of more recent origin. Furthermore, as new e-commerce platforms in the form of wearable computing and virtual reality are emerging, we will see fresh media formats that may be used for marketing communication (Figure 3.10).

There is a shift to digital formats but traditional media are here to stay—at least for a while. Looking back over the last 80+ years, newly introduced communication mediums have never fully replaced existing ones. The radio, once predicted to be replaced by the TV, is still around. The TV is still here despite the internet. Desktops

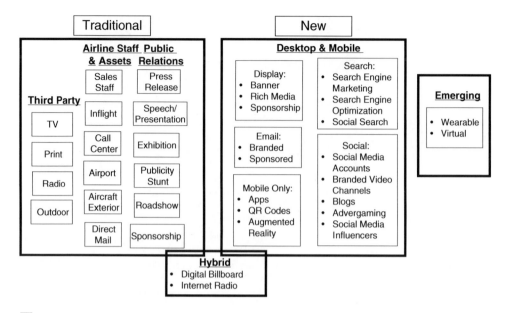

**Figure 3.10** *Traditional and new communication media formats in airline marketing*

have not been fully substituted by mobile devices. In other words, there will be more fragmentation ahead.

Managing its brand across this diverse landscape with so many formats in a consistent, integrated, and speedy manner is a challenge for any airline. Our following section provides for insight into these formats and how airlines can use them for the benefit of their e-commerce activities. Discussed are some best practices and showcased are numerous carriers that have managed this challenge well.

## 3.7 TRADITIONAL MEDIA DEPLOYED IN AIRLINE E-MARKETING

### 3.7.1 TV advertising

The TV was introduced in the late 1940s and has quickly become a source of news, information, and entertainment. The world's first official, paid television advertisement was broadcast in the United States on July 1, 1941, over a New York station before a baseball game between the Brooklyn Dodgers and Philadelphia Phillies and involved an announcement for Bulova watches.[25] Today, it is the single largest media format in the world accounting for around $200 billion or over 40% of global media spending.[26]

TV carries great appeal due to its combination of sight, sound, motion, and mass audience reach. Nevertheless, it faces several challenges. It continues losing attraction with the younger demographic that increasingly prefers the interaction with digital media. In 2014, Americans aged 18 to 24 watched TV for four hours less every week than in 2013 (from 22.5 hours per week to 18.5 hours).[27] At the same time, more traditional TV content is available online while digital

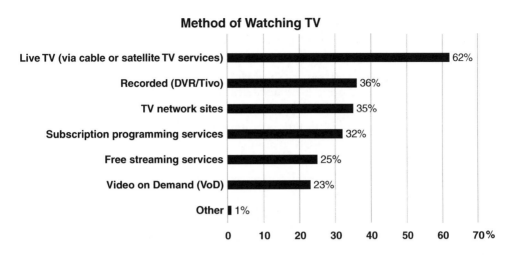

**Method of Watching TV**

**Figure 3.11** *1 in 3 travelers watch their favorite programs outside of live TV*

Source: Google (2014)[28]

video recorders (DVRs) and video-on-demand (VOD) have also shifted habits toward ad avoidance. Travelers are part of this overall trend. Many of them watch live TV but have started to interact with other TV-related formats (Figure 3.11).

TV advertising is very expensive and its cpm is significantly higher than that for other media formats. Cable TV, unlike its broadcast counterpart, has fared better although it faces a similar challenge when it comes to appealing to younger viewers. Nevertheless, from humble beginnings in the 1980s, it boasts large penetration rates today. In the United States, for example, over 90% of all households have it.[29] The average cable home has access to over 120 channels with nearly 3,000 programs available each week.[30] Equally important, its cpm is lower than those of broadcast TV. This makes it much more affordable to companies that want to air their ads on local cable TV services. The downsides include its smaller audience reach, its higher fragmentation, and the higher number of commercials per hour.

Airlines have a long history with TV commercials that first appeared in larger numbers in the 1950s and 1960s. The themes initially focused on history and safety but over time changed and emphasized aircraft types and fleet size, speed, network coverage, and inflight service. With the launch of airlines' first websites in the late 1990s, digital brands found their ways into TV ads as well. Airlines often feature their website domain name at the end of an ad. Illustrative examples are TWA's vintage TV commercial from 2000[31] and Southwest Airlines' TV commercial from 2012 and 2013 always signed off with a prominent display of www.southwest.com.[32] Another common tactic is to have the voiceover ad narrator call out the website address with an action item such as "Go to airline.com for more details." This also helps increase awareness for an airline's digital brand, TV's primary ad objective.

There are also TV commercials where the airline website or related online features are actually the main story. British Airways' 40-second TV ad "Have you clicked yet?" from 2005 is an example where numerous benefits for web travelers are high-lighted when using ba.com. These included at the time online check-in, seat selection, and booking change. Others were the ability to book ancillary travel such as hotel and rental car while the low fare guarantee was also emphasized.[33] Another example of a digital brand ad is Air France's one-minute TV commercial from 2014 "Your trip at your finger tips." It introduced the company's mobile features such as online fare shopping, check-in, and boarding pass.[34] In Spring 2015, UK LCC easyJet spent £2 million on two TV commercials, one showcasing its mobile boarding technology.

Overall, TV advertising has been remarkably resilient over the years. It looks like any significant changes in how TV is used for advertising are neither imminent nor large scale. Data on how much airlines invest in this media format are not publicly available. However, considering its high cost, airlines are not very active with this format. OTAs actually dominate the travel spending on TV. For example, in the United States in 2014, $624 million was invested by travel brands but the Top 10 spenders were all OTAs (Delta Vacation was actually on rank 10 with $2.3 million).[35]

Occasionally, of course, there is a carrier that goes full force with TV advertising. An example is Etihad Airways with its "Reimagined Flying" campaign from March 2015. With the objective of strengthening its global brand recognition, the carrier decided to hire actress Nicole Kidman as the airline's new brand ambassador. In the TV commercial, aired in 12 major markets around the world, she showcased "The Residence, a first-class three-bedroom suite on the company's flagship Airbus A380". Areas where the company expected a concrete return on what it called a "sensible investment" included uptakes in social media traffic and increased website sales.[36] Initial results were encouraging: Within two days of the release, the TV commercial already garnered close to 360,000 views on YouTube. Not to be left behind in such global advertising brand push, Emirates followed suit and announced a $20 million TV and digital channel campaign starring Jennifer Aniston in August 2015. The first commercial aired on October 5, 2015, and within 24 hours attracted over 450,000 views on YouTube and close to 1.2 million views on Facebook.

### 3.7.2 Developments in TV advertising to watch out for

One key development is related to the emergence of "social TV." It involves second screen usage by viewers who watch TV and are plugged into their mobile devices at the same time. Gone are the days when "social TV" meant younger generations shared the living room with their parents and had to agree what to watch and sat in front of a big and non-mobile TV. Change in consumers' TV viewing behavior today means simultaneous interaction with multiple screens including TV. In the United States, for instance, 75% of smart phone and tablet users are engaging with second screen content more than once a month as they watch TV. About half of those people are engaged with second screen content daily—that is about 50 million people.[37]

This development has picked up since Twitter introduced in 2013 conversation targeting and TV advertising capabilities. This was specifically created to meet the needs of TV advertisers and broaden the reach and power of their ads.[38] A travel industry example comes from Expedia's TV 2013 campaign "Find Your Spontaneity" that promoted mobile booking via its travel application with a television ad campaign and sweepstakes giving anyone who downloads the app that same day a chance to win a free trip.[39]

The future of TV advertising is intertwined with how the medium itself and consumer preferences change. This is clearly illustrated when we look at the other kind of social TV—TV viewing on social networks. If one website has come to define this trend, it is YouTube. It is the world's most famous and largest video-sharing site that was founded in 2005 and is today owned by Google. For many younger generations, TV means YouTube. The irony is that while TV viewers will skip commercials, they will go out of their way to seek inane YouTube clips. The popularity and ongoing growth of YouTube indicates that traditional TV networks may not be needed any longer as they used to. Figure 3.12 shows that the most popular channels watched on YouTube. They cater undoubtedly to more niche audiences and thus keep the risk of annoying a primetime audience low. However, they can certainly also attract million-strong audiences.

Another development is the growing presence of smart TVs that are connected to the internet, also referred to as interactive TV or ITV, this is a form of TV viewing that airline marketers should pay attention to because it is a platform that allows precise targeting and measurability. Unlike traditional TV advertising that is a mass medium with minimal feedback on how it actually performs, ITV involves so-called addressable advertising. Addressable advertising provides marketers with targeting that is better attuned to individual households. Furthermore, the interactive component that is part of digitally delivered ads allows advertisers to view in real time whether ads are being viewed, clicked, and accessed. It is also possible to change ads on the spot depending on the success of an ongoing campaign. In short, ITV provides a better way to reach the right audience, and gives a whole new view of advertising performance.[40]

American Airlines, in the wake of an interactive banner ad campaign called "The New American," used ITV ads in the UK. It claims to have achieved significantly higher brand favorability and purchase intent rates than in instances where such exposure to TV viewers did not take place.[41]

### 3.7.3 Radio advertising

Radio is the original mass medium and advertising via this format started in the 1920s. Radio is always on and its reach crosses demographics, ethnicities, and geographies. Over 90% of people in the United States are reached via the 16,000 radio stations with audio listening amounting to 2.5 hours per day.[42]

Although the medium is restricted to audio, it carries some attraction with advertisers including airlines. Airlines generally purchase airtime from a station or network

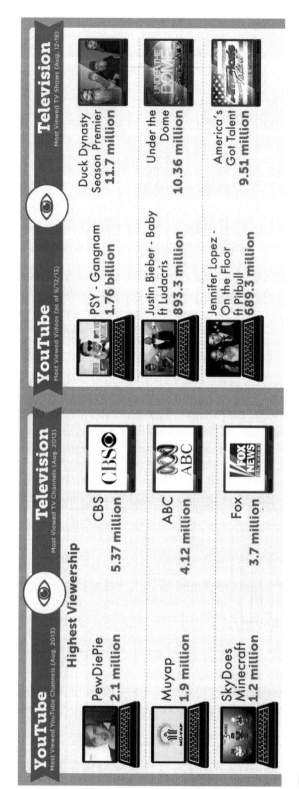

**Figure 3.12** *YouTube vs TV: Viewership of Top 3 channels and shows*

Source: Kelly (2013)[43]

in exchange for broadcasting their commercials. Typical are 60 second-long spots, although smaller intervals like 30 seconds are also used. Content of these radio commercials typically involves a type of fare promotion, although brand-focused messages occasionally are also broadcast. An example for the latter is Ethiopian Airlines' 30-second radio commercial on South African station 5FM highlighting the carrier's route network to Asia (their radio advert can be checked out on YouTube).[44] In an attempt to drive listeners to the branded airline website, it is common to conclude the broadcast with a reference to the respective website address. In Ethiopian Airlines' case, it was flyethiopianairline.co.za.

Besides buying airtime for commercials, airlines also advertise on radios by becoming a sponsor for individual programs. In this case, there is a brief mention of the carrier's name at the beginning and end of the show. An example of this arrangement is American Airlines and Chicago-based Jazz station WNUA 95.5. As part of its Trip-A-Day giveaway promotion that ran for over 10 years since 1997, American Airlines was featured daily on the show with its website address also mentioned. Observers stated that this was one of the most enduring contests in the history of radio with more than 5,500 listeners having won a chance to fly on the carrier's network.[45]

Looking ahead, however, the future for radio as an advertising format, particularly in its terrestrial form, is cloudy. In the United States, for instance, it claims an 8.9% share of the total ad spend in 2014. This number is expected to gently decline to 7.1% in 2018[46] largely as a result of the ad spending shifting toward digital media. Major arguments against radio advertising are its limitations in terms of personalization, trackability, measurability, and interactivity. These are all traits that advertisers have come to expect in today's digital age.

In this regard, the emergence of internet radio is worth mentioning as it addresses these issues. As of March 2014, in the United States, internet radio accounts for almost 10% of the total radio market.[47] The top player is Pandora Internet Radio or simply Pandora, founded in 2000 and currently available in Australia, New Zealand, and the United States. It holds a 70% share of the internet radio market and boasts over 250 million users of which 77 million are active listeners.[48] Its service plays songs based on the online user's artist selection. The listener provides for positive and negative feedback on the songs and future song selections are offered accordingly.

Pandora's advertising pitch for audio advertising and website banner placements is simple. It claims to be able to micro-target consumers by accounting for their postal code, age, and gender, to mention a few factors.[49] Airlines that have signed up with Pandora as local advertisers include Alaska Airlines and Virgin America.[50] Evidence shows that internet radio can increase the effectiveness of online advertising as consumer recalls of online ad placements by an advertiser on a website are higher when done in combination with online radio ads (Figure 3.13).

Other internet radio companies offering a personalized listening experience include Spotify, a European online streaming music service, and US-based iHeart Radio. One has to see how much market share these companies capture from terrestrial radio in the future but it seems reasonable to state that radio advertising overall is going to remain a niche format.

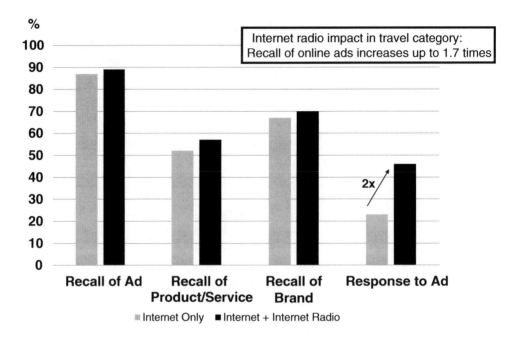

**Figure 3.13** *Cross-media consumer advertising: Recall with and without internet radio advertising*

*Source:* targetspot.com (2011)[51]

### 3.7.4 Print advertising

Print advertising has a long history with the airline industry and goes back to the 1920s when airline branded print ads first began to appear. Figure 3.14 illustrates some early examples.

The principal forms of print advertising that airlines apply today include:

- newspapers
- magazines
- trade journals
- direct mail
- brochures/leaflets.

As far as newspapers, magazines, and trade journals are concerned, the scope for each of these varies. It can be broad with readership bases on a national and international level for major titles or rather narrow when using local publications and trade journals covering very specialized topics. Audiences in relevant business print publications including the *Financial Times* and *The Economist* are carefully targeted for trumpeting an airline's business and first-class convenience features via brand ads. Fare promotion and even destination ads are more common in mainstream newspapers. Despite an overall shift to digital media in recent years, print advertising is still a sizeable component in most carriers' marketing portfolio.

**KLM Poster (1925)**

**TWA Magazine Ad (1946)**

**Eastern Airlines
Classified Ad (1952)**

**Figure 3.14** *Early print advertising by airlines*

*Source:* thedesignair.net (2012),[52] reminisce.com (2014)[53]

For example, when United launched its web presence in markets outside the United States, it deployed plenty of print media to drive up awareness for its new digital brand. In the UK, daily newspapers including the *Daily Telegraph* and *Financial Times* were used in addition to magazines such as *The Economist* and *New Scientist*. Clearly, there was a correlation between beating the advertising drum and the increase in online bookings on the new local UK website (Figure 3.15). Of course, there are those LCCs that largely shun print advertising. Take LCC Tiger Airways as an example that almost spends nothing on print and instead prefers investing in social advertising.[54]

For most airlines, however, print advertising continues playing a role. Of all print media, direct mail is the one that allows an airline to deliver the most personalized message. Airlines often use direct mail for communication to retain or reward their frequent flyers, although it is occasionally also used to recruit new customers. It can

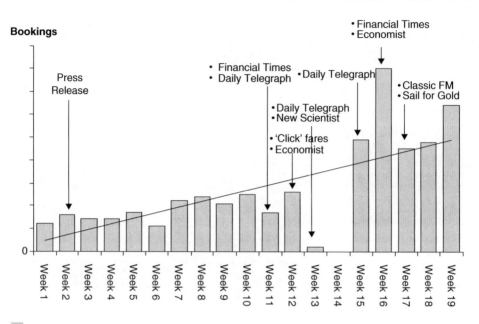

**Figure 3.15** *Online booking development on unitedairlines.co.uk\**

\* There were no online bookings due to a United Airlines' pilot strike in week 14.

*Source:* Author analysis[55]

be argued that direct mail takes an airline's message one step further and involves an individual more than other forms of media. Some studies show that despite a more digitally focused world, there are consumers that still have a preference for traditional marketing communication such as direct mail. Reasons include direct mail's portability (one can read it now, later, or pass it along to others) while consumer trust for the postal channels also appears to be higher than for email or social media.[56]

Airline print advertising today typically features the carrier's website address. It does not matter what the specific marketing message is, the website brand's domain name is also displayed. Some airlines produce print ads and leaflets specifically advertising their website and promoting the benefits of going online. Figure 3.16 shows an example of Air China's print advertising campaign to promote its digital brand.

In recent years, airlines have been focusing on raising awareness for their new mobile products. An example of a print ad showcasing a mobile website is EgyptAir (Figure 3.17).

Other than airline print ads featuring a website address or dedicating the ad message to the carrier's digital products, does print do anything else in cyberspace? The answer is yes. Print has also gone digital in the sense that it allows a new interactivity with an individual via mobile devices that has not existed before. Two areas are worth mentioning: Quick Response (QR) codes and Augmented Reality advertising also referred to as ARvertising. Both are discussed in greater detail in section 3.17 on mobile advertising.

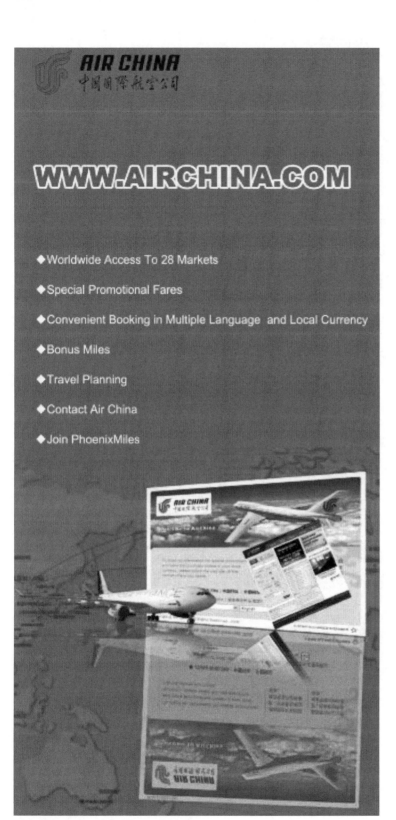

**Figure 3.16** *Airport/inflight brochureware promoting airchina.com*

*Source:* Air China (2008)[57] with kind permission of Air China

**Figure 3.17** *Print Ads by Egyptair promoting its mobile service*

*Source:* deviantart.com (2010)[58] with kind permission of Egyptair

*Figure 3.18* Swissair outdoor advertising: Agricultural creative

*Source:* Swartzonmedia (2008)[59] with kind permission of Swiss International Air Lines

### 3.7.5 Outdoor advertising

Any advertising done outdoors that publicizes a company's products and services is considered outdoor advertising. It is a widespread practice among airlines to place outdoor ads near and on the way to airports. Billboards and the exterior of brick-and-mortar locations are common, although transit media placements involving the interiors and exteriors of buses, taxis, and business vehicles are also popular. The idea is to expose the airline brand on the routes taken by travelers whenever going to or coming from an airport.

Airlines use outdoor advertising also to promote their digital brands. An interesting example involves Swiss International Air Lines. They designed a landscape to draw attention to www.swissair.com (this is now www.swiss.com). This agricultural advertisement (Figure 3.18) could be seen in its entirety from the air on approach to or after take-off from Zurich Airport. Because of its originality, it is certain that the ad generated some viral buzz.

Outdoor advertising can also be literally connected to cyberspace. British Airways garnered much attention with its 2013 digital billboard campaign called "Look Up." The digital billboards showed a young boy or girl pointing to the sky. Following the path of the finger, one would see an actual BA airplane above. The billboard updated in real time and displayed the flight number and origin. In Figure 3.19, the flight involved was BA 431 arriving from Amsterdam. BA used three locations in London whose positions allowed a juxtaposition with BA airplanes upon landing at Heathrow.[60]

**Figure 3.19** *British Airways' digital billboard "Look Up" campaign*

*Source:* Blogspot.com (2014)[61] with kind permission of British Airways

The selling point of digital billboards is their interactivity with the environment. In BA's case, it involved airplanes in the sky. BA's campaign played on the theme that people often wonder where planes are going to or coming from, thus thinking about a different place or even daydreaming about a vacation. The billboard uses custom-built surveillance technology to answer that question and thereby managed to engage people.[62]

When looking at some interactive outdoor campaigns of other organizations and companies, we obtain a glimpse of things that may also be used by airlines in the future. Take for example the outdoor campaign "Because I am a girl" by British charity organization Plan UK. They used bus shelters ads in London that detected the gender of people and targeted different messages at women and men. For instance, female viewers saw a short video while men were shown some statistics.[63] In another digital billboard campaign by UK retailer Marks & Spencer for Valentine's Day, augmented reality was used. The billboard featuring an attractive model encouraged people to download an app and point their mobile device to the billboard. The model would spring to life and the billboard would transform into a live fashion show of M&S's selections of Valentine's Day delicates.[64]

An outdoor campaign can involve traditional formats like static billboards but still create buzz in cyberspace. In August 2014, Emirates took down a huge 208 square meter outdoor banner it had displayed at Zurich Airport and repurposed it into 300 reusable shopping bags. This was captured on YouTube and Twitter to demonstrate the company's innovation in the area of recycling.[65]

Our discussion on outdoor advertising will not be complete without mentioning the "flying billboard": The aircraft itself and specifically its fuselage. The uptake in the airline industry, particularly among legacy carriers, to paint anything except for their brand name on the airplane has been slow. There are exceptions to this. Take the Pepsi Concorde from 1996 when an Air France Concorde was painted in Pepsi's brand colors and flew around the world to boost the soda maker's brand image.[66]

In the context of digital brand promotion, the question is whether an aircraft fuselage may be used to feature an airline's website domain name. This kind of exposure helps increase awareness for a carrier's digital brand. Interestingly, there are many carriers that still do not do this. In particular, legacy airlines often mention concerns over diluting their traditional brand or fear of alienating their traditional travel agency partners.

However, as online shopping is becoming more and more a mainstream activity, this concern appears to be waning. Accordingly, some of these airlines have started to feature their website domain (Figure 3.20). LCCs, as part of their internet-based sales and distribution business model, are generally much more aggressive and show off their domain names rather boldly. Paradoxically, some of them are so synonymous with their presence in cyberspace that they do not need to promote their digital brand this way.

**Figure 3.20** *Website domains on aircraft*

With kind permission of airBerlin, Emirates, Lufthansa, and Wizz

### 3.7.6 Airline staff and airline media assets

Airlines own a variety of traditional media that existed long before the advent of e-commerce in the mid-1990s. Since the launch of the first airline websites, carriers have sought to utilize their own media assets to promote their digital brand with the traveling public. Table 3.2 gives more detail of these main assets and how they can be purposed.

Fully utilizing traditional media assets for the purpose of increasing the traveling public's awareness of a carrier's digital brand requires some internal "heavy lifting" at an airline. Specifically, the organizational entity in charge of running the airline's e-commerce activities needs to collaborate closely with other departments. It is not uncommon to start this cross-departmental approach with some form of internal education in order to ensure that other corporate stakeholders fully understand and appreciate the value of e-commerce. This approach helps turn other departments over time into important contributors and owners of the digital brand.

### 3.7.7 Public relations

The traditional formats used for public relations (or PR in short) are manifold. They include press releases/conferences, speeches, and seminars. Furthermore, exhibitions, roadshows, sponsorships, and publicity stunts are also covered by PR. As a reminder, PR falls into the category of earned media. This means that an organization engaging in PR has no control over the information once released to the public. Most airlines employ a PR agency that assists them in the management of public relations.

*Table 3.2* *Staff and airline media assets*

| Staff/Media asset | Ways to grow awareness for digital brand |
|---|---|
| Frontline staff | ■ Website address on business card<br>■ Website address in email sign-off stamp<br>■ Word of mouth<br>■ Handing out of website branded brochures/leaflets<br>■ Personal demonstrations |
| Call center | ■ Taped welcome greetings with reference to website address<br>■ On-hold/after-hour messages referring to website and its benefits<br>■ Call center agent conversational script to include website address |
| Inflight | ■ Inflight announcements after take-off/before landing referring to website address<br>■ Ambient media (napkins, coasters, seat covers, cups, meal tray cards) branded with website address<br>■ Inflight magazine feature articles and ads promoting airline website<br>■ Special feature before inflight movie program |
| Airport | ■ Check-in counter TV monitors featuring website address<br>■ Ticket wallets and lounge invitations branded with website address<br>■ Lounge PCs featuring website address as screensaver<br>■ Display banners and posters in terminal promoting airline website |

Table 3.3 illustrates the various forms of PR and how they are often used to promote the airline's digital brand.

One popular PR event that is exclusively dedicated to the internet is the Webby Awards. Founded in 1995, it awards webbies for excellence on the internet. The award is also referred to as the Oscar of the internet. The ceremony is hosted annually by the International Academy of Digital Arts and Sciences in New York. Among

**Table 3.3** *Supporting a carrier's digital brand with PR*

| PR format | What it is | How it can be used |
|---|---|---|
| Press release | Invented in 1906 in the United States, a press release is an announcement to the news media with the objective of sharing information with the public. An airline could either self-publish by creating the content itself and being responsible for the distribution via email and other web venues. Alternatively, a hired PR agency is in charge of writing the press release and sharing it with news wires and journalists. | ■ Publicize new e-commerce products and services. In recent years, common were announcements covering the launch of new mobile services and social media platforms.<br>■ Alert the traveling public to special promotions, competitions and prizes, and milestone achievements related to e-commerce. |
| Executive speeches and presentations | Formal address delivered by airline senior executives to a particular target audience. Typical venues include conferences, chambers of commerce, and industry bodies. | ■ Provide for details on an airline's e-commerce strategy and/or share certain corporate positions and viewpoints.<br>■ Similar to press releases, announce imminent product and service introductions. |
| Exhibitions | Public display of products/services during trade fairs. ITB Berlin and WTM London are examples although other public venues like airport galleries are also used. Beneficial for face-to-face interactions. | ■ Demonstrate in person actual use of airline e-commerce products and services to traveling public.<br>■ Hand out of brochureware informing about carrier's digital brand. |
| Roadshow | A touring show by company officials who visit different geographic locations and meet with partners and customers to promote a product and service/garner support for them. | ■ Promoting airlines' digital brand as part of an overall company roadshow.<br>■ Similar to exhibitions, opportunity for actual use demonstration of online products and services to end users. |
| Publicity stunt | A staged and unusual event meant to gain public attention for a company, product/service or cause. Since the company drives the stunt, it is an attempt to control what the media end up reporting. | ■ Typically inexpensive way of drawing attention to airline's digital brand. |
| Sponsorship | In return for brand exposure via traditional and online media formats, a company offers financial support to other organizations. Sports sponsorships are most common (Figure 3.21). Other areas of sponsorship include the arts and charity. | ■ When used in conjunction with airline's web address displayed on media formats, awareness for digital brand is created and increased.<br>■ Leverages airlines' digital brand due to association with sponsored organizations. |

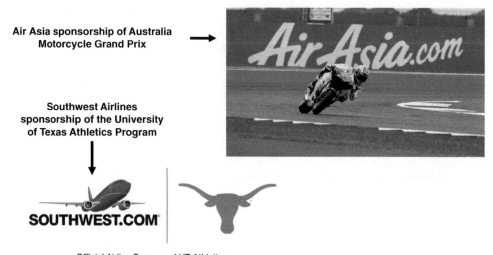

**Air Asia sponsorship of Australia Motorcycle Grand Prix**

**Southwest Airlines sponsorship of the University of Texas Athletics Program**

SOUTHWEST.COM

Official Airline Sponsor of UT Athletics

**Figure 3.21** *Public relations formats to promote airline digital brands: Sports sponsorships by Southwest Airlines and Air Asia*

With kind permission of AirAsia and Southwest Airlines

the categories are also websites and mobiles. Past winner airlines include KLM, which won in 2014 for its social customer care program, and United Airlines for its newly designed mobile website and app in 2015.

## 3.8 DIGITAL MEDIA DEPLOYED IN AIRLINE E-MARKETING

### 3.8.1 Search marketing

General search engines including Google, Yahoo!, and Bing have become important gateways to cyberspace. Some commentators even refer to them as the "Hubble of the internet galaxy that enables online users to navigate through this space and find the information they are looking for."[67] Any airline that looks into leveraging this form of digital advertising successfully needs to have a good understanding of how search engines work and what specific role they play for web travelers.

In our discussion of airline e-commerce, we consider search marketing as the process of gaining traffic to and visibility of an airline's digital properties from search engines. The goals of search marketing are to reinforce a carrier's digital brand and support direct online sales with web travelers. This is accomplished through both paid efforts (also referred to as "sponsored" or "biased" search) and unpaid efforts ("natural," "unbiased," and "organic" are frequent labels as well). Specifically, search marketing covers two key areas:

■ Search engine marketing (SEM) which attracts online traffic to an airline's digital properties through paid search results.
■ Search engine optimization (SEO) which earns an airline online traffic via unpaid search results.

Search marketing, in particular SEM, is the most important digital media format for airlines. Search marketing receives most of an airline's digital marketing budget—and for good reasons. Search is what most of online users do as part of their navigation in cyberspace. It has been one of the top activities on the internet for years (the other one is reading email) and it is likely to retain this status for years to come. In the United States, for instance, over 90% of the online population uses search throughout any given day.[68]

For web travelers, even the ones that are relatively loyal to particular airline digital brands, search engines are an indispensable tools to manage their online travel activities. Leisure travelers and business travelers differ slightly in their prioritization but both value search engines highly. For 60% of leisure travelers, it is the top online source used for travel planning. In the case of business travelers, 55% see it as a top source (Figure 3.22).

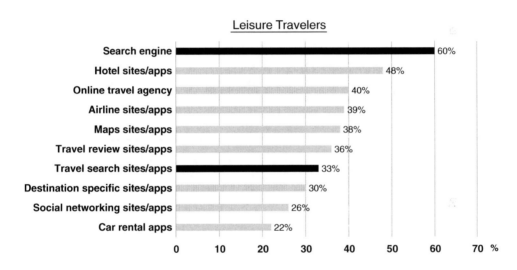

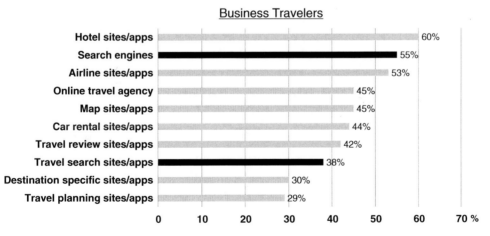

*Figure 3.22* Search engines are among the most popular online planning sources for travelers

Source: Google (2014)[69]

Common reasons for web travelers to use search engines include:

- obtaining information about destinations;
- seeing if special offers or promotions are available;
- finding out about fare rates;
- learning which airline serves a particular market;
- finding picture about a destination;
- learning of other travelers' experiences.

The importance of search engines is also reflected in the significant amount of traffic that flows from them to airline websites. Table 3.4 shows a snapshot for the month of November 2014 for ten airlines operating a website in the United States. The number one source of website traffic by far to any of these carriers' website in all cases is a search engine. Google to be exact. Google's traffic share can be as high as 46% as in Virgin Atlantic's case and still claims over a quarter of Virgin America's at the low end. For most carriers' websites in this sample, the Top 2 website traffic source is also a search engine—Bing, although a distant second in single digits. If on average a third of an airline's web traffic originates from a search engine, it is

**Table 3.4** *Top 2 websites visited before the airline website*

| Airline | Airline website | Top 2 websites | Traffic share of top 2 websites |
|---------|-----------------|----------------|----------------------------------|
| Virgin Atlantic | www.virgin–atlantic.com | ■ Google<br>■ Delta | ■ 46%<br>■ 4% |
| Jetblue | www.jetblue.com | ■ Google<br>■ Bing | ■ 34%<br>■ 5% |
| Frontier Airlines | www.flyfrontier.com | ■ Google<br>■ Bing | ■ 33%<br>■ 6% |
| Delta Airlines | www.delta.com | ■ Google<br>■ Gmail | ■ 31%<br>■ 5% |
| American Airlines | www.aa.com | ■ Google<br>■ Bing | ■ 30%<br>■ 4% |
| United Airlines | www.united.com | ■ Google<br>■ Gmail | ■ 29%<br>■ 6% |
| Hawaiian Airlines | www.hawaiian.com | ■ Google<br>■ Bing | ■ 29%<br>■ 6% |
| Air Canada | www.aircanada.com | ■ Google<br>■ Bing | ■ 29%<br>■ 6% |
| British Airways | www.ba.com | ■ Google<br>■ Facebook | ■ 28%<br>■ 14% |
| Virgin America | www.virginamerica.com | ■ Google<br>■ Gmail | ■ 26%<br>■ 9% |

*Source:* Hitwise (2014)[70]

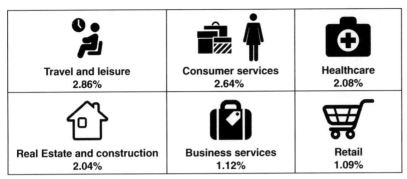

| | | |
|---|---|---|
| **Travel and leisure** <br> **2.86%** | **Consumer services** <br> **2.64%** | **Healthcare** <br> **2.08%** |
| **Real Estate and construction** <br> **2.04%** | **Business services** <br> **1.12%** | **Retail** <br> **1.09%** |

**Total across all Verticals: 1.60%**

*Figure 3.23* US paid search click-through rate by industry

*Source:* Kenshoo (2015)[71]

crucial to pay close attention to this very source. The goal is to use it to an airline's competitive advantage as much as possible.

Another reason for an airline to focus on search marketing is the fact that it works relatively well. Customer response to this digital advertising format has been solid over the years and the click-through rates (CTRs) range between 1% and 5%. In the United States, the CTR for travel and leisure averages 2.86%, the highest when compared with other key industries (Figure 3.23).

*Who are the key search engine providers?*

For both SEM and SEO, airlines work with general search engine providers. There are some regional nuances but the overall global picture is dominated by Google. Worldwide, by the end of 2014, it commanded a search market share on desktops of almost 90%. The picture is similar for searches on tablets and smart phones.[72] Without simplifying things too much, Google has risen to such prominence since the early 2000s because its services have been faster and produce more relevant search results than others. Today, Google handles over 1.1 billion unique search visitors[73] and over 114 billion searches on a monthly basis.[74] Airlines engaged in search marketing really have no choice but to work with Google—at least for now.

A distant second are Yahoo and Bing with a combined share of around 9%.[75] Both companies are also frequently found in an airline's search marketing portfolio. Notable countries where none of these three are the top search engine player include China (Baidu is the number one search engine there), Russia (Yandex), and South Korea (Naver). In order to capture the largest possible online audience, airlines operating in these markets have cooperated with such local key search engine providers. One search engine provider that is often forgotten but should be mentioned also is YouTube. It may not fit the profile of a general search engine provider but it nevertheless handles significant search traffic: 3 billion searches on a monthly basis and 1 billion unique visitors.[76] This makes YouTube the second largest search engine provider.

*How do search engines work?*

Essentially, a search engine is one big answer machine to questions. After typing a search query, a web traveler is presented with a list of web pages identified by the search engine as providing the best match to the query. It is important to understand that each search engine provider works differently and keeps the methodology of how its engine works proprietary. The methodology is actually considered a trade secret, and similar, say, to the recipe of Coca Cola, only known to selected senior people in the Coca-Cola company.

No matter what algorithms these search engines apply in their crawl through cyberspace to find matches to the queried search terms, they work incredibly fast and produce plenty of results. Typing "Flights to Rio" in Google, for example, generates 114 million search results in 0.25 seconds. Upon submitting this query, a web traveler sees two types of listings: Those sponsored by an advertiser and the ones that are organic and the result of a company's search engine optimization efforts (Figure 3.24).

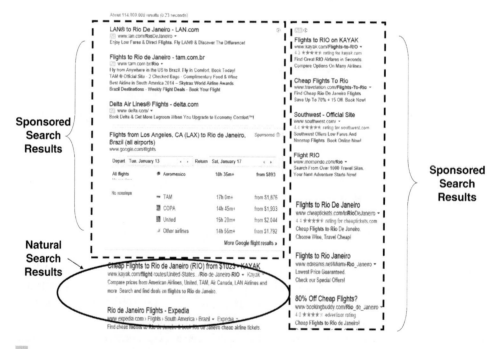

**Figure 3.24** *Google search results for query "Flights to Rio"*

*Source:* Google (2014)[77] Google and the Google logo are registered trademarks of Google Inc., used with permission

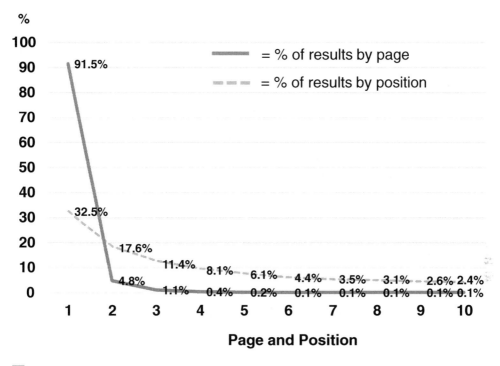

*Figure 3.25 Percentage of traffic by Google results position and page (June 2013)*

Source: IronPaper.com (2013)[78]

In our example, the paid listings show several airlines including LAN, TAM, and Delta Airlines. They are at the top of the result page above the organic listings. On the right hand side, there are more sponsored listings featured in a vertical bar. Some are paid for by meta-search search engines like Kayak, others by online travel agencies such as eDreams. The natural results include Expedia. The box containing the word "AD" is an indicator that these results are sponsored by the advertiser. Their display is a legal requirement.

For a search marketing campaign of an airline to be successful, it needs the right exposure to the eyeballs of web travelers. In this respect, "visibility," "rank," and "position" all point to the same critical question: How important is it to be on top of a search result page? The short answer is "very." The large majority of online searchers including web travelers rarely go beyond the first page. In the case of Google, for example, over 91% of their search traffic goes to the first page and almost a third of that very traffic involves the first position on that page (Figure 3.25). Once we venture off the first page, the traffic declines dramatically. The right position makes all the difference in search engine marketing. Being on the first search result page and as high as possible needs to be the top priority of an airline's search marketing efforts.

After our introductory discussion of search marketing, let us elaborate in more detail on how airlines manage their SEM and SEO activities with search engine providers.

*Search engine marketing (SEM)*

SEM encompasses three types of paid digital advertising: Paid inclusion, keyword advertising, and context advertising. All three are perfect illustrations of how the value of the search process has been monetized. In Google's case, this means $50+ billion in annual revenue from digital advertising.[79] The payment models involved include fees that airlines pay to the search engine providers as a result of guaranteed listings, keyword biddings, and pay-per-click (PPC) performance on text ads.

- *Paid inclusion.* In return for paying a fee, the airline is guaranteed an inclusion on the search result page. By law, these ads are identified as "sponsored links" or "sponsored results." This is done so that a viewer knows that a given company has bought the placement and position of the ad text on the web result page. Paying for the inclusion of text ads goes back to 1998 when Yahoo first started this type of advertising.
- *Keyword advertising.* The airline purchases keywords as part of a competitive 24/7 bidding process. The more it offers for keywords, the higher its rank and visibility on the text-based ad on a web page. Besides the bidding amount, the popularity of an ad measured in terms of clicks can also drive the ranking position. Google's Adwords is the most popular keyword advertising program and was introduced in 2002.
- *Context advertising.* Also referred to as network keyword advertising, an airline has the opportunity to place its ads on third party websites that have joined an advertising network like Google's Adsense. The idea is to do an in-text or contextual placement of an ad on a web page. The airline has no control over where its ads appear but relies on the search engine provider to determine the relevant and appropriate placement.

The travel sector's investment on sponsored search is significant. In 2013, for instance, it amounted to almost $750 million in the United States on Google alone. This makes it the seventh highest spending category (shopping was number one). In other countries, paid search related to travel ranked even higher. In Australia, Canada, and the UK, it was the second highest spending category. In France and Germany, it was on spot three.

The "big guns" in paid travel search are OTAs, not airlines. OTAs control huge digital marketing budgets and dominate the scene as far as reaching out to web travelers is concerned. Their reach, measured in terms of impressions paid for, is shown in Table 3.5. Among the companies, Priceline is the real giant. In combination with its two other online booking properties—Booking.com and Kayak—it alone accounts for over a third of the total 5.9 billion impressions purchased in this Top 10 group.

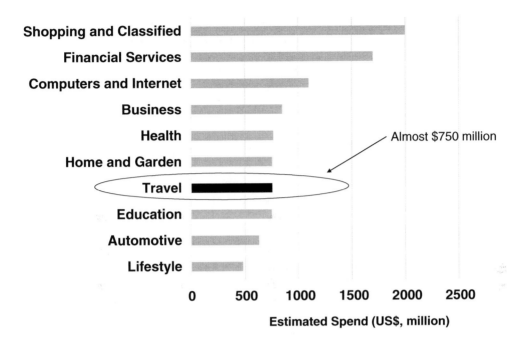

Estimated Spend (US$, million)

**Figure 3.26** *Top categories by spend on paid search (Google 2013)*

Source: Leicheko (2014)[80]

**Table 3.5** *Top 10 travel advertisers in paid search (US, 2013) Google Adwords, desktop/tablet*

| Advertiser | Impressions | 2013 rank | 2012 rank |
|---|---|---|---|
| Booking.com | 793 million | 1 | 7 |
| Tripadvisor | 781 million | 2 | 4 |
| Priceline | 724 million | 4 | 6 |
| Expedia | 662 million | 4 | 6 |
| Kayak | 604 million | 5 | 1 |
| Orbitz | 546 million | 6 | 3 |
| Cheapoair | 497 million | 7 | 5 |
| Travelzoo | 492 million | 8 | 8 |
| Bookingbuddy | 445 million | 9 | 9 |
| Hotels.com | 357 million | 10 | 10 |

Source: Leichenko (2014)[81]

Although airlines have a smaller exposure reach in SEM because they bought less impressions from search engine providers, they nevertheless command a brand recognition by web travelers that is noteworthy (Table 3.6). Among the most clicked travel keywords in paid search, besides the generic "cheap flights" on rank 2, we find

**Table 3.6** *The 20 most clicked travel keywords in paid search (US, January–April 2014)*

| Rank | Company | Rank | Company |
|---|---|---|---|
| 1 | Expedia | 11 | Delta Airlines |
| 2 | Cheap flights | 12 | Enterprise |
| 3 | Travelocity | 13 | Carnival Cruise |
| 4 | Southwest | 14 | Hotwire |
| 5 | JetBlue | 15 | Alaska Airlines |
| 6 | Priceline | 16 | VRBO |
| 7 | Orbitz | 17 | Malaysia Airlines |
| 8 | USAirways | 18 | Cheaptickets |
| 9 | Amtrak | 19 | AirBnB |
| 10 | Southwest Airlines | 20 | Royal Carribbean |

*Source:* Marvin (2013)[82]

familiar brand names including Southwest Airlines, JetBlue, US Airways, Delta, and Alaska Airlines. Malaysia Airlines is an anomaly in this list and its presence is likely the result of web travelers clicking on ads in search of information about the airliner's Flight MH370, which has been missing since March 2014.

*Search engine optimization (SEO)*

SEM is largely contingent on how deep an airline's pockets are to buy its placement on a search result page. Search engine optimization, however, deals with the natural or unsponsored display of text ads. SEO is the practice of improving and promoting a website so that its placement in organic search results is improved.[83]

This is achieved through the process of building web pages in a manner so that the web pages are enabled to rank highly in algorithmically determined search results.

From our previous screen shot in Figure 3.25, we will recall that natural search results are displayed on the left hand side of a web search result page. Again, these algorithms are confidential and differ across search engine providers. When calculating the search results in fractions of seconds, these algorithms use over 100 factors.[84] Some are off-page such as a website's popularity and number of links pointing to the website. Others are concerned with on-page issues such as content topics, words used, their location, repetition, and others.[85]

Without going into too much computer science detail here, search engines are effectively text browsers and index HTML code, the standard language used to create web pages. If the HTML code is not designed with search engine accessibility in mind, an airline website cannot be "seen" or "read" by a search engine. This in turn means that a website cannot be indexed and is therefore not displayed to a searcher.

The author himself has seen a number of airline website designs with a trendy look and feel. Unfortunately, because they had not accounted for search engine accessibility, they often ranked poorly in natural search engine results and had to be improved later at great expense. When an airline launches a brand new website design, considerations for search engine accessibility should therefore play a role.

Additional aspects to consider for competitive SEO efforts include the integration of social media and application of mobile devices. SEO is both an art and a science. Airlines typically work with two main external parties on SEO efforts. One includes the so-called human indexers. These are experts provided by search engine providers who sit down with an airline's IT staff and/or whoever manages the airline's website architecture and content. Furthermore, it is not unusual for a carrier to hire an outside expert such as a digital media agency with expertise in the SEO field.

It is crucial to understand that although an airline does not pay a search engine provider any fee for natural search results, it does not mean that SEO is free of charge. On the contrary. The initial analysis to determine the SEO quality of an airline website—one typically would start with 15–20 key pages—requires a few weeks of full-time work and can easily exceed $20,000. Common areas that need fixing include broken links, duplicated web pages, missing tags, and HTML validation errors. Nevertheless, this is a worthwhile investment because the improved search result rankings are often remarkable. It is not uncommon to see a carrier move from backward search result pages like 12 or 15 to page one or two.

Besides the initial SEO set-up, the optimization of secondary web pages and ongoing SEO maintenance requires work. Search engine providers such as Google do between 500 to 600 changes to their search algorithms every year.[86] Some of these are major and may have a big impact on the search result listings of a company. For instance, as a result of Google's algorithm update "Panda" in 2011, travel aggregator websites received less organic search priority and reported damages to their visitors' numbers.[87] In 2012 when Google release the "Penguin" update, Expedia reportedly lost 25% of its organic search result visibility.[88]

We should emphasize that Google does not release these algorithm updates to intentionally harm a website. Google is not perfect and is simply trying to keep their search process as relevant and up to date as possible to maintain the quality of the information presented to customers. The takeaway for an airline from this is to continually make adjustments to its website in order to make sure it does not deteriorate in its SEO rankings.

*What about the search behavior of web travelers?*

Search engine providers and airlines are not the only parties that are evolving in their search practices. Web travelers do not stand still either in their search behavior. More than ever, when conducting a travel-related search, they anticipate being presented with more detailed information and engaging content. Examples in this regard include reviews, ratings, photos, and even videos. In the past, this kind of content

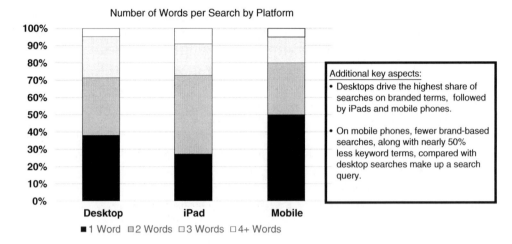

**Figure 3.27** *Search behavior varies by platform*

*Source:* Sullivan (2011)[89]

used to be offered to web travelers more toward the end of their purchase cycle. Today, the expectation is to see it earlier.

Another important shift in the search behavior of web travelers is the result of the proliferation of mobile technology. Today, search is increasingly conducted via smart phones and tablets. Mobile search is different from desktop search because it often involves circumstances that are:

- on-the-go (traveling, price comparison, reviews)
- in-the moment (weather, location, traffic)
- immediate in information needs (news, social, questions).

In this environment, people generally use shorter search terms (Figure 3.27). Furthermore, more generic and less branded search terms are applied. An airline that does not adjust its search engine activities accordingly is not competitive and produces inferior search engine results.

It is also crucial to highlight the difference between smart phones and tablets. Many airlines often lump both into a single "mobile" category. However, research shows that online users do not engage with them the same way. Examples of areas where these differences are noted include search query categories, click and browsing patterns, and time spent.[90] For more effective e-marketing via mobile devices, an airline needs to account for these behavioral variances by users. We come back to this issue in more detail in section 3.17 on mobile advertising.

Another development that an airline should be aware of is the rise of intelligent search. Also referred to as semantic search, this form of search accommodates a user's personal interest, emotions, and other background.

Finally, one can only speculate how search will evolve in connection with wearable computers like Google Glass and smart watches but retailers including airlines need to be on the lookout for these developments.

*Criteria in successful search marketing: Composition of keywords and managing the long tail*

The starting point for an airline when it comes to search marketing is the compilation of keywords and sentences. What search terms should be used for an SEM campaign to be effective? What search words and phrases should be considered for SEO? A person such as a web marketer actually has to sit down and put a list together containing words and sentences that the airline deems critical for a competitive search listing. Typically, an airline's digital media agency assists in this task, although the final decision of what stays on the list or not remains with the airline.

Search terms are differentiated between branded and generic terms. Each of them plays a role and contributes to the success or failure in a carrier's search marketing campaign. Web travelers rely on both branded and generic search terms throughout their travel planning stages. Figure 3.28 shows leisure travelers in the United States and the significance of their search terms usage. It is therefore crucial that an airline manages both categories with sufficient attention.

*Branded search terms*

Branded search terms are those that reference the carrier's trademark company name, related products and services, and possibly some variation of them. An example of branded search terms would be "Air Malta," its frequent flyer program "Flypass" or its subsidiary "Air Malta Holidays." Branded search terms can also be hybrids containing branded and generic words. People refer to these hybrids as the "long tail"

| Search terms that leisure travelers use in planning | | | |
| --- | --- | --- | --- |
| | When first starting to plan | When considering multiple possibilities | When ready to book/reserve |
| Destination-related terms | 51% | 48% | 20% |
| Price-related terms | 41% | 49% | 23% |
| Specific brand or website terms | 31% | 48% | 30% |
| Activity-related terms | 36% | 49% | 20% |
| Terms related to specific needs or wants | 32% | 43% | 22% |

**Figure 3.28** *Travelers rely on generic and branded search across planning stages*

*Source:* Google (2014)[91]

search terms. For Air Malta, examples are "Buy Air Malta low fares," Flypass promotion, and "Travel with Air Malta Holiday."

Branded search terms generate more traffic and have high value in terms of click-through and conversion rates. This is because branded keyword searches are undertaken by web travelers who are already familiar with the airline brand. Their typing of branded key terms is generally navigational in nature. In other words, web travelers may be looking for a particular airline website because they have been exposed to the carrier before and are simply typing the branded search term to find the website. In a way, this is the equivalent to typing the airline's website domain name directly into the internet browser. It is also important to point out that a web traveler's use of branded search terms is more likely toward the end of their buying cycle when they are getting ready to complete their online purchase.

Can Google or other search engines sell branded keywords that happen to be part of registered trademarks? For example, can British Airways buy the keywords "Virgin Atlantic"? This means that every time a web traveler enters them in a search engine, the text ads/links of British Airways actually show up in the sponsored part of the search result page next to Virgin's text ads/links. The answer to the question is yes. A company may purchase keywords that are related to a rival's registered trademark.

An example of this is shown in Figure 3.29 and involves Air India. Upon entering "Air India" as a search term, the result page shows a sponsored ad by an OTA called makemytrip.com. Their ad displays right above the link to Air India's official website in the natural result section.

As one can imagine, this issue is contentious. Several companies including American Airlines actually sued Google over the sale of keyword ads to competitors

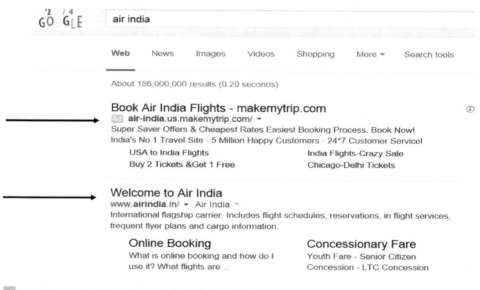

**Figure 3.29** *Competitive bidding for trademark search terms*

*Source:* Google (2014)[92]

triggered for display when search terms related to American's trademark had been submitted. These lawsuits were all ruled in favor of Google. The explanation? A trademark does not give its holder complete control of the use of the word. A competitor may use it for competitive advertising as long as it is not confusing a consumer.[93]

Airlines usually do not bid on search terms related to a competitor's trademark. Nevertheless, in regards to travel intermediaries, the situation appears to be different. The earlier example of Air India is by no means unique and many other carriers are equally impacted. E-Commerce savvy airlines contractually prevent distribution partners such as online travel agencies or affiliate program members from bidding on key terms related to the airline's brand. If such an agreement had been put in place between Air India and makemytrip.com, the latter's ad would not have appeared. What are the benefits of this type of agreement? First, the carrier's brand is not infringed upon by a third party. Second, the airline itself captures the website traffic and a potential customer as opposed to having them handled through an intermediary at a higher cost. Third, the competitive bidding for key terms with search providers is not artificially inflated and unnecessarily driving up fees.

*Generic search terms*

Unlike branded terms, generic search terms do not include any brand name related to the airline. They can include phrases like "cheap tickets to Toronto," "Paris flight deals," and "China fare promotion." Figure 3.30 displays a word cloud with the top 25 generic search words used in the United States in connection with air travel in

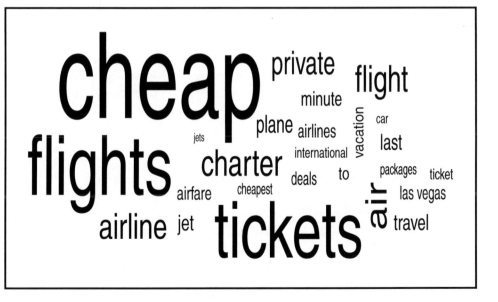

**Figure 3.30** *Top 25 generic search terms in air travel (US market)*

*Source:* Kenshoo.com (2015)[94]

**105**

2014. The more frequent the use, the larger the font size. Based on this chart, the focus among web travelers is apparently on cheap flights and tickets. An airline should continuously analyze and monitor the website traffic captured as a result of non-branded search terms. The reason is because the majority of an airline's new website business stems from this type of traffic.

In order to compile an effective list of generic search terms, one needs to understand the search behavior of web travelers. What are the most common travel-related search terms? How many words do they typically type? How do search terms differ by trip purpose? Can search terms be simply translated from one language to another or do they require adjustments to be truly localized for a particular market?

The list with generic key terms is generally longer than that with branded terms. It may contain hundreds if not thousands of search terms. Managing these requires dedicated resources, and at larger airlines that are active in search marketing, this often involves a full-time job. At the same time, the performance of individual generic search terms is typically not as strong as what we see from branded key terms. The reason why generic search terms generate less traffic has to do with web traveler behavior. They type generic key terms because they are usually not familiar with a particular airline brand. Moreover, they are most likely early in the buying cycle where research and checking out options are prevalent activities. This kind of web traveler is more of a prospect than a customer.

However, despite the weaker performance of an individual generic search term, *collectively* they account for a huge volume in traffic and as such generate click-through and conversion rates similar to those of branded terms. This is where the so-called "long tail" of search marketing enters the scene.

The concept of long tail is not unique to search marketing. It is often described in conjunction with the success of online retailer Amazon. The long tail was first coined by *Wired* magazine editor Chris Anderson in 2004. He argued that products in low demand or with low sales volume collectively can constitute a market share that rivals or even exceeds top-selling items, provided that the store or distribution channel is large enough.[95] The following section elaborates on the long tail concept for airline search marketing.

*The long tail and search marketing*

Figure 3.31 sheds more light on this phenomenon. On the horizontal axis are individual search terms while on the vertical axis is the website traffic (measured in terms of visitors) that results from each search term.

An airline (and ideally the involved digital agency responsible for handling search marketing) that analyzes the performance of its search term portfolio will come across important findings. It will realize that only a few search terms, probably not more than 10 to 20, generate the bulk of traffic from search engines to the carrier's website and that they perform relatively strongly. This is the so-called head area that is dominated by company branded terms. At the same time, the tail area is largely populated by many generic search words and phrases that each contribute relatively little to

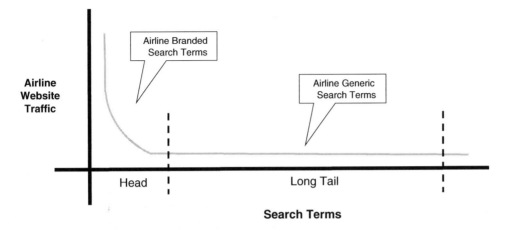

**Figure 3.31** *The long tail for search terms*

driving traffic to the airline's website. According to research in this area, travel search terms that are branded drive 35% of the click traffic, yet they only account for 4% of all search terms displayed and only 7% of the search word spending (Figure 3.32).

From this insight, we can ask a few key questions for a carrier's search marketing activities:

■ Is the number of branded search terms sufficient to drive much of the search traffic?
■ How many generic search terms are accommodated in the tail section?
■ Are there any surprises in the performance of key search terms?
■ What changes should be considered to improve the search term portfolio?

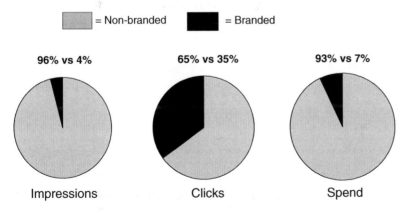

**Figure 3.32** *Comparison of branded and non-branded travel search terms*

*Source:* Kenshoo.com (2015)[96]

- What is the budget split between brand and generic search terms?
- What should be the budget split between SEM and SEO?

Keeping in mind that the collective impact of many individual generic search terms can be as powerful as a few branded key terms, the focus when developing a framework for search marketing should be on generic search terms. This is because an airline that wants to capture web travelers who are in the early stage of the booking cycle when they still evaluate various options has an opportunity to expose its brand early on to new customers. In other words, if an airline intends to grow its online business and attract new web travelers, it is crucial to be more engaged with generic search terms.

For many airlines, however, it is not uncommon to find that they actually emphasize branded search terms. Their SEM budget is spent heavily on this category of search terms. This ensures that a branded search term such as "Air Malta" shows up on the first result page in a sponsored top position but the funds left to bid on the more expensive, generic search terms including "flights to Malta" are small. Probably too small to allow an airline to be a competitive bidder among many other companies such as OTAs and meta-search engine providers that are active in this space.

The result of this is that an airline is not exposed to web travelers early on in their buying cycle. This in turn means that it most likely misses out on capturing these prospects later and the opportunity to turn them into a customer is gone. Studies have shown that airlines with higher spending levels in search generally benefit from higher click-through rates (Figure 3.33). It seems a reasonable policy for an airline to apply these economics to the generic category of search terms where it then has a higher chance to establish early on a connection with new online shoppers.

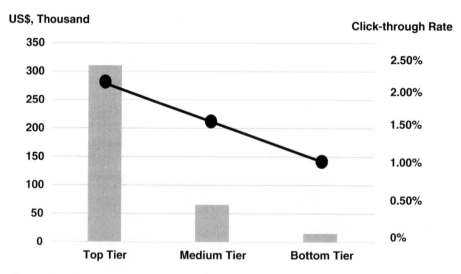

Tiers are determined by overall spend levels on keywords receiving at least five clicks from more than one competitor. Averages are calculated for Top 10 competitors in each tier.

*Figure 3.33* Higher spending levels in search correspond to higher click-through rates

Source: Kenshoo.com (2015)[97]

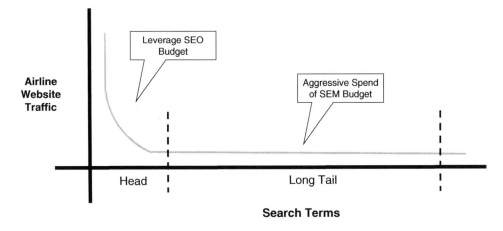

*Figure 3.34* *Optimizing budget allocation between SEM and SEO*

Naturally, an airline needs to be concerned about the ranking of company branded terms. However, the question is whether this is best addressed by using the SEM budget or actually the SEO budget. Differently asked, what is the optimal budget use for SEM and SEO?

Based on our above discussion, a more suitable budget allocation between SEM and SEO should be achieved (Figure 3.34). Accordingly, an SEM budget is better spent bidding on generic terms in the tail section while SEO budget dollars are used to optimize brand terms in the head section.

An example of a carrier pursuing this approach is LCC Ryanair. According to Google Adwords data for the airline's website (www.ryanair.com), the Top 20 paid search terms it bids for on Google.ie in Ireland are all generic. One example is "Flights to Faro from Dublin" accounting for 7.75% of the paid search traffic. Each of these generic search terms do not account for much traffic to the airline's website. However, the total traffic of the Top 20 keywords amounts to over 80%. At the same time, the top organic search term for the airline is "Ryanair." It generates over 73% (!) of the search traffic alone. Interestingly, with one exception, all organic search terms are Ryanair branded. Clearly, Ryanair does not need to buy branded terms—the organic results are strong enough (Figure 3.35).

An airline that spends its SEM budget aggressively on generic search terms in the tail section realizes several important advantages:

- It shows up higher when web travelers search with generic terms—sticking out is crucial as there are many other competitors.
- The likelihood of capturing a web traveler's business is improved because the airline is more exposed in the early stages of the person's buying cycle.
- The same SEM budget can be stretched further by also bidding for generic niche search terms. Generic search terms are generally costly because they attract many bidders but niche search terms are less expensive. An airline may therefore also include many additional search terms in its portfolio.

**109**

## Top 20 paid search terms

| Keyword | Traffic [%] |
| --- | --- |
| Flights To Faro From Dublin | 7.75 |
| Flights From Dublin To Bristol | 6.38 |
| Flights From Dublin To Barcelona | 6.38 |
| Dublin To Barcelona Flights | 6.38 |
| Dublin To Glasgow Flights | 6.38 |
| Flights To Glasgow From Dublin | 5.01 |
| Flights From Dublin To Malta | 5.01 |
| Flights From Dublin To Glasgow | 5.01 |
| Flights From Dublin To Faro | 5.01 |
| Flights Dublin To Glasgow | 3.19 |
| Cheap Flights To Barcelona From Dublin | 3.19 |
| Dublin Barcelona Flights | 3.19 |
| Dublin To Bristol Flights | 3.19 |
| Flights Dublin To Faro | 3.19 |
| Flights Dublin To Malta | 3.19 |
| Shannon To Paris | 3.19 |
| Cheap Flights To Malta From Dublin | 2.28 |
| Flights From Dublin To Faro Portugal | 2.28 |
| Flights From Dublin To Nice | 2.28 |
| Flights From Dublin To Salzburg | 2.28 |

**Total: > 80%**

## Top 20 organic search terms

| Keyword | Traffic [%] |
| --- | --- |
| Ryanair | 73.83 |
| Ryanair IE | 1.90 |
| Ryan air | 1.27 |
| Ryanair.com | 1.04 |
| www ryanair com | 1.04 |
| www.ryanair.com | 1.04 |
| Ryanair Flights | 0.57 |
| Ryanair IE | 0.52 |
| Ryanair Check In | 0.46 |
| Ryanair IE | 0.36 |
| Ryan air | 0.35 |
| Ryanair Ireland | 0.31 |
| Ryanair.com | 0.28 |
| www ryanair com | 0.28 |
| www.ryanair.com | 0.28 |
| Ryanair IE | 0.28 |
| Ryanair | 0.25 |
| Ryan air | 0.24 |
| Cheap Flights [The only non-branded keyword!] | 0.24 |
| Ryanair Online Check In | 0.20 |

***Figure 3.35*** *Top 20 search keywords on Google.ie by traffic generated*

*Source:* Tnooz.com (2015)[98]

An airline's SEO budget is most effectively leveraged when optimizing the head area with branded search terms. The benefits from this are:

- Simplification of SEO activities by focusing on a few key branded terms and not hundreds of other generic terms.
- The airline shows up in high-ranking positions when web travelers search with branded terms.
- The budget is not overspent on web travelers that already know the airline brand.

*A word on search spending and search cost*

We have touched a few times on the issues of budget and costs. Let us take a closer look at some actual numbers to develop an appreciation for what is involved.

Paid search in the travel sector appears to becoming more expensive. When looking at how cost per click is trending for the US market, we see a year–over–year increase from $1.08 to $1.72 (Figure 3.36). This 59% hike is remarkable when compared with the cost–per–click changes for other industries. Some like healthcare and business services even showed a decline during the same timeframe. It appears that the competition for travel search terms is heating up.

We need to remind ourselves that there are some formidable players with deep pockets in the travel space, above all the online travel agencies. In 2013, for example, Expedia and Priceline spent $82.3 million and $71.6 million, respectively, on Google alone just for search terms displayed on desktop computers. Both companies are among the Top 5 spenders when it comes to SEM and reportedly account for a combined "astounding 5% of Google's total advertising revenue."[99] Other companies in this group include Amazon with $157.7 million, AT&T with $81.9 million, and Microsoft with $ 67.1 million.

| Search Category | Q 4 2012 | | Q 4 2013 |
|---|---|---|---|
| Healthcare | $4.63 | → | $3.68 |
| Travel & Leisure | $1.08 | → | $1.72 |
| Retail | $1.28 | → | $1.65 |
| Real Estate & Construction | $1.03 | → | $1.13 |
| Consumer Services | $0.63 | → | $0.86 |
| Business Services | $0.91 | → | $0.68 |
| **Total** | **$1.04** | → | **$1.33** |

**Figure 3.36** *Development of cost per click by industry*

*Source:* eMarketer.com (2014)[100]

**Table 3.7** *SEM budgets: Selected US carriers vs top OTAs*

| Airline | Total 2013 US marketing budget | Estimated digital budget* | Estimated SEM spending** | OTA |
|---------|-------------------------------|---------------------------|--------------------------|-----|
| JetBlue | $204 million | $61 million | $24 million | Expedia: $82 million |
| Southwest | $199 million | $60 million | $24 million | Priceline: $72 million |
| American | $51 million | $15 million | $6 million | |

*Based on assumption that digital spending is on average 30% of total budget, $ amounts are rounded.

**Average of 40% of digital marketing spending goes to SEM based on author's assessment.

In comparison with these numbers, airlines pale in significance. For instance, American Airlines total marketing budget in 2013 for the United States amounted to "only" $51 million. Even JetBlue ($204 million) and Southwest Airlines ($199 million), the Top 2 marketing spenders among US carriers, do not even come close. The breakdown of airline marketing budgets by digital format is not publicly available information but we can work with some basic assumptions to obtain some insight into what airlines are up against (Table 3.7).

OTAs outspend airlines significantly in SEM. For example, Expedia's spending is more than three times higher than that of JetBlue and over 13 times higher than that of American. It can therefore afford to bid higher on a wide spectrum of generic search terms than JetBlue or any other airline for that matter. This is one reason why a large number of sponsored ads we see on search result pages come from OTAs and not from airlines.

Can airlines narrow this resource gap versus OTAs and increase their digital marketing spending? Lately, ancillary sales have provided new profit streams for airlines. At least theoretically, a portion of these could be used to compete more effectively against OTAs also in the area of digital marketing. However, it remains to be seen how this will play out in the future. Other e-commerce savvy players with huge marketing budgets are destined to join the digital travel space. One such example is Amazon, which launched a booking platform for independent hotels in spring 2015. Another example is TripAdvisor, which has recently morphed from a travel review website to a full-blown intermediary meta-search engine platform like Kayak. Both companies are likely to be very active in digital marketing including SEM. Travel search terms are therefore likely to become more expensive. This development should be a call to action for any carrier to leverage its SEO search activities while fine-tuning SEM as much as possible. Moreover, the increased competition in the SEM area may also lead to the channeling of marketing funds to other online formats—some of which are still at an infant stage including online video—or even into existing offline formats such as print and radio.

*Writing the ad copy for paid search*

An aspect often forgotten in SEM deals with the ad copy. The traditional offline advertising formats and also a number of online formats have more space and allow

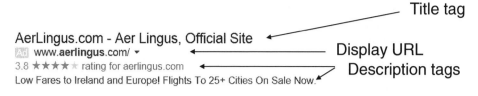

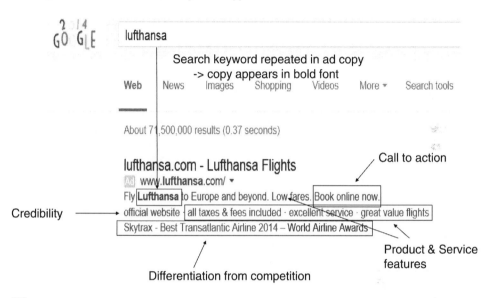

**Figure 3.37a** *Elements that make up the ad copy…*

**Figure 3.37b** *…and how to make an ad copy effective*

*Source:* Google (2014)[101, 102] Google and the Google logo are registered trademarks of Google Inc., used with permission

an airline to use multiple lines of text and possibly even paragraphs and images. In the world of SEM, real estate comes at a premium. An airline advertising paid search via Google Adwords has typically 130 characters or less in most languages to work with to accommodate the title tag, display URL, and description tags. Against this limitation, the writing of a strong ad copy is crucial. Airlines that want to be competitive with search ads needs to pay attention to a few key aspects. We exemplify these with an ad copy of Lufthansa (Figure 3.37).

- *Use of search copy.* Repeating the search keyword in the ad copy means that the ad copy is partially bold because it matches the keyword. This draws additional attention to the ad copy since it sticks out more.
- *Feature a strong call to action.* A strong call to action like "Book Now!" in the airline ad often means to encourage web travelers to go to the airline website and perform particular tasks such as booking a ticket or enrolling in the FFP.
- *Include product and service features.* Highlighted are the carrier's offerings. From non-stop flights and best fare guarantee to friendly inflight service and particular

aircraft types (like the B787 Dreamliner), this additional information emphasizes the carrier's unique selling position.

■ *Establish credibility.* As a means of establishing trustworthiness and authority, airlines often display service ratings from third parties such as Skytrax, awards, and other accolades. "Official website" is another label occasionally used.

### The emergence of social search

Search has always been social at its core. A person that is looking for answers to questions—by virtue of reaching out to other people for information, inputs, and thoughts—is social after all. This fundamental aspect has not changed in today's digital world. Web travelers check out travel review sites, engage with social networks, pay attention to recommendations by friends and relatives, and may also be exposed to sponsored ads that include social popularity ratings (Figure 3.38).

The question is if these social aspects in travel search can be captured by a formal social search engine. The objective of such a search engine would be to generate results based on the so-called social graph of a person. A social graph is understood as the algorithmic depiction of social contacts and personal relations that an online user has with other online users. In other words, a social search engine is fundamentally a search engine that combines algorithm-based technology with social filters such as recommendations, preferences, historical website uses, and other factors. Arguably, social search engines produce more relevant results because they come from sources that are deemed more trustworthy than those generated by a general search engine.

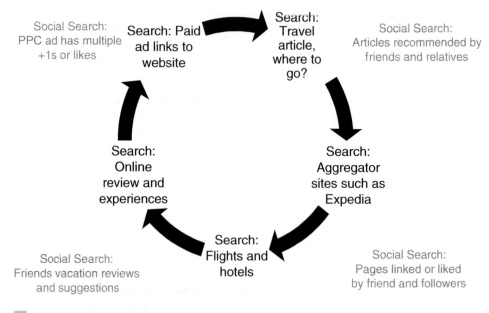

**Figure 3.38** *Social search in travel planning*

*Source:* TugAgency (2013)[103]

None of the major search engine providers have fully implemented a social search engine that captures the universe of online users' social circles with all their personal likes and preferences. One of the challenges is that generating or interacting with social media content often occurs in real-time. There is literally no time lag between composition and publishing (postings on Twitter are a good example). Because these pieces of information are not indexed by current search engine providers, they are not shown in search results. Nevertheless, there are some noteworthy developments that search engine providers have become more social in recent years:

- Search engine providers have added social factors to their SEO menu. They largely influence the organic search results of a company today. Based on one analysis, seven out the Top 10 factors critical to SEO-driven search results are now social in nature and include popularity with social networks like Google+1, Facebook, Pinterest, and Twitter.[104]
- Search engine providers have launched their own social network services including Google with Google+ and Bing with its social column.[105] For example, one feature of Google+ is the Google+1 button that allows a web traveler to put +1 next to websites that they find helpful and therefore recommend for future use. Friends of this web traveler are automatically notified by this recommendation and if they engage in a similar search themselves, the +1 recommended websites will rank higher on the result page. (Facebook's "Like" button operates similarly.)
- Search engine providers and social networks have entered partnerships in the form of reciprocal account linkings. For example, web travelers activating their "Social Bar" setting on Yahoo automatically share via feeds activities such as articles read about an airline or videos watched about a destination with friends on Facebook. This feature allows members to view and share news and updates across multiple networks faster and more conveniently.[106]

Airlines have to determine what specifically of these developments they want to make part of their overall social media strategy. At the same time, an airline may consider working more closely with social media networks for the purpose of tapping into social search. This could make sense because some of the social media networks have also become a venue for web travelers to conduct travel-related search in varying degrees. Let us remember from our introductory section that social networking sites play a role and they are among the Top 10 online resources for search. Facebook, LinkedIn, and Twitter are examples. However, although web travelers tap into social networks for inspiration and advice, they are not necessarily offered a rich choice of formal social search tools for travel. Probably most commonly known is Facebook's Like button whereby one Facebook user recommends a website and thereby turns into a trustworthy source of content to friends.

In December 2014, Facebook launched Facebook search. This feature is a keyword-based search option that digs up previous news feed posts by friends. Keywords such as "travel" or an airline-specific brand name that otherwise was buried deep in people's profiles or news feeds are now easily found.[107] This is certainly a powerful search tool but it is internal and limited to Facebook. LinkedIn and others also offer their own internal search engines. All these cannot be equated with a social search engine that accounts for the universe of reviews, preferences, and recommendations existing in cyberspace and that displays them in a Google-like fashion.

The closest thing to a social search engine currently in the travel sector is the tie-up between Facebook and TripAdvisor, the world's largest travel review site with over 100 million travel reviews. In 2010, they launched a travel search application called TripFriends that makes use of the social graph concept. The goal is to offer visitors to TripAdvisor the ability to ask their friends on Facebook about a hotel or other service featured on TripAdvisor. In 2012, this was further expanded to also include the friends of friends.[108] According to TripAdvisor, Facebook-connected people write a quarter of all reviews submitted on TripAdvisor. On average each of these travelers has about 190 people in their friends network, thus enlarging the circle of social contacts to thousands of people.[109]

How does TripFriends work? When engaging in research on a hotel or other attraction offered on TripAdvisor, a user will see their friends' reviews first, followed by reviews of their friends' friends. They can use the platform's built-in private message feature to ask anyone in this network for further advice. TripFriends is an illustrative example of how well the social network landscape has integrated travel and how—although not with an exclusive focus on airline brands—it can impact the performance of a travel supplier and get seen on TripAdvisor or not. Maybe we might see a similar cooperation between Facebook and an airline review/rating website such as Skytrax in the future.

An airline "lite" version of Facebook's TripFriends was introduced by KLM in 2013 with its "Must See Map" product. It is a smart use of a map and list of things to do in certain destinations in a  social graph context. Specifically, a web traveler chooses a destination and is served a Google Map that looks like a paper city guide travelers carried in their pockets and used in the offline days of travel. Through their Facebook account that is the entry point, a web traveler could receive tips from friends and family who populate the web traveler's map with ideas. Any replies are automatically placed on the map and also shared back on Facebook and Twitter. The effort to create such a product is certainly not small but it can improve an airline's footprint in cyberspace which in turn helps increase brand awareness and engagement.[110]

*Moving forward with search marketing*

Search marketing is expected to continue playing a formidable role in airlines' digital marketing activities in the foreseeable future. For better or worse, this means dealing above all with Google, a single company that overwhelmingly dominates this space currently. It certainly does not help that factors influencing organic search engine results are largely shrouded in mystery while money spent on sponsored search results only goes so far to secure a particular placement. An airline that aims at a successful search marketing program needs to:

- engage in continuous fine-tuning of organic and sponsored search activities—key is to pursue a holistic approach and address both forms of search marketing at the same time
- deploy sufficient and qualified resources in this area even when a third party digital agency is involved to manage the full cycles of SEM and SEO campaigns
- plan for more budget because of the possible costlier competition for keywords
- accommodate the shift in web traveler search behavior that is increasingly oriented toward social, mobile, and semantic search.

### 3.8.2 Display ads

Display ads comprise four different kinds of formats: Banner ads, rich media, sponsorships, and video ads. Our discussion below shares more details on each of them.

*Web banners*

Web banners are the oldest form of digital display ad. They go back to 1996 when the US web magazine *Hotwired* featured its first banner ad for US telecom AT&T. Upon clicking on a banner, a user is linked to the advertiser's website where they can browse or potentially even shop. Over the years, we have seen the introduction of various banner sizes that airlines have come to adopt (Figure 3.39). Most of these are not static but are typically animated as they rotate through two to three frames with interrelated messages.

Airlines engaging in banner advertising consider a number of factors when deciding what banner size to use. These include the target audience the airline wants to reach, the content environment, and also the carrier's marketing budget. The Top 3 banner sizes currently in use—they account for almost 80% of all banners served in the world—are the medium rectangle, the leaderboard, and the skyscraper.[111]

The number of ads served is truly remarkable: Measured in terms of impressions (the number of times a web ad is displayed), over 5 trillion in the US alone[112] while the average online user is served more than 1,700 banners every month.[113] When reviewing some statistics provided by Google Display Network (GDN), the world's largest advertising network, we can gain some insight into the scale of the travel industry. An ad network is an entity that connects advertisers such as airlines with companies that want to host digital ads. According to GDN figures for the third quarter 2012, travel companies deployed over 2.14 billion ads in the marketplace—this makes travel the second largest category after finance with 5.32 billion ads for the same time frame.[114] The volume of web ads a single airline serves in a given calendar year may easily involve a few million. This is the case when a carrier operates in multiple markets that are e-commerce mature and where the carrier seeks to support its various online campaigns.

At the time banner ads were introduced, customer response measured in terms the so-called click-through rate (CTR) exceeded 30% and more. However, the novelty factor with them quickly wore off and CTRs declined significantly.

Skyscraper
(120 x 600)

Wide
Skyscraper
(160 x 600)

Half Page
(300 x 250)

Half Banner
(234 x 60)

Leaderboard
(728 x 90)

Large
Rectangle
(336 x 280)

Square
(125 x 125)

  **Figure 3.39** *Common banner formats:* * *Example KLM*

\* Size is expressed in pixels

With kind permission of KLM

Today, the worldwide average CTR for banners hovers around 0.1%[115] while the travel sector is not much higher with 0.18% (this figure is for the United States).[116]

A number of carriers apply more innovative formats that invite a higher level of engagement by web travelers. One example is Air New Zealand. For some campaigns in the past, they used web "smart" banners (Figure 3.40). These were already prepopulated with essential travel details (origin/destination, dates, number of travelers) that a web traveler could modify. Upon clicking on the "book now" button, the person then was deep linked into the carrier's website booking page with all travel details carried over from the banner. Standard banners without deep links involve

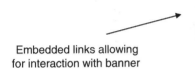

Embedded links allowing for interaction with banner

**Figure 3.40** *Air New Zealand banner with embedded deep links*

*Source:* Schiff (2013)[117] with kind permission of Air New Zealand

**119**

more clicks and require a web user to enter more information. What further stimulated interaction with the carrier's banner was a sweepstake promotion to win tickets and attend the movie premiere of *The Hobbit* in Wellington, New Zealand.

Another example involves web banners with embedded video ads. The video ad, once clicked upon, plays within the banner although it may expand outside the banner also. A carrier using this type of banner is ULCC Spirit Airlines (Figure 3.41). The embedded video ad is one minute and 43 seconds long. It explains the carrier's no-frills business model and lays out the trade-offs between its rock bottom "bare fare" and no free bags or drinks, less leg room, and no reclining seats.[118]

Web banners are going to remain a staple in any airline's digital campaign portfolio. One key reason is that they are relatively cost efficient vehicles when it comes to creating brand awareness and communicating a call for action. Additionally, thanks to the emergence of programmatic advertising, individual web travelers can also be targeted with highly relevant messages. All of this ensures that web banners are part of the next generation of an airline's digital advertising activities.

*Rich media*

Another display format, arguably more creative, covers rich media. The Interactive Agency Bureau (IAB) defines rich media ads as those an online user can interact with.

**Figure 3.41** *Spirit Airlines embedded video ad*

*Source:* www.adweek.com (2014)[119] with kind permission of Spirit Airlines

Common formats include so-called transitionals and a variety of over-the-web page ads such as floating ads and tear-backs.[120] Rich media play a large role in today's online advertising. With broadband connectivity becoming more common and technology constantly improving, rich media are a good option for attracting online traffic to an airline's digital property and growing its brand awareness. Click-through rates for rich media are said to be up to five times higher than for non-rich media ads.[121]

A transitional is a kind of interstitial ad shown to an online user as they move from one web page to the next. The idea is to kill the dead time between pages and bridge it by integrating an advertising message into the navigation flow. Airlines place interstitial ads not only on third party websites but also on their own to expose web travelers to mostly brand-related messages. Figure 3.42 shows Air Mauritius deploying an interstitial banner to promote its frequent flyer program Kestrelflyer as a user navigates from the carrier's homepage to the flight/class of service selection page. An interstitial is typically only displayed for a one- to three-second period.

Over-the-top web page ads, as this label implies, are superimposed on an existing web page. A floating banner ad appears uninitiated by the web user over a web page and blocks part of it. The ad might automatically disappear after a few seconds or may also provide a means of escape with a close button. The basic form of a floating ad shows a static text/image while more sophisticated versions feature sound, animation, and interactive components. Admittedly, a floating ad is intrusive but if it is well created and executed, it can grab a web user's attention and generate a high degree of brand awareness for an airline. Figure 3.43 features a floating ad of Orange-jet, a fictitious airline.

Unlike the floating ad, a tear-back (or peel-back) banner requires the action of a web user. Typically, upon clicking on the banner, it expands its size and may cover a substantial part of a web page. The banner tears back from the upper right-hand corner and reveals an advertising message. It typically also features a hyperlink back to the carrier's website for further engagement.

### Sponsorships

Sponsorships are a venue for airlines to create and reinforce awareness for their brand. In regards to digital display media, the placement of a carrier's logo in the form of a static banner on the sponsoree's website is common. Figure 3.44 provides an example of Aeroflot sponsoring the soccer club Manchester United.

Furthermore, sponsorships can also materialize with advertorial content. This is a combination of editorial content and an advertising message. The principal aim of advertorials is to make the communication with a particular target audience more valuable and attractive.

Figure 3.45 displays a social media form of advertorial. It involves Singapore Airlines and American Express sharing information about their newly launched co-branded credit on a Singaporean blog.

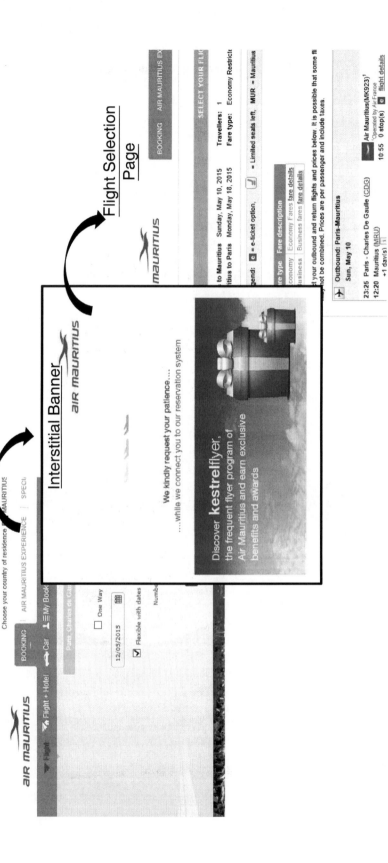

**Figure 3.42** *Interstitial banner on Air Mauritius website*

Source: airmauritius.com (2014)[122] with kind permission of Air Mauritius

**Figure 3.43** *Rich media online advertising: Float and tear-back banner ads*

Source: Ajc.com

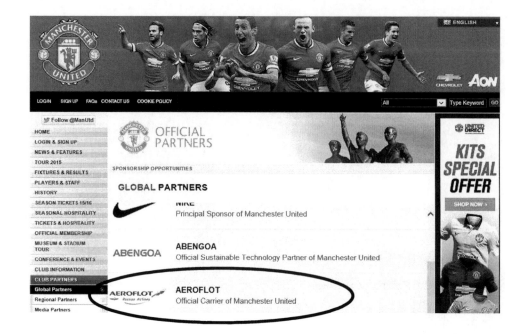

**Figure 3.44** *Airline display banner on sponsored sports clubs' websites*

*Source:* manutd.com (2014)[123]

*Behind the scenes of digital display ads: The role of advertising networks*
*and the rise of programmatic advertising*

Through the early 2000s, it was not unusual for airlines, especially the larger ones, to work directly with a few popular websites to place digital display ads with them. Of interest then was (and still is today) an audience with an affinity for travel. The author himself recalls attending meetings on behalf of united.com with companies including news organizations, weather channels, and large internet portals to negotiate United Airlines banner display ad placements on their respective websites.

Fast forwarding to today, the situation has changed significantly. There are now hundreds of thousands of websites that an airline can choose from for banner advertising. Managing this much larger pool of websites is a challenge for any airline that wants to take care of this on its own.

Enter the so-called ad networks. These are highly specialized digital marketing entities that are capable of managing the entire process of display ad buying and selling quite efficiently and effectively. They act as intermediaries between airlines and those thousands of websites where airline banner ads are placed. Popular ad networks include DoubleClick which is part of the Google Display Network (GDN) and 24//7 Real Media by WPP, the world's biggest advertising firm. There are still companies that manage this process bilaterally. Let us think of an airline and car rental company that agree to display the other company's banners on its own website. However, such an arrangement has become rare. The standard today is that

**Enjoy Great Travel Privileges with American Express Singapore Airlines Krisflyer Ascend Credit Card**

May 25th, 2013

❝ This post is a reprint of a post by Zhiqiang & Tingyi that originally appeared at Singapore Travel Blog.

**Advertorial**

American Express and Singapore Airlines are taking the success of their exclusive cobrand card partnership in Singapore of 13 years to a new high, with the announcement of their latest cobrand card, **American Express Singapore Airlines KrisFlyer Ascend Credit Card (Ascend)**.

*Figure 3.45* *Advertorial content by airlines: Example—Singapore Airlines*

Source: Singapore Award Blog (2014)[124]

ad networks acquire banner placement inventory from a number of third-party websites that offer space to advertisers such as airlines. In the event there is a business transaction—be it a click on a banner or a conversion by a web traveler to a ticket purchase—the third party receives a payment from the ad network.

The way ads are served to the end-consumer including web travelers has undergone significant changes lately. One of them deals with so-called real-time bidding (RTB) facilitated by ad exchanges. RTB does not target broad segments with generic messages but instead focuses on individuals with more specific communications. This is possible because of the high degree of data intelligence applied. By using e-tags such as cookies that track the movements of online users in cyberspace, ad networks develop a sophisticated insight into web travelers. The data collected on online behavior, past purchases, prior clickstreams, demographics, and psychographics are all utilized to serve relevant web ads to an individual. Via an ad exchange that is managed through an ad network, an airline can bid on serving a web traveler its ads. If the carrier is not outbid by a company also interested in pitching an ad, then the ad network serves the carrier's ad throughout the time the web traveler is online.

Airlines bring two of their own data sets to this mix. One data set contains data on FFP, a web traveler's past purchases, and data on their behavior based on the e-tags the airline has also installed on its digital properties. The other data set includes data from revenue management in order to adjust pricing.[125] Equipped with this insight, airlines can then decide to bid or not on a web traveler presented to them via the ad exchange. Depending on the value of the web traveler, an airline bids higher or lower to serve its ads to an individual. This entire process generally takes place in less than 150 milliseconds and is entirely managed by computers, hence the term of programmatic advertising.[126]

Figure 3.46 illustrates how RTB advertising through an ad exchange works. In our hypothetical example, we have an online user that checks on the British BBC website for travel news. Unbeknownst to them, the BBC website is a member of an ad network (like DoubleClick for example) that has implanted e-tags on the online user's computer. Upon accessing the BBC website, the BBC server connects to the ad network server.

The ad network server checks against a database on the profile of the user. The information then is passed on to the ad exchange. Airlines, in our example, Virgin and American, have an interest in serving a display ad to this online user and promoting their services to London. Depending on what information they have internally available on this user (FFP, website data) and their revenue management situation, they may decide to bid. In our case, Virgin outbids American and the ad network shows Virgin's display to the online user.

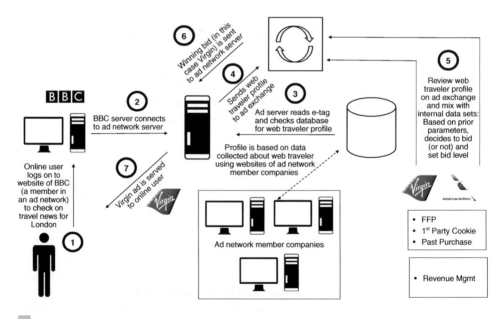

**Figure 3.46** *How does an ad exchange work?*

*Source:* Author based on Rice (2014),[127] Laudon and Traver (2013)[128]

It is estimated that 20% of global display advertising in 2015 is programmatic and handled in real-time bidding. The forecast for 2017 is 50% as more countries outside the United States are likely adopt it and mobile ads and online videos are also increasingly traded in this system. Other platforms including TV, radio, and the Internet of Things could eventually be included as well.[129] In today's data-driven marketplace, it is difficult for an airline to ignore this type of advertising in the long run. Some already participate through a popular programmatic advertising tactic called "re-targeting." In this case, web travelers are served ads by a particular carrier whose website was accessed during a prior visit but no ticket was purchased.

## 3.9 EMAIL MARKETING

Originally designed to carry text-only messages, emails today also allow for the transmission of multi-media content with audio and video files as well as digital photos. Since the early 1990s, email has not only evolved to become a highly popular medium for personal communication but also for business communication.

In analogy with Mark Twain's famous quote, the death of email has been exaggerated. With the number of worldwide email users in 2014 being an estimated 2.5 billion[130] and the daily email traffic amounting to 204 billion,[131] it is still by far the most widely used internet-based communications channel in the world. These impressive statistics should put the ongoing hype on social media into a certain perspective.

It is fair to refer to email marketing as the "workhorse" of all digital marketing media formats. In the United States, 86% of all digital marketers used email marketing in 2014 regularly—the most commonly used format.[132] At the same time, in the UK, for example, slightly over 60% of internet users indicated that email was the most preferred media format for receiving marketing communication from retailers.[133] This is far ahead of other methods of communication such as direct mail (20.8%) or social media (2.5%).[134]

Equally important, when compared with other digital formats, email marketing appears to be the single most effective way of achieving all principal marketing goals including customer awareness, acquisition, conversion, and retention. Email marketing is a more effective way to acquire customers than social media—nearly 40 times that of Facebook and Twitter combined while emails are also found to prompt purchases estimated to be three times higher in value than those of social media.[135] At the same time, email is highly effective when it comes to customer retention and leads by almost 20 percentage points over social marketing as the next effective format (Figure 3.47).

These figures are not airline industry specific but we can reasonably assume that they play out similarly for airlines to some extent. Many of them are custodians of email marketing communication through various vehicles including e-newsletters, frequent flyer programs, and to a lesser extent customer service notifications. For instance, while subscription rates naturally vary by country, it is common for a third to a quarter of leisure travelers to receive email newsletters from airlines. In markets like Australia and Brazil, the share of local web travelers subscribing to email

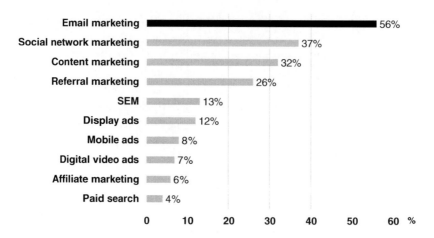

*Figure 3.47* *Effectiveness of digital marketing programs for retention (US, Q2 2014)*

*Source:* eMarketer.com (2014)[136]

newsletters is 38% and 52%, respectively (Figure 3.48). Airlines should be careful shifting their budgets away from email marketing too quickly and rushing into social media and mobile formats.

### 3.9.1 Email marketing: Getting started

E-Commerce savvy airlines have long realized that multiple aspects must be tackled when it comes to effective email marketing. Deciding where and how to collect email addresses, managing the cross-departmental/inter-company process of creating email content, handling the logistics of email distribution and the reporting/analysis

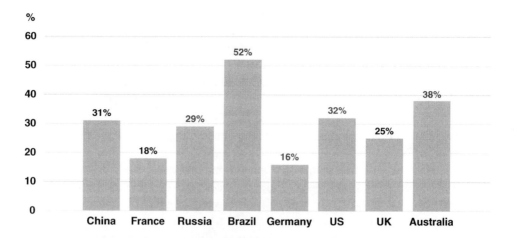

*Figure 3.48* *Email newsletter subscription among leisure travelers in selected markets*

*Source:* Phocuswright (2015)[137]

of email campaign results are all key activities. A lot needs to go right in order for email marketing to be successful. Our discussion below sheds some light on these areas that all need to be integral parts of email management.

*Qualified email addresses and types of airline emails*

Not every email address is a good email and can be considered "qualified" for the purpose of digital communication. An airline, as part of an email policy, needs to have a clear understanding of what constitutes an email address for it to be eligible for marketing communication.

A qualified email address should meet all of the following criteria:

- Web traveler has given permission to receive communications from the airline.
- Web traveler may unsubscribe at any time.
- The email address collection process adheres to proper global and industry legal and standards and regulations.
- The web traveler's email address is active and deliverable.
- An email address is considered active when the airline has successfully sent an email in the last 6 months (some airline use a 12-month timeframe) and it was not returned as undeliverable.
- After several unsuccessful delivery attempts, an email address should be classified as a "bad address."

In essence, there are two types of emails which an airline uses for communication with web travelers: Marketing emails and customer service emails (Figure 3.49).

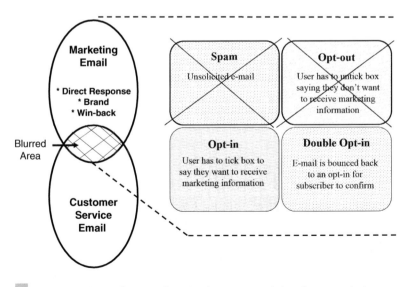

**Figure 3.49** *Email types and associated customer permissions for communication*

MARKETING EMAILS

These comprise promotional or informational messages that the airline sends to a list of web travelers. Fare sales, FFP promotions, and new product and service announcements are examples of the email content web travelers see. Based on the content involved, it is common to differentiate between two major types of marketing emails: Direct response and brand emails. Some observers consider the "win-back" email as a third type of email. It is common when attempting to regain a lapsed customer who has abandoned the carrier.

Out of respect for a web traveler's privacy and to be in compliance with legal requirements, an airline can engage only in the sending of marketing emails when the web traveler has given permission to do so. Sending unsolicited email communication or so-called spam to customers is illegal. Furthermore, legal provisions in some countries, an example is the European Directive on Privacy and Electronic Communication from 2002, do not allow the practice of "opting out" whereby an airline pre-checks a consent box for web travelers indicating agreement to receive email communication. It has to be the travelers themselves who provide for an "explicit" opt-in by ticking the consent box. Some airlines are still lacking compliance in this area and ultimately hurt their brands because they are often viewed as spammers.

Other than unsubscribing, people receiving irrelevant emails from airlines may take a few more drastic steps. These include blocking the senders' email address, reporting the company to authorities, or punishing the business by not buying from them. In order to ensure that they received consent from a traveler for email communication, some airlines not only look for an explicit opt-in by a web traveler, but also ask for additional confirmation in a separate email whether the web traveler truly agrees with receiving email communication. This is the so-called "double opt-in" and one airline following this approach is Lufthansa in Germany.[138]

CUSTOMER SERVICE EMAILS

All airlines use email communication for a variety of customer service purposes and we elaborate on this area extensively in Chapter 5. However, the reasons for bringing up customer service emails in the context of marketing communication has to do with an interesting trend. In recent years, a growing number of airlines have started to blur the boundaries of customer service emails by including sales and branding messages that in the past had been strictly confined to email marketing communication.

Take for example a confirmation email that an airline is legally mandated to provide to a web traveler after an online ticket booking on the carrier's website is completed. Another example is the alert for an online check-in sent out 24 hours prior to a web traveler's departure. These emails are all automatically triggered by a web traveler's activity and an airline does not require an explicit permission to use them because the nature of the communication involved is not related to marketing.

From an airline perspective, the inclusion of up-/cross-sell offers is tempting because service emails traditionally enjoy very high open rates and greater engagement with customers. This could potentially generate additional revenue streams. However, no matter how "soft" the sale communicated in a customer service email, it is a fine line to cross. Some web travelers may view this as a violation of their privacy and it could even be questionable from a legal perspective. Therefore, an airline needs to be careful not to overstep and engage in marketing communication under a service pretext.

The author is aware of such a campaign involving Air France several years ago. At the time, the airline followed up with customers after their trip was completed and thanked them for having chosen Air France. In the same email, the carrier also offered social media engagement, an FFP enrollment, and a city guide (that eventually led with several clicks to a booking engine).[139]

### 3.9.2 Finding subscribers: Methods and sources to acquire email addresses

There are three principal methods for an airline to acquire email addresses: Build, rent, and buy. Each method is associated with a number of specific sources that are discussed in more detail in Figure 3.50.

*Building an opt-in email list*

Growing a permission-based email list to a significant size takes time and effort. A main reason is the increased wariness of consumers. Despite better spam filters, there are still issues in cyberspace involving communication clutter and inundation with marketing messages. People have become more selective with whom they share their email address (some individuals alleviate this situation by maintaining multiple email accounts and designating one for marketing communication from companies only).

The early days when email addresses were volunteered without second thoughts are gone. Companies today often have to offer incentives in return for obtaining a

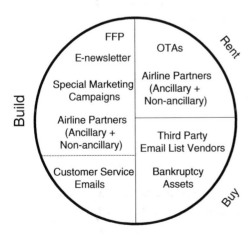

*Figure 3.50 Methods and sources to acquire email addresses*

consumer's email address. A popular tactic applied by airlines is a mileage bonus for web travelers who sign up for the company's e-newsletter. In order to boost customer response rates, some companies have even offered incentives when emails were opened or clicked through to the airline website. When sharing their email address, web travelers do so because of interest and trust to receive valuable and helpful communication from the carrier.

Another reason why building an email list is often a challenge is found in the airline itself. Some carriers do not even have an explicit email address acquisition goal. At best, they may view it as a by-product of other objectives such as increasing the number of FFP memberships. An airline should grow its email database annually by a minimum of 3% to 5%. This compensates for natural attritions resulting from travelers unsubscribing for various reasons including switching loyalties to other carriers. Furthermore, conducting special promotional campaigns such as sweepstakes and auctions should also be conducted with email address acquisition goals in mind. There are other internal factors why the increase of email address lists is often suboptimal is because of a lack of clear organizational ownership, roles, procedures, inadequate resources, and often insufficient know-how in using existing technical data management applications.

There are several sources an airline can tap into for building up a permissible email address list. They include an airline's:

- frequent flyer program
- e-newsletters
- special online marketing campaigns
- opt-in email lists from airline marketing partners
- customer service emails from PNR feeds (although contested).

## FREQUENT FLYER PROGRAMS

One of the richest sources for an airline to collect email addresses is through its frequent flyer program. Web travelers who sign up and become FFP members are relatively familiar with and loyal to the airline brand. Of all audiences targeted for email communication, they are likely to be most receptive and therefore will share their email address readily.

Ideally, every single FFP member should be on an airline's record with an email address for marketing communication. This can be achieved by requiring web travelers to share their email address as part of the enrollment in an airline's FFP. This ensures that members receive FFP account updates and promotional information. Airlines that do not make it mandatory for FFP members to share their email address miss out on an important low-cost communication opportunity with their most loyal customers.

In instances where a web traveler's email address is not in an airline's FFP database, a follow-up with an appropriate cover letter by the airline can always be done via regular mail to collect it. An incentive in the form of bonus miles may be used to encourage web travelers to share their email address. Airlines have applied this tactic before in a similar situation when they wanted to ease the transition for their FFP members from paper account statements to e-statements. "Carrots" offered to FFP members included bonus miles while "sticks" involved extra fees if an FFP member insisted on receiving traditional paper statements. For example, United currently charges $25 for sending out FFP statements in paper form.[140]

## E-NEWSLETTERS

Most airlines maintain an e-newsletter program that web travelers can sign up for. In some cases, multiple email newsletters are offered. For example on Emirates.com, one can select a special offers email and a newsletter (the carrier even shows examples of these so people have an impression what they would receive).

The sign-up process can be as simple as providing a name and an email address. Some airlines take the opportunity to collect more information in order to gain additional insight into the individual they are communicating with. Among other things, this allows some degree of personalization in the email communication. For instance, Air Canada offers a sign-up for surveys and its inflight magazine while KLM also asks for a person's date of birth. Interesting about Virgin Australia is how prominently they promote a newsletter enrollment. On their website homepage, a large float ad appears making it impossible for a web traveler to ignore. As in other airline cases, they also seek FFP and airport departure information from a web traveler (Figure 3.51).

## SPECIAL ONLINE MARKETING CAMPAIGNS

Sweepstakes are one popular example of a special marketing campaign that many airlines conduct for different occasions throughout the year. In return for the possibility of winning one of the many airline prizes such as free tickets or bonus miles, a web traveler who wishes to participate has to register with their contact details including email addresses. Carriers often build special microsites to handle the registrations involved. Figure 3.52 shows such an example of Finnair.

Assuming the web traveler agrees to receive marketing communications, their email address is added to the airline's data permission-based email list. If an airline conducts a co-marketing campaign with another company, the email addresses collected are typically owned by both parties.

A sweepstake campaign often features a viral marketing component. In this instance, an airline relies on web travelers to pass on details about the campaign to other people including friends, relatives, and peers who in turn may register with their email address as well. This could further boost the number of possible opt-in emails.

## OPT-IN EMAIL LISTS FROM AIRLINE PARTNERS

Airlines collect opt-in emails indirectly via travel and non-travel related companies. For example, a web user on a car rental company's site may be in the process of signing up for that company's e-newsletter and is also asked if they agree to receive

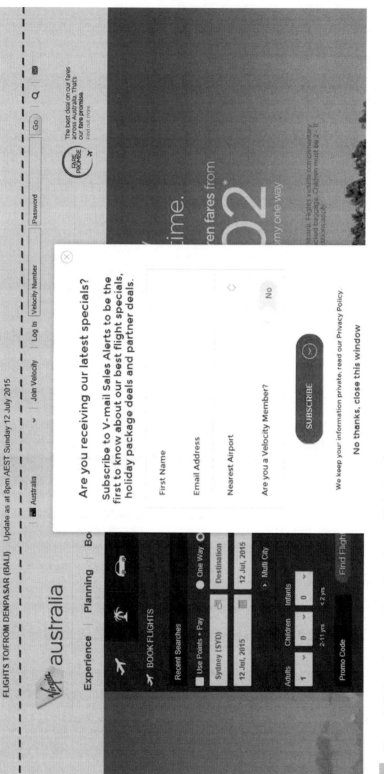

**Figure 3.51** *Promoting an email newsletter sign-up: Virgin Australia*

Source: virginaustralia.com (2015)[141] with kind permission of Virgin Australia

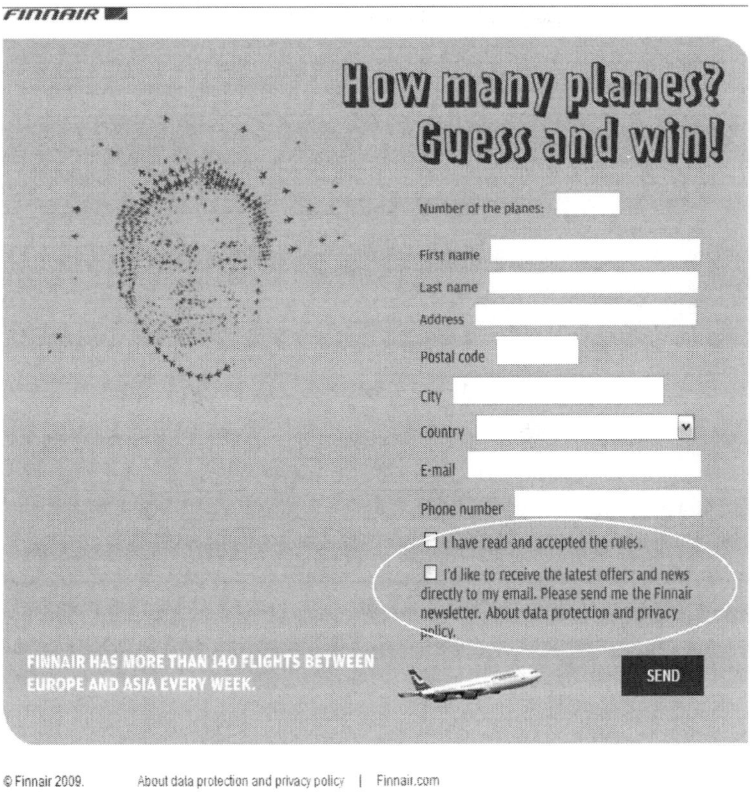

FINNAIR

# How many planes? Guess and win!

Number of the planes:

First name

Last name

Address

Postal code

City

Country

E-mail

Phone number

☐ I have read and accepted the rules.

☐ I'd like to receive the latest offers and news directly to my email. Please send me the Finnair newsletter. About data protection and privacy policy.

FINNAIR HAS MORE THAN 140 FLIGHTS BETWEEN EUROPE AND ASIA EVERY WEEK.

SEND

© Finnair 2009.      About data protection and privacy policy   |   Finnair.com

*Figure 3.52* *Email address collection as part of a sweepstake—Finnair: How many planes?*

*Source:* finnair.com (ca 2009)[142] with kind permission of Finnair

emails with promotional information from other selected partners of the company. One of these "selected partners" could be an airline. If web users give their consent to receiving marketing emails from third parties, the airline can now add their email addresses to its opt-in list for future communication. The airline typically pays a fee for this email acquisition unless there is another agreement with the partner in place.

## CUSTOMER SERVICE EMAILS REPURPOSED FOR MARKETING COMMUNICATION

We have mentioned earlier the borderline case where some airlines repurpose customer service emails for the inclusion of marketing communication.

Web travelers share their email address with an airline for customer service reasons. For example, upon completing an online ticket purchase on a carrier's website, web travelers also have to provide an email address. If an airline wants to use it also for marketing communication, the correct policy to follow is to contact the web traveler (via the customer service email address or even the postal address) and ask for permission.

Another instance where customer service contact information comes into play is when an airline's FFP and non–FFP database shows customers with no email address at all. The only record available may be the customer's postal address and phone number. In this case an airline needs to contact the customer via regular mail to check on their interest in receiving email marketing information. Customers often share their email address in this instance, especially when offered an incentive.

*Buying third party email lists*

Buying email addresses in the open market is generally not a good idea. There are hundreds of companies claiming to offer "qualified" email addresses at incredibly attractive prices (a simple Google search "buy email addresses" shows the corresponding results) but the truth is that such lists are of extreme low quality. This is because their email addresses often contain misspellings, are inactive, or are generic (for example, info@abcbusiness) and not tied to a particular user name because a web crawler compiled them.

Unsurprisingly, the performance results in terms of email delivery and customer response rates are weak. It is not unusual to see a non–delivery rate of 90% or more. The unwelcome consequences from all of this is that the few good email addresses in this list are blocked or treated as spam. Worse, the email transmitter such as AOL, Yahoo, or Google ends up blacklisting the IP address of the company having used this low-quality list. In essence, a purchased third party email list is a poor match for an airline's needs.

There is one exception to this: The acquisition of email address databases from bankrupt travel organizations such as tour operators/travel agencies, cruise ship companies, and airlines. Their customer loyalty programs and membership bases are highly sought after in the event of a liquidation sale of corporate assets. In the wake of the Australian carrier Ansett Airlines' demise in September 2001, for example, several airlines including United Airlines looked into bidding for the airline's frequent flyer program member database. Other airlines that went out of business since then and that also operated FFP databases include Maxjet Airways in 2007, EOS in 2008, and Mexicana in 2010. An airline should always look out for such a rare opportunity to expand its qualified email database with people that have been doing business with other travel brands before.

*Renting third party email lists*

Besides acquiring email addresses and adding them to the their own database, carriers also tap into the permissionable email list of third parties. Preferred are companies with customers who have some affinity for travel. Airlines often work with ancillary travel partners including hotels and car rental companies. The databases of online travel agencies are also frequently used (Figure 3.53 shows an example of Icelandair renting Expedia's e-newsletter database). Occasionally, mobile phone and credit card companies may be part of the mix.

Renting an email database from another company is not cheap. During past negotiations with OTAs for inclusion of airline marketing information, this author has seen

**Figure 3.53** *Expedia newsletter with Icelandair promotion*

*Source:* Expedia Newsletter (2014)[143] with kind permission of Expedia

fees of up to $10,000 during a three-month period involving two to three email drops. A caveat when communicating to the marketplace under another company's brand is that the email content conveys a generic rather than an individualized message. Nevertheless, communicating to a third-party travel-minded audience helps increase the airline's digital brand exposure and may ultimately stimulate online revenue.

When an airline uses the email database of another company, there are four key aspects that should be taken into account in order to maximize the campaign performance:

- *Opt-in.* The airline's email drop should only go to people who have agreed to receive information from third parties.
- *Recency.* People should be targeted that have signed up for receiving news within the last 1–6 months.
- *Competition.* The airline should ensure that the email drop does not feature a competitor's offer and that the target audience has not been emailed a similar offer recently.
- *Relevance.* The email message should be focused on a specified interest.

### 3.9.3 Managing the email cycle

Starting with the collection of content and finishing with the follow–up reporting, Figure 3.54 illustrates a typical email management cycle with the specific steps and actors involved. The whole cycle typically takes a week. Efficiencies can be created by re-using email templates so that an email does not have to be created from scratch all the time and handling routines can help speed things up. The information below shares more details on each of these steps.

The handling of this cycle occurs largely within the infrastructure of an email management platform. Some carriers have deployed inhouse or hybrid solutions while others revert to an outsourced provider entirely. There are pros and cons for these different approaches but an elaboration is beyond the scope of our discussion. Essentially, budget issues as well as staff resources and their quality play a huge role.

*Managing email content*

Content is king with email marketing communication. Content can accomplish the following:

- it builds awareness of and a relationship with the carrier's digital brand
- it drives page views to an airline's website
- it may create viral awareness of the carrier through email forwards.

Generally, for a carrier's email content to be compelling in the eyes of a web traveler, it has to address topics that touch on fares, frequent flyer program, and company news and updates. Depending on the nature of the email (direct response vs brand), one topic is emphasized over others or it may be the only one featured.

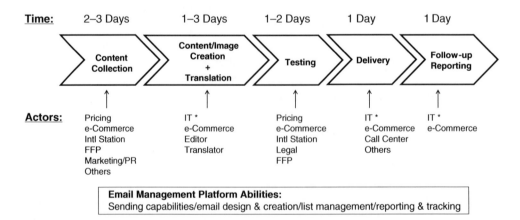

**Figure 3.54** *A typical e-mail management cycle*

\* The involvement of an airline's IT department is largely contingent on whether an internal or outsourced email management platform is utilized. If outsourced, their necessary interaction during the various steps in the email management cycle is small.

Considering that the vast majority of email messages are direct response focused and therefore involve a fare promotion, the presentation of price points with a call to action ("book now") is supremely important. The fare specials are typically for economy class but occasionally are for business class as well. The airline head office's pricing department, often in coordination with local management in different markets, takes charge of determining the fare levels and associated terms and conditions.

If a fare sale is not the key message, frequent flyer program information is often a focus in an airline e-newsletter. Larger carriers typically operate a separate email product in the form of an FFP newsletter providing information on a web traveler's person's account while also sharing marketing information. Common FFP topics are one-time and ongoing promotions. They could also be about important program adjustments such as the addition of new airline partners for mileage collection/redemption. A carrier's FFP department is responsible for sponsoring this kind of e-newsletter input.

Lastly, overall company news and updates generally include information on routes, aircraft purchases, schedule changes, and others. The input comes from the head office including PR, marketing, and sales as well as local offices in other countries.

One comment on segmentation. Early on in the email management cycle, a decision needs to be taken on how targeted the email drop should be. It may be by demographics or by geography. It is also common to look at the so-called consumer state which is active or passive. For some carriers, a web traveler is considered active if they have traveled with the airline in the last 6 months or they have opened an email in the last 12 months. Accordingly, a web traveler's consumer state may also play a role when an airline decides whom to target with their email communication.

*Dealing with email format*

Besides content, managing an email's format also requires attention in order to ensure that the performance of the email communication is maximized. Four aspects have to be addressed:

- file size
- copy writing
- subject line
- viral.

What is the ideal file size of an email? Taking into account that about three-quarters of emails are accessed via mobile devices and how expensive data access via these devices can be, the answer is as small as possible. For an HTML email, the limit is currently 102 kilobyte (excluding images that do not count toward this number).[144] Not paying attention to file size leads to a delayed email download or clipped message. Either scenario is not good and any issues must be ideally addressed by the carrier during the initial crafting phase or resolved at the latest during the email testing stage.

Email content needs to be written by a professional copywriter. They create compelling content that is brief, catchy, and call-to-action oriented. Moreover, there has to be a healthy balance between text and images. When opening an email, the average reader spends approximately 15 seconds on a mobile device and just over 36 seconds on desktops.[145] There is not much time for an airline to bring its email marketing message across. Another issue a professional copywriter looks out for is minimizing, if not avoiding phrases such as "for free" and "get it now" that set in motion spam filters by email service providers. There are approximately 200 words/phrases on this list.[146] Not managing this carefully means that the airline email may end up in the subscriber's spam folder. Also, good copywriters mark any links in the text clearly and visibly. This allows a reader to be directed seamlessly from the email to one of the carrier's digital platforms such as the desktop website or mobile site. All of this happens only provided that the email is opened in the first place.

This brings us to the email's subject line. Most web travelers are inundated with emails so they might have developed an "anti-headline" defense to some extent. Therefore, if the subject line is not convincing, the reader will move on. Importantly, the subject line has to fit the recipient's view panel or at least give enough information so that a reader has a clue what the message is about. Furthermore, similar to content, subject lines are also picked by spam filters. Words such as "free" or "discount" must be avoided since they are associated with spam. Common email subject lines of airline newsletters touch on the themes of urgency or fascination although news, seasonality, issue-based, and even personalized subject lines are also applied (Figure 3.55).

**Theme: Urgency**

**JetBlue Subject Header: "Two Days Only!"**

A way of creating anxiety and playing on the issue that some web travelers respond better to the threat of losing out on a fare sale. "Last chance" is also used.

**Theme: Personalized**

**Lufthansa Subject Header: "A Birthday Surprise To You, Michael Hanke"**

Targeted email and calling out the web traveler's name for increased attention, often in conjunction with fascination or urgency theme.

*Figure 3.55* *Airline email newsletter samples*

With kind permission of Cathay Pacific, JetBlue, airBerlin, Croatia Airlines, Lufthansa, and Ukraine International Airlines

**Theme: Seasonality**

**Croatia Airlines Subject Line: "Happy Easter"**

Reference to seasonality or time of year
that tries to catch reader's attention

**Theme: Issue-based**

**UIA Subject Line: New York-Kiev $806**

Subject line simply announces the content of
the email, no further details required

**Theme: News**

**Cathay Pacific Subject Line:
"Website Refresh for Cathay"**

Offering something new to web travelers
that they have not experienced before.

**Theme: Fascination**

**airberlin Subject Line:
"Discover the East"**

Exploiting the reader's curiosity and a
motivation to find more information in the email.
"Discover," "Explore," "Amazing"
are related words applied.

**Figure 3.55** *continued*

Concerning the viral aspect of email communication, the question is whether the email's content is attractive enough to expect pass-ons. It is a good policy for an airline to integrate viral components in its email communication. They help increase brand awareness in the marketplace and potentially generate incremental revenue. If the content involves a great offer, is humorous, or twisted, the chances for a pass-on by a web traveler to others are high. Another factor has to do with the ease for the recipient of sharing an email with friends and relatives. Featuring links to social networks including Facebook and Twitter and offering easy-to-use subscription forms where people can share their email address are crucial.

Once the email is created and a prototype review is completed by several stakeholders—for example, the pricing department checks on the accuracy of the fare levels advertised and the legal department ensures that the email content promoted is in accordance with applicable regulations—it is test-sent through the delivery system. This may be the airline's own inhouse logistics system or a third-party emailer infrastructure that manages the email drop. Testing is important because it reveals any possible shortcomings particularly in the email design. For example, an airline's email templates react differently to gmail, Yahoo, and hotmail. If the email is test-delivered without issues, it is time to prepare its drop to customers.

*Timing of the email drop*

Some carriers decide on an adhoc basis for the timing of their email communication. This approach may be justified occasionally. An example is the promotion of last-minute fare specials because an airline has too much distressed seat inventory. However, it should not be a policy. E-Commerce savvy airlines establish an annual online media calendar and email campaigns have their confirmed spot on it with a pre-determined frequency. Three factors should be taken into consideration for the airline's email drop:

- week day of the drop
- time of the day
- frequency.

As a general rule of thumb, email deliveries are more successful when they avoid the beginning or end of a working week. In most countries, this counts Monday and Friday out because people are either just coming off the weekend or about to enter the weekend. Several studies have proven that email open rates are generally best between Tuesday and Thursday. According to one survey in the UK involving the analysis of 200 million emails sent, close to 60% of all emails are opened between Tuesday and Thursday.[147] In terms of time of day, it appears that regular working hours between 9 am and 5 pm account for almost 70% of all emails opened. Within this timeframe, a peak apparently occurs around 11 am with another spike in the evening.[148] Airlines operating successful email marketing programs have typically run a few campaigns and know their statistics in order to determine best weekday and time for certain target audiences.

Lastly, frequency speaks to the number of times an airline contacts a web traveler. In the context of an attention marketplace, an airline should aim at sending ideally three or four emails during a calendar month. Anything less is likely to harm a carrier's brand because web travelers tend to overlook it in an otherwise crowded cyberspace. Conversely, airlines considering any frequency significantly above this number could be perceived as spammers, especially if messages are rather similar in nature. Of the airlines shown earlier in Figure 3.55, the author receives on average one email per week from each carrier.

*Follow-up reporting*

Within a couple of days after the email delivery, the e-marketer at an airline should have a good idea on the performance of the email campaign. There are a few key metrics to look out for that reflect the relative success (or failure) of the campaign (Table 3.8).

***Table 3.8*** *Key metrics for email marketing campaigns*

| Metric | Commentary |
|---|---|
| Email list size | This goes back to an airline's email campaign starting point: The original list size used. Depending on how small or large the list involved, the results should be interpreted accordingly. |
| | For example, if an airline sends an email to a small group such as its top tier FFP members, one could expect the campaign's performance results to be overall stronger as these flyers are more brand committed. Conversely, an email drop to the entire FFP database would lead to a weaker performance due to the more general population with less brand supportive members. |
| Delivered rate | This metric indicates the number of email delivered including those that end up in spam folders. The Delivered Rate also shows the proportion of bad addresses where emails bounced back. |
| | Delivery rates of 90% or more are an indicator that the carrier's email address database is in a good condition. If more than 15% to 20% of the emails dropped could not be delivered, we have a warning sign for an overdue email data hygiene action item. There may be too many bad addresses (misspellings, inactive email accounts) that drive this number and an airline should clean these out. This step not only avoids undue attention by ISPs who might blacklist the airline if this is an ongoing issue but also saves the company money if an external email sender is involved who typically earns a fee for the emails sent. |
| Open rate | How many recipients opened the email? The Open Rate provides for insight and the higher the number, the better. The travel sector enjoys a good email open rate with around 22%. In comparison with other sectors like the public sector (34%) on the high end and event (16%) on the lower end of the spectrum, this performance is therefore competitive.[149] |
| Click-through rate | This metric shows the number of people who interacted with the airline's email and clicked on a link that directed them back to the airline's website. |
| | The average click-through rate is almost 3%. This means than 3 out of 100 web travelers who actually have opened the email click on a hyperlink within the email and are then directed to the carrier's digital platform. Again, this number puts the travel sector in the middle field.[150] |

**Table 3.8** *continued*

| Metric | Commentary |
|---|---|
| Conversion rate | The conversion rate is the ultimate indicator for an email's performance. How many tickets were purchased or how many FFP enrollments were registered as a result of the email campaign? Email management platforms do not handle this metric. Some carriers use open source tools including Google Analytics while others apply proprietary applications. |
| Number of unsubscribes/ spam complaints | If the email drop triggers a high number of unsubscribes or even spam complaints, a carrier has to review the quality of its email content and/or re-assess the frequency of email communication. The objective of an email campaign is not to reduce the number of subscribers or hurt the airline's reputation. The lower this metric, the better. |

*Source:* Based on Author and Neely (2014) [151]

If an airline email campaign's performance metrics are not as good as one might have expected, it is crucial to do a follow-up review. Factors that could have led to weak results include:

- *Unattractive offer.* "The fare special was just not special enough."
- *Inadequate execution.* "Poor branding, too much text or images, broken links."
- *Weak email design.* "Unclear path to click-through, non-optimized landing pages, not optimized for mobile devices."
- *Poor deliverability.* "Usage of uncleansed email list."
- *Unrealistic goals.* "Conversion expectations are too high, dead email list with customers tired of same or similar offers."

### 3.9.4 The future of email marketing

Email marketing is here to stay. Carriers have a reasonably good opportunity to continue deploying this online mass media format. Its benefits in terms of low cost, segmentation, personalization, and high speed are too compelling to ignore. However, dealing with "standard" challenges such as providing sufficient resources and finding new subscribers is not easy. Furthermore, airlines need to watch out for maintaining the relevance of their email communication by optimizing it for mobile devices. It is estimated that almost three-quarters of people in the United States access email via mobile devices, yet many companies have not configured their email marketing communication for mobile platforms.[152] Any airline that may fall into this group of companies needs to set aside resources in order to upgrade for mobile-optimized email marketing communication.

### 3.10 SOCIAL MEDIA MARKETING

Social media marketing (SMM) refers to the use of social media websites by companies to increase awareness for their brand and grow their sales.

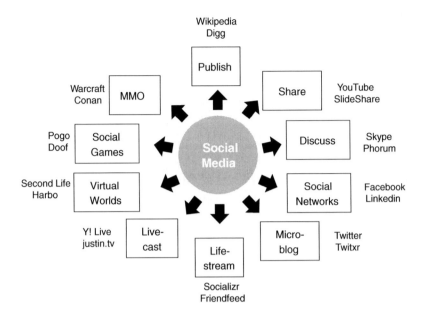

**Figure 3.56** *The social media landscape*

Source: Based on Fredcavazza.net (2015)[153]

The landscape comprising social media is highly diverse with many potential options for an airline to choose from. We have social networks including Facebook, multi-sharing websites such as YouTube, microblogs (Twitter), social games (Pogo), virtual worlds (Second Life), and many other categories (Figure 3.56).

Worldwide, advertisers spend an increasing amount in this area. By 2016, the spending is estimated at almost $26 billion, almost four times higher than it was in 2012 (Table 3.9). North America is taking a clear lead over other regions with Facebook being by far the most common platform where marketers advertise.

The speed by which the social media landscape keeps on changing is amazing. Simultaneously, the adoption of social media websites by consumers continues being pushed due to the proliferation of mobile technology. In essence, the demand side for social networks is strong in key travel markets around the world (Figure 3.57).

Social media marketing is a highly dynamic field which can easily puzzle any airline. It may allocate too many marketing resources to a handful of social media platforms, it may attempt to keep up with most, or it may shy away from doing enough.

Before we go into a more specific discussion on the objectives that an airline has to keep in mind for social media marketing, it is important to remember what we emphasized at the outset of this chapter. Besides the various types of *paid* and *owned* media formats that airlines deploy in their communication with web travelers, there is also an *earned* aspect to marketing. This is particularly true for social media marketing. By way of mouth, a trusted communication channel for people are family, friends, and colleagues. They are the top offline source for almost 50% of leisure travelers and for 35% of business travelers.[154] In a way, this trust aspect has been

**Table 3.9** *Social network ad spend by region (2012–2016, $ millions)*[*]

| Region | 2012 | 2013 | 2014 | 2015 | 2016 |
|---|---|---|---|---|---|
| North America | $3,393 | $4,951 | $7,164 | $9,205 | $11,154 |
| Asia Pacific | $2,015 | $3,199 | $4,632 | $6,135 | $7,637 |
| Western Europe | $1,555 | $2,202 | $3,283 | $4,428 | $5,580 |
| Latin America | $237 | $350 | $523 | $612 | $716 |
| Central & Eastern Europe | $230 | $315 | $390 | $453 | $508 |
| Middle East & Africa | $39 | $66 | $108 | $165 | $221 |
| Worldwide | **$7,470** | **$11,083** | **$16,100** | **$20,998** | **$25,815** |

[*]Includes display, search video, and other forms of paid advertising appearing within social networks, social games, and social applications. Excluding spending on development and maintenance of social network pages or branded applications. Numbers may not add up to total due to rounding.

*Source:* eMarketer.com (2014)[155]

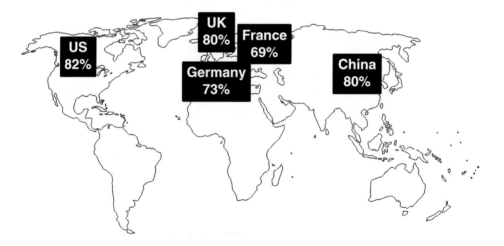

**Figure 3.57** *Percentage of travelers active with social networks at least monthly*

*Source:* Quinby and Gasdia (2014)[156]

extended to today's social media platforms such as Facebook and Twitter. They are the modern forms of conducting word of mouth. Over three-quarters of social media users agree that online travel reviews give them insight knowledge not available elsewhere while close to 70% state that online travel reviews give them the confidence they need to book.[157]

Word of mouth is more trusted than whatever messages come through via paid or owned communication channels. Moreover, because of their popularity and omnipresence, the power of social media as a means of persuasion cannot be underestimated. Its power exceeds by far that of owned and paid media formats. For an airline, the implication of this is to break with tradition and not only be concerned with paid and owned media. Today, through the participation and monitoring of social media, an airline can amplify the original marketing message and enhance its delivery to the marketplace. This in turn creates larger word of mouth and an opportunity for awareness, consideration, and purchase by other web travelers of the airline's products and services (Figure 3.58).

Airlines that are effective players in the social media sphere are those that turn web travelers into brand advocates. Some 77% of leisure travelers are undecided on the airline brand when initiating their travel planning activities.[158] Against this background, an airline should seek brand advocates wherever it can because they are surely needed. At the same time, we need to remember that we live in a sharing economy. Today, consumers including web travelers want their voices heard. Airlines need to show that they are good listeners who seek input in a variety of topics. This requires relinquishing control. This is not an easy thing to do but absolutely essential if a carrier wants to be successful in this space.

### 3.10.1 A framework for successful social media marketing

How can an airline achieve brand advocacy with social media marketing? The answer is to establish a framework with organizing principles on which successful social media marketing rests.

In analogy with the so-called "T-principles" proposed by Andy Sernovitz, president emeritus of the Word of Mouth Marketing Association, our framework for an airline's social media marketing activities is based on the following:

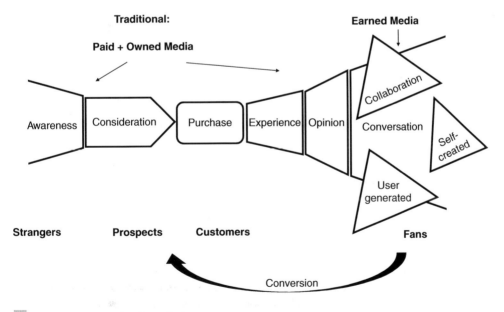

*Figure 3.58 Social media marketing*

Source: Based on Edwards (2011)[159]

1. *Topics*. Build a marketing message that is simple, interesting, and invites being shared with others.
2. *Talkers*. Finding web travelers who have social influence and talk about a carrier.
3. *Tools*. Make sure that social media web travelers can interact with the message.
4. *Taking part*. Engagement with web travelers by providing them with new information on an ongoing basis and answering their questions.
5. *Targets*. Identify objectives and metrics that a carrier should establish and monitor to gauge progress.

*Topics*

Attention magnets are not so much fare promotions or other direct sales topics. This is because social media, at least in North American and European travel markets, are not widely used to buy tickets. Instead, web travelers' interaction with social media is about engagement with an airline and other web travelers. Typical topics that trigger engagement include:

- special events (an example is Qatar Airways' Airbus A350XWB inaugural flight to London Heathrow in January 2015 that attracted huge crowds on Facebook)
- a brand message conveyed in a twisted and funny way (think of Turkish Airlines' ongoing YouTube campaign with basketball player Kobe Bryant and footballer Lionel Messi)
- unique contests (Cathay Pacific's "Travel the World in 80 days" campaign on Facebook);
- areas that highlight an airline's involvement in social causes (an example is JetBlue's "FlyItForward" campaign).

For topics to trigger web traveler engagement, they also need to have local relevancy, otherwise the intended audience tunes out.

*Talkers*

Talkers are not big groups but few in numbers. The first step is to identify these key influencers and tap into them to replicate word of mouth on a large scale. Since key influencers are considered authentic and trustworthy, their involvement in the creation or distribution of a message can help in the promotion of an airline brand. As we will see later in our discussion, several airlines including American Airlines and Japanese ANA have struck important relationships with social influencers.

*Tools*

A carrier has to ensure that the topic always invites a response. It is therefore important to design them with a viral component. Encouragement to pass on the topic is crucial for further distribution to a wider audience. Part of the tool kit is also a strong and dedicated social media team. Airlines that excel in social media including Jet-Blue, KLM, and Qatar Airways employ full-time staff who are exclusively focused on this area. Furthermore, managing across multiple social media platforms, possibly in several countries, requires attention to making sure that the topic is connected and the brand is presented consistently.

*Taking part*

Airline social media marketers must seek the informal social media dialogue with their target audience. It is often difficult to manage these conversations. Airlines have to invest in training and resources to be able to participate and not only speak the social media language but also fix problems. Moreover, the communication has to be in real time.

*Targets*

The framework for social media marketing has to be tied into the identification of social media marketing objectives. This process involves three key steps that an airline should consider.

STEP 1: SETTING UP OBJECTIVES

It is important to acknowledge that launching a presence on selected social media platforms "just because other competitors are doing it" is not a viable long-term perspective. When an airline engages in social media marketing, there needs to be clarity on what the objectives are. They may include:

- brand reputation monitoring
- development of brand awareness and public relations
- insight on web traveler behavior via analytics
- higher level of web traveler brand engagement
- conversions such as ticket purchases or FFP enrollments.

This cannot be accomplished all at once but involves a gradual process over time.

When engaged in the objective setting process, it is crucial to make sure that the objectives reflect the appropriate stage the airline is in when it comes to social media marketing. If this is not properly handled, a carrier may have a mismatch between what the company can realistically achieve versus where it is in the evolutionary stage of social media marketing. A smart approach in the setting of objectives for social media marketing is to see this as a four-stage evolution. One typically starts with activity-based objectives and then moves on to audience-building, engagement, and finally return on investment (ROI) objectives (Table 3.10).

The objectives are intertwined with the level of an airline's commitment to social media. Successful social media marketing involves much work. Managing blog posts,

**Table 3.10** *The stages in social media marketing objectives*

| Stage | Commentary |
|---|---|
| Stage 1: Activity-Based Objectives | The carrier decides on the number of blog posts per month, tweets per day, and status updates per week that can be managed. Furthermore, there needs to be clarity on the types of topics covered in these activities. |
| Stage 2: Audience-Building Objectives | The carrier manages some degree of consistency in social media activities. Next is to attract an audience and appeal to strangers, prospects, customers, influencers, and even employees. Typical metrics include the number of email subscribers to a blog and the followers/fans on Facebook and Twitter for example. |
| Stage 3: Engagement Objectives | At this stage, web travelers are starting to regularly share the airline's blog posts, retweet and like and comment on LinkedIn status updates. An airline now can concern itself with improving the level of engagement. Metrics such as likes, shares, retweets, mentions, and comments are important. At the same time, the airline should identify social media influencers and engage them. |
| Stage 4: ROI Objectives | ROI of social media efforts can be measured now as a result of the carrier's consistent and growing social media activity. An engaged audience is starting to drive website traffic and landing page clicks. |

status updates, tweets, and videos on a daily or weekly basis is an area that requires time, money, and people.

## STEP 2: DECIDING ON WHICH SOCIAL MEDIA PLATFORM TO FOCUS ON FOR MARKETING

The decision where and how to participate in the social media world can be guided by a few questions including:

- Where do web travelers spend their time?
- What are they sharing?
- How do they share it?

For example, if web travelers are active on Facebook, Twitter, and YouTube, an airline needs to be there as well. Is it worth being on Google+, Instagram, and Flickr? The platforms an airline is active on not only depend on the target audience but also on what an airline's competitors are up to, what the carrier's objectives are, and what its resource availability is. Some airlines overstretch themselves and participate in too many venues. Dormant accounts, outdated content, and infrequent engagement with web travelers are evidence of this. Instead, a better approach is to focus on a few main social platforms and manage them really well. Helpful in this regard is also to remember where social media fit in the travel life cycle of web travelers. For the US market, for instance, social media play a strong role during the inspiration, research, and sharing stages. Less important are social media for shopping aspects.[160]

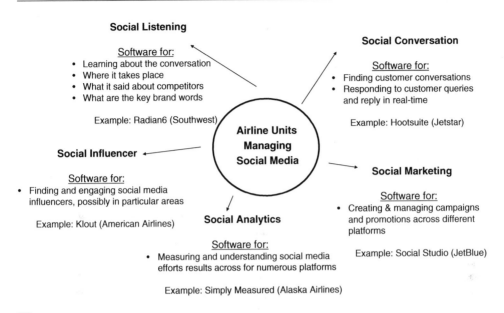

**Social Listening**

Software for:
- Learning about the conversation
- Where it takes place
- What it said about competitors
- What are the key brand words

Example: Radian6 (Southwest)

**Social Influencer**

Software for:
- Finding and engaging social media influencers, possibly in particular areas

Example: Klout (American Airlines)

**Airline Units Managing Social Media**

**Social Conversation**

Software for:
- Finding customer conversations
- Responding to customer queries and reply in real-time

Example: Hootsuite (Jetstar)

**Social Marketing**

Software for:
- Creating & managing campaigns and promotions across different platforms

Example: Social Studio (JetBlue)

**Social Analytics**

Software for:
- Measuring and understanding social media efforts results across for numerous platforms

Example: Simply Measured (Alaska Airlines)

**Figure 3.59** *Critical tools for the management of social media*

*Source:* Dyer (2013)[161]

## STEP 3: TRACKING AND MEASURING PROGRESS

There are a number of tools available that an airline can use. Depending on what is tracked, Klout, Google Analytics, Bitly, Crowdbooster, and many other tools are all beneficial and can be used to report on the relevant metrics. This area still is a challenge because we are dealing with an organic kind of feedback from travelers and purely ROI-focused performance metrics are insufficient.

Figure 3.59 shows what specific areas an airline has to look out for. They include social media software tools for listening, conversation, marketing, influencers, and analytics. Information about what each of them cover and a sample of airlines using them is also displayed.

### 3.10.2 Popular social media websites for airlines

In 2015, the Top 3 social media websites for brands around the world were Facebook, Youtube, and Twitter.[162] They accounted for more than 2.7 billion active users each month. Their popularity with airlines is high and many of them have a presence on all three platforms and others.

Travel market research firm Phocuswright has looked closely at the popularity of social media with travel brands including airlines. Specifically, they designed a chart to measure popularity in terms of usage (on which social media platform do travel companies actually have a presence?) and importance (what is the value of being present on a specific platform?). In an ideal scenario, usage and importance are

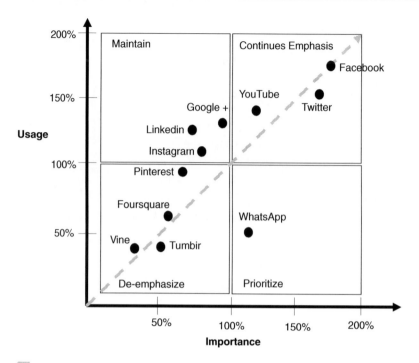

**Figure 3.60** *Social media utility in travel use versus importance*

*Source:* Quinby and Gasdia (2014)[163]

perfectly lined up. As is graphically illustrated in Figure 3.60, many travel companies use Facebook, Twitter, and YouTube *and* they view these very platforms as highly important. In the case of Facebook, for example, which is graphically speaking exactly on the diagonal, we have perfect match between usage and importance. For Twitter, not all travel companies use it, yet those that do, see it as very important. This explains its location below the diagonal.

We take this chart as guidance to focus in our following discussion on a few key social media platforms. Specifically, we look at how carriers use Facebook, Twitter, YouTube, Google+, LinkedIn, and Instagram for their social media marketing.

### 3.10.3 Facebook marketing

With approximately 1.5 billion monthly active users, Facebook is *the* global social network. It dominates in most countries although there are a few exceptions such as China where QZone is the top player, Russia (VKontakte), and Iran (Facenama). Nevertheless, if Facebook were a country, it would be the largest in the world followed by China and India with their billion+ populations (Table 3.11).

Equally noteworthy is that Facebook is a declared mobile company. For the first time in March of 2014, the company reported over one billion mobile active users.[164]

**Table 3.11** *Country population vs Facebook active monthly users*

| Country | Population Size |
|---|---|
| Facebook | 1.49 billion* |
| China | 1.36 billion |
| India | 1.27 billion |
| USA★★ | 323 million |
| Indonesia | 253 million |

*Facebook second quarter 2015;

**in the US, internet users spend on average 6.35 hours on Facebook, almost twice the time as on the next popular network Google+ with 3.2 hours (these figures apply to desktops only).

*Source:* Spredfast (2014),[165] Worldometers (2014)[166]

Facebook is a must-have social network platform for an airline's digital marketing activity. The platform's geographic coverage, the significant time users spend on it, and the ever-growing importance of Facebook in the mobile space are all aspects difficult to ignore by any airline.

Travel is a highly popular topic on Facebook. Some 50% of Facebook users have liked a travel brand, with airlines and hotels being most popular.[167] According to a Facebook study, travel as a category is among the Top 3 posts and outnumbers those related to other categories including nights out, music, food, pets, babies, and weddings.[168] Figure 3.61 shows how much Facebook influences the engagement of its users in all stages of travel.

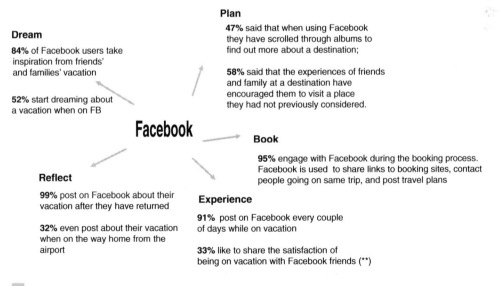

**Plan**

**47%** said that when using Facebook they have scrolled through albums to find out more about a destination;

**58%** said that the experiences of friends and family at a destination have encouraged them to visit a place they had not previously considered.

**Dream**

**84%** of Facebook users take inspiration from friends' and families' vacation

**52%** start dreaming about a vacation when on FB

**Facebook**

**Book**

**95%** engage with Facebook during the booking process. Facebook is used to share links to booking sites, contact people going on same trip, and post travel plans

**Reflect**

**99%** post on Facebook about their vacation after they have returned

**32%** even post about their vacation when on the way home from the airport

**Experience**

**91%** post on Facebook every couple of days while on vacation

**33%** like to share the satisfaction of being on vacation with Facebook friends (**)

**Figure 3.61** *The role of Facebook in travel★*

★ Based on a Facebook survey involving 3,000 participants in Germany, Scandinavia, and the UK.

*Source:* FreshBuzz Media (2013);[169] ★★ *Source:* Deloitte.com (2014)[170]

From the "Dream" and "Plan" stages to the "Book," "Experience," and "Reflect" stages, Facebook is an integral part. An airline is therefore well advised to maintain a presence on Facebook in order to increase brand awareness and online sales.

### The Facebook website: An overview

Before going into airline-specific Facebook marketing insights, let us first take a glance at the basic "what is what" on this website. This insight allows us to understand better how Facebook works and what aspects require a carrier's attention. Figure 3.62 provides an overview.

It is not uncommon that an airline maintains multiple Facebook accounts. Besides the main corporate Facebook page, country specific pages are popular. For instance, Turkish Airlines, among the most active carriers in the world of social media, maintains over 20 local Facebook pages. Other corporate Facebook pages are dedicated to a particular topic. "Careers" or employee groups such as cabin crews are examples. In order to ensure brand consistency across these multiple accounts, an airline needs to apply an overarching management policy with standards and guidelines as a framework.

Like for any social media platform—and Facebook is not an exception—content postings by the owner of the account are highly critical for the quality of an airline brand's communication. Although Facebook users may "Like" an airline brand's page because they feel a connection to it, they will stop following it if the content it posts does not meet their expectations in terms of frequency, relevance, and quality.

In essence, there are four different types of content posts on Facebook that an airline can share:

- text-only posts
- link posts
- photo posts
- video posts.

Each of these has its unique advantages and challenges. For example, text-only posts are quick and easy to do but are ineffective when exceeding 80–100 characters, especially in today's mobile device world. However, link posts feature a URL and are concerned with driving traffic to a website. However, users are typically not keen to leave Facebook at that particular moment and therefore may not click on the link. Photo posts have gained more significance in the wake of the growing popularity of photo sharing sites such as Instagram.

Photo posts, similar to text posts, aim at creating engagement. They need to be of high quality and catchy, otherwise people turn off their attention. The same can be said for video posts, the smallest but fast-growing post format on Facebook.[171] They appear to have great growth potential considering that for the first time in December 2014, there were more videos posted on Facebook than on YouTube for certain categories including for brands.[172]

Airlines generally mix up all four post types, although one occasionally sees a single post type only. The key for an airline is to not randomly feed content posts

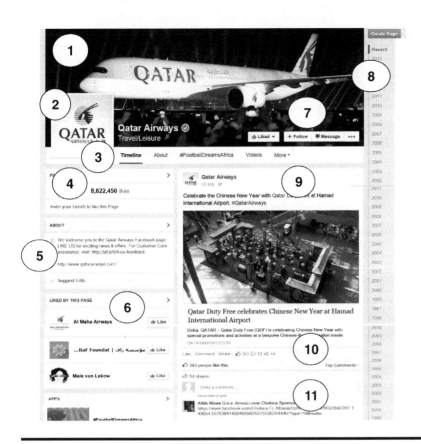

| Facebook page component | Commentary |
| --- | --- |
| 1. Cover photo | This photo captures the essence of the company's business and showcases a carrier's products and services. |
| 2. Profile picture | Display of corporate logo associated with the airline. |
| 3. Menu bar | Links to different content areas on the Facebook page. The "More" Button also features links to external sites like YouTube and Instagram. |
| 4. Page title, Likes, and People Talking About This | Provides for high-level Facebook statistics including the number of Likes and People Talking about This (PTAT). |
| 5. About | Informs the world who the airline is. |
| 6. Endorsement of third parties | Shows third parties that the airline Facebook page likes. |
| 7. Admin panel | User section to manage interaction with Facebook page including communication, edits, and preference for "Like" and "Following." |
| 8. Date selector | Navigation tool to different sections of the airline's page timeline. |
| 9. Pinned post | Information sharing by airline with the audience. This shows up in the so-called "Newsfeed" section of a Facebook user. |
| 10. Composer | To drive engagement means to invite web travelers to interact (like, compose, share) with a post. |
| 11. Viewer activity | A person can see how other people interact with a carrier's posts. |

*Source:* Based on Facebook.com (2015)[173] permission from Qatar Airways

**Figure 3.62** *Facebook page key components: Example—Qatar Airways*

into Facebook. Depending on what objectives an airline attempts to fulfill, there has to be a rationale plan that not only rotates the types of posts but also the message (Figure 3.63). It could involve a product/service announcement, a special fare sale, a famous quote, a question, an image caption, or even a meme.[174] Maintaining a mix and fine-tuning it over time ensures that the posts do not become boring. This secures a higher degree of web traveler engagement with the brand.

*Airline Facebook marketing insights*

Size alone does not translate into big numbers on Facebook. American Airlines and Delta Airlines as the world's two largest airlines in terms of passenger volume handled do not have an equivalent presence on Facebook as far as the number of "Likes" is concerned. The act of "liking" is de facto a recommendation or endorsement of an airline's activity. This can be as basic as being impressed with the news updates an airline shares on Facebook and thereby trigger a web traveler to "like" an airline.

Figure 3.64 provides for an overview of the Top 10 most socially active airlines on Facebook. The number one social airline on Facebook is Qatar Airways with 10.4 million Likes. KLM is second with 9.9 million Likes. The fact that just four of

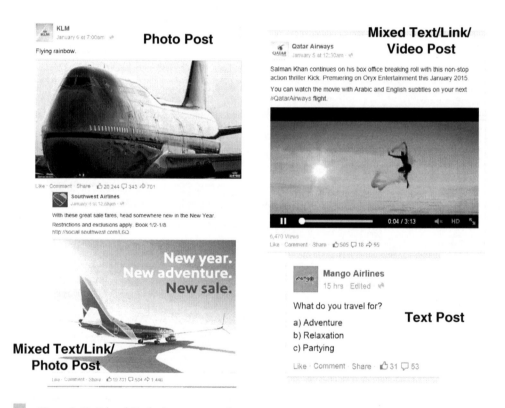

**Figure 3.63** *Selected Facebook post types and messages*

*Source:* Facebook.com (2015)[175] with kind permission of Southwest Airlines, KLM, Mango, Qatar Airways.

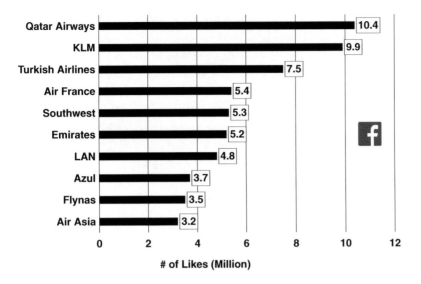

**Figure 3.64** *Top 10 most "liked" airlines on Facebook (December 2015)*

*Source:* Facebook.com (2015)[176]

these Top 10 airlines are LCCs (Southwest, Azul, Flynas, and Air Asia) shows that traditional network carriers are also successful in attracting a sizeable social audience in cyberspace. Qatar Airways' Likes are more than twice the volume of what Southwest Airlines has attracted.

These fan bases are impressive but unfortunately do not say much about how *engaged* users are when it comes to their interaction with an airline. Gauging the level of interaction between users and Facebook is not an uncontroversial topic. Many expert opinions exist about what should be measured and how it should be measured. Nevertheless, (at least for now) there appears to be some common ground on two indicators: The page engagement rate and the post engagement rate. Utilizing these allows an airline to have some insight into the overall effectiveness of its social media marketing efforts with Facebook. The following section sheds some light on both.

*Page engagement rate and post engagement rate*

The page engagement rate works with a metric called PTAT (People Talked About This [Page]). "People Talked About This" is simply a proxy for a user's activities in regards to an airline Facebook page post in the past seven days. These activities include but are not limited to the following interactions:

- shares (any shares of airline page's updates, videos, images, and activities)
- likes (every instance when Facebook users click "Like" on an airline page or posts)
- comments (comments on an airline's Facebook posts and updates).

The engagement rate is calculated as = (PTAT/total number of page likes) x 100. This rate indicates the share of followers overall engaged with the airline brand on Facebook. It is easy and straightforward. If an airline's Facebook content is not resonating with web travelers who have explicitly declared their interest in the brand, it may be time to review one's marketing tactics.

When accounting for the page engagement rate of our Top 10 social airlines, a slightly different pictures emerges. Figure 3.65 shows a snapshot for a 7-day period in December 2015. The leader is Emirates with an engagement rate of 2.3% followed by KLM and Air France with 1.5% and 1.4%, respectively.

Clearly, being able to attract a large following does not necessarily translate into an equally engaged audience. Azul is an illustrative example. Despite its 3.7 million strong fan base, it managed to engage 800 users only leading to 0% engagement rate.

What is a good engagement rate for airline brands on Facebook? If we relate to the page engagement rate of the US airline industry, most of our Top 10 socially active carriers are actually performing well. The average Facebook engagement rate for US carriers in 2014 was 0.57% and was on rank three after the industry categories automobile and alcohol (Figure 3.66).

However, when compared against the page engagement of individual brands, possibly even from outside the airline industry, the picture is different. For Apple, arguably the world's most famous brand, the calculated engagement rate is 2.7% (based on Facebook data from January 2015). For other brands it is as follows: Mercedes-Benz (1.4%), Coca-Cola (1.1%), Starbucks (0.3%), and Nike (0.2%).

Then of course, there are personality brands. Take for instance the Facebook page of actor/film director George Takei. He is widely known for his role as Hikaru Sulu,

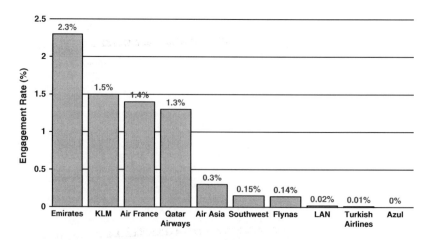

**Figure 3.65** *Facebook page engagement rate*

*Source:* Based on Facebook December data (2015)[177]

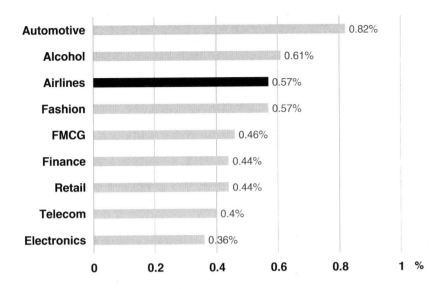

**Figure 3.66** *Average page engagement rate by industry*

Source: Guglielmelli (2014)[178]

helmsman of the USS *Enterprise* in the US television series *Star Trek*. Mr Takei is liked by more than 8.3 million Facebook users and has a page engagement rate of 52%. This is apparently one of the highest found today on Facebook. If a carrier indeed applies benchmarking to any of these non-airline brands, its Facebook page engagement rate looks correspondingly better or worse. Most estimates for brands with a large, several million-people strong following point to a 1% to 2% engagement rate.[179] In order to be considered truly socially engaging, a carrier should strive to be in this range at a minimum. Ideally, however, should frequently monitor how rivals and even leading non-airline brands perform in this area.

Is the page engagement rate a perfect indicator to measure how socially active web travelers are on Facebook? Obviously not. Like all statistical indicators, the page engagement rate and in particular the metric PTAT need to be put into perspective. PTAT is supposed to be terminated. Facebook announced in July 2014 the discontinuation of PTAT as a metric[180] and its split into three separate metrics. One of them is People Engaged (the number of unique people who have clicked on, liked, commented on, or shared posts).[181] PTAT still displays on numerous brand websites including those of airlines in spring 2015. We just need to be aware that its lifespan appears to be limited at this point. However, as long as it is still used, the following needs to be kept in mind about PTAT:

- *Some engagement is not captured by PTAT.* A perfect example is a user that looks at an airline's post but does not click on it.
- *PTAT includes page Likes.* This means that a unique promotion or event posted during the last seven days can cause a significant spike in traffic liking a page.

**159**

This increases the PTAT for a brief period but it is typically not a reflection of a user's engagement over the longer term. In the case of Qatar Airways, this is what actually happened. Its Facebook coverage on the inaugural of the Airbus A350XWB starting on January 6, 2015—Qatar Airways was the global launch customer for this aircraft—received an enormous level of customer response on Facebook throughout the rest of the month. Its engagement rate was temporarily boosted to 8.6%!

■ *Interaction for promoted posts and ads are included in PTAT.* Conducting Facebook marketing campaigns may involve advertising that is paid for by the airline. Therefore, when looking at a page engagement rate, it is good to ask if some of the social interaction has actually been purchased or not.

■ *PTAT is page and not post based.* This point is important. An airline Facebook page that posts multiple times a day versus one with only a single post a day can reasonably be expected to display a higher page engagement rate. The page engagement rate we discussed above ignores this particular aspect. Therefore some observers advocate focusing on the so-called post engagement rate. It would be calculated as = (PTAT/number of posts/total number of page likes) x 100.

Table 3.12 gives us more insight on the weekly frequency of Facebook posts by Qatar Airways, KLM, and Southwest. During a random sample week from January 7 to January 14, 2015, Qatar Airways generated 16 posts while KLM managed 8 and Southwest 4. The total engagement with over 152,000 for Qatar Airways is four times higher than that of KLM with slightly over 38,000. At the same time, Southwest's 16,000 engaged users is less than half the engagement volume of KLM's. More posts appear to pay off with more engagements by Facebook users. Studies have shown that the sweet spot for the number of posts per week is somewhere between five and ten. Anything significantly less or more means losing a connection with a Facebook user or becoming too invasive.[182] Each airline needs to find its own optimal schedule. The only way to achieve this is by trial and error.

Besides post frequency, the level of engagement is also driven by the post type. We remember from our discussion that there is a wide spectrum of different posts used by airlines. Apparently, photos are key for Facebook-user engagement. For example, Qatar Airways' best performing post with over 20,500 engagements is a photo post covering the airline's A350 arrival in London Heathrow. The carrier's worst performing post is a global fare sale triggering 15 engagements only. Looking at KLM, we see a similar picture. Its best performing post is a photo post with 31,301 engagements while the post with the lowest engagement—79—involved a fare sale as well. Snapshot surveys by other observers have also proven that photos are a key influencer for engagement.[183]

This confirms our earlier statement that social media do not appear to be an ideal venue for ticket sales—at least not right now and not when a network carrier is involved. Southwest as an LCC fares better in this area. One of its best (but also worst) performing post was about a fare sale.

**Table 3.12** *Facebook postings and engagements (January 7—14, 2015)*

| Airline | No. of weekly posts | Total no. of engagements | Highest engagement with single post* | Lowest engagement with single post* |
|---|---|---|---|---|
| Qatar Airways | 16 | 152,105 | 20,523 | 15 |
| KLM | 8 | 38,060 | 13,301 | 79 |
| Southwest | 4 | 16,054 | 9,507 | 1,088 |

* As a benchmark, the average number of engaged users per post for the US airline industry in 2014 was 515.[184]

*Source:* Author analysis based on Facebook.com (2015)[185]

Our coverage of Facebook airline marketing activities is incomplete without introducing some carrier-specific campaigns. The next section showcases what some airlines have done.

*Facebook marketing campaign objectives and advertising formats*

The marketing objectives for Facebook vary by airline. What appears to be often on the top of the list is the promotion of the carrier's Facebook page. This makes sense considering that one can communicate to millions of Likes via a simple status update, an efficient and well-leveraged marketing approach. However, there are other objectives that also deserve attention. They include the direction of web traveler traffic to an airline's website, the promotion of Facebook apps, and the capture of web travelers. Figure 3.67 shows in more detail what specific aims are associated with each of these.

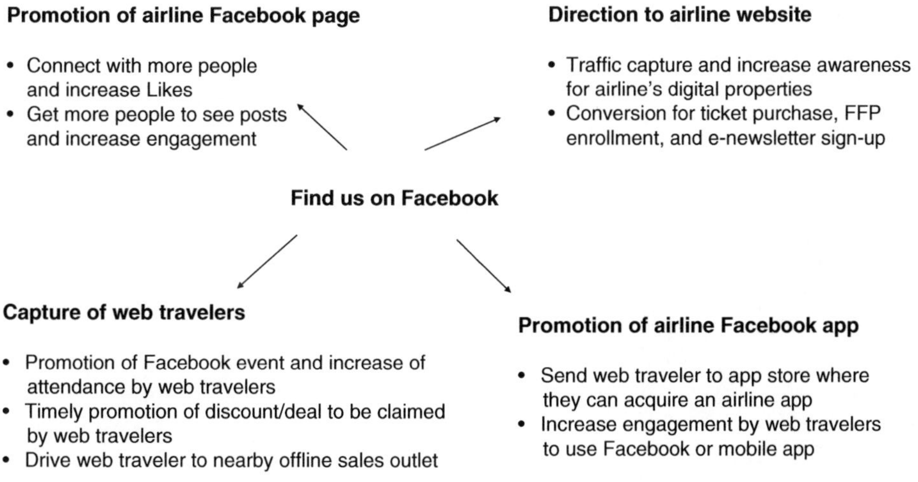

**Promotion of airline Facebook page**

- Connect with more people and increase Likes
- Get more people to see posts and increase engagement

**Direction to airline website**

- Traffic capture and increase awareness for airline's digital properties
- Conversion for ticket purchase, FFP enrollment, and e-newsletter sign-up

**Find us on Facebook**

**Capture of web travelers**

- Promotion of Facebook event and increase of attendance by web travelers
- Timely promotion of discount/deal to be claimed by web travelers
- Drive web traveler to nearby offline sales outlet

**Promotion of airline Facebook app**

- Send web traveler to app store where they can acquire an airline app
- Increase engagement by web travelers to use Facebook or mobile app

**Figure 3.67** *Common Facebook marketing objectives*

*Source:* Based on Facebook.com (2015)[186]

Once a carrier has clarity on its Facebook marketing goal(s), the next step is to focus on the communication with the Facebook target audience. An airline should be concerned with the posts that are entered in the newsfeed of a Facebook user. These Facebook posts can be viewed as owned media because the carrier has full control over them. Specific decisions cover the types of posts, their topics, and their frequencies. For example, if the goal is web traveler engagement, photo posts with an appealing caption and displayed in the newsfeed with a high frequency are effective. Airlines often buy advertising on Facebook to target a group of customers. Depending on their objective and budget, they may go full scale and deploy a number of different formats over a longer timeframe or pursue a specific campaign for a short period with a single format only.

Facebook offers sponsored advertising for three areas: In the right-hand column of a Facebook page, in the newsfeed, and for mobile devices. The advertising formats an airline can buy range from the different post types (text, link, video, etc.) to page likes, mobile ads, and event/special offer announcements. The most common of all Facebook ads types is the page post link. Airlines use it to promote their external website. Entered into the newsfeed, it should show a large image to catch attention. Figure 3.68 illustrates an example of Facebook ads sponsored by British Airways and Southwest.

Considering that Facebook is increasingly focused on mobile users, a carrier needs to ensure that its advertising activities accommodate mobile formats. A web traveler clicking on ads that an airline deployed for Facebook mobile should link to a landing page optimized for mobile devices. Not doing so could turn off web travelers. BA's mobile ad below was not optimized as it linked to its standard desktop website.[187]

*Figure 3.68* *Facebook ads sponsored by British Airways and Southwest*

*Source:* Lopez (2014),[188] FourthSource (2014)[189] with kind permission of British Airways and Southwest Airlines

After our coverage of airline Facebook marketing objectives, the following section presents a sample of some airline Facebook campaigns that involve both owned and paid Facebook advertising.

*Selected Facebook marketing campaigns*

## SCOOT: "NAME OUR BABIES"

*Background*   Singapore-based LCC Scoot wanted to create a buzz and an awareness of its brand and drive ticket sales (including via physical stores) for its new Japan service. A "Name our Babies" campaign asked fans on Facebook to christen two airplanes in the Scoot fleet. Entries were collected on Facebook. A Facebook app allowed people to win different Scoot prizes, such as discounts for flights and Scoot underwear.

*Facebook advertising used*

- Mobile placements
- News feed placements
- Apps

*Results*[190]

- Created awareness for new service to Tokyo
- Growth in Facebook Likes and user engagement
- Created 14x return–on–investment for the Japan launch campaign
- Some 9,000 entries to the "Name our Babies" campaign
- More than 60% of new fans across Scoot's Pages came from mobiles

## LUFTHANSA: "LIFE IS A JOURNEY, INSPIRED BY TRAVEL"

*Background*   Lufthansa wanted to engage with well-travelled millennials in the US and Germany. Knowing that brand loyalty of 18–30 year olds is generally low, Lufthansa wanted to reach out to this generation of travellers via a Facebook campaign that emphasized an emotional theme.

The campaign's focus was on inspiring content in the form of small documentary stories about real-life people and their travel experiences all over the world. Over an 11-week timeframe, eleven people were accompanied by a camera crew on their trips to places they had never been before.

*Facebook advertising used*

- Page publishing
- Mobile placements
- News Feed placements
- Boosted posts

*Results[191]*

- A 14.8% increase in brand affinity in the core target group
- A total of 25% of the brand's sceptics changed their stance as a result of the campaign—the number of people who responded that they did not like Lufthansa declined by more than 530,000
- Lufthansa created an emotional connection to the target group and made the brand more relevant to younger audiences
- Some 16.3 million well-travelled people reached
- Of the people reached, 81% were in the defined target group of 18–30 year olds (7 million in Germany and 6 million in the USA)
- Over 2 million video views on Facebook alone
- EUR 0.10 cost per view for the videos via optimised ads on Facebook

## SAS: "LOW FARE CALENDAR CAMPAIGN"

*Background*

Following up on a previously successful geo-targeted Facebook campaign, SAS embarked on a new, major multi-channel campaign to boost awareness of its new fare sale.

*Facebook advertising used*

- Right-hand ads on desktops
- Mobile placements
- Newsfeed placements

*Results[192]*

- Created 54x return on ad spending directly attributable to Facebook activity
- A total of 15% above average order value for Facebook conversions
- Created 15–20x return on ad spending for geographically segmented page post ad campaign in Norway in 2012

In closing, as we have pointed out at the beginning of our Facebook marketing discussion, this social platform is absolutely critical for any airline. Facebook, be it for B2C or B2B marketing purposes, is powerful in amplifying a carrier's communication in cyberspace.

### 3.10.4 Twitter marketing

Twitter is the world's largest micro-blogging platform. It allows for the exchange of messages with up to 140 characters. Since 2012, not only text but also pictures and even video (not exceeding six seconds) can be tweeted. It averages over 300 million active users every month and close to 80% of its account users are outside the United

States.[193] In a number of emerging markets, Twitter is highly popular. For instance, in the Philippines, Twitter is the second most used social media application while in places including Brazil, Nigeria, and Vietnam, it ranks third.[194] Considering its size and geographic spread, it is difficult for an airline to ignore advertising opportunities via Twitter.

For several years now, airlines have acknowledged the value of Twitter in their communication with web travelers. Fare promotions, product updates, and new route announcements are examples of what is communicated. Today, most carriers have an active Twitter account, a few also operate multiple company accounts to address specific topics and audiences. It is interesting to note that some carriers' senior executives even maintain Twitter accounts and communicate with the public on company matters. Examples are Tony Fernandes, CEO of Air Asia, and Marty St. George, SVP Marketing and Commercial at JetBlue. Another area where Twitter plays a huge role is web customer service. We discuss this aspect of Twitter in Chapter 5.

It is easy for any airline to set up a Twitter account. This is why there are over 250 airlines worldwide that are found on Twitter. However, being simply present on Twitter is one thing, being competitively present another. As pointed out before, there are plenty of airlines that are quick in launching a new digital property but lack the mindset, focus, and resources to manage it on an ongoing basis.

Twitter is no exception. Of those 250+ Twitter airlines, around 100 are active and of these an estimated 30 accounts are really busy and create content.[195] This

| Airline | # of Followers |
|---------|----------------|
| 1. KLM | 1.99 million |
| 2. JetBlue | 1.98 million |
| 3. Southwest | 1.93 million |
| 4. Air Asia | 1.85 million |
| 5. Philippine Airlines | 1.25 million |
| 6. American | 1.23 million |
| 7. Aeromexico | 1.16 million |
| 8. Delta | 1.07 million |
| 9. TAM | 0.94 million |
| 10. British Airways | 0.79 million |

*Figure 3.69* Top 10 global Twitter airlines (December 2015)

*Source:* Twitter.com (2015)[196]

shows that there is no shortage of airlines with a weak Twitter presence. This is reflected in their accounts' outdated content, low number of followers, and old tweets—some of which are as "recent" as from 2010. The number of players really committed to Twitter and doing an effective job is small.

Who are the star performers on Twitter? As of December 2015, there are only eight airlines in the world with more than 1 million followers. KLM, JetBlue, Southwest, and Air Asia are the undisputed social airlines on Twitter with each soon to pass through the two million follower threshold. It is obvious from these impressive numbers that all carriers in the Top 10 category are seriously committed to Twitter for marketing and customer service purposes.

*Selected case studies of airline Twitter campaigns*

Airlines use Twitter for various types of marketing activities. Some are outright campaigns aimed at attracting new customers, others are more brand focused and some even have a strong personal touch and highlight a particular social cause. Below are some selected airline Twitter campaigns.

TWITTER CASE STUDY: #DEAL 30 (AMERICAN AIRLINES)

To celebrate the thirtieth anniversary of AAdvantage, American Airlines ran a Twitter contest and offered any follower the chance to become one of 30 people to win 30,000 miles. To enter the sweepstake, contestants had to enter their AAdvantage number, tweet the branded hashtag and follow AAdvantage on Twitter (Figure 3.70).

Within one week, the campaign's microsite garnered almost 18,000 clicks on Twitter while the @AAdvantage Twitter account saw a 70% increase in followers from the campaign. Importantly, the campaign went viral to some extent and retweets increased 43%. The Deal 30 microsite ended up with over 27,000 registrations.[197]

**Figure 3.70** *American airlines Twitter campaign*

*Source:* With kind permission of BoardingArea.com (2011)[198]

The takeaways:

- A campaign where people can win something attracts attention.
- Higher visibility of campaign due to use of branded hashtag like American's Deal 30.
- Increased brand exposure as participants were required to follow the company's Twitter account.
- Stronger web traveler engagement from integrative campaign that uses multiple digital platforms like a microsite.

## TWITTER CASE STUDY: # FLY2MIAMI (KLM)

KLM announced the re-opening of Amsterdam–Miami on Twitter. Dutch DJ/producer Sied van Riel (@SiedVanRiel) and film-maker Wilco Jung (@WilcoJung) replied that this would be just too late for the great spring break events, including the Ultra Music Festival. Sied and Wilco said they could easily fill up a plane if KLM flew a few days earlier. KLM decided to challenge them and tweeted its willingness to move up the flight schedule (Figure 3.71).

Specifically, KLM was looking for 150 people booking the flight within seven days. Sied and Wilco launched a special website www.fly2miami.nl and Twitter account @Fly2Miami. Various media picked up on the story and within five hours, Sied and Wilco collected the 150 commitments to book. Result: KLM changed its flight schedule. Deploying an aircraft following a customer request on Twitter was a 'first' for the company.

The takeaways:

- Social media are key to share information with customers about products and services.
- Listening to customers can really pay off.
- Increased revenue for airline.
- Energized consumers who engaged with others.

## TWITTER CASE STUDY: #FLYITFORWARD (JETBLUE)

JetBlue launched a campaign called "Fly It Forward" that provides people worthy of admiration with a free flight on JetBlue. They then in turn can pass on this chance

**KLM** Royal Dutch Airlines

@WilcoJung You try to fill the plane, we'll try to fly! RT i bet we could fill a plane of house music dutchies who go to WMC miami

12 Nov

*Figure 3.71 KLM's Twitter challenge*

Source: Drimmelen (2011)[199]

 **JetBlue Airways** ✔
@JetBlue

What story would you tell? We're helping people like you #FlyItForward. See who's already taken flight & get inspired: bit.ly/1oRmdQG

↩  ↻  ★  •••

| RETWEETS | FAVORITES | |
|---|---|---|
| 12 | 11 |  |

11:15 AM - 5 Nov 2014

**Figure 3.72** *JetBlue's "FlyItForward" campaign on Twitter*

*Source:* Wegert (2014)[200] with kind permission of JetBlue

to other people who could also fly for free. JetBlue started the campaign with the profiles of four people selected by its crew members and a planning team by looking online for deserving stories. In a next step, they turned to Twitter and asked people to nominate their "Fly It Forward" candidates (Figure 3.72).

Within a few days of this open-ended campaign, JetBlue received already close to 1,200 nominations.

The takeaways:

- Highlights that Twitter can also be used for campaigns to showcase a carrier's compassionate side, ranging from corporate social responsibilities to improving an individual's life.
- Increased engagement by people with the airline that shows its "human side."
- Boosted consumer sentiment including more trust toward carrier brand.

*Paid marketing on Twitter*

Twitter started offering advertising services in 2010 and today features three main advertising venues for companies including airlines. These include promoted tweets, promoted accounts, and promoted trends.

- *Promoted tweets.* Airlines pay Twitter to have their sponsored tweets show up in the research results of a web traveler. An "Ad" logo indicates that a particular tweet is sponsored. Virgin American was among the first carriers to apply this

**LeaderChat** Blanchard LeaderChat
4 Ways To Handle Rejection In Business -- Learn from rejection and
use it to your advantage. http://ow.ly/5Tz2¯
15 minutes ago

 **VirginAmerica** Virgin America ↺ 78 Retweets
Time flies when you're flying fun! Enjoy fares starting from $59
(+taxes/fees/restr). Book by Aug 8. http://vgn.am/6015Rz4X
#VXFlyDeals
30 Jul

 Promoted by Virgin America

**Figure 3.73** *Example of promoted tweet by Virgin America*

Source: Lansystems (2010)[201] with kind permission of Virgin America

type of Twitter advertising in 2010 (Figure 3.73). The pricing for promoted
tweets is based on an auction that runs behind the scenes on a Twitter platform.
A carrier pays Twitter only if the sponsored tweet is engaged with (clicked,
replied, re-tweeted, favored). In 2014/2015, the cost for this ranged between
$0.50 and $4.00.

■ *Promoted accounts.* They allow an airline to have its branded account move to
the top of the Twitter homepage. The idea is to position the airline's Twitter
account as one among the "who to follow." Figure 3.74 displays an example with
Lufthansa. Targeting based on gender, geography, and interest is possible. The
price for a new follower fell between $0.50 and $4.00 in 2014/2015.

■ *Promoted trends.* In this case, the airline is charged for a prominent listing of its
hashtag to the top of Twitter's Trend List. This is featured on the left-hand side
of the Twitter homepage. The alternative is to default to Twitter's search engine.
However, only those hashtags are found that are organically popular and make it
to the Trend's List in the first place. Figure 3.75 indicates the specific area where
an airline sponsored hashtag would be featured if it decided to use this format.
The price tag for an ad placement in this area is not small and in 2014/2015 went
for around $200,000 per day.

The answer to the question as to whether it is worth advertising on Twitter varies
from airline to airline. In essence, the attraction of new followers and the number of
retweets gained are certainly beneficial for web traveler brand advocacy. Furthermore, when running Twitter ads, an airline can gain valuable insight about its followers and the performance of its tweets because of the analytics made available.

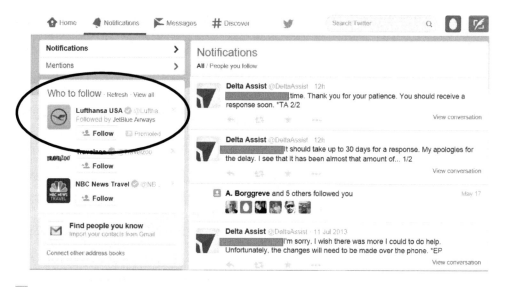

**Figure 3.74** *Example of Twitter promoted account*

*Source:* Twitter.com (2015)[202]

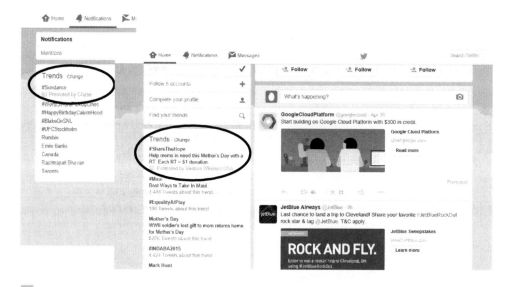

**Figure 3.75** *Area on Twitter reserved for promoted trends*

*Source:* Twitter.com (2015)[203]

## Tactics for a successful airline Twitter campaign

For a more effective Twitter campaign, there are a few tactics that a web marketer at an airline needs to pay attention to. Besides the marketing-related aspects we have already highlighted in our Twitter campaign case studies above, there are also a number of "operational" factors that play a role. They are:[204]

- *Tweets should be less than 140 characters.* Shorter tweets appear to receive 17% higher customer engagement. Reason: When people have room to retweet, they can insert their own comments. An airline tweet using all 140 characters is less likely to go viral.
- *Tweeting should occur during daytime hours.* Tweets sent out between 8 am and 7 pm have a 30% higher interaction. A tool like Tweriod can be used to analyze when the target audience in a particular timezone is most active. User engagement with tweets is also high on weekends and airlines should not take a break.
- *Image sharing.* Broadcasting so-called rich tweets (the ones with images and videos) translates into higher levels of engagement. For example, images increase retweets by 150%. Apparently, a good picture–text ratio is 70/30.
- *Boost the number of retweets.* The user engagement with a tweet is short. About half of a tweet's retweet occur within 18 minutes.[205] Therefore, the opportunity to outrightly ask people for retweets should not be missed. It is important to spell out the word "retweet" in its entirety as opposed to using the "RT" abbreviation. Including links in a tweet can also boost the retweet rate by 86% according to some studies.
- *Hashtags are crucial.* Hashtags double a user's engagement, have a higher visibility on Twitter and are viewed as an implicit call to action.
- *Refrain from tweeting too often.* Therefore, tweeting a few times is acceptable but should not exceed four times, otherwise users will disengage and perceive the brand to be too pushy.
- *Twitter analytics.* Running regular analytics on tweet popularity and user engagement are key for optimizing Twitter campaigns on an ongoing basis.

Southwest Airlines is among the most successful users of Twitter marketing. One analysis over a 90-day period in fall 2014 showed that among the major US carriers, no airline does a better job with posting tweets that triggered engagement and were then retweeted. For instance, the most retweeted post during the timeframe showed the airline's new exterior airplane design. It was retweeted over 491 times[206] (Figure 3.76). Without solid operational management of Twitter's marketing aspects, the airline clearly would not be as successful as it is in cyberspace.

### 3.10.5 YouTube marketing

Over the years, many airlines have introduced their own presence via "channels" on YouTube to promote their brand. One such example is German carrier Condor Airlines. In 2013, under the name of "Condor TV", it launched a YouTube channel where it showcases videos about the company and numerous promotional clips.[207]

Online videos are popular with travelers. Over half of both leisure (53%) and business travelers (64%) place value on videos by travel brands.[208] Moreover, a presence on social network TV can improve the bottom line. Several years ago, Air New Zealand did a YouTube advertising campaign called "Kiwi Sceptics." In a series of videos, each around five minutes in length, the carrier aimed at raising the awareness

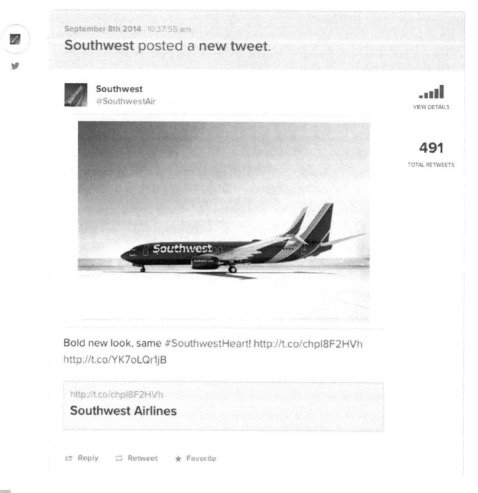

September 8th 2014 10:37:55 am

**Southwest** posted a **new tweet**.

**Southwest**
@SouthwestAir

VIEW DETAILS

**491**
TOTAL RETWEETS

Bold new look, same #SouthwestHeart! http://t.co/chpl8F2HVh
http://t.co/YK7oLQr1jB

http://t.co/chpl8F2HVh
**Southwest Airlines**

↩ Reply    ⟳ Retweet    ★ Favorite

**Figure 3.76** *Southwest's Twitter post on its new airplane design*

*Source:* Grant (2014)[209] with kind permission of Southwest Airlines

of New Zealand as a destination. The results included a return on investment of over $2 per advertising dollar spent and a 31% sales boost.[210]

Among the top players on YouTube are Turkish Airlines, KLM, and Air New Zealand. This is measured by the volume of video uploads, although the number of subscribers is also of consideration for some observers (Table 3.13). As a reminder, the current ranking is a snapshot and can change rather quickly depending on what a carrier does next on Youtube. Nevertheless, Turkish Airlines has earned an undisputed "rockstar" status among its peers. With 436 million video uploads and over 103,000 subscribers, it outperforms other top airlines by a wide margin. Contributing to this have been several unique video campaigns including the one featuring basketball player Kobe Bryant and footballer Lionel Messi. The "Selfie Shootout" video alone was uploaded over 140 million times (Figure 3.77).

**Table 3.13** *Top 5 popular YouTube airlines vs other brands and celebrities (on December 13, 2015)*

| Category | Brand/Celebrity | Video Uploads | Subscribers |
|---|---|---|---|
| Airlines | Turkish Airlines | 436 million | 103,110 |
| | Air France | 95 million | 38,308 |
| | KLM | 85 million | 69,180 |
| | WestJet | 74 million | 51,393 |
| | Air New Zealand | 66 million | 78,832 |
| Other Consumer Brands | Red Bull | 1.3 billion | 4.8 million |
| | PlayStation | 862 million | 3.9 million |
| | Nike Football | 491 million | 2.3 million |
| Celebrities | Rihanna | 7.6 billion | 18.1 million |
| | Justin Bieber | 7.4 billion | 16.1 million |
| | Taylor Swift | 7.3 billion | 17.3 million |

*Source:* Socialbakers (2015)[211]

**Figure 3.77** *Turkish Airlines YouTube "Selfie Shootout"*

*Source:* Youtube.com (2015) with kind permission of Turkish Airlines[212]

The reasons why this December 2013 video campaign was so successful and literally crushed other brand campaigns including by YouTube and Google when it was released are worth noting:[213]

- First, it features not only one but two celebrities. Messi is a four-time world footballer of the year, and Bryant has started in the NBA All-Star game 15 consecutive times, not to mention the five NBA championship rings he has at home. Both athletes draw major attention for viewers—Bryant in the United States and Messi abroad.
- Second, it has a great story. Similar to the 2012 "Legends on Board" video campaign, the two are again featured in a friendly rivalry. This time, they are trying to take the most impressive selfie. In this attempt, they are traveling around the world and visit different places. This showcases Turkish Airlines' far-flung route network and is a departure from the standard airline campaigns focusing on service or delays.
- Third, the campaign's theme—the selfie—was perfectly timed. In 2013, one of the hottest trends was the selfie (like planking in 2012). Since then, it has caught up and even heads of states, the pope, and royalty came out with selfies. Turkish Airlines was at the right place at the right time.

To put things into perspective, when compared with other consumer and celebrity brands, airlines pale in significance as far as their popularity is concerned. Energy drink provider Red Bull has attracted 1.3 billion video uploads while those of celebrities such as female artist Rihanna or singer/songwriter Justin Bieber exceed 7 billion.

As the magazine *The Economist* stated: "Even if its content is not yet as striking as its form, YouTube presents a promise of a genuine revolution. It offers transparent advantages over TV for any younger audiences and creators not married to the comforts and conventions of the senior art form."[214]

*Video ads on YouTube*

Video ads in the travel space are aspirational and truly lend themselves to airlines as an advertising format. In a way, they can be considered the ultimate multi-media format because audio, video, and text are combined. In other words, video ads are a lucrative venue for an airline to tell a story because they offer creative opportunities for growing awareness of its brand while growing viewer demand.

Also important is the fact that they can be updated dynamically with whatever the relevant message has to be. Furthermore, there are new performance metrics in place that allow advertisers to closely monitor the effectiveness. The typical length of the video ads range from anywhere less than 15 seconds to more than 30 seconds. The 15–30 seconds timeframe accounts for 51% of all video ads shown.[215]

In relation with other industries, the travel sector is currently underrepresented in its use of video ads. Figure 3.78 shows for the US market that leisure travel as an

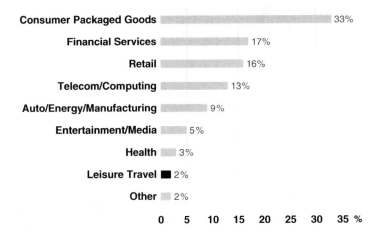

*Figure 3.78* US digital video ad share by industry category (Q2, 2014)

*Source:* eMarketer (2014)[216]

industry category only claims a 2% share of the entire video ad market (the top share with 33% is taken up by consumer packaged goods).

It is reasonable to assume that this share is poised for some growth in the near future. Already, other than mobile advertising, video is the fastest-growing advertising medium and it is expected to grow by almost 20% through 2016.[217]

There are four major types of video ads used by airlines today: In-banner video ad, linear video ad, non-linear video ad, and stand-alone video ad (Table 3.14).

A platform such as YouTube is an attractive advertising venue for airlines. This is because of the format's mass audience. According to company statistics, almost 4 billion videos are watched every day and the 800 million unique worldwide visitors upload 72 hours of video every minute.[218]

*Table 3.14* Types of airline video ads

| Video format | How does it work | Deployment |
|---|---|---|
| Banner-embedded video ad | Once clicked upon, video ad plays within banner although it may expand outside the banner also | Part of a banner ad that is placed on web page with relevant content |
| Linear video ad | Video ad takes over the video an online user wants to watch for a short period of time | Typically shown at the start of a video—the pre-roll—an online user watches on a social network such as YouTube or Hulu |
| Non-linear video ad | Video ad is overlayed on existing screen. Does not take over full screen | Featured during, over, or within a video |
| Stand-alone video ad | Branded video ad is separately featured and does not interact with other videos | Placed at top of YouTube result page and clearly marked with "AD" to identify them as advertising |

Linear or pre-roll video ads made their debut on YouTube in 2010 when the social network launched a new form of advertising vehicle called "TrueView." With TrueView, people have the option to watch an ad played at the beginning of a video (the so-called "pre-roll") or skip it and go straight to the video. From the standpoint of airlines that want to advertise, this does not seem appealing although they would only have to pay YouTube if their ad, typically 10–30 seconds in length, was watched. YouTube claims that 30% of users watch video pre-roll ads.[219]

At the same time, by giving the viewer complete control over the experience, it means that ads would have to be really capturing someone's attention and be entertaining/intriguing if they are to be watched. The choice for an airline is to show an ad to all consumers, no matter what their level of engagement is, or opt for a smaller audience that is more interested. This in turn may translate into a ticket purchase.

Some airlines have decided to pursue this TrueView opportunity for their brand and placed some pre-roll video ads on YouTube. For instance, pre-roll video ads were involved in an October 2014 advertising campaign with unscripted 30-second videos by JetBlue titled "Ground Rules" featuring the shortcomings of other airlines in the area of customer service.[220] Jetstar of Australia used 15-second long pre-roll ads on YouTube in 2013 to promote spring fare specials to various destinations (Figure 3.79).

It might be hard for some people to watch even a five-second pre-roll; one can therefore only imagine what their reaction is to the pre-roll video ad released by Virgin America in October 2014. Titled "Have you been flying BLAH airlines?," this pre-roll ad is five hours and 45 minutes long (this is correct: five hours and 45 minutes) video and can be watched in front of other videos unless one decides to skip this, of course. Specifically, the Virgin America video ad takes the viewer inside BLAH Airlines flight 101 to San Francisco, where one experiences all the things that travelers hate most about flying: Babies crying non-stop, children bouncing around

*Figure 3.79* Jetstar pre-roll video ads on YouTube

Source: Youtube.com (2014) with kind permission of Jetstar[221]

in their seats, someone humming way too loudly, the plane being seventh in line to take off, someone watching a show constantly laughing out loud, the person next to you stealing your armrest, and so forth. The video shows an impressive amount of boring detail and takes a stab at competing airlines that have no personality and excitement. The ad's basic message is how good a choice Virgin America would be.[222] Virgin America even set up a website at www.blahairlines.com and a Twitter account (@BLAHairlines). This particular ad certainly resonates with many web travelers but it is doubtful that its full length is ever watched by many viewers. Nevertheless, the creative concept behind it is interesting and may win this ad all kinds of prizes. It already was honored by the Webby Awards for best ad writing.

Video ads are typically placed on other commercial videos including movies, documentaries, and news. Airlines are currently cautious about putting ads around non-professional videos, although there are plenty with a travel theme that could be of interest. A common reason cited is that non-professional videos—another term is user-generated videos—are less glamorous, do not feature paid actors, and are rarely flawless. All of this can hurt a carrier's brand. However, they do capture a significant number of viewers' attention because they are raw, simple, and honest. Furthermore, the quality of these videos is constantly improving thanks to the ever-growing availability of better and low-cost recording/production tools. Millennial travelers are known to have used quadcopters to shoot high-quality travel destination videos.[223] This development is likely to gain further traction. All of this means that an airline should not categorically disregard this type of video as a venue for placements as they can give a boost to a business.

One last comment on YouTube relates to its future. It is undoubtedly in a dominating position currently but this status is not written in stone. We have already alluded to the rising popularity of Facebook videos in our Facebook marketing discussion. Apparently, for the first time in November 2014, brands uploaded more videos on Facebook than on YouTube. The gap between the two appears to be widening with Facebook posting 20,000 more brand videos than YouTube in December 2014. Equally important is the fact that brand videos posted on Facebook pages involve many more interactions than those on YouTube. Facebook received 80% of all video interactions.[224] Against this background, it is likely that we will also see an increased deployment of branded videos on Facebook by airlines. Moreover, other video formats such as offered via Instagram or Twitter's Vine for short format videos should not be overlooked either.

### 3.10.6 Google+ marketing

With Google+ being part of Google, this is also a social network difficult to ignore. In 2015, with over 340 million active monthly users, it was the second highest active social network after Facebook.[225]

We have talked at length about the importance of search marketing including SEO. With Google+, an airline's ranking when it comes to socially based SEO can be strengthened. At the same time, a web traveler's search efforts are improved because they can follow and view an airline's brand right from the Google search results. Considering

**Figure 3.80** *Singapore Airlines Google+*

*Source:* Google (2015), Google and the Google logo are registered trademarks of Google Inc., used with permission[226]

the dominating presence of Google in search marketing, Google+ is an effective way to introduce or highlight an airline's brand on prime search real estate.

There are two key reasons why an airline might consider Google+ in its social media portfolio:

- *Better brand presence on Google.* With Google+, a web traveler can view any recent post activity by a carrier while detailed brand information and the number of followers are also shared. As an example, Figure 3.80 shows the improved brand presence of Singapore Airlines. In addition to the regular search results in Google, Singapore Airlines' G+ account is also shown on the right side along with an image, follower count and a verified check. A web traveler that happens to be a G+ follower even sees additional content in this space. Lastly, if someone that the web traveler trusts has recommended Singapore Airlines, this information shows up as well.
- *Deeper brand engagement.* Google+ Hangouts is one feature that can help an airline brand to engage with web travelers on a more personal level. In G+ hangouts, an airline can chat with web travelers via video anywhere in the world or host any kind of event. Some carriers deploy hangouts to foster their brand reputation as an industry leader and innovator by sharing their opinions and connecting with other specialists in the field. For example, Virgin America, when celebrating the launch of a new flight to New Jersey in 2013, used several social media campaigns. They also included an invitation to web travelers to join a live Google+ hangout onboard an airplane with Mashable CEO & founder Pete Cashmore and Virgin founder Richard Branson.[227] Virgin America appears to stepping up its

**Followers (Million)**

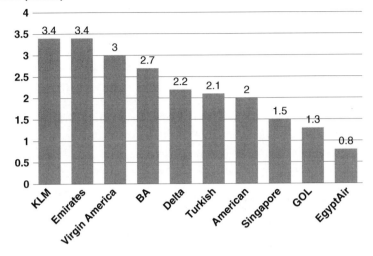

*Figure 3.81* Top 10 Google+ airlines (December 2015)

*Source:* Socialbakers (2015)[228]

involvement with Google+. In the second half of 2015, it grew the number of followers from 1.9 million to three million. This is an impressive performance.

A Google+ presence is not widespread among airlines. According to statistics by Socialbakers, there were close to 70 carriers worldwide on Google+ in December 2015. Figure 3.81 shows the Top 10 airlines on Google+ in terms of their followers. KLM and Emirates are in a tie with 3.4 million followers. Both carriers gained traction with Google+ as they each added over 400,000 new followers between May and December 2015. Singapore Airlines was equally strong with 300,000 new followers. The number of followers is one indicator of how popular the airline Google+ profile is with web travelers (another one, as we discussed in the search marketing section is how many people gave +1 to the carrier's profile). Despite the strong showings among the Top 10, the number of followers quickly falls off from rank 20 and is less than 100,000. Among them, for example, are well known brands including United Airlines (22,000 followers), Cathay Pacific (7,000), and airBerlin (472). In the case of EVA Air, the number of followers was as low as 284 with only two postings done through the entire year of 2015. In these instances, a strategic review of the carrier's approach for Google+ is highly recommended. Not doing so means continuing a weak digital brand presence on this platform and wasting valuable corporate resources.

### 3.10.7 LinkedIn marketing

Contrary to some beliefs that LinkedIn is only a hub for people seeking a job, it is actually the world's leading B2B website. In 2015, it averaged approximately 100 million active monthly users. One in three professionals globally is on LinkedIn and

43% of them use mobiles.[229] This is a powerful social media platform that can be utilized for more than the announcement of job openings and the recruitment of talent. A number of airlines have found creative ways to use their official company pages for building engagement with web travelers and for expanding their brand's visibility. While airlines' fan bases on LinkedIn are smaller when compared with those of Facebook and Youtube, some of them have nevertheless attracted sizeable audiences. They include Emirates as the largest player with over 491,000 followers (these are December 2015 figures) and KLM with 348,000. Other notable carriers are Etihad with 265,000 and Qatar Airways with 222,000. The major airlines from Europe and the US fall somewhere between 100,000 to 200,000 followers.

Common marketing tactics airlines use on LinkedIn include:

- Status updates. These are tied into ongoing campaigns such as special promotions or, better, into contests that allow followers to enter and qualify for special prizes. All of this creates great potential for going viral. Other status updates cover company news including special anniversaries, product/service announcements, and even travel tips  (Figure 3.82 shows examples of KLM).
- The use of captivating visuals. Without them, a LinkedIn page does not look too appealing. KLM's opening display banner showcasing several aircraft at Amsterdam Shiphol Airport can draw a web traveler's attention quickly.
- Cross-promotion of an airline's other social media platforms. For example, banner placements with embedded links under the Products/Services tab could be deployed to invite a web traveler to join the airline in Facebook or Twitter.
- Purchase of paid media on LinkedIn including display banners, text advertising, email campaigns, sponsored polls, and recommendation ads.

In addition to these "standard" marketing tactics, a handful airlines have started unique programs on LinkedIn. One example is Delta's "Innovation Class". Launched in 2014, this is an inflight mentoring program whereby LinkedIn users are offered the chance to meet with a thought leader from a different field on a designated Delta flight. Specifically, a LinkedIn user selects an upcoming flight and shares their credentials. Delta then creates a shortlist of candidates based on their LinkedIn profiles. If chosen, the leader would use their air time to share their knowledge and experience with the up-and-coming LinkedIn user.

Another interesting LinkedIn-based initiative involves ANA. Recognizing that professional networking is important to LinkedIn users, in 2015, ANA launched "Flight Connections" to turn online connections into face-to-face meetings. How does this work? Once a visitors to the Flight Connections website is logged in with their LinkedIn profile, the platform creates a personalized "flight map" visualization of the LinkedIn's connections and overlays them with the ANA route network where geographically applicable (Figure 3.83). The idea is to show how easily a LinkedIn user could meet other LinkedIn users whom they might have never met. Flight Connections allows one to reimagine a LinkedIn user's network via the additional dimension of ANA's route network.

**Travel Tips**

**Product & Service Announcement**

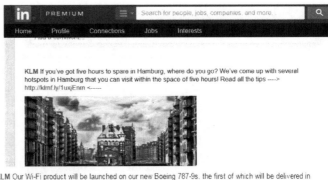

**Fare Sale**

*Figure 3.82* *KLM's social marketing use of LinkedIn*

Source: linkedin.com (2015),[230] with permission of KLM

Our above discussion shows that LinkedIn is more than just a site to look up jobs. It continues to evolve with newly added features and functionalities. Through the application of new innovative marketing concepts, it certainly is one important pillar for an airline's future social media marketing activities.

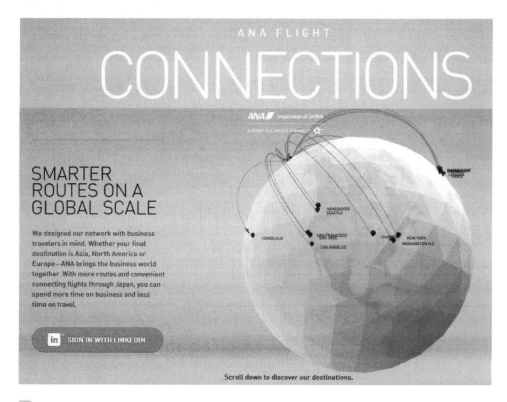

**Figure 3.83** *Flight Connections by All Nippon Airways on LinkedIn (March 2015)*

*Source:* ana-flight connections.com (2015), with kind permission of All Nippon Airways[231]

### 3.10.8 Instagram marketing

Launched in 2010, Instagram is an online photo-sharing and social networking service. In 2015, it counted over 400 million active users worldwide who take pictures, apply filters to them and then share them across social networks such as Facebook (which acquired Instagram in 2012), Twitter, and Flickr. Instagram is available as an app for iPhone, iPad, and Android devices. Popularity of individual Instagram photos is measured in terms of Likes, and Instagram account holders such as airlines rely on the number of followers to gauge the size of their fan base. Early Instagram adopters include Southwest Airlines and KLM. By year end 2015, they boasted 170,000 and 254,000 followers, respectively. However, the large Instagram fan bases today are found with the Gulf carriers including Emirates with 895,000 and Qatar Airways with 629,000 followers.

For the most part, it lends itself to serving as a branding platform for the airline by posting intriguing shots of its airplanes. After all, a picture of an airplane says a thousand words. Figure 3.84 shows examples of common posting themes found on airline Instagram accounts, for increasing the fan base and securing web traveler engagement is to establish an effective policy framework. It must address the following factors:

**Figure 3.84** *Selected airlines' posts on Instagram*

*Source:* Instagram.com (2015)[232] with kind permission of Air Asia, Southwest Airlines, KLM, Sony, and Aeroflot Russian Airlines.

- posting frequency
- photo themes
- allowing members to post their own photos
- photo quality.

Benchmarking against these factors, the Instagram presence of some airlines is weak. For example, Aeromexico had a total of five posts for the entire year of 2014. This largely explains why the carrier had only 4,500 followers that year (in 2015, it improved its presence on Instagram remarkably by a much higher posting frequency). Several Thai Airways photos were not properly formatted showing black frames around the images (the "black bar syndrome"). Taking into account today's high-quality camera in mobile devices and the numerous filters that can be applied to enhance the quality of images, there is no excuse for a carrier to feature sub-standard pictures. Some carriers avoid this situation by only posting their own images. However, the downside of this approach is a lower level of web traveler engagement. This is because social media including photo-sharing sites work best when they are set up for engagement with users as opposed to being one-way posting platforms for companies.

How engaged this photo-sharing community is becomes clear when we look at a conversational trail among Instagram members regarding a photo post on the Virgin Australia page. At hand is a debate about what two aircraft types are actually seen in

**Figure 3.85** *Instagram conversation: "When Boeing met Airbus"*

*Source:* Instagram.com (2015),[233] with kind permission of Virgin Australia and photo credit to @sydney_airport_airplanes

the photo post. As controversial as the debate may appear—people are connecting (Figure 3.85). An interesting approach for user engagement is also used by Emirates. They deploy so-called "Instagram Ambassadors" who do postings on the carrier's behalf. This allows for both leveraging the ambassador's followers and adding a personal touch to the postings.

## 3.11 THE ROLE OF SOCIAL MEDIA INFLUENCERS

In an attempt to stand out from the social media ad clutter and improve on their brand advocacy with web travelers, airlines may use social media influencers. The idea is to leverage them and increase the airline's brand within their identified following, sometimes also referred to as "tribe."

Social media influencers have their roots in "mom bloggers" who were paid to promote food, homewares, and baby products.[234] The practice of using social influencers has been in place for a few years now and appears to grow in importance.

There are many different forms that social influencers can take. They include:[235]

- celebrities and personalities with a significant social presence
- brand ambassadors
- events/activities/sports
- bloggers and instagrammers
- journalists

- individuals that have received social notoriety purely from their social activities (for example YouTube videos)
- industry analysts and consultants
- product review sites (e.g. App Store).

It is unclear how much money is spent on this type of advertising. This is because, as a category, it is not broken out yet from the multi-billion spending in social media. Existing advertising media agencies including Ogilvy have established new inhouse units to manage this area. At the same time, there are also agencies such as US-based 247Laundry Service that are exclusively focused on dealing with influencer marketing. In Waggener Edstrom's case, a media company based in Singapore, they even track the popularity of individuals outside their own network across a wide range of earned media channels.[236]

Considering the high level of trust people place on word of mouth, it is not surprising that social influencers have gained such prominence in recent years. Some of them have followers that go into the millions, an audience size that exceeds that of some TV shows and magazine circulations. Brands including airlines capitalize on the popularity of these social media gurus and thereby take word of mouth to a much larger scale.

Carriers all have individual approaches in their deployment of social influencers. In the case of Japanese airline ANA, for example, a social media influencer—actually titled as "Brand Ambassador"—comes from a group of people that are very active in social media and relevant to the carrier's brand.[237] American Airlines, however, goes by a more (arguably) objective metric such as the Klout score that represents influence in social media circles. The score ranges from 1 to 100 and the higher it is, the more influential the individual. American requires a Klout score of 55 to be considered an influencer. In return for lending support to the airline, an influencer can earn perks such as free airport lounge access.[238]

There are some issues an airline needs to watch out for when dealing with social influencers. One is related to how much an influencer should be allowed to create their own message. An airline may feel uncomfortable losing this kind of control. At the same time, however, one needs to realize that part of an influencer's authenticity is exactly what makes the social media influencer influential. A middle ground needs to be struck. Another issue deals with the disclosure of compensation. Laws vary by country but an airline also needs to be careful not to come across as a party that simply paid a social influencer to broadcast a handed-down message. This is detrimental to its brand. Furthermore, related to compensation is the question of how much an influencer should be paid. Standard online metrics including impressions served and click-throughs applied to paid advertising cannot be used. For now, most companies rely on the size of an influencer's following.[239]

As airlines become more active in the area of social media marketing, it is likely that social influencing will also gain more importance. Airlines that have not been active in this area yet may want to start exploring opportunities to see how they can become more engaged. Some observers have even suggested that an airline may invite customers to connect their social media account with their frequent flyer membership. Positive interactions such as downloading the carrier's app or promoting the company's website could translate into benefits such as earning bonus miles or even being awarded premium tier status.[240]

## 3.12 AIRLINE BLOGS

A blog, or web log, is maintained by an individual or a company with regular entries of commentaries on literally anything that the blog owner deems important and worthy. The blog owner controls the communication flow about a chosen topic with other online users.

For airlines, we differentiate between internal and external blogs. The former are accessible via an airline's intranet and are developed and maintained by employees for employees. The objective is to engage in informal communication among each other. In the case of external blogs, which is our focus in the following discussion, a group of employees communicates with the traveling public on a wide variety of topics.

Some have more of a marketing aspect such as the announcement of a fare promotion or new route. Others are clearly more social where employees share insider tips about certain destinations and others even engage by inviting web travelers to share input for topics such as a carrier's new website design. Airline blogs are owned media and are a great venue for reinforcing the carrier's brand, engaging with web travelers, and also for generating leads for more online sales. Company communication on external blogs is subject to corporate censorship and release guidelines. However, true to their nature, the communication tone and style are typically informal and personal.

Launching and, more importantly, maintaining such a digital property is not a small effort. For example, Southwest Airlines, one of the early adopters of an airline blog, has over 30 employees that contribute to its blog "Nuts About Southwest."[241] It takes resources (often full-time), know-how, and a certain open corporate culture to operate a corporate blog. If these crucial factors are absent, an airline should think twice before entering the world of blogging.

Several airline blogs are introduced below in order to provide some insight of what is going on with these platforms. Importantly, they differ substantially and do not fit in a single mold—an indication of the creative freedom applied to them.

*Southwest Airlines*

One of the first airline blogs around and launched in 2006, it features a new post almost every day. They touch on a wide spectrum of topics including contests, destination information, travel tips, employee volunteering work in the community, personal stories, flight operational insights, and historical flashbacks. Over the years, this blog has collected several prizes for being among the leading corporate blogs. A feature called "Luv Mail" shares customer letters that acknowledge the work of Southwest employees. The blog also showcases links to podcasts and videos (Figure 3.86).

**Figure 3.86** *Southwest blog "Nuts about Southwest"*

*Source:* southwestairlines.com (2015)[242] with kind permission of Southwest Airlines

*Vueling*

Started in 2011, "My Vueling City" appears to be a hybrid between a destination guide and booking portal. It features information on over 130 destinations served by the carrier. Highlighted is information on food, weather, and sightseeing. A booking engine enables online reservations and ticket purchases while a web traveler can also sign up for the carrier's newsletter. Live Twitter feeds are also displayed (Figure 3.87).

*Air New Zealand*

Air New Zealand offers an amazing variety of topics and functionalities. This is probably why it labels its blog the "The Flying Social Network" or "TFSN." The blogs cover topics from lifestyle and food to health and education. Its Instagram like-wall for photos and the Air NZ Fairy that grants travel-related wishes to social network users ensure a high level of engagement with web travelers on this platform. Interestingly, the carrier's news is localized by key markets. It even offers a Chinese language section for the Chinese community.

## 3.13 AIRLINES AND THIRD PARTY BLOGS

In addition to their own corporate blog, some carriers also manage a presence on third party blogs. Blogging in this case involves senior managers personifying the company.

**187**

**Figure 3.87** *Vueling blog "MyVuelingCity"*

*Source:* vueling.com (2015)[243] permission of Vueling Airlines

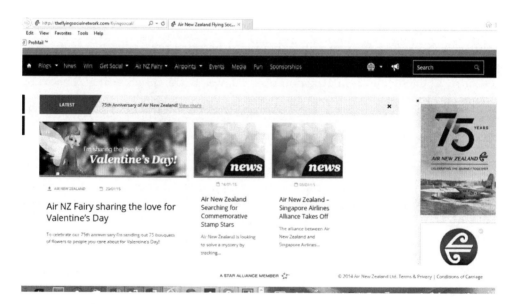

**Figure 3.88** *Air New Zealand blog "The Flying Social Network"*

*Source:* airnewzealand.com (2015)[244] with kind permission of Air New Zealand

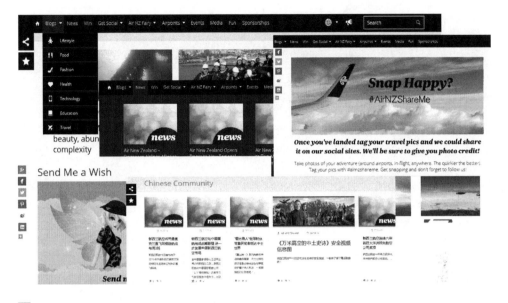

**Figure 3.88** *continued*

An example is Alan Joyce, the CEO of Qantas. He joined LinkedIn's Influencer Program in 2013. The program originally operated on an invite-only basis and was restricted to approximately 300 people worldwide. The idea for his participation was to create awareness of the airline CEO's leadership by contributing blogs about the airline industry and general business issues.[245] A post from this exclusive group averages around 31,000 views with 150 Likes and 80 comments. It therefore is a suitable social media venue to also raise the brand awareness of a carrier, in this case that of Qantas. Richard Branson of the Virgin Group is another prolific member of this group with almost 8 million followers. In 2014, LinkedIn decided to expand on the program and enabled around 25,000 LinkedIn members to blog as well.[246]

In addition to LinkedIn, Twitter as the premier microblog also offers opportunities for brand exposure and web traveler engagement. Take for instance Tony Fernandes, the CEO of Air Asia, who maintains a Twitter account and has close to 1 million followers (Figure 3.89).

## 3.14 GAME ADVERTISING

The integration of advertising by companies into games has a long tradition and goes back to the early days of the video game industry. There are four major types of game advertising:

- in-game display of advertising such as billboard ads
- in-game product/service placements
- game sponsorships
- branded games (also referred to advergames).

**Figure 3.89** *High-profile airline bloggers*

*Source:* linkedin.com (2015)[247] with kind permission of Qantas, Twitter (2015)[248] with kind permission of Air Asia

As a result of the continuous growth of the internet, advergaming in particular has taken off and become popular with online users. Advergames are sponsored games by companies to promote their brands. A number of airlines are active in this area because they see advergaming as a fit to their other social media activities. At a minimum, advergames help an airline reinforce its brand. In addition, contingent on the game design, an airline can collect user data. In this regard, a common tactic is to offer prizes upon registration for the game. Lastly, some games include a viral component and allow users to invite others to participate. Below are listed selected airline advergames.

### 3.14.1 Air France: "Fly Further" (released in spring 2014)

*Game walk-through*    The objective is to fly an Air France plane as far as one can while keeping passengers comfortable. A bar at the top of the PC screen works as indicator of the passenger comfort level. The comfort level decreases over time and when the comfort bar is fully depleted, the game has come to an end.

*Advergaming goals*

- News lettter promotion
- Customer engagement
- Highlighting of Air France route network

*Execution*

- Free ticket prize offerings to any Air France destination (only offered during the initial release of the game)
- Customer email address collection
- Display of sample Air France destinations
- "Send to a friend" viral component

### 3.14.2 JetBlue: "Get Away With It" (run in summer 2012 during five-day period)

*Game walk-through*    Combination of retro game show elements including live host and beautiful assistant with digital way for participants to play. Contestants had to provide game host with correct answers about travel and JetBlue's "Getaway" vacation package.

*Advergaming goals*

- Build awareness for JetBlue's "Getaways" vacation package program
- Customer engagement
- Data collection

*Execution*

- Online game show featured on JetBlue.com via microsite
- Cross-format advertising support with print, outdoor, inflight, and online ads
- Show takes place in real-time with real people 5x/day for 5 days
- Prize offerings for JetBlue's Getaways and gift certificates
- Can be also played on one's own (without prize and certificates)

### 3.14.3 KLM: "Aviation Empire" (summer 2013) and "Jets" (spring 2015)

*Game walk-through "Aviation Empire".*    Players manage their own airline. While playing through KLM's 95+ year history, one can acquire airports and planes and establish

**191**

routes. The task is to manage a well-maintained, up-to-date fleet, create a profitable network with international destinations, and upgrade airports with all kinds of facilities to keep passengers satisfied.

*Game walk-through "Jets"*. A mission-based endless flyer for mobile devices in which players lead their paper plane safely through an obstacle-ridden cardboard world. The first missions of Jets are set in a cardboard version of Amsterdam. Players have to avoid cars, trams, and boats while flying their paper plane through the center of the old city and over the famous canals. Jets operates in a single player mode, but other players can be invited via their social media accounts.

*Advergaming goals*

- Strengthening KLM's already significant involvement with social media via Facebook, Twitter, Linkedin, and Google+ even further by adding games with fun and challenges
- Cementing KLM's reputation as a brand seriously committed to social media
- Growing relationship between airline and web travelers with help of gamification

*Execution*

- Availability of games via mobile devices from app stores
- No prizes such as bonus miles, upgrades or free flights offered and no special online registrations required
- Press conferences and special online announcements including Twitter and YouTube trailers[249]

## 3.15 THE ROLE OF GAMIFICATION IN AIRLINE E-MARKETING

Our above discussion of advergaming touches on a rising phenomenon in travel: Digital gamification. Gamification is the concept of incorporating game design elements and techniques into otherwise ordinary, non-game activities. These therefore become more interesting and engaging. Gamifying an activity in the context of airline e-commerce means to make a web traveler's interaction with an airline's digital properties fun and engaging.

Gamified services for consumer goods marketing and customer retention are estimated to become as important as Facebook, eBay, or Amazon, and more than 70% of Global 2000 organizations will have at least one gamified application.[250]

Gamification taps into the basic desires and needs of people to achieve status and achievement for things they do. Airline frequent flyer programs are often quoted as an early form of gamification since they reward customer loyalty with discounted travel, upgrades, and other amenities. Some airlines have expanded this concept to involve internet-based technology, mobile devices, and social media.

Gamification can help an airline:

- educate and familiarize a web traveler with the airline's products and services
- stimulate further engagement by a web traveler with an airline in cyberspace
- create long-term loyalty.

Besides social media savvy carriers such as Jetblue and KLM, other airlines have also become active in this area. One example is Turkish Airlines that sent people on a scavenger hunt through London during the Summer Olympics in 2012. The airline transformed 73 country flags into QR codes and displayed them on 94 digital bus shelters. The campaign was linked to the company's Facebook and Twitter account and participants could win free tickets by scanning the QR code with their mobile device.[251] However, gamification does not always have to involve a competition as Virgin America's seat-to-delivery program shows.[252] It encourages travelers to make contact to a person by sending one another cocktails and messages through the entertainment system touchscreens on seatbacks.[253]

An airline that wants to apply gamification can benefit from increased brand awareness and web traveler engagement. At the same time, gamification concepts are not a light undertaking. Our examples have shown that these types of programs must be designed and thought through from beginning to end similarly to when creating a loyalty program for web travelers, otherwise they will fail.

## 3.16 AIRLINE SOCIAL MEDIA COMMUNITIES

The idea to establish crossovers between an airline's customers including its FFP members and social media is not new. A few airlines have been active in establishing their own communities in this area for a few years. Some of these are hosted on third party social media platforms including Facebook and LinkedIn, others are on a carrier's own website such as "SoFly" of JetBlue. With social being such an integral part of today's web travelers, these types of connections are likely to proliferate. Several examples are introduced in Table 3.15.

## 3.17 AIRLINE MOBILE MARKETING

Mobile marketing is (at least currently) marketing done on or with a mobile device including smart phones and tablets. Other mobile devices like wearables are already making their initial forays into the mainstream so this definition is a bit fluid. It does not matter what data source is consulted these days, all signs point to solid growth of mobile advertising over the next years. With an ever-increasing number of people using smart phones and tablets, mobile advertising budgets worldwide are going up accordingly.

Global mobile advertising as a share of total digital advertising is predicted to increase from 25% in 2015 to over 36% in 2017. During the same timeframe in North America, the world's most evolved mobile market, advertising spending on mobile formats is likely to increase its share of the total digital advertising spending

**Table 3.15** *Airline social network crossovers*

| Carrier program | Commentary |
| --- | --- |
| British Airways: "MetroTwin" | Introduced in 2008, the site was designed to link people in London and New York. Mumbai was added in 2009. With the twinning theme, main feature was blogging content about places to see and things to do in either city. BA discontinued the sites in 2011 and repurposed the concept for Facebook under "Perfect Days" for key cities in the BA/Iberia network. |
| JetBlue: "SoFly" | "SoFly" (short for Social Fly) was launched in 2013 on Jetblue.com. JetBlue travelers can leave tips for other travelers and shares photos of their travel experience. The carrier also features many fun facts about its business. |
| Lufthansa: "MySkyStatus" and "MemberScout" | Launched in 2009, MySkyStatus application enables web travelers to send automatic status updates about their flights to their friends on social networks. The MemberScout app has been live since 2010 and Miles and More participants share travel tips through it. |
| KLM: "Meet & Seat" | With "Meet & Seat," web travelers can learn details of people on their upcoming flight. Once participants in this program have established a link from their Facebook and LinkedIn accounts to Meet & Seat, they can check prospective seatmates by browsing their various social media profiles. Next step: The web traveler can request to sit next to somebody of particular interest, meet up in-flight or at the airport, or share landside transportation upon arrival. |
| Virgin America: "Here On Biz" | Web travelers access this app via a LinkedIn sign-up and login when they arrive at the gate or while in-flight. It is possible then to connect with passengers on their flight and other passengers on currently airborne Virgin America flights, or heading to the same destination. "Here On Biz" is supported on all Virgin America domestic flights. |

*Source:* Lufthansa (2015),[254] Del Nero (2014),[255] Fox (2011)[256]

from 33% to almost 50%.[257] The travel industry is part of this seismic shift in budget allocation and has been among the Top 10 global mobile advertising spenders for a few years (Figure 3.90).

As more web travelers use mobile devices for various stages of their travel activities, airlines also have to follow their target audience to ensure that they stay relevant in this changing environment. The goals of building brand awareness and stimulating direct sales by opening up and pursuing new, mobile-based advertising opportunities in order to reach web travelers are crucial for any carrier.

Mobile advertising media are attractive to airlines for several powerful reasons:[258]

- mobile is a mass medium
- mobile is a private medium
- mobile is a two-way interactive medium
- mobile is always on
- mobile is immediate
- mobile is locally relevant.

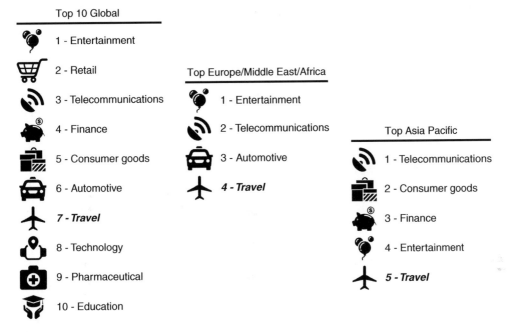

**Figure 3.90** *Top 10 global spenders for mobile advertising and regional spotlights (by industry category, 2013)*

*Source:* Millennial Media (2014)[259]

Against this background, the following section introduces several mobile key advertising formats and shares information on how airlines engage with them.

### 3.17.1 Mobile marketing formats

The most common mobile advertising formats that play a role today include search, display, and various forms of messaging. Table 3.16 shows for the US market that mobile advertising is a solid multi-billion dollar business. By 2017, mobile advertising is predicted to be at almost $25 billion. The breakdown by format shows that the spending is skewed toward mobile search and mobile display. Both claim over 90% of the total. The reason why display advertising is so strong is because it includes social media-related advertising spending that by itself is on an up-swing trajectory. Although not airline industry specific, these figures nevertheless provide some indication of the relative importance of each mobile ad format to some carriers.

*Mobile search advertising*

Many airlines deploy this advertising format extensively because web travelers use their smart phones and tablets frequently for travel search. Flight-related information is actually the second most commonly researched content with 69% of smart phone

**Table 3.16** *US mobile (smartphone and tablet) ad spending, by format 2012, 2014, 2016 ($ millions)*

| Category | 2012 | 2014 | 2016 |
|---|---|---|---|
| Search | $2,241 | $6,661 | $12,229 |
| Display* | $1,848 | $5,988 | $11,571 |
| SMS/MMS/P2P | $223 | $223 | $209 |
| Other (Classified, email, lead generation) | $50 | $214 | $695 |
| Total | $4,363 | $13,086 | $24,705 |

*Includes* ads on Facebook's sponsored stories and Twitter's promoted tweets

*Source:* eMarketer.com (2013)[260]

and 65% of tablet users doing this.[261] Figure 3.91 gives us a more detailed insight into what specific content is searched for.

There are some unique aspects an airline should pay attention to when developing a mobile search campaign. One has to do with SEO again. Some practices here are similar to what we know from our earlier discussion about desktop-based SEO. However, others are unique to the mobile format and need to be observed to ensure top organic search result listings with the major mobile search providers.

Another aspect we have already mentioned earlier includes the number of words per search involved in the various computing platforms. The more mobile the device, the shorter the search query. This is not a surprise considering that entering search terms on a smart phone qwerty keyboard obviously creates a different need than tapping the glass on a tablet's touchscreen or using a PC's standard keyboard. In this environment, the majority of online users submit one or two search words. Tablets involve two search words for the most

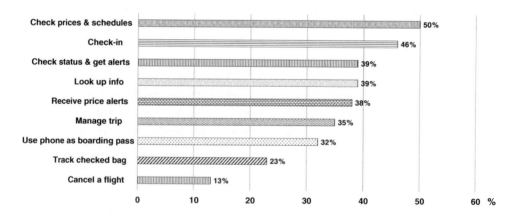

**Figure 3.91** *Smartphone search for flight activities*

*Source:* Millennial Media (2014)[262]

**Table 3.17** *Airlines and flights: Top word combos*

| PC/Tablet | | Smartphone | |
|---|---|---|---|
| *Title* | *Tag description* | *Title* | *Tag description* |
| Hotels | Online | Airlines | Travel |
| Online | Hotels | Discount/Deals | Last Minute |
| Online | Travel | Discount/Deals | Destination |
| Price/Pricing | Tickets | Airlines | Destination |
| Compare | Airlines | Airfares | Business |

*Source:* Gagnon (2011)[263]

part. We have also pointed out that online users generally tend to apply more generic rather than brand-specific search terms on their mobile devices. The implication from this insight is that airlines need to adjust the combination of words they apply in the copy text that is displayed to mobile users. Specifically, the title and tag description require close attention.

An example of what word combination appears to be more effective around holiday travel is displayed in Table 3.17. In the case of PC/tablet users, they often want to put together travel packages. Therefore, when searching for airlines and flights, the term "hotels" is of relevance. Additionally, the price comparison shopping aspect also plays a role as indicated by keywords such as "price" and "compare." For mobile searchers, the picture looks different. An airline that wants to earn a higher engagement with them should include words such as "save," "discount," and "deals" in its copy text. This is because mobile searchers typically look for last-minute specials. There is one situation when mobile searchers respond well to airline and flight ads that include the name of the carrier in the title tag and destination in the description tag. This is when the mobile searcher is accessing the airline for pre-check-in or to verify flights that have already been booked.[264] However, in order to capture a mobile searcher's attention and earn their business, an airline needs to stay focused on generic search terms.

An important issue that should also be mentioned deals with location-based search targeting. The "where" of a web traveler takes importance with mobile users and search results must take this geographic aspect into account. Ensuring that a mobile web traveler receives a message at the right place (and often also at the right time) is crucial for the search result to be relevant. Apparently, carriers in the United States are active users and account for 27% of location-based mobile ads (Figure 3.92).

*Mobile display ads*

Mobile display ads also play a major role in mobile advertising for airlines. The most common formats are graphical banners with or without text links. They have been

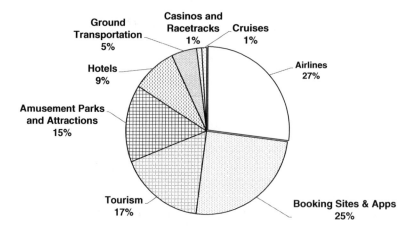

**Figure 3.92** *Travel categories using location-based targeting in mobile ad campaigns*

*Source:* Millennial Media (2014)[265]

around for several years and one may say that they are coming of age. Their performance in terms of customer responses has been very moderate with the average CTRs reported to be around 0.09%.[266] There are several reasons why conventional display ads are not working effectively. In many cases, they do not display well on mobile devices and people do not look at them. This is because they are often very tiny and this is not inviting for interaction.

As a counter measure, the Interactive Advertising Bureau (IAB) introduced a variety of new mobile ad formats in 2012. Dubbed as the "rising stars" of new mobile advertising, they have proven the point that bigger can mean better. The five new mobile formats are Filmstrip, Slider, Adhesion Banner, Full Page Flex, and Push (Figure 3.93). Each of them is a creative way to engage users without fully interrupting the browsing experience of an online user.

The initiative by the IAB should help increase the effectiveness of these new formats. Based on a 2013 benchmark report involving the analysis of more than 100 billion impressions served, the rising stars reported on average a CTR of 0.16%, significantly higher than the 0.09% for the traditional standards we have mentioned earlier.[267] An airline looking into increasing its digital advertising activities via mobile needs to embrace these new innovative formats.

However let us not forget that the advertising industry has been at this point before. In the early 2000s, people were concerned about the rapidly declining CTRs for the then existing banner ads—and along came the bigger skyscraper banner that brought "relief" but not for long. Some observers are therefore cautious with their optimism regarding the new mobile formats. Instead they argue that the future of mobile advertising lies with apps. We will come back to apps advertising shortly.

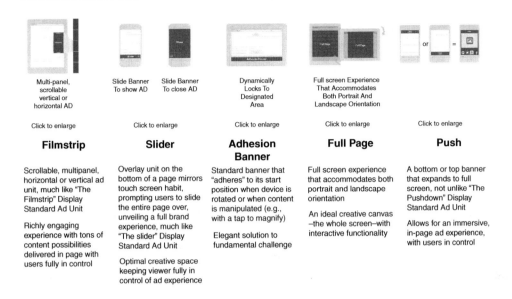

| Filmstrip | Slider | Adhesion Banner | Full Page | Push |
|---|---|---|---|---|
| Multi-panel, scrollable vertical or horizontal AD | Slide Banner To show AD    Slide Banner To close AD | Dynamically Locks To Designated Area | Full screen Experience That Accommodates Both Portrait And Landscape Orientation | |
| Click to enlarge | Click to enlarge | Click to enlarge | Click to enlarge | Click to enlarge |
| Scrollable, multipanel, horizontal or vertical ad unit, much like "The Filmstrip" Display Standard Ad Unit

Richly engaging experience with tons of content possibilities delivered in page with users fully in control | Overlay unit on the bottom of a page mirrors touch screen habit, prompting users to slide the entire page over, unveiling a full brand experience, much like "The slider" Display Standard Ad Unit

Optimal creative space keeping viewer fully in control of ad experience | Standard banner that "adheres" to its start position when device is rotated or when content is manipulated (e.g., with a tap to magnify)

Elegant solution to fundamental challenge | Full screen experience that accommodates both portrait and landscape orientation

An ideal creative canvas –the whole screen–with interactive functionality | A bottom or top banner that expands to full screen, not unlike "The Pushdown" Display Standard Ad Unit

Allows for an immersive, in-page ad experience, with users in control |

**Figure 3.93** *The five rising stars in mobile advertising formats*

*Source:* Weborama.com (2014)[268]

## A CLOSER LOOK AT JETBLUE'S MOBILE ADVERTISING ACTIVITIES

One airline that has been active in the area of mobile banner displays is e-commerce savvy JetBlue. Over the years, they have developed a reputation for sophisticated digital campaigns including mobile formats. An example is their "Air on the Side of Humanity" campaign that was rolled out in New York and southern Florida in spring 2014. It essentially touted the carrier's theme to make traveling more enjoyable. What is interesting about this campaign is that JetBlue for the first time took a user device-conscious approach and created mobile-specific messages and display formats. By targeting smart phone and tablet web travelers separately, the airline decided that it could no longer view them as the same platform.[269]

This approach makes perfect sense considering that each device is consumed differently. They are typically used during different times throughout a given working week day and in different environments. Smart phones are more popular when people are literally on the go while tablets are the preferred platform for "downtime on the sofa." We have mentioned this issue at the beginning of this chapter when discussing digital consumer profiling. Figure 3.94 highlights this phenomenon for the UK as an example. The type of ad message and web content an airline presents to a web traveler needs to take this aspect into account and modify its mobile ads accordingly.

With this market intelligence, JetBlue mostly displayed smart-phone geared ads in the mornings, emphasizing its claim to offer more leg room than other airlines— when consumers are likely traveling on crowded public transportation during their

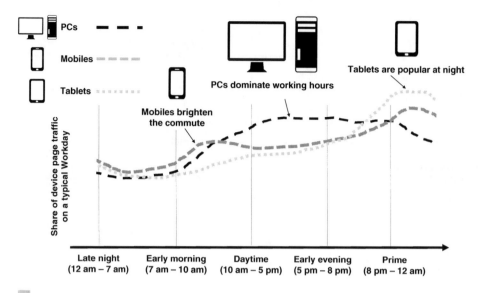

**Figure 3.94** *Device preferences throughout the day*

*Source:* Bosomworth (2015)[270]

commute to work. Knowing that smart phones are frequently used for travel research, the carrier's calls-to-action and push for sales were subdued while its brand was more highlighted.

For tablets, the ads were different. In recognition that web travelers have more time to engage with web content when using tablets, JetBlue used a rich media game that allowed online users to interact with the pigeons featured in JetBlue's video spots. In both cases, the engagement with the display ads was enriched by linking the web traveler to the campaign's microsite at www.jetbluecentralperch.com where additional information including videos was shared (Figure 3.95).

JetBlue's campaign provides valuable lessons. For mobile campaigns to increase their effectiveness, they have to be geared toward specific mobile devices. This requires two important measures by an airline: The application of responsive website concepts whereby the display ads served to web travelers are automatically adjusted according to the mobile device's screen size and the consideration of a web traveler's behavorial patterns. There is some indication that a larger number of players in the travel industry apply some device differentiation in their execution of mobile campaigns. According to one benchmark study for the US market, 64% of all mobile travel ads were run on smart phones versus 34% on tablet.[271]

Another example where JetBlue differentiated its mobile ad efforts in the marketplace goes back to 2013. That year, the airline partnered with a company called Mobile Theory and introduced a voice-activated mobile campaign—the first of its kind in the United States.[272] Web travelers saw a collapsed ad that expanded once clicked on. An image of a pigeon then popped up and a voice-over prompted the web traveler to learn how to speak like a pigeon by clicking through on the mobile

*Figure 3.95* JetBlue mobile ad display and campaign microsite ("*Air on the Side of Humanity*" campaign)

Source: JetBlue (2015),[273] Johnson (2013)[274] with kind permission of JetBlue

*Figure 3.96* Mobile JetBlue display ad

*Source:* Johnson (2013)[275] with kind permission of JetBlue

ad (Figure 3.96). Sounds and words scrolled across the screen when a user said a specific prompt, creating an entire sentence. Once the web traveler completed two sentences, they earned a medal and could choose to replay the game. When clicking on the ads, web travelers were prompted to tap on the screen to start a conversation with a pigeon. This technology is obviously still relatively new in the context of being integrated into a mobile display ad campaign. It therefore needs to be seen if other mobile campaigns are going to integrate a voice-activation feature. JetBlue deserves credit for experimenting with new formats to engage the web traveler in a two-way conversation.

The "Air on the Humanity" campaign also played out via video, the other digital mobile display format. The videos were an extension of the carrier's TV campaign and run on both tablets and desktop properties.

*Short message service (SMS)*

SMS text advertising represents the smallest of the mobile ad formats. We need to differentiate between permission-based and non-permission-based SMS texting. In the former case, the web traveler has agreed to become a subscriber and to receive SMS ad text from an airline. Non-permission-based SMS involves the delivery of mobile advertising without prior approval from the online user. Considering today's various digital privacy protection laws in most countries, it is illegal for airlines to engage in this practice.

Besides conveying an attractive direct response message and targeting the right audience, it is critical for a successful SMS campaign to maximize the interactivity feature of SMS. This is achieved by making the web traveler:

- reply to the SMS ad because it involves a polling, voting, or possibly a question and answer set-up
- click-to-call by inserting a phone number in the ad
- click-to-browse and feature a link to the carrier's mobile site—ideally, the SMS ad text serves as an entry point to a richer experience with more engagement for the web traveler.

An example of an interactive ad campaign that leveraged the SMS format to reach thousands of consumers in a short time span involves Southwest Airlines. They partnered with a radio station in Boston and promoted a flyaway trip for two to attend the NBA Finals game in Los Angeles. Within a few minutes of the campaign being live, Southwest managed to collect over 10,000 entries, a remarkable result (Table 3.18).

*Mobile app advertising*

Apps on smart phones and tablets are a relatively new venue for mobile advertising. There are two forms of app advertising that bear relevance for airlines:

- in-app advertising
- indirect app advertising.

In-app advertising concerns the placement of airline ads inside the apps of other brands. It may seem challenging for an airline to select the right app because there are over 1 million each in Apple's iTunes App store and Google's Play. However, the actual number of apps people generally interact with on a monthly basis did not exceed more than 26 in 2013. This number is only a slight increase over the 23 recorded for 2011. Interestingly, the time online users spent with apps went up significantly: From around 18 hours to right over 30 hours a month.[276] When compared with mobile sites where people spent only around six hours each month, mobile apps are clearly the platform of choice in the mobile world. It is this very aspect that makes apps so appealing to advertisers including those from the travel sector.

**Table 3.18** *Southwest Airlines SMS text ad campaign*

| Marketers | Southwest Airlines & WEEI Sports Radio Network, Boston |
|---|---|
| Campaign/program name | Southwest NBA Finals Getaway Text-2-Win Contest |
| Target audience | Fans of the National Basketball Association's Boston Celtics |
| Call-to-action | Win a flyway trip to the NBA Finals in Los Angeles, including a pair of tickets to a 2010 NBA Finals game, round-trip airfare, and hotel accommodations. |
| Common short code and keywords used | Text FINALS to 850850 |
| Bounce-back message | "WEEI: Thanks for entering the Southwest Airlines LA giveaway! We will contact winner of the contest. Good luck! Message & data rates may apply. Text HELP 4 help" |
| Tactics | WEEI partnered with Southwest Airlines to give Celtics fans an opportunity to win a trip for two to the NBA finals in Los Angeles. |
| | Leading up to the giveaway, WEEI promoted the contest heavily through a number of promotional vehicles, including on-air promos, live talent reads, station newsletters, social media and website exposure. |
| | Listeners tuned into the Dennis & Callahan Show, WEEI's morning show, on Friday, June 4, to get a special SMS keyword—"Finals"—and then had 10 minutes to text it in to WEEI's short code, 850850. |
| Results | After 10 minutes, 10,154 total entries and 4,220 unique entries |

*Source:* Butcher (2011)[277]

The types of app categories travel companies consider for in-app advertising are shown in Table 3.19. The Top 10 list with different app categories highlights four (games, productivity and tools, dating, and shopping and retail) that show the highest visitation and engagement levels for travel campaigns.

Is in-app advertising more effective than mobile site advertising? It depends. The mobile web is large and in markets where Apple or Google do not dominate as platform providers, ads on mobile sites can still be accessed by any smart phone. In this instance, mobile advertising could have an edge over mobile apps in terms of CTRs,[278] otherwise ads on apps appear to outperform ads on mobiles by more than two to one.[279] Airlines, especially those operating in multiple markets, need to pay close attention to what environment is more conducive to a particular format. Some carriers pursue a dual approach and place ads on both mobile sites and in apps at the same time.

As far as indirect app advertising is concerned, it is important not to underestimate the impact a downloaded airline app has. Its presence among the other dozen or so apps found on average on a web traveler's mobile device serves, according to Henry Hardeveldt, a prominent commentator on travel e-commerce topics, "as a constant advertising reminder that the airline exists."[280] Equally important for the indirect

**Table 3.19** *Top 10 mobile app categories for travel campaigns*

| Categories | Rank |
|---|---|
| Games* | 1 |
| Music/Entertainment | 2 |
| Social | 3 |
| Productivity Tools* | 4 |
| Communications | 5 |
| News | 6 |
| Weather | 7 |
| Dating* | 8 |
| Shopping and Retail* | 9 |
| Books and Reference | 10 |

*Top engaging

Source: Millennial Media (2014)[281]

advertising effect of airline apps is their expansion into social networks. For example, Delta offers a feature on their "Fly Delta App" that allows web travelers on Facebook to broadcast the fact that they travel on Delta and what their itinerary details are. Sharing this kind of information in a public forum also raises a carrier's brand recognition.

*Quick response codes (QRs)*

QR codes have been popping up over the last five to six years on almost any kind of object including printed material. Examples are business cards, brochures, posters, and newspapers/magazines. A QR code is a two-dimensional barcode consisting of black modules that are arranged on white background. This barcode can be read by QR scanners, mobile phones with a camera, smart phones, and tablets. The barcode contains alpha–numeric text and hyper-links that allow users to access/download additional information linked to a specific article and advertisements.

Airlines are mainly using QR codes for mobile boarding passes but they are also applied to extend their static print ads. This allows for a new kind of interaction between a web traveler and an airline's print ad. For instance, Swiss carrier Helvetic Airways conducted a QR code-based campaign. It involved airport advertising boards, in-flight magazines, and on-door drop vouchers which were printed to look like the airline's tickets. When the web traveler scanned the QR code, they were directed to a downloadable voucher allowing them to claim their free return flight from a number of European destinations (Figure 3.97). The airline also applies QR codes in its destination guide.

**Figure 3.97** *Helvetic Airways' QR code for promotions and destination guides*

*Source:* Coupmedia (2014)[282] with kind permission of Helvetic Airways, Helvetic Airways Destination guide (2015)[283]

Lufthansa used QR codes for a promotion of its new business class seats in 2012 on several print ads (Figure 3.98). Upon scanning, a user was linked to a mobile site where they could watch a 30-second video of how the seats work. This was followed by a call to action showing the carrier's website address. The web traveler then could replay the video or be directed to another mobile site for completing a booking.

*Augmented reality and print advertising*

The essential idea of augmented reality (AR) is to enhance or supplement reality by superimposing graphics, video, audio, and other sensory elements over a real-world environment in real time. Current main devices used to experience AR include smart phones and tablets. In addition, normal eyewear glasses are likely to produce the enhanced environment in the future.

**Figure 3.98** *Lufthansa's print ad in* Esquire *magazine with QR code*

Source: Johnson (2012)[284] with kind permission of Lufthansa

ARvertising, the concept of applying AR to advertising, has been around for several years and some airlines have been dabbling with it. It offers airline brands the opportunity to unexpectedly integrate the digital world with the real world. An example of applying AR to print advertising involves Firefly, a subsidiary of Malaysian Airlines. By holding a smart phone over the print ad, the web traveler can watch a 50-second video involving an onboard aircraft tour accompanied by music and additional information (Figure 3.99).

Our discussion on QR codes and ARvertising in the context of print shows that print advertising can bridge into cyberspace and therefore does not need to be a static one-way medium.

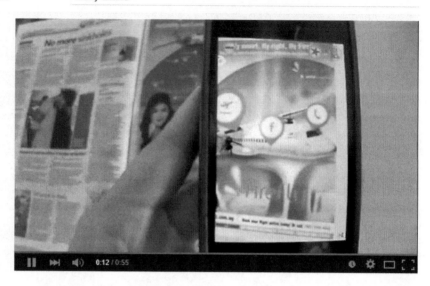

**Figure 3.99** *Firefly print ad enhanced by augmented reality*

*Source:* Youtube.com (2014)[285] permission of FireFly

## 3.18 COMPUTING WEARABLES: THE NEXT FRONTIER FOR MOBILE MARKETING?

With smart watches and smart glasses likely to go mainstream in the near future, the question is what new advertising opportunities could emerge for airlines. Wearable computer providers are apparently already working on various advertising models.

An example is Google that was granted a patent in 2013 for a Google Glass-based ad system. Labelled as "pay-per-gaze," advertisers would be charged any time a person looked at their ad. The ad involved would be displayed on some form of smart Google billboard or it simply would be a traditional media format such as a print ad. As per their filed patent, Google also considers a second phase to the "pay-per-gaze" called "pay-per-emotion." Accordingly, an advertiser would pay more if there was an emotional reaction to an ad. This would be measured in terms of a person's pupil dilation which according to the patent correlates with emotional states.[286] If an airline ad is supposed to make a viewer laugh, this reaction now would be captured. In other words, wearables become electronic mood rings and advertisers for the first time have real-time feedback from users.

The above information highlights one of the main benefits of wearables (at least from an advertiser's perspective—a consumer simply might feel more creepy about this development): The tracking of an individual and the collection of their personal data. Having access to this kind of data could enable advertisers including airlines to fundamentally alter the way they market and possibly even develop new products and services for web travelers. As a result, an airline's future advertising may be impacted by two changes: contextual advertising and emotive advertising.

### 3.18.1 Contextual advertising

By collecting data from wearables, airlines would have much greater insight into a web traveler's current condition and circumstance including their bio state. Ads would be served according to a web traveler's location, interests, and emotional state. These ads would not only be served on a web traveler's personal devices. As a result of cloud computing, they may also appear elsewhere near the environment of the web traveler. An example would be an outdoor advertising venue, including a talking billboard or bus shelter, where the web traveler would be pitched an ad just made for them. Anybody who may have watched the 2002 Tom Cruise movie *Minority Report* would have already seen back then plenty of these types of personalized interactive ads where the advertisement "would recognize you—not only recognize you, but recognize your state of mind," according to Jeff Boortz, creative director for ads in that movie.[287]

### 3.18.2 Emotive advertising

Advertisers including airlines would have for the first time in history an opportunity to gather real-time emotional feedback on their ads. Some observers would argue that today's ads are often "flat" because advertisers do not want to risk alienating the viewers. For example, if an airline decided to run an ad featuring a same-sex couple and display it to people with conservative values, the feedback would probably indicate a preference for more of a mainstream ad. Conversely, a more progressive viewer might tolerate such as an ad and the airline would know that it could share similar ads like this in the future.

In closing, it is reasonable to ask the question whether there will ever be a line in the future that technology companies are not going to cross in the name of advertising. The future will tell but it is safe to state that advertising as we know it today is in the midst of a fundamental transformation—and airlines are part of this.

## 3.19 THE MANAGEMENT OF WWW.AIRLINE.COM DOMAIN NAMES

Domain names play a crucial role in the communication and marketing activities of an airline. They establish a location in cyberspace—a digital address where web travelers can go and interact with the airline. Equally important, domain names give a name to the airline's digital brand. The effective use of a domain name—or rather a portfolio of domain names since an airline typically owns a few (Figure 3.100)—means that an airline is likely to attract more relevant web travelers who access its website for purchases and self-servicing. E-Commerce savvy airlines view domain names as an integral part of the airline's overall brand and treat them as valuable assets to acquire and manage.

**Figure 3.100** *Which domain name?*

### 3.19.1 What is in a domain name?

The location of an airline's administrative offices, sales, and service outlets in the physical world has a digital equivalent that is assigned a unique numerical internet protocol (IP) address. An example of such an IP address is 217.31.410. However, since numerical IP addresses are difficult to remember, they are expressed in natural language and referred to as domain names. The web domain name behind the above IP numerical address is virgin-atlantic.com.

Helping in this process is the so-called domain name system (DNS) which has a record for each website's domain name and IP address. Upon entering a website name in a web browser or clicking on a link, a request is transmitted to the DNS database to resolve the website to the corresponding IP address. In analogy with a telephone book that matches the name of an individual or company to a phone number, the DNS allows a web traveler to use the domain name of an airline as an address locator in cyberspace.

As a digital addressee, it is the airline that selects the domain names used. The conventional approach is to replicate the existing trademark name of the airline and those of its products for a presence in the online world. For example, the domain name for Lufthansa is lufthansa.com while British Airways' FFP Avios uses avios.com. The key is to make domain names intuitive so that web travelers are brought directly to the airline's site. This way, they do not waste valuable time surfing through third party sites such as search engines.

Some domain names represent an abbreviated version of the airline's standard name. American Airlines uses aa.com while ba.com stands for British Airways. The old real estate adage "location, location, location" applies also to two-letter domain names. They are considered prime real estate in cyberspace. Two-letter domains, especially with the popular .com suffix, are special in several ways:

- They are rare—there are only 676 = 26 x 26 of them in the world.
- They are easy to remember and often reflect how consumers refer to the brand—think of GE for General Electric or BA for British Airways.
- They are more likely to capture so-called type-in traffic from web users who go directly to a browser bar and type in the website address (this approach bypasses search engines hence saving an airline money otherwise spent on SEO and SEM).
- They are extremely easy on eyes and finger typing, especially on mobile devices.

Any airline considering an acquisition of a two-letter domain name (the two-letter IATA code would be ideal), needs to think again, however. All 676 two-letter domain names are taken up. If available, they are only traded in the secondary market where an original owner may offer one for sale. Two-letter domain names command a price premium. For instance FB.com was sold for $8.5 million to Facebook in 2010. At least 108 of the two-letter domain names are in the hands of global brands and there are only four airlines in the world among them.[288] They include American Airlines (aa.com), British Airways (ba.com), Lufthansa (lh.com), and French carrier XL Airways (xl.com).

American Airlines made domain name history. It was not only the first airline to acquire a two-letter domain name in 1997 but also the first company ever that purchased a domain in the secondary market. The original owner of aa.com was Architech & Arts. The purchase price in each transaction remained confidential although it is reasonable to assume that the amounts involved could be millions of dollars. Airlines that missed out on their two-letter.com registration did so because the domain name was either already in possession of a strong holder or its management simply failed to buy the domain name. Two airlines occasionally mentioned in this regard are Air France—af.com went to a company called Domain Investor—and Iberia that lost ib.com to IB Domains.[289]

In the context of our naming conventions, airline names clearly have become less geographically oriented in recent years. We have moved from the likes of Japan Airlines and Air Canada to today's rather catchy themes such as Tigerair, Mango, and Vanilla. The purpose for their use is to reflect an airline's unique persona and also distinguish them from the established legacy airlines. It therefore should not be a surprise that even internet-related airline names have surfaced. Barcelona-based Clickair that was founded in 2006 and merged with Vueling in 2009, web*jet* of Rio de Janeiro which operated from 2005 to 2012, and Zimbabwe-based LCC Flyafrica.com are all examples. These carriers tout their close affiliation with the web via their company names.

### 3.19.2 ICANN and the domain name system

The organization responsible for managing the internet's worldwide domain name system is called ICANN (Internet Corporation for Assigned Names and Numbers). It is a non-profit entity that was created in 1998 and is based in Los Angeles, California. According to ICANN nomenclature, domain names are divided into different hierarchies following the dot ("."). The dot is also referred to as the root of the name space. The whole structure of the domain name system can be broken down by what comes before, between, and after the dot.

The first hierarchy distinguishes between generic top-level domains (gTLDs) and country code top level domains (ccTLDs) (Figure 3.101). Based on the latest data available by Verisign, a US internet infrastructure company, the total number of domain name registrations worldwide for both categories stood at 296 million in the second quarter of 2015. This is a 5.9% year-over-year growth.[290] The second hierarchy refers to second level domains. The second level is the name to the left of the top-level domain in an internet address. For example, in AirFrance.com, the second level domain name is AirFrance.

It is important to recognize that two identical second-level domain names cannot exist under the same top level domain. This is where domain name disputes between different companies arise (how these disputes are typically resolved is discussed later in this chapter). For example, while Delta Airlines, Delta Tools, and Delta Financial all may want to own the domain name delta.com to guide online shoppers to their respective website, only one company can actually possess it.

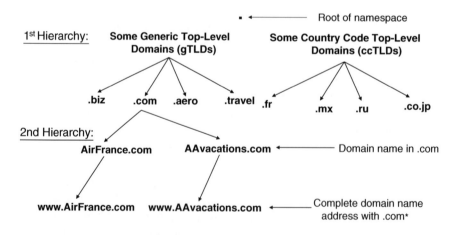

**Figure 3.101** *The structure of the DNS naming hierarchy*

* "Complete" does not mean that the domain name address has to feature the prefix "www." However, if a web traveler leaves the prefix off and the web browser stalls, this is an indication that the DNS record does not contain the short version of the domain name (the version without the "www"). Most airlines ensure that both the short and long version of their website domain names are recorded. The entire string prefaced by the Hyper Text Transfer Protocol abbreviation (http) is also referred to as the uniform record locator or URL.

Before Delta Airlines acquired delta.com, it was legitimately registered to and owned by Delta Financial. Delta Airlines bought it for a large amount, presumably for more than $1.6 million.[291] Other travel-related domain names that made headlines due to their high price tag include privatejet.com selling for $30 million and vacationrentals.com that fetched $35 million, the highest ever amount paid for a domain name.[292]

The acquisition of domain names is governed by ICANN's "first-come, first-served" principle. Some domain names are subject to certain prerequisites as to who can acquire them and when the acquisition can take place. However, many domains, especially the popular .com one, face no such restrictions. If available, they can be acquired by an individual or company for a fee and the ownership is typically locked in for one or two years before a possible renewal.

The reasons why individuals and companies acquire another third party company's domain names has often to do with cybersquatting. We will address this topic later in this chapter in more detail. Airlines that have missed out on a timely acquisition for their company domain names typically resort to registering domains with other generic extensions. This is because being without an address, an airline literally does not exist in cyberspace.

For example, if the .com extension is not available, some carriers use their brand name with the .net suffix instead. Korean LCC Jeju with jeju.net is such an example. Another alternative is to create a domain name that is similar to the airline's brand name. Popular with airlines is to preface their brand name with "fly." Korean airline Asiana uses this approach with flyasiana.com. Airlines that are not in possession of a domain name of their initial interest often try to gain ownership. This is done either via legal means or some form of out-of-court dispute resolution process. Trademark infringement is frequently used as an argument by an airline to win its case.

### 3.19.3 The airline domain name portfolio

From an airline perspective, the universe of domain names comprises the names owned by the airline (the so-called domain portfolio), those in possession by a third party, and those that are not claimed yet (Figure 3.102). Managing domain names effectively means to deal with all three areas.

### 3.19.4 The domain names owned by an airline

The domain names owned by an airline constitute the domain name portfolio. Its size and make-up vary by carrier. However, there are six essential factors that an airline should consider when putting it together:

1. The airline brand
2. The company's sub-brands
3. Other airline organizational entities and their respective brand names
4. The geographic coverage of markets served
5. The languages the (sub)-brands domain are to be expressed in
6. The areas crucial for brand protection reasons.

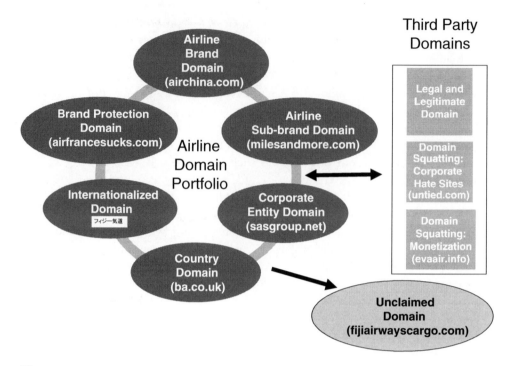

*Figure 3.102* *Domain names relevant for a carrier's digital brand*

The domain name portfolio of an airline that is serious about its digital brand can easily contain a few dozen names. For a large carrier with an international route network and multiple product/service offerings including FFP, cargo, and vacation package, it is not unusual to manage several hundred domain names. However, only a handful of domain names are typically used by an airline for interaction with web travelers.

The large majority of domain names in an airline's portfolio are acquired purely for brand protection against third party abuse. They are not used by airlines for communication with web travelers.

### 3.19.5 Domain names owned by third parties or unclaimed

Besides its own portfolio, the other key area of domain names an airline should be concerned with involves third parties. These domain names are owned by third parties and an airline may eye them for acquisition. This is because it wants to use them for marketing communication or for brand defensive reasons. Third party domain names can be segregated into two groups:

- legitimate and rightful domain names
- domain names used for squatting.

Lastly, there is the category of domain names that are currently in what is called unclaimed territory. In this area of domain names, no one has claimed ownership of a domain name. Subject to the first-come, first-served rule and regulations governing the domain name system, such a domain name can be acquired by an interested party at any time.

## 3.20 BUILDING A SOLID AIRLINE DOMAIN NAME PORTFOLIO

An airline that aims at building and maintaining an effective domain name portfolio should be guided by three key questions:

1. What domain names to acquire and publicize for interaction with web travelers?
2. What domain names to obtain for brand protection purposes?
3. How to deal with third party domain name abuse?

### 3.20.1 Airline domains commonly used for public communication

For communication in cyberspace, an airline typically wants to use the exact same name of its already established brand from the offline world. The reasons for this are the shoppers who are familiar with it. Of primary interest is the airline name in conjunction with the popular .com extension. Examples are airFrance.com and country-specific domains such as www.airfrance.fr (France), www.airfrance.ae (United Arab Emirates), and www.airfrance.mx (Mexico).

For an airline's key sub-brands, the investment in the registration and publication of domain names is equally important. For example, considering the crucial role FFPs play in developing and maintaining an airline's customer loyalty, it is no surprise that many airlines use the name of their FFPs in domain names with both generic and country code suffixes. An example is Lufthansa with www.milesandmore.com and www.milesandmore.de.

Another category for which airlines often register and publicize domain names is related to a company's holding name and the names of a subsidiary. For instance, the holding company of the Scandinavian airline SAS is the SAS Group and the related domain name is registered under www.sasgroup.net. This type of website is geared toward investors and representatives from the media. Similarly, carriers that operate subsidiaries—tour/holiday package companies and air cargo are common—frequently purchase and publicize domain names for these respective entities. Examples include the air cargo websites of Singapore Airlines (www.siacargo.com) and Japan Airlines (www.cargo.jal.co.jp) as well as www.aavacations.com for American Airlines' holiday arm.

Finally, in order to target web travelers more successfully in non-Western language markets, an airline should consider the acquisition of domain names in non-Latin characters. Of increasing importance for airlines are the so-called internationalized domain names in Chinese but also in Arabic and Cyrillic.

### 3.20.2 The importance of generic top-level domains for airlines

Between 1985, the birth year of domain names, and 2012, when ICANN abolished the old domain name system, the world of cyberspace dealt with 22 gTLDs in total. They included the popular .com and less familiar ones such as .net, .info, and .biz. The world's most common gTLD is .com. Introduced in 1985, it initially had been designed for use by commercial entities with an online presence but it also came to serve personal websites. It is the single largest top-level domain with close to 119 million recorded registrations and still growing.[293]

For airlines, the .com extension so far has been the top choice. They make it part of their website's domain name whenever feasible because of its popularity with consumers. No other gTLD enjoys as much international prestige and worldwide recognition as .com. Airlines make little if any use of other particular gTLDs. If some of them do, it is because they got squeezed out of registering for the highly demanded .com version. A gTLD often used as a .com alternative is .net which is a distant second to .com 15 million registrations.[294] Another reason why an airline may acquire any of these non-dotcom gTLDs is for defensive purposes in order to protect its trademark and brand.

Are there airline or travel industry specific gTLDs? The answer is yes. ICANN had wanted to de-emphasize the .com gTLD and to be more appealing to distinct online audiences by giving them access to websites whose domain names are indicative of a specialized online business focus. The domain .aero was the first ever industry-specific gTLD created. Intended for use by air transport-related businesses, it was sponsored by SITA and introduced in 2002. However, with less than 9,000 registrations, its actual use is minor. Most commercial airlines still stick to the more popular .com domain or other generic domains. Libyan carrier Afriqiyah is one airline applying the .aero domain for its cyberspace presence. Another example is the reborn Miami-based Eastern Airlines with easternairlines.aero.

Another example of an industry-specific gTLD is .travel. It was created in 2005 and sponsored by the Travel Partnership Corporation. The idea was to support the website activities of travel agencies and tourism authorities. The first website launched with the .travel domain was in 2006 by the Egypt Tourism Authority for their web portal www.egypt.travel. However, the overall acceptance by the travel industry for this domain is very still small. Of the top one million websites in the world, less than 200 carry the .travel domain.[295] In 2014 the top two .travel domains were travelagency.travel (this domain redirects to the French online travel agency Govoyage.com) and rurubu.travel (a Japanese online travel agency).[296]

### 3.20.3 The role of country code TLDs for airlines

Country code TLDs are two-letter indicators and designed for use by countries and territories. Examples include .ae for United Arab Emirates, .cl for Chile, and .in for India. In 2015, there were approximately 126 million ccTLDs and the registration for most of them is limited to individuals and companies located in their home country. There are only a few countries allowing domain registration to anyone in the world (the UK with .uk is one of them). Among the top 5 largest ccTLDs are .de (Germany), .uk (UK), and .cn (China).[297]

The reason why an airline should be concerned with ccTLDs is to tap most effectively into the business with web travelers in local markets. This is especially the case for an airline that operates an international route network and therefore needs to offer a truly localized website experience. A country-specific website address is one important step in this direction. Many web shoppers, despite the overwhelming popularity of the .com TLD extension, generally use the localized domain name when accessing a website.

For instance, in recognition that Chinese web shoppers default to websites with a .cn suffix, Hawaiian Airlines when commencing its new service between Honolulu and Beijing in April 2014, advised web travelers residing in China to access the carrier's local website at www.hawaiianairlines.com.cn. At the same time, United States-based travelers were directed to www.hawaiianairlines.com.[298]

Interestingly, there are some airlines that maintain a country-specific website presence with a localized domain name even though they do not offer flights to/from that country. Air Botswana is such a case. Although the airline maintains a route network exclusively in southern Africa, it nevertheless has a web presence in the UK with its local website www.airbotswana.co.uk. This website is tailored for British web travelers who would find it understandably difficult to guess Botswana's country code .bw and access www.airbotswana.co.bw.

There are several notable country code TLDs that resemble well-known words or abbreviations. Examples include .fm (the domain name of the Federated States of Micronesia) but used by FM radio stations with an online presence, .la (Laos) that is marketed as the unofficial top level domain of Los Angeles, and .me (Montenegro) used for personal websites. By renting out their ccTLD to commercial entities, some of these countries have simply decided to cash in on the interest of web users for domain names other than the standard gTLD such as .com.

An illustrative case of a ccTLD that has been acquired by some airlines because of its repurposed deployment as a commercial domain name is .tv. The ccTLD .tv represents the Polynesian island nation of Tuvalu that earns several millions US dollars every year for the use of its domain space.[299] Air France uses www.airfrance.tv to feature a simple welcome page where web travelers can select country specific websites for further interaction with the carrier's digital brand while Lufthansa redirects the www.lufthansa.tv domain name to www.lufthansa.com. Obviously, these current uses of the .tv domain name may change. For example, it is possible that airlines in the future could deploy websites with the .tv domain name to feature video content specific to their brand. In other words, while some domain name applications still have to find a better fit depending on future technology developments and web user preferences, their acquisition today nevertheless is important.

One comment on .us and .ca, the country code for the United States and Canada, respectively. Airlines based in either country rarely use them in their communication with web travelers because the .com TLD has literally become synonymous with a

**217**

local web presence in North America. Air Canada and WestJet, Canada's two largest airlines, for instance, own the .ca domain names but redirect the traveling public to their .com website addresses.

Of the major US carriers, Delta, has acquired the delta.us domain (this web address is also redirected to delta.com) while American and United, for example, have not even bothered with the registration of the .us domain name. Foreign airlines serving the US market prefer a .com domain name as well. In the rare event that a local web traveler in the US types a .us web address in the web browser, they find themselves on a .com website. Emirates, for instance, resolves www.emirates.us to www.emirates.com.

---

## SNAPSHOT: THE NEW GENERIC TOP LEVEL DOMAIN PROGRAM AND ITS IMPACT ON AIRLINE E-COMMERCE

In June 2011, ICANN announced, after several years in the making, a huge change to the gTLD system. As of 2012, most restrictions on the then existing 22 gTLDs were ended and anybody was allowed to create arbitrary gTLDs. Domain names could now refer to:

- a specific company (an example would be .canon by the Japanese electronics company Canon that expressed interest early on)
- a geographic location (.berlin of the German capital city of Berlin is an example)
- a legal profession such as .attorney
- any word such as .life or even common abbreviations including .rsvp are now possible.[300]

Furthermore, the use of non-Latin characters (e.g. Arabic, Chinese, and Cyrillic) in gTLDs would also be permitted.

After some initial delays, the first new gTLDs went live in fall 2013 and approximately 1,000 are estimated to have come into existence in 2014. This equates to more than one new gTLD every day. The internet as we know it thus will expand vastly and quickly. ICANN ultimately expects around 1,300 new generic domains to be established in the next few years.[301]

Among the pool of almost 2,000 initial applicants that submitted their bids to ICANN in June 2012, we find the usual suspects such as Google with 101 applications including .fly and Amazon with 76 applications for new gTLDs. Another company called Donuts, which had been specifically set up with more than $100 million to make the new gTLDs its business, expressed interest in 307 new domains including .flights.[302]

Several airlines have also applied for gLTDs under the new scheme. They include Avianca, Delta, SAS, Swiss International Air Lines, and Virgin. Examples of other companies from the travel and transportation industry that have submitted their bids for brand-specific TLDs involve Airbus, FedEx, TUI (a travel and tourism company based in Germany), and WebJet (an Australian online travel agency).[303]

## Advantages of the new generic TLD program for airlines

Does the new gTLD program bear any relevance for airlines? One key argument in favor is the more innovative branding and new level of customization airlines could offer via commercial gTLDs. Specifically, the combination of an airline name in a top-level domain with a meaningful second hierarchy level domain could significantly increase the sense-making value of the digital brand.

In its application to ICANN for the gTLD .virgin, for example, Virgin stressed the possibility of creating on-demand second hierarchy-level domain names such as geographicnames.virgin for country specific websites, function.virgin for websites highlighting particular features, and product.virgin to showcase unique website products.[304] Branding on such granular level in cyberspace allows an airline to better inform online users what to expect on a website before they access it. Again, this saves time in navigation as one could bypass search engines.

Similarly, Swiss International Air Lines, in its bid for the .swiss TLD, suggested among other things the possible creation of personal accounts for valuable flyers that could be accessible via unique web addresses (an example would be John.Smith.swiss).[305] This idea may also partially explain their anticipated volume of .swiss gTLDs amounting to almost 5,000 within ten years.[306]

Delta and SAS highlighted in their applications the need to make the overall interaction between a web traveler and the airline's digital brand easier, more memorable, and more secure. These are valuable points. Let us not forget how crowded cyberspace has become with over 296 million domain names. Of this total, the popular gTLD .com alone accounts for almost 119 million website registrations (over 20% of the .com websites just being one-page holding sites and 15% are "parked" or inactive).[307] Using the airline brand in the gTLD and combining it with product-specific names in second-level domains thus could offer an opportunity for their digital brand to stick out better in this overflowing environment. At the same time, as already mentioned, web travelers are sent directly to particular parts of the airline website, hence making their navigation more efficient.

Furthermore, there are the ongoing issues with online fraud and domain name squatting. Domain name squatting is the use of domain names in bad faith. This is done by capturing website traffic meant for another website because of its reputation and trademark's goodwill. Against this background, airlines understandably want to take stronger control of their digital brand. Using the airline name in the gTLD is a guarantee that the website is controlled by the airline and that web travelers have secure access through direct, trusted, and authentic connections.

A closing argument supporting the new gTLD system involves search engines, particularly the area of search engine optimization (SEO). We discussed SEO earlier in this chapter and it should suffice to state that e-commerce savvy airlines are deeply engaged in making it as easy as possible for search engines to find their brand. Google has publicly stated that the new gTLDs would not receive a preferential display over the .com TLD. This announcement deflated initial beliefs that some kind of boost in search engine ranking would be possible but one has to see how this plays out in the mid- to long term.

Let us remember that search engines can change their search algorithms at will any time. For example, Google not long ago added selected country code TLDs including .co (Colombia), .tv (Tuvalu), and .la (Laos) to the same category as generic TLDs such as .com. This adjustment led to increased web traffic to the very sites using the country code TLDs. It is a bit difficult to imagine that Google would not undertake some re-arrangement of its search algorithm in the future to accommodate the new gTLDs in its search rankings. A .airlinebrand TLD could have a better search result position and capture more relevant, qualified traffic.

## Disadvantages of the new generic TLD program for airlines

Critics point to the huge fees involving the registration of gTLDs: $185,000 per application plus an annual fee of $25,000. This is before any other legal and administrative resource costs that very likely have to be added. This is not a light investment for any airline. The benefits and costs of adopting new airline branded TLDs had better be clear to all stakeholders involved.

Another argument often tabled against new gTLDs is the ingrained behavior of web users. Their preference for .com websites is still high[308] and one of the key reasons why previously launched gTLDs by ICANN including .mobi and .travel never really took off with the public. Therefore, it could be argued that .com will remain the top gTLD for many years to come.

Additionally, people rarely type the full website addresses anymore. Apparently even common ones such as Facebook.com are accessed via search engines and web browsers also. This follows the lead from Google Chrome's "omnibox," which combines the web address bar and search field into one.[309]

Finally, and not a small issue to ignore, is the growing significance of apps that users install on their mobile devices. Apps do not have website addresses and are not rendered in a browser. In other words, there is no need for a domain name.

Fact is right now that there is no firm insight yet as to how the public including web travelers will adjust to the TLD system changes. However, when taking into account the enormous investments in terms of time and money by ICANN and key cyberspace players, one is tempted to say that this new gTLD program is bound to succeed rather than being a white elephant.

The face of the internet as we have known it so far is thus likely to change for good. For airlines, at a minimum, it is prudent to actively monitor these developments. The rapid speed and large scale of the new gTLD program's roll-out simply cannot be ignored. If initial signals throughout 2014 and 2015 point to a market acceptance of the new commercial gTLDs by web travelers, an airline cannot afford to ignore this. It should then embark on re-structuring its digital brand presence for the new internet. This needs to be a cross-departmental process with stakeholders from e-commerce, IT, marketing, legal, and other key departments.

### 3.20.4 Country codes and the use of shortened URLs

Some carriers use a country code such as .ly (Libya) and .be (Belgium) in links on their social media websites including Twitter, Linkedin, or YouTube. Figure 3.103 shows examples of Qantas, JetBlue, and British Airways.

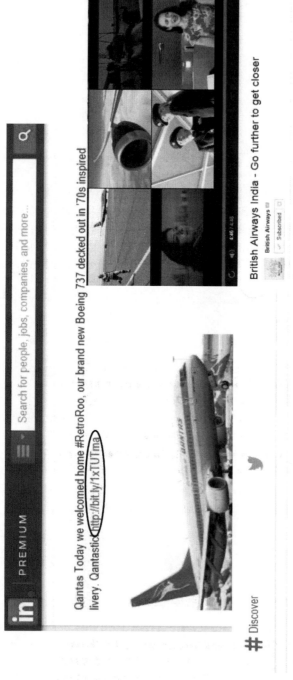

*Figure 3.103*   The use of shortened URLs on social media

Source: LinkedIn (2015),[310] Twitter (2015),[311] YouTube (2015)[312] with kind permission of British Airways, JetBlue, and Qantas

In recent years, companies including airlines with a social media presence have started to use so-called shortened uniform record locators. These URLs are significantly shorter than the standard URLs that can contain many, sometimes hundreds, of characters. Thus, for the simple reason to save space—which is especially a premium on mobile devices and with micro-blogging platforms and instant messaging services—these shorter URLs are applied. Furthermore, because of their brevity, they are easier to remember. Finally, another use for them is the tracking of the number of clicks a link receives. A main URL shortening service provider is the company Bitly. They are typically found on Twitter. Google as the owner of You-Tube decided to launch its own URL shortening application with YouTu.be.

### 3.20.5 Airline domain names critical for brand protection

E-Commerce savvy airlines not only concern themselves with those domain names that are used in communication with the traveling public, but also look out for those that provide for protection of their digital brand. These domain names typically remain un-publicized and are not applied to regular, if any, cyberspace communication with web travelers. They are nevertheless of crucial importance to a successful presence in cyberspace. This is because they help minimize third party infringement on the airline's digital brand and they ensure that web travelers are directed to the appropriate site(s) owned by the airline and not by someone else.

*Domain name squatting*

The practice of domain name squatting can cause significant infringement issues on an airline's digital brand. Domain name squatters exploit the first-come, first served nature of the domain name registration system. They register domain names that are identical or confusingly similar to an airline's trade/servicemarks or to important people from a carrier with which they otherwise have no legal or legitimate affiliation. Depending on the motives that drive them, there are essentially four categories of domain name squatters:

1.  *Ransom artists.* They simply want to sell the domain name back to the company involved for a price that far exceeds the cost of original registration.
2.  *Sneaky competitors.* This category of squatters operates in the same or related industry and they capture existing customers or new prospects to their own websites.
3.  *Bad faith advertisers.* They lure traffic to specially built websites to either monetize for advertising purposes the web traffic flows they capture or to promote some personal agenda.
4.  *Corporate haters.* They claim to be the voice of alienated, frustrated constituents in cyberspace and thus use the domain name for operating a corporate hate website to publish negative information on the company and thereby tarnish the brand.

It is impossible to achieve a 100% digital brand protection. However, an airline can delimit the business damage from domain name squatters by adopting several measures in a few key areas. These are described in the next section.

*Enhancing an airline's brand protection in cyberspace*

An airline may register domain names of its (sub)-brands with a variety of generic suffixes such as .net, .biz, and .info that mirror its domain name portfolio already used for public communication with the .com extension. These domain names then, if actually typed by a web traveler simply point to the currently active website domain name.

Air China applies this approach. The domains www.airchina.info, www.airchina.biz, www.airchina.org, for instance, all direct to the main digital brand www.airchina.com. An airline missing out on this type of domain name registration runs the risk of losing valuable website traffic to other third party sites while at the same time exposing itself to brand dilution. Take the example of Taiwanese airline EVA Air. It owns evaair.com but it has failed to re-acquire or cancel other relevant domain names to adequately protect its digital brand. For instance, the domain name evaair.info (this redirects to an online travel agency site in Germany called Asia Travel that sells tickets on a variety of Asian carriers) is clearly in possession of other third parties that use the EVA Air trademark to their financial advantage. The same is true for evaair.mobi (a website that offers loans and insurances), and evaair.org (a site operated by a travel agency in Vietnam). All these examples are evidence of domain name squatting (Figure 3.104).

E-Commerce leading airlines frequently go after domain names containing a derivative of their brand. Common is to combine "fly" with the company name or also use "airlines" or "airways," occasionally even with a hyphen. Take for example the domain names www.flyemirates.com, www.flyqatar.com, and www.flyklm.com. They all redirect web travelers to www.emirates.com, www.qatarairways.com, and www.klm.com, respectively, the official domain names used in public communication. Likewise, www.air-france.com, www.airfranceairlines.com and www.airfranceairways.com all point to www.airfrance.com, the official company website address of Air France.

Other domain names that an airline should consider for registration comprise those where their application for a commercial website currently is still unclear but could play a role in the near future in light of emerging technology. For instance, given the increasing possibilities for online consumers to "build" their website via personalization tools, it is not too surprising that companies pursue a more individualized approach for their domain name registrations as well. Domain names in the form of myamazon.com, mygoogle.com, and myyahoo.com have already surfaced years ago and have recently found their way into the airline industry as well. Examples include Lufthansa and Air France that have acquired mylufthansa.com and myairfrance.com, respectively. Both domain names currently point to the main .com websites but it is likely that they may be applied to new, yet to be developed, unique website products in the future.

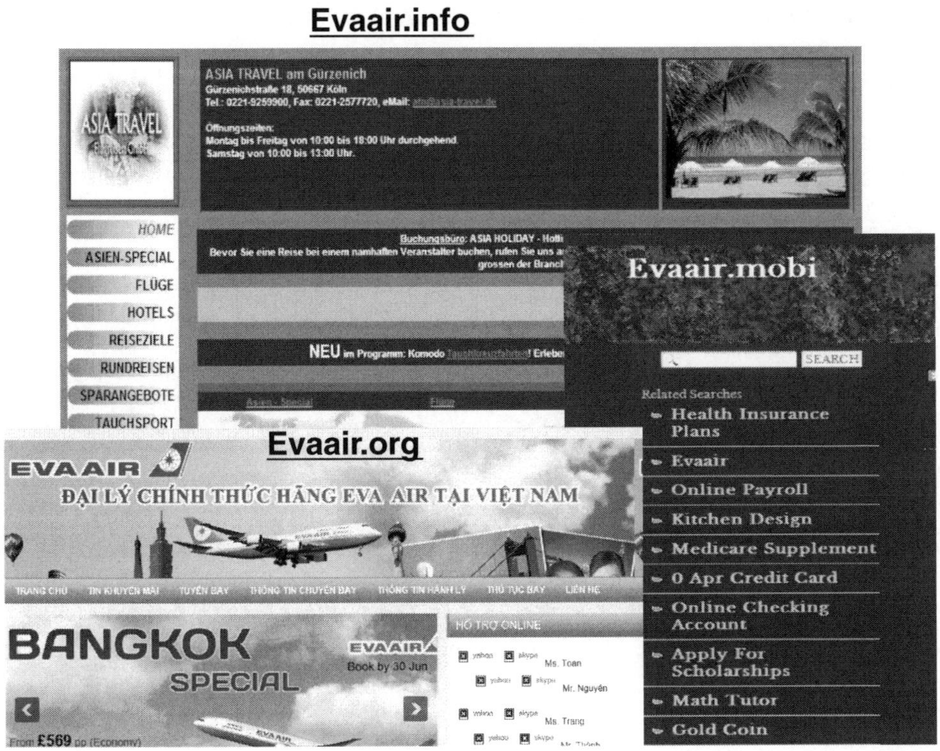

*Figure 3.104* Lack of digital brand protection: Example—EVA Air

Source: evaair.mobi (2015),[313] evaair.org (2015),[314] asia-travel.de (2015)[315]

The discussion on brand derivatives in domain names is incomplete without mentioning the importance of registering and redirecting misspelled names. Web travelers might do an accidental typo when typing on a keyboard or they simply do not know how a certain word is correctly spelled. Some third parties exploit this situation commercially, commonly referred to as typo-squatting. In this situation, the incorrect domain name is acquired in the hope of monetizing the web traffic drawn to a specially built site.

As a category, the airline industry, after gaming, is considered one of the most saturated with typo squatters. Web travelers, when mistyping the website address of a carrier, have an 11% chance to end on a typo-squatter website.[316] Airlines can protect themselves against this form of brand infringement by acquiring the most common misspelled versions of an airline's (sub)brands. However, unlike several mainstream websites such as www.amazon.com for instance, that have registered the most frequent misspellings of their respective company names (e.g. Amazon has registered aamazon.com and ammazon.com), many airlines have failed to establish a proper domain name portfolio. In this regard, an exception is easyJet, for instance, that has acquired the misspelled eeasyjet.com domain name and links online users to easyjet.com.

*Domain name registrations that correspond to current events: Mergers and emergencies*

The practice of acquiring domain names that correspond to current events has been around for some time. These current events are admittedly outliers, but they are nevertheless worth registering domain names for in order to protect an airline's digital brand. The cost of registration is far less than the cost of brand infringement by third parties. Two outlier scenarios where brand protection would be crucial include airline mergers and emergencies.

## MERGERS

Merger advisors typically recommend the pro-active registration of selected domain names in the run-up to the merger. Some people even opine that the first step in a merger today is the purchase of domain names.[317] US Airways, for instance, registered domain names weeks before its official merger announcement with American Airlines including American-USAirways.com, AmericanUSAirways.net, and USandAA.com. The reason for this step was that it would help minimize any backlash and negative impact from third parties on the two brands involved.[318] Against this background, it is not unreasonable to expect the registration of merger-related domain names prior to an official announcement if an airline considers a merger with another carrier. In the United States, for example, Alaska Airlines is frequently mentioned in this regard.

## AIRLINE EMERGENCIES

Another outlier scenario involves that of an airline emergency situation. An emergency situation could range from a natural disaster to an aircraft accident or a terrorist attack. Airlines generally default to their main website to communicate any information related to the emergency. Nevertheless, it may still be beneficial to register several domain names in conjunction with the company name such as accident.com or emergency.com. Even hijacking.com or terroristattack.com, although a bit farfetched for some people, should be added to an airline domain name portfolio for defensive reasons. This measure prevents third parties from using these domain names to operate their own website and engage in public communication on the situation that could hurt the airline's brand.

The author, having been closely involved in managing UA's international websites on September 11, has first-hand experience dealing with these third parties. He was notified by the company's registrar that day about unusual domain name registrations including www.unitedairlineshittheworldtradecenter.com. However, this and other domain names were quickly re-acquired from the individuals at no extra fee upon threatening legal action. On a more positive note, United Airlines received unsolicited assistance from Air France on September 11 which had been registering several relevant domain names that were eventually transferred to United's possession. This was a welcome gesture and helpful because at one point all telecommunication infrastructure was completely non-operational, thus making a domain name registration via phone or email for United impossible.

The interest in domain names related to airline emergencies has certainly not abated. This became clear again in a more recent situation involving Malaysia Airlines—twice to be exact. In the case of Malaysia Airlines flight MH 370 that disappeared on March 8, 2014, on its way from Kuala Lumpur to Beijing, the domain name MH370.com gained some notoriety in cyberspace. After an individual's unsuccessful attempt to auction off the domain name on March 9 via ebay for $5,000,[319] it was registered with a person in Australia who published a website featuring a combination of politically and religiously related topics. Considering that the rescue efforts by the Malaysian government had already been subject to wide criticism, a third party website boasting the ill-fated flight number with what many people viewed as questionable content certainly did not help Malaysia Airline's brand. In another tragedy on July 17, 2014, when Malaysia Airlines flight MH17 was accidentally shot down over Ukrainian airspace, several domain names were registered that same day. They included mh17movie.com, mh17disaster.com, malaysiaflightmh17.com, and mh17planecrash.com.[320] Some of them do not link to a website but are simply parked on a domain server, a clear indication that their current owner wants to sell.

Third parties obtained these domain names for various reasons such as expressing their sympathy to the victims on specially built websites. In other cases, commercial reasons such as re-selling the domain or even launching websites with the flight numbers are drivers. For example, law firms soliciting business from the victims' families via specially created websites are particularly known to be active in the registration of domain names related to airline flight numbers.

The conclusion from the above examples is that an airline's domain management should pro-actively extend to emergency situations. It is impossible to register all variations of emergency-related domain names but it is prudent to at least acquire the airline's flight number(s) and the .com extension. By doing so, a carrier's digital brand is protected at least to some degree. E-Commerce leading airlines have agreements in place with their domain name registrars whereby flight-based domain names are automatically acquired in the event of an emergency.

## 3.21 DEALING WITH DOMAIN NAME SQUATTERS

In those instances where a domain name is already owned by a squatter, an airline committed to preserving the integrity of its digital brand could essentially pursue three options to achieve the possession or cancellation of the domain name at stake:

- Apply a "carrots and sticks" approach. In this case, the airline reaches out to the third party and looks for an amicable arrangement to transfer the domain name.

Typically used are alerts of possible legal action (the "sticks") due to trade/service marks infringement combined with a purchase price offer for the domain name (the "carrot").

■ Involve lawyers and the court system. The caveat is that embarking on legal proceedings is often lengthy and costly.

■ Initiate measures under the so-called Uniform-Domain-Name-Dispute Resolution Policy (UDRP). The UDRP is an ICANN-based, international arbitration process applied to resolve domain name disputes. Airlines that seek to settle the dispute without resorting to expensive litigation often apply the UDRP approach. The process can take several months and is paper intensive. However, its ruling is adopted by accredited domain name registrars and is therefore binding for the parties involved (Figure 3.105).

For example, easyJet used the UDRP process to complain about the bad faith use of easyjet.net whose owner had been operating a website that also linked to two of easyJet's competitors. The result was that easyJet was successfully awarded the transfer of easyjet.net.[321] The domain name now resolved to easyjet.com. Similarly, Delta Airlines followed the UDRP process and filed a complaint via the World Intellectual Property Organization (WIPO) against the bad faith use of the domain name delta-tickets.com. An individual had been using the domain name in question for a website with links to third party websites promoting the sale of airline tickets and other services. Furthermore, at one point the website had been claiming to be an affiliate of Delta selling tickets for Delta's flights. The arbitration led to the transfer of delta-tickets.com to Delta Airlines.[322]

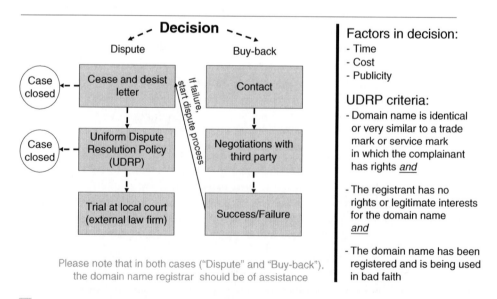

*Figure 3.105* Options to re-acquire or cancel airline domain names

## 3.22 ANTI-BRANDING SITES: THE ULTIMATE BRAND INFRINGEMENT?

A final group of domain names to register for purely brand defensive reasons includes those commonly used for anti-branding sites. Anti-branding sites are also popularly known as corporate hate sites. Most famous in this regard, at least in the English language, is a domain name containing the verb "sucks." It is typically acquired by individuals who want to operate a website that features complaints about their experience with a particular airline. Cyberspace is littered with "airline sucks" websites although many "I hate" airline-related sites on social media also exist. Figure 3.106 shows some examples.

Many of the anti-branding websites are weak in terms of design and editorial content. However, a few are of good quality and actually attract a following among web travelers. Some carriers, unless they have already purchased a few standard domain names that could be used for an anti-branding website, undertake an effort to re-acquire relevant domain names.

An example is Air France that went before WIPO in 2005 and initiated UDRP proceedings to be awarded airfrancesucks.com. Its then owner who had been maintaining a website under this domain since 1999, while claiming freedom of

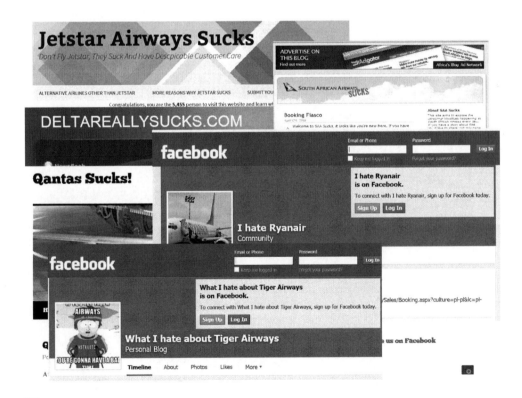

**Figure 3.106** *Selected anti-branding websites*

*Source:* Various websites (2015)[323]

expression and not using the domain name in bad faith, had to transfer it as two of the three arbitration panelists ruled in favor of Air France.[324] When airlines are able to acquire an anti-branding site domain, they typically park it on their domain name server and do not point to any website. This is what Air France did with airfrancesucks.com. It is noteworthy that decisions in domain name disputes involving "sucks" websites appeared to be trending in favor of the original trademark holders.[325] This means that if an airline sees its brand infringed upon by a "sucks" website, it stands a fair chance of winning its case.

Anti-branding websites do not always involve "sucks" domain names. There are those that play a twist on a company's brand name. One example is shipping and logistics company United Parcel Service (UPS) that at one point dealt with unitedparcelsmashers.com. Another example of a domain name in this regard is untied.com. Its owner Jeremy Cooperstock has been maintaining untied.com since 1997 for the purpose of providing both passengers and employees a digital platform to air their concerns, experiences, and complaints as they related to United Airlines (Figure 3.107). United Airlines has been unsuccessfully trying for years to shut this website down. Clearly, untied.com plays on united.com. However, it is apparently not considered a trademark infringement—its use predates united.com by several years—otherwise United Airlines would have probably succeeded in canceling this website address or at least changing it.

*Figure 3.107* untied.com and glenntilton.com: Examples of United Airlines anti-branding website

*Source:* untied.com (2015)[326] with kind permission of Jeremy Cooperstock, author e-commerce archive (2008)[327]

It has also become a common practice within anti-branding circles to dedicate a website to high-ranking executives. Featuring negative information on them translates into hurting the company's brand. It is thus advisable to acquire domain names related to the names of key airline senior officers including CEO, president, and chairman. An example where United Airlines missed out on a timely registration is the domain GlennTilton.com in reference to its former CEO. The domain name, owned at the time by the United Airlines ALPA union group, directed to this website and asked for the resignation of Glenn Tilton while simultaneously not leaving out any opportunity to highlight company's mis-management and customer disservice issues on this website.

## 3.23 SOMETHING TO WATCH OUT FOR: THE RISE OF SOCIAL SQUATTING

Our discussion on digital brand protection via smart domain name management is incomplete without visiting the issue of social squatting. Social squatting, sometimes also labeled as "username squatting", refers to a situation where an unknown party sets up and uses a mock account with a social media platform related to a company or product/service although it is not owned by the company. It is registered by an unknown party and a company can be either brandjacked by negative social communication or approached to buy back the account for a hefty price premium.

All this is reminiscent of domain name squatting. There is a big difference, however. Individuals do not need to prove, justify, or even legitimize the selection of their username. Most social media platforms apply little if any screening when it comes to a user's account creations and usernames. Like with the domain name registration, social media user name registrations work on a first-come, first-served basis.

Airlines are known to be exposed to this issue as well. Numerous cases have surfaced in recent years with unknown third parties faking a particular airline on popular social platforms including Facebook, Instagram, and Twitter. Qantas, in September 2014, alerted the public in Australia to a fake Facebook page playing on the carrier's birthday theme and offering users a chance to win AU$1,500 voucher upon sharing financial details.[328] Philippine carrier Cebu Pacific reported bogus Facebook pages where alleged sales representatives offered to handle bookings for travelers.[329] Likewise, fake Instagram accounts for several US carriers popped up on a large scale in 2012. These accounts looked real with @americanairlines_giveaways, @united_giveaways, @jetbluegiveaways, and @delta_giveaways. They all work similarly and promised a free airline ticket or round-trip ticket to the first several thousand followers. The scary part is that the accounts apparently worked well in terms of attracting interest. Delta's fake account garnered 21,000 followers after it promised a free trip for the first 20,000 people who followed and shared the account. Likewise, the Jet-Blue account had 20,000 followers.[330]

What defensive moves can an airline adopt to deal with these situations? Unlike with domain names, there is unfortunately not much. One remedy is to complain to the owner of the service and request that usernames infringing upon their trademarks be turned over. However, if the owner of the service does not engage, the only recourse may be costly litigation. Some observers believe that trademark law should apply. This is especially the case when the unknown party impersonates a company brand and makes false statements of identity and authorship that lead to an increase in customer search cost and encourage customers to their detriment on wrong information.[331]

At the same time, one can do what American Airlines did in the case of Twitter: They registered every possible Twitter name that could be associated with them.[332] In today's digital era where word of mouth via increasingly popular social media platforms is important, an airline can clearly not afford to have their digital brand infringed upon by a third party that impersonates the carrier for whatever reason.

## 3.24 CRITICAL SUCCESS FACTORS FOR MANAGING AN AIRLINE DOMAIN NAME PORTFOLIO

The ongoing proliferation of new generic top-level domains and the many domain names an airline may want to acquire for different countries and brand protection reasons means that the management of domain names has become rather complex. For an airline to stay on top in this area, several key considerations should come into play (Figure 3.108).

### 3.24.1 Engagement of a domain name registrar

Keeping track of the ever-growing list of new domain names and re-registrations is more efficient when done by an outside expert company. This is the so-called domain name registrar. Main players in this space include Corporation Services Company (CSC), GoDaddy, Netnames, and NetSolutions. All of them work with clients from the travel industry. When an airline selects a domain name registrar, it should make sure to partner with a company that fulfills a number of important requirements (Figure 3.109).

*Establishment of single point of contact*

The interaction with a domain name registrar is most successful when a single point of contact is established within the airline. Billing settlements and overall account management are more efficient and the airline's diverse domain name needs, including those of other organizational entities such the holding and various subsidiaries such as cargo, vacation/tour package, and aircraft maintenance are channeled through a single point.

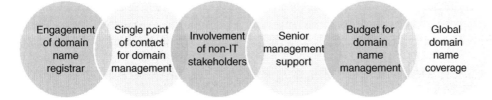

*Figure 3.108* Crucial aspects in domain name management

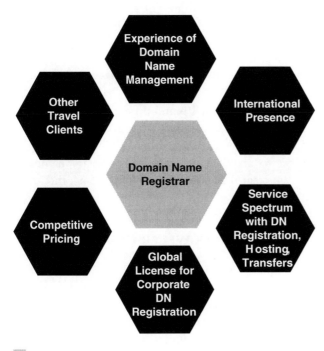

*Figure 3.109* What to look for in a domain name registrar

*Involvement of airline non-IT department stakeholders*

The early days of e-commerce when an IT department was the principal entity for managing a handful of domain names are gone. Today, in recognition of the increased scope and scale of domain name management, a cross–departmental approach with stakeholders from sales, marketing, legal, IT, and other relevant departments makes more sense. Decision makers from these corporate functions can contribute valuable input in the management of domain names.

*Digital brand protection is a senior management level issue*

The presence in the online world today is a pivotal part of an airline's overall brand. For example, domain name squatting and corporate hate websites can seriously harm an airline's digital brand. This in turn should increase awareness among senior level managers including board members for the need (and financial support) of the company's brand protection.

### Funds to be made available for domain name management

Above and beyond the expenses for standard registrations of relevant domain names, an airline should be prepared to allocate an additional budget to hire a variety of external services to manage its domain name portfolio. For example legal services may be necessary to negotiate the acquisition of crucial domain names currently owned by third parties or to fight trade/servicemarks infringements.

### Global coverage of domain name registration

Country specific domain names are a crucial digital brand differentiator. The registration for ccTLDs often involves comprehensive administrative processes with local government authorities. Domain name registrars should be considered who have the expertise and legal permit to acquire and re-register domain names in multiple countries. Furthermore, registrars that also operate their own office network are well-suited partners for airlines.

## 3.25 AIRLINE WEBSITE DESIGN AND WEB TRAVELER USER EXPERIENCE

### 3.25.1 Introduction

When web travelers open an airline website, the first thing that happens is they look at the page as a whole. They quickly scan how the content is presented. Specifically, they scan how the text and images look, the size of the letters, the length of the lines, the colors on the web pages, and the overall page layout. Within a few seconds, an unconscious judgment determines the likelihood of finding the solution to their issues.

During this brief but crucial moment, the quality of the airline website's design is judged. Undoubtedly, interacting with a website is inherently subjective and the design's impact thus differs from person to person. Nevertheless, if an airline wants to make its website compelling and engaging for web travelers, it should pay attention to a few universally important aspects in website design.

What is website design? Depending on who is asked in an airline, the design of a website can take on different meanings. IT staff, stressing the technical side, focus on the IT systems architecture while marketers are more concerned with devising advertising and promotion messages.

For an airline web design site to be "consumed" well and create a positive user experience (UX) with the web traveler, it needs to be concerned with two areas: Visual presentation and ergonomics.

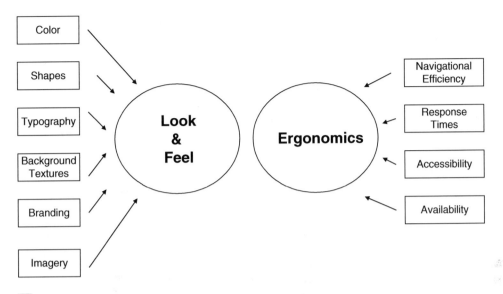

**Figure 3.110** *Determinants in airline website design*

Visual presentation works with colors, shapes, typography, background textures, branding, and imagery. These elements are all part of what is often referred to as a website's digital look and feel (Figure 3.110). It plays an important role in establishing and maintaining trust with web travelers. On the other hand, ergonomics deals with a website's ease of use. Issues addressed in this area include navigational efficiency for tasks and workflows, response times, accessibility from multiple internet-enabled devices, and for users with different abilities, and lastly, availability of content and function.

Generally, complaints by web travelers mentioned in these two areas touch on the following:

- search, menus, click paths, and links
- information (product, destination, location, offers, and promotions)
- booking process (time outs, security concerns, redundant forms).

According to one user experience survey from 2013 covering nine travel sites including those of five major US carriers, visual appeal was mentioned most when participants were asked what areas to fix.[333] Comments by participants were clear about what would need to be addressed:

- United Airlines: "Cleaner look. There are so many different colors on the main page that it's distracting to look at and takes longer to figure out which part of the site is relevant."
- United Airlines: "The homepage looks extremely cluttered. It is daunting."
- Delta: "Under the 'Book a Trip' section, the flights should be better sorted with additional options (such as total flight time, rather than just connection time)."

- Southwest: "More easily changing the dates once you get to the selection screen after choosing destination."
- American: "Sometimes actually too much info. I wish it would just give me the top 5 flights within my time/price parameters with the option to expand if it doesn't meet my requirements."

The following discussion provides for some insight into what it takes to present a visually appealing and user-friendly website to the traveling public.

### 3.25.2 Airline website design: Then and now

The design of airline websites has not stood still over the years. The web pages of most websites in the early 2000s were almost completely HTML-table based and involved a grid-based design. When viewed through today's lenses, they look rather crude. Figure 3.111 is an example of the look and feel of two airlines' digital brands: American Airlines' aa.com and Ryanair's ryanair.com from 2002. Looking at both carriers' website homepage in 2015 clearly shows how much more modern and sophisticated contemporary website design has become.

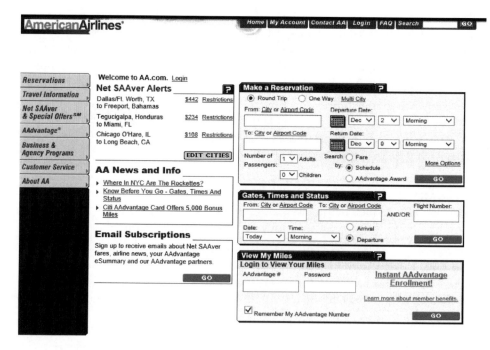

**Figure 3.111a** *aa.com in 2002*

*Source:* aa.com (2014)[334] permission of American Airlines

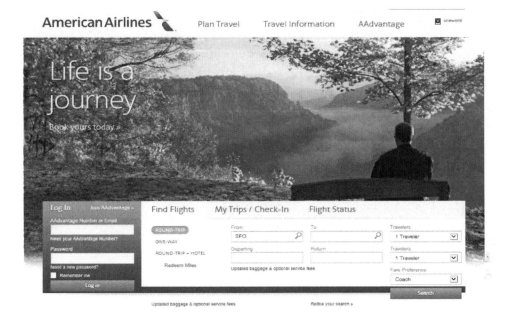

*Figure 3.111b* aa.com in 2015

*Source:* aa.com (2014)[334] permission of American Airlines

*Figure 3.111c* ryanair.com in 2002

*Source:* aa.com (2014)[334] with kind permission of Ryanair

*Figure 3.111d ryanair.com in 2015*

*Source:* ryanair.com (2014)[335] with kind permission of Ryanair

Airline websites back then were typically designed for the lowest common denominator with fixed widths for small screens. Web travelers had a slow internet connection and a 640 x 480 screen resolution. The layout of web pages of most airlines' websites at the time was dominated by three major columns in which various content containers were featured. One of the biggest challenges with this particular approach has often been the lack of information hierarchy because website content was typically presented to prospective web travelers with equal weight.

For example, booking functionalities were mixed with self-service tools and form fields for different applications had similar if not equal size. Furthermore, promotions for fare specials or ancillary services could be rather loud. This situation was often exacerbated by three issues. First, the random use of color that challenges the human eye to stay focused. Second, as a result of airlines squeezing more and more content into their pages, cluttered real estate that made it difficult for web travelers to find the content they were looking for. Third, most designs left a lot to be desired from a branding perspective. They seemed to emphasize more the utility aspect than the human touch.

Fast forward to contemporary airline website designs. With many airlines, gone is the HTML/grid-based page layout with three main columns. Airlines today can choose from hundreds of different design patterns. "In" right now appears to be the use of imagery carousels that rotate large images of either photographic or abstract nature that stretch across the homepage and on which menus float. Hawaiian Airlines was among the early adopters in the United States in 2007 of this more sophisticated design pattern and many other airlines around the world have embraced it for their current websites. Clutter is also less of an issue because a lot of content considered to be secondary is now found on real estate below the website centerfold where web travelers scroll down to. In terms of branding, some carriers appear to be much more expressive about what they stand for.

It cannot be emphasized enough that website design has matured as a result of technological developments. Complex interactions ranging from ancillary bookings and interactive information retrieval to social interaction can now be handled thanks to broadband internet with Ajax and Flash technologies. Website design has even gone "intelligent" in the sense that it can respond now to a user's browser for the size of their screen. Depending on which internet access device is used by a web traveler—desktop, smartphone, tablet, the three main screens considered so far—so-called "responsive design" adapts the layout of the web pages to the viewing environment. Air Namibia highlights this aspect of its new website design launched in 2014 for airnamibia.com (Figure 3.112).

### 3.25.3  Goals in website design: Airline vs web traveler?

One objective for an airline in web design is to transfer its brand attributes to the airline website. Whatever an airline's brand looks like and stands for in the offline world, the idea is to extend it to cyberspace with a digital brand.

Most airline websites do a relatively good job in this regard. At the same time, however, there often appears a shortfall in the delivery of a web experience that caters to what web travelers want—otherwise we would not have the common design-related complaints we have mentioned above. Against this background, the question has to be raised of how aligned airlines and web travelers really are when it comes to website design.

Today, a growing number of airlines behave much more like online retailers. Therefore, one key question of web design from a company perspective should be: How much can the airline.com website be optimized for selling, marketing, and customer servicing? And how could this be done in an emotionally engaging way?

Website design affects business and it should therefore be focused on addressing these specific questions. Airlines that are successful in e-commerce recognize this and they

**Figure 3.112** *Responsive airline website design: Air Namibia*

*Source:* airnamibia.com (2014)[336] with kind permission of Air Namibia

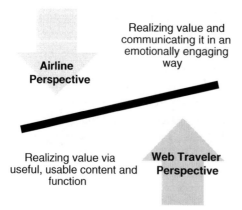

**Figure 3.113** *Website design: A balancing act between the airline and web traveler*

establish specific goals so that the effectiveness of changes can be measured. The goals may include a boost in ticket purchase conversion rates, a reduction of customer support costs, and an increase in web traveler satisfaction. Soft goals such as "we just want to introduce a more modern look" are not sufficient. Another incentive for establishing specific goals is the fact that website design typically involves a sizeable investment. It ranges between $100,000 and $1 million and this requires a proper return.

At the same time, web travelers have their own perspective. They interact with airline websites for a host of reasons including looking for attractive airline fares, buying a ticket or an ancillary service, getting help, or simply retrieving information as easily and quickly as possible (Figure 3.113).

The first step in managing this balancing act is to clearly identify the website design goals for both the airline and the web traveler and then align them with each other (Table 3.20). The ultimate objective for an airline should be to reduce friction in the airline website funnel in order to provide an online user experience that creates/maintains loyal web travelers. Loyalty should be understood up to what degree a web traveler is willing to place their reputation on the line by recommending an airline site to other people.

**Table 3.20** *Alignment of website design goals*

| Airline Website Business goals | Web Traveler goals |
|---|---|
| ■ Offer product and service information | ■ Conduct research |
| ■ Sell airline tickets and ancillary services | ■ Buy online |
| ■ Provide for customer support | ■ Get help |
| ■ Generate business leads for business partners | ■ Learn of promotional offers |
| ■ Reduce costs | ■ Save time and money |
| ■ Increase loyalty | ■ Complete online tasks efficiently anywhere any time |

**Figure 3.114** *Tools and techniques to evaluate airline website design*

### 3.25.4 Ways to identify barriers encountered by web travelers because of web design

An airline has multiple tools and techniques at its disposal to identify what specifically needs to be improved for its website design (Figure 3.114).

*Customer feedback*

This includes information provided to an airline via feedback forms featured on specific website pages and surveys. Measured against established benchmarks, the feedback gives an indication of the quality of the performance of the website. Other sources include complaint/compliment emails and commentaries shared among web travelers via social media. Some carriers even solicit input from web travelers through social media such as their own blog or Facebook site that are used as venues to share mockup versions of new website designs. The note of caution is that there is often a discrepancy between customer feedback and customer behavior. Other airlines feature multiple live versions of their website for a temporary period and gather feedback on market acceptance. Ethiopian Airlines applied this approach in 2015 (Figure 3.115).

Another possibility is to deploy the new website in parallel to the live site under a separate domain name address. For instance in May 2015 United Airlines unveiled a preview of its newly designed website under http://beta.united.com.

*Site analytics tools*

Vendors including Omniture provide for tools that can accurately determine what is happening on specific website pages. For example, if there is a drop-off in web

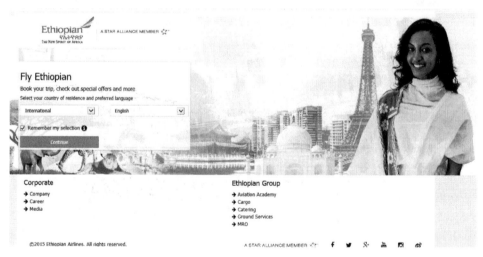

**Figure 3.115** *Old vs new website design: Ethiopian Airlines*

*Source:* ethiopianairlines.com (2015)[337] permisson from Ethiopian Airlines

traveler traffic beyond the homepage or on the payment page, site analytics tools will capture this. The downside is that the cause for the drop-off is not identified. Thus, site analytics do not turn up solution, they are merely another indicator of potential problems.

*Expert reviews*

An expert or so-called heuristic review can quickly identify shortcomings in website design. A company such as Human Factors International (HFI), for example, is well equipped to remedy poor online user experiences based on their comprehensive research from usability studies. A heuristic review typically involves two or more people. They assess an airline website in a couple of days based on certain usability criteria and then produce a report with their findings. Figure 3.116 shows an excerpt of a heuristic review. It was conducted on the former Air Mauritius website and influenced the design of the carrier's new site.

*Usability labs/focus groups*

This type of evaluation in a closed environment allows website design developers and other stakeholders to view real customers using their website. This provides for valuable insight on what portions of the website work well and which areas need further refinement.

Participating should be 5 to 15 web travelers who are recruited based on criteria such as gender, age, frequency of travel, online tenure, and FFP status. A test

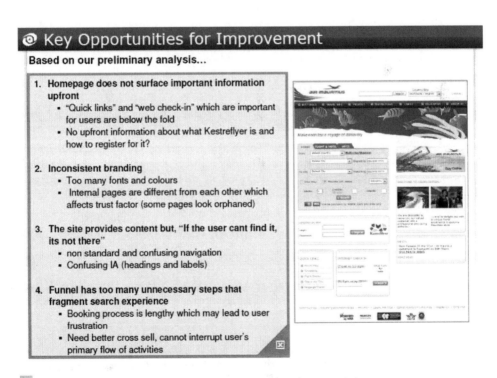

**Figure 3.116** *Heuristic feedback on previous Air Mauritius homepage design*

*Source:* airmauritius.com (2012)[338] with kind permission of Air Mauritius

protocol administered by a moderator outlines the usability tests to be conducted. They often involve two critical exercises. One is the so-called card sorting. This is a technique to gain insight into an optimal website navigation structure and menu labels by gathering feedback from web travelers about how content and functionality on a website should be organized. The other involves user testing. During user testing, the web traveler is asked to accomplish certain online tasks on a website prototype. Occasionally, the focus group may also be asked to execute tasks on secondary websites such as those of competing carriers for benchmarking. It is not uncommon to watch these sessions live through one-way mirrors, although they are generally recorded for a post-mortem analysis.

An unusual but nevertheless effective approach for a focus group was applied by United Airlines. In 2013, the carrier wanted to redesign its mobile app. However, as opposed to inviting users and conducting focus group session on its premises, it decided to go on the road and accompany more than 100 of its customers on their trips. This was done in order to better understand the habits of their fliers. The company watched their online shopping habits, rode along in the taxi, went through security, and sat next to them on the flight. The feedback was helpful for United redesigning its then existing app.

The new mobile was launched in spring 2014. The final outcome was a more modern look with a less crowded interface, the top of which is largely blank to reserve space for displaying important details. The bottom features a touch-friendly design with critical activation options including check-in and airport maps. Crucially, key information access points were now enabled by single hand use.[339]

*Website persona*

E-Commerce leading airlines also apply another technique that involves the personification of demographics that are common to major market segments. Website personas are not real people. They are invented on paper and are hypothetical. Nevertheless, their composition is very detailed in terms of their background and online tasks they aim to accomplish on the airline website.

An example of a user scenario of such invented person could be an online ticket booking for a family, the enrollment in an airline's FFP, or the checking on some website information. Table 3.21 illustrates a specific instance featuring two different web personas. One is a tourist traveler going from London to Cape Town with his family. The other is on a multi-city business trip from Mumbai to South Africa. These two parties have obviously very different goals to pursue on an airline website.

Involving web persona reveals quickly how (un)successful the interaction scenarios play out. How difficult is it to locate a certain section on the website? How many clicks does it take to accomplish a task? The insight gained from using web persona is valuable as it shows how well an airline's website serves the various needs of web travelers.

**Table 3.21** *Website persona for a hypothetical trip to South Africa*

| Traveler Type | Persona Name | Persona Background | Persona's User Scenario |
|---|---|---|---|
| Tourist | John Q (UK) | John Q from London is planning a one-week vacation for him and his wife and two children (1.5-year-old daughter, 5-year-old son) in Cape Town<br><br>John Q is looking for a non-stop flight and wants to know if there is a fare premium when flying on weekends. He wants to know about kids' fares and what the policy is for infants: What is the age cut-off for having the baby fly seated in his wife's lap vs having to buy an extra seat?<br><br>Also, John wants to find out about more flexible fare options in case they have to cancel the trip last minute if the children get sick, and he is interested in buying travel insurance in case the flexible fares are too costly.<br><br>Given the age of the children and the travel distance involved, John Q wants to know what choices exist to reserve seats together in advance.<br><br>Finally, John Q wants to look into four- to five-star hotel properties where his family can stay for a week for full room and board. | John Q's primary goal is to research and book Y-class round-trip tickets from London to Cape Town. Additionally, his goals include finding information on infant/children fares, advance seat reservation, travel insurance and booking an ancillary hotel. |
| Corporate | Kailash M (India) | Kailash M, 32, from Mumbai, is looking for a multi-city trip from Mumbai to Johannesburg (two days) and Durban (two days) in C-class. He uses both a desktop and a tablet for his online shopping.<br><br>This is his first trip to South Africa, thus he needs destination and visa information.<br><br>He also needs to work in the airport lounges before departure and needs to know if there is internet/fax access. He typically buys his wife items from the inflight duty free shop. He wants to know about the airline inflight service<br><br>Finally, since he intends to use his laptop inflight for work, he needs to know about onboard power outlets. | Kailash M's primary goal is to research a round-trip business class ticket for a multi-city itinerary. Also, he needs information on visa, destination, airport lounge services and inflight services. |

*Third party website benchmarking*

Another useful source when dealing with website design involves third parties. Monitoring the websites of peers and a handful of other leading online retailers for clues and ideas is an essential activity for successful website design that should be conducted on a regular basis.

Having introduced the above methodologies to improve on website design, it becomes clear that stakeholders from an airline's external environment play a crucial role. This is important to acknowledge since many airlines make the mistake of designing from the "inside out" whereby only employees are involved. In some extreme cases, an airline website is designed to please first and foremost the taste of a senior manager. Disregarding input from customers and experts runs the great risk of designing a website that adversely impacts an airline's performance in cyberspace. From online revenue losses and service cost increases to resource waste and web traveler dissatisfaction, the price of poor website design is significant.

### 3.25.5 Factors in airline website design affecting conversion

As pointed out earlier, there are various elements that account for the visual appearance and ergonomics of an airline's website design. The discussion below shares more details on some of them in order to provide a better understanding of what role they can play to achieve increased conversion rates by web travelers on airline websites.

*Visual appearance: Color*

The perception of color is inherently subjective. Above all reasons, this is due to the fact that people have different physical attributes. Their vision can be farsighted, nearsighted, or color blind. Some people's eyes tire easily and they become more photosensitive, other have serious vision impairment or no vision at all. Equally important, color preferences change with people's age. Color perception is also subject to cultural, religious, political, and social influences. Even gender plays a role. For example, women not only respond to colors differently from men but they also have a more diverse taste.

The principal colors of an airline's digital brand originate with whatever the airline's brand colors are in the offline world. In this regard, an airline cannot be completely deliberate when choosing colors for its website designs. If Colombia-based airline Avianca uses a combination of dark orange and white as principal colors of its corporate branding, these are the same colors found on the website www.avianca.com.

Colors should not be used without a purpose and be appropriately selected with the target audience in mind. Why? Colors provide sites with meaning without having to use descriptive words. They exert significant impact and create emotions and values that help show online users what the company is all about and what the types of products and services are that they are selling.[340]

For example, orange is considered an "inexpensive" color in the sense that it signifies discounted products and services. It is probably not an accident that LCCs including easyJet (UK), GOL (Brazil), Mango (South Africa), and Jetstar (Australia) all have made orange one of their prominent corporate branding colors. At the same time, as one industry observer stated, standard colors such as blue, red, white, and yellow already had been taken by the legacy carriers. Thus, a better way to stand out and signify the break with tradition is to resort to unconventional color choices.

Red is often used to stimulate/alert shoppers to pending sales. An example is the "Red Sale" British Airways often features on ba.com to highlight its special fare promotions. When combined with white, red in Eastern cultures stands for joy. The corporate brand of LCC Air Asia makes use of this color combination.

The color black, other than for text and lines, rarely finds greater application on airline websites. An exception is Air New Zealand that uses black intensively as a result of a corporate re-brand in 2013. Black in this respect can be understood to underscore the elegance and sophistication of the carrier's products and services.

Purple is an interesting color as it is also used to promote creativity, sophistication, and feminine qualities. LCCs Wizz (Hungary) and Peach (Japan) feature purple on their websites while Virgin America also applies various shades of purple for illustrative images, text, and background.

### Typography

Simply put in the context of our discussion, typography pertains to the arrangement and appearance of characters, letters, and numbers on a website page. An airline should be concerned with typography because the typical airline website is text heavy. Therefore, hitting the correct mark for the site's typography is an important element in successful web design.

From a branding perspective, typography typically allows an online retailer to add personality and style to its website design. In this regard, however, airlines do not differ much from each other. When looking at some airline website's type style, for example, Helvetica, Arial, and Verdana seem to be common. Their use underlines a rather formal appearance. This is likely a reflection of the airlines' desire to maintain credibility and convey a certain sense of business mindedness to the traveling public. Noteworthy also is that there does not appear to be too much mixing of font types going on with most airline websites. They keep the different font types to a minimum and feature one or two main types. This is in line with good typography principles because too many different type styles reflect a fragmented personality of the digital brand.

Informal type styles including Comic Sans or AR Blanca are applied to airline websites but these are mostly an exception. Figure 3.117 shows that they are typically found in connection with temporary promotions to make them stick out more from the rest of the text. One example is the "Space Seat Option" promotion by Peach. Another one shows Lufthansa promoting in a more casual conversation style

**Figure 3.117** *Informal font styles on airline websites*

*Source:* flypeach.com (2014)[341] permission from Peach; lufthansa.com (2014)[342] with kind permission of Lufthansa

a free app because the target audience is children or "little passengers" as Lufthansa calls them.

It is important to point out that reading speed and legibility are impacted by the type style used. It seems that text presented in Times New Roman and Arial are read the fastest while Arial and Courier are among the most legible font type.[343] Besides the type style, does text size matter? Apparently so, with a point size of 12 being preferred by online users, although an accepted minimum could be 10-point.[344, 345]

It appears that several airlines present some of their key information below this minimum. They therefore fail to feature text that would be large enough for all audiences to read. For example, on lufthansa.com, a lot of body text from essential content such as FFP account information, product descriptions, and flight booking details range between 8 and 9 point size. The issue of illegibility due to small text size can be further exacerbated when there is a lack of contrast from the background color. Light grey text used on white background, for example, is known to make reading difficult.

Other core typographic principles such as text line length, leading, kerning, positive/reverse type, and typographic hierarchy all come into play when talking about how to maximize text readability and also reinforcement of an airline's brand attributes. For people in charge of managing an airline website, the conclusion from the brief discussion above is that typography does matter. It should be well thought out as opposed to being thrown together randomly.

*Imagery*

Imagery deals mainly with photographs, illustrations, and videos. In order to successfully build a digital brand, imagery should do two things:[346]

- It should help web travelers accomplish their online goals on the airline website. For example, if an airline wants to increase its ancillary revenue from last-minute upgrade sales, a detailed photographic close-up showing the class of service and seat may influence a web traveler's purchase decision. Today, many airline websites typically show an unenticing pop-up box with text and a price point. Digital agency Fantasy interactive (F-i.com) illustrates how this could be presented differently (see Figure 3.118).
- It should reinforce key brand attributes of the airline. The right imagery can create strong triggers that help define the brand. For instance, if an airline touts its customer service orientation and stresses its human touch, images with friendly customer service representatives (CSRs) can play a crucial role strengthening this impression (Figure 3.119).

In comparison with the early days of airline e-commerce, the imagery featured on today's airline websites overall has improved significantly. Airlines appear to use it more generously throughout their sites and the quality is better. Nevertheless, much,

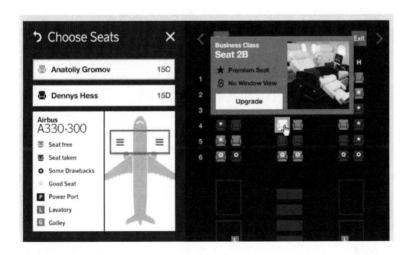

**Figure 3.118** *Using imagery to sell*

*Source:* F–i.com (2014)[347] with kind permission of F-i.com

**Figure 3.119** *Imagery used in customer service: Example Myanmar Airways Intl*

*Source:* maiair.com (2015)[348] permission of Myanmar Airways International

arguably too much, content on airline websites is still text. Airlines should look into making their websites more "social" via rich imagery.

It is important to recognize, however, that effective imagery on an airline website is not a small task. Airlines that excel in this area maintain a vast image and high-quality library and even work with exclusive photographers/video producers/illustrative artists that tailor imagery to a specific brand. They also understand that imagery is not only about happy smiling CSRs. The mission is to strike a balance between imagery establishing a human touch and evoking an emotional response to the brand and imagery that helps web users understand the products and services. This point is crucial for a positive online user experience by the web traveler, particularly so in the area of web customer service.

Furthermore, a review of all imagery for compliance with brand attributes and consistency should be done before it is published. After publication, regular reviews take place to ensure that the airline website's imagery is still in accordance with the corporate brand attributes. If this is not the case, the necessary adjustments are made. One of several airlines deploying imagery successfully is Etihad from Abu Dhabi. Its website features high-contrast photos and videos to showcase rich product details of its Airbus A380 premium first classes such as "The Residence" and "First Apartment" (Figure 3.120).

*Shapes*

Shapes are another essential element that plays a role in website design. They relate to the figures and forms that are geometric, organic or abstract and make up all the other elements in design.

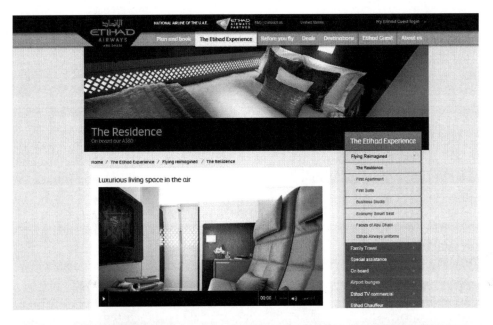

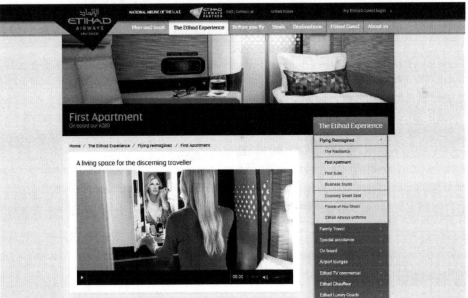

*Figure 3.120* *Imagery on Etihad.com*

*Source:* Etihad.com (2014)[349] permission of Etihad Airways

When used properly, shapes can successfully create an outstanding and effective graphic design. The mood and message of the design may be enhanced by altering its shape in terms of form, color, and size. Shapes each convey a different type of mood or emotion. They may be used in a variety of ways, such as organizing, connecting, or separating elements and content. Shapes may also symbolize or represent a concept, create movement, provide depth or texture, and a lot more.

The shapes used for airline website designs are largely homogeneous. Rectangles, and to a lesser degree squares, dominate if not overwhelm the picture. Differences exist in terms of how sharp, rounded, or angled they are but this is it. The user experience when viewed from the angle of website design shapes is rather similar, if not boring, from airline website to airline website. It is not argued that alternate shapes should be used just for the sake of being different. Nevertheless, it would be refreshing to see a break with this generic mold and shapes such as circles, triangles, and even natural shapes accommodated into designs to make them more interesting and possibly thematic. Shape creation has become much easier and faster these days with the help of modern graphic design tools. It is therefore a bit surprising that airlines have not pursued more out of the ordinary shapes to differentiate themselves in this rather commoditized website design landscape.

The airasia.com and the vanilla-air.com websites move a bit in this direction by having adopted some circular shapes and trapeziums, shapes, respectively (Figure 3.121).

However, this can hardly be viewed a break with tradition considering that rectangles and squares still account for the principal shapes on their respective websites. Figure 3.122 provides some examples of website designs that are bolder in their

*Figure 3.121* Non-standard shapes on airline websites: Example—airasia.com and vanilla-air.com

Source: airasia.com (2014)[350] with kind permission of Air Asia; vanilla-air.com (2014)[351]

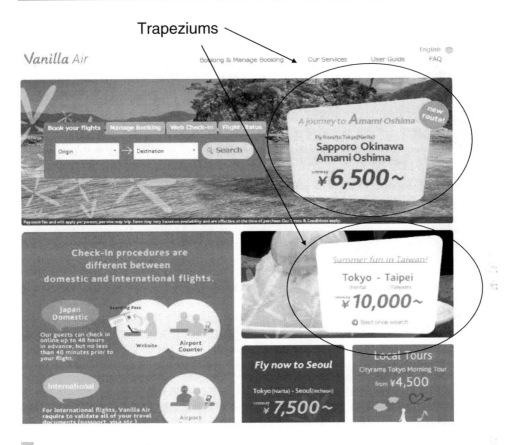

**Figure 3.121** *continued*

creative approach. It may be useful for airlines to look outside their industry for some fresh design ideas.

## 3.26 ERGONOMIC FACTORS

### 3.26.1 Navigation system basics

Website navigation is also a crucial area that affects the success or failure of a web traveler's experience on an airline's website. In a way, the website's navigation system could be viewed as a road map to all the different areas and information contained within the website.

Navigational patterns vary according to the type of website involved but there are some commonalities that are literally found on all sites no matter what their genre is:

■ *Tabbed navigation.* This is widely accepted because tabs as used for notebooks and binders in the offline world have proven useful to identify new sections of content, something that text or buttons could not do so well.

**Figure 3.122** *Other ways of delivering website content and functionality: Diagonals, polygons, circles, and rhombus elements*

*Source:* Klementi (2014)[352]

- *Header navigation across the top of the website.* Online users are familiar with checking out the header for navigation links. This pre-determined behavior paves the way for an airline to design its website in a user-friendly way.
- *Footer navigation.* Most online users look in the website's bottom section for navigation links if they cannot be located elsewhere. Airline websites generally place links including "sitemap" or those of subsidiaries such as "cargo" in this area. Social media logos and links are also often featured here. An illustration of these navigational elements is shown in Figure 3.123.

Beyond these commonalities, an airline needs to select the navigational pattern that makes most sense for the specific website on hand.

For example, a social media website such as an airline blog with large volumes of content is typically navigated in reverse-chronological order. The most recent content contribution is shown first while older content is available further below on a website page. Furthermore, a combination of pagination and archive page, sidebar navigation for categories and/or tags, and header and footer navigation is commonly used.

However, the navigation on an airline e-commerce website with its focus on online retailing is different. Involved are hundreds (if not thousands) of web pages for booking, product, and service information. The navigational pattern applied may be hierarchical, task oriented, by category, search and browse, or a combination. In this environment, navigational efficiency on a website is key. It is achieved if an airline pays attention to best web design principles. More information on this subject is presented in the next section.

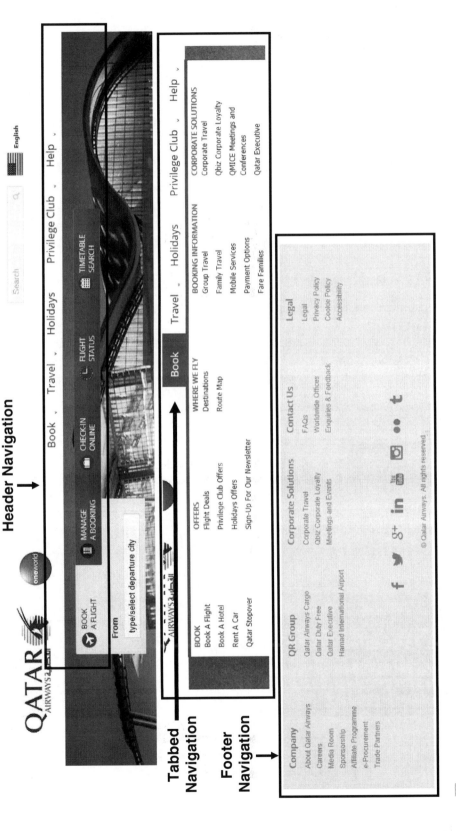

**Figure 3.123** Common navigation elements on airline websites

Source: qatarairways.com (2014)[353]

### 3.26.2 Best website design principles

The following discussion presents information on several website design principles. Taking them into account enables an airline to offer ultimately a better user experience to web travelers on its website.

*Be upfront with most information and use descriptive labels*

In order to capture a web traveler's attention right away when it comes to the carrier's website home page, the most important information should be presented prominently (Figure 3.124). Key is also to avoid generic labels. Airlines should aim at saving web travelers clicks by designing their website navigation in more descriptive ways.

*Avoid clutter with navigation tools*

Some airline websites present a navigation system that is too crowded and even assembled arbitrarily.

Take for instance Angolan airline TAAG that features ten items in the header navigation bar alone. They are visually not distinguishable from each other and seem to carry all the same topical weight. "Book Now" and "Customer Service" are mixed in with "Austral" (the carrier's inflight magazine), "About Angola," and other

**Figure 3.124** *Considerations for homepage designs and navigation labels: Most of the important information that web travelers may be interested in is provided upfront*

*Source:* emirates.com (2014),[354] cathaypacific.com (2014),[355] with kind permission of Cathay Pacific, virginaustralia.com (2014)[356] with kind permission of Virgin Australia, ba.com (2014)[357] with kind permission of British Airways

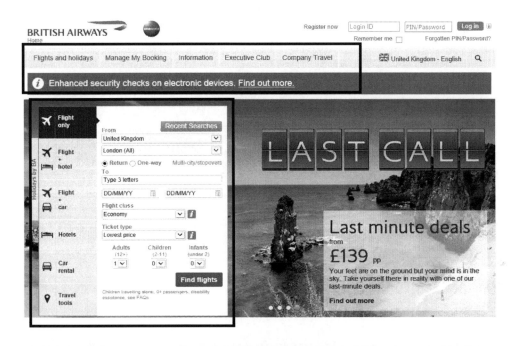

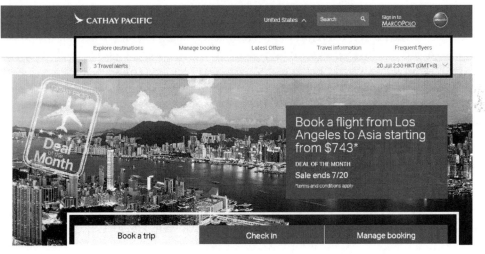

**Figure 3.124** *continued*

labels (Figure 3.125). A better solution is not only to consolidate some of these items under different labels but also to place them in less valuable real estate such as the footer area.

There is no right or wrong number but it is important not to spam web travelers with too many labels and links. This is particularly the case for the header area of a website where a web traveler's navigation often begins. Here, prevalent are between

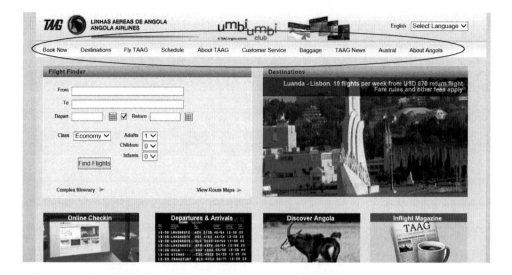

**Figure 3.125** *Too many items in the header navigation area of TAAG.com*

*Source:* taag.com (2014)[358] with permission from TAAG Angola Airlines

five and nine navigation items. This website design arrangement has a connection to the 7 +/- 2 rule. It was devised by American psychologist George Miller in the 1950s as part of his work on human being's short-term memory retention and attention span.[359] This rule is questionable to some in a web design context—the main argument is that website navigation systems are featured throughout a website and therefore make short-term memory an insignificant issue[360]—but many airline websites appear to accommodate this concept so far.

*Be consistent in navigation tool presentation*

Another crucial aspect of successful navigation systems is consistency. Some choices that airlines make may not be perfectly logical but they can get away with them as long as it is consistent across the entire website. As a web traveler moves throughout a website, a different presentation from one page to the next is expected and reasonable. However, unpredictable and baseless design changes in the middle of the website should be avoided since they prove highly disruptive to a web traveler's user experience. Changes in icons, terminology, and colors should be kept at an absolute minimum if not avoided altogether.

One website where the "principle of least astonishment" is broken involves fijiairways.com. This website's homepage navigation header almost completely disappears on subsequent booking pages. A web traveler looking for certain navigational links during the booking process such as "Experience Fiji" or "Flight Information" is at a loss and has to return all the way to the homepage (Figure 3.126).

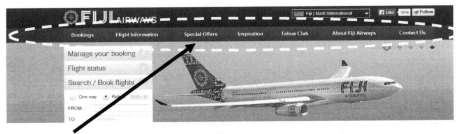

Homepage Header Navigation Bar Disappears on Subsequent Web Pages

*Figure 3.126* *Degradation of user experience due to inconsistency in navigation system*

Source: fijiairways.com (2015)[361]

## Finding the right balance

Efficient navigation systems also strike the right balance between visible navigation elements featured on a single web page (the breadth) versus navigation elements spread over multiple pages in a hierarchical fashion (the depth). The trade-off is clear: The fewer navigation items on one web page, the deeper the website structure and the more a web traveler has to submerge into a website. Conversely, more navigation items on a web page result in a shallow website structure. In this case, a web traveler does not need to "drill" deeply into a website to locate information.

Research strongly suggests that broader structures perform more successfully than deeper structures in general. Online users are better able to navigate and find information in shallow hierarchies. Many airline websites have adopted a multi-level navigational system with main, secondary, and tertiary navigation elements on a single page. The separation among these levels is achieved by position on the page, font size and type, color, and menu type applied such as drop-down, collapse/expand, and rollover menus (Figure 3.127).

## Arranging for the right order of navigation

Getting the items used for navigating a website in the right order is also important for a positive online user experience. Research of online users' eye-tracking movements has shown that websites are scanned in certain ways. For example, following the reading gravity of Western cultures from the upper left to the lower right, website

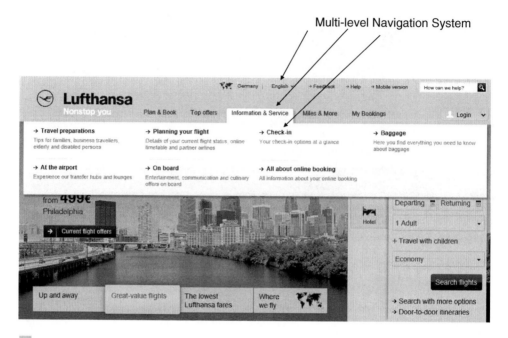

**Figure 3.127** *Multi-level navigation system in header area on lufthansa.com*

Source: lufthansa.com (2015)[362] with kind permission of Lufthansa

design has incorporated a few key scanning patterns of online users. One is the so-called Z-pattern.

In the case of an airline website, a web traveler's scan starts in the upper left of the web page, moves horizontally across to the right, scoops diagonally across the web page to the lower left and terminates in the lower right. If one ever wondered why airlines targeting Western travelers feature the online booking function in the upper left of their website homepage, the Z-pattern has something to do with it. Selling tickets on its website is a top priority for an airline, hence placing the booking function at the very beginning of a web traveler's scanning path in the upper left-hand corner makes perfect sense. In the case of Arabic and Asian language websites, the scanning path is reversed and starts in the upper right corner. Figure 3.128 illustrates an example with Tunisair.com for both English and Arabic.

Deviating from the general Z-pattern is certainly possible and a web traveler can be taken on an alternative navigation path. Different colors, font sizes, and shapes should be introduced then to create visual weights that support non–Z based website navigation. However, one has to be careful when adopting this approach. If not executed well, it most likely leads to an awkward impression with many online users. Occasionally, this occurs by "accident" when an airline simply globalizes its non-Western, domestic market website design version. It is good policy to accommodate website user patterns of other cultures and adjust the design of an airline website accordingly. A better user experience and increased likelihood to convert an online shopper into a booker should be compelling enough reasons.

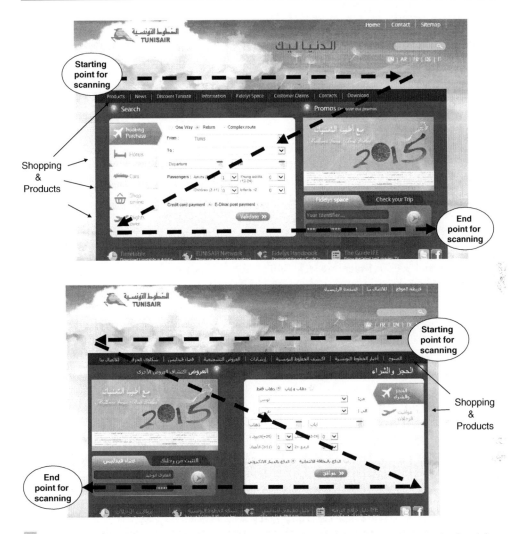

**Figure 3.128** *Scanning a website based on the Z-pattern: a) English language version, scanning from left to right; b) Arabic language version, scanning from right to left*

*Source:* tunisair.com (2015)[363] with kind permission of Tunisair

## Use a responsive web design approach

Web traveler use of mobile via smartphones and tablets is on the rise. In order to provide for a positive user experience, offering digital properties that are mobile friendly is a must. For many airlines, this is not an issue because they have designed one website for desktops and another one especially for mobile users. However, this dual approach may be increasingly questionable because it is not cost efficient and marketing effective. Some carriers therefore have decided to adopt web design principles that equally favor desktop and mobile users. We have referred to this concept earlier as responsive web design whereby content, images, and structure remains the same for

**261**

any device. Web travelers using a desktop get the full view of an airline's website and a retracted view fit to smaller screens when accessing a smartphone or tablet.

Maintaining web designs for different devices is costly. For example, for search marketing, an airline has to run separate campaigns for each. This is not the best use of developers and marketing managers. Furthermore, search engine providers such as Google give preferred ranking results to websites with responsive web design. It is more efficient for Google to crawl one site and index it as opposed to two sites with different urls and html pages. Also, let us think of a web traveler's user experience. It is easier to share, engage, and interact with one website and url than with two or more. Imagine a web traveler sharing a mobile site's url on Facebook with other users who access it on their desktops. They would experience a sub-optimal product. This in turn results in lost leads and lower conversion rates with customers.

Considering the advantages of responsive web design, it is a bit surprising that not more carriers have embraced it (see Table 3.22 for a sample).

The most likely reason is that the effort involved is not small. In most cases, a new site would have to be built from scratch as opposed to reworking existing pages. For carriers operating large websites such as Air China, American, or Emirates, this would be a particularly large undertaking and would need to be tied into a website re-launch project. Some carriers, in order to address this issue, have decided to be selective and only convert the top visited information and transactional web pages while the remaining pages are not touched. This approach certainly buys some extra time but does not avoid the eventual step to deal with responsive web design for the company's digital properties.

In this respect, however, we should mention that some industry observers actually reject the idea of just scaling a web presence to different screen sizes. They point to the new emerging platforms such as wearables, smart TVs, and virtual

*Table 3.22* Who uses responsive web design? A snapshot across different regions (Fall 2015) (*)

| Carrier/Region | US | Europe | Middle East | Asia Pacific | Latin America |
|---|---|---|---|---|---|
| | American – No | Austrian – Yes | Emirates – No | Air China – No | Aeromexico – Yes |
| | Delta – No | Air France – No | Etihad – No | Cathay – Yes | LAN – Yes |
| | JetBlue – No | BA – No | Turkish – No | JAL – No | |
| | United – No | easyJet – No | Qatar – No | Qantas – No | |
| | | KLM – Yes | | | |
| | | Lufthansa – Yes | | | |
| | | Ryanair – No | | | |
| | | Swiss – Yes | | | |

(*) = Carriers indicated with a "yes" may not have configured the entire web content but only selected pages for responsiveness

reality that require design to be adaptive and not responsive. Adaptive design is the idea of consuming web content in a way that it connects seamlessly with whatever device people use. Stated differently, fitting the device rather than the screen size could be the way of the future for web design. Airlines need to stay tuned in this area so they take a smart decision how to move forward with their next website redesign.

### 3.26.3 Navigational efficiency

The discussion of website navigation systems is incomplete without mentioning another key aspect: Navigational efficiency. Specifically, how many clicks does it takes to accomplish an online task? The fewer clicks it takes to complete a task on a website the better, because more clicks translate into more screens which means more time. And more time means a higher risk of task interruption or failure with the ultimate result of a poor user experience by the web traveler.

Ever since e-commerce took off in the mid-1990s, there has been a widespread interest in reducing the number of clicks, particularly after Amazon introduced its "1-click purchase" button in 1999. One estimate puts the financial impact of this feature at over $2 billion in incremental annual revenue for Amazon.[364] As the term implies, one-click buying is a technique that enables online shoppers to complete website purchases with a single mouse click. This is possible by storing a customer's profile including their address and payment information.

As a means of improving the booking/purchasing experience for web travelers and minimizing the number of clicks involved, an airline should aim at simplified processes and more intuitive navigation. If a standard online booking requires more than four or five clicks, it is advisable to take a look at what can be streamlined. LCC Ryanair was notorious for its cumbersome booking process. It took 17 clicks(!) until it released a new website design in 2013 that decreased it down to five.[365] Qantas made click efficiency a highlight when it announced in March 2015 the roll-out of its new "three-click" Auto Check-in service via mobile devices for domestic flights.[366]

Features to improve navigational efficiency are those that increase the situational understanding of the web traveler. Via geo-location, for instance, website content can be adapted to the closest airport to the traveler's current location. There are still too many airline websites that lack basic options for customizing search. In the screenshot of Korean Air's US homepage (Figure 3.129), why are the origin and destination fields still blank and need to be clicked on or filled out? The website should "know" the nearest departure airport—Los Angeles in this case where the author was at the time of accessing the site—and also offer a logical default destination such as Seoul.

Furthermore, also mentioned should be the use of repositories where information on web travelers such as payment, billing address, FFP member profile, and purchase history is stored. For web travelers who are authenticated by the website through their FFP login or website registration, the information can then be used to auto-populate

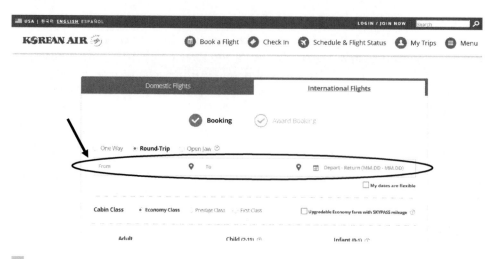

**Figure 3.129** *Korean Air's US homepage*

*Source:* koreanair.com (2015)[367]

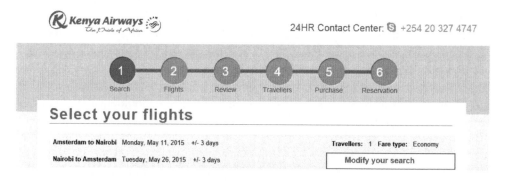

**Figure 3.130** *Where on the website am I? Example—Kenyairways.com featuring six steps of progression*

*Source:* kenyaairways.com (2014)[368] with kind permission of Kenya Airways

various entry fields. How about customizing search options that account for a web traveler's budget and calendar? All of this in turn saves clicks and time.

A fair number of websites share information on the steps of progression for the booking process (Figure 3.130). Giving web travelers a better understanding of how far they have come and how much further they have to go is important. This is especially the case in situations where questions arise or last-minute changes are necessary.

At the same time, however, one needs to be realistic about how much efficiency gain can be achieved. Take for example the continuous increase of ancillary product and service offerings on airline websites. By requiring web travelers to engage in additional opt-ins/opt-outs, the clickstream on some websites has actually become longer. This means that the navigational efficiency gains mentioned above may be partially offset in some cases.

### 3.26.4 Speed and availability of websites

A website should be designed to deliver fast response times. Studies have shown that there is a strong relationship between speed of response and shopping conversion rates. In the United States, for instance, 51% of online shoppers abandon a website because it is too slow. The so-called performance poverty line—the level where a website literally ceases to matter to a web user because it is too slow—is approximately eight seconds for most websites.[369] In a study of OTA Travelocity's website, it has been shown that ticket purchase conversion rates could be increased by 55% as a result of cutting website response times by over 30%. This translated in improved airline ticket revenue of more than $12 million per year.[370]

Website speed not only matters in terms of user experience by web travelers but also as a marketing effectiveness issue for an airline. In 2011, search engine provider Google introduced "Panda," which is an update to the company's search algorithm and specifically how sites are ranked. Since then, speed is also a key performance metric that has a direct impact on the ranking position of an airline website on search engine result pages.

A study by Compuserve in spring 2013 has demonstrated that the differences between airline websites in their response time can be significant. The average speed for downloading a site page on a desktop and mobile device was 3.261 seconds and 14.006 seconds, respectively. Chilean carrier LAN was the fastest for desktops with 0.764 seconds while Air France was the slowest with 7.864 seconds. For mobile sites, US Airways earned the top spot with 7.767 seconds while KoreanAir was the slowest with almost 40 seconds (Table 3.23).

This study also shows the substantial performance difference between desktop/laptop sites and mobile sites. This is a concern when taking into account that a large majority of web users—85% in the United States to be exact—have come to expect mobile site speed to be as good as desktop/laptops, if not better. Over 60% of web users insist on mobile sites downloading pages in less than four seconds.[371]

Besides speed, a website's availability is another performance parameter an airline should look out for. Availability refers to the "uptime" of a website, which is often directly related to the uptime of the web servers. The availability of a website is often expressed as a percentage. For instance, JetBlue's website availability in our study was 99.98%. The 0.02% when the website was not available comes down to about 20 minutes when it could not be reached by visitors that month.

Any downtime has an adversarial impact on an airline's business. Losing ticket sales, damaged credibility, and even poorer search engine rankings are some of the consequences. Leading e-commerce carriers monitor their performance in this area constantly. Ideally, a 100% uptime (Southwest was the only airline that achieved this) should be in place but an airline should strive for a minimum of 99.5%.

### 3.26.5 Website accessibility: Legal challenges to website design

The design of airline websites is a topic that has found increasing interest in the courtroom and the press in recent years. Contrary to popular perception that an

*Table 3.23* Response times and availability of airline websites (desktops and mobile) in the United States (selected carriers, January 1–February 1, 2013)

| Desktops | | | | Mobiles | | | |
|---|---|---|---|---|---|---|---|
| Site Speed | (seconds) | Availability | (%) | Site Speed | (seconds) | Availability | (%) |
| LAN | 0.764 | Southwest | 100 | US Airways | 7.767 | US Airways | 99.12 |
| Aeromexico | 1.196 | Air Canada | 99.99 | American | 8.405 | American | 98.95 |
| Alaska | 1.678 | LAN | 99.99 | JetBlue | 8.700 | Alaska | 98.91 |
| Southwest | 2.301 | JetBlue | 99.98 | Lufthansa | 13.224 | United | 98.47 |
| JetBlue | 2.323 | Volaris | 99.97 | Air France | 13. 294 | Southwest | 97.70 |
| Hawaiian | 2.358 | BA | 99.95 | **Average\*** | **14.006** | **Average\*** | **97.53** |
| Cathay | 2.859 | Alaska | 99.90 | United | 14.169 | Lufthansa | 96.53 |
| **Average\*** | **3.261** | **Average\*** | **99.56** | Qatar | 20.339 | Korean | 97.93 |
| Air Canada | 4.329 | Cathay | 99.36 | Korean | 39.923 | JetBlue | 94.92 |
| Volaris | 4.593 | Korean | 99.35 | | | | |
| Korean | 4.975 | Lufthansa | 99.31 | | | | |
| BA | 5.495 | Air France | 98.95 | | | | |
| Qatar | 7.470 | Aeromexico | 98.55 | | | | |
| Air France | 7.864 | Qatar | 97.93 | | | | |

*Please note that this average is based on a total sample surveyed by Compuware, not on the number of carriers listed here. The total sample included 24 carriers for the desktop and 12 carriers for the mobile site analysis.

Source: Tnooz.com (2013)[372]

airline can design its website any way it wishes, this is not the case. The reason for this lies in website accessibility requirements for people with disabilities. As carriers have moved more services online, from booking flights to checking on flight status, equal access for users that suffer from visual, auditory, tactile, and cognitive disabilities has become more important. A growing number of countries are looking into making this a legal–regulatory requirement for online retailers including airlines.

The number of people affected is not small. It is estimated that there are over 650 million people in the world with disabilities. Together with their families, that means approximately 2 billion people are directly affected by disability, representing almost a third of the world's population.[373]

In today's modern society, making travel accessible for people with disabilities is first and foremost a social responsibility. However, one cannot deny the fact that there is also a compelling business case for companies to make their digital properties available to disabled users. Unfortunately, providing disabled users with equal access to websites has not always been the common way of thinking. In the United States, for example, a court ruling in a case brought against Southwest

Airlines in 2002 stated that the accessibility requirements of the Americans with Disabilities Act (ADA) did not apply to websites but to the physical places of business only.[374] Over time, other law suits were filed under the ADA that challenged businesses in what the involved plaintiffs called discriminatory practices on the basis of disability. Specifically, the bone of contention was the fact that websites lacked the necessary coding in website content to support various technologies that could be used by disabled people to interact with a website and complete online transactions.

In November 2013, the US Department of Transport (DOT) announced that the Air Carriers Access Act (ACAA) of 1986 that prohibits discrimination by US and foreign air carriers on the basis of physical or mental disability would apply to websites as well. Specifically, airlines with a seating capacity of more than 60 passengers would be required to upgrade their websites in two phases: First, by December 2015, all web pages that provide for core travel services and information (e.g. booking engine, frequent flyer account) would have to be compliant with the widely accepted Web Content Accessibility Guidelines (WCAG), Level AA criteria. Second, by December 2016, all remaining web pages that cover non-core travel areas such as the "About us" section must have been adjusted.[375] (At the time of reviewing this book before its print, the DOT announced in December 2015 a postponement of the first deadline to June 30, 2016, as apparently too many carriers struggled to be ready on time. Considering that the deadline was known for two years and even exempted mobile platforms, advocates of disability organizations are understandably frustrated with the slow pace of this initiative's implementation).

Another requirement of the ACAA is that all online discounts or opportunities must be given to persons with disabilities whose disability makes online access impossible. If an airline charges an extra fee when contacting the call center to make a booking, a person with a disability does not need to pay extra because the airline's website is inaccessible.

The amended ACAA is significant as the new website accessibility standards are likely to reverberate outside the United States. Government agencies of the EU and of countries including Australia, Canada, and New Zealand have already adopted the WCAG standard. It is therefore reasonable to assume that airlines in other international markets will also work with it in some shape or form to provide equal access to their websites.

At this stage, the DOT has refrained from imposing a web accessibility standard on mobile devices and applications and other means of electronic communications such as email and text messaging. This is largely because of the absence of wider accessibility standards for these technologies and the need to focus carriers' resources first on achieving accessibility compliance for their websites.[376] Nevertheless, it is only a question of time when corresponding guidelines will be introduced and airlines need to be ready for this upgrade as well.

We do not want to leave this discussion on website accessibility with the impression that the airline industry has been completely inactive on this subject. A number of carriers have voluntarily launched website features to accommodate disabled users. For example, some carriers in the United States have converted their websites in recognition of Section 508 of the Rehabilitation Act that mandates federal agencies in the United States to make their website accessible. British Airways is working with a UK charity organization called AbilityNet to make ba.com accessible to users with disabilities (Figure 3.131).

### 3.26.6 The significance of a web style guide

Style guides originated in the print world and have found their way into cyberspace as well. A web style guide is a document that establishes a framework for a company's standards on the digital look and feel of, as well as navigation on, its own website and its website properties on external website types.

A web style guide is a living document that is periodically updated to reflect the latest changes to the digital brand's look and feel. Major updates occur if the airline undergoes a so-called website refresh that typically involves a complete re-arrangement of the digital brand's content and navigation.

Based on the author's consulting experience with several clients, the record with website style guides is spotty: Some carriers have only fragmented pieces, others have an outdated version. A web style guide is an indispensable tool to ensure the stylistic integrity of the digital brand. Any person touching the airline website for updates and changes should have a copy and be familiar with it. Some of the areas typically featured in a style guide are introduced in Table 3.24.

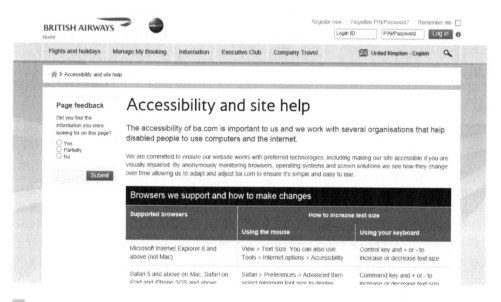

**Figure 3.131** *Website information on accessibility access for disabled web travelers*

*Source:* ba.com (2014)[377] with kind permission of British Airways

*Table 3.24* Website style guide

| Key component | Explanation |
| --- | --- |
| Logo/Trade-Service Mark/Copyright symbols | The airline's logo and other symbols should be defined and examples should be provided in various formats including full color, black and white, transparent, or on different backgrounds. If the logo is associated with a tagline, there must be rules around placement, font, color, and size in relationship to the logo. |
| Color palette | Color values should be provided for all different areas on the website such as text, hyperlinks, navigation tabs/breadcrumbs, homepage, navigation area of portal and IBE pages. |
| Writing style and typography | Plain language should be used that is clear, succinct, relevant and informative. The tone and voice on the airline website should sound straightforward and welcoming.<br><br>Typography: The definition must be in place for the font families, sizes, kerning, line spacing, colors for various content types, header, sub-head, paragraph, cite, block quote, labels, form headers or any other formatted text that will be used. |
| Layout | The layout addresses where and how HTML and other elements are positioned on the page and how they relate to each other. Defined are margins, padding, gutters or grid patterns of the overall layout as well as any specific elements if different. So-called container modules define the layout of the website pages. |
| Photography and illustrations | Photography and illustrations literally speak a thousand words and can help lighten up communication dominated otherwise by too much text. Crucial for photography is the use of quality images that can be obtained sometimes for free or, more likely, due to usage rights, for a fee through image libraries. Some airlines even create their own inhouse image library.<br>Questions to address: What is the style of imagery? Color or black and white? Should one display different ethnic and demographic groups? What should these people be doing? |
| Links/Buttons | The colors and styles for all links and buttons that will be used should be defined. |
| Promotional tiles | Promotions highlight "call to action" items such as information on vacation packages and encourage customers to visit areas of the site that they might not be aware of otherwise. |
| Graphics/Icons | The type, sizes, file sizes, dimensions, and styles used for graphics and icons on the site should be defined. |
| Navigation/Visual hierarchy | A definition of the main and sub-navigation styles as well as the interactivity of them is important. Particularly crucial is the definition of the click stream. |

## 3.27 THE ROLE OF DIGITAL MEDIA AGENCIES

### 3.27.1 Introduction

By the time commercial air transport transformed itself into becoming a mass market in the 1960s, the airline industry found a well-established, modern-day advertising agency system operated by numerous intermediaries. They offered a wide range of media services to any company able and willing to hire them. Looking at the situation today, this system, apart from the introduction of digital media formats and some new compensation forms for agencies, has really not changed much.

In the following section, we introduce digital advertising agencies and their role in e-marketing. In our context, a digital advertising agency is defined as an intermediary that provides services to airlines in order to manage their e-marketing activities for online media formats in cyberspace.

### 3.27.2 The competencies and services of digital advertising agencies

The competencies and services available through digital agencies are hugely diverse, yet highly specialized. Figure 3.132 provides for an overview of agency activities and specifically illustrates both what they offer and what digital formats are managed. Most airlines today involve digital advertising agencies in some shape or form for managing various aspects of their e-marketing activities. These agencies play a role in how savvy and strong (or not) an airline's digital brand is that is presented to web travelers.

On one end of the spectrum we find mega players, so-called full-service digital agencies. The full-service advertising agency presents itself as a one-stop shop where an airline receives comprehensive support, ranging from the initial planning stage to the post-execution analysis and optimization stage. Other, somewhat more unconventional, services even include research to cover competitive monitoring and industry benchmarks and so-called onboarding whereby a digital agency provides an airline with training and familiarization in the management of online media. This is done across a diversity of online media formats in advertising and promotion and PR that we discussed earlier in this chapter. The other end of the spectrum features the niche agency that specializes in one or a few online media formats covering selected services. The buying of adwords from search engine providers is one example.

### 3.27.3 Who are the players?

Today's main full-service digital advertising agencies are actually the traditional advertising agencies. The world's Top 5 media companies/holding companies owning advertising agencies in terms of annual advertising revenue in 2014 are shown in Table 3.25.

These companies operate in multiple countries and also work with many airlines around the world. All of them have their origins in the pre-internet era with some being over 100 years old. For example, Interpublic Group (IPG) was founded in 1870. The advent of digital media in the late 1990s presented several challenges to them. Due to their roots in the offline world and long history with traditional media formats, there was an initial lack of understanding of how to deal with digital media. Specifically, dealing with the growing number of choices and flexibility when it comes to the timing, placement, and type of media formats that online advertising offer was new.

270

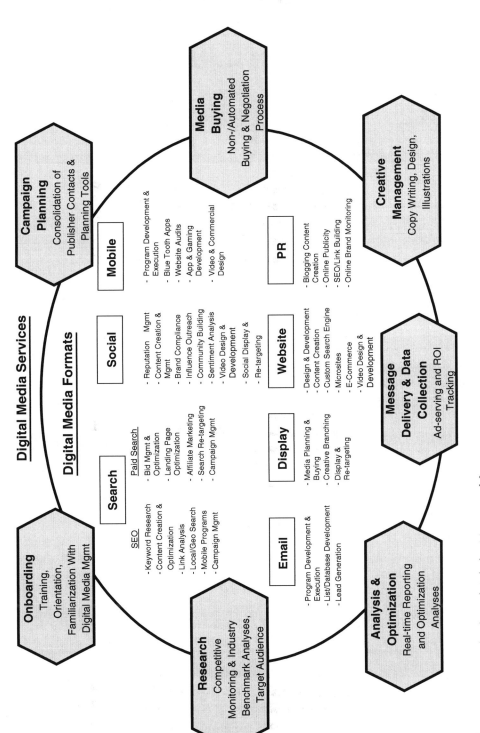

**Figure 3.132** *What does a digital advertising agency do?*

**Table 3.25** *World Top 5 advertising companies*

| Advertising/Holding company | Estimated Annual Revenue (2014) | Number of employees |
| --- | --- | --- |
| WPP (UK) | $19.0 billion | 165,000 |
| Omnicom Group (USA) | $15.3 billion | 70,600 |
| Publicis (France) | $9.6 billion | 60,000 |
| Interpublic Group/IPG (USA) | $7.5 billion | 7,494 |
| Dentsu (Japan) | $6.0 billion | 14,898 |

*Source:* Adage (2015)[378]

Moreover, the new powerful capabilities for measuring the behavior of web users and tracking customer responses to specific campaigns also represented unfamiliar dimensions. In order to keep up with the growing shift of marketing budgets to online media by their clients including airlines and also to strengthen their digital know-how, these companies have gone on a shopping spree ever since and have spent billions of dollars acquiring digital specialist agencies. For example, in July 2012, Dentsu from Japan, the world's fifth largest ad agency, bought UK-based Aegis for $4.9 billion, which in turn had been buying up numerous digital companies since 2004. Likewise, WPP acquired digital agency AKQA for $550 million while IPG snapped up digital agencies in the UK and Brazil between 2010 and 2012.[379]

So what is the reaction in the marketplace to these merger/acquisition developments? Although not airline industry specific, a 2013 survey among senior marketing executives in the United States revealed the view that almost three-quarters of them are apparently not impressed by the way traditional agencies are transforming themselves to adopt digital marketing capabilities. Queried to describe how traditional agencies are managing to adjust to cyberspace, 48% state that agencies "are struggling to transition their business models," while another 26% say that agencies "are acquiring assets, but are having difficulty integrating digital capabilities."[380]

If there is indeed a lack of integration among *and* between offline and online media formats, a holistic approach to engage with consumers is very difficult to achieve for a company. Some 68% of the survey participants indicated that integrated marketing is the most important area to them and it even ranks ahead of effective advertising (65% voted for this). Furthermore, it is also among the key reasons that marketers dismiss an agency and look for a new one. It is also a pivotal factor in selecting a particular agency in a pitch.[381]

### 3.27.4 The (rising) complexity of digital advertising—and inefficiencies

In fairness to the media companies, today's management of digital media is complex— and this is still rising. One should not have the impression that we are dealing with a straightforward value chain when it comes to airlines, advertising agencies, and media format owners. Some people may argue that this value chain has always been "complicated," even just for traditional media formats. However, the digital dimension has added more complexity to the game. This is because of the application of all the sophisticated technology and ever proliferating online formats. Furthermore, there is an unprecedented involvement of many players including the media agency's various subsidiaries, sister agencies, and other digital partners that each specialize in their respective field.

A glimpse of this situation for an airline can be gained from JetBlue's interaction with digital media agencies. JetBlue, one of the leading e-commerce carriers in the industry, works with about 40(!) advertising-technology companies to broadcast its messages to web travelers on desktops and mobile devices. The specific types of companies partnered with include:[382]

- agencies that are specialists in geo-targeting, helping campaigns focus their ads on specific geographic regions
- social-analytics and listening firms that can follow and interpret what people are talking about on social-media sites
- dynamic-ad-serving companies that enable an advertiser to customize ad content based on consumers' web-browsing behavior
- demand-side platforms, or firms that allow advertisers to buy ads through multiple ad exchanges
- A mobile-analytics company, which can track user behavior on mobile apps.

In light of new emerging online media formats, one can only imagine what type of specialist agency would have to be added to this list in the future. Clearly, most of these agencies are data driven and apply heavily proprietary technology. Because of this, it seems more appropriate to speak of them as "techno-advertising agencies" as opposed to just digital agencies. As a side comment, the organizational impact on an airline of this technology-ization of marketing should not be underestimated. If one adds to the above mix of ad agencies other technology providers that are also involved when deploying an online ad campaign—think of suppliers managing the airline's website portal, booking engine, and payment service platform, for example—it becomes apparent that digital advertising is not easy.

Today, airlines can certainly enjoy the power of significantly improved insight and therefore obtain a better understanding of the "other half of advertising" that the famous John Wanamaker was talking about. However, there needs to be the realization that this very power comes at the price of increased complexity that in turn is often fertile breeding ground for inefficiencies in the management of digital media.

Focusing on the agency side in our discussion for a moment, empirical data confirm the issue of inefficiencies. Apparently, advertising agencies suffer from more than 25 inefficiencies and pain points in the planning-to-billing cycle. On average, many agencies engage only in one day of value-creating activities during a five-day working week when working on a campaign. The remaining four days are wasted with waiting time, redundancies, and reworks.[383] An airline has to pay attention to how an agency runs its business and specifically what the degree of efficiency in its business processes is.

A lean process and a unified technology platform that can handle multiple online media formats can make the life of an airline easier (or at least not more complex than it already is). This is because it contributes to strengthening a competitive position in the marketplace that requires fast and effective advertising campaigns. Wasting four days out of a five-day period with non-value creative activities is not an option for any company including those from the airline industry.

The author has witnessed his share of inefficiencies with several airline clients. In one case, different digital media agencies for different geographic regions had been hired for alleged cost-saving reasons. However, a cost benefit analysis quickly showed that this led to an increased workload for the airline staff. This was the result of the many interactions with two agencies' respective technology solutions and partners. With this downside far outweighing any cost savings in terms of agency commissions, the consolidation of all global digital marketing activities under one digital agency was implemented. In another client's case, they insisted on extending an already existing offline agency relationship into the online world and to manage the carrier's digital formats. However, this agency not only levied a higher commission fee structure than other agencies but also applied very little coordination among the four subgroups involved in digital media management. It was eventually decided to introduce a dedicated account manager as single point of contact for the airline in order to increase the quality of interaction.

We cannot only focus on the demand side whereby the airline simply requests its agency partners to be on top of their game and apply the most efficient technology and processes in their work. An airline is equally responsible for keeping inefficiencies in the working relationship with the agency at a minimum. Therefore, an airline needs to engage in a self-assessment that covers the objectives it plans to achieve by working with an agency. Additionally, it needs to address its own strengths and weaknesses in digital know-how and technology, resources, and processes. Some typical issues to focus on include:

- Organizational ownership of the relationship. A quarrel often exists between departments such as E-Commerce and Marketing on one side and the airline's IT Department on the other side. This situation adversely impacts how efficiently work is completed.
- Quality and amount of organizational resources to support e-marketing including the interaction with one or, more likely, multiple digital advertising agencies.
- Specific advertising targets that need to be reached in certain time frames and how performance is measured. Data overload is a common challenge leading to the question as to how much insight is really needed from techno-advertising agencies before benefits from their data granularity become too marginal and have little impact on digital media decisions.
- Type of digital agency to be hired (full-service versus specialist).

Establishing clarity on these issues helps an airline apply a more productive inter-action between an airline and its advertising agencies.

An opportune time for an airline to structure the relationship with a digital advertising agency is when it is looking for new and/or additional agency partners or re-arranging an existing contract. Considering that the establishment and mainte-nance of a relationship with a digital agency is a significant investment for an airline, a better understanding of how one should go about selecting the appropriate digital advertising agency in the first place is crucial. The following section sheds light on this issue.

### 3.27.5 Selecting the digital advertising agency

Finding the right digital agency requires a meticulous and structured assessment of the airline's and agency's business in terms of objectives, resources, and cultures. After an airline's self-assessment, the next step is to draw up a list of crucial factors that eventually become part of a so-called request for proposal (RFP) or request for information (RFI). Both are process tools that many airlines use in order to go more or less methodologically through an evaluation of a vendor. Doing so increases the probability of partnering with an agency that makes best sense. Due to the complex-ity involved, some airlines even hire outside specialists that manage an entire RFP from beginning to end for them. For instance, when ULCC Spirit Airlines in the United States was looking for a new full-service agency starting in early 2014, it involved a consulting firm during the summer the previous year in order to assist in the review of advertising agencies.[384] The principal criteria to apply in the selection process are shown in Figure 3.133 and further discussed.

*Type of media formats*

Does the agency have the competency to manage a single or multiple forms of digital media? This depends on what the airline needs. One has to distinguish between the

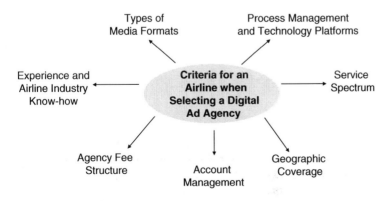

**Figure 3.133** *What to look for in a digital agency?*

AOR (Agency of Record) that handles all of the airline's advertising needs versus a specialist agency. If just one area is targeted, say search marketing, one may look for a specialist agency in this area. If multiple digital formats are supposed to be managed, a full-service, one-stop agency may make more sense in order to realize marketing message consistency among different formats as well as cost savings from increased efficiencies.

*Experience and airline industry know-how*

Some aspects such as the creative side in airline advertising may be better served by industry outsiders for a fresher perspective. At the same time, having an in-depth understanding of the airline industry structure, the characteristics of its shoppers, and the unique selling positions of airlines cannot hurt and should be considered an asset rather than a liability for an advertising agency.

*Agency fee structure*

The fee structure can vary significantly. It is not uncommon to even find more than one type applied for a single agency depending on the airline's media formats chosen. In the interest of managing a sound digital marketing budget, an airline must have a clear approach in mind as to how it pays its digital advertising agency. Table 3.26 illustrates the most popular approaches and the respective up- and down-sides involved.

In addition to the above fee types, it is possible that an agency levies a one-time set-up charge for the initial implementation of the carrier's account and third party

**Table 3.26** *Common digital agency compensation types*

| Fee structure type | Common media | Benefits | Challenges |
|---|---|---|---|
| Percentage of total media spending | Paid media (PPC, display) | High degree of predictability in expenses | Agency might increase media buy to reap higher pay while advertising effectiveness diminishes at the same time |
| Time-based | Earned, owned media (SEO, mobile, social) | Only paying for actual work done for airline account | Campaigns could overrun, efficiency of account management could be questionable |
| Retainer/fixed | Earned, owned media (SEO, mobile, social) | Predictable expenses | Cost overruns could trigger re-negotiations, questions on efficiency of account management |
| Performance | Paid and earned (paid search, display, some social) | Agency shares risk for campaign performance | Frequent re-negotiations due to under-/over performances, agency might stick to tactical initiatives to guarantee revenue rather than long-term strategy |

*Source:* Third Door Media (2014)[385]

software fees because some applications are outsourced for development. The airline should have clarity on who is doing what.

*Account management*

Depending on the size of the advertising business, there is either a dedicated account executive for the airline or agency staff that are shared with other agency clients. Airlines with larger budgets typically require a dedicated account set up. Advertising agencies appoint a single contact to liaise with the airline clients. This arrangement is important for an effective interaction including the handling of the creative brief of a campaign or settling the payment of invoices. It is key for the account executive to be fully aware of the airline's requirements that can be conveyed to other stakeholders in the agency who work on particular e-marketing aspects for the carrier.

*Geographic coverage*

Depending on the airline's operational size, the scope for a digital advertising agency's geographic coverage can be more or less important. Larger agencies generally have a presence in multiple countries with local offices and staff. Their expertise and insight on local markets are important when it comes to calibrating e-marketing activities more effectively. Sometimes smaller agencies, in order to satisfy the global needs of their airline clients, offer a partner agency network where regional specialists are involved to enrich the main themes of a marketing message and adapt it to local market conditions.

*Service spectrum*

What specific services does the agency offer and does the airline need? If a carrier looks for an end-to-end solution starting with the initial set-up and research for e-marketing activities all the way to their execution and post-campaign analysis and optimization, an airline is better matched with a digital agency equipped to do so.

We have already introduced earlier what the service spectrum of a digital agency could entail and thus do not repeat it here. If the airline can manage several of these service activities on its own through inhouse resources, it obviously may opt for a smaller scope arrangement.

*Process management and technology platforms*

With efficiency in the management of digital media a main concern, an airline should include its process management and technology platforms in any assessment of a digital advertising agency. Ideally, as already mentioned before, a unified approach can be offered for multiple media formats in order to minimize any complexities in the day-to-day interaction between the airline and its advertising agency.

## SNAPSHOT: AIRLINE—DIGITAL ADVERTISING MODELS AND WHO IS WORKING WITH WHOM

A review of some airlines in terms of their arrangement with advertising agencies shows a variety of agency models are in place, from full-service to specialist, and even a mix between the two. Our discussion below sheds more light on these arrangements for both legacy and LCC carriers.

### Legacy airlines

The selection of Firstborn (a Dentsu company) by All Nippon Airways (ANA) to become the airline's global lead agency, starting 2014, is an example of a single ad company managing numerous media formats for its airline client. However, what is interesting in this case is the fact that the assignment goes outside Firstborn's scope as a digital agency and includes also offline collateral including print, TV, and social media. One has to see whether this kind of agency crossover becomes more widespread. Possibly the more important message is the realization of crucial benefits in the form of marketing message consistency between different formats as well as cost savings. In this regard, ANA differs from other traditional full-service airlines that have entered into multiple agreements with a host of players.

We find an example in Lufthansa that partnered with the agency MRM (a company of IPG) in February 2014 for a single campaign on Facebook only in India. It involved the design of an online game to promote the airline's Airbus A380 aircraft.[386] This is an adhoc version of the specialist agency model. In this case, an airline works with a particular advertising agency for a unique occasion and/or market for a limited time. Such an arrangement is not that unusual to find with other airlines. The reason behind this approach is to complement already existing relationships with other advertising agencies that are longer-term (typically two to four years) and cover multiple countries.

South African Airways expands on the usage of the specialist agency model by working for the UK/Ireland alone with an array of specialists for different areas such as PR, social, and creative media. Digital media are handled by specialist agency UM (part of IPG).[387]

The specialist agency model can also work on a global basis and not just for a particular market. An example of this is Lufthansa. For instance, the company Wunderman of WPP is responsible for direct marketing, Mindshare (another WPP company) handles the media planning and buying, while the independent agency Kolle Rebbe manages the creative side for Lufthansa as of 2012. To add more complexity (and confusion), Kolle Rebbe also became responsible for all of the airline's online media in 2013 and covers global markets via a five-partner agency network.[388],[389] Lufthansa reportedly spends annually €100 million worldwide for its advertising in 40 markets.[390]

Between the full-service agency and specialist agency, we find a few airlines that borrow elements from both, hence the hybrid agency approach. British Airways (and possibly United Airlines) fall into this category. In 2012, Ogilvy (a WPP company) became BA's lead agency for all digital matters in a number of areas including digital innovation, strategy, e-commerce, social media, display, and mobile.

Unique about Ogilvy's approach to win the three-year contract from BA is that it created "The 12th Floor," a consortium of four digital specialist agencies including:

- eCommera (e-commerce retail consulting and data experts)
- Imano (mobile)
- Ravensbourne (innovation and design college)
- Decision Technology (behavioural scientists and academics).

They are all handled under the leadership of Ogilvy to take care of BA's global digital advertising needs across a variety of digital formats.[391] The "12th Floor" works alongside other BA agencies that manage specialist tasks such as brand communication agency Bartle Bogle Hegarty (Publicis) and global media planning and buying entity Carat (Dentsu).

United Airlines appeared to be interested in a similar approach following the lead agency model pitch by WPP in December 2013.[392] Unlike BA's digital "The 12th Floor" agency consortium, however, WPP would manage both offline and online media formats and involved only WPP owned specialist agencies. These agencies comprise:

- Wunderman for direct mail (whose founder Lester Wunderman, the godfather of modern direct marketing with innovations such as the toll-free 1-800 number and reward loyalty programs, coined the term "direct marketing" first in 1967)[393]
- KBM for data management
- MEC for media planning and buying
- Landor Associates for brand consulting
- Kantar for research and data handing.

A final decision by United Airlines, which spent $60 million in 2012 on advertising, for this agency concept, was expected in early 2014 but has not materialized so far.

The above discussion involved globally operating airlines with relatively well-known brands in many markets. Maybe the sheer size of their operations and the fact that they are traditional full-service airlines targeting multiple customer segments with all kinds of communication explain their often eclectic assembly of digital agencies. The only exception was ANA with a single agency partner.

## LCCs

Are LLCs different when it comes to handling their advertising activities via agencies? To some extent, the answer seems to be yes. The budgets involved are significantly smaller and consequently limit the option to spread monies across multiple agency accounts.

For example, Spirit Airlines, in line with its ultra-low-cost approach, has a total annual advertising budget of $5 million. In November 2013, ULCC Spirit Airlines appointed Barkley, one of the United States's largest independent and employee-owned advertising agencies, as its new agency of record and one-stop shop. Barkley covers all of Spirit's advertising media needs including those for cyberspace across its entire markets.[394]

Then, of course, there is Ryanair. They did all their advertising work inhouse for twenty years and rejected the merits of working with advertising agencies altogether. However, although its CEO Michael O'Leary who went on record for stating that "bad publicity sells more seats" and considered advertising agencies as "useless, expensive and prone to producing identikit campaigns for their clients,"[395] there has been a change. The reason is the company's late 2013 image shakeup that now conveys the message of a customer-friendly airline. The annual advertising budget for 2014 was increased from the previous €15 million to €40–45 million with part of this budget going to TV advertising.[396] The company selected the agency Dare to handle its advertising activities including online in 2014.

Jetstar of Australia is also known for doing much advertising work inhouse and it only works with one advertising agency (Maxus of WPP). Maxus covers Jetstar's media buying activities in Australia and the Asia Pacific region[397] estimated to be worth up to AU$40 million (Figure 3.134).[398]

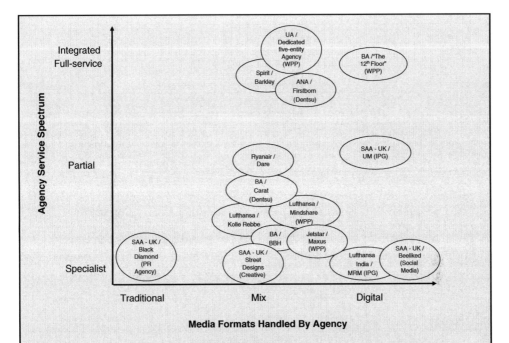

**Figure 3.134** *Airlines and their media agencies* *

* Unless indicated, the media agencies work with the airlines across all their international markets.

*Source*: Based on media sources quoted in snapshot section

## Closing comments

The above discussion tables the issue of what the scope of an airline's arrangement with digital agencies should be. Taking into account that digital advertising is already complex enough with all the technology specialists involved, the aim should be to reduce the number of parties a carrier works with. Therefore, the consolidation into a smaller number of agencies, possibly even just into one, can be beneficial. This is especially the case in terms of efficiency gains, communication consistency across different formats, and cost savings realized.

A pure digital advertising outfit in the form of BA's "The 12th Floor" is more the exception than the rule. It is an option only for a few, globally operating and large airlines with deep pockets.

When it comes to the choice of full-service versus specialist agency, a trade-off has to be made. A full-service agency is not necessarily the best of class for every single online media format. However, these potential concerns may be outweighed by the benefits just mentioned earlier.

> Agency bundling could translate into a competitive advantage for an airline. At the same time, airlines also need to strengthen their internal competencies in order to effectively involve themselves in digital advertising and establish institutional memory on digital know-how. Not doing so risks the carrier being reduced to an observer status rather than an active (and competent) participant in managing its digital advertising affairs.

### 3.27.6 The interaction between an airline and a digital advertising agency

A systematic planning process between the carrier and the ad agencies is key for performing—if not outperforming—competitively in the area of e-marketing. The process is intended to facilitate an on-time/in-budget development and deployment of specific online campaigns. Specifically the process outlines:

- the responsibilities of the carrier and the ad agency
- the lines of communication between the two
- the e-marketing agency and partner agency engagement.

The expected outcomes of this process are to engage the e-marketing agency and partners more efficiently and appropriately. Further, a logical process to systematically roll out e-campaigns must also be defined at the same time. A well-designed process is a key ingredient for successful e marketing campaign management in cyberspace. The rather common urge to skip steps to shorten timelines (and save money) should be resisted as this adversely impacts on campaign results.

Figure 3.135 illustrates the four specific steps (set-up, creative process, integration, launch) generally involved in the interaction between an airline and digital advertising agency. The discussion below shares more details in the context of a search engine marketing campaign by an airline. The process for the initial set-up to launch covers a three-week timeframe. Anything shorter than this jeopardizes the quality of the campaign by the carrier.

*E-marketing calendar*

The airline's engagement for media placements in cyberspace is embedded in the company's annual integrated e-marketing calendar (IEMC). The IEMC maps out the year's planned e-marketing activities and is prepared under the leadership of the airline's e-marketing department and relevant stakeholders from the commercial side. They include sales, pricing, the offline marketing department, and FFP. Operational representatives from inflight or airport may be pulled in as well. Specific projects for each key market are identified. The IEMC provides for a visual time line view of e-marketing project description, project timing, project objectives, and project costs.

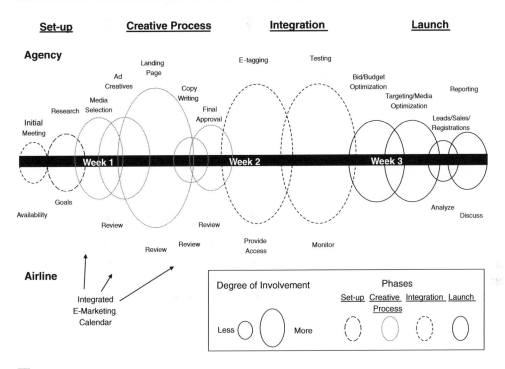

**Figure 3.135** *Action items and timelines in interaction between airlines and digital advertising agency: Example—search engine marketing campaign*

*Source:* Based on initial concept by SearcherMagnet (2014)[399]

The airline's e-marketing department approves and shares the IEMC with digital media agency and other stakeholders. In its approved and finalized form, the IEMC serves as the basis for the airline e-marketing department and other stakeholders to commence sequentially the deployment of e-marketing activities.

### Set-up

During the set-up phase, the carrier and digital ad agency agree on an initial meeting to explore the possibility for online marketing initiatives. In our case, it involves a search engine campaign. The airline e-marketing department and possibly other department representatives define the business issue, develop a project brief, and define success metrics. The e-marketing department's approval puts the project on calendar and notifies the digital agency that a project is in the pipeline.

For the carrier's communication to be effective, it is recommended to develop an e-campaign marketing brief. Presented by the airline e-marketing department, it contains detailed information previously discussed internally such as purpose of the search engine campaign and related business goals. The digital agency in turn engages in further research. One action item for example is the identification of popular search words/sentences used by web travelers. If the campaign takes place in several countries, this would have to be done for different languages.

The search might extend beyond key search terms and also include tag lines promoted to web travelers on search engines. Furthermore, information is gathered on the competitive situation, resources required, and cost and timelines involved for the campaign. It is likely that some consultation between the two parties will take place during this process.

*Creative process*

The media agency reviews creative and e-marketing plans and ensures that suggested solutions meet quality/strategy/executional criteria before a presentation is made to the airline's e-marketing department and related stakeholders.

Generally, key during this step is to assess what digital format (single or part of a mix) is most suitable to support the airline's direct response and/or brand goals. Since our examples involves a search engine campaign, the focus at this point is on selecting specific search terms and copywriting associated tag lines. Other action items for the digital agency include the development or optimization of existing landing pages to secure higher web traveler response rates (click-throughs specifically). This information is shared with the carrier's e-marketing department for continuous feedback on the creative suggestions presented.

Assuming that there are no further changes, final authorization to proceed to integration as the next step is granted.

*Integration*

A crucial next step is the set-up of e-tags that allow for the tracking of customer clickstreams to/from and on the carrier's websites. Carriers have to provide for back office access to their digital platforms in order to enable the placement of these tracking applications. Normally involved are the airline's web portal and ticket booking engine. Since these may be operated by other third parties, the airline would have to coordinate the interaction with the digital ad agencies. This step, depending on the number of parties involved and where they are geographically located, can be time-consuming and involve a few days.

Once the e-tags are deployed, the new set-up needs to be tested. If all tracking is properly installed and operational, testing conducted by all parties involved should go well. This confirms that the campaign can proceed to the next stage.

*Launch*

The e-campaign goes live and the bidding for selected search engine terms begins. First results are available quickly and allow the ad agency to gauge the initial performance of the campaign. Fine-tuning is the natural next step and a standard procedure applied by all ad agencies. This is done in order to stretch the associated budget for their airline client further if possible. Results are compiled, analyzed, and shared with the airline's e-marketing for next steps. Again, more optimization of the media format(s) might be done by the ad agency during the remainder of the campaign.

### 3.27.7 Crowdsourcing a media agency

Airlines do not only engage digital media agencies when it comes to crafting advertising creatives. Advertising crowdsourcing, another term is "user-generated advertising", has also found its way into some airlines. The idea goes back to 2007 when PepsiCo allowed people to create their own ads during the Super Bowl as part of the "Crash the Super Bowl" contest.

Since then, a number of online platforms have emerged that host user-generated advertising competitions on behalf of a company. One such player is Zoopa, an Italy-based player that has managed crowdsourced advertising for Alitalia.

Zoopa works with a staff of only 20 people and manages a platform that connects over 270,000 filmmakers and graphic artists worldwide with clients. The clients post a brief on what is required along with the prize that a successful submission attracts. Zoopa charges the client a flat fee of $50,000. This is significantly less than what a media agency costs and the client retains the rights to all submissions. Typically submitted are hundreds of ready-to-go ads by people with in-depth knowledge of the marketplace and above-the-average care of the brand involved.[400]

In Alitalia's case, the carrier had asked for the creation of several 60-second-long videos touching on themes like service quality, well-trained staff, and social media milestone achievements (Table 3.27). Each of the themes offered a prize of $5,000 for the successful submission.

*Table 3.27* Alitalia's crowdsourced advertising campaign

| Theme | Description provided by Alitalia to Zoopa |
| --- | --- |
| "Excellence to Fly" | Alitalia has one of the best teams of pilots in the world, try putting yourself in the place of one of the pilots of the company and tell us a story of his life, imagining being in his shoes. |
| "The Heart of Innovation" | Advanced technology, innovation and safety are the key concepts that represent the core values of Alitalia and that make it excellent among airlines. |
| "Great Care" | Describe the attention and care that Alitalia has implemented in all phases of aircraft maintenance and overhaul.<br><br>(You can use metaphors or resort to funny and paradoxical situations to show the attention to detail that distinguishes Alitalia.) |
| "Magnificent Preparation" | For the third consecutive year, Alitalia has won the Best Airline Cuisine for its inflight menus.<br><br>(Describe the attention to detail in the preparation, the careful selection of ingredients, combinations of flavors, the pleasure of enjoying a good Italian dish even at 10,000 meters flight altitude.) |
| "Flight Attendants Prepare for Take-off" | Tell us the funny situations that have happened to you or you directly witnessed during a trip and how they would be resolved by the professionalism and ingenuity of an Alitalia flight attendant. |

**Table 3.27** *continued*

| Theme | Description provided by Alitalia to Zoopa |
|---|---|
| "Social Alitalia" | Alitalia has reached one million Facebook fans: It is in the global top ten for number of fans in Italy and first in the category "Socially Devoted Brands" and in the top five among the world's "Most Socially Devoted Airlines." |
| | (With the use of a video format, tell the success story of Alitialia with social media and the reputation it has earned in this area.) |
| "Good Morning, how can I help?" | Tell the life of operators at Alitalia who are available 24 hours a day for all necessary support, their work and the readiness with which they always respond to all requests, even the most strange and desperate. |
| "Be a Frequent Flyer" | Describe the journey of an Alitalia frequent flyer, his characteristics, and his first-hand travel experience. |
| | (Describe what it means to access exclusive airport lounges and be able to make the travel experience with Alitalia even more comfortable and memorable.) |

*Source:* Tiragraffi.it (2013)[401]

## NOTES

1  Miklos On Media (2013) "Global advertising spend in 2013.," http://miklosonmediaandmarketing. blogspot.co.uk/2013/06/global-advertising-spend-in-2013.html (accessed March 24, 2015).

2  eMarketer.com (2014) "Global Ad Spending Growth to Double This Year," www.emarketer.com/ Article/Global-Ad-Spending-Growth-Double-This-Year/1010997 (accessed March 24, 2015).

3  Ibid.

4  eMarketer.com (2014) "Direct-response spending flying high in US travel industry," www. emarketer.com/Article/Direct-Response-Spending-Flying-High-US-Travel-Industry/1010859 (accessed March 24, 2015).

5  Ibid.

6  MarketingMag.com.au (2013) "Infographic: the history of online advertising," www.marketingmag. com.au/news-c/infographic-the-history-of-online-advertising/#.UqW9tM0o4qR (accessed March 24, 2015).

7  eMarketer.com, "Direct-response spending flying high in US travel industry."

8  Outdoor Advertising Association of America (2014) "Major media CPM comparison," www.oaaa. org/portals/0/Images/Major%20CPM%20Comparison%20Chart.jpg (accessed March 24, 2015).

9  Evans, P.B. and Wurster, T.S. (1997) "Strategy and the new economics of information," *Harvard Business Review*, September–October, 70: 71–82.

10  Roberts, M. and Zahay, D. (2014) "The elements of content marketing strategy," www.slideshare. net/fullscreen/zahayblatz/content-marketing-roberts-and-zahay/6 (accessed March 24, 2015).

11  Gasdia, M. (2014) "Touch and go: travel planning across channels," www.phocuswright.com/Free-Travel-Research/Touch-and-Go-Travel-Planning-Across-Channels#.VRHKWhDF-7A (accessed March 24, 2015).

12 Ibid.

13 Weps, F. (2014) "Use analytics to take advantage of online travel trends," www.trainingaid.org/news/infographic-use-analytics-take-advantage-online-travel-trends (accessed March 24, 2015).

14 CatapultRPM (2012) "Segmenting customers by technology preference," http://catapultrpmfrontier.blogspot.com/2012/07/segmenting-customers-by-technology.html (accessed February 25, 2014).

15 Yahoo! Advertising Solutions (2013) "What are gen Z kids up to online?" http://news.yahoo.com/blogs/advertising/gen-z-kids-online-202822575.html (accessed March 24, 2015).

16 PBT Consulting (2013) "The Mobile, social, and web connection preferences of gen Zers (18–23 Years) and how this affects brand marketing strategies," http://tommytoy.typepad.com/tommy-toy-pbt-consultin/2013/04/gen-z-trusts-mobile-social-content-more-than-other-generations-do.html (accessed March 24, 2015).

17 TourismIntelligence.ca (2014) "Generation Y, the new face of business travel," http://tourismintelligence.ca/2014/06/30/generation-y-the-new-face-of-business-travel/ (accessed March 24, 2015).

18 Boston Consulting Group (2014) "Traveling with millennials," www.bcgperspectives.com/content/articles/transportation_travel_tourism_consumer_insight_traveling_with_millennials/?chapter=4#chapter4 (accessed March 24, 2015).

19 Sverdlov, G. (2012) "The state of US consumers and technology," www.forbes.com/sites/forrester/2012/12/19/the-state-of-us-consumers-and-technology/ (accessed March 24, 2015).

20 TourismIntelligence.ca, "Generation Y, the new face of business travel."

21 Boston Consulting Group, "Traveling with millennials."

22 Clark, C. (2014) "Turkish Airlines' social media journey," https://d3bg2441si4wp3.cloudfront.net/prod/wp-content/uploads/2014/01/Turkish-Airlines-Social-Media-Journey.pdf (accessed March 24, 2015).

23 Boston Consulting Group (2013) "The digital road to earning travelers' trust," www.bcgperspectives.com/content/interviews/transportation_travel_tourism_digital_economy_bolden_dylan_digital_road_to_earning_travelers_trust/ (accessed March 24, 2015).

24 Corcoran, S. (2009) "Defining earned, owned and paid media," http://blogs.forrester.com/interactive_marketing/2009/12/defining-earned-owned-and-paid-media.html (accessed March 24, 2015).

25 Wikipedia (2015) "Television advertisement," http://en.wikipedia.org/wiki/Television_advertisement (accessed March 24, 2015).

26 Miklos On Media, "Global advertising spend in 2013,"

27 Marketingcharts.com (2015), "Are young people watching less TV?" http://www.marketingcharts.com/television/are-young-people-watching-less-tv-24817/ (accessed April 30, 2015).

28 Google (2014) "1 in 3 travelers watch their favorite programs outside of live TV," www.slideshare.net/fullscreen/fracanz/google-the-2014-travelers-road-to-decision/44 (accessed March 24, 2015).

29 Outdoor Advertising Association of America (2015) "OAAA," www.oaaa.org/ (accessed March 24, 2015).

30 Ibid.

31 Youtube.com (2011) "10 TWA TV ads," www.youtube.com/watch?v=JRjaKoX4I_Q (accessed March 24, 2015).

32 iSpot.tv (2015) "Southwest Airlines TV commercials," www.ispot.tv/brands/A5a/southwest-airlines?view-all=true (accessed March 24, 2015).

33 Youtube.com (2005) "British Airways' website ba.com TV Ad—Have you clicked yet?" www.youtube.com/watch?v=fHI9Mo8OKZA (accessed March 24, 2015).

34  Youtube.com (2014) "Air France Mobile (English version)," www.youtube.com/watch?v=WxnTJpjm57g (accessed March 24, 2015).

35  Schaal, D. (2014) "Travel booking sites spent $624 million on TV advertising in 2014," http://skift.com/2014/12/31/booking-sites-spent-624-million-on-tv-advertising-in-2014-expedia-dominated/?utm_source=Skift&utm_campaign=567767190a-UA-28362693-1&utm_medium=email&utm_term=0_fe7fb4248c-567767190a-63938597 (accessed March 24, 2015).

36  Spary, S. (2015) "Nicole Kidman signing will accelerate Etihad's global appeal, says marketing chief," www.marketingmagazine.co.uk/article/1338379/nicole-kidman-signing-will-accelerate-etihads-global-appeal-says-marketing-chief?dcmp=emc-conmarketingdailybulletin&bulletin=marketingdaily (accessed March 24, 2015).

37  Nielsen (2013) "Nielsen TV: second screen use is a boon for TV advertisers," www.nielsen.com/us/en/newswire/2013/nielsen-tv-second-screen-use-is-a-boon-for-tv-advertisers.html (accessed March 24, 2015).

38  Davis, B. (2013) "Twitter and TV: ignore the stats and focus on best practice," http://econsultancy.com/blog/63959-twitter-and-tv-ignore-the-stats-and-focus-on-best-practice (accessed March 24, 2015).

39  Tode, C. (2013) "Expedia drives mobile bookings via TV campaign, trip-a-day giveaway," www.mobilecommercedaily.com/expedia-drives-mobile-bookings-via-tv-campaign-trip-a-day-giveaway (accessed March 24, 2015).

40  Nelson, J. (2013) "Guess what, marketers? Interactive TV is actually here," www.forbes.com/sites/onmarketing/2013/05/20/guess-what-marketers-interactive-tv-is-actually-here/ (accessed March 24, 2015).

41  Digital Strategy Consulting (2013) "Rise of connected TVs: American Airlines sees strong results for interactive TV campaign," www.digitalstrategyconsulting.com/intelligence/2013/06/rise_of_connected_tvs_american_airlines_sees_strong_results_for_interactive_tv_campaign.php (accessed March 24, 2015).

42  Nielsen (2014) "State of the Media: Audio Today 2014," www.nielsen.com/us/en/insights/reports/2014/state-of-the-media-audio-today-2014.html (accessed March 24, 2015).

43  Kelly, M. (2013) "TV's not dead yet: A comparison of YouTube and the boob tube (infographic)," http://venturebeat.com/2013/10/14/youtube-tv/ (accessed March 24, 2015).

44  Youtube.com (2014) "Ethiopian Airlines Radio Advert 2," www.youtube.com/watch?v=mtJRv7A1278It (accessed March 24, 2015).

45  O'Dell, R. (2012) "Smooth Jazz News," http://chicagosmooth.typepad.com/my-blog/smooth-jazz-news/page/7/ (accessed March 24, 2015).

46  Hill, B. (2014) "Mobile advertising will surpass radio and print this year," http://rainnews.com/mobile-advertising-will-surpass-radio-and-print-this-year/ (accessed March 24, 2015).

47  Pandora.com (2014) "Pandora announces May 2014 audience metrics," http://investor.pandora.com/phoenix.zhtml?c=227956&p=irol-newsArticle&ID=1937243 (accessed March 24, 2015).

48  Ibid.

49  Sisario, B. and Vega, T. (2012) "Pandora courts local advertisers, by offering well-defined listeners," www.nytimes.com/2012/04/16/business/media/pandora-courts-local-advertisers-by-reaching-a-narrow-audience.html?pagewanted=all&_r=0 (accessed March 24, 2015).

50  Pandora.com, "Pandora announces May 2014 audience metrics."

51  Targetspot.com (2011) "Target Spot Inc. ad impact study white paper," www.cdn.targetspot.com/pdfs/TargetSpot-Inc_Ad_Impact_Study_White_Paper-2011.pdf (accessed March 24, 2015).

52  Thedesignair.net (2012) "1925 Poster," http://thedesignair.net/2012/05/21/klm-the-first-airline-poster-boy/#jp-carousel-447 (accessed March 24, 2015).

53  Reminisce.com (2014) "The jet set: vintage airline ads," www.reminisce.com/1940s/the-jet-set-vintage-airline-ads/ (accessed March 24, 2015).

54  The New Zealand Herald (2011) "Budget airlines turn to social media," www.nzherald.co.nz/business/news/article.cfm?c_id=3&objectid=10702700 (accessed March 24, 2015).

55  United Airlines (2000) Author's analysis based on online booking data e-for UK market. Data from author's e-commerce archives.

56  Marketing Strategies Blog (2013) "Direct mail still preferred over email, social and mobile marketing," http://marstrategiesworld.blogspot.com/2013/10/direct-mail-still-preferred-over-email.html (accessed March 24, 2015).

57  Air China (2008) e-commerce promotional brochures, from author's e-commerce archives.

58  DeviantArt (2010) "Egyptair," www.deviantart.com/art/Egyptair-153219880 (accessed March 24, 2015).

59  Swartzonmedia (2008) "Artfield1," https://swartzonmedia.files.wordpress.com/2008/01/artfield1.jpg (accessed March 24, 2015).

60  Sass, E. (2013) "British airways billboard ads interact with planes," www.mediapost.com/publications/article/213912/british-airways-billboard-ads-interact-with-planes.html?edition= (accessed March 24, 2015).

61  Blogspot.com (2014) "British airways digital outdoor advertising," http://4.bp.blogspot.com/-WMyh3Fnqbeo/UoyercVrU8I/AAAAAAAACRQ/VhZlHTAAv_c/s1600/british-airways-digital-outdoor-advertising.png (accessed March 24, 2015).

62  MacLeod, I. (2013) "British Airways unveils digital billboards to remind customers how magical flying can be," http://www.thedrum.com/news/2013/11/19/british-airways-unveils-digital-billboards-remind-customers-how-magical-flying-can (accessed March 24, 2015).

63  Fera, R. (2012) "The 14 Most Arresting Interactive Outdoor Ads: From Vibrating Benches to Geofencing," www.fastcocreate.com/1680513/the-14-most-arresting-interactive-outdoor-ads-from-vibrating-benches-to-geofencing#7 (accessed March 24, 2015).

64  Ibid.

65  Ying, L. (2014) "Emirates upcycles its outdoor advertising posters into reusable shopping bags," http://designtaxi.com/news/368786/Emirates-Upcycles-Its-Outdoor-Advertising-Posters-Into-Reusable-Shopping-Bags/ (accessed March 24, 2015).

66  Mengus, A. "Pepsi Concord—F—BTSD," www.concordesst.com/history/events/pepsi.html (accessed March 24, 2015).

67  Fesenmaier, D. (2009) "An analysis of search engine use for travel planning," www.panb.people.cofc.edu/pan/Analysis_Search_engine_Use_Travel_Planning.pdf (accessed March 24, 2015).

68  Pew Research Center (2012) "Search engine use over time," www.pewinternet.org/2012/03/09/main-findings-11/ (accessed March 24, 2015).

69  ThinkWithGoogle.com (2014) "The 2014 traveler's road to decision," www.thinkwithgoogle.com/research-studies/2014-travelers-road-to-decision.html (accessed March 24, 2015).

70  Hitwise (2014) "Website traffic based on US internet usage, November 2014," from author's e-commerce archive (accessed November 30, 2014).

71  Kenshoo.com (2015) "INFOGRAPHIC: Kenshoo industry spotlight: air travel," http://kenshoo.com/airtravelspotlight/ (accessed March 24, 2015).

72 Lloyd, A. (2014) "Search engine statistics October 2014," www.clicky.co.uk/2014/11/search-engine-statistics-october-2014/ (accessed March 24, 2015).

73 eBizMBA.com (2015) "Top 15 Most Popular Search Engines," www.ebizmba.com/articles/search-engines (accessed March 24, 2015).

74 Sullivan, D. (2013) "Google still world's most popular search engine by far, but share of unique searchers dips slightly," http://searchengineland.com/google-worlds-most-popular-search-engine-148089 (accessed March 24, 2015).

75 Ibid.

76 Mushroom Networks (2015) "YouTube—the 2nd largest search engine (Infographic)," www.mushroomnetworks.com/infographics/youtube---the-2nd-largest-search-engine-infographic (accessed March 24, 2015).

77 Google.com (2014) "Search results for query 'Flights to Rio'," www.google.com (accessed December 28, 2014).

78 IronPaper (2013) "How important is being on the top of Google?" www.ironpaper.com/current/2013/06/how-important-is-being-on-the-top-of-google/#.VKBtqsCcNA (accessed March 24, 2015).

79 Statista (2014) "Google's advertising revenue from 2001 to 2014 (in billion U.S. dollars)," www.statista.com/statistics/266249/advertising-revenue-of-google/ (accessed March 24, 2015).

80 Leicheko, J. (2014) "Travel advertisers and paid search," www.adgooroo.com/resources/blog/travel-advertisers-and-paid-search/ (accessed March 24, 2015).

81 Ibid.

82 Marvin, G. (2013) "Is Google poaching clicks from travel advertisers? Spend trends down even as advertisers increase (study)," http://searchengineland.com/is-google-poaching-clicks-from-travel-advertisers-spend-trends-down-even-as-advertisers-increase-study-160553 (accessed March 24, 2015).

83 Knight, M. (2014) "What is SEO? A beginners guide," http://midasmedia.co.uk/what-is-seo-a-beginners-guide/ (accessed March 24, 2015).

84 SearchMetrics (2014) "Ranking factors 2014," www.searchmetrics.com/wp-content/uploads/seo-ranking-factors-2014.png (accessed March 24, 2015).

85 SearchMetrics (2014) "SearchMetrics ranking factor study," http://pages.searchmetrics.com/rs/searchmetricsgmbh/images/Searchmetrics_Ranking_Factor_Study_2014.pdf (accessed March 24, 2015).

86 Moz.com (2014) "Google algorithm change," http://moz.com/google-algorithm-change_ (accessed March 24, 2015).

87 Tnooz.com (2013) "Three years on from Google Panda, many travel sites struggle with traffic," www.tnooz.com/article/google-panda-travel-sites-struggle#sthash.Ns3IgCw4.dpu (accessed March 24, 2015).

88 Tober, M. (2014) "SEO analysis: Why Expedia.com lost 25% of their visibility (update)," http://blog.searchmetrics.com/us/2014/01/22/seo-analysis-why-expedia-com-lost-25-of-their-visibility/ (accessed March 24, 2015).

89 Sullivan, L. (2011) "Mobile, tablet, desktop varies search behavior," www.mediapost.com/publications/article/146347/mobile-tablet-desktop-varies-search-behavior.html (accessed March 24, 2015).

90 Gagnon, J. (2014) "Words that work for the holiday travel season," www.clickz.com/clickz/column/2370614/words-that-work-for-the-holiday-travel-season (accessed March 24, 2015).

91 ThinkWithGoogle.com, "The 2014 traveler's road to decision."

92   Google.com (2014) "Search results for query 'Air India'," www.google.com (accessed December 30, 2014).

93   TechDirt (2008) "American Airlines and Google settle keyword advertising spat," www.techdirt. com/articles/20080720/1929561737.shtml (accessed March 24, 2015).

94   Kenshoo.com, "INFOGRAPHIC: Kenshoo Industry Spotlight: Air Travel."

95   Anderson, C. (2006) *The Long Tail*. New York: Hachette Book Group.

96   Kenshoo.com, "INFOGRAPHIC: Kenshoo Industry Spotlight: Air Travel."

97   Ibid.

98   Tnooz.com (2015) "Ryanair doing its thing on the web [INFOGRAPHIC]," www.tnooz. com/article/ryanair-30-years-infographic/#utm_source=Tnooz+Mailing+List&utm_ medium=email&utm_campaign=09dde11cc7-RSS_EMAIL_CAMPAIGN&utm_term=0_ c691357c44-09dde11cc7-137333989 (accessed March 24, 2015).

99   eMarketer.com (2014) "7 travel trends for 2015—how digital will drive new opportunities for revenue and distribution," www.Revenue-Distribution/4000097 (accessed March 24, 2015).

100  Ibid.

101  Google.com (2014) "Search results," www.google.com (accessed December 31, 2014).

102  Ibid.

103  TugAgency (2013) "Social search SES 2013," www.slideshare.net/TugSearch/social-search-ses-2013 (accessed March 24, 2015).

104  SearchMetrics, "SearchMetrics ranking factor study."

105  Ulanoff, L. (2012) "Bing reinvents social search and discovery," http://mashable.com/2012/05/10/ bing-social-search-discovery (accessed March 24, 2015).

106  TugAgency, "Social search SES 2013."

107  Constine, J. (2014) "Facebook brings graph search to mobile and lets you find feed posts by keyword," http://techcrunch.com/2014/12/08/facebook-keyword-search/ (accessed March 24, 2015).

108  May, K. (2012) "TripAdvisor unveils next phase of Facebook tie-in, friends of friends included in reviews," www.tnooz.com/article/tripadvisor-unveils-next-phase-of-facebook-tie-in-friends-of-friends-included-in-reviews/#sthash.lbgVfzE5.dpuf (accessed March 24, 2015).

109  Sawers, P. (2012) "TripAdvisor deepens Facebook integration with 'Friend of a Friend,' recommendations," http://thenextweb.com/insider/2012/04/11/tripadvisor-deepens-facebook-integration-with-friend-of-a-friend-recommendations/ (accessed March 24, 2015).

110  Tnooz (2013) "KLM is at it again—combines the social graph, things-to-do and maps", http:// www.tnooz.com/article/klm-is-at-it-again-combines-the-social-graph-things-to-do-and-maps/ (accessed December 12, 2015).

111  Google (2015) "What's trending in display for publishers?" www.google.com/doubleclick/pdfs/ display-business-trends-publisher-edition.pdf (accessed March 24, 2015).

112  Ha, A. (2013) "ComScore says 5.3 trillion ads shown in 2012, but 3 in 10 are never seen," http:// techcrunch.com/2013/02/14/comscore-digital-future-2013/ (accessed March 24, 2015).

113  New Media and Marketing (2014) "The average person is served over 1700 banner ads per month," www.newmediaandmarketing.com/the-average-person-is-served-over-1700-banner-ads-per-month/ (accessed March 24, 2015).

114  Koetsier, J. (2012) "How Google makes $100 million a day—and how GOOG lost $21 billion last week (infographic)," http://venturebeat.com/2012/10/25/how-google-makes-over-100-million-a-day-and-how-goog-lost-21-billion-last-week-infographic/ (accessed March 24, 2015).

115 Sizmek.com (2014) "Sizmek benchmarks report 2014," www.sizmek.com/assets/pdf/Sizmek_2014-03_Benchmarks_report.pdf (accessed March 24, 2015).

116 Koetsier, "How Google makes $100 million a day."

117 Schiff, A. (2013) "Interactive ads to rule them all," www.dmnews.com/interactive-ads-to-rule-them-all/article/296696/ (accessed March 24, 2015).

118 O'Leary, N. (2014) "Spirit Airlines launches new ad strategy," www.adweek.com/news/advertising-branding/spirit-airlines-launches-new-ad-strategy-157526 (accessed March 24, 2015).

119 Adweek (2014) "Spirit 101 HEADER," www.adweek.com/files/imagecache/node-detail/news_article/spirit-101-hed-2014_0.jpg (accessed March 24, 2015).

120 Iab.net (2007) "Rich media measurement guidelines," www.iab.net/guidelines/508676/guidelines/Rich_Media_Measurement#sthash.S4UsvN4c.dpuf (accessed March 24, 2015).

121 Sharma, R. (2011) "Benefits of rich media ads," http://insights.marinsoftware.com/rich-ads/benefits-of-rich-media-ads/) (accessed June 28, 2015).

122 Air Mauritius (2014) "Air Mauritius," www.airmauritius.com (accessed December 22, 2014).

123 Manchester United (2015) "Manchester United—official site," www.manutd.com./ (accessed December 14, 2014).

124 Singapore Award Blog (2014) "Singapore award blog," http://sgblogawards.omy.sg/ (accessed December 23, 2014).

125 Rice, K. (2014) "Fueled by data, individualized ads changing travel sales," www.travelweekly.com/Travel-News/Travel-Agent-Issues/Fueled-by-data-individualized-ads-profoundly-changing-travel-sales (accessed March 24, 2015).

126 The Economist (2014) "Buy, buy, baby: The rise of an electronic marketplace for online ads is reshaping the media business," www.economist.com/news/special-report/21615872-rise-electronic-marketplace-online-ads-reshaping-media-business-buy (accessed March 24, 2015).

127 Rice, "Fueled by data, individualized ads changing travel sales."

128 Laudon, K.C. and Traver, C.G. (2013) *E-commerce: Business, Technology, Society*, Edinburgh: Pearson Education.

129 Ibid.

130 The Radicati Group (2014) "Email statistics report, 2014–2018," www.radicati.com/wp/wp-content/uploads/2014/01/Email-Statistics-Report-2014-2018-Executive-Summary.pdf (accessed March 24, 2015).

131 Ibid.

132 eMarketer.com (2014) "Email: the old kid on the block's still got it," www.emarketer.com/Article/Email-Old-Kid-on-Blocks-Still/1011047 (accessed March 24, 2015).

133 eMarketer.com (2013) "Email marketing still relevant for UK consumers," www.emarketer.com/articles/print.aspx?R=1010251 (accessed March 24, 2015).

134 eMarketer.com, "Email: the old kid on the block's still got it."

135 McKinsey & Company (2014) "Why marketers should keep sending you e-mails," www.McKinsey.com/insights/marketing_sales/why_marketers_should_keep_sending_you_emails (accessed March 24, 2015).

136 eMarketer.com, "Email: the old kid on the block's still got it."

137 Phocuswright (2015) "The mobile effect: disrupting the competitive landscape in the digital travel market," www.criteo.com/media/2187/phocuswright-criteo-the-mobile-effect-travel.pdf (accessed July 3, 2015).

138 EmailMarketingTipps.de (2012) "Double opt-in in Germany—is it legally mandated?" www. emailmarketingtipps.de/2012/05/11/double-opt-in-in-germany-is-it-legally-mandated/ (accessed March 24, 2015).

139 Air France (2012) "Thank you email," from author's e-commerce archive (accessed July 16, 2014).

140 United Airlines (2014) "United Airlines," www.united.com (accessed April 24, 2014).

141 Virgin Australia (2015) "Virgin Australia," www.virginaustralia.com/au/en/ (accessed June 29, 2015).

142 Finnair (ca 2009) "Finnair," www.finnair.com/, from author's e-commerce archive (accessed March 15, 2014).

143 Expedia (2014) "Expedia newsletter," from author's e-commerce archive (accessed June 27, 2014).

144 Hodgekiss, R. (2011) "What's the maximum file size for an HTML email?" www.campaignmonitor. com/blog/post/3610/maximum-file-size-for-html-email/ (accessed March 24, 2015).

145 Marketing Charts (2013) "How long do mobile owners spend reading the b2c emails they open?" www.marketingcharts.com/online/how-long-do-mobile-owners-spend-reading-the-b2c-emails-they-open-35936/ (accessed March 24, 2015).

146 Rubin, K. (2012) "The ultimate list of email SPAM trigger words," http://blog.hubspot.com/ blog/tabid/6307/bid/30684/The-Ultimate-List-of-Email-SPAM-Trigger-Words.aspx (accessed March 24, 2015).

147 Vieira, H. (2014) "When is the best time to send my email marketing campaign?" https:// signupto1.zendesk.com/hc/en-gb/articles/201828978-When-is-the-best-time-to-send-my-email-marketing-campaign- (accessed March 24, 2015).

148 Ibid.

149 Signup.to (2014) "The 2014 UK email marketing benchmark report," www.signupto.com/assets/ email-benchmark-2014.pdf (accessed March 31, 2015).

150 Ibid.

151 Neely, P. (2014) "11 email marketing metrics ranked in order of importance," http:// webmarketingtoday.com/articles/113354-11-Email-Marketing-Metrics-Ranked-in-Order-of-Importance/ (accessed April 3, 2015).

152 eMarketer.com, "Email: the old kid on the block's still got it."

153 Fredcavazza.net (2015) "Social media landscape," www.fredcavazza.net/files/Q2-08/ SocialMediaLandscape.jpg (accessed March 24, 2015).

154 ThinkWithGoogle.com, "The 2014 traveler's road to decision."

155 eMarketer.com (2015) "Social ad network spending worldwide, by region," https://media.licdn. com/mpr/mpr/p/2/005/07e/3e8/0e79bcf.jpg (accessed March 24, 2015).

156 Quinby, D. and Gasdia, M. (2014) "The state of social media in travel featuring Facebook travel analytics," www.phocuswright.com/Free-Travel-Research/The-State-of-Social-Media-in-Travel-Featuring-Facebook-Travel-Analytics#.VVY-kGfbLIU (accessed February 23, 2015).

157 Deloitte.com (2015) "Quick facts on travel infographic," www2.deloitte.com/content/dam/ Deloitte/global/Documents/Consumer-Business/gx-cb-thl-facebook-digital-channels-travel-infogr.pdf (accessed March 24, 2015).

158 ThinkWithGoogle.com, "The 2014 traveler's road to decision."

159 Edwards, S. (2011) "A social media mindset," http://jiad.org/article148.html (accessed March 24, 2015).

160 Quinby and Gasdia, "The state of social media in travel featuring facebook travel analytics."

161 Dyer, P. (2013) "50 top tools for social media monitoring, analytics, and management," www. analytics-and-management (accessed July 3, 2014).

162 Statista (2014) "Facebook is a must for brands around the world," https://d28wbuch0jlv7v. cloudfront.net/images/infografik/normal/chartoftheday_2942_Brand_use_of_social_media_ platforms_n.jpg (accessed March 24, 2015).

163 Quinby and Gasdia, "The State of Social Media in Travel Featuring Facebook Travel Analytics."

164 Popper, B. (2014) "Facebook now has more than a billion mobile users every month," www. theverge.com/2014/4/23/5644740/facebook-q1-2014-earnings (accessed March 24, 2015).

165 Spredfast (2014) "14 stats inform your 2014 social marketing strategy," www.spredfast.com/social-marketing-blog/14-stats-inform-your-2014-social-marketing-strategy (accessed March 24, 2015).

166 Worldometers (2014) "Countries in the world (ranked by 2014 population)," www.worldometers. info/world-population/population-by-country/ (accessed March 24, 2015).

167 Deloitte.com, "Quick facts on travel infographic."

168 FreshBuzz Media (2013) "Facebook travel survey shows influence of engagement," https:// freshbuzzmedia.com/2013/11/facebook-travel-survey-shows-influence-of-engagement (accessed March 24, 2015).

169 Ibid.

170 Deloitte.com, "Quick facts on travel infographic."

171 Ayres, S. (2014) "Here's what you should post on your Facebook page to get more likes & shares," www.postplanner.com/facebook-page-posts-goals-expectations/ (accessed March 24, 2015).

172 James, A. (2015) "Facebook video is now bigger than YouTube for brands," www.socialbakers.com/ blog/2335-facebook-video-is-now-bigger-than-youtube-for-brands (accessed March 24, 2015).

173 Facebook.com (2015) "Qatar Airways Facebook page," www.facebook.com/qatarairways (accessed January 13, 2015).

174 Campbell, K. (2013) "8 Facebook post types for boosting engagement," http://webmarketingtoday. com/articles/109397-8-Facebook-Post-Types-for-Boosting-Engagement/ (accessed March 24, 2015).

175 Facebook.com (2015) "Facebook," www.facebook.com (accessed January 13, 2015).

176 Ibid.

177 Facebook.com, "Facebook."

178 Guglielmelli, C. (2014) "Finding the right engagement rate for your Facebook page in 2014," www.socialbakers.com/blog/2137-finding-the-right-engagement-rate-for-your-facebook-page-in-2014 (accessed March 24, 2015).

179 Creamer, M. (2012) "Brand engagement rate still 1%, but Facebook is ok with that," http://adage. com/article/digital/brand-engagement-rate-1-facebook/238317/ (accessed March 24, 2015).

180 Facebook.com (2014) "Removal of PTAT metric," https://developers.facebook.com/docs/apps/ migrations/pages-api-changes-2014-07-02 (accessed March 24, 2015).

181 Ibid.

182 Lee, K. (2014) "The social media frequency guide: how often to post to Facebook, Twitter, LinkedIn, and More," www.fastcompany.com/3029019/work-smart/the-social-media-frequency-guide-how-often-to-post-to-facebook-twitter-linkedin-a (accessed March 24, 2015).

183 Pal, S. (2012) "How airlines and airports can dramatically increase engagement on their Facebook pages through one simple action," http://simpliflying.com/2012/how-airlines-and-airports-can-dramatically-increase-engagement-on-their-facebook-pages-through-one-simple-action/ (accessed March 24, 2015).

184 Guglielmelli, "Finding the right engagement rate for your Facebook page in 2014."

185 Facebook.com, "Facebook."

186 Facebook.com (2015) "Advertise on Facebook," www.facebook.com/ads/create/ (accessed March 24, 2015).

187 Vadgama, S. (2013) "Facebook puts mobile first, so should advertisers," www.fourthsource.com/news/facebook-puts-mobile-first-so-should-advertisers-13772 (accessed March 24, 2015).

188 Lopez, M. (2014) "The Facebook mirror challenge," http://quickresultscopywriting.com/2014/05/the-facebook-mirror-challenge/ (accessed March 24, 2015).

189 Fourth Source (2014) "British Airways sponsored story on Facebook," www.fourthsource.com/wp-content/uploads/2013/04/British-Airways-Sponsored-Story-on-Facebook-192x300.png (accessed March 24, 2015).

190 Facebook For Business (2014) "Success story: marketing with audience participation," www.facebook.com/business/success/scoot (accessed March 24, 2015).

191 Facebook For Business (2014) "Success story: inspiration lift-off," www.facebook.com/business/success/lufthansa#u_0_a (accessed March 24, 2015).

192 Facebook For Business (2014) "Success story: getting new customers on board," www.facebook.com/business/success/sas (accessed March 24, 2015).

193 Twitter (2015) "About," https://about.twitter.com/company (accessed March 24, 2015).

194 Jana.com (2014) "Twitter has bright future in emerging markets," www.jana.com/blog/twitter-has-a-future-in-emerging-markets/ (accessed March 24, 2015).

195 Petrucci, T. (2014) "Flying high: airlines on social media," www.mycleveragency.com/blog/2014/10/social-media-cloud-9/ (accessed March 24, 2015).

196 Twitter (2015) "Twitter," www.twitter.com (accessed January 9, 2015).

197 Escudero, N. (2013) "Twitter resources," www.slideshare.net/NickiEscudero/twitter-bible-32712-2 (accessed March 24, 2015).

198 BoardingArea.com (2011) "Tweet for a chance to win 30,000 miles," http://dealswelike.boardingarea.com/wp-content/uploads/2011/04/aa-day-4.png (accessed March 24, 2015).

199 Drimmelen, J. (2011) "Fly2Miami—First ever twitter-filled aircraft," https://blog.klm.com/fly2miami-first-ever-twitter-filled-aircraft-2/ (accessed March 24, 2015).

200 Wegert, T. (2014) "JetBlue pays it forward through a social storytelling campaign with no end in sight," http://contently.com/strategist/2014/11/13/jetblue-pays-it-forward-through-a-social-storytelling-campaign-with-no-end-in-sight/ (accessed March 24, 2015).

201 lansystems (2010) "Promoted tweets: lead or gold?" http://lansystems.com/business-strategiespromoted-tweets-lead-or-gold (accessed April 22, 2014).

202 Twitter, "Twitter."

203 Ibid.

204 Patel, N. (2014) "10 Twitter tactics to increase your engagement," www.socialmediaexaminer.com/twitter-tactics-to-increase-engagement/ (accessed March 24, 2015).

205 Lee, "The Social Media Frequency Guide."

206 Grant, G. (2014) "Which airline is soaring above the competition with killer content?" http://trackmaven.com/blog/2014/11/airlines-soaring-above-competition-with-content/ (accessed March 24, 2015).

207 CAPA (2013) "Condor launches own YouTube channel," http://centreforaviation.com/profiles/airlines/condor-flugdienst-de#news (accessed January 30, 2013).

208 ThinkWithGoogle.com, "The 2014 traveler's road to decision."

209  Grant, G. (2014) "Which airline is soaring above the competition with killer content?" http://trackmaven.com/blog/2014/11/airlines-soaring-above-competition-with-content/ (accessed March 24, 2015).

210  ThinkWithGoogle.com (2014) "Air New Zealand increases awareness and sales using YouTube," www.thinkwithgoogle.com/case-studies/air-new-zealand-increases-awareness-sales-using-youtube.html (accessed March 24, 2015).

211  SocialBakers.com (2014) "All Youtube Channels," www.socialbakers.com/youtube-statistics/ (accessed November 24, 2014).

212  Youtube.com (2015) "Turkish Airlines," www.youtube.com/user/TURKISHAIRLINES (accessed February 14, 2015).

213  Russell, M. (2014) "3 reasons Turkish Airlines' 'Selfie Shootout' was so darn popular," www.imediaconnection.com/content/35765.asp (accessed March 24, 2015).

214  The Economist (2013) "Screen Grab," www.economist.com/blogs/graphicdetail/2013/10/daily-chart-20 (accessed April 7, 2015]

215  Google, "What's trending in display for publishers?"

216  eMarketer (2014) "Digital video, which is under-represented in the travel category, is poised for growth," www.slideshare.net/fullscreen/eMarketerInc/emarketer-webinar-7-travel-trends-for-2015how-digital-will-drive-new-opportunities-for-revenue-and-distribution/27 (accessed March 24, 2015).

217  Hoelzel, M. (2014) "Online video advertising is growing many times faster than TV, search, and most other digital ad markets," www.businessinsider.com/digital-video-advertising-growth-trends-2014-5 (accessed March 24, 2015).

218  GoogleUserContent.com (2012) "Youtube trueview video ads: let the audience choose you," http://static.googleusercontent.com/media/www.youtube.com/en/us/yt/advertise/medias/pdfs/trueview-onesheeter-en.pdf (accessed March 24, 2015).

219  Fisher, L. (2011) "Only 30% of YouTube users skip pre-roll ads [correction: 30% in fact WATCH the ads]," http://thenextweb.com/socialmedia/2011/06/12/only-30-of-youtube-users-skip-pre-roll-ads/#!vUcAU (accessed March 24, 2015).

220  PR Newswire (2014) "JetBlue launches new advertising and marketing campaign: you above all™," www.prnewswire.com/news-releases/jetblue-launches-new-advertising-and-marketing-campaign-you-above-all-104955079.html (accessed March 24, 2015).

221  Youtube.com (2014) "Search results for query 'jetstar pre-roll ad'," www.youtube.com/results?search_query=jetstar+pre-roll+ad (accessed December 25, 2014).

222  McClellan, S. (2014) "Virgin Airlines launches unusual campaign using a fake airline," www.bmielite.com/virgin-airlines-launches-unusual-campaign-using-a-fake-airline/ (accessed March 24, 2015).

223  Prabu, K. (2014) "Generation Y travellers and the future of travel technology," www.technology/ (accessed March 24, 2015).

224  James, "Facebook video is now bigger than YouTube for brands."

225  Statista (2015) "Leading social networks worldwide as of March 2015, ranked by number of active users (in millions)," www.statista.com/statistics/272014/global-social-networks-ranked-by-number-of-users/ (accessed March 24, 2015).

226  Google.com (2015) "Search results for query 'singapore airlines'," www.google.com/#q=singapore+airlines (accessed January 20, 2015).

227  Virgin America (2013) "Fly like a Boss: Virgin America invites New Jersey travelers to ask for more in a business airline," www.virginamerica.com/cms/about-our-airline/press/2013/virgin-america-invites-travelers-to-ask-for-more-in-a-business-airline (accessed March 24, 2015).

228 SocialBakers.com (2015) "Brands Google+ stats—airlines," www.socialbakers.com/statistics/ google-plus/profiles/brands/airlines/ (accessed March 24, 2015).

229 Cohen, H. (2014) "Is your business tapping into the full power of LinkedIn?" http://heidicohen. com/linkedin-business-tactics/ (accessed March 24, 2015).

230 LinkedIn (2015) "LinkedIn," www.linkedin.com (accessed January 22, 2015).

231 All Nippon Airways (2015) "ana-flight-connections," https://www.ana-flightconnections.com/ (accessed on December 13, 2015).

232 Instagram.com (2015) "Instagram," https://instagram.com/ (accessed January 27, 2015).

233 Instagram.com (2015) "Virgin Australia," https://instagram.com/virginaustralia (accessed January 27, 2015).

234 Kuchler, H. (2015) "Advertisers ride wave of social media influencers," www.ft.com/intl/cms/s/0/ cffd04ba-8256-11e4-a9bb-00144feabdc0.html#axzz3PoWxyf5 (accessed March 24, 2015).

235 Von Muenster, S. (2015) "Social influencers and the law—where does it stand on disclosure?" http://mumbrella.com.au/social-influencers-law-stand-disclosure-270908 (accessed March 24, 2015).

236 Waggener Edstrom Communications (2014) "Waggener edstrom launches mobile, real-time influencer intelligence solutions for Asia-Pacific," http://apac.waggeneredstrom.com/blog/news/ waggener-edstrom-launches-mobile-real-time-influencer-intelligence-solutions-for-asia-pacific/ (accessed March 24, 2015).

237 Schaffer, N. (2011) "Social media influencer outreach brand ambassador case study—all Nippon Airways #ANALAX," http://maximizesocialbusiness.com/social-media-influencer-outreach-brand-ambassador-case-study-all-nippon-airways-analax-5338/ (accessed March 24, 2015).

238 Highfield, V. (2013) "American Airlines rewards popular social media influencers," www. totalcustomer.org/2013/05/08/american-airlines-rewards-popular-social-media-influencers/ (accessed March 24, 2015).

239 Kuchler, "Advertisers ride wave of social media influencers."

240 WorkingThree.com (2014) "How Qantas can become a digital leader," http://workingthree. com/uncategorized/qantas-can-become-digital-leader/ (accessed March 24, 2015).

241 Drell, L. (2011) "How airlines have taken flight with social media [INFOGRAPHIC]," http:// mashable.com/2011/09/16/airlines-social-media-infographic/ (accessed March 24, 2015).

242 Southwest Airlines (2015) "Nuts about Southwest," www.blogsouthwest.com/ (accessed January 25, 2015).

243 Vueling Airlines (2015) "My Vueling City," www.myvuelingcity.com/en?LGCD=1 (accessed January 27, 2015).

244 Air New Zealand (2015) "Flying social," http://theflyingsocialnetwork.com/flyingsocial/ (accessed January 25, 2015).

245 Fitzsimmons, C. (2013) "Qantas CEO Alan Joyce joins LinkedIn Influencer program, but is it worth the time?" www.brw.com.au/p/marketing/qantas_time_alan_joyce_joins_linkedin_9hlxQ BTd2oKakF0ukL7SVP (accessed March 24, 2015).

246 Loeb, S. (2014) "Now everyone can become a LinkedIn Influencer," http://vator.tv/news/2014-02-19-now-everyone-can-become-a-linkedin-influencer (accessed March 24, 2015).

247 LinkedIn, "LinkedIn."

248 Twitter, "Twitter."

249 Youtube.com (2015) "Trailer of KLM"'s new game Jets," www.youtube.com/watch?v=xraHHJ8-_ lM&feature=youtu.be (accessed March 24, 2015).

250  Gartner (2011) "Gartner says by 2015, more than 50 percent of organizations that manage innovation processes will gamify those processes," www.gartner.com/newsroom/id/1629214 (accessed March 24, 2015).

251  Mickens, D. (2012) "Turkish Airlines asks Olympics goers to fly QR flags," www.clickz.com/clickz/news/2197313/turkish-airlines-asks-olympics-goers-to-fly-qr-flags (accessed March 24, 2015).

252  Youtube.com (2015) "Sir Richard Branson's guide to getting lucky," www.youtube.com/watch?v=M_Bes6P2isY&feature=youtu.be (accessed March 24, 2015).

253  Ibid.

254  Lufthansa (2015) "Blue legends: New Lufthansa app connects frequent flyers," http://newsroom.lufthansa.com/news/blue-legends-new-lufthansa-app-connects-frequent-flyers (accessed March 24, 2015).

255  Del Nero, J. (2014) "Making connections in the sky: 4 apps that make flights more social," www.frequentbusinesstraveler.com/2014/03/making-connections-in-the-sky-4-apps-that-make-flights-more-social/ (accessed March 24, 2015).

256  Fox, L. (2011) "Goodbye Metrotwin, BA social network axed in favour of Facebook," www.tnooz.com/article/goodbye-metrotwin-ba-social-network-axed-in-favour-of-facebook/ (accessed March 24, 2015).

257  eMarketer.com (2013) "Mobile internet as spending share of total digital ad spending, by region 2011–2017," www.emarketer.com/Article/Mobile-Expands-Its-Share-of-Worldwide-Digital-Ad-Spend/1010170 (accessed March 24, 2015).

258  M-Stars.net (2009) "Mobile media workshop at Fre Sh community," www.slideshare.net/italo.gani/mobile-media-workshop-at-fre-sh-community (accessed March 24, 2015).

259  Millennial Media (2014) "Mobile travel audience," www.slideshare.net/fullscreen/corinnewan1/mobile-insights-for-travel-brands-millennial-media/4 (accessed March 24, 2015).

260  eMarketer.com, "Mobile internet as spending share of total digital ad spending, by region 2011–2017."

261  Millennial Media, "Mobile travel audience."

262  Ibid.

263  Gagnon, "Words that work for the holiday travel season."

264  Sullivan, "Mobile, tablet, desktop varies search behavior."

265  Millennial Media, "Mobile travel audience."

266  Boris, C. (2014) "Study shows one third of Google ad conversions happen on mobile," www.marketingpilgrim.com/2014/10/study-shows-one-third-of-google-ad-conversions-happen-on-mobile.html (accessed March 24, 2015).

267  Nanji, A. (2014) "Digital advertising benchmarks: performance metrics by format," www.marketingprofs.com/charts/2014/24821/digital-ad-benchmarks-performance-by-format (accessed March 24, 2015).

268  Weborama.com (2014) "iab Mobile Rising Stars," www.slideshare.net/fullscreen/fernandocomet/display-advertising-visual-guide/61 (accessed March 24, 2015).

269  Johnson, L. (2014) "JetBlue tailors mobile ads to target tablets and smartphones separately," www.mobilemarketer.com/cms/news/advertising/17518.htm (accessed March 24, 2015).

270  Bosomworth, D. (2015) "Statistics on mobile usage and adoption to inform your mobile marketing strategy," www.smartinsights.com/mobile-marketing/mobile-marketing-analytics/mobile-marketing-statistics/ (accessed March 24, 2015).

271  Millennial Media, "Mobile travel audience."

272  Johnson, "JetBlue differentiates mobile ad efforts via voice recognition."

273  JetBlue (2015) "Central perch," www.jetbluecentralperch.com (accessed January 4, 2015).

274  Johnson, L. (2013) "JetBlue differentiates mobile ad efforts via voice recognition," www. mobilemarketer.com/cms/news/advertising/16191.html (accessed March 24, 2015).

275  Ibid.

276  Perez, S. (2014) "An upper limit for apps? New data suggests consumers only use around two dozen apps per month," http://techcrunch.com/2014/07/01/an-upper-limit-for-apps-new-data-suggests-consumers-only-use-around-two-dozen-apps-per-month/ (accessed March 24, 2015).

277  Butcher, D. (2011) "SMS case study—Southwest Airlines and Entercom's WEEI," www. mobilemarketer.com/cms/resources/case-studies/8891.html (accessed March 24, 2015).

278  Harris, J. (2010) "Case study: mobile web ads more effective than mobile apps," http://techcraver.com/2010/01/21/case-study-mobile-web-ads-more-effective-than-mobile-apps/ (accessed March 24, 2015).

279  Hof, R. (2014) "Study: mobile ads actually do work—especially in apps," www.forbes.com/sites/roberthof/2014/08/27/study-mobile-ads-actually-do-work-especially-in-apps (accessed March 24, 2015).

280  M. G. (2013) "Appy days are here," www.economist.com/blogs/gulliver/2013/07/airline-apps (accessed March 24, 2015).

281  Millennial Media, "Mobile travel audience."

282  Coupmedia (2014) "Helvetic Airways," www.airways/ (accessed December 1, 2014).

283  Ibid.

284  Johnson, L. (2012) "Lufthansa seals airline bookings via QR codes," www.mobilecommercedaily.com/lufthansa-seals-airline-bookings-via-qr-codes (accessed March 24, 2015).

285  Youtube.com (2014) "Firefly Airlines: print advertisement with augmented reality," www.youtube.com/watch?v=JT9DjE9fB-Y (accessed November 15, 2014).

286  Taylor, C. (2013) "The future of advertising: 'Pay-Per-Gaze,' is just the beginning," http://mashable.com/2013/08/15/the-future-of-advertising-pay-per-gaze-is-just-the-beginning/ (accessed March 24, 2015).

287  Parker, P. (2002) "Interactive ads play big role in 'Minority Report'," www.clickz.com/clickz/news/1718239/interactive-ads-play-big-role-minority-report (accessed March 24, 2015).

288  VB.com (2011) "These 108 famous brands own their 'two letter' domain," www.vb.com/fame.htm (accessed March 24, 2015).

289  VB.com (2011) "Famous brands are becoming UNcompatible with a more and more internet minded world," www.vb.com/shame.htm (accessed March 24, 2015).

290  Verisign, Inc. (2015) "Verisign News Releases: Internet grows to 296 million domain names in second quarter of 2015", http://www.verisign.com/en_US/internet-technology-news/verisign-press-releases/articles/index.xhtml artLink=aHR0cDovL3ZlcmlzaWduduLm13bmV3c3Jvb20uY29tL2FydGljbGUvcnNzP2lkPTE5ODUwMzk%3D (accessed December 4, 2015).

291  Airliners.net (2000) "Price of delta.com domain," www.airliners.net/aviation-forums/general_aviation/read.main/281632/ (accessed March 24, 2015).

292  Lock, T. (2014) "Introduction to the new gTLDs generic top level domain names," http://todlock.com/introduction-to-the-new-gtlds-generic-top-level-domain-names/#.U0wdbRYaV6d (accessed March 24, 2015).

293  Verisign, "Verisign News Releases: Internet grows to 296 million domain names in second quarter of 2015".

294  Ibid.

295  DomainTyper (2015) "Top websites with .travel," http://domaintyper.com/top-websites/most-popular-websites-with-travel-domain/page/1 (accessed March 24, 2015).

296  Ibid.

297  Centr (2014), "Centr Domain Wire, Domain Name Stat Report", https://centr.org/system/files/share/domainwire_stat_report_2014_1.pdf (accessed December 5, 2015).

298  CAPA News (2014) "Hawaiian launches Beijing Service," http://centreforaviation.com/profiles/airlines/hawaiian-airlines-ha#news (accessed April 17, 2014).

299  Higgins, C. (2012) "The weird world of country-specific web domains," http://mentalfloss.com/article/30583/weird-world-country-specific-web-domains (accessed March 24, 2015).

300  Voice of America (2014) "New Internet name rule opens door to huge changes," www.voanews.com/content/new-internet-name-rule-opens-door-to-huge-changes-124180874/141045.html) (accessed March 24, 2015).

301  ICANN (2015) "New generic top level domains," http://newgtlds.icann.org/en/program-status/delegated-strings (accessed March 24, 2015).

302  qz.com (2014) "The biggest land rush in the history of the internet starts on February 4." http://qz.com/165238/the-biggest-land-rush-in-the-history-of-the-internet-begins-on-february-4/ (accessed May 3, 2014).

303  ICANN (2015) "Current application status." https://gtldresult.icann.org/application-result/applicationstatus (accessed March 24, 2015).

304  Ibid. (check application detail section for .Virgin).

305  Ibid. (check application detail section for .Swiss).

306  Ibid. (check application detail section for .Swiss).

307  Lock, "Introduction to the new gTLDs generic top level domain names."

308  Allemann, A. (2009) "Study questions if consumers want new top level domains." http://domainnamewire.com/2009/06/09/study-questions-if-consumers-want-new-top-level-domains (accessed March 24, 2015)

309  Ibid.

310  Linkedin, "Linkedin."

311  Twitter, "Twitter."

312  YouTube, "YouTube."

313  Evaair.mobi (2015) "evaair.mobi www.evaair.mobi (accessed November 11, 2014).

314  Evaair.org (2015) "evaair.org," www.evaair.org (accessed November 11, 2014).

315  Asia Travel (2015) "asia-travel.de," http://asia-travel.de (accessed November 11, 2014).

316  Kee, T. (2007) "McAfee: Gaming, airlines sites most likely typo-squatter targets," www.mediapost.com/publications/article/73092/mcafee-gaming-airlines-sites-most-likely-typo-sq.html?edition (accessed March 24, 2015).

317  Hobson, J. (2012) "The first step to merger: Buying domain names?" www.marketplace.org/topics/business/mid-day-update/first-step-merger-buying-domain-names (accessed March 31, 2015).

318  Lee, R. (2012) "US airways buys domain names, hinting at merger with American," www.ibtimes.com/us-airways-buys-domain-names-hinting-merger-american-424378 (accessed March 24, 2015).

319  BBC Trending (2014) "#BBCtrending: How the MH370 website ended up on eBay," www.bbc.com/news/blogs-trending-26515165 (accessed March 24, 2015).

320 Silver, E. (2014) "Malaysian airlines crash domain names already being registered." www.domaininvesting.com/malaysian-airlines-crash-domain-names-already-registered/ (accessed March 24, 2015).

321 Harvard Law "Analysis of Key UDRP Issues," http://cyber.law.harvard.edu/udrp/analysis.html (accessed March 24, 2015).

322 WIPO Arbitration and Mediation Center (2009) "Administrative panel decision: Delta Air Lines, Inc. v. Jannie Blazek," www.wipo.int/amc/en/domains/decisions/html/2009/d2009-1172.html (accessed March 24, 2015).

323 Various corporate hate websites set up by individuals under their real name or pseudonym.

324 WIPO (2005) "WIPO domain name decisions"—Arbitration and Mediation Center, www.wipo.int/amc/en/domains/decisions/html/2005/d2005-0168.html (accessed February 4, 2014).

325 Our-Law.com, www.our-law.com/page-5781 (accessed March 24, 2015).

326 Untied.com (2015) "Untied.com," www.untied.com (accessed November 12, 2014).

327 Author e-commerce archive (2008) "GlennTilton.com," http://glenntilton.com (accessed in 2008).

328 Hills, M. (2014) "Facebook investigates a fake Qantas page using the airline's 'birthday celebrations' to convince customers to hand over personal details for the chance to win a $1500 travel voucher," www.dailymail.co.uk/news/article-2757328/Fake-Qantas-Facebook-page-using-airline-s-birthday-celebrations-convince-customers-hand-personal-details-chance-win-1500-travel-voucher.html (accessed March 24, 2015).

329 ABS-CBNNews.com (2014) "Cebu Pacific warns vs fake airline reps on Facebook," www.abs-cbnnews.com/business/11/25/14/cebu-pacific-warns-vs-fake-airline-reps-facebook (accessed March 24, 2015).

330 Cheng, R. (2012) "Beware: Fake airline Instagram accounts promise free flights," www.cnet.com/news/beware-fake-airline-instagram-accounts-promise-free-flights/ (accessed March 24, 2015).

331 Buffalo Law Review (2010) "Brandjacking on social networks: trademark infringement by impersonation of markholders," www.buffalolawreview.org/past_issues/58_4/Ramsey.pdf (accessed March 24, 2015).

332 Public Relations Society of America (2009) "PR blotter: Twitter users have caused an uproar by impersonating celebrities on the popular micro-blogging service, but now businesses are also targets of fake Twitter profiles — sometimes from competitors," www.prsa.org/Intelligence/Tactics/Articles/view/6C-080913/101/PR_Blotter_Twitter_users_have_caused_an_uproar_by#.VIuamWd0xgU (accessed March 24, 2015).

333 Sauro, J. (2014) "The user experience of airline & aggregator websites," www.measuringu.com/blog/airline-benchmarks.php (accessed March 24, 2015).

334 American Airlines (2002) "www.aa.com," http://web.archive.org/web/20020920071525/www.aa.com/ (accessed March 24, 2015).

335 RyanAir (2002) "www.ryanair.com," http://web.archive.org/web/20020928092451/www.ryanair.com/ (accessed March 24, 2015).

336 Air Namibia (2014) "Fly to Namibia—Air Namibia," www.airnamibia.com/ (accessed November 24, 2014).

337 Ethiopian Airlines (2015) "Ethiopian Airlines website homepage," www.flyethiopianairlines.com (accessed May 23, 2015).

338 Air Mauritius (ca 2012) "Initial findings from heuristic study." Author's e-commerce archive.

339  Saettler, M. (2014) "United Airlines plots new course to ramp up on mobile," www.mobilemarketer.com/cms/news/software-technology/17862.html (accessed March 14, 2015).

340  Noack, S. (2010) "A look into color theory in web design," http://sixrevisions.com/web_design/a-look-into-color-theory-in-web-design/ (accessed March 24, 2015).

341  Peach (2014) "Peach," www.flypeach.com/home.aspx (accessed July 7, 2014).

342  Lufthansa.com (2014) "Lufthansa," www.lufthansa.com/us/en/homepage (accessed July 7, 2014).

343  Bernard, M. (2002) "A comparison of popular online fonts: which size and type is best?" http://usabilitynews.org/a-comparison-of-popular-online-fonts-which-size-and-type-is-best/ (accessed March 24, 2015).

344  Ibid.

345  Drego, V.L. et al. (2008) "Best and worse of B2C Site Design," www.forrester.com/Best+And+Worst+Of+B2C+Site+Design+2008/fulltext/-/E-res45718 (accessed August 25, 2014).

346  Rogowski, R. (2008) "Website imagery that builds brands," www.forrester.com/Web+Site+Imagery+That+Builds+Brands/fulltext/-/E-res46945 (accessed August 25, 2014).

347  F-i.com (2014) "Fi," www.f-i.com/ (accessed July 15, 2014).

348  Myanmar Airways International (2015) "Myanmar Airways International," www.maiair.com/ (accessed July 7, 2015).

349  Etihad Airways (2014) "Etihad Airways," www.delta.com/ (accessed July 7, 2014).

350  Air Asia (2014) "Air Asia," www.airasia.com/ (accessed July 7, 2014).

351  Vanilla Air (2014) "Vanilla Air," www.vanilla-air.com/en/ (accessed July 7, 2014).

352  Klementi, K. (2014) "Geometric web design 2014. Revision of the most-used shapes," http://blog.templatemonster.com/2014/01/29/geometric-web-design-2014-most-used-shapes/ (accessed March 24, 2015).

353  Qatar Airways (2014) "Qatar Airways," www.qatarairways.com/us/en/homepage.page?iid=ALL29109910 (accessed December 13, 2014).

354  Emirates (2014) "Emirates," www.emirates.com/us/english/index.aspx (accessed June 16, 2014).

355  Cathay Pacific (2015) "Cathay Pacific," www.cathaypacific.com (accessed June 23, 2015).

356  Virgin Australia (2014) "Virgin Australia," www.virginaustralia.com/au/en/ (accessed June 16, 2014).

357  British Airways (2014) "British Airways," www.britishairways.com/travel/home/public/en_us (accessed June 16, 2014).

358  Angola Airlines (2014) "TAAG a Sua Companhia de Semre," http://taag.com/ (accessed July 15, 2014).

359  Vitello, P. (2012) "George A. Miller, a pioneer in cognitive psychology, is dead at 92," www.nytimes.com/2012/08/02/us/george-a-miller-cognitive-psychology-pioneer-dies-at-92.html?pagewanted=all&_r=0 (accessed March 24, 2015).

360  Kalbach, J. (2002) "The myth of 'seven, plus or minus 2'," www.drdobbs.com/web-development/the-myth-of-seven-plus-or-minus-2/184412300 (accessed March 24, 2015).

361  Fiji Airways (2015) "Fiji Airways," www.fijiairways.com/ (accessed January 30, 2015).

362  Lufthansa, "Lufthansa."

363  Tunisair (2015) "Tunisair," www.tunisair.com/site/publish/content/default.asp?lang=en (accessed January 30, 2015).

364  Arsenault, M. (2012) "How valuable is Amazon's 1-click patent? It's worth billions," http://blog.rejoiner.com/2012/07/amazon-1click-patent/ (accessed March 24, 2015).

365  Tnooz.com (2014) "The evolution of the RyanAir website," www.tnooz.com/wp-content/uploads/2015/02/ryanair-30-FULL.jpg (accessed March 24, 2015).

366  FutureTravelExperience.com (2015) "Qantas rolling out auto check-in across domestic network," www.futuretravelexperience.com/2015/03/qantas-rolling-auto-check-across-domestic-network/?utm_source=Future+Travel+Experience+Newsletter&utm_campaign=c45409b0da-fte_otg_nl_190315&utm_medium=email&utm_term=0_c306aa3edf-c45409b0da-89609589 (accessed March 24, 2015).

367  Korean Airlines (2015) "Korean Air," www.koreanair.com/global/en.html (accessed January 30, 2015).

368  Kenya Airways (2014) "Kenya Airways," www.kenya-airways.com/?gclid=CP-s0fHXzMQCFRSVfgodt0gASQ (accessed December 14, 2014).

369  Everts, T. (2014) "55 web performance stats you'll want to know," http://blog.radware.com/applicationdelivery/applicationaccelerationoptimization/2014/01/55-web-performance-stats-youll-want-to-know/ (accessed March 24, 2015).

370  Smith, B. and Darrow, R. (2007) "Travelocity becomes a travel retailer," www.math.washington.edu/~billey/classes/honors.350/articles/Week.7.pdf (accessed March 31, 2015).

371  Everts, "55 web performance stats you'll want to know."

372  Tnooz.com (2013) "Speed demons and slowpokes: These are the travel industry benchmarks," www.tnooz.com/article/speed-demons-and-slowpokes-these-are-the-travel-industry-benchmarks/ (accessed March 24, 2015).

373  European Commission (2015) "Accessible Tourism," http://ec.europa.eu/enterprise/sectors/tourism/accessibility/index_en.htm (accessed March 24, 2015).

374  American Foundation for the Blind (2014) "Access Now, Inc. v. Southwest Airlines, Co," http://afp.org/Section.asp?SectionID=49&TopicID=262&DocumentID=2410 (accessed March 24, 2015).

375  Department of Transport (2013) *14 CFR Parts 382 and 399, 49 CFR Part 27, Non-Discrimination on the Basis of Disability in Air Travel: Accessibility of Websites and Automated Kiosks at US Airports*, Federal Register, Vol. 78, No. 218.

376  Ibid.

377  British Airways, "British Airways."

378  Adage (2015) "Ad Age: Agency family trees," http://adage.coverleaf.com/advertisingage/201505 04?pg=72#pg72 (accessed on October 2, 2015).

379  Third Door Media (2014) "Market intelligence report: digital advertising agencies 2014: a buyer's guide," http://downloads.digitalmarketingdepot.com/rs/thirddoormedia/images/MIR_1304_DigAgenc13%20_2.0.pdf?mkt_tok=3RkMMJWWfF9wsRoksqXBZKXonjHpfsX77%2BksUa%2BwlMI%2F0ER3fOvrPUfGjI4FRMRgI%2BSLDwEYGJlv6SgFTbLCMbpx37gNXxU%3D (accessed March 24, 2015).

380  Dan, A. (2013) "What are 10 great ad agencies of 2013, according to CMOs?" www.forbes.com/sites/avidan/2013/12/04/ten-great-agencies-of-2013/ (accessed March 24, 2015).

381  Ibid.

382  Vranica, S. (2013) "Why does it take so many companies to produce one digital ad?" www.wsj.com/articles/SB10001424052702304672404579181621467692940 (accessed March 24, 2015).

383  Field, D. and Rehse, O. (2013) "Cutting complexity, adding value, efficiency and effectiveness in digital advertising," www.bcgperspectives.com/content/articles/media_entertainment_marketing_cutting_complexity_adding_value_efficiency_effectiviness_digital_advertising (accessed April 8, 2015).

384  McMains, A. (2013) "Spirit Airlines selects a new lead agency," www.adweek.com/news/advertising-branding/spirit-airlines-selects-new-lead-agency-153515 (accessed March 24, 2015).

385  Third Door Media, "Market intelligence report."

386  Naidu, V. (2014) "Lufthansa India invites fans to park the A380 on facebook," http://lighthouseinsights.in/lufthansa-india-park-the-a380-facebook-campaign.html (accessed March 24, 2015).

387  Magee, K. (2014) "South African Airways hands digital media to UM London," www.campaignlive.co.uk/news/1228758/ (accessed March 24, 2015).

388  Jacob, E. (2012) "Kolle Rebbe: Internationales Team für Lufthansa hebt ab," www.horizont.net/agenturen/nachrichten/-Kolle-Rebbe-Internationales-Team-fuer-Lufthansa-hebt-ab-108031 (accessed March 24, 2015).

389  Amirkhizi, M. (2013) "Kolle Rebbe erhält auch den Online-Etat von Lufthansa," www.horizont.net/agenturen/nachrichten/Buendelung-Kolle-Rebbe-erhaelt-auch-den-Online-Etat-von-Lufthansa-116694 (accessed March 24, 2015).

390  Jacob, E. (2013) "Mindshare muss wieder in den Pitch-Ring steigen," www.horizont.net/agenturen/nachrichten/Lufthansa-Mindshare-muss-wieder-in-den-Pitch-Ring-steigen-116192 (accessed March 24, 2015).

391  Ogilvy & Mather Group UK (2012) "OgilvyOne UK wins British Airways digital business," http://ogilvy.co.uk/agencies/ogilvy-one2012/03/19/ogilvyone-uk-wins-british-airways-digital-business/ (accessed March 24, 2015).

392  Faull, J. (2013) "WPP looking to create a new agency dedicated to servicing United Airlines," www.thedrum.com/news/2013/12/07/wpp-looking-create-new-agency-dedicated-servicing-united-airlines (accessed March 24, 2015).

393  Wikipedia (2015) "Lester Wunderman," http://en.wikipedia.org/wiki/Lester_Wunderman (accessed March 24, 2015).

394  O'Leary, N., "Spirit Airlines launches new ad strategy."

395  Irish Times (2014) "Ryanair Trebles ad budget as O'Leary embraces TV," www.irishtimes.com/business/sectors/media-and-marketing/ryanair-trebles-ad-budget-as-o-leary-embraces-tv-1.1656350 (accessed March 24, 2015).

396  Ibid.

397  mUmBRELLA.com (2013) "Maxus retains JetStar." http://mumbrella.com.au/maxus-retains-jetstar-142448 (accessed March 24, 2015).

398  Campaign AsiaPacific (2012) "Maxus wins pitch for Jetstar's $40 million media account," www.campaignasia.com/Article/334729,Maxus+wins+pitch+for+Jetstars+$40+million+media+account.aspx (accessed March 24, 2015).

399  SearcherMagnet (2014) "Internet advertising: a timeline," www.searchermag.net/internet-advertising-timeline/ (accessed March 24, 2015).

400  Goldsmith, S. (2014) "Zooppa summons global online creativity to make ads a very different way," www.bizjournals.com/seattle/print-edition/2014/09/26/zooppa-summons-global-online-creativity-to-make.html?page=all (accessed March 24, 2015).

401  TiraGraffi (2013) "Zooppa contest and the new Alitalia: 6 ways to tell excellence in flight," http://translate.google.com/translate?hl=en&sl=it&u=www.tiragraffi.it/segnalazioni/bandi-e-concorsi/2013/01/zooppa-e-il-nuovo-contest-alitalia-8-modi-per-raccontare-leccellenza-in-volo/&prev=search (accessed March 24, 2015).

# Chapter 4

# Airline e-sales and distribution

Convenience drives demand.

Unknown author

## 4.1 E-SALES MARKET SIZE AND REGIONAL ASPECTS

Global online travel sales are big and exceeded $533 billion in 2015. This corresponded to almost half of the world's total travel sales. It is expected that online sales will continue rising through 2019 reaching $762 billion.[1] As previously discussed in the introduction of Chapter 1, a combination of factors is responsible for this continuous growth. Among them are inexpensive access to an ever more ubiquitous internet, online travel's mass market appeal, changing shopper behavior, favorable demographics, and the arrival of new large marketing and technology-savvy companies in the travel space. When looking at specific geographic regions, Europe and North America account for today's lion's share of global online travel with 34% and 28%, respectively. Other parts of the world including the Middle East /Africa with 5% and Central and Eastern Europe with 2% claim a much smaller share. However, despite their small size, they grew strongly in 2015 with 18% and 10%, respectively (Figure 4.1).

With Europe and North America becoming more mature online markets, their growth rates will slow down and be in the single digits in the years ahead (Western Europe with an 8% growth in 2015 is already plateauing although the $186 billion in e-sales for 2019 are still formidable). What is the implication of this development for airlines operating in these markets and looking for sustainable growth of their online business? It essentially means that they have to increasingly go after web travelers who are currently doing business with other players including competitors and online travel agencies. A unique selling position, for example by offering personalized products and services, will therefore be crucial more than ever before in order to attract new customers and maintain their loyalty. This is particularly the case for the up and coming millennial travelers who will account for a significant share of the future online travel demand. In markets with double-digit growth rates, the focus for a large part will still be on enticing existing offline shoppers to cross over to online. Additionally, there are also new bookers from generation Z who have never purchased travel before and will fuel the demand for airlines' online travel products and services.

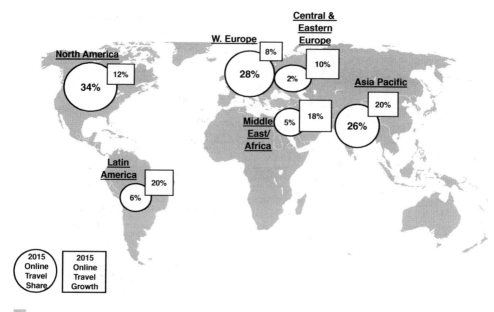

**Figure 4.1** *E-travel sales share and e-travel sales growth by region (2015)*

*Source:* eMarketer (2015)[2]

There are a number of regional facts and figures worth mentioning (Figure 4.2). For example, the United States is the world's single largest source country for online travel. In 2014, it generated $145 billion in e-travel sales. Interestingly, $26 billion

## Global Online Travel: From $534 Billion in 2015 to $762 Billion in 2019

### USA
$145 Billion (2014)
Mobile accounted for:
- $26 billion (+60% vs 2013)
- 18% of all online travel sales
- 38% of US shoppers used mobile for buying online travel (vs 25% in 2012)

### Latin America
+25% growth in 2014
Markets where online travel accounts for significant share of general B2C:
- Mexico with over 65%
- Brazil with over 35%
- Brazil is predicted to spend $10 billion on online travel in 2016

### Europe
Almost 50% of all EU travelers book online
UK: 50% of leisure travel booked online
Italy & Spain: Fastest growth with 10%+ through 2016

### Middle East
UAE: 46% of all airline tickets are sold online
Kuwait: 34%
Saudi Arabia: 23%
OTAs reached $14 billion in 2014

### Asia Pacific
Japan: Largest online market, accounting for 32% of total
China: 61% growth (2013 vs 2015) reaching $29 billion
India: 25% growth, 2nd fastest growing market

| Region | 2015 | → | 2019 |
|---|---|---|---|
| North America | $179B | → | $220B |
| Western Europe | $152B | → | $186B |
| Asia Pacific | $139B | → | $243B |
| Latin America | $30B | → | $55B |
| Middle East/Africa | $24B | → | $45B |
| Central/Eastern Europe | $10B | → | $14B |

**Figure 4.2** *A snapshot of online travel sales developments by region (rounded figures)*

*Source:* Weps (2014),[3] Del Rosso (2014),[4] Etc-digital.org (2013),[5] TripInfo.com (2015),[6] Arabian Travel Market (2014),[7] eMarketer (2015),[8] Tnooz (2015)[9]

of this volume came from mobile sales alone. This represents an increase of almost 60% versus 2013 and 18% of the country's total e-travel sales.

Western Europe as a region has the highest online travel penetration with almost 50%. The most active online travel shoppers are in the UK where over 50% of leisure travelers book online. At the same time, both Italy and Spain show the largest increases in online travel growth. Latin America is the fastest growing region. In 2014, its online travel sales grew by over 25% with 2015 posting another strong year with a 20% increase. Brazil and Mexico largely drive this trend.

For 2015, Asia–Pacific reached $139 billion. It is the fast growing online travel region and is poised to overtake the US in a few years and become the world's largest market for online travel. For 2019, it is forecasted that $243 billion of online sales will be generated. The biggest single source market in the Asia Pacific region is currently Japan. It accounted for over 30% of the region's total. However, as China keeps on growing its e-sales thanks to a burgeoning middle-class with more disposable income to spend on travel, Japan's dominant position will decrease. In 2015, China reached $29 billion which equated to a 61% growth over its e-sales volume in 2013. Not to be discounted is India that is the second fastest growing market.

## 4.2 SETTING THE STAGE: A BRIEF HISTORY OF E-SALES AND DISTRIBUTION

The roots of today's electronic marketplace in the airline industry go back to the 1964 launch of American Airlines' in-house computer reservation system (CRS) called SABRE. It enabled American Airlines to electronically manage the growing volume/complexity of seat inventory and pricing data much more efficiently and effectively. Other airlines around the world followed suit and built similar systems.

In the 1970s, the airlines' in-house CRSs were externalized and installed with travel agencies via special desktop terminals. The industry's first B2B information exchange and industry-wide electronic marketplace were born. Through the airline CRSs, travel agencies realized similar efficiencies as airlines when researching and booking tickets for their clients. Providing travel agencies access to their CRSs gave airlines additional influence with their top sales partners.

Throughout the 1980s, the CRSs evolved into more complex Global Distribution System (GDS) companies. The emergence of electronic data interchange (EDI) standards enabled real-time communication with the former airline CRSs that now featured different types of multiple travel suppliers such as airlines, hotels, and car rentals. Travel agencies engaged in comparison-shopping for their customers and checked on prices and other travel information across many suppliers.

In the 1990s, several significant developments occurred. The advent of the worldwide web coupled with the release of the first internet browser ushered in the era of the commercial internet. Airlines launched their official websites and gave web travelers direct access to their reservation systems for the first time. This development empowered shoppers to an unprecedented level as they could now manage on their own crucial steps of the travel life cycle including search and purchase. Another new player, the online travel agency, embodied by Expedia and Travelocity, entered the marketplace.

During the 2000s, other important online entities became integral parts of the e-sales and distribution system. Among them were LCCs, meta-travel search engines and social media companies. Alternative GDSs, the so-called GNEs, arrived on the scene and marketed themselves as new low-cost distribution intermediaries. Airlines leveraged them in their ongoing battle with GDSs from which they extracted discounts on distribution fees. Furthermore, with the release of Apple's iPhone, consumers' adoption of mobile devices entered the mainstream. Moreover, airlines started turning into retailers by unbundling their products/services. This was supported by internet XML-based communication standards and marked the beginning of the airline industry's era of merchandising. Some airlines also started distributing in a so-called direct connect approach.

Travelers who in the past interacted with and relied largely on a single source— their trusted travel agent—have now themselves become very engaged in the research, planning, and shopping stages of the travel cycle. Multi-device usage (PC/ laptop, smart phone/tablet) and multi-website type access (airline/OTA/referral/ social websites) have become common and trump the traditional face-to-face/phone channels between the airline/travel agent and traveler. Traditional travel agencies handling the leisure side of air travel have significantly declined in numbers and the ones remaining today mostly play a niche role. At the same time, for corporate travel, traditional agencies still hold their position as the primary handler of travel arrangements and bookings. Some LCCs, in their attempt to capture a share of the business travel market, have even entered relationships with them despite the higher cost of doing business in this segment.

Noteworthy is also the trend of consumerization of corporate travel. Business travelers increasingly demand access to the same kinds of booking features from their corporate booking tools that they can find today on OTAs and airline websites. Unless corporate travel departments upgauge their platforms, so-called "open bookings" whereby business travelers book outside the corporate system, are likely to increase. This could be beneficial for an airline that comes up with an innovative solution to capture this business. The challenge is to extend specific fare discounts negotiated with a corporation to open booking platforms.

In our following discussion, we will come back to many of the developments and issues touched on in our high-level, historical run-through of e-sales and distribution.

## 4.3 MARKETPLACE STRUCTURES FOR AIRLINE E-COMMERCE

The marketplace structure for airline e-commerce describes how airlines sell and distribute their products and services to web travelers. It is important to highlight that e-sales and distribution is increasingly diverse. We do not any longer only deal with the "standard" topics such as revenue generation, distribution costs, types of sales outlets used, and the choices made for behind-the-scene GDS distribution intermediaries.

Today, e-sales and distribution has to be viewed in a wider context of how an airline is shopped for, perceived, booked, and rated across the entire travel ecosystem. In this regard, an airline's own social media presence, the impact of social media influencers, travel reviews, and likes and followers cannot be underestimated. The same goes for the crucial role of referral channels in the form of travel meta-search engines and affiliate programs. Airline e-sales and distribution is becoming more intertwined with e-marketing. For the lack of a better word, one may refer to this development as the "marketing-ization" of e-sales and distribution. Airlines treating e-sales and distribution in a silo and not recognizing their close relationship with e-marketing run the risk of not connecting the right dots when managing this area.

### 4.3.1 E-sales and distribution: A high-level overview

There are different ways to categorize the venue where an airline ticket sale is handled. One approach is to refer to direct and indirect channels depending on whether a shopper goes through an airline-owned outlet or a third party. With e-commerce, an additional differentiation between online or offline channels has also become popular. We discuss these venues in more detail below.

*Retail channels*

They can be direct, airline-owned such as a city ticket office, or a call center. They can also involve indirect, third-party-owned retail channels including travel agencies. A further differentiation is between offline and online channels. Offline channels have their origins in a pre-internet era and most of them have been in existence for a long time. Examples are airline call centers that entered the scene in the 1970s and modern travel agencies that date back to the 1840s. Online channels are internet based and were introduced in the marketplace as of the mid-/late 1990s. Airline websites and online travel agencies such as Opodo and Orbitz are examples.

Most companies that operate travel retail channels today are hybrids. This means they conduct business via both offline and online channels. However, depending on their corporate roots and how they started out, one of the two typically outweighs the other, in some cases by a wide margin. LCCs, for example, are known to handle the large majority of their business online. Carriers such as Ryanair produce over 90% of their revenue through ryanair.com. Conversely, the Germany-based TUI Group, the world's largest travel company, has its origins in a pre-internet era and largely built its business in the offline world. Over the years, they have also expanded into cyberspace but their online business is significantly smaller. Reverse migrations of pure online players to the offline world are rare but they do occur. An example is Expedia that opened physical sales outlets in India as part of its partnership with Air Asia in 2013.[10]

*Referral and social channels*

Referral channels including general search engines, travel meta-search engine providers, and affiliates literally refer web travelers to a selected group of airlines and

OTAs. Referrers do not handle the sale themselves. However, they are often one of the first points of contact for web travelers and they generate important leads by passing the web traveler on to retail outlets that manage online bookings. In the case of travel meta-search engines, it is possible that they do not operate under their own brand but power another one from behind the scenes. An example of this arrangement is the online portal Yahoo that uses meta-search engine provider Hipmunk to handle travel queries for Yahoo Travel.

Social media are another important online-only player in the e-sales and distribution system. As in the case of referral channels, social media platforms do not handle a sale themselves—an exception is when a carrier offers booking engine features through social media platforms (KLM is currently one of those few companies using Facebook and Twitter for online bookings). Nevertheless, an airline's own marketing and even customer service activities through social media create and reinforce brand awareness. This in turn could be of benefit or detriment to an airline's e-sales and distribution system.

Traditional network carriers, because of their legacy, generally use a mix of direct/indirect and offline/online channels. In recent years, they have been increasingly focused on shifting their sales toward direct/online channels. LCCs, on the other hand, have always cultivated the direct relationship with their target audience. They largely use direct online retail channels such as their websites for their sales, although some of them have also become involved with travel agencies and travel meta-search engines.

### Airline computer reservation systems and global distribution system intermediaries

An airline's supply is the product or three ingredients: seat inventory, fares, and flight schedule. Various airline departments feed all three in the company's reservation system. From there the supply is electronically distributed in real time to the retail channels on the sales frontline. An airline also shares individual supply ingredients with other third parties. They include the Airline Tariffs Publishing Company (ATPCO) for fares and the Official Airline Guide (OAG) for flight schedule. These parties in turn are sourced by GDSs for fares and flight schedule. They are bundled with seat inventory from the airlines so GDSs can now also offer the airline supply through their platforms to retail channels as well.

An airline CRS comes essentially in three forms:

- A proprietary system exclusively built and customized by a technology provider for an airline. Examples of technology companies are IBM and Hewlett Packard. Both Air Canada and American Airlines have gone for such an arrangement.
- A standard, on-the-shelf system with some customization supplied by a CRS provider like Navitaire (used by AirAsia) and Radixx (FlyDubai is one of their clients).

■ A system hosted uniquely for the airline by one of the major GDSs. With this set-up, an airline's relevant CRS information is partitioned from the general GDS so there is no mix with other information available through the GDS. Amadeus, for example, powers the CRS for British Airways.

When it comes to GDSs, aside from a few regional players, there are three global companies: Amadeus, Sabre, and Travelport. They operate in key travel markets around the world, generate billions of dollars in revenue, and feature supply content of hundreds of airlines and other travel providers such as hotels, car rentals, and travel insurance companies (a more detailed profile on GDS is provided in section 4.6.5 in this chapter).

Computer reservation systems are the key supply source for a carrier's direct retail channels (both offline and online). GDSs on the other hand are linked to indirect retail channels, first and foremost to travel agencies. The GDS-based distribution set-up has come under increasing strain and a growing number of airlines do business (or are at least looking into this) with indirect retail outlets without GDSs. Airlines' primary reason for bypassing GDSs is cost savings they can realize by not using this distribution intermediary. At the same time, another increasingly important driver to pursue a GDS bypass has to do with airlines wanting to price and brand their supply uniquely. Ancillary sales play a large role in this. GDSs still have limitations to accommodate this development (although they are catching up) while airlines tapping into their CRSs do not. We come back to this issue in later sections of this chapter.

Figure 4.3 is an overview of the airline e-commerce marketplace structure.

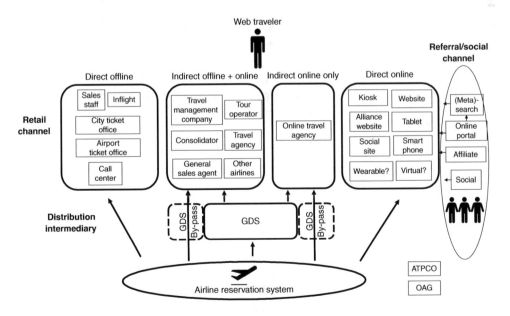

**Figure 4.3** *The airline e-commerce marketplace*

## 4.4 SELLING DIRECTLY VS SELLING INDIRECTLY

Direct sales is about sales activities that an airline manages through its own channels. As discussed earlier, they comprise both offline and online outlets. Today, for many airlines, the website has emerged as the number one direct sales channel, ahead of the call center that used to be the primary direct sales outlet. Figure 4.4 shows airlines from different geographies and business models their typical e-sales shares.

An LCC generates the bulk of its sales online. The key platform is the carrier's own website accounting for an estimated 70% to 80%. So far, mobile sales are a small fraction of total sales with another 5% to 10% but are poised to grow at the expense of an airline's website. One key driver of this development is the demand by the "mobile first" generation, the millennial travelers. Several LCCs including JetBlue and easyJet also work with OTAs such as Expedia that produce another 5% to 10% of total sales. Working with OTAs—and therefore most likely also with GDSs—increases distribution cost. However, LCCs justify this with their strategy to penetrate the corporate travel market that still works with middlemen including travel agencies and GDSs. Ironically, as LCCs become increasingly involved in this market segment, their own website share will decline a bit. Any remaining contribution to sales comes from offline channels including call centers, airport offices, and even traditional travel agencies.

A typical legacy airline based in Europe and the United States produces today somewhere between 55% and 75% in total online sales. These are markets with highly evolved online demand for domestic and international travel. Generally, between 30% and 40% come from the carrier's website while OTAs account for a

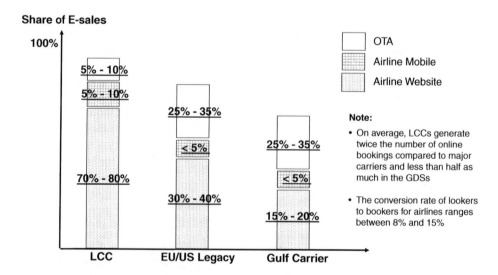

**Figure 4.4** *Typical e-sales for airlines (2015)★*

★ Author assessment based on public and private data.

significant, albeit smaller portion ranging from 25% to 35%. OTAs used to be higher but airlines have been pushing away from them in recent years as they aim to capture more business through their own digital properties. Mobile sales are less than 5% at this stage. At the same time, sales through traditional offline channels still account in some cases for 30%–40%. This is a reflection of carriers' still existing legacy in the offline world, their relatively larger share of managing corporate travel bookings, and the lower degree of customer readiness for online travel shopping in certain international markets. For example, United Airlines still operates over 40 city ticket offices in Latin America because the majority of local travelers are accustomed to doing business offline, specifically face to face, for service and shopping.

One exception of a legacy carrier that does not fit this mold and has managed to generate online sales in size and make-up similar to that of an LCC is Irish airline Aer Lingus. Faced with possible bankruptcy in 2001 and suffering major financial losses due to competition from LCC Ryanair, then CEO Willie Walsh turned the company around within two years. Among the key decisions taken was to position aerlingus.com as the primary sales channel and compete with Ryanair on LCC terms and not as a legacy airline. Within four years, the carrier's online sales grew from 4% in 2001 to 70% in 2005.[11] This was further increased and today the carrier's website is responsible for over 80% of total sales, among the highest of any legacy airline in the world.

Gulf carriers currently produce 15% to 20% of sales through their own websites.[12] This is relatively low but the result of several factors. First, Gulf airlines serve many markets in their global route network that are still evolving in terms of e-commerce and online travel. Even in their immediate neighborhood, the culture of shopping in the Gulf States still favors offline outlets. Second, in order to capture market share from established airlines and build their fifth freedom traffic, early on Gulf carriers partnered with traditional travel agencies. These were (and still are) often paid commissions and overrides—compensations that otherwise have largely disappeared for offline agencies by US and European airlines in their efforts to save distribution costs. Third, Gulf carriers are also active in the corporate travel market that generally involves travel agencies, both offline and online. Fourth, the Gulf carriers comprise many long-haul routes that are essentially (at least for now) not exposed to LCCs.

No what matter the geography or business model, airlines will continue striving for more control over their sales and distribution activities. This means shifting as much business as possible to direct online channels because the resultant benefits in the form of cost savings, new direct 1:1 relationships with customers, and unprecedented branding and pricing opportunities are just too compelling to ignore. In this development, a carrier's website as a booking platform will continue playing the dominant role. Figure 4.5 shows how the airline industry sees the relative importance of individual direct sales channels beyond 2015.

Noteworthy is the rapid rise of the mobile channel. It is the fastest growing method of online travel booking and is predicted to be a close second to the website channel. In Europe and the United States, mobile bookings for travel are estimated to double their share of total online bookings within two years from 2013 to 2015

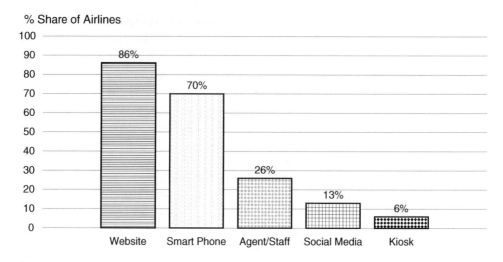

% Share of Airlines

***Figure 4.5*** *Dominant direct sales channels beyond 2015*

Source: SITA (2012)[13]

(Figure 4.6). If this trend continues, it is likely that the majority of travel search and booking will be done on mobile devices within the next four to six years. Thus, the concept of mobiles as a separate channel will eventually disappear in the future.

The picture with social media is very different. Their role as a sales channel in the airline industry is significantly smaller. This is because web travelers use social media primarily to connect/engage with other travelers and airline brands. The purchase of

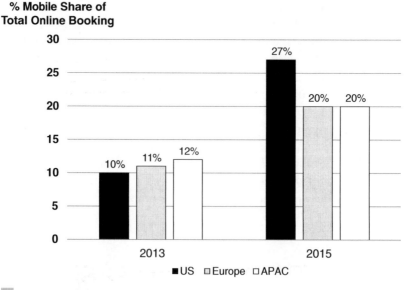

% Mobile Share of
Total Online Booking

***Figure 4.6*** *The rise of mobile travel bookings*

Source: Sileo (2014)[14]

airline tickets is not a top consideration for them. At the same time, airlines have yet to introduce tools that make social purchases for web travelers possible or more attractive. In this respect, one may be reminded again of the scaled-down Facebook booking engines that several carriers including Delta had launched in 2010. They were quietly discontinued after a few years because of lack of demand by web travelers.

Interestingly, KLM has recently demonstrated that social channels can generate revenue for a carrier provided that a tool optimized for a social environment is used. With the airline's new social pay feature that was launched in February 2014, web travelers can now pay for their tickets, upgrades, and rebookings via Facebook and Twitter. In 2014, this service generated €25 million in social sales, a number they plan to double during 2015.[15] This is an admittedly small fraction of the carrier's overall revenue but it is substantial enough to warrant attention and other airlines should take notice of such application. If and when more carriers decide to adopt similar socially optimized features, social sales may have more sales potential than currently estimated.

### 4.4.1 The issue of disintermediation, re-intermediation, and counter-mediation

The arrival of the internet and the application of internet-based technology has forced airlines to redesign the relationship with their target audience. In this regard, one specific development and one that has received much attention—is the so-called disintermediation. There are other redesigned relationships, among them re-intermediation and counter-mediation (Figure 4.7). Our following discussion covers each of them in more detail.

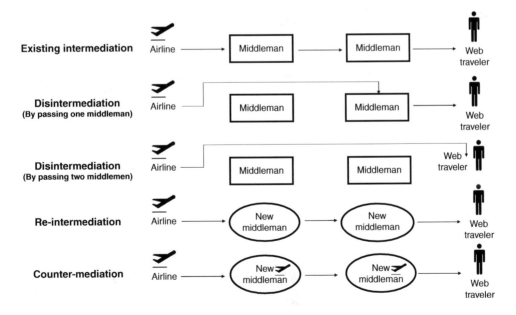

*Figure 4.7* *The relationship between an airline and middlemen*

*Disintermediation*

With disintermediation, middlemen who are expensive and inadequate for an airline's business model are cut out of a company's e-sales and distribution system. Modifying or breaking up an existing intermediary relationship is not easy especially when considering that some of them have been in place a decade or more and even date back to a pre-internet era. An airline deciding to lessen or completely discontinue its relationships with e-sales and distribution partners such as travel agencies (offline and online) and GDSs typically encounters some form of channel conflict. This may play out in retaliation such as a boycott or even lawsuit by middlemen against the airline. Emirates experienced this when it cut the travel agency commission from 7% to 5% in 2008 in Hong Kong and local agencies shifted bookings to other carriers. In the early 2000s, United Airlines, when offering an online booking bonus on its local Belgian website, was taken to court by the Belgium Travel Agents Association over alleged discrimination against offline bookers.

In some cases, channel conflicts are dealt with through re-negotiations. We saw this a few years ago when several airlines confronted GDSs and pushed for lower booking fees. With airlines threatening to switch to alternative GDSs or reduce their participation in existing GDSs, they eventually were able to settle better terms. At the same time, GDSs, secured continuous access to a carrier's full fare content. This included web exclusive fares that could also be distributed to travel agencies as opposed to being only available through an airline's website. In other situations, negotiations between an airline and a middleman are not fruitful. A case in point is American Airlines' decision to pull all its fares from OTA Orbitz in 2014 because the relationship was too costly and it could not extract booking fee reductions.

Disintermediation—and the accompanying channel conflict—is for the most part the story of legacy airlines. Unlike the LCCs, legacy airlines have a large footprint in the traditional sales and distribution system. Disintermediation focuses on reducing this arrangement and dealing directly with the web traveler. From a carrier's perspective, primary benefits of disintermediation include:

- cost savings that can be passed on to the web traveler in the form of lower fares
- higher profile and brand awareness in the marketplace
- improved opportunities for airlines to uniquely brand and price their otherwise commoditized supply
- data capture from web travelers' use of the airline's digital properties allowing for enhanced digital profiling that can be applied to tailoring 1:1 offerings
- higher control over sales channel and distribution.

Where does disintermediation currently stand with airlines? It has been a focus of many carriers' e-sales and distribution activities and continues playing a role. However, one can foresee that it is somewhat slowing down. Reason for this development:

- Carriers find it increasingly difficult to shift to direct online sales in non-home markets.
- Certain geographies (Africa, the Middle East, and parts of Asia and Latin America) are harder to disintermediate because they still favor traditional intermediaries.

- Some market segments including corporate and bundled travel products still require middlemen due to complexity (multiple PNRs, expense/travel policy management).
- Economic incentives to disintermediate are weakening as the costs of middlemen are coming down.
- LCCs as key drivers for disintermediation operate in market segments such as leisure travel that are direct-sales mature. For LCCs to tap into new segments including corporate travel requires adjustment to indirect sales and distribution approach. Some LCCs also have adopted hybrid business models (two-class cabin, interlining) that are more complex.
- GDSs/OTAs and other intermediaries embrace NDC XML-messaging standard and become more efficient in distribution. This translates into lower cost and capability to distribute airline ancillaries.

*Re-intermediation*

Much discussion focuses on disintermediation but it is equally important to mention re-intermediation. Although airlines, especially legacy carriers, have gone through plenty of break-ups with sales partners and near break-ups with GDSs in recent years, they have also entered a variety of relationships with new, mostly cyberspace-based middlemen.

A good example are online travel agencies (OTAs) that have become a main sales channel intermediary for many airlines. Simultaneously, we have also seen the rise of brand new online entities that have not existed before. One of these is the search/meta-search engine provider that offers valuable search and comparison functions to web travelers. Furthermore, working through virtual communities found on social media is another way of using an intermediary. Most carriers have established their own accounts with major platforms including Facebook and Twitter to interact with them as part of their sales and distribution activities. A few airlines even deploy social media influencers, persons who have large fan bases, to connect with web travelers in order to generate qualified shopping visits.

Lastly, another instance where we have seen re-intermediation in recent years involves LCCs and GDSs. After shunning GDSs for years because of their high cost, easyJet, JetBlue, and even Ryanair are examples of low-cost airlines that have become re-engaged with these traditional distribution intermediaries. The driver behind this move has been to support the airlines' growth into the corporate travel market which still books more traditionally via corporate travel agencies and GDSs.

Our above discussion on re-intermediation highlights the key benefits involved:

- It removes inefficiencies between airlines and web travelers because a web traveler can only interact with a limited number of different airlines when looking for flight and fare options. A middleman performs an evaluation across multiple sites more efficiently.
- Despite initial set-up and ongoing maintenance costs, it opens access to new markets and customer segments, thereby increasing sales potential.

The consequence of an airline embarking on re-intermediation is deciding on the specific areas which work with middlemen, integrating them into the existing e-sales and distribution infrastructure system, and managing this new relationship on an ongoing basis. One key aspect an airline needs to be concerned about is how it is positioned in relation to other competitors. In the case of OTAs, for instance, an airline should look out for how competitive its fare levels are versus those of other airlines. For social media, the focus should be on how many fans a carrier has and what their engagement level with the company is.

### Counter-mediation

The last issue to touch on in this discussion deals with counter-mediation. This involves a situation where the supplier is the one who sets up a new intermediary in response to a competitive threat or unfilled market demand. The OTAs Orbitz, Opodo, and Zuji are all examples of counter-mediation. Orbitz, for example, was launched in 2001 by the five US carriers American, Continental, Delta, Northwest, and United. They feared that both Expedia and Travelocity could become too powerful as an intermediary in the travel space. For similar reasons, Opodo and Zuji were originally established by a group of European and mainly Asia Pacific carriers, respectively.

### 4.5 PROFILE: THE MARKET SEGMENTS IN AIRLINE E-SALES AND DISTRIBUTION

The travel market is generally split into leisure and corporate segments. In order to target these segments and relevant decision makers in cyberspace more effectively, an airline should take a deeper dive for an indepth understanding.

Let us start with the travel sub-segments. Corporate could be broken down into four sub-segments based on enterprise type while leisure is commonly segregated into six sub-segments according to a traveler's profile and trip purpose (Table 4.1).

It is also useful to look more closely at who the actual decision makers in these sub-segments are. Doing so means that the airline engages the right person for its e-sales initiatives. For example, in the corporate sub-segments, the web traveler is certainly one but often not the most important decision maker an airline should target (Figure 4.8).

Part of this deeper dive should also provide airlines with more insight on a number of areas as they relate to each of the corporate and leisure segments. Specifically, a carrier should have an understanding of:

- What the customer's needs are.
- What the offering requirements are for an airline that intends to target these segments.
- What the competitive dynamics are and who the major players are vying with to get the business.

Table 4.2 provides for more details on each of these issues.

**Table 4.1** *Primary travel segments*

| Corporate | Market segment | Additional background |
|---|---|---|
| | 1. Large Market | Companies with annual air spend of $50 million and more |
| | 2. SMEAD (Small–Medium Enterprises Agency Driven) | Small and mid-size companies with annual air expenditure of $5–$50 million |
| | 3. Small Corporate | Small companies with air spend of $250,000 to $5 million per year |
| | 4. SOHO (Small Office, Home Office) | Small offices and entrepreneurs with yearly air spend of $250,000 or less |
| Leisure | Market segment | Additional background |
| | 1. High End Leisure | Airline brand loyalist |
| | 2. College | Student who is potential brand loyalist |
| | 3. Senior | Price-sensitive vacation/leisure traveler |
| | 4. Bargain Hunter | Price-sensitive traveler who trades off various elements (time of travel, time) for price |
| | 5. Honeymooners | Couples seeking special vacation |
| | 6. Adventurer | Traveler seeking active and exciting vacation |

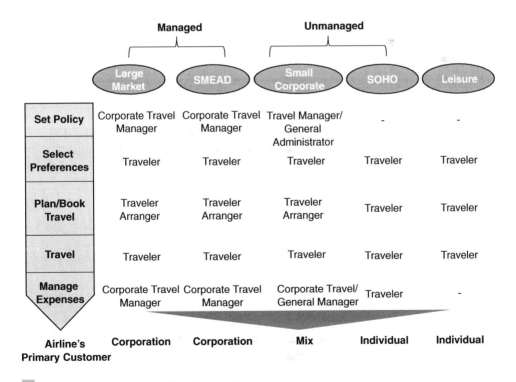

| | Managed | | Unmanaged | | |
|---|---|---|---|---|---|
| | Large Market | SMEAD | Small Corporate | SOHO | Leisure |
| **Set Policy** | Corporate Travel Manager | Corporate Travel Manager | Travel Manager/ General Administrator | - | - |
| **Select Preferences** | Traveler | Traveler | Traveler | Traveler | Traveler |
| **Plan/Book Travel** | Traveler Arranger | Traveler Arranger | Traveler Arranger | Traveler | Traveler |
| **Travel** | Traveler | Traveler | Traveler | Traveler | Traveler |
| **Manage Expenses** | Corporate Travel Manager | Corporate Travel Manager | Corporate Travel/ General Manager | Traveler | - |
| **Airline's Primary Customer** | Corporation | Corporation | Mix | Individual | Individual |

**Figure 4.8** *Decision makers for airline travel*

**Table 4.2a** Profile of travel market corporate sub-segments

| Market Segment | Customer Needs | Offering Requirements | Competitive Dynamics | Examples of Players |
|---|---|---|---|---|
| Large Market | ■ Requires specialized providers for best-in-class service<br>■ Demands high degree of support in value-added service like expense and supplier management; development and maintenance of travel policies | ■ Convenience and personalized attention to provide for the travel needs of company employees (Fulfillment operators, customer service) | ■ Many competitors look for serving this segment<br>■ Requires resources, coordination, and capabilities that most airlines lack | ■ Large agencies (American Express, Carlson Wagonlit, Rosenbluth)<br>■ Mid-tier agencies (Omega World Travel, McCord Travel Management)<br>■ Technology providers (Boeing Travel Management Company, Oracle e-Travel) |
| SMEAD | ■ Relies on intermediaries to provide for end-to-end solutions in travel management<br>■ Focus on cost containment | ■ Management of company's cost (expense management, supplier relations, payment services) | ■ Always looking for opportunities to leverage buying power and deal directly with suppliers<br>■ Requires resources, coordination, and capabilities | |
| Small Corporate | ■ Seeks managed online solution at low cost to promote travel policy compliance leading to greater savings<br>■ Support to purchase travel effectively | ■ Web-based tools for expense management<br>■ 24/7 customer service<br>■ Incentive and discount programs | ■ The number of online offerings is small<br>■ Segment is large and unaddressed in many markets | ■ Corporate travel agency<br>■ Specialized websites (Amex RezPort)<br>■ OTAs (Expedia, Opodo)<br>■ Biz OTAs (Egencia, OFB)<br>■ Airline websites |
| SOHO | ■ Focuses on online tools that offer more features and functionality than leisure segments<br>■ Very interested in perks received in return for generating certain revenue | ■ Broad inventory access<br>■ Range of web-based tools for expense tracking; itinerary/refund management<br>■ 24/7 customer service<br>■ Incentive and discount programs | ■ SOHO tailored offerings exist but are not comprehensive<br>■ Attractive segment due to large size and capturability | ■ OTAs<br>■ Airline websites |

**Table 4.2b** *Profile of travel market leisure sub-segments*

| Market Segment | Customer Needs | Offering Requirements | Competitive Dynamics | Examples of Players |
|---|---|---|---|---|
| High End Leisure | ■ Exceptional service and recognition<br>■ Advisory services<br>■ Quality travel experience | ■ Booking capability to cover vast number of different suppliers<br>■ Variety of customer service options (online self-service assisted service plus traditional tools<br>■ Content including fare promotions, destination info, and travel management tools) | ■ Very competitive<br>■ Crowded with many players and numerous strategies | ■ Airline websites<br>■ OTAs<br>■ Traditional agencies<br>■ Consolidators/Discounters<br>■ Niche agencies |
| College | ■ Low fares<br>■ Travel-related products (i.e. Eurail passes, guidebooks)<br>■ Destination information (i.e. hostel listings) | | | |
| Senior | ■ Senior fare discounts<br>■ Tour packages | | | |
| Bargain Hunter | ■ Fares specials and promotions | | | |
| Honey-Mooners | ■ Destination information<br>■ Advisory services<br>■ Package deals | | | |
| Adventurer | ■ Destination information<br>■ Suggested trips/trip planning<br>■ Package deals (biking, kayaking, scuba diving, etc.) | | | |

## 4.6 PROFILE: THE PARTICIPANTS IN AIRLINE E-SALES AND DISTRIBUTION

The participants in airline e-sales and distribution are an eclectic group. Besides airlines and GDSs, they also include various types of travel agencies such as traditional travel agencies, OTAs, consolidators, niche players, corporate agencies, and travel management companies (TMCs).

Table 4.3 shows the distinct features associated with each of these participants in terms of their economic model, product offerings and customer service needs. An airline that wants to build and maintain a competitive web presence needs to have a good understanding of who exactly these other players in the travel ecosystem are and how they operate.

### 4.6.1 Travel agencies

Intermediaries in the travel industry have a long tradition. Travel advisors called *entrepreneurs* first appeared in France, Germany, and Italy in the 1700s. Their task was to provide travelers with information on prices and attractions for their journeys. From UK-based Thomas Cook, which is considered the first modern travel agency and started in 1841, there are today over 60,000 travel agencies worldwide. The essential mission of travel agents, traditional and online, has not changed. They provide for critical advice by aggregating information from a universe of travel suppliers and thereby enable travelers to shop more efficiently.

Focusing for a moment on traditional travel agencies, they had risen to occupy a major role for airlines as a third party sales channel. By the early 1990s, just before the advent of the commercial internet, they had become the primary sales channel for most airlines and generated over 80% of the industry's revenue.

How was it possible that travel agencies had become so prominent? There are four major reasons:

- By the time airline travel was about to become a mass market in the 1950s, modern travel agencies already had been around for 100+ years. This was because of their engagement with customers for other modes of transport, mostly maritime shipping and trains. Airlines gladly tapped into this network and pool of travel expertise for representation of their own services.
- Airlines could not cost efficiently replicate the vast scope of travel agencies' geographic coverage and have their own city ticket office at every corner in every town.
- Airlines could not offer the same wide spectrum of numerous travel products and services from multiple travel suppliers.
- Airlines could not provide travelers with independent advice thereby positioning travel agencies more as an unbiased intermediary.

Depending on their business model, travel agencies target one or a combination of sub-segments in the corporate and leisure markets (Table 4.4).

**Table 4.3** Participants in the airline e-sales and distribution system

| | Airline | OTA | Traditional Agency | Consolidator | Niche Player | Corporate Agency/TMC | Meta Search Engine | GDS |
|---|---|---|---|---|---|---|---|---|
| Description | Emphasis on fare availability, service standards, ancillary sales, matching or exceeding offline offerings to increase share | Prominent online players focusing on fare availability and service standards | Companies with offline and online presence reaping the benefits of both environments | Bulk purchases and distressed inventory, engaging agents who are transaction focused and compete on price | Specialists who provide wide range of in-depth services to small, well defined market segments | Aiming at offering many different suppliers, competing on service and travel policy mgmt | Referral to selected number of airlines and OTAs, focus on price sensitive shoppers | Electronic B2B platform provider that aggregates content including seat inventory, fare info, and flight schedules plus limited ancillaries |
| Focus of Economic Model | ■ Distribution cost savings<br>■ Revenue share | ■ Commission/ Fee/GDS incentive, other<br>■ Advertising<br>■ Affiliates | ■ Commission/ Fee/GDS incentive, other | ■ Markups | ■ Commission/ Fee<br>■ Affinity deals<br>■ Advertising | ■ Commission/ Incentives/ Service and Mgmt fees | ■ Cost per click, cost per action, cost per thousand | ■ Booking segment fees<br>■ IT consulting and technology solutions |
| Offering | ■ Online/Phone/ CTO/ATO<br>■ Broad and standard | ■ Online<br>■ Broad and standard | ■ Online/ Phone/ Retail<br>■ Broad and standard | ■ Online/ Phone<br>■ Narrow | ■ Online/ Phone<br>■ Narrow and custom | ■ Online/ Phone/ Retail/Implant<br>■ Broad and custom | ■ Online<br>■ Broad and standard | ■ Mainframes and EDIFACT messaging<br>■ Broad and standard |
| **Customer Needs:** | | | | | | | | |
| - Offering Breadth | Medium | High | High | Low | Low | High | High | Medium/High |
| - Customer Service Level | High | High | High | Low | High | High | Low | Low |
| - Price Sensitivity | Medium/Low | Medium/High | Low | High | Varies | Low | High | High |

**Table 4.4** *Types of travel agencies*

| Travel agency type | What they do |
| --- | --- |
| Leisure Agency | Services the price-sensitive leisure market. Some leisure agencies focus on certain niches such as visiting friends/relatives (VFR), medical/wellness, adventure, golf/sports, and seniors. They often work with consolidators and tour operators. |
| Corporate Agency | Deals with the corporate travel needs of business entities such as SMEADs. Primary travel products include air, hotel, and car. |
| General Purpose Agency | Caters to both leisure and business travelers. Business travelers could come from SMEs and even SOHOs. |
| Travel Management Companies (TMCs) | Provides full suite of travel management and services to large corporate clients that go beyond the standard travel agency services like bookings and customer service. Common examples are the management of travel supplier contracts and procurement programs, travel expense reporting, and even the development and oversight of travel policies. |
| Consolidator | Generally does not sell directly to the traveling public but to retail agencies only. The consolidator purchases bulk inventory from travel suppliers including airlines and re-sells it with a mark-up to individual retail agencies. |
| Tour Operator | Acquires inventory from core travel suppliers (air, car, hotel, others) and bundles them for packages that are re-sold to retail agencies or directly in the marketplace. |

For several decades, the top product sold by the travel agency community was "flight," far ahead of other core travel products such as hotel and car rental. However, this has changed significantly. As a result of missing out on the shift to the online travel market starting in the mid-1990s, traditional leisure agencies have lost a significant share of their flight-only sales. Today, the ones still in business operate in a variety of niche roles. For the most part, this business has been captured by airlines and OTAs. The reason why traditional travel agencies still play a role in selling flight at all is because of TMCs/corporate agencies that handle a large portion of airline bookings for corporate travel.

### 4.6.2 The rise of online travel agencies

The era of OTAs began with the launch of Expedia and Travelocity in 1996 in the United States. Over the years, other OTAs have sprung up in travel markets around the world. Today, OTAs comprise global actors including US-based Expedia and eDreams ODIGEO from Spain, regional players such as DNATA offering its services in UAE and Saudi Arabia, and in-country players like Oktogo from Russia (Figure 4.9).

The current global OTA landscape is quickly consolidating. This development is mostly driven by Expedia and Priceline that have been buying up or investing in

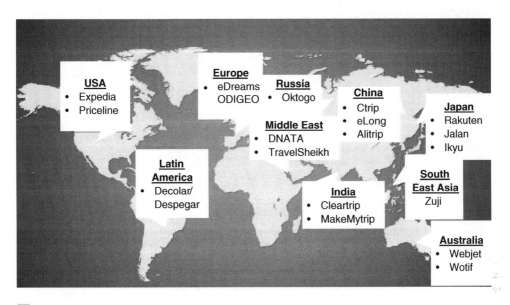

**Figure 4.9a** *Major OTAs around the world selling air travel...*

**Expedia digital properties and investments**

**Expedia**

Based in Bellevue, WA, USA
Employees: 18,000

- Expedia.com:           Full service OTA in 31 countries
- Hotels.com:            Hotel specialist in 60 countries
- Hotwire:               Opaque discount site in 12 countries
- Egencia:               5th largest corporate TMC
- Venere.com:            Online hotel reservation specialist in Europe
- Trivago":              Hotel meta search in 49 countries
- Wotif Group:           OTA in Asia Pacific based in Australia
- Expedia Local Expert:  Online & in-market concierge service
- Classic Vacations:     Top luxury travel specialist
- Expedia Cruise Ship Center:  Provider of expert advice for travelers booking
  cruises
- CarRentals.com:        Online car rental booking company
- Decolar/Despegar       Minority equity stake (< 20%)
- Orbitz.com and Travelocity   Full service OTAs

*Together, both OTAs control over 50% of the global OTA booking share*

**Priceline digital properties and investments**

**The Priceline Group**

Based in Norwalk, CT, USA
Employees: 9,000

- Booking.com:      Online hotel booking company
- Priceline.com:    Full service OTA
- Agoda.com         Hotel booking site in Asia Pacific
- Kajak:            Travel meta search engine
- Rentalcars:       Booking site for car rental
- OpenTable:        Restaurant reservation
- Ctrip             Up to 10% stake

**Figure 4.9b** *....and the two online travel giants: Expedia and Priceline*

a wide variety of online travel players. For instance, in 2015, Expedia acquired both Travelocity and Orbitz in the United States. At the same time, the company also invested $270 million for a minority stake in the Latin America OTA Decolar. Priceline committed in August 2014 to a $500 million investment in C-trip, one of China's major OTAs. With these additions, both companies command today a global OTA booking share of well over 50%. If one considers in this mix also the two European OTA heavyweights (eDream Odigeo and the Bravofly Rumbo Group), these four OTAs alone control 70% of the global OTA market that is currently worth around $170 billion.

Size is clearly a priority for Expedia and Priceline. The drivers for them to bulk up have a lot to do with turf defense. One key point is that airlines have managed to attract more web travelers directly to their own websites. Also, hotels that traditionally have been the largest revenue generators for OTAs have reduced their commission payments over the years from a high of 25% down now to 16%. Finally, there is the anxiety over a large entrance to the online travel market by the likes of Google.

The presence of OTAs has become visible across multiple digital platforms including websites, mobile sites, and apps. In some cases, their cyberspace participation extends to meta-travel search engines. For instance, Priceline owns Kayak while eDream ODIGEO acquired Liligo several years ago. Furthermore, several of them also operate in the offline world with call centers and physical retail stores.

In terms of growth measured by gross bookings, OTAs are outpacing the overall travel market. In 2015, while total global travel was predicted to increase by 6%, OTAs were expected to grow by 12% as a result of developments in emerging markets. In the more mature United States, OTAs' growth is more in line with the country's overall growth of close to 6% (Figure 4.10). The largest OTA market in 2013 was Europe with slightly over $83 billion in revenue, followed by the United States, and the Asia/Pacific region with close to $45 billion and $29 billion, respectively.

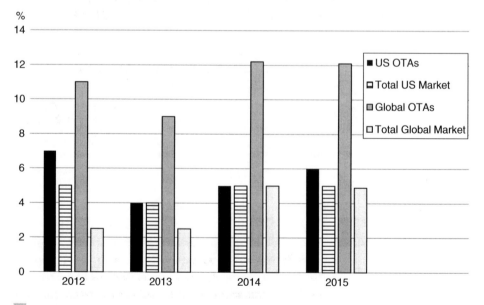

**Figure 4.10a** *Gross bookings growth (%) of OTAs and total market…*

**$ Billion**

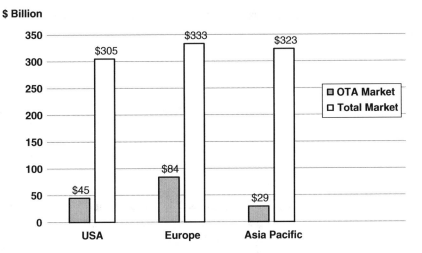

*Figure 4.10b* ...*OTA market size vs total market ($, by region 2013)*

*Source:* Sileo (2014)[16]

*The different OTA types and their contribution to online travel*

OTAs can be segregated into three main groups:

- *Retail.* Most OTA bookings for airlines originate from retail OTAs. They deliver relatively low yields with a focus on predominantly leisure and VFR bookings. Examples include Expedia, Webjet, and Despegar.
- *Opaque.* Opaque OTAs hide the names of the airlines on their website until a web traveler completes their booking. Opaques typically generate the lowest yield for airlines that provide for fixed quantities of distressed inventories. Opaques pay airlines upfront for the seats they acquire. This means they bear the economic risk of selling the airline seats in the marketplace. Opaque players include Priceline, Hotwire, and Site59.
- *Corporate.* Business OTAs serve corporate airline customers. Companies from the large market and SMEAD segments are able to pre-load their negotiated rates in the GDSs or take advantage of private fares previously negotiated with the business OTAs. Major OTAs serving this market segment comprise Expedia's Egencia, Orbitz for Business (OFB), Travelocity Business (TBiz), and Odigeo's Travelink.

OTAs overall are highly technology and marketing savvy travel companies. To their credit, they have made enormous contributions to the online travel market—and airlines also have benefitted greatly. Without these contributions, today's online travel market would have probably evolved more slowly, would be less price transparent and less convenient. Even airlines themselves have admitted this publicly.[17]

The groundbreaking innovations that have become standard because of their new efficiencies and conveniences created for online travel shopping include:[18]

- *Air fare matrix display*. Orbitz first launched this feature that allows web travelers to click on any cell within a matrix and sort airline search results by airline, price, and number of stops.
- *Dynamic packaging*. This feature enables web travelers to buy bundled offerings including "Flight+Hotel" in a single search and realize savings as opposed to shopping for these travel components individually and paying a higher price.
- *Flexible and alternative date search*. A web traveler can compare flight options across multiple departure/return dates to find the lowest possible fare. Some OTAs have expanded on this concept with a calendar-based display allowing for price comparison across a range of dates.

Other innovations include low fare alerts and alternative airport search.

OTAs not only serve airlines as an intermediary for selling but also to do marketing. Carriers deploy a variety of paid digital media formats including display ads, microsites, and email newsletters via OTA digital platforms. Moreover, OTAs also play a role as a quasi-search engine. Web travelers' first stop in their comparison-shopping is often an OTA from where they proceed to check out other travel websites including those by airlines.

### OTAs: Partners or competitors to airlines?

OTAs are key players in the online travel space and they account for a significant share of airline bookings in most markets. In the United States, for example, OTAs currently handle about one-third of airline bookings. However, the overall trend points to a decline. Over a ten-year timeframe between 2002 and 2012, OTAs' share of 44% went down to 33%. As a matter of fact, 2012 marked a watershed year as US carriers, with 36% for the first time, posted a larger share of airline bookings than OTAs.[19]

Largely responsible for this development is the OTAs' increasing focus on selling hotels. In Expedia's case, for example, 74% of their revenue in 2012 came from hotel bookings while flights only accounted for 8%. In 2005, air still generated 22% while hotels were at 63%[20] (one of the drivers for Expedia to acquire Orbitz in 2015 was to re-balance and strengthen its air portfolio). Additionally, airlines did a good job in attracting shoppers to book directly with them. Popular tactics to support this shift included offering incentives. Examples are advance seat reservation, lower ticket change fee, and full mileage credit. All of these are typically not available for web travelers booking via OTAs. Low fare guarantees and airline website-exclusive fares are other measures airlines often use.

In an ideal world from an airline perspective, all bookings would come through the carrier's website and third party middlemen such as OTAs would not be needed. However, even LCCs that otherwise handle most bookings through their own digital properties, work in some areas with OTAs. If we want to understand the underlying dynamics in the competitive–cooperative relationship between OTAs and airlines better, we need to take a closer look at several key areas. These include web traveler behavior, pricing activities by OTAs and airlines, and OTA product qualities.

*Web traveler behavior and OTA / airline pricing activities*

Both leisure and business travelers appreciate OTAs. Above all, their attractive fares and their one-stop shop booking capabilities for air, car, hotel, and packages are appealing. Furthermore, OTAs offer access to a vast database of supplier, destination, and travel information. Importantly, the up-and-coming millennial travelers have a greater affinity for OTAs than for airlines (Figure 4.11).

The relationship between OTAs and airlines is influenced by each party's pricing activities and corresponding impact on web traveler shopping behavior. With air travel being considered the most familiar, most commoditized, and lowest margin online travel product, price has obviously a big switching effect. OTAs have generally a reputation for being a great search source and offering good value for money. In this regard, OTAs are more competitive than airlines and are therefore of greater appeal to web travelers. Findings from research firm Phocuswright even suggest that OTAs and airlines appear to increasingly attract different web travelers. OTAs seem more relevant to the infrequent leisure traveler who takes only one to three trips per year and is much more price elastic. Airline websites, however, appear to attract the more frequent traveler who is somewhat less concerned with price and more interested in schedule, convenience, and additional booking incentives.[21] If this

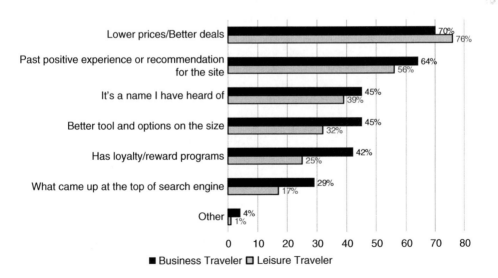

**Figure 4.11a** *Reasons for booking on OTAs...*

*Source:* Google (2014)[22]

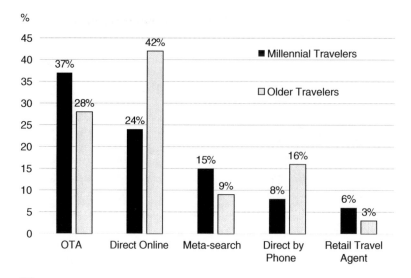

**Figure 4.11b** *...with millennial travelers gravitating to OTAs*

Source: Quinby et al. (2015)[23]

assessment still holds true, the commonly mentioned competitive aspect between OTAs and airlines then seems overplayed and the two are actually more complementary to each other.

From a partnership perspective, airlines are generally concerned with two aspects when it comes to OTAs: Cost of doing business with them and their product quality. We do not want to jump start our discussion on the cost of e-sales and distribution here—we elaborate on this in a separate section later—but it suffices to say that doing business with OTAs has its price. Airlines pay them bookings fees, and also fees to the GDSs which handle these very bookings on the backend. Airlines want to contain if not eliminate these fees as much as possible. If an agreement for what an airline thinks is fair compensation cannot reached, it is not uncommon for a carrier to simply pull its inventory from an OTA site.

American Airlines had a couple of high-profile run-ins with Orbitz and Expedia on this subject. The most recent occurred in August 2014 when the carrier decided to stop Orbitz from selling its flights over a dispute on the agency's compensation. This "going dark" lasted for three days when a last minute agreement was reached before American was about to withdraw US Airways flights from Orbitz.

What is the consequence for an airline of pulling its flights from an OTA? Assuming that we are not talking about a second- or third-tier agency but a major one such as Orbitz, the most immediate impact for an airlines is not just booking fee savings but certainly also revenue losses. The revenue losses can be significant because it is unlikely that an airline can compensate for them by re-directing the OTA web traffic straight to its own website. No airline brand, unless we talk about a Southwest, JetBlue, or Ryanair—and they capture most of their bookings directly anyway—is that strong.

330

This issue touches on what is an OTA's hidden but powerful role as a quasi-search engine. We know from our discussion in Chapter 3 on e-marketing how important it is to be visible on a search engine when web travelers engage in price-comparison shopping. One study shows that 41% of web travelers that visited Expedia or Orbitz actually linked to aa.com where they ended up buying their ticket (Figure 4.12).[24]

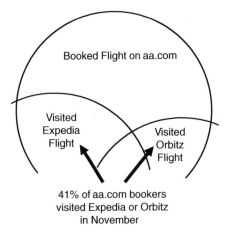

Booked Flight on aa.com

Visited
Expedia
Flight

Visited
Orbitz
Flight

41% of aa.com bookers
visited Expedia or Orbitz
in November

**Figure 4.12** *The role of OTAs in direct bookings on a carrier's website: Example—American Airlines*

*Source:* Malone (2011)[25]

It is clear that as much as a traditional network carrier including American wants to build its own direct online channel, a large number of web travelers still make a stop first at an OTA. Without a presence on them, a purchase on the airline's website appears less likely. That same study also highlighted how much stronger web travelers were attached to the Southwest brand: Close to 70% of all web travelers visiting southwest. com ended up booking on that website. Furthermore, for 56% of Southwest's flight bookers, southwest.com was the *only* airline website they visited that month. American, however, captured just 36% of total flight bookings made by people who had come to aa.com and saw less than one-third of its bookers display single-site loyalty.[26]

Besides cost of sale, airlines also look out for an OTA's product quality. Let us take the area of online vacation packages. For more complex multi-component travel itineraries involving vacation packages and combinations (e.g. air + hotel or air + car bought in a single purchase), OTAs appear to have a significant edge over airlines. In the UK and United States, for example, web travelers visit OTA websites much more. For instance, in 2013 in the UK, OTAs claimed a 28% share of all websites for vacation package bookings versus 12% by airlines. For the United States, 47% of web travelers booking a vacation package visited an OTA website versus 11% going to airline websites.[27]

It remains to be seen whether airlines are going to invest as heavily as OTAs in this type of online product. Some airlines feature vacation packages online, www. aavacation.com and www.virginholidays.com are examples. However, these products appear often only peripherally on the airline's websites and are most likely only marginal revenue contributors when compared with what these carriers sell online for their core product. If and when airlines decide to enter this segment more aggressively, the resulting offering overlaps with what OTAs feature on their sites so are predicted to heat up the competition between the two.

A key area where airlines have started differentiating their online presence versus that of OTAs deals with fare merchandising. With à la carte fares, fare families, and branded fares, a new form of branding has been introduced to an otherwise highly commoditized marketplace. This is not widespread yet but has been gaining momentum with an increasing number of airlines. Figure 4.13 illustrates this "breadth versus depth" situation as exemplified by Air New Zealand and Orbitz. When searching for an economy class fare from Los Angeles to Auckland, airnewzealand.com displays

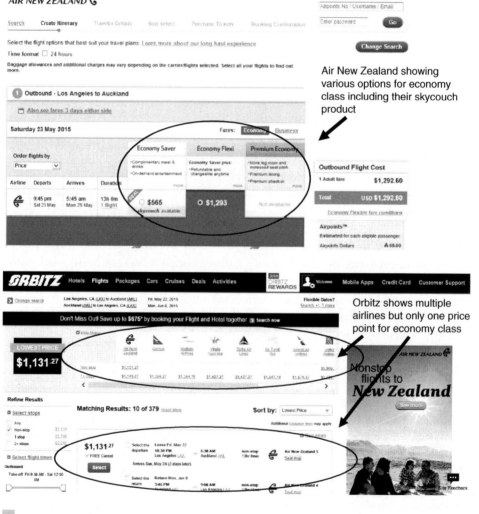

*Figure 4.13* Breadth vs depth: Booking LAX-AKL on *airnewzealand.com* and *orbitz.com*

*Source:* orbitz.com (2015),[28] airnewzealand.com (2015)[29] with kind permission of Air New Zealand

three economy class fare products. The website also allows a web traveler to book the airline's economy class Skycouch, a row of three economy class seats that can be turned into a couch. All these fare products are currently not featured on OTAs. In the case of orbitz.com, a web traveler can choose from ten different carriers for this booking, but each airline is only featured with a single price point for its economy class.

In order to maintain their attractiveness as viable sales partners to airlines, OTAs should seek the integration of fare merchandising on their websites. As we will discuss below in section 4.7 on ancillaries, fare merchandising is a major revenue generator for airlines and essential for improving their profitability. OTAs would need to work with GDSs that manage the relevant distribution platforms in order to be able to offer it. Alternatively, OTAs may directly access the airline reservation system via a GDS-bypass set-up. One thing seems sure: Not engaging in fare merchandising is not an option in the long term for an OTA.

Finally, other forms of website innovation, both content and functionality related, have an impact on web travelers' preferences where they shop. Social media content, mobile applications, alternative forms of payments, web customer service, and personalization features are all examples that provide for a richer and "stickier" website experience. Assuming that OTAs continue investing in new travel technology and web applications— they are known for being innovative and aggressive in this area—there is no reason why they should not be able to excel in the marketplace. One recent example in this regard is the customized app for the Apple Smart Watch launched by Orbitz in April 2015.

Essentially, airlines have reasons to be ambivalent toward OTAs. They add to sales and distribution costs that airlines try to minimize so desperately. They also occupy a powerful middle man position that makes it more difficult for airlines to develop and own direct relationships with end-consumers. Furthermore, they have been slow with the adoption of featuring airline ancillary offerings on their websites. While GDSs have their fair share in this, airlines are also frustrated with OTAs because they lose out on potential incremental revenue streams from web travelers in this area.

Despite all of this, airlines should nevertheless be careful to discard OTAs as sales partners. As we have pointed out earlier, OTAs have great appeal to both business and leisure travelers. Additionally, OTAs have entrenched positions in most key online markets worldwide and have huge marketing budgets at their disposal. Against this background and considering the consolidation of the global OTA market, airlines will face a formidable challenge if they decide to compete head-on with major OTAs. It seems that the cooperative-competitive relationship between airlines and OTAs is to stay with us for some time to come.

### 4.6.3 Meta-search engine providers

*Overview*

A travel meta-search engine, also known as referral website or aggregator website, is a second-generation search engine that essentially applies the Google model merged with a travel context. A travel meta-search engine is a one-stop site where a web traveler enters a single search request including travel dates and origin/destination. It then runs simultaneous searches on multiple airline and OTA websites. The aggregated search results are displayed in the form of qualified leads on a single result page according to their source. When connecting to any of the recommended shopping sites, a web traveler typically deep links. This means that they bypass the first web pages where one typically enters the routing and travel dates and land deeper in the website. Data fields on flight routing and travel dates are already pre-populated. What is left to do for the web traveler is provide their personal details including name, address, and payment information.

Any meta-search engine including those for the travel space operate on the premise that more comprehensive search results can be obtained by combining the results from several websites and efficiently presenting them on one page. Since travel meta-search engines aggregate from both suppliers such as airlines and intermediaries such as OTAs, they are also considered meta-mediaries. Travel meta-search engines, although not shopping channels in their own right, have emerged as significant players and captured their fair share among web travelers looking to buy airline tickets. In the United States, almost one-quarter of travelers search for airline tickets via travel meta-search sites (Figure 4.14).

Meta-search engines emerged because of a market need for more efficient searches for low fares among the proliferating number of airline and OTA websites. So many websites have sprung up since the mid-1990s and the fare differences from site to site were large enough that the average web traveler looking for a good fare deal was really challenged to decide which websites to engage with.

Aggregator websites promised to resolve this dilemma by not requiring the web traveler to use multiple websites separately. Since the early 2000s, meta-search

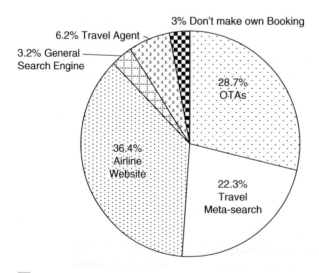

**Figure 4.14** *Websites used by travelers when searching for airline tickets (June 2014)*

Source: Wellman (2014)[30]

**Table 4.5** *Selected meta-search engine providers in the travel space (home country/year founded)*

| Europe | USA | Asia Pacific |
| --- | --- | --- |
| Cheapflights (UK/1996) | Kayak (US/2004) | Qunar (China/2005) |
| Skyscanner (UK/2002) | Mobissimo (US/2004) | Wego (Singapore/2005) |
| | Hipmunk (US/2010) | |
| | Google Flight Search (US/2011) | |

engine players have appeared in all parts of the world and established a local presence in many countries (Table 4.5). The most high-profile addition to this group is Google with its Google/Flights product in 2011.

Any money made by travel meta-search engines comes from a referral fee for ticket purchases paid by whatever site ends up fulfilling the ticket purchase and an advertising fee collected from third party advertisers.

No two travel meta-search engine work alike. Each applies its own unique search approach when crawling through the universe of websites and gathering data. Some have a strong focus on domestic markets, others have deeper access to international markets, while other travel meta-search engine companies neglect lesser known brands in their search. The result: There is no such thing as a truly complete search that covers all the flight options and all the providers. No single site finds every flight option, every fare, or every seller. There are three main methods of going about producing search results:

- A faring engine such as used by Google/ITA relying on a unique, highly guarded (and typically patented) search algorithm.
- An XML direct connect link between the aggregator and airline and/or OTA.
- Screen scraping that is based on robotic search.

*Screen scraping airline websites: A contentious issue*

Screen scraping continues to cause ill will with airlines. Unless there is a commercial agreement in place with the meta-search engine, they consider it a form of electronic trespassing and violation of property rights. Screen scraping is defined as a process by which a software program simulates a user's interaction with a website to access information stored on that site. A screen scraper can not only enter the information a human user would but also capture the website's replies. It is also possible that some screen scrapers extract substantial data portions stored on the site. Screen scraping can overload a website and slow it down, an issue any airline should be concerned with.

There are several ways to respond to screen scraping. Airlines can apply IP address blocking but it is commonly understood that screen scraping companies are savvy enough to circumvent such technical countermeasures. Many airlines therefore often resort to legal actions but even these can be difficult to enforce because some of the screen scraping companies are in jurisdictions outside the reach of country-specific laws.

One of the first law suits brought against a meta-search engine by an airline took place in 2003. American Airlines took Farechase, a company owned at the time by Yahoo, to court over its scraping of content from aa.com. American viewed its website content as personal property of the airline. The court concluded Farechase's screen scraping was not only adversely impacting the performance of the aa.com website infrastructure but also constituted an interference with the airline's efforts to reduce its distribution costs and position its website as a platform for attractive web fares. Farechase ultimately had to stop the screen scraping of aa.com.[31]

Screen scraping is still an issue. For example, in 2014, Ryanair brought a case before the European Court of Justice (ECJ) against PR Aviation, a Dutch company operating aggregator sites. A previous ruling by a Dutch court had already made clear that a publicly accessible database such as flight information posted on a website was not protected under EU database copyright laws. In other words, screen scrapers cannot be prohibited from accessing ryanair.com. However, Ryanair still fought its case.[32] It specifically argued that the comparison company had checked a consent box to gain access to ryanair.com agreeing to its terms and conditions. These, amongst other things, did not allow the use of an automated system to extract data from the website for commercial purposes. The ECJ ruled in Ryanair's favor and PR aviation had to stop its screen scraping of ryanair.com.[33]

---

## SNAPSHOT: GOOGLE'S ACQUISITION OF ITA

In July 2010, Google announced its intent to acquire ITA Software for $700 million. ITA, founded in 1996 as a faring engine provided data on multiple websites including Kayak, Orbitz, Expedia, TripAdvisor, and Microsoft's Bing. Despite heavy lobbying against this deal, including by Kayak with backing from Expedia to buy ITA itself, the Department of Justice cleared the deal in April 2011. Some restrictions such as not influencing the flight displays and rankings of other ITA users were put in place. In September 2011, Google then launched Google.com/flights and this is when general search transformed into meta-search.

Why is this such a big deal? It is important to highlight the large role of general search engines when it comes to the online purchase of airline tickets. We have learned from our discussion in chapter 3 on booking behavior by web travelers that general search engines and meta-search engines are among the Top 10 sources used for travel planning. Any company combining general search with meta-search is therefore able to command a significant share of the search market.

How does the Google Flight product work? When launching a flight search in Google, say "Low fares from New York to Los Angeles," a "Flights" link will appear on the left side of Google's search page (Google Flight Search can also be accessed directly at google.com/flights). This is the first time a general search is combined with flight schedule specifics, air fares, and a web traveler's budget. Google shows a shortlist of flights based on price and total travel time, including various departure times and airlines. Filters are set for "reasonable" price and duration, but users can manipulate them to show additional flights. Other features include a map to identify flights where one could travel based on one's budget constraints from a specific origin city, and a calendar view to find out when lower fares are available. First offered only for US domestic flights, the product expanded to include international destinations served from the United States. The next step is to offer google.com/flights also outside the United States. This makes the product also relevant for airlines based in other markets.

It is interesting that Google Flight Search does not work with OTAs but airlines only. It is not clear if this is Google's principal policy or just a negotiation tactic to extract more advertising revenue from these players—after all, they already are major ad spenders with Google. Unless this situation changes, airlines capture the business directly on their website—an uncomfortable scenario for OTAs and travel meta-search engines.

Equally important about Google Flight Search is the new quality of travel search results that can be generated. The current Google Flight Search product may still look basic to many people. However, let us remember that Google has an unparalleled, if not unrivalled, omnipresence on the internet with its products and services such as search, cloud computing, software, and advertising technologies. In combination with all the data collected and mined about a web user's general digital footprint and whatever they do in a travel context, a user is much more transparent to Google. This provides for search results that are more relevant and contextualized for an individual web traveler than what is currently offered by the existing meta-search engines. Airlines need to be aware of how they are positioned with Google in this new meta-search engine environment and what they can do to optimize their presence and improve revenue.

The formation of a closer relationships between general and travel meta-search engines is by no means limited to the United States. Similar crossovers occurred in other markets such as in China between search engine provider Baidu and travel search entity Qunar.

*Meta-search engines moving forward*

Even before Google entered the scene with its ITA acquisition, the travel meta-search engine market had not been standing still. A few key developments should be mentioned that give an indication of how things may evolve:

PRODUCT GROWTH AND INTERNATIONAL EXPANSION

The majority of meta-search engines started out as pure air fare aggregators. However, today, they also offer non-air travel products including hotels, car rentals, and even prepackaged vacation deals and cruises to popular destinations. What is missing at this stage are dynamic vacation packages such as air + hotel, air + car, and individual vacation packages that web travelers have been offered for some time now on most airline websites.

Interesting is the launch of a facilitated booking feature. Accordingly, rather than being transferred to an OTA or airline website, the web traveler actually stays "in-app" for the completion of the booking. Meta-search engines are unlikely to turn into transaction handlers themselves but they have stepped closer with this feature where the OTA or supplier stays in the background. For instance, in June 2015, Google announced the "Book on Google" initiative in a partnership with GDS Sabre. This is a beta for North America and allows its hotel partners to choose to pay commissions to Google and Sabre for credit card transactions that Google handles right on Google platforms. With web travelers now being able to book some hotels directly on Google Search, Google Maps, and Google+, the company has the potential to play an even more central role for the online travel industry. This is because it can offer a hotel booking functionality to its large base of users on desktop and mobile, in search and maps. It is only a question of time when Google will offer a similar application for flight bookings.

In terms of geographic growth, there are still opportunities in the international arena. Large companies such as Kayak and Travelzoo from the United States and Skyscanner and Cheapflights from the UK, for example, have already established a local presence in several countries. This expansion is likely to continue for a while as a result of the combined growth of demand for air travel and customer readiness for online travel shopping in Africa, Asia, and the Middle East.

This development provides for growth opportunities. This is not only of significance for existing players but also for travel companies that have watched the meta-search business from a distance but decided to crossover. One example is TripAdvisor. Since its inception in 2001, it had been a pure travel review site but adopted a meta-search engine function in 2009 on its website and thus overnight became a big participant in this field. The OTAs themselves are not sitting on the sidelines either. Take for example one of the largest OTAs in Europe, Spain-based Odigeo, which acquired travel meta-search engine Liligo in 2013.

It is also noteworthy that some of the US-based OTAs accept advertising placements on their websites by companies that offer comparisons of air fare results with those from other OTAs and travel meta-search engines. Figure 4.15 is an example of

**Figure 4.15** *Air fare comparison on Expedia*

*Source:* expedia.com (2015)[34] with kind permission of Expedia

such an advertising placement on Expedia. When clicking on the ad sponsored by travel meta-search engine provider Bookingbuddy.com, a web traveler is linked to a booking buddy landing page. There, the air fare of the original query submitted on Expedia could be checked on other sites such as Cheapoair, Orbitz, and Priceline.

In essence, competition among travel meta-search engines remains intensive and this can only translate into better search and products and lower costs—a good thing for airlines.

## LEISURE TRAVEL VERSUS CORPORATE TRAVEL

Travel meta-search has been largely confined to leisure travel. Some web travelers with a SOHO and SME background display similar psychographic and technographic characteristics as leisure travelers and use travel meta-search engines in their search for low air fares. However, the corporate world so far has shied away from an official adoption. If and when corporate web travelers compare air fares quoted by meta-search engines with those from the primary venues for handling corporate travel—self-booking tools and travel agencies are key examples—and find better deals through meta-search engines, there could be friction, among others, between airlines and their corporate clients to provide more attractive fares.

## MOBILE

Travel meta-search engine companies, as most other travel players, have as much as possible optimized their website products for mobile devices. However, content and navigation set-ups otherwise featured on desktop websites are broken up and fragmented for a mobile environment. The user experience is not ideal for a continuous engagement by a web user and interacting with mobile travel meta-search engine sites still means scrolling across multiple websites.

Side-by-side comparison of multiple OTAs and airlines is hampered by the smaller screens. If meta-search engine players do not come up with genuinely user-friendly applications for mobile devices, their role as intermediaries could diminish over time because web travelers continue shifting to mobile for self-servicing and air fare purchasing.

The new seamlessness between mobile devices and PC search is interesting. For example, Hipmunk offers this feature whereby web travelers can start their search on one device and can continue on another and vice versa.

## PERSPECTIVE OF AIRLINES ON META-SEARCH ENGINES

It is a gray area and up to an individual airline to view aggregators as partners or as competitors. Generally, airlines in their efforts to capture more direct business through their own websites are not overly excited about any new middlemen and this includes travel meta-search engines.

However, can they afford to ignore the traffic and business they generate for them? Not really. The fact remains that aggregators have inserted themselves in the travel value chain and today are an established intermediary capturing significant website traffic among the travel players.

### 4.6.4 Affiliate programs

Affiliate programs enable an airline to extend the reach of its online sales network. They are performance-based programs where an airline rewards affiliates for their efforts to generate business such as bringing a web traveler to the carrier's website or producing an online ticket purchase. Some people view an affiliate program as an e-marketing tool because of the online advertising and promotion methods applied. These include SEM, SEO, email, and display marketing. However, because an airline's compensation scheme for affiliates often involves pay per sale—similar to a commission paid to a travel agent—we can introduce affiliate programs also in the context of our e-sales and distribution discussion.

Affiliate programs involve four core players: The airline, the affiliate network that contains the offers by various suppliers and also manages the administrative side including payments, the online retailer, and the web traveler. There are many affiliate networks that airlines can choose from to work with. For an airline to be effective in this area and recruit the right partner(s), a few aspects should be considered. Above all, the affiliate network should have experience and know-how of the travel industry. This makes it easier for an airline to work with the online retailers in the network to distribute its promotions and offers. Other aspects including critical mass, technology used to manage the program, revenue potential, and customer service should also be of consideration (Figure 4.16).

Some of the key affiliate networks that airlines have entered partnerships with include:

- *Commission Junction.* They claim to power half of the top 500 web retailers' affiliate programs and appear to have the largest and most diversified travel supplier

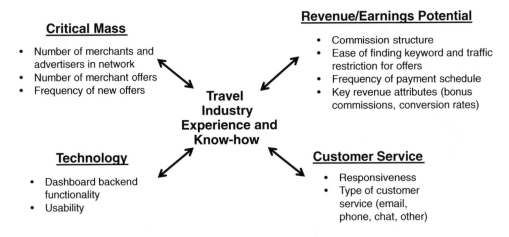

**Figure 4.16** *Key criteria for selecting an affiliate network*

portfolio. They work with over 200 travel suppliers including Air France, LAN Chile, and Lufthansa. OTAs including Expedia, Travelocity, and Priceline are also their clients.

■ *Rakuten Linkshare.* Large in scale and scope, it works with Orbitz, Hotwire, Delta, and Enterprise Car Rental.

■ *Google Affiliate Network.* Formerly Perfomics, it was acquired by Google in 2008 via DoubleClick. Rebranded as GAN (Google Affiliate Network), it typically works with high volume suppliers. Candidates apply for acceptance, match GAN's quality standards and can be subject to lengthy pre-qualification interviews.

■ *Affiliate Future.* Based in London, it has a large presence in Europe. It has plenty of travel experience and is currently working with BA, Virgin, and RUI Hotels.

Some airlines have gone into the affiliate program business themselves in recent years. Information on these very programs is found on their websites and ranges from featuring a generic overview to specific details on commission rates. Examples are the affiliate programs of Hawaiian Airlines and Turkish Airlines (Figure 4.17). Typically, airlines are open to a wide range of companies joining them. They include social media platforms, cashback sites, coupon/rebate sites, and even price comparison sites.

In the future, airlines are likely to continue using affiliate programs to leverage their online sales activities. This is because affiliate programs:

■ increase revenue as a result of more traffic driven to the carrier's site
■ extend the reach of the digital brand by tapping into additional outlets that have in-depth knowledge and access to local markets and shoppers
■ allow for an effective use of budgetary resources thanks to the performance-based aspect.

However, one area of concern moving forward deals with mobiles. With the ongoing shift toward mobile shopping, an airline has every reason to insist

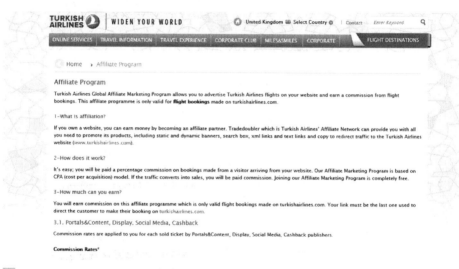

**Figure 4.17** *The affiliate program of Hawaiian Airlines and Turkish Airlines*

*Source:* hawaiianairlines.com (2015),[35] with permission from Hawaiian Airlines, turkishairlines.com (2015)[36] with kind permission of Turkish Airlines

that affiliates in a network have optimized their web presence for smart phones and tablets. Issues such as slow downloads and user–unfriendly consumer interfaces are counterproductive and make affiliate networks less attractive to airlines.

### 4.6.5 Profile: Global distribution systems (GDSs)

GDSs perform a number of critical functions. As a behind–the–scene distribution intermediary, they link electronically in real-time third party retail channels in the marketplace with the supply of airlines and other travel suppliers. The databases of

**Table 4.6** *Overview of the main global distribution systems*

| GDS Parent Company | Amadeus | Sabre | Travelport | Abacus* |
|---|---|---|---|---|
| Operation | Amadeus | Sabre | Apollo, Galileo, Worldspan | Abacus |
| Ownership | Several investors including BC Partners and Cinven, Air France, Lufthansa | Silver Lake, Texas Pacific Group | Several investors including Blackstone Group | Sabre + 11 Asia Pacific airline consortium |
| Head Office | Spain | USA | UK | Singapore |
| Approx. Employees | 12,000 | 10,000 | 3,400 | N/A |
| Revenue (2014) | $2.9 billion | $2.6 billion | $1.6 billion | $335 million (2013) |
| Region | Global presence, focus on Africa, Europe, Middle East, Asia Pacific | Global presence with focus on United States and Asia Pacific | Global presence, United States and Europe | Asia Pacific |
| Estimated Air Market Booking Share (2013) | 40% | 29% | 26% | 5% |

*A total of 35% of Abacus has been owned by Sabre since 1998. In May 2015, Sabre announced the acquisition of the remaining 65% for $411 million.

GDSs are vast and contain literally billions of pieces of information. Airlines participating in GDSs include their information on airline fares (fare levels and fare terms and conditions), flight schedules, and seat inventories. In addition, GDSs feature information for other areas such as travel insurance, destination information, and sightseeing. GDSs also conduct critical back office functions including feeding travel data to other parties both internally and externally for accounting and reporting purposes.

There are currently four major GDS parent companies in the world that operate six GDSs (Table 4.6). They include Amadeus, Sabre, Travelport, and Abacus. There are also country-specific GDSs such as Axxes/Infini (Japan), Sirena (Russia), Topaz (South Korea), and Travelsky (China). The main players including Amadeus, Sabre, and Travelport are wholly or partially owned by private equity groups.

The core business of GDSs is huge and they feature content of hundreds of airlines. Amadeus as the largest GDS accommodates close to 700 airlines' flight schedules for instance. The main GDSs also provide for IT consulting services and technology solutions to airlines including website booking engine platforms. In some cases, they were or even are investors in online travel start-ups and OTAs. An example is Amadeus' investment in Yapta, a travel meta-search engine. It also had owned a stake in OTA Opodo before it sold it to Odigeo in 2011. Over the last couple of years, Sabre sold OTAs it owned including lastminute.com, Travelocity, and Zuji.

It is crucial to highlight that GDSs can only aggregate and display information that is fed to them. For example, if a carrier decides not to share certain information such as fare specials with GDSs and only makes them available via its own direct channels, GDSs simply cannot distribute them to the other retail channels on the frontline. GDSs try to avoid this situation because it puts them at disadvantage for several reasons. They lose out on potential revenue in the form of booking fees that carriers pay them when flights (or flight segments to be exact) are booked via GDSs. Additionally, it weakens their partners, the third party retail channels, because they cannot offer attractive fares to the traveling public.

In order to address this issue, GDSs typically insist on contractual clauses applying the so-called "MFN" (Most Favored Nation) status. This gives them full content access to all of a carrier's fares. MFN is a concept borrowed from international trade relations whereby one nation grants another special trade status such as importing goods at reduced tariffs in order to increase the overall trade between the two countries. It is easy to imagine how quickly this causes contentious feelings in the relationship with a GDS if an airline wants to offer fare specials exclusively through its own lower cost online channels.

Equally important to point out is that GDSs can only aggregate and share information that the GDS platform itself is technologically enabled to handle. As part of their new fare merchandising strategy, a growing number of airlines have unbundled their fares and today offer a variety of add-ons on their own digital properties. Most GDSs are challenged to display this type of full content in their current systems. Due to the limitations to merchandising their products through GDSs, airlines have thus increasingly made the case for favoring distribution directly through their own sales outlets. This has caused tension in the travel ecosystem and we address this issue in more detail in our following discussion of ancillaries.

## 4.7 ANCILLARIES: AIRLINES TURNING TO MERCHANDISING AND BECOMING RETAILERS

Revenue generation beyond the actual ticket sale has existed for many years in the airline industry. It commonly included the fees levied for excess baggage, ticket changes, prepaid tickets, and unaccompanied minors. With the emergence of LCCs in the late 1980s, however, a whole new and wider perspective was brought to this extra or ancillary revenue.

In their strategy to compete against established legacy carriers, LCCs offered drastically lower fares by removing components of the airline fare product that were traditionally included in the base fare. In the past, airline customers have never considered these elements as part of a bundle since airlines have always marketed products, not bundles of components. This clearly changed when LCCs started unbundling fares and introduced à la carte fares.

An à la carte fare product essentially features separate and itemized elements of the airline fare product for which an airline customer now pays extra. In recent years, carriers have enhanced the à la carte menu with a variety of travel-related items. They include airport lounge vouchers, inflight wi-fi passes, priority boarding, and mileage boosters, to name a few examples. Besides offering à la carte products and services, several airlines have also started to re-package items and now market fare families and

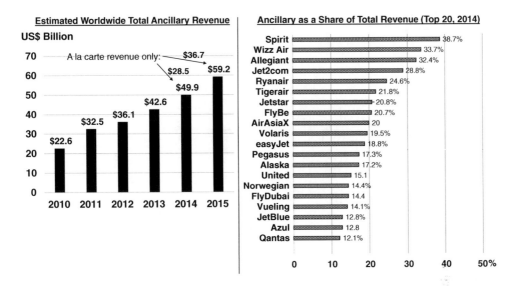

**Figure 4.18** *The growing importance of ancillary revenue★*

★Ancillaries defined: It includes à la carte, commission-based, frequent flyer, and advertising revenue

*Source:* Sorenson (2015)[37]

branded fares. Therefore, when referring to fare merchandising, we need to keep in mind that it involves a rather expanded concept. Importantly, while LCCs are still the main adopters of fare merchandising, legacy carriers have come to embrace it as well. In October 2015, Lufthansa became the first European legacy airline to unbundle services by introducing a three-tier fare system. This allows the company to not only compete more directly on the actual fare but also charge more for non-ticket items including checked bags and seat reservations. Introducing such services incur minimal costs and can therefore be an additional profitable revenue stream for airlines. The revenue importance of fare merchandising cannot be underestimated: Today, they are a major contributor to the airline industry's ancillary revenue generation. For 2015, the estimate was $36.7 billion out of a total ancillary revenue volume of $59.2 billion. ULCCs/LCCs are clearly leading in this area (Figure 4.18).

Airline websites are the main venue for generating ancillaries for now, although mobiles and airport kiosks are catching up (Figure 4.19).

By selling merchandise fares, an airline acknowledges that a seat is not any longer just a seat but actually a unique product. The days are gone when a seat was viewed as a commodity with the fundamental differentiator being whether the seat was in economy, business, or first class. Each airline will have to develop its own approach as to how to unbundle/repackage its fare products and price the different components.

Air Canada, a pioneer in fare merchandising—it unbundled fares and created branded fare families already back in 2002—currently features five fare products for its two-cabin service: Three in economy class branded as Tango, Flex, and Latitude, and two in business class (Business Class Lowest, Business Class Flexible). Associated

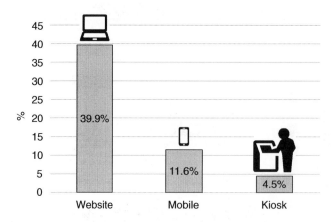

**Figure 4.19** *Where are ancillaries sold?*

*Source:* SITA (2014)[38]

with these fare products are various components ranging from fare refundability to baggage allowance (Figure 4.20). Depending on what fare components are important to online bookers, they opt for a particular fare product accordingly. One customer may appreciate Latitude's fare refundability and the option to check in two bags free of charge while another traveler may be drawn to Tango mostly because of its attractive price and the fact that other fare components such as full mileage credit or priority boarding are less critical.

### 4.7.1 Benefits of fare merchandising

Fare merchandising offers an airline several benefits. Importantly, it allows an airline to achieve three main objectives further discussed below.

*Product differentiation and brand enhancement*

With the ability to offer more choices in actual merchandising, an airline not only differentiates itself in the marketplace from the competition but also provides a unique value proposition for web travelers. Fare merchandising allows the "de-commoditization" of the airline seat, morphing airline into marketers and making it possible to strengthen their brand. This point is important because much, arguably too much, discussion revolves around the incremental revenue streams that come from fare merchandising. These are certainly beneficial but equally crucial should be the realization that fare merchandising is also about earning trust with web travelers, matching fares of competitors (most often LCCs), and providing for additional value.

*Revenue maximization*

The revenue streams from fare merchandising can be significant for a carrier. For example, in 2014, United Airlines realized $5.8 billion in revenue from

Fare
Products

| Fare Components | Economy class | | | Business Class (lowest) | Business Class (flexible) |
|---|---|---|---|---|---|
| | Tango | Flex | Latitude | | |
| Refundability ? | Non-refundable | Non-refundable | ✓ | Non-refundable | ✓ |
| Any-time change ? | $75 CAD + fare difference* | $50 CAD + fare difference* | fare difference* | $50 CAD + fare difference* | fare difference* |
| Same-day airport change fee ? | $150 CAD $75 CAD on Rapidair routes and flights between Calgary, Edmonton and Vancouver | $75 CAD | ✓ | $75 CAD | ✓ |
| Same-day airport standby ? | | Available on Rapidair routes and flights between Calgary, Edmonton and Vancouver Learn more | ✓ | Available on Rapidair routes and flights between Calgary, Edmonton and Vancouver Learn more | ✓ |

Fare
Components

| Mileage Accrual and Altitude Benefits | Tango | Flex | Latitude | Business Class (lowest) | Business Class (flexible) |
|---|---|---|---|---|---|
| Aeroplan Miles Accumulated ? | 25% | 100% | 125% | 150% | 150% |
| Altitude Qualifying Miles Accumulated ? | 25% | 100% | 125% | 150% | 150% |

| Travel Experience | Economy class | | | Business Class (lowest) | Business Class (flexible) |
|---|---|---|---|---|---|
| | Tango | Flex | Latitude | | |
| Priority check-in, baggage handling and boarding ? | | | ✓ | ✓ | ✓ |
| Access to Maple Leaf Lounges ? | | +$50 CAD | +$25 CAD | ✓ | ✓ |
| Complimentary checked baggage allowance ? | 1st bag $25 CAD (per direction) 2nd bag $25 CAD (per direction) | 1 Check a 2nd bag for only $25 CAD | 2 | 2 | 2 |

All Economy fares - Tickets issued before September 18, 2014 or travel before November 2, 2014: 1st bag free / $20 CAD (per direction)

Fare
Components

**Figure 4.20** *The fare products of Air Canada*

Source: Reproduced with the permission of Air Canada (2015)[39]

various ancillary sources including fare merchandising. Delta Airlines generated $350 million alone from Comfort Plus, its re-branded extra legroom economy class seats.[40] Further insight in how an ULCC maximizes revenues from fare merchandising is provided by Spirit Airlines. With almost 40% of their total annual revenue coming from ancillaries, they are among the world's leading carriers in this field. They have found the price elasticity of the primary purchase (the ticket) to increase significantly for fare levels of $99 and higher. If the base is less than $99, concern for the price levels of secondary add-ons is much less significant. With this approach, the carrier not only increases its loadfactor but also generates substantial ancillary revenue.[41] Figure 4.21 further illustrates the hypothetical revenue scenarios of a carrier with and without a fare merchandising process.

When discussing revenue maximization from fare merchandising, one should not ignore the opportunity for an airline to offset other cost increases quickly. Let us think of think of fuel price upswings that make à la carte fares also attractive to airlines. During the 2008 fuel crisis, for example, many US carriers swiftly introduced charges for checking a second bag.

*Distribution cost savings*

Certain fare merchandising products, à la carte fares for example, are offered primarily (at least currently) via airlines' direct online channels. This not only drives more web travelers to the airlines' digital properties but also saves distribution cost because of not merchandising via third party channels. However, one may also argue that not using the wider net of third party channels to attract more business limits the sales potential with shoppers who are undecided on the airline brand. This issue is clearly a trade-off and is different from airline to airline.

**Scenario 1:**
Traditional revenue management without ancillary revenue process. Carrier focuses on fare revenue maximization.

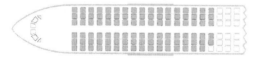

**Result:**

| | |
|---|---|
| Final booked load factor (*): | 84% |
| Final booked average fare: | $130 |
| Fare revenue: | $13,130 |
| Ancillary revenue: | $3,030 |
| Total revenue: | $16,160 |

**Scenario 2:**
Revenue management with ancillary revenue process. Carrier focuses on fare revenue maximization while increasing load factor.

**Result:**

| | |
|---|---|
| Final booked load factor (*): | 93% |
| Final booked average fare: | $115 |
| Fare revenue: | $12,834 |
| Ancillary revenue: | $3,520 |
| Total revenue: | $16,354 |

* = Aircraft has capacity of 120 seats

**Figure 4.21** *The ancillary revenue impact*

### 4.7.2 Challenges in fare merchandising

Introducing and managing fare merchandising on an airline's digital properties is not without challenges and it does not happen overnight. If it was easy, a larger number of carriers would have adopted a merchandising approach by now. There are several issues often encountered by carriers that should be highlighted.

*Damage to airline reputation*

Some carriers fear that their reputation could suffer by taking back something that people think they are already paying for. However, when we look at the impressive development of ancillary revenue, this fear appears largely unfounded. There is a willingness among web travelers to pay the extras provided they have real value, top quality, and help drive the base fare lower.

The key is to apply a sales and marketing concept that determines which web traveler type is to be attracted with fare merchandising in the first place. In this regard, a clear distinction between premium and leisure/VFR web travelers is required. This is because economy class is naturally the class of service to tackle with à la carte fares for example, without sacrificing the image of airlines, particularly that of legacy carriers. Once this is accomplished, an airline can embark on specific steps such as determining the base fare and the price points for the add-ons.

*Technological challenge of an airline's internal CRSs*

Many carriers still operate reservations and inventory platforms with legacy features dating back to computer mainframe infrastructures built in the 1960s. This kind of stale IT framework makes the introduction of fare merchandising in a web-driven environment difficult. The solution is a substantial upgrade of the existing legacy infrastructure or a switch to a new platform with tailor-made features that could also handle fare merchandising. Leading airlines in this field including Air Canada, American, and Spirit all have deployed unique IT platforms to support fare merchandising.

*Difficult to re-orient company culture*

LCCs have internalized fare merchandising but a large number of legacy carriers still struggle. This is because they manage their pricing activities based on old airline industry business models rather benchmarking themselves against companies such as Amazon and Apple to learn about their unrivalled best practices as online retailers. Also, the lack of dedicated resources to managing fare merchandising across sales, marketing and pricing/distribution departments can cause problems. Lastly, the lack of knowhow, experience, and training to pursue a more general retailer-oriented strategy also contributes to the challenges.

*Financial and other challenges*

The price to pay for entering the world of ancillaries varies by airline but there needs to be clarity on how much this costs and how fast this investment can be recouped. Investments are required for upgrading inhouse technology, integrating with third parties, supplying dedicated resources, and conducting ongoing training.

In addition to these internal challenges, there are issues that require attention in the external environment. There are several third party intermediaries in the picture including ATPCO, GDSs, and travel agencies. We need to remember that these companies' interactions among each other and with airlines for the purpose of fare communication and distribution follow technical formats and standards that were established in the 1960s and have not much changed.

Standard published fare products are available through this infrastructure. However, bundled, unbundled, and hyprid fare products that have increasingly become a standard offer on individual airline websites are still hard to find on GDS platforms and with travel agencies. One of the reasons is because they lack the required open XML web-based environment. For example, if we try to book Air Zealand's economy class Skycouch on an OTA website, this is currently impossible to do and one has to visit airnewzealand.com to book this product. It took GDSs eight years to create an infrastructure so that Air Canada's fare family, originally made available in 2002, finally could be accessed via GDS in 2010.[42]

It is therefore not surprising that many airlines are unhappy about the GDSs' lack of vision and slow uptake on this topic. A survey of several airlines provide for some clear comments in this regard:[43]

> **Our website presents multiple fare families. We have improved the user interface to help with upselling and how we present ancillary products. Take-up rates for some of our ancillary offers exceeds 20%. We get none of that—zero—on the OTAs.**
> **(Director e-Commerce US-based network airline)**

> **GDSs and travel agencies that can't or won't sell our ancillaries products the way we want will find that they have become invisible to us.**
> **(Managing Director, e-Commerce, European network/flag airline)**

GDSs have started to invest in their systems to handle merchandising products but the overall picture still looks patchy. Clearly, this is less of a technical and more of a commercial issue for GDSs. The investment in upgrades and training of agencies is not a small matter but needs to be addressed. In fairness to the GDSs, the continuous posturing by many airlines and then providing full content access on a selective basis only has not helped to resolve this dilemma more quickly. The recent IATA New Distribution Capability (NDC) initiative that also involves the adoption of an important XML-based messaging standard should help establish a base for a distribution of ancillaries on a consistent basis and large scale.

## SNAPSHOT: XML, OPEN AXIS GROUP, AND IATA'S RESOLUTION 787 FOR A NEW DISTRIBUTION CAPABILITY (NDC)

XML (eXtensible Markedup Language) is *the* language of communication between self-contained business applications that operate over the internet. In an analogy, English is a common language spoken by people all over the world (this makes English the lingua franca in the physical world actually), XML is the equivalent as the most common language of communication used by internet-based business applications.

The reason why XML is so popular and has acquired universal acceptance is mainly due to two aspects:[44]

■ XML has enabled different computer systems and databases containing data in incompatible data formats to talk to each other by prescribing a simple and common format.
■ XML is a so-called "meta-language," a language for describing other languages which allows for the design of one's own customized markup language for different types of documents.[45]

These two aspects allow for the development of a specific vocabulary for an industry such as travel and hospitality.

In 2010, one consortium called the Open Axis Group was created by North American carriers and technology companies. The purpose was to develop and advance XML vocabulary unique to the travel industry. The growing standardization of internet-based business applications and the standardization efforts around XML paved the way for different service providers to use standard interfaces. Via these interfaces, they could interact with each other and with the traveling public as there was no semantic gap between the various parties, be it airlines, travel agencies, or other participants.

Examples of internet-based business applications of importance in the airline travel space include:

■ those allowing for direct access to a travel supplier's inventory system
■ those enabling the bundling of fares and service offerings from single and multiple providers and personalizing these offerings based on a web traveler's value.

Without these internet–based applications, the aggregation, personalization, and direct access delivery is not possible. The IBM TPF (Transaction Processing Facility) platforms of the GDS mainframes from the 1950s/1960s were not built for the decoupling of data such as separating a passenger's transaction from his itinerary. With the new business applications on the market, this is now feasible.

As a result of pressure from member airlines, IATA had been looking for quite some time to address carriers' limitations in terms of distributing new internet–enabled differentiated product/service offerings and providing access to full and rich air content. The existing GDSs had been focused on delivering standard, commoditized content to travel agencies and therefore could not (or would not) accommodate the retailing solutions airlines wanted to offer. Against this background, IATA launched the NDC program with IATA Resolution 787 in fall 2012 (Figure 4.22).

The NDC program advocates an XML-based transmission standard that enables a modernization of the way airlines distribute their offerings. Specifically, airlines are provided with the ability to de-commoditize their supply. At the same time, third party channels including travel agencies, travel content aggregators such as meta–search engines, and

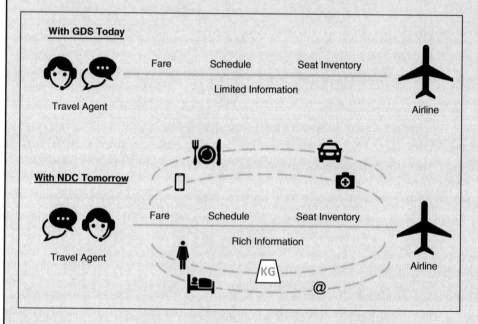

*Figure 4.22* De-commoditizing airline distribution: The impact of IATA NDC

corporate buyers are offered new rich airline content they can access. In spring 2013, after evaluating several XML standards, IATA opted for the one originally developed by the Open Axis Group.[46]

In essence, IATA's 787 Resolution for NDC has four mandates at its core to overcome the industry's current distribution gap:

- Allow individual airlines to determine their own prices and the nature of those products/services offered depending on who the requestor is and what they are requesting.
- Facilitate the implementation of a shopping basket capability a shopper to add or remove items from their basket as they choose. The different choices may trigger a re-pricing of the products offered by a carrier.
- Support the distribution of new products and the changes and amendments of existing orders.
- Facilitate a transparent display of products being offered and enable comparison among different products.

IATA's NDC program still makes some third parties nervous. For obvious reasons, GDSs are worried about the impact on their business by being bypassed in some direct connect scenarios. Likewise, corporate travel organizations such as the Business Travel Coalition (BTC) in the United States have gone on record with their concerns. Among the issues they claim one needs to watch out for include:[47]

- diminished price transparency due to airlines' individual ancillary programs that make an apple-to-apple product and service comparisons across different carriers almost impossible
- invasion of consumers' privacy as a result of collecting data that airlines require for their 1:1 product and service offerings.

Despite these concerns, the NDC program is progressing. An important boost for the NDC program came from the approval of the US DOT in August 2014.

The NDC program and associated XML standard is voluntary and no IATA member has to adopt it. Anyone wishing to continue using the existing transmission standard EDIFACT can do so. In 2014, ten airlines had signed up for participating in an NDC pilot including Aer Lingus, American, Hainan Airlines, Qatar Airways, and Swiss International.[48] The program is planned to be rolled out in 2016. In the meantime, issues such as who will ultimately pay for the adoption and ongoing operation of this technology standard by many of the worldwide 60,000 travel agencies still need to be settled. This means that NDC is not a guaranteed success. If NDC fails to catch on, it is likely that airlines will simply move forward individually with building platforms that enable the offering of ancillaries and personalized products and fares.

The introduction of airline merchandise fares has wide-ranging consequences. It represents a radically different way of distributing and selling airline fare products. Considering that this amazon.com retailing approach continues to garner momentum, it is difficult to imagine the industry will ever go back to the previous standard booking process for fares. Table 4.7 provides for an overview of what the implications are for specific players.

*Table 4.7* Implications of fare merchandising

| Entity | Impact |
| --- | --- |
| Web Travelers | The number of fare choices has certainly gone up and web travelers need to decide for various aspects of each booking what they want (or not). Web travelers would be challenged in their comparison shopping as an "apple-to-apple" comparison has become more difficult and time consuming. |
| Travel Agencies (off and online) | Traditional travel agencies and OTAs would be required to upgrade or replace their current technical systems in order to integrate the merchandise fare products and move away from offering standard, non-merchandise fare products to the traveling public. Part of this upgrade would involve the decision whether or not to "direct connect" to an airline's internal reservations system and/or modified GDS that could also handle merchandise fares. Like web travelers, travel agencies are likely to spend more time on the booking process due to the increased number of choices. |
| Global Distribution Systems | GDSs would need to invest in platform technology upgrades/training to be able to handle airline-specific merchandise fare products for further distribution among travel agencies. |
| Travel Meta-search Engines | Low fare search results may not be accurate, thus a modification of search algorithms reflecting a web traveler's search for merchandise fare products would seem critical. |
| Travel Management Companies | They might have to modify their corporate client databases and profiles as well as upgrade their booking platforms and technical systems to handle merchandise fare products. The booking process, as in the case for regular travel agencies, is likely to take longer and increase cost. |
| Airlines (and other ancillary suppliers like Hotels) | Suppliers need to overhaul their internal reservations platforms to offer merchandise fare products, re-orient their company culture, and adjust intra/inter-departmental processes to adopt a retailing approach. |

*Source:* Based on PhocusWright.com, 2008[49]

**Web Traveler Touchpoint:**

**Web Traveler Experience:**

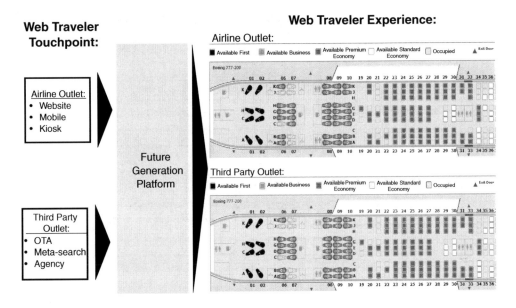

**Figure 4.23** *Consistency in customer experience across multiple touchpoints*

If and when merchandised products are available beyond an airline's own digital properties, web travelers can expect a more "apple-to-apple" consistent experience in terms of what specific ancillaries are offered and at what price. How this could look like is illustrated in Figure 4.23. It shows an example of an interactive aircraft seat map made available through an airline's digital properties and third party outlets including OTAs. Web travelers would experience a consistent product in both cases. For instance, buying a premium economy class seat or changing an existing business class seat would be feasible through either outlet. This is different from today where web travelers can do this on some carriers' websites but not on most other third party website.

## 4.8 THE COST OF AIRLINE E-SALES AND DISTRIBUTION

The airline industry is notorious for generating insufficient profits. When looking at the big picture, the overall return on capital has been improving in recent years and is predicted to be at 5.4% for 2014. However, this is still below the cost of capital and inadequate returns for the industry are the norm, not the exception (Figure 4.24). Furthermore, when reviewing the current cost situation for individual airlines, the legacy network carriers still have a long way to go to be more competitive.

Nevertheless, legacy airlines have made great strides in tackling costs in recent years. They reduced staff costs, benefits and pensions, they outsourced a number of operations, they cut down on inflight amenities, and they introduced new fees for high touch bookings. The problem: Most carriers still lost money. It was therefore only a matter of time before airlines addressed their high costs of distribution.

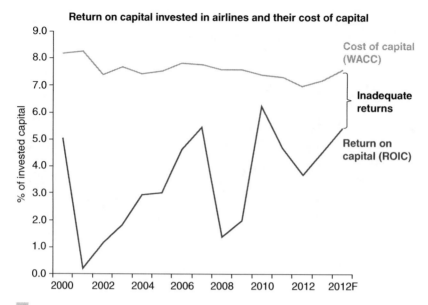

**Figure 4.24a** *Airline industry cost: Capital and return on capital…*

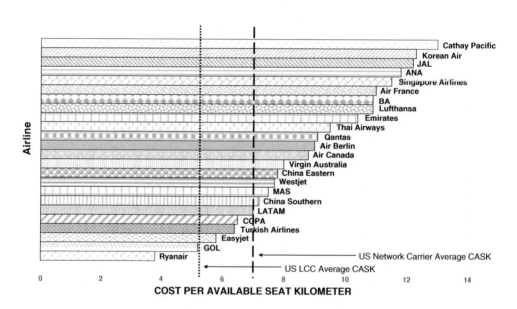

**Figure 4.24b** *…and cost per available seat kilometer for international carriers (adjusted to stage length of 2,126 km, average of group)\**

\* The CASK information shown here is useful for indicating the relative difference between airlines and should not be used for precise benchmarking or other analysis.

*Source:* Based on data by IATA (2014)[50] and Hazel and Stalnaker (2014)[51]

E-sales and distribution is expensive. According to one estimate, airlines world-wide pay annually around $7 billion in GDS fees alone.[52] Today, distribution accounts for 10% and less of gross revenue. LCCs have pushed this down even further.[53] Many airlines have managed to slash their distribution costs by half in a 10–15 year timeframe. This is a remarkable achievement but distribution costs nevertheless still weigh heavily on the mind of airline executives today (Figure 4.25).

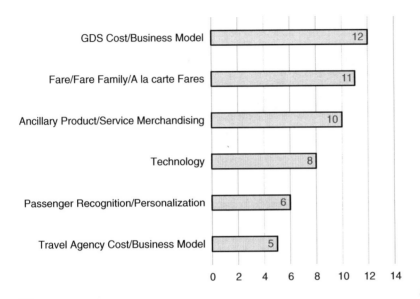

**Figure 4.25** *Distribution business issues frustrate airline executives more than technology*

Source: IATA (2015)[54]

This situation is understandable. From the airlines' perspective, they are the main service provider in the air transport value chain yet achieve small profits only. In 2014, a major carrier such as Lufthansa generated €30 billion in annual revenue with a profit of €55 million. At the same time, other participants including GDSs produce significantly by less revenue but show a much better profit picture. For example, the 2014 profit of GDS Amadeus was €632 million on revenue of €3.4 billion.[55] Amadeus' gross profit margin is 44%—even Apple with a 39% profit margin did not manage to achieve this.

It is in this context that Lufthansa embarked on an initiative that has received significant attention in the marketplace. In June 2015, the carrier announced that the Lufthansa Group would apply a so-called distribution cost surcharge of €16 (almost $18) per ticket as of September 1, 2015.[56] Thus, any leisure and corporate agency handling bookings via a GDS would have to either absorb this extra charge or pass it on to the traveler.

Initial market reactions to Lufthansa's announcement ranged from "the airline has gone mad" to "this was overdue." Not surprisingly, GDSs and many travel agencies are particularly concerned about loss of income as a result of this move. However,

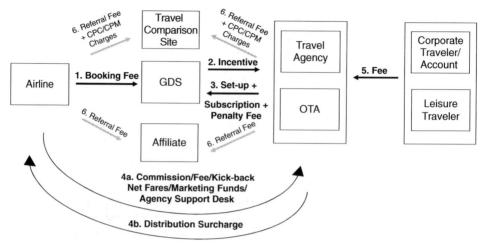

Excluded from this illustration:
- Booking engine provider fees
- Payment service provider fees
- Form of payment commissions

**Figure 4.26** *The system is expensive: The cost of sales and distribution*

this needs to be seen in the light of the airline's attempt to gain a higher share of the profits. According to the carrier, 70% of its tickets are handled through indirect distribution. Also, a direct booking with Lufthansa costs €2 versus €18 for bookings through third party channels that involve a GDS.[57] Against this background, the incentive to shift ticket sales to direct distribution and save on cost—the carrier spends a three-digit million Euro amount in payment to GDSs each year—is understandably strong.

In order to appreciate this whole cost sales and distribution discussion better, let us take a closer look where these costs actually originate and who is paying who for what. Figure 4.26 provides for an overview of this "web of costs" while Table 4.8 shares more details on each of the cost items involved.

**Table 4.8** *Who is paying who for what?*

| Who is paying who | Cost category | What is it? |
|---|---|---|
| 1. Airline to GDS | Booking Fee | It is a segment fee which means that each leg in a flight itinerary is charged. A typical airline booking contains three to four segments. The fee level is influenced by numerous factors and varies by carrier. Factors that come into play include the length of the contract with a GDS, a carrier's booking volume, and aspects such as how keen a GDS is to break into a market. A booking fee can be around $2 on the low end and exceed $10 on the high end. Typically, a booking fee is even paid when a traveler cancels their itinerary. |

**Table 4.8** *continued*

| Who is paying who | Cost category | What is it? |
|---|---|---|
| 2. GDS to Travel Agency/ OTA | Incentive | This fee is a legacy from the days when GDSs in their early days as CRSs were still owned by airlines. Back then, to incentivize the sign-up of a travel agency to its respective CRS, an airline offered a payment for every booking by the travel agent. Today, GDSs share part of the booking fee collected from the airline with the travel agency. |
| 3. Travel Agency to GDS | Set-up/ and Subscription/ Penalty Fee | One-time installation for GDS connection plus a monthly maintenance fee. Depending on the contract, the set-up can range from being free to a few hundred dollars, same for subscription. A penalty fee could kick in if a travel agency does not meet its share quota of bookings on a particular GDS. Bookings done on another GDS can be penalized with a payment of around $2 per booking segment by the agency to the main GDS. |
| 4a. Airline to Travel Agency | Various | *Commission*: A percentage of the airline fare. Most of the United States and Europe today are commission free but airlines still pay them in many other markets around the world such as in Africa, Asia/Oceania, and Latin America. Commissions are also common for tour packages of which airlines could be part. |
| | | *Service Fee*: Paid for travel agency booking. |
| | | *Kick-back*: An override payment for having achieved certain revenue volume hurdles. |
| | | *Net Fare*: A deep discount applied to fare that the travel agency can mark up and sell at a level of its choosing. |
| | | *Marketing Funds*: Cash contribution to travel agency's marketing activities that promote the airline. |
| | | *Travel Agency Support Desk*: An airline help/Q&A desk dedicated to a particular agency in order to handle its queries. |
| 4b. Travel Agency to Airline | Distribution Surcharge | A surcharge levied by some carriers on agencies (traditional and OTAs) when going through a GDS for their bookings. The surcharge can be as high as $18 per ticket as in the Lufthansa case. It aims at stimulating direct bookings with the carrier's sales outlets including website/ mobile, and ATO/CTO that bypass GDSs. |
| 5. Traveller to Travel Agency/ OTA | Fee | *Management Fee*: Paid by corporate accounts for having managed their travel policy. This could also include part or all of any commission that an airline pays to corporate clients. |
| | | *Service Fee*: Paid by traveler for travel agency service including bookings. The service could be a flat fee or a transaction paid for particular activities. |
| | | Either fee may include a distribution surcharge that some airlines apply when a booking is done via a channel that uses a GDS. |
| 6. Airline and OTA to Travel Meta-search Engine and Affiliate | Referral Fee | *Affiliate Fee*: Cost per Action (CPA) paid for qualified booking that originates on affiliate website. Can be flat amount or percentage based. |
| | | *Travel Meta-search Fee*: CPA coupled with Cost per Click (CPC) or Cost per Thousand (CPM). |

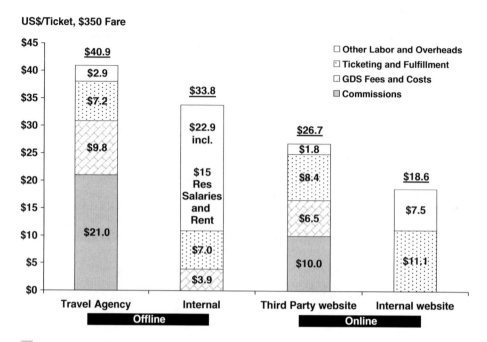

**US$/Ticket, $350 Fare**

*Figure 4.27* Distribution cost by channel

Source: Author analysis[58]

For an airline to be able to bypass middlemen translates into significant cost savings as illustrated by cost of channel analysis involving a major US carrier. For instance, an average ticket price of $350 involves over $40 in distribution costs when sold through a travel agent receiving a commission and a GDS earning a booking fee. On the other end of the spectrum, if the same ticket was sold on a carrier's website bypassing third parties such as travel agencies and GDSs, the distribution costs could fall below $19 (Figure 4.27). These savings naturally vary by carrier. However, they emphasize the general significance of direct distribution and in particular the role of an airline's website as a low-cost distribution channel.

Admittedly, some internet channel-specific cost items are excluded. One example is a carrier's distribution costs associated with advertising and promotion. They are likely to increase because the carrier would have to make up for some of its brand disappearance on third party sales and distribution platforms. An airline would have to engage in a full-cost channel analysis to gauge where its various channels stand in relation to each other.

If the direct distribution costs approached those of indirect channels (this is unlikely but let us assume this for a moment), one would have to raise the question of whether the quality of these other channels was the same. If, for example, third party sales channels and distribution intermediaries cannot offer the same travel ancillaries and fare merchandising as available on the carrier's digital properties, the answer is no because the carrier probably loses out incremental revenue streams. Likewise, if selling direct enables an airline to gather data for digital profiling about web travelers that would otherwise be not available, one could argue that this benefit is worth a premium. Lufthansa's motive to levy a distribution surcharge is undoubtedly also driven by these aspects.

It is unknown how the marketplace will eventually deal with Lufthansa moving forward. As planned, the carrier implemented the fee on September 1, 2015, and throughout spring 2016, the company has been sticking to its strategy. A reported 16% market share drop in Europe for Lufthansa with the main GDSs[59] is too early (and too distorted since Lufthansa also suffered from a two-day pilot strike that month) to indicate if the company's financial performance will be hurt or the result will be impact neutral because shifted booking patterns are made up for by increased direct bookings. Other major carriers around the world including British Airways and the KLM-Air France Group operating in Lufthansa's immediate neighborhood are likely to follow this development closely. One thing seems sure: Lufthansa has put a stake in the ground for direct distribution.

---

## SNAPSHOT:ONE AIRLINE'S EXPERIENCE (US AIRWAYS)—AIRLINE DISTRIBUTION THROUGH TIME

1993    Close to 80% of US Airways' revenue comes from the traditional travel agency sector. The company even owned 11% of the Galileo GDS at the time. Like other US carriers, US Airways pays a 10% standard commission on the ticket price.

1995    US carriers decide to keep the 10% commission paid to travel agencies but caps it at $50 for a round trip. Agencies respond with lawsuits claiming that airlines illegally collude. US Airways closes its call center in Reno, Nevada. A PC-based booking tool called Priority TravelWorks was introduced. Two new technologies are explored e-ticketing and airport kiosks.

1997    US Airways lowers its standard commission to 8% while caps on payout remain in place.

1998    USAirways.com is launched and replaces Priority TravelWorks.

1999    E-ticketing represents half of the carrier's sales. It sells its stake in Galileo and online sales amount to 6% with half coming from young OTA Priceline.com. Travel agency commission drops from 8% to 5%.

| 2000 | Majority of bookings still comes from travel agencies but online revenue climbs to 11%. |
|------|------------------------------------------------------------------------------------------|
| 2002 | Airline eliminates travel-based commission of 5% completely but leaves intact overrides provided agencies achieve certain revenue targets. Not surprisingly, commission as a percentage of overall operating expense drops to less than 2%. |
| 2003 | Internet bookings rise to 20%. E-tickets make up 90% of all tickets boosted by a $25 surcharge for non-elite members still using paper tickets. Carrier comments on the fact that while traditional travel agencies are becoming less expensive, OTA bookings actually are becoming more costly. OTAs could charge extra for preferential display, unlike the regulated GDSs. |
| 2004 | GDS deregulation opens new opportunities to negotiate lower transaction fees, especially after US Airways' merger with America West that has now more bargaining power. First travel meta-search engine in the form of Kayak.com enters the market. |
| 2005 | Alternative lower cost GDSs (GNEs) emerge. Airlines leverage them to push GDSs to accept lower fees as more carriers threaten to otherwise withdraw fare content from them. GDSs also agree to new pricing models including extending fee discounts on low fare bookings and differentiation by geographic region. |
| 2007 | US Airways announces launch of mobile site. Distribution cost as of percentage of total cost stands at 4%. |
| 2008 | The carrier levies surcharges for bookings done via its call centers or city ticket offices. USAirways.com reaches 25% of total sales with OTAs contributing another 32%. The airline also offers "Choice Seats" as an online ancillary for customers who want the option to reserve certain seats on the airplane. |
| 2010 | US Airways is developing the capability for travel intermediaries to sell ancillary services through a direct connection, bypassing the GDSs. |
| 2013 | US Airways generates 61% of its revenue online—33% come from its website and 28% from OTAs. It also introduces a mobile app. |

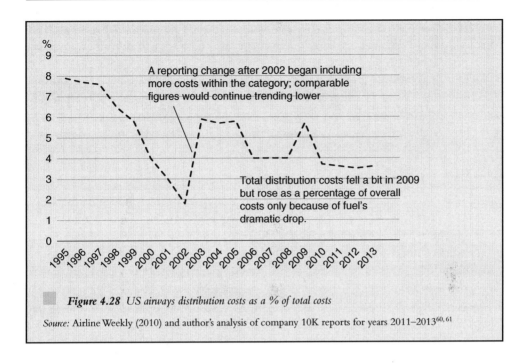

*Figure 4.28* US airways distribution costs as a % of total costs

*Source:* Airline Weekly (2010) and author's analysis of company 10K reports for years 2011–2013[60, 61]

## 4.9 THE ISSUE OF DIRECT CONNECT

Direct connect describes a sales and distribution arrangement where a direct relationship between the airline and a travel agency exists and the GDS is bypassed. However, direct connect can also involve a GDS and even an aggregator (Figure 4.29). Direct

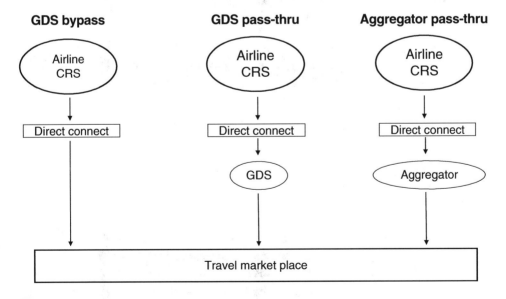

*Figure 4.29* Direct connect scenarios

connect is about a link that directly taps into an airline's inhouse reservation system. This link uses XML internet-based technology that allows for more robust and flexible transactions including those related to merchandising and ancillaries.

Over 30% of airlines already had this type of set-up in place in 2012 and another 30% planned to do so by the end of 2015 according to a SITA survey.[62] Even if only half of this materializes, this is a significant enough development in the marketplace with huge implications for all stakeholders of the e-travel ecosystem.

### 4.9.1 GDS bypass

There is no GDS involved in this distribution scenario. A direct link exists between the airline's inhouse reservation system and travel agencies. For a travel agency, the upside of this relationship is full access to an airline's suite of fares and ancillary products/services, identical with what is offered on the airline's website. Furthermore, dynamic pricing and offerings of personalized ancillary services based on a web traveler's value are possible.

Some airlines promote their direct connect solutions under particular brand names. An example is Delta and its SPRK platform. Travel agencies and TMCs can sign up for it on delta.com in order to have full access to the carrier's fares and ancillary options. A high profile airline that has recently implemented direct connect set-ups is Lufthansa. In November 2015, it revealed that several German travel agencies would be using a new interface that provides for direct access to the Lufthansa Group's reservation system. This arrangement allows for the booking of fares as available on lufthansa.com (and on the websites of the other member airlines of the Lufthansa Group) but without the application of the distribution cost charge of €16 otherwise levied when bookings involve GDSs.

The GDS bypass set-up entails a 1:1 relationship between an airline and a travel agency/TMC. This also means whatever the cross-selling product limitations of the airline are in terms of selling hotels and cars, for example, the travel agency/TMC faces the same limitations. It therefore should be of genuine interest to an indirect retail outlet to enter a direct connect relationship with multiple airlines and other core travel suppliers. It is not uncommon for a travel agency to maintain both direct connect with selected airlines and relationships with other airlines via GDSs at the same time. The challenge for a travel agency is to engage some interface that allows efficient toggling back and forth between the two set-ups. However, this may be the lesser evil if one wants to have access to both deep content and wide content from airlines at the same time.

Importantly, companies including small corporates and SOHOs are also often engaged in direct relationships with airlines. However, this should not be confused with direct connect because there is no travel agency/TMC involved. Instead, it is another form of direct distribution. In this case, the corporate may have signed up for one of the online corporate travel incentive programs that most airlines offer today through their websites. In return for generating a certain volume of business through an airline's website, the companies could become eligible for a variety of perks such as fare discounts, special mileage bonuses, upgrades, and other benefits. Air New Zealands'

"CompanyAdvantage", British Airways' "On Business", and Singapore Airlines' "SQCorporate" are program examples offered to small–medium sized companies.

### 4.9.2 GDS pass-thru

In this set-up, the GDS is fully integrated and a direct connect exists between the airline inhouse reservation system and the GDS. The GDS then acts as a central aggregator and distributor of the content provided by airlines and, further, shares it with travel agencies and other indirect sales intermediaries. This all sounds like what we are already familiar with from the traditional GDS in its role as a distribution intermediary. However, the big difference is that the connection between the airline's reservation system and GDS is XML-based—as opposed to an EDIFACT connectivity—and involves web traveler authentication.

With the GDS pass-thru, content with fares and ancillary products/services is "pulled" from the airline reservation system and delivered in a tailored fashion according to the web traveler's value. Companies that have adopted this approach include Air Canada that partnered with airline technology provider Farelogix to offer its direct connect product "AC2U" linking to the Travelport GDS.[63]

### 4.9.3 Aggregator pass-thru

An aggregator in this case is understood to be a company with a platform that assembles fares and ancillary products/services from multiple sources and provides them to the traveling public. An example would be an OTA like Priceline.com that actually has had this arrangement with American Airlines since late 2010.[64]

With aggregator pass-thru, no GDS is involved. Whatever content resides in the airline's reservations system is channeled through its direct connect product straight to the aggregator for further distribution to the marketplace. B2B corporate travel solutions provider Concur is another company that uses this set-up for its business. It currently has a direct connect arrangement with Aer Lingus, Air Canada, Southwest, and Virgin Australia.[65] Interestingly, Lufthansa has brought a new twist to the aggregator based direct connect. In a first for any legacy carrier in the world, Lufthansa has struck a direct connect partnership with Google. Web travelers using Google Flight Search would now be able to secure their tickets directly with the airline via a Book On Google button featured in the search results (Figure 4.30). The feature is currently only offered to web travelers in the US and is on both desktop and mobile versions of Google Flight Search.

Table 4.9 provides a high-level comparison between GDS and direct connect distribution.

### 4.10 OPEN BOOKING: A KIND OF CORPORATE VERSION OF DIRECT CONNECT

With online leisure travel being continuously revolutionized by new internet-based devices and applications, it should not come as a surprise that the way corporate

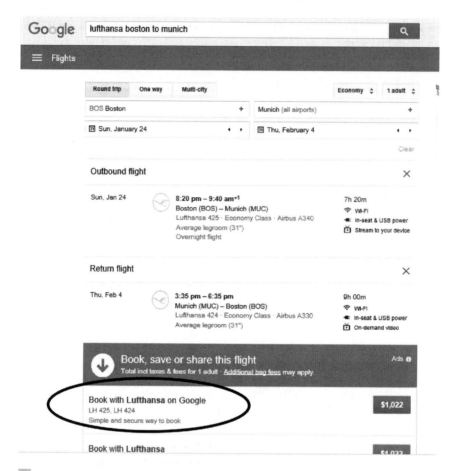

***Figure 4.30*** *A new form of direct connect: Lufthansa's partnership with Google*

*Source:* Google (2015)[66]

Google and the Google logo are registered trademarks of Google Inc., used with permission

travel is booked and sold is also undergoing significant changes. Open booking is one of them. Open booking surfaced as a popular term in 2012 in regards to corporate travel. Essentially, it is a concept which frees a business traveler from having to arrange their bookings through specifically designated channels as part of a company's travel management policy. Large market and SMEAD (Small and Medium Enterprise Agency Driven) companies generally have these travel management policies in place. As long as the traveler stays within budget and does not violate travel program criteria, they may book wherever they want. Some companies including Yahoo and Google have abandoned traditional corporate agencies/TMCs already years ago but these were more exceptions than the rule.

The purpose of corporate travel programs is to enforce defined travel policies such as booking with certain travel suppliers and through certain agencies. The overarching aim is to control travel expenses. However, numerous studies for the US business travel market have shown that booking compliance with company travel policies is not

**Table 4.9** GDS distribution vs direct connect

| Issues | GDS<br>Collect and offer airline supply but not all price and ancillary options | Direct connect<br>Offers deeper 1:1 access to an airline's CRS with all price and ancillary options |
|---|---|---|
| Balance of power | GDS | Airline |
| Airline data control/capture | Poor | Good |
| Ability to merchandise | Poor–Medium | Excellent |
| primary technology | Mainframes and proprietary terminals using EDIFACT messaging | Internet-based technology with XML messaging |
| Consequence of direct connect | *Short-term*: GDSs agree to fee reductions and new more competitive pricing models for airlines, possible lawsuits and airline product boycotts.<br><br>*Long-term*: Sustainability of GDS business model based on booking segment fees questionable.<br><br>Massive investments in technology upgrades necessary to operate in internet-based environment and also handle merchandising (some of this is already underway). Battling with new distribution intermediaries such as Google is increasingly likely.<br><br>*Key question*: Are GDSs moving fast enough? | Cost savings, increase of brand equity due to direct interaction with traveler, full data capture for digital profiling, increase of revenue from merchandising. |
| Relationship with travel agency | Some travel agencies may put pressure on GDSs to sustain current business model and thereby attempt to protect their income streams. Others, particularly corporate agencies and TMCs, continue favoring GDSs due to their one-stop access to multiple suppliers (for them the GDS reach is "one to many"). However, these agencies will also push for GDS platform upgrades to offer dynamic pricing based on travel client value and ancillaries. | *Upside*: Travel agency has access to full suite of fares and ancillaries of individual airline.<br><br>*Downside*: Travel agency loses booking incentives from GDSs. Also, the reach to many airlines and other core travel suppliers is more limited due to lack of central access system such as GDS (the direct connect reach is one to one).<br><br>*Key question*: What are carriers' incentives for selling ancillaries? Impact on corporate agencies/TMCs due to open booking? |

consistent and is falling short. For instance, 40% of business travelers do not consistently book through their company's TMC.[67] Furthermore, only 21% of US companies have a mandated travel program. The rest either run a lightly managed program with guidelines and a recommended travel agency or have a completely unmanaged travel program where employees book through any website or travel agency that they prefer.[68]

The marketplace has changed and "do it yourself" bookings by corporate travellers outside the company program have grown in popularity. Booking out-of-program is generally done for valid reasons. They include having found a lower rate on the internet and wanting to save money for their company. At the same time, today's business travelers have access to a wide array of well developed leisure travel booking tools by OTAs and airlines. They therefore look for the same kind of features on their company's booking platforms. Absent these, the consumerization trend of corporate travel is likely to gain more momentum in the future. Against this background, companies have been looking for tools to still track a corporate traveler's booking/trip expenses and also receive the corporate discounts previously negotiated with an airline and other travel providers. One such tool is provided by Concur, a travel technology and expense management company (Figure 4.31).

A carrier that has entered a partnership with Concur is United Airlines. In 2014, they announced a deal whereby companies that are clients of both United and Concur and book flights on united.com would still receive the corporate discounts that their companies have negotiated with the airline. Under this arrangement, employees of Concur clients that have negotiated airfare deals with United and, using TripLink, can link their Concur profiles with their United MileagePlus FFP accounts, and then shop for flights on united.com instead of being required to use the approved corporate booking tool. In addition to still getting the corporate fare discount on the United website, the travelers can also view their consolidated itinerary in Concur's TripIt itinerary manager and have their flight bookings automatically flow into their expense reports.

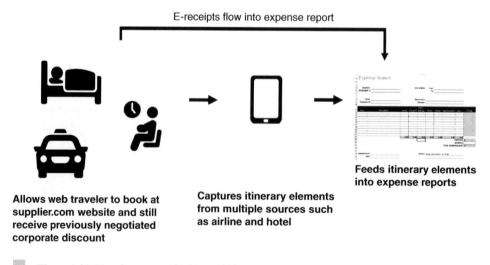

E-receipts flow into expense report

Feeds itinerary elements
into expense reports

Allows web traveler to book at
supplier.com website and still
receive previously negotiated
corporate discount

Captures itinerary elements
from multiple sources such
as airline and hotel

*Figure 4.31 How does an open booking tool like Concur work?*

## 4.11 AIRLINE ONLINE PRICING: AN INTRODUCTION

Airline online pricing deals with the methods and processes a carrier deploys to set prices for the fares it offers to the traveling public. Online pricing is developed against the background of the overall corporate pricing policy and objectives of an airline. As such they are an integral part of what the company should seek to achieve: The generation of an adequate profit after the recovery of its costs related to the production of the transport service, associated advertising and promotion, and utilization of certain sales and distribution channels.

Is online pricing different from offline pricing? The answer to this commonly posed question is that it depends. When looking at the inherent service characteristics of air transportation, the answer is no. This is because they equally apply to pricing via offline and online channels. Let us recall what these inherent characteristics are:

- First, the demand for air transport is a so-called derived demand because it depends on the demand for other goods and services. This interdependence means that pricing for it to be effective needs to be cognizant of developments of a socio-economic, political–legal, and technological nature that determine a market's demand for goods and services.
- Second, air transportation is a fairly undifferentiated service with a high degree of homogeneity. Features associated with the delivery of service such as aircraft type, flight schedule, and seat comfort are largely viewed by the traveling public more as a commodity. An airline typically seeks to avoid this commoditization with branding efforts. The role of pricing is to help recover these costs.
- Third, in air transportation, production and consumption take place at the same time and a seat not filled at take-off means lost revenue forever. This instant economic perishability introduces a time utility dimension that has a twofold impact on an airline's pricing decisions. One is that it will attempt to account for the various time utilities of different market segments by price discriminating accordingly. The other is that if a seat appears to be left empty at departure time, an airline will usually undertake every effort to at least sell the seat at a price to cover its marginal costs. This contributes to recouping some of its fixed costs.

There are other factors known to exert influence on an airline's pricing activities. One is related to the market demand for airline services and how this very demand changes as a result of price level adjustments. The relationship between the two is inverse: When prices goes up, demand declines and vice versa. Depending on the character traits of a person and their travel context (e.g. is the purpose of the trip for business or personal reasons and who is absorbing the trip expenses, when is the trip scheduled and how long is it?), everyone has a different reaction to price changes even at different points in time. This is all captured by a concept called price elasticity of demand.

Demand-based pricing, also referred to as charging what the market can bear, seeks to set fare levels according to the value perception and elasticity of travelers. Against this background, maximizing a carrier's revenue is achieved by optimizing the mix of seats allocated to each passenger segment and charging each segment the highest possible fare. The concept of price elasticity does not care if the channel through which fares are offered is digital or analog.

The same is true for competition, another factor that plays a key role in airline pricing activities. The industry is known for oligopolistic pricing behavior where pricing by one airline is managed with a close eye on the effect on its competitors. This is particularly the case for markets and industries with a relatively small number of competitors offering a fairly undifferentiated service.

Is there a difference between offline and online pricing because of government influence? There are instances where countries have bilateral aviation agreements that require the prior approval of fares by government authorities from both sides before airlines can offer them. Furthermore, governments in many countries are concerned with the protection of the traveling public against collusive pricing behavior by airlines that attempt to charge higher fares by secretly coordinating their pricing activities. Another aspect of consumer protection extends to the transparency of price information and specifically how airlines communicate their fare information to the public. In all these instances, again, it does not matter if we deal with fares distributed offline or online.

### 4.11.1 Fares on the web or web fares?

Due to competitive pressures and customer demands, many incumbent carriers rushed into an online presence and did not have a chance to appreciate the complexities of multi-channel pricing. If there was anything such as an online pricing strategy, it mirrored what was going on in the traditional world of airline pricing:

- Fare transparency was limited to airlines and travel agencies.
- Fares were available everywhere (hence the term "published fare") via airlines and travel agencies. Exceptions were the so-called negotiated fares, specially discounted fares that an airline offered to a few designated travel agencies and corporate accounts only (negotiated fares are also referred to as "private fares").
- Airlines reacted quickly to industry fare changes and matched fares competitively as appropriate.
- Minimization of low yield fare products including opaque and net fares.

In the first few years of airline e-commerce, most airlines simply transferred their offline fare products to the online world. In other words, they published fares on the web. However, this "copying and pasting" of fares from the offline to the online world was about to change with the introduction of web-exclusive fares.

LCC easyJet is credited with having created the world's first web discount in 1998. The web fare level was set below that of fares sold via the call center, then the company's primary sales channel. With this action, web fares were born. One may argue that the emergence of the internet has given rise to a new sales channel consciousness within an airline that had not existed before. In the past, a carrier would not have thought about pricing fares differently when selling through its call center or CTO. The cost of sales of these internal channels was similar and business was done for the most part anyway with trusted partners such as travel agencies. However, with the advent of the commercial internet, airlines now could sell directly and more cost efficiently. The emergence of web-exclusive fares therefore was only a question of time.

### 4.11.2 Airline web fares and services

From the first web discount in 1998 by a single LCC, online pricing by airlines has come a long way. For example, most carriers today are able to segregate lower internet-only fares from the published fare inventory. Among other things, the introduction of new inventory booking classes dedicated to web fares and the application of new fare filing mechanisms have made this possible. With this, an airline can manage the allocation of seat inventory to web fares more effectively. Additionally, over the years, there has been a proliferation of web-based fare products and services. Many airlines today offer a wide range of them (Figure 4.32). Our following discussion provides for more details.

*Web fare specials*

These are fare specials offered to offload last minute distressed inventory or promote a particular occasion. They are sporadic in nature. The airline's website is the principal sales platform for this type of fare. Examples include Virgin Atlantic's midnight fares that web travelers could only purchase online within brief windows (e.g. Friday evening between 10 pm and midnight) and Cyber Monday deals in the United States

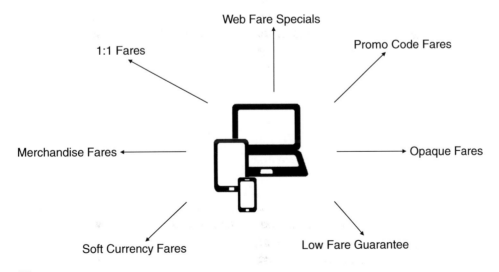

*Figure 4.32* Major airline web fare products

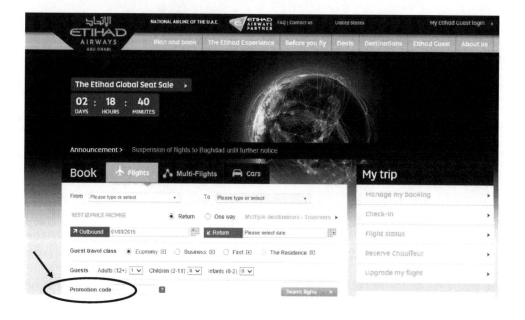

**Figure 4.33** *Promo-code fare on etihad.com*

Source: etihad.com (2015)[69]

when airlines offer extremely discounted web fares. Occasionally, third party platforms including auction websites are also used for the promotion of airline web fare specials.

*Promo code fares*

The airline issues an alpha-numeric code that is provided by private communication, typically email. Upon entering this particular code in a promo code field on the airline website during the reservations/purchase process, the shopper receives a discount (a percentage or a certain dollar amount) on whatever the otherwise published fare level is (Figure 4.33). Carriers use them in three ways:

- To address post-flight customer service issues. The tool is used for compensation purposes and involves a discount for the next flight within a certain time period. The code is communicated via email by customer service.
- To increase web revenue with leisure/VFR travelers with one-time codes. Market communication is low profile and this is the closest thing to a truly private fare because the airline determines the target audience and level of discount. Frequent target customers are FFP members and other high-value travelers. A wider non-FFP audience may also be engaged but the fare communication is then less shielded from the larger public and could invite competitors' to counter.

■ To manage business with corporate accounts (mostly with SME, SOHO but also large corporations) where online discounts are offered on a 365-day basis. The code is generally shared with the travel arranger in a company.

## Opaque fares

Airlines offer unbranded fares via third party opaque operators including Hotwire59 and Priceline which sell them at their own economic risk. Opaque fares are from distressed inventory and airlines like to offer them during weak demand periods while still protecting their brand and reputation as a premium/high- or full-service carrier in the marketplace.

A buyer of an opaque fare does not know until payment completion/receipt of reservation confirmation with what airline they will fly. Opaque fares are private fares and offered via a selected number of online travel agencies.

## Merchandise fares

Merchandise fares are considered the industry's single biggest strategic initiative in airline pricing. By selling merchandise fares, an airline acknowledges that different web travelers have different needs (and even the same web traveler has different needs at different times) and they do not need all components of a trip. One web traveler may accept no or fewer miles in return for a lower fare while another may be willing to pay an extra fee for a premium seating or a wi-fi pass.

Merchandise fares come in three main forms: Branded fares, fare families, and à la carte fares.

■ *Branded fares.* These are typically promoted under particular names to make it easier for web travelers to understand what they are paying for. An example is American Airlines that offers three fares under an umbrella brand that deals with several travel options: "Choice", "Choice Essential", and "Choice Plus". Essentially, a branded fare is a fare product that offers basic amenities but a web traveler has the option to upgrade to higher-end bundles with additional extras. Branded fares are always available and the price differentials among them are fixed. For instance, in American's case, this means that the "Choice" fare is offered on each flight and the upgrade charge from "Choice Essential" to "Choice Plus" is the same with $20. Jetstar is another example of a carrier applying a similar fare concept as American, although their fares may not be considered by some observers as branded because of the rather generic labels applied (Figure 4.34). Branded fares do not always have to be part of an airline's standard fare suite. Some carriers also brand fares for temporary special promotions. United Airlines' E-fares are an example.
■ *Fare families.* Similar to branded fares, they are linked to existing fare categories whereby higher fares mean more benefits for the web traveler. However, unlike with branded fares, once their lower fare options are sold out on a flight, web travelers have only limited choices. An example of a fare family is Air Canada's with Tango, Flex, Latitude fares.

**Figure 4.34** *Fare merchandising on jetstar.com*

*Source:* jetstar.com (2015)[70] with kind permission of Jetstar

■ *À la carte fares.* With this fare type, a web traveler may opt to purchase add-ons to the base fare. Standard extras could be premium seating, boarding priority, and inflight wi-fi pass. The lower fare options may sell out as demand increases but the add-ons are always available for purchase.

*Low fare guarantee (LFG)*

This is not really a fare product but more of a service. LFG programs are offered by many airlines today. Started by Continental Airlines in August 2004 in the United States and replicated by other airlines around the world, it is typically promoted on an airline's website homepage. Figure 4.35 shows Polish airline LOT promoting its LFG on lot.com.

An LFG is essentially an airline's promise to the traveling public to match a lower fare for the same itinerary offered on third party websites. The purpose of an LFG is twofold:

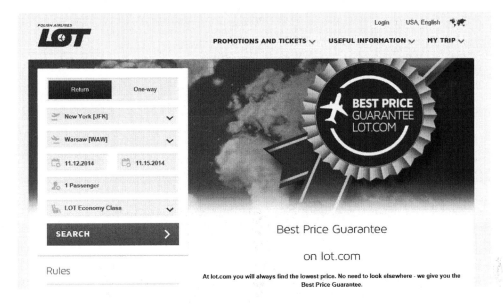

**Figure 4.35** *Low fare guarantee on lot.com*

*Source:* lot.com (2015)[71] with kind permission of LOT Polish Airlines

- To enhance the airline website's traction with price-sensitive web travelers known to check out multiple websites before their final purchase decision and capture more of their wallets.
- To position an airline website as a competitive shopping alternative to OTA websites that traditionally have a larger appeal with price-sensitive leisure travelers due to their wide selection of different airline suppliers and attractive fare levels.

The burden of proof is with the web traveler who needs to submit a claim form and provide for a screenshot of the site with the lower fare or contact the airline's customer service. If the claim is legitimate, the fare differential is redeemed in the form of a credit for a future ticket purchase or even refunded. Whatever the redemption process is, an airline needs to ensure that it is fast and uncomplicated to maintain the LFG's credibility in the marketplace.

A LFG is typically fenced in by tight terms and conditions. The lower fare has to be found 24 hours after a purchase on the airline's site has already been made. Additionally, it only applies to the same airline, date, class of service, and flight. In other words, the applicability of the program is relatively narrow and airlines have consciously stayed away from matching anything else (especially fares of other carriers).

From the perspective of price-sensitive web travelers engaging in aggressive comparison shopping and normally purchasing on OTA websites, the current LFGs may have some appeal. It dismisses the general perception that suppliers do not offer the best rates themselves. As such, LFGs probably offer some peace of mind for shopping on specific airline websites. At the same time, unless the scope of the current LFGs is enlarged to include matching fares of competing airlines, an LFG by itself is not a game changer. LFGs may play a more important role for carriers in emerging online travel markets where the online purchase of airline tickets is not firmly established yet and the "offline-to-online channel shift" is still in its early stages.

### Soft currency fares

Soft currency fares are generally offered in situations where airlines face limitations in discounting online fare levels. This could be because the airline wants to avoid a confrontation with sales and distribution middlemen. Another reason can be regulatory related. For example, Japan throughout the early 2000s, was one of the world's last major travel markets prohibiting the introduction of lower web fares. All carriers operating in this market had to file their web fares at the same offline fare level out of protection for Japan's traditional travel agencies.

In such a situation, some airlines resorted to offering additional benefits in the form of online booking bonuses and gifts-with-purchase such as travel destination guides, duty free vouchers or lounge passes. Saving airport check-in queue time and allowing online bookers, even though they might have purchased an economy class ticket, to check at a business class counter or increasing a web traveler's maximum luggage weight are also popular tactics.

### One-to-one fares: The future web fares?

This type of fare would be truly private and offered by an airline to a particular individual. Enabled by computer databases and internet monitoring technology, airlines can track the website surfing behavior and purchase patterns of web travelers. Equipped with this new insight, it would be possible for airlines to micro-segment and offer web travelers unique fare products at specific price points based on their "assets" such as FFP status, past ticket buys, and price sensitivities. One may call these one-to-fares also "big data fares." This brings tailored pricing to a whole new, rather personal level and is probably the most illustrative example of "pull-pricing." With pull-pricing, a fare is literally built based on a web traveler's unique demand profile.

One-to-one fares would only be possible via web traveler authentication such as an FFP number or some other form of login so that the web traveler is recognized. One-to-one fares can be offered on airline websites and via travel agencies provided that they have a direct connect relationship.

From an airline perspective, a closer match of a customer's demand is expected to create benefits in the form of incremental revenue streams, closer customer relationships, and stronger brand improvements. Not insignificant is the fact that this type of fare is impossible to match and different from today's focus on "Best Fare" (Figure 4.36).

The implications of this one-to-one pricing model would be far reaching. In essence, it is about using all the information a carrier has about a web traveler and turning this insight into incremental sales. The infrastructure and management of one-to-one pricing is undoubtedly complex and there are external issues to look out

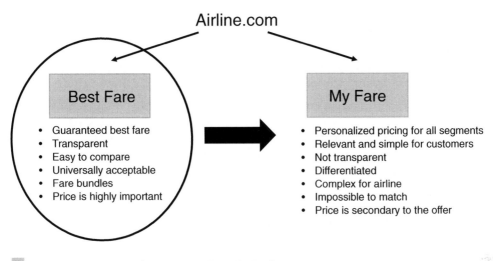

**Figure 4.36** *Migrating from "Best Fare" to "My Fare"*

for. Privacy concerns and the systematic limitation of economic choices presented to different groups, otherwise known as price discrimination, are among them. These issues are likely to stir debates. Not to be taken lightly either is the possibility that supplier transparency that we have become accustomed to over the last few years would become increasingly a thing of the past.

### 4.11.3 A word on airline web pricing and consumer regulation

Over the last few years, many countries have introduced laws to ensure that online ticket selling does not involve misleading advertising or unfair practices. A particular concern of these legislative efforts is to ensure that people are made aware of any additional charges levied on the ticket price. This issue arose from the practice of airlines to advertise rock bottom headline fares that are then subject to all kinds of mandatory taxes and fees. In 2007, the EU Commission had to mandate 137 airline websites to become compliant with consumer protection rules in this area.[72] It is now commonly required by law to include mandatory charges in any advertising and specify a single price as opposed to breaking them out separately.

Recently, legislation in the United States and the EU appears to be focusing more on the practice of merchandising and pricing fare products on an à la carte basis. This is because of the airline industry's drive toward fare merchandising and in particular the introduction of à la carte fares. Web travelers can enjoy a larger choice for customizing their purchase but, at the same time, they have also become more confused as to what the final purchase price at the time of payment is. Apple-to-apple price comparison across multiple airlines is becoming increasingly difficult.

An all-in fare is more honest but airlines naturally resist this as they are concerned that higher fares discourage web travelers from buying tickets on their websites. However, the equally important question to ask is whether it is practical (and actually possible) to pursue an all-in fare approach in the first place when dealing with non-mandatory fees. Let us keep in mind that they not only seem to be growing by the day but they could still vary from person to person.

Take for example a web traveler who is eligible for a first checked-in free bag because of their premier FFP status while another web traveler has the first checked bag fee waived because of using their airline-issued credit card for the ticket purchase. In this regard, one suggested solution whereby an airline would advertise by starting with a top price and then deduct the add-on charges according to a web traveler's choice would only be a limited remedy. In the United States, for example, since 2012, all airlines are required to have an explicit link from their home pages to a page showing all their optional fees for things such as checked bags and change fees.

Against the background of growing concerns in the marketplace, especially from consumer advocacy groups, the topic of how and when to display non-mandatory fees on airline websites (and any third party website showing airline fare products) is likely to garner more public attention. This in turn may lead to additional or new legislative action. Airlines should stay tuned on this topic.

### 4.11.4 Myths in airline e-pricing

A discussion of airline online is incomplete without addressing a few myths about online pricing that have emerged over the past few years.

*Myth 1: The internet has ushered in an era of unprecedented transparency in airline pricing*

Reality: this is true.

In the past, fare transparency was limited to airlines and travel agencies. Travelers often had only very few options, many times just one, in their selection of airlines and fares. The pre-internet logistics involving physical travel agents and airline sales outlets were just too time consuming and cumbersome to allow a broader search. The lack of travelers' control over the entire airline ticket search and purchase process should be also mentioned.

Today, travelers are more sophisticated. They use internet-based tools to engage in efficient comparison shopping. With a few mouse clicks, a web traveler can access multiple websites and compare hundreds of fares by different airlines in one instant. Additionally, they can track price changes over time. An example is Kayak's feature "Show chart of fare history." They can even rush or delay a ticket purchase and receive special email alerts such as offered by Yapta or Hotwire's Tripwatcher based on their prior itinerary/price baseline criteria. All this insight has never been available to the traveling public before.

Nevertheless, transparency as we know it today might disappear because of two reasons. First, the growing merchandization of the airline product where comparison across multiple airlines becomes more difficult. What is actually included in an air fare? Unless new rules are devised, this question cannot be answered easily. Second, in a world of one-to-one web fares, customers are going to be created unequally and served their individual fare product that no one else is offered. In this scenario, to maintain pricing transparency is challenging.

At the same time, the discussion on the new transparency of supplier pricing often neglects to mention the other side of the equation: The new level of customer transparency. Gone are the days when an airline needed to invest significant time and money to conduct price elasticity tests. These typically involved only a small set of fare products over a narrow range of price levels in order to find out how a target audience responded to fare level changes. Today, an airline can use its website to do continuous, real-time price testing, and change the fare levels to gauge the reaction of web travelers instantly and at literally zero cost.

*Myth 2: New transparency in airline pricing means finding lower fares is simpler*

Reality: Not true.

Despite the new transparency in airline pricing as a result of web travelers' new search powers, there is still a great deal of fare variation. A case in point is the search for the lowest fare, a common objective of web travelers when shopping online. Although the itinerary starts with the same data in terms of travel dates and class of service on each site, the fare results may vary substantially. This is due to different technologies that sort through the airline schedules, fares, rules, inventory, and the application of varying business rules. Take for example the application of a ticketing fee or the offering of a discount voucher because of a layover of more than four hours. As there is not one consistently low price quotation by a single site, it appears that web travelers still need to shop around and check out multiple websites before settling on the best fare.

Figure 4.37 illustrates the above issues in an analysis of three routes (JFK–LAX, LAX–Sydney, Singapore–Tokyo Narita) for an economy class round trip in May 2015. Checked were 14 websites including travel meta-search engines, OTAs, and airline websites for the lowest fare. Besides the fact that travel meta-search engines quote less expensive fares while airlines are on the high end, there is not one single site offering consistently the lowest fare.

*Myth 3: Selling online pushes average fare levels down*

Reality: It depends.

The discussion of a possible relationship between an airline's growing online sales volume and declining fare levels first publicly emerged in connection with Continental Airlines. The company showcased its impressive shift to selling tickets online (from less than 5% in 1998 to almost 40% in 2005) while suffering from a fall in average yield (revenue generated per mile) from $0.15 to less than $0.12 during the same timeframe.[73]

If there is an inverse relationship between a legacy airline's increasing internet penetration and decreasing average yield, then the question is whether an airline has altered its approach to pricing because of the internet. The underlying assumption is

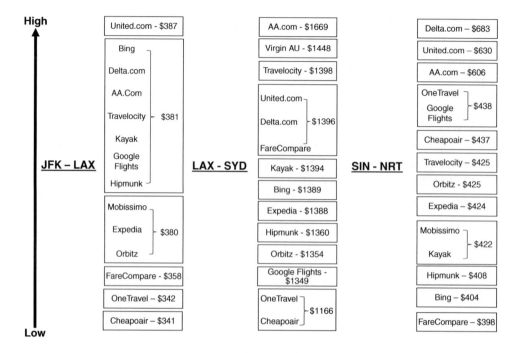

**Figure 4.37** *Who has the fairest fare? (Round trip, Y-class, May 1/15, 2015)*

that markets have become so much more transparent therefore that airlines introduced lower fares to stay competitive. Is this really the case?

On the surface, one may be led to say yes. Low fare guarantees and competition with OTAs for highly price-sensitive web travelers are genuine elements of today's online environment and could exert downward pressure on fare levels. However, the flexibility for most carriers to offer web exclusive fares, certainly those distributing through GDSs, is limited. We need to remember the MFN clauses applied by GDSs in their agreements with airlines: These stipulate that all airline fares are to be made available to third party retailers such as travel agencies. Research has shown that in situations when fares were identical for online channels, online shoppers paid on average 11.5% less than customers buying their tickets offline.[74]

If the downward pressure on average yields is not the result of airlines' lower *offered* fares exclusively available through online channels, the answer may lie in the fares *paid* by web travelers. In this regard, it is important to emphasize the increased search power of web travelers. By using shopping agents in the form of general referral sites such as Google, meta-search engines, airline sites and OTAs—all are literally available at zero cost and are both the result and cause of a growing internet penetration—today's shoppers have unprecedented transparency. We can say that lower fares have always existed and undoubtedly were available in the pre-internet era. The challenge then was to find them because of a lack of efficient search tools. In a way, the internet has put a cap on an airline's ability, certainly with the traditional network carriers, to levy a price premium on their tickets.

Are there any factors in the e-commerce environment that relieve the downward pressures on average yield and could even contribute to a rise? The answer is yes. First, airlines, even the ones operating in small domestic markets, today deal with a global audience. Therefore, their customer base is larger than ever before. For example, unsold airline seats a few days prior to departure have little value if only offered via offline sales outlets. Going online means that not only the chance to find a buyer has increased, but also the airline could even levy a slight price premium and sell a fare at a higher level because one deals with a larger customer base of buyers willing to pay a higher price.

Second, in times when the airline seats are in strong demand—around popular holidays, for example—airlines can increase their fare levels and this is done for online sales outlets as well.

Third, we should look at the advent of the deregulation of GDSs in the United States in 2004 and the expanding deployment by airlines of XML-based direct connect technology. In the name of revenue maximization, not all sales and distribution partners have the same access to fare products any longer. Some airlines can decide selectively what part of their content to share with what sales and distribution partner. Furthermore, with the growth of ancillary and the possibility of one-to-one pricing models, we are moving away from a push-based, "one-price-fits-all" pricing approach. Instead, price is about to become secondary to the offer provided the offer is uniquely tailored to an individual. Against this background, airlines will be able to levy price premiums, hence boosting their average yields.

*Myth 4: Web pricing is faster than traditional pricing*

Reality: Yes and no.

Generally, web pricing is associated with shorter timeframes when it comes to responding to market changes and adjusting price points. This may stem from the fact that the lead times to manage price changes in the offline world are traditionally longer. We can think of some print material or even radio/TV ads for which price points are commonly set significantly in advance that make later revisions logistically impossible or very costly. Web pricing, however, allows for instantaneous adjustments and depends on the market situation. An airline can change price levels to benefit from fluctuations such as changes in customer demand and competitor behavior.

In the context of the airline industry, however, the logistics of creating, filing, and distributing some kind of e-fare product are not that different from regular fares. As such, the production process takes about the same amount of time. Table 4.10 displays some of the typical steps involved in a bare bones e-fare product creation marketed on an airline website.

Considering the number of stakeholders involved and the respective processes applied, a two- to three-day timeframe is common before the fare product is live. However, this can easily grow into a five- to six-day timeframe if fare testing turns up any errors, re-filings with ATPCO are necessary, the marketing of e-fares is extended beyond the airline's web/mobile sites such as sending a special email alert

*Table 4.10 Production process of e-fare promotion*

| Activity | Stakeholder |
|---|---|
| 1. Identification of markets with distressed inventory | Commercial Depts (Rev Mgmt, Internet Rev Mgmt, Pricing/e-Pricing) |
| 2. Create fare filing and develop sheet with specific fares and markets | Commercial Depts (Rev Mgmt, Internet Rev Mgmt, Pricing/e-Pricing) |
| 3. Internal stakeholder feedback | Legal, Sales, e-Commerce |
| 4. Send fares to ATPCO for transmission to GDSs | Commercial Depts (Rev Mgmt, Internet Rev Mgmt, Pricing/e-Pricing) |
| 5. Fares live in GDSs | ATPCO/GDSs |
| 6. Testing of fares on airline test and production website | Commercial Depts (Rev Mgmt, Internet Rev Mgmt, Pricing/e-Pricing, e-Commerce), QA |
| 7. Publication of e-fares (airline website) | e-Commerce |

to FFP members. If other players including code/alliance partners are involved, the process can become even more complex.

Despite all of this, we should remember that the pricing process even before the advent of the commercial era in the mid-1990s had already been relatively fast. Thanks to the combination of a deregulated market environment and the heavy automation/computerization applied in day-to-day pricing, the average lifespan of an airline fare then was less than two weeks and the number of price changes per week amounted over 270,000. This all reflects a rather dynamic environment.

## 4.12 ISSUES TO LOOK OUT FOR IN AIRLINE E-SALES AND DISTRIBUTION

### 4.12.1 The rise of new e-sales and distribution players: Watch out for "CAFGAA" with Concur, Apple, Facebook, Google, Amazon and Alibaba

Over the last few years, a new breed of players has joined, dabbled, or expressed interest in the online travel space. Airlines are well advised to watch out for these companies, a group collectively referred to as CAFGAA (Concur, Apple, Facebook, Google, Amazon, and Alibaba). The degree of their engagement varies but what they all have in common is a powerful brand recognition in the marketplace, a large customer base, a thorough understanding of technology coupled with marketing savviness, and deep pockets. They are all known to be highly effective disruptors and certainly have the potential to re-write the rules of the game for e-sales and distribution as we have come to know it so far. One particular aspect to look out for is the power of these companies' proprietary ecosystems that make it relatively easy to integrate and expand travel products and services (Figure 4.38).

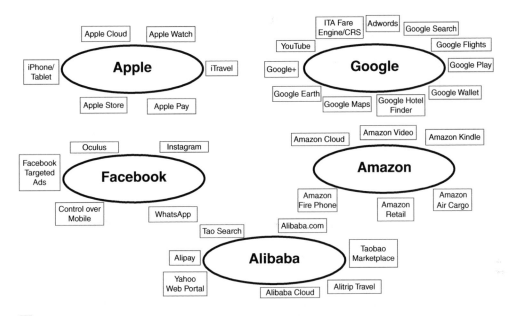

**Figure 4.38** *Managing online travel within proprietary ecosystems*

*Concur*

As a result of its acquisition of TripIt in 2011, Concur could become an intermediary between an airline and web travelers. TripIt can build a so-called "Super PNR" of its users' trips. A super PNR contains consolidated information on a web traveler's multiple reservations for flight, hotel, car, and trip components. Moreover, since Concur also operates an expense reporting application, it has access to massive travel data that could be extremely valuable to airlines. Market share data, insight on purchase channels, and fares paid are all examples.[75]

*Apple*

In 2012, iTravel was granted as a patent to Apple. Among other things, it covers travel services such as boarding pass and express check-in. The Near Field Communication (NFC) is another aspect of this patent. Ticketing and identification information can be stored on the iOS device and transmitted via near field communication to another electronic device. A handheld device such as a smart phone or even wearable computer could be used to check into flights, hotels, and car rentals. Furthermore, web traveler ID information could be transmitted electronically to allow for faster security verification.[76]

In combination with Apple's Wallet (formerly Passbook) feature, a mobile wallet, the iTravel patent could disrupt the airline–traveler relationship. Apple is known to have a knack for user-friendly application designs and thus could quickly find a large number of fans among travelers who enjoy better utility. It is speculation that Apple could become a travel retailer but it could use Wallet as a "toll booth" and airlines would have to pay if they wanted to reach their passengers.[77]

*Facebook*

Facebook boasts over 1.5 billion active users worldwide and is the premier social network on desktop and mobile devices. People use it to search for friends and information on brands, interests, and destinations. It is possible that Facebook could introduce a booking feature for travel at some point and handle the cycle from inspiration to reservation and beyond within its eco system. Moreover, it has powerful insight into people's behavior due to its data collection. The data could be monetized by offering airlines (or other travel players including OTAs) the opportunity to engage in highly targeted marketing campaigns.[78]

*Google*

Google participates in every aspect of sales and distribution in cyberspace via a number of power digital properties. These include its general search and meta-search engine services, Google+ as a social network, and YouTube. Other valuable travel-related properties comprise Google's ITA software reservation system, mobile wallet, Google Flights, Google Maps, and Google Earth. Arguably, the only item missing are airplanes. It is doubtful that Google wants to own/operate physical assets (although this may change if they build Google cars) but it can severely disrupt or facilitate the interaction between airlines and web travelers. Even if facilitation is chosen, it could come at a high price for airlines that want use certain products and reach their customers.[79]

*Amazon*

As the largest online retailer in the world, Amazon is bound to enter the travel space. The company actually already attempted to manage travel offerings in the past but achieved only moderate success. For example, in 2012, it launched flash sales and discounts for hotel rooms through Amazon Local. In spring 2015, it upscaled this to "Destinations" which tried to formalize agreements between Amazon and hotels to offer more comprehensive listings. This would have put it on a more equal footing with major OTAs. In return, hotels would gain more bookings with exposure to Amazon's 280 million shoppers. Besides the hotel deals, Amazon Destinations also included maps and user reviews of restaurants in the area. Then in October 2015, Destinations was abruptly and quietly folded. Among other reasons, entrenched competitors including Expedia and Priceline apparently proved to be too formidable to take on.

Nevertheless, Amazon, like Apple and Google has a captive audience, take as an example its Prime members (they may have up to 80 million of them as of 2015), so an expansion into travel products is likely to occur over time. Of the CAFGAA group, Amazon is the closest to managing traditional airline assets such as airplanes. In December 2015, news surfaced that Amazon seeks as many as 25 planes including B767s in an effort to take greater control of its shipment delivery operations. This foray into airplane operations might open the door for transporting passenger at some point in the future (UPS did this in the past and used modified B727s for weekend charter flights).

*Alibaba*

Alibaba is a Chinese e-commerce company that manages a variety of B2C, B2B, and C2C platforms. Its handles over 250 million mobile users across its platforms that include prominent products and services such as the China Yahoo! portal, its Tao search engine, the Taobao marketplace (similar to eBay), Alibaba cloud computing, and the Alipay online payment service.

In October 2014, the company added Alitrip, an online travel agency, to this mix of e-commerce companies. In its first year already, Alitrip managed 50 million travelers and has become one of China's leading online travel sites. It can leverage the entire Alibaba ecosystem to attract online travelers and use the digital data collected on them to enhance customer experiences. Unlike other players discussed, Alibaba has clearly signaled its intention to establish a new playing field for the online travel market in mainland China (and possibly beyond) via Alitrip. Their massive data insight is very valuable for any airline serving this market and they could also ask for an "access fee" if an airline wants to reach customers in this ecosystem.

### 4.12.2 Co-existence of multiple e-sales and distribution arrangements

Over the next few years, it is likely several e-sales and distribution arrangements will exist side by side. Airlines will continue working in traditional ways with intermediaries including agencies (off- and online) and GDSs. At the same time, there will be more set-ups in place for direct distribution. They include an NDC-based direct connect with third party retailers and facilitated by airline technology providers such as Farelogix and others that offer applications to bridge the different platforms involved. Direct distribution will also mean that airlines are going to look for ways to make their own direct online presence more competitive with increased ancillaries and personalization features (Figure 4.39). In this regard, the role of merchandising engines will be significant.

All three e-sales and distribution arrangements will be governed by a cost control imperative whereby airlines will look to accomplish the following:

■ re-negotiate more favorable terms with existing partners including GDSs and agencies
■ shift volume to lower cost channels (direct connect and direct online sales)
■ reduce costs through increased efficiencies like cloud computing.

It should be emphasized that e-sales and distribution are not only about cost efficiency, but also involve important value addition. This is because more airlines and intermediaries will be able to offer ancillary sales and they can use enhanced big data insight to do more targeted offerings.

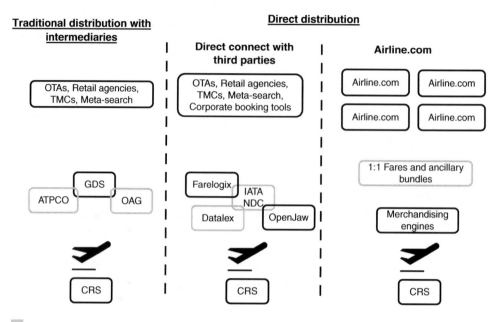

**Figure 4.39** *Co-existence of multiple e-sales and distribution arrangements*

### 4.12.3 Business aviation: Competitor or partner in the future e-sales and distribution of airlines?

The subject of travelers flying on private airplanes has gained some attention in the airline industry in recent years. Due to an increasing demand in the private travel segment, a few carriers have decided to tap into this niche. Most common is the mixing of commercial and private flights on the same itinerary. Arrangements to offer this type of service vary: For instance, Lufthansa's "Private Jet" is offered in partnership with NetJets Europe while Delta Airlines uses its wholly owned subsidiary Delta Private Jets, which operates close to 70 business jets of various sizes. Emirates, in a league of its own, operates "Emirates Executive" with an Airbus A319 that can accommodate up to 19 passengers in a full-flat bed configuration. The private flight portion can be booked either individually for point-to-point itineraries or for seamless connections with long-haul flights in the global route network operated by the carriers.

Besides being part of a customer's airline itinerary, private flights are also operated on a stand-alone basis for commercial reasons. Typically, these are on-demand charters that account for a significant share of what is called "business aviation". The largest markets for business aviation are the US and Europe. The price system for private flights, and it does not matter if they are mixed with commercial flights or not, is generally based on the aircraft size and route but independent of the number of passengers.

E-commerce for business aviation is essentially handled through a digital front-end with companies featuring informational product/service content and online request/price quote forms on their main websites. By phone and brokers are still the main channels for checking aircraft availability and making a booking. This offline system is in many ways reminiscent of the airline sales and distribution set-up from the 1980s. In comparison with their commercial airliner cousins, the vast majority of business aviation operators appear significantly less digitized and are in many cases years behind the airline industry's e-commerce curve. Sophisticated online booking platforms, the application of savvy digital marketing strategies, and the use of big data for enhancing both operational aspects and customer experiences are examples of areas that are still mostly at an infant stage, if they exist at all. Noteworthy exceptions are a handful companies including XOJet and Jetsuite from the US, whose web presence is more on par with what web travelers are accustomed to from airlines.

Also interesting is the arrival of a new breed of players who both bring significant resources and digital know-how to this market segment and have the capability to drive its digitization at an unprecedented speed and quality. Examples of these companies include Silicon Valley-based Stellar and Stratajet from the UK (Figure 4.40). Airlines should take notice of these companies for several reasons, as their activities are reminiscent of past developments in the airline industry that had a huge impact on its sales and distribution system. Let us take the introduction of the airline GDS, starting with American Airlines' SABRE in 1964, that allowed carriers to electronically manage their vast volume/complexity of seat inventory and pricing data much better. In the case of Stellar, business aviation operators are provided with a backend platform that captures, among other things, operational, client demand, and aircraft inventory data and optimizes their business to an unprecedented level. Improved scheduling – resulting in the minimization of notorious empty legs (empty outbound or return flights as a result of a client's one-way charter) – and more competitive pricing via yield management techniques are just some examples. Equally important is Stellar's platform aggregator function for the end-consumer. Similar to the impact that Expedia and Travelocity had in 1996 when they entered the travel market, these new platforms consolidate a widely dispersed supply with thousands of aircraft operators and airplanes and make it available in a user-friendly way to end-consumers. Real-time access to aircraft availability, transparent price and (even branded) product information, and instant booking functionalities coupled with new alternative forms of payment are some of the key features.

An interesting question is also how the digitization of the business aviation market will impact the suppliers participating in the business aviation market segment. One scenario is that they will take this development as an opportunity to upgauge their own digitalness. Among other things, this means deploying an inhouse digital booking platform that bypasses traditional brokers and new digital middlemen to establish a "direct connect" relationship. The investment and know how required to do this are not a light undertaking, thus only a few companies are likely to follow this path any time soon. The other more likely scenario is that many will join one of the new third party digital platforms. For better or worse, this will perpetuate their reliance on middlemen at least in the short-term but they might eventually also operate in parallel a digital end consumer booking platform on their own. Time will tell.

Undoubtedly, these new disruptive digital platforms that function as a hybrid between an OTA and a GDS will accelerate the consumerization trend of the

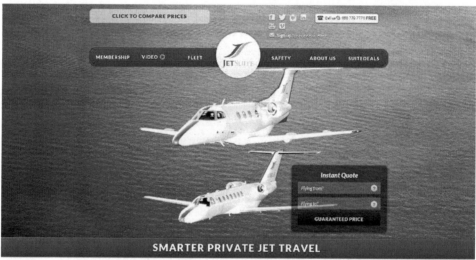

**Figure 4.40** *The new e-commerce players in business aviation*

*Source:* JetSuite.com (2015)[80] with kind permission of JetSuite, XOJet.com (2015)[81] with kind permission of XOJet, Stellar.aero (2015)[82] with kind permission of Stellar, Stratajet.com (2015)[83] with kind permission of Stratajet

business aviation market. This in turn raises the question whether private flying can achieve parity with premium class airline fares.

Recently, this topic has made some headlines in advertising and newspaper articles suggesting that private flying can rival first-class airline fares and even economy class fares. On some routes in certain circumstances such pricing may be available, but not nearly as easily or often as some these headlines might suggest. However, it appears that private flying has become accessible to more consumers beyond an ultra-wealthy

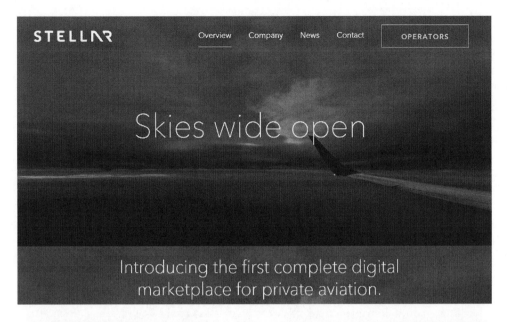

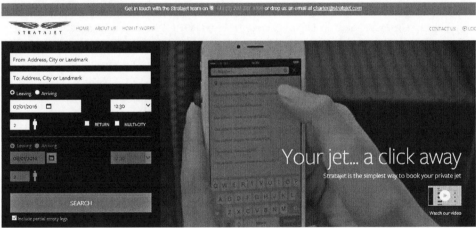

**Figure 4.40** *Continued*

demographic. This is in no small thanks to the new digital platforms such as Stellar's that provide for improved levels of price/product transparency and online shopping convenience in business aviation that web travelers have come to expect based on their cyberspace experience with airlines. At the same time, new business aviation pricing models, think of all-you-can-fly membership services such as offered by Rise, a Texas-based company that offers a three-tiered monthly membership program that ranges from $1,650 to $2,650 and allows for unlimited flights between Dallas, Austin, and Houston, have also garnered attention with travelers, especially from the corporate sector. Furthermore, not to be discounted is the high level of convenient access travelers are offered by business aviation operators. For example, in the US, business aviation serves over 5,000 public use airports (versus 500 used by commercial airlines).

Our above brief discussion has shown that airlines should pay attention to the digitization evolution in business aviation. This is because this development is likely to contribute to the opening of the private travel segment to a broader end-consumer base. Particularly premium class travellers who are currently booking with commercial airlines directly or via leisure/corporate travel intermediaries might be attracted – an issue that an airline targeting these types of customers can ill afford to take lightly.

## NOTES

1 emarketer (2015) "Worldwide Digital Travel Sales Will Total More than $533 Billion in 2015" http://www.emarketer.com/Article/Worldwide-Digital-Travel-Sales-Will-Total-More-than-533-Billion-2015/1013392#sthash.KXqCzX8T.dpuf (accessed Dec 29, 2015).

2 Quinby, D. et al. (2015) "The year ahead in digital travel," www.phocuswright.com/Free-Travel-Research/The-Year-Ahead-in-Digital-Travel#.VVD4yGd0zIU (accessed February 12, 2015).

3 Weps, F. (2014) "[Infographic] Use analytics to take advantage of online travel trends," www.trainingaid.org/news/infographic-use-analytics-take-advantage-online-travel-trends (accessed March 29, 2015).

4 Del Rosso, L. (2014) "Consumer trends 2014: Explosion in mobile bookings," www.travelweekly.com/Travel-News/Travel-Technology/Explosion-in-mobile-bookings/ (accessed March 29, 2015).

5 Etc-Digital.org (2013) "Travel Booking," http://etc-digital.org/digital-trends/ecommerce/travel-booking/regional-overview/europe/ (accessed March 29, 2015).

6 TripInfo.com (2015) "Digital travel sales growth worldwide, by country, 2012-2017," www.tripinfo.com/ITM/Articles2014/images/6118a.jpg (accessed March 29, 2015).

7 Arabian Travel Market (2014) "OTA sales in Middle East to reach US$ 3 billion this year," www.arabiantravelmarket.com/news-and-media/ATM-Press-Releases1/OTA-sales-in-Middle-East-to-reach-US-3-billion-this-year---/ (accessed March 29, 2015).

8 emarketer (2015) "Worldwide Digital Travel Sales Will Total More than $533 Billion in 2015".

9 Tnooz (2015) "The state of online travel in Asia," www.tnooz.com/article/erevmax-asia-online-travel/#utm_source=Tnooz+Mailing+List&utm_medium=email&utm_campaign=b02e4546b1-RSS_EMAIL_CAMPAIGN&utm_term=0_c691357c44-b02e4546b1-137333989 (accessed July 4, 2015).

10 MyDigitalFC.com 2014(2013) "Expedia partners with AirAsia in India," www.mydigitalfc.com/news/expedia-partner-airasia-india-452 (accessed March 29, 2015).

11 Coleman, Maurice (2005) "reGaining Control of Distribution and Costs," Aer Lingus Presentation, EyeForTravel, Travel Distribution Summit USA, Chicago.

12 Author assessment based on information provided to him by carriers based in the Gulf region.

13 SITA (2012) "2012 SITA Airline IT Trends Survey," page 5.

14 Sileo, L. (2014) "Online TRAVEL AGENCIES: More than a distribution channel," www.phocuswright.com/Free-Travel-Research/Online-Travel-Agencies-More-Than-a-Distribution-Channel#.VVFWiWd0zIU (accessed February 18, 2015).

15 Simson, M. (2015) "KLM aims to double social media ROI after Euro 25 million haul in 2014," www.runwaygirlnetwork.com/2015/02/17/klm-aims-double-social-media-roi-e25-million-haul-2014/ (accessed April 24, 2015).

16 Sileo, "Online Travel Agencies."

17 Steenland, D. (2008) "Statement of Douglas M. Steedland." www.judiciary.senate.gov/imo/media/doc/08-04-24SteenlandTestimony.pdf (accessed March 29, 2015).

18 ETTSA (2012) "Technology and independent distribution in the European travel industry," www.slideshare.net/fullscreen/MarinetLtd/travel-distribution/1 (accessed March 29, 2015).

19 O'Neill, S. (2013) "A new problem for OTAs: Airline websites are outselling them in the US," www.tnooz.com/article/a-new-problem-for-otas-airline-websites-are-outselling-them-in-the-us/#sthash.JBcRMUtH.dpuf (accessed October 10, 2014).

20 Expedia, presentation at ATPCO conference in Miami, April 2013.

21 Quinby et al., "The year ahead in digital travel."

22 ThinkWithGoogle.com (2014) "The 2014 Traveler's Road to Decision," http://storage.googleapis.com/think/docs/2014-travelers-road-to-decision_research_studies.pdf (accessed March 24, 2015).

23 Quinby et al., "The year ahead in digital travel."

24 Malone, K. (2011) "American's GDS gamble," https://blog.compete.com/2011/01/26/american%e2%80%99s-gds-gamble/ (accessed March 29, 2015).

25 Ibid.

26 Ibid.

27 Expedia (2013) "The traveler's path to purchase," http://info.advertising.expedia.com/travelerspathtopurchase-1-3-0-0?utm_campaign=Path%20to%20Purchase%20UK%202014&utm_medium=PR&utm_source=Other%20Campaigns (accessed November 14, 2014).

28 Orbitz (2014) "Orbitz," www.orbitz.com/ (accessed September 9, 2014).

29 Air New Zealand (2015) "Air New Zealand," airnewzealand.com (accessed February 22, 2015).

30 Wellman, K. (2014) "OTAs & meta-search engines: It's not just about trip planning," http://blog.flightview.com/ota-metasearch-trip-planning-traveler-survey (accessed March 29, 2015).

31 Adler, K. (2008) "Controversy surrounds 'screen scrapers': Software helps users access web sites but activity by competitors comes under scrutiny," http://corporate.findlaw.com/law-library/controversy-surrounds-screen-scrapers-software-helps-users.html (accessed March 29, 2015).

32 Out-law.com (2014) "EU Ryanair 'screen-scraping' case could affect biz models," www.theregister.co.uk/2014/11/12/cjeu_case_on_screenscraping_has_potential_to_affect_business_models_says_expert/ (accessed March 29, 2015).

33 Baker, J. (2015) "Top EU court: Ryanair data barrel must be left unscraped," www.theregister.co.uk/2015/01/15/the_bottom_of_ryanair_data_barrel_must_be_left_unscrapped/ (accessed March 29, 2015).

34 Expedia.com (2015) "Expedia travel," www.expedia.com/ (accessed February 27, 2015).

35 Hawaiian Airlines (2015) "Hawaiian Airlines – official site," www.hawaiianairlines/ (accessed February 8, 2015).

36 Turkish Airlines (2015) "Turkish Airlines – official site," www.turkishairlines.com/ (accessed February 8, 2015).

37 Sorenson, J. (2015) "The cartrawler yearbook of ancillary revenue," www.ideaworkscompany. com/wp-content/uploads/2015/09/2015-Ancillary-Revenue-Yearbook.pdf (accessed September 26, 2015).

38 SITA (2014) "2014 SITA Airline IT Trends Survey."

39 Air Canada (2014) "Air Canada – official site," www.aircanada.com/ (accessed February 16, 2014).

40 Sorenson, "The cartrawler yearbook of ancillary revenue."

41 Cavaliere, Marc (2005) VP Sales and Distribution Spirit Airlines, remarks during presentation "The Great GDS Debate," EyeForTravel, Travel Distribution Summit USA, Chicago.

42 O'Neill, S. (2013) "The real NDC: Decoding the planned (r)evolution in airline distribution by IATA and airlines," www.tnooz.com/article/the-real-ndc-decoding-the-planned-revolution-in-airline-distribution-by-iata-and-airlines/ (accessed March 29, 2015).

43 Harteveldt, H. (2012) "The future of airline distribution: A look ahead to 2017," www.iata.org/whatwedo/stb/documents/future-airline-distribution-report.pdf (accessed March 29, 2015).

44 Amdekar, J. and Padmanabhuni, S. (2006) "Future of travel & tourism industry with the adoption of web services in electronic distribution," www.infosys.com/industries/hospitality-leisure/white-papers/Documents/webservices-adoption-travel-tourism.pdf (accessed March 31, 2015).

45 Ibid.

46 May, K. (2013) "IATA opts for Open AXIS as technical standard for NDC initiative," www.tnooz.com/article/iata-opts-for-open-axis-as-technical-standard-for-ndc-initiative/ (accessed March 29, 2015).

47 Kelly, G. (2013) "BTC says opposition to IATA's," www.travelpulse.com/news/features/btc-says-opposition-to-iatas.html (accessed March 29, 2015).

48 IATA (2015) "New distribution capability," www.iata.org/whatwedo/airline-distribution/ndc/Pages/default.aspx (accessed March 29, 2015).

49 Phocuswright (2008) "The Air Canada effect: How to unbundle your commodity product to maximize revenue," Analysis.

50 IATA analysis quoted in: Hazel, B. and Stalnaker, T. (2014) "Airline economic analysis," www.oliverwyman.com/content/dam/oliver-wyman/global/en/2014/nov/Airline%20Economic%20Analysis_Screen_OW.pdf (accessed April 8, 2015).

51 Hazel and Stalnaker, "Airline economic analysis."

52 Ibid.

53 The Economist (2012) "The ineluctable middlemen," www.economist.com/node/21560866 (accessed March 29, 2015).

54 IATA, "New Distribution Capability."

55 Ebner, C. (2015) "Streit um GDS Gebuehr. Lufthansa legt sich mit Vetriebspartnern an," www.aero.de/content/pics/p 4876jpg (accessed July 20, 2015).

56 McDonald, M. (2015) "Luftansa to add hefty surcharge to GDS bookings," www.travelmarketreport.com/articles/Lufthansa-to-Add-Hefty-Surcharge-to-GDS-Bookings (accessed June 4, 2015).

57 Ebner, "Streit um GDS Gebuehr."

58 Author analysis of selected distribution cost data of a US carrier.

59 May, K. (2015) "Lufthansa takes GDS booking tumble with new surcharge, rival carriers benefit," www.tnooz.com/article/lufthansa-takes-gds-booking-tumble-with-new-surcharge-rival-carriers-benefit/?utm_source=Tnooz+Mailing+List&utm_medium=email&utm_campaign=fcdd98845f-RSS_

EMAIL_CAMPAIGN&utm_term=0_c691357c44-fcdd98845f-137333989 (accessed September 30, 2015).

60 Airline Weekly, Special Report, June 2010, author's analysis of US Airways' 10K Filings.

61 Ibid.

62 SITA (2012) "2012 SITA Airline IT Trends Survey," page 5.

63 Business Travel Executive (2014) "Air Canada and Travelport Ink multi-year Extension," www.askbte.com/RedlineNews/RedlineNews1/Air_Canada_and_Travelport_Ink_Multiyear_Extension_72566.aspx (accessed March 29, 2015).

64 Schaal, D. (2011) "Priceline: Ticketing milestone with American Airlines direct connect," www.tnooz.com/article/priceline-ticketing-milestone-with-american-airlines-direct-connect/ (accessed March 29, 2015).

65 Concur.com (2015) "Direct connect suppliers," www.concur.com/en-us/partners/travel-suppliers/direct-connect-suppliers (accessed March 29, 2015).

66 Google.com (2015) , search query "Flights Boston to Frankfurt" on Google Flight (accessed December 28, 2015).

67 Laub, E. (2014) "How open booking can benefit managed travel," www.ciswired.com/insight-and-opinion/entry/open-booking (accessed March 29, 2015).

68 Ibid.

69 Etihad Airways (2015) "Etihad Airways," www.etihad.com/en-us/ (accessed March 1, 2015).

70 Jetstar (2015), "Jetstar.com website", www.jetstar.com (accessed March 24, 2015).

71 LOT (2015) "LOT Polish Airlines," www.lot.com/us/en/ (accessed January 13, 2015).

72 Europa Press Releases (2009) "Consumers: Airlines move to clean up ticket selling websites," europa.eu/rapid/press-release_IP-09-783_en.pdf (accessed March 12, 2015).

73 Brunger, W. and Perelli, S. (2008) "The impact of the internet on airline fares: Customer perspectives on the transition to internet distribution," www.palgrave-journals.com/rpm/journal/v8/n2/pdf/rpm200831a.pdf (accessed March 29, 2015).

74 Ibid.

75 IATA, "New Distribution Capability."

76 PatentlyApple.com (2012) "Apple wins a major patent for iTravel & More," www.patentlyapple.com/patently-apple/2012/07/apple-wins-a-major-patent-for-itravel-more.html (accessed March 29, 2015).

77 IATA, "New distribution capability."

78 Ibid.

79 Ibid.

80 Jetsuite (2015) "Jetsuite - official website", www.jetsuite.com (accessed on December 30, 2015).

81 XOJet (2015) "XOJet - official website", www.xojet.com (accessed December 30, 2015).

82 Stellar (2015) "Stellar - official website", www.stellar.aero (accessed December 30, 2015)

83 Stratajet (2015), "Stratajet - official website", www.stratajet.com (accessed December 30, 2015).

# Chapter 5

# Airline web customer service

The future of customer service is no customer service.

Bill Price, architect of Amazon customer service

## 5.1 INTRODUCTION

With product and price no longer providing the competitive edge they used to, customer service has gained increasing importance as a key differentiator in competitive market conditions and as an opportunity to improve the understanding of a customer's true value. Good customer service is good for business and can lead to higher rates of buying and loyalty. Some 87% of consumers state that good customer service influenced their decision to do business with companies again.[1] The annual impact on the airline industry in the United States from additional purchases, reduced customer churn, and word-of-mouth as a result of good customer service is an estimated $590 million.[2]

Successful e-commerce airlines pursue a multi-channel approach when it comes to servicing web travelers. Multi-channel web customer servicing involves the combined and coordinated offering of traditional channels—examples are an airline's call center and city/airport ticket offices—and online channels allowing customer service via email, website, mobile, and social media. In the context of our discussion, web customer service is defined as the delivery of multi-channel assistance offered to web travelers that encounter an issue and require a resolution.

Managing traditional and online service channels as a cohesive portfolio can easily be overwhelming for an airline. This is not only because new service tools arrive on the market all the time but also because existing ways of customer servicing face ongoing changes themselves. However, when it is done right, the benefits in the form of increased cost efficiencies in web customer service operations and higher customer satisfaction that lead in turn to more loyalty and repeat business are compelling and hard to ignore. Not accommodating the new customer service channels and not taking a holistic view in their management puts an airline at a competitive disadvantage.

When is web customer service "good"? People have divergent views on this topic but there are some cornerstones that are pivotal for delivering high-quality web customer service at an airline:

- *Timeliness.* Web travelers need to be serviced promptly. It does not matter whether this is done in person, via email, on the website self-help area, over the phone, or involving any other service channel. Waiting several days for an email reply, being on hold for ten minutes when contacting the call center, and coping with slow web page downloads are all examples of what an airline should not do.
- *Effectiveness.* The carrier's communication with web travelers should be clear and conducted by skilled and trained people who know what they are talking about. It must offer a solution that remedies the web traveler's issue.
- *Personalization.* The solutions offered should be individualized rather than standard responses. This means that the company-web traveler relationship history as well as the value of the web traveler should be known to the airline.
- *Contextualization.* Knowing who the customer is, their past interactions and circumstances of the web traveler leading up to their service request with the airline, the physical situation of the web traveler in terms of time, place, and setting (is the web traveler chatting with the airline while on the airplane?) are part of contextualization. Finally, what is the web traveler's context, specifically what words are used and what kind of language is selected (questions, answers, or insults)?
- *Flexibility.* A web traveler should be offered a range of different service channel options to contact the airline. Also, the crossing from one service channel to another should be seamless and intuitive.
- *Consistency.* No matter what service channel the web traveler engages, the information supplied should be the same and the interaction with the airline should be standardized.

An airline resolving service issues with this perspective in mind will boost a web traveler's satisfaction while it strengthens its web-based value proposition and also develops a better insight into a web traveler's wants and needs.

For over 60 years since the 1920s/1930s, customer service in the airline industry was principally conducted in-person, by phone, and through traditional mail. Travelers who required assistance from an airline consulted an employee at the company's CTO/ATO, picked up the phone or simply sent a letter. Brochureware in the form of timetables, (although they are rare species nowadays) catalogues, leaflets, and special pages in inflight magazines has also been around for some time. It is used to provide information about the company's products/services so that customers may use it for so-called self-service.

With the advent of the commercial internet in the early 1990s, a variety of new customer service channels surfaced. One game changer was the adoption of email as a communication channel for business purposes. This was followed by other developments such as the use of company websites, social media, and mobile for customer service activities. Today, it seems more the norm than the exception for customers to use multiple channels. A total of 74% use at least three channels while almost a quarter engage five or more (these are so-called "high velocity" users) (Figure 5.1).

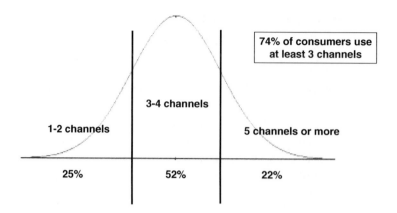

**Figure 5.1** *Consumers demand more channels*

*Source:* Genesys (2015)[3]

This development is remarkable considering that it only occurred within the last 10–15 years—and there is no end in sight to what new channels might arrive in the marketplace next. More channels lead to more communication. For an airline, this means the number of transactions—and complexity—in customer service goes up.

The proliferation of service channels has been mainly consumer led. Specifically, it has been fuelled by changes in behavior and channel usage patterns as well as by changing demographics in the emerging net generation. At the same time, the desire/need by companies to increase their business efficiencies has also played a role. We will address each of these issues in our following discussion.

## 5.2 WEB TRAVELER PREFERENCES IN CUSTOMER SERVICE

The fragmentation of today's customer service channel landscape is an indication that customers want to use more channels and not less. Although not airline industry specific, we can obtain insight on user preferences for service options and how they have changed over time based on a Forrester Research survey from 2013 (Table 5.1).

The survey shows:

- The span of service channels used by customers today is wide.
- Each channel receives its share of requests.
- There have been some significant changes toward the adoption of cyberspace-based service channels.

Web traveler preferences for service options are driven by several factors. These include familiarity with the service option, the expected time to resolve an issue, and

**Table 5.1** *The changing customer service preferences (2012 vs 2009, US market)*

|  | Service Option | 2012 | 2009 |
|---|---|---|---|
| **Traditional Options:** Preference for them is almost constant | Phone | 73% | 73% |
|  | Email | 58% | 56% |
| **2nd Wave Options:** Growing in importance | FAQ | 67% | 37% |
|  | Online Communities | 32% | 23% |
|  | Instant Messaging/Chat | 43% | 30% |
|  | Twitter | 22% | 11% |
| **3rd Wave Options:** Did not exist in 2009 but now used substantially | Click-to-call | 33% |  |
|  | Co-Browsing | 30% | – |
|  | Avatars | 28% | – |
|  | Sending SMS/ mobile messaging | 24% | – |

*Source*: Moxiesoft and Forrester Research (2013)[4]

past experience. Another key aspect relates to demographics. Web-based service options are often associated with younger users such as the millennials and generation Z. Table 5.2 shows that the preference for using online options is unsurprisingly skewed toward younger users. Web travelers belonging to the baby boomer and golden generations have more of an affinity for the traditional service options. However, noteworthy is the significant uptake in the adoption of new web-based service options among older generations. The perception that web-based customer service options are not used by older web travelers therefore does not hold true. Key for an airline is to offer a mix with both traditional and new web-based service options to appeal to web travelers from different demographics.

**Table 5.2** *Service option usage by demographic segment (percentage of US adults that have adopted online customer service channels)*

| Service Option | 2012 Overall | Golden Gen | Boomers | Millennials | Gen Z |
|---|---|---|---|---|---|
| Phone | 73% | 71% | 71% | 71% | 75% |
| FAQ | 67% | 52% | 60% | 64% | 76% |
| Email | 58% | 44% | 51% | 60% | 69% |
| IM/Chat | 43% | 29% | 28% | 47% | 57% |
| Click-to-call | 33% | 19% | 22% | 34% | 50% |
| Online Communities | 32% | 11% | 17% | 33% | 56% |
| Avatars | 28% | 20% | 20% | 31% | 46% |
| Co-browsing | 30% | 14% | 15% | 30% | 46% |
| Sending SMS/mobile messaging | 24% | 7% | 9% | 27% | 44% |
| Twitter | 22% | 8% | 9% | 25% | 43% |

*Source:* Moxiesoft & Forrester Research (2013)[5]

A common question frequently asked is which of the two types of web customer services—traditional or web-based—is more important. The answer is both. An airline needs to strike a balance between the two and manage a portfolio of web customer service options. This is the basis for an effective multi-channel approach. An airline's presence in cyberspace is more competitive when it offers a wider range of service options that appeal to customers with different demographics. Additionally, by incorporating web-based service options, an airline can realize significant cost savings.

## 5.3 WEB CUSTOMER SERVICE ISSUES: WHY THEY EXIST

In order to be successful with web customer service, an airline needs to ask two essential questions: Why do web travelers seek assistance? How are their issues resolved? Not all customer service issues a web traveler faces are the same. Some require a swift resolution while others are less time sensitive. Some are technical in nature or have a business reason.

A web traveler typically seeks assistance from the airline in any of the following four situations (Figure 5.2):

- They face a problem during the online purchase process.
- They run into an issue while engaged in a non-purchase activity.
- They encounter a website usability problem.
- They deal with a major disruption in the airline's operations

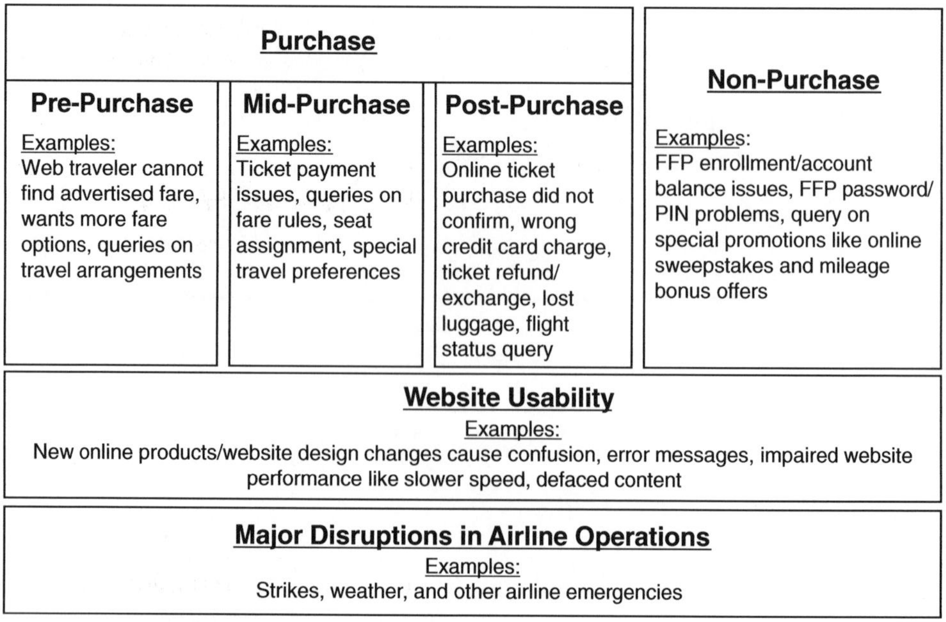

| **Purchase** | | | **Non-Purchase** |
|---|---|---|---|
| **Pre-Purchase** | **Mid-Purchase** | **Post-Purchase** | Examples:<br>FFP enrollment/account balance issues, FFP password/PIN problems, query on special promotions like online sweepstakes and mileage bonus offers |
| Examples:<br>Web traveler cannot find advertised fare, wants more fare options, queries on travel arrangements | Examples:<br>Ticket payment issues, queries on fare rules, seat assignment, special travel preferences | Examples:<br>Online ticket purchase did not confirm, wrong credit card charge, ticket refund/exchange, lost luggage, flight status query | |
| **Website Usability** | | | |
| Examples:<br>New online products/website design changes cause confusion, error messages, impaired website performance like slower speed, defaced content | | | |
| **Major Disruptions in Airline Operations** | | | |
| Examples:<br>Strikes, weather, and other airline emergencies | | | |

*Figure 5.2* *Reasons why web travelers require web customer service*

### 5.3.1 Online purchase process

To obtain insight as to where in the online purchase process the assistance for the web traveler is required, it is also useful to look at the specific phase of the purchase process: Pre-purchase, mid-purchase, and post-purchase.

During the pre-purchase phase, web travelers are exploring different options and looking for information that could help firm up their purchase decision. However, if the information on the carrier's website is not clear enough or not available, web travelers may seek customer service (unless they decide to abandon the website). Common issues include not being able to find an advertised fare or checking on additional fare options.

The mid-purchase phase generally triggers the majority of requests for customer service. Here, web travelers often need assistance because they have questions on fare rules or they want to manage their travel preferences. These could range from selecting a specific aircraft seat to arranging a multi-city stopover itinerary. Also, online payment issues such as the credit card not being accepted fall into this category. Web travelers in the mid-purchase phase have a need for precise information and help.

The same can be said for post-purchase problems that also typically cause a large number of customer service requests. Making changes to an existing reservation, applying for a ticket refund or exchange, complaining about an inflight/on-the-ground disservice, and reporting damaged or lost luggage are several post-purchase examples.

Web customer service is also sought by web travelers when they interact with an airline's website for non-purchase activities. Common issues that surface are related to the frequent flyer program (FFP). Specific examples include forgotten passwords/PINs, inaccurate mileage account information or problems in completing the FFP enrollment process. On other occasions, the web traveler may seek additional information to obtain clarity on special promotions including mileage bonus specials and online sweepstakes.

Another area frequently triggering requests for web customer service has to do with web usability. Often, web travelers run into navigational issues and get lost on the website. This could be because the airline has just launched a new website design or introduced new online products. In those situations, e-commerce savvy airlines staff up their support channel in order to provide the extra help needed. At the same time, it could be that web travelers see error messages that may be cryptic and require further clarification from the airline. Website malfunctions such as slow page response times, internet booking engine outages, and defaced website content also cause a web traveler to reach out for help.

Finally, web travelers might seek web customer support due to major disruptions in the operations of the airline. This could be weather related, because of a strike, or as a result of another emergency situation.

For any of the above issues, leading e-commerce airlines do not ask what service channel is appropriate for help. Instead, they look at the root cause of the issues in order to the get to the bottom of a web traveler's site abandonment, excessive use of self-service channels, and "bad" emails or phone calls. In his book *The Future of Customer Service Is No Service*, Bill Price, architect of Amazon's customer service, suggests that the value of customer service is not about being able to handle more queries more efficiently, but about shifting the focus on eliminating the upstream root causes that lead customers to seek assistance.[6]

For example, if web travelers encounter a problem such as not being able to find an advertised fare special, this could indicate a lack of synchronization between the Pricing/Marketing Department activities and the internet booking engine. This can be fixed by adjusting certain business processes including the proper loading of fare specials on the website booking engine. Another area where customer issues frequently occur is on the website payment page. Is the payment console for the website not properly set up? Is the design of the payment page confusing? As part of an ongoing quality control policy, airlines should constantly monitor the performance of their website. This helps detect any possible malfunctions or deficiencies that could be the source of problems.

Web travelers should also be viewed as a valuable source of information. When a live CSR is contacted by a web traveler via phone or email ("I was just on your website and had a problem..."), the airline should take notice as valuable insight can be learned about current shortcomings that cause these issues. Gathering feedback, storing and analyzing it for the purpose of improving a web traveler's interaction experience is crucial. Leading e-commerce airlines perform these measures systematically as part of a Voice-of-the-Customer (VoC) program. We cover VoC programs in section 5.12.2.

## 5.4 RESOLVING WEB CUSTOMER SERVICE ISSUES

What is the "journey" of a web traveler when seeking assistance? Web travelers are typically time constrained. When encountering an issue, they are likely to stay on the same site only provided they find a resolution quickly. They scan web page content for help and an airline should offer trigger words to provide the motivation to continue interacting with the carrier. It is not uncommon for a web traveler to engage several service channels and bounce back and forth between them before a resolution is found. Figure 5.3 illustrates the life cycle of a web customer service issue. It shows succinct points of decision-making by a web traveler as to what service channel to start the resolution with, where to cross over to another channel, or to leave for a competitor.

In a typical scenario, the web traveler, upon countering a problem on an airline website, may use a self-service tool such as a site search feature for resolving it. If no resolution is found, the web traveler could retry another self-service option or transition to another service channel. If this still does not produce the desired result, the web traveler could give up or escalate the issue to a supervisory/senior manager level. No single service channel should be viewed in isolation but be seen as part of a larger whole portfolio that a web traveler engages for a resolution.

Resolving a web traveler customer service issue is a journey in itself that often involves more than a single service channel. For an airline to manage multi-channel web customer service successfully means to offer a seamlessness between the different

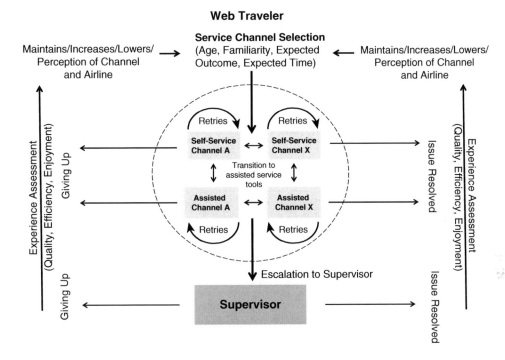

**Figure 5.3** *The life cycle of customer service issues*

service channels. Only this approach delivers an integrated experience to the web traveler. Therefore, the question "Should we adopt chat?" or "Should we engage in social customer service?" misses the point that mastering web customer service is not about deploying a particular technology. It is about resolving a problem for a web traveler who has a blended view of the individual customer service channels.

Service channels are not created equal when it comes to their ability to help customers accomplish tasks. Some may work well in certain situations while others may not help at all. An airline needs to analyze the types of customer service interactions to ensure proper channel availability and alignment. For example, a web traveler who seeks information about an airline's inflight service should be encouraged to use a self-service tool such as the frequently asked questions (FAQ) section. However, customer service issues with a higher degree of complexity may be better handled in real-time via phone or interactive secure chat. An example would be the resolution of a payment problem a web traveler might have encountered on the airline's website.

The deployment of new web-based services is not about the displacement of traditional options including phone and email services. Above all, it is about a smart expansion of an airline's service options to satisfy the demand of today's web travelers for additional (self-)service tools. An airline that is not aligned with web travelers in this regard runs the risk of losing business to those competitors who do offer a wider choice. This is an important argument because there is often concern among customer service representatives (CSRs) and their managers that self-service tools are geared to replace them ("job killers"). This explains the hesitation occasionally observed at some airlines when it comes to supporting the introduction of new web-based service options.

## 5.5 THE COST OF CUSTOMER SERVICE

Airlines do not make data on the cost of customer service publicly available. Confidentiality is a key reason although some carriers do not even track them in the first place. Another challenge is that airlines have their individual approaches for how to account for the cost of customer service. Therefore, data comparability is an issue. Nevertheless, general information published on the subject of customer service costs provides for some valuable insight (Figure 5.4).

The cost of handling a phone call via a CSR ranges between $6 and $12 per interaction, depending if a general CSR or a technical support specialist is involved. At the low end of the cost spectrum is social customer service at around $1 and web self-service at $0.10 or less. Assisted customer service is expensive because it is the airline that provides for the resources to help. With self-service, it is the web travelers who do the work and help themselves.

Phone service is by far the most expensive assistance. This is because the average number of customers a call center CSR can handle in a given time period is lower than the number of customers handled by a CSR who provides assistance via chat, email, or social media. In other words, the ratio between the airline employee and the number of customers supported plays a role.

For example, a typical call center CSR could interact with 7–10 individual callers during one hour. A chat CSR is likely to manage 12–20 customers during the same timeframe. The explanation for this is the chat tool's inherent multi-tasking feature that

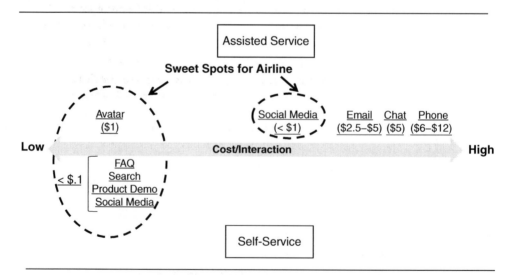

**Figure 5.4** *Estimated cost by customer service channel*

*Source:* Data by Clarkson (2009),[7] Gartner (2012)[8]

allows for dealing with several customers simultaneously. An email CSR could deal with 10–20 customers per hour because email is not real-time and does not tie up an agent in lengthy live one-on-one conversations. The efficiency of an email CSR can be further increased with an auto-reply email system. It notifies the sender that an email has been received and that a response will be provided within days.

When it comes to social customer service, a single CSR uses one-to-many platforms including forums, blogs, and social networks. Hundreds or thousands of web travelers can be reached at once. At the same time, if social customer service is provided by an online community, an airline can also realize cost savings. A set-up whereby customers assist other customers can help deflect phone calls and emails. Companies that integrate online communities in their customer assistance are estimated to realize cost savings between 10% and 50%.[9]

For airlines, the deployment of virtual agents (or avatars) can also be compelling. Avatars engage in one-on-one interactions, they are available around the clock, and they have become very sophisticated in recent years. Importantly, the cost of using them for customer service is very low at less than $1 per interaction.

## 5.6 WEB CUSTOMER SERVICE CHANNELS: DETAILED OVERVIEW

Airline web customer service falls into two categories: Assisted service and self-service. Each category features a wide variety of service options (Figure 5.5). With assisted service, an airline deploys CSRs, typically through a call center/help desk, airport/city ticket office, or back office. These people interact with the web traveler and assist them in whatever the issues are. Assisted customer service is not only provided by human beings but also available by artificial means. One example involves the avatar. This is an artificial, virtual person representing a live person that can offer support on a website to a web traveler, albeit in a limited fashion. Another example is the intelligent personal assistant (IPA) particularly popular on mobile devices. When it comes to the category of self-service, airlines do not provide the support. It is the web travelers who help themselves and rely on tools that do not require interaction with a CSR or artificial intelligence.

Another aspect should be pointed out when discussing web customer service: Assisted customer service is not only reactive in nature where the airline provides for support because the web traveler has reached out. Assisted customer service can also be "pre-emptive" as it is initiated by the airline. The idea of performing pre-emptive web customer service is to pro-actively notify a web traveler of an issue. This is often done to ensure that the issue does not become a problem. Examples of pre-emptive customer service that have become standard in the airline industry include:

- a reminder of an upcoming flight by an IPA or SMS
- a frequent flyer account alert informing about the expiration of FFP miles, sent generally by email or regular post
- a pop-up window on a web page offering to accept chat service
- a flight status notification advising of flight delays/cancellations, typically sent via IPA or SMS.

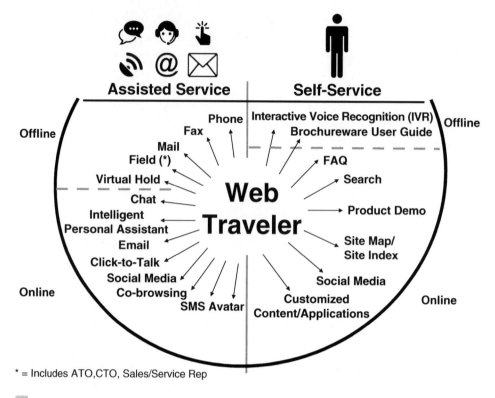

**Figure 5.5** *When encountering a problem, which of the following service options could web travelers use?*

Web customer service is largely responsive in nature which means it is the web traveler themselves who initiates the service request. By using a "Help" or "Contact" link/button, they are guided to a special landing page where information is featured on how to obtain support from the airline either through CSR assistance or via self-service.

The service options used for customer service are wide ranging. Depending on the variety of factors including a web traveler's preferences and the context at hand, one tool might be more suitable to get the necessary support than another. Our following discussion introduces the various options available in more detail.

### 5.6.1 Self-service options

From an airline point of view, the benefits of web customer self-service are compelling and cover a wide range. They can include 24/7 availability, cost savings, acquisition of web traveler usage data, and the ability to provide web travelers with immediate responses to their queries (Figure 5.6).

Moreover, for web travelers, especially from the millennial generation, "do-it-yourself" when interacting with an airline website and other third parties has always been attractive and important. By 2020, it is estimated that a customer will own 85% of a transaction without speaking to anyone.[10] This is more evidence that the previously mentioned 3Cs of web travelers—control, convenience, and choice—will

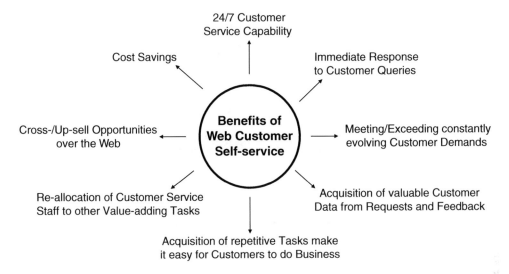

**Figure 5.6** *Why is web customer self-service important for airlines?*

even play a more important role in the future. Our discussion below introduces the major self-service options web travelers use today.

*Search*

| What is it | General benefits | General challenges |
| --- | --- | --- |
| Web crawler that matches a customer's query with site content | Low cost, tracking data from search logs, instantaneous | Match not always suitable due to engine algorithm |

Search is a widespread self-service option offered by airlines on their websites. With a search application, customers can initiate a query on the airline website. The search engine then matches the query containing keywords with content found on the website. A list of the best matches is displayed to the web traveler. Web savvy airlines offering search make sure that even common misspellings (e.g. "trip insurnce") are auto-corrected ("Did you mean 'trip insurance'?") or they are also tagged as key-words and included in the search results. Some carriers use an inhouse application while others work with outside suppliers like search engine provider Google that embed their search solutions in an airline website (see ba.com in Figure 5.7).

Search generates instant answers and is one of the preferred self-service tools of the younger "net" generation. Airlines simultaneously can also gain valuable insight about a web traveler's needs from analyzing the search logs.

Search, as in the case for the other self-service tools, is not self-maintaining. In order to facilitate a fast and accurate information retrieval for web travelers, certain key tasks

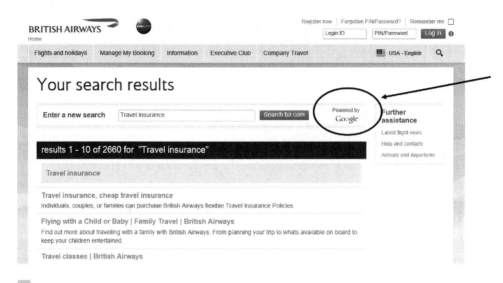

**Figure 5.7** *Google powers search on ba.com*

*Source:* British Airways (2013)[11] with kind permission of British Airways

need to be performed on an ongoing basis. This is because websites constantly change and grow in terms of content and functionality. These tasks include the so-called search engine indexing that allows for a much quicker search of web pages and documents as well as the selection of precise keywords and sentences tagged for display. The organizational responsibility for this type of work cuts across different departments such as IT and e-commerce. It typically also involves outside players such as search engine providers, e-media agencies, and even web travelers. All of them might be sourced for inputs.

*Frequently asked questions (FAQs)*

| What is it | General benefits | General challenges |
|---|---|---|
| Website information presented in a Q&A format on commonly asked customer queries | Low cost, tracking data, instantaneous | Not personalized or contextualized, need constant updating, growing in volume |

FAQs are a list of commonly asked customer questions with answers. They provide companies with a simple way to address repetitive customer queries on their website. Airlines started featuring FAQs on their websites in the early 2000s. FAQs are not personalized and any out of the ordinary question requires the use of another service tool, most likely one with CSR assistance. FAQs are not only one of the oldest forms of web self-service tools but are also considered one of the least expensive methods of providing help to web travelers. Today, FAQ sections are found on most airline websites, some containing a large number of questions and answers (see www.united.com with over 100 FAQs). Only a few airlines like Jazeera Airways from Kuwait do not have a FAQ section at all.

A small or large number of FAQs on an airline website is not on its own an indicator of the quality of self-service that web travelers can perform. One of the dangers to the quality of FAQs is their neglect. In order to keep the FAQ section on its website up to date and relevant, an airline should collect inputs from several sources. These include:

- Web travelers who are invited/encouraged to submit on-the-spot feedback on an FAQ web page ("Did you find the information you were looking for? Yes, No, Partially") or who partake in a relevant focus group/customer panel.
- CSRs from an airline's call center and customer relations department. These people should have excellent insight into commonly asked questions due to their frequent interaction with customers.
- Airline e-commerce department employees, especially those involved in managing web customer services.
- Web customer service experts.
- Other websites both from within and outside the travel industry.
- Website data tracking applications that can provide insight into web traveler's search queries.

Airline FAQ sections seldom shrink. As an airline adds content and functionality to its website, FAQ sections often grow proportionally over time. In this case, a common practice by airlines with large FAQ sections is to present the Top 10 questions on a single page. Additional FAQs then are accommodated on the same web page in sidebar menus under different categories and sub-categories such as "Making A Reservation," "Lost Baggage," and "Refund Policy," for example. This is a sound policy that should be followed more widely.

Navigating through FAQ sections can be challenging for web travelers because it often involves significant page scrolling and the scanning/reading of small font size text. A clear and user-intuitive presentation of the various FAQ topics, possibly combined with the use of images of CSRs representing the "human touch" in customer service is crucial if an airline wants web travelers to embrace this form of self-help and use it extensively. If a particular question does not appear in the FAQ section or the answer to a web traveler's questions is insufficient, it is important for the airline website to collect feedback at the point of experience from the web traveler for future FAQ section improvements. Furthermore, the carrier needs to ensure that a seamless transition to other service options is offered. These ideally should prioritize customer self-service ahead of more expensive CSR-assisted service options such as the telephone. The help section on swiss.com is an illustrative example how this can all be displayed (Figure 5.8).

A future possibility for FAQs is personalization. As previously stated, airline FAQ sections are currently not personalized or "smart" to recognize a particular user, although the technology already exists in other website applications. For example, the capabilities that can be used to predict what kind of book a person may want to buy when shopping on www.amazon.com could also be applied to web travelers encountering certain issues while on an airline website.

Specifically, based on a web traveler's previous purchases and those by other web travelers, a list with most likely FAQs could be generated on the airline website.

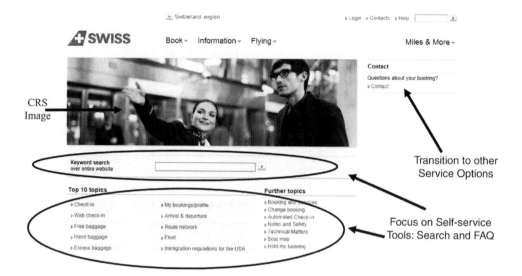

**Figure 5.8** *The help section on swiss.com*

*Source:* swiss.com (2014)[12] with kind permission of Swiss International Air Lines

These could be displayed through a pop-up window with a virtual agent, thereby addressing questions a web traveler might have. This approach requires the use of real-time analytics and dataware such as used for CRM applications. So far they have been deployed only in a sales context to manage up- and cross-sell campaigns and not in web customer service. Additionally, technology providers like Siebel, Kana, and E.piphany offer solutions that allow FAQ lists to be pre-filtered by customer data so that only FAQs display that pertain to a web traveler's specific product purchase.

Overall, FAQ sections on airline websites still have room for improvement when it comes to being channel applications that are user friendly and personalized.

*Site map / Site index*

| What is it | General benefits | General challenges |
|---|---|---|
| List of web pages accessible to online users and search engine | Low cost, tracking data, instantaneous | Organization of map/index not always intuitive for users |

The pages in the site map section are typically organized in a hierarchical fashion providing for a top-down view of the content. This is so that web travelers and search engine crawlers can find specific content on particular airline web pages. However, this hierarchical organization is often not intuitive for web travelers and specific content can be often difficult to find.

Many airlines treat site maps more as an afterthought so they are often buried in a website footer section. There are airlines, however, that not only prominently display the site map link on their website but also make it an integral part of their web customer service section. They offer a user-friendly presentation of the site map content which features large and bold font size headers and even an alphabetical arrangement of the various areas on the website (see Japan Airlines and JetBlue in Figure 5.9). It is a policy that should be more widely adopted.

*Figure 5.9* *The site map on jal.com and jetblue.com*

*Source:* jal.com (2014)[13] with kind permission of Japan Airlines, jetblue.com (2014)[14] with kind permission of JetBlue

*Customized web pages*

| What is it | General benefits | General challenges |
|---|---|---|
| Web content/applications "built" by user according to their preferences | User-friendly interaction by user with website, more conducive to self-service | Development of several web page content templates, investment in and integration of new technology |

Some airline websites allow web travelers to customize individual web pages. These pages can be used to display certain content such as destination information. They can also record purchases of airline tickets, and store travel preferences. Building one's own website (or at least a portion of it) is a form of self-service because it allows a web traveler quick access to highly relevant information. This in turn translates into an improved interaction with the airline's website.

The idea of offering users the ability to configure their own website is not new and features like "MyYahoo" have been around since the early 2000s.[15] An airline website example is lufthansa.com. Via a feature called "Your personal homepage," web travelers have the ability to choose from several pre-configured template pages and tailoring web pages according to their individual needs (Figure 5.10).

There is a range of choices with templates for recurring trips and booking fields with entries such as origin, destination, and travel dates that are already linked to booking histories and FFP status information.

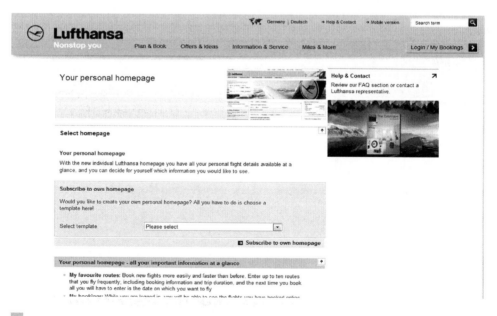

**Figure 5.10** *Customization on lufthansa.com*

*Source:* lufthansa.com (2014)[16] with kind permission of Lufthansa

*Product demo*

| What is it | General benefits | General challenges |
|---|---|---|
| Presentation of how products work under actual use conditions | User self-driven demos with audio, text, and video | Adoption of user perspective, investment in/integration of new technology |

Common examples of product demos include:

- how to purchase a ticket on the airline website
- how to use the airline's web check-in and airport kiosk
- how to use the airline's mobile website
- how to manage award bookings.

These online product demos are presented by some airlines as static text on web pages that web travelers read on their own. Such an application is shown on southwest.com (Figure 5.11). They also offer web animation and video. With web animations, web travelers can follow a demonstration through various website screens showing specific cursor movements and mouse clicks to accomplish certain online tasks. This type of product demo uses mostly text pop-ups to illustrate each step. Occasionally, audio is applied as well. A broad selection of products demos is found on qantas.com. This site also does a good job in featuring "Online Tutorials" in its help section next to FAQ, contact us, and site map.

*Interactive voice response (IVR)*

| What is it | General benefits | General challenges |
|---|---|---|
| Menu-driven phone system allowing self-service via phone keypad or speech recognition | Deflection of customer calls, instant answers to simple queries | Quality of IVR content, user-friendly navigation, and voice presentation/production |

IVR systems respond with prerecorded or dynamically generated audio messages to direct users on how to proceed and retrieve information about simple queries. IVR systems can be useful because they allow web travelers to receive up-to-date information immediately without having to speak directly to a person. IVR technology is also used to gather information from web travelers. Telephone surveys offered after a conversation with a live CSR to rate their performance are a prime example. In these, one is prompted to answer questions by pushing the numbers on a touch-tone telephone.

IVR technology is common among US carriers but is also used by airlines in other parts of the world. It is often applied to areas such as flight arrival/departure

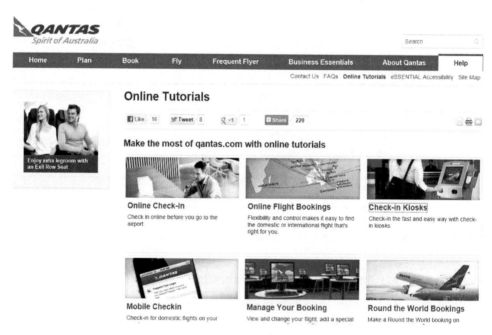

information, FFP account status, ticket bookings including for FFP redemption bookings, and check-in (see Figure 5.12).

Critical elements for a superior IVR system are:

- *Quality of content.* Is all relevant content presented to a web traveler that allows them to access the necessary information for self-service?
- *Ease of navigation.* Is it intuitive and user friendly for guiding the customer through the IVR menu and retrieving information?
- *Voice presentation/production.* Can the caller's voice easily be understood by the IVR voice recognition system? How clear and audible is the IVR voice to the caller?[19]

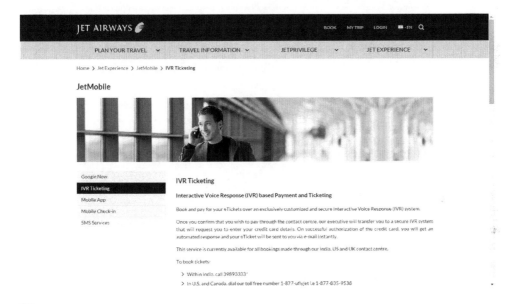

**Figure 5.12** *IVR application promoted on jetairways.com*

*Source:* jetairways.com (2014)[20] with kind permission of Jet Airways

Airlines use IVR technology because of its cost-saving possibility. This largely results from call center deflection. US Airways, for example, claims a 5% reduction in call volume in the wake of a new IVR system implementation in 2011.[21]

Among the self-service channels, IVR is popular. Although not airline industry specific, data show that IVR ranks second only to web usage as the most offered self-help path. It is concerning, however, that 50% of contact centers do not schedule any regular reviews of their IVR systems. Worse still, nearly three-quarters (72%) are apparently unnecessarily frustrating their customers by not passing information collected in the IVR through to agents.[22]

*Brochureware user guide*

| What is it | General benefits | General challenges |
|---|---|---|
| A printed manual intended to provide for assistance on how to use a particular feature on a digital property | Illustration of use via clear and simplified diagrams and associated screenshots/images, portability | Matching language use with target audience, content dates quickly |

Offering travelers printed manuals to illustrate the use of airline products is a common practice, even in today's digital driven environment. We just need to think of safety instruction cards and amenity cards in aircraft seat pockets as examples. When airlines launched their first generation websites, they produced brochureware in the form of leaflets and flyers that were handed out to travelers upon check-in or inflight. Besides promotional aspects, their purpose was to introduce the airline's website and illustrate how its features work. Nowadays, such printed material is rare but airlines use their inflight magazines to share on dedicated pages "how to" information for their digital properties. If an airline really wants to show each and every positive aspect of a particular website feature, a good user manual is an important component in the mix of self-service options. Readers are typically presented with imagery such as screenshots and (hopefully) user friendly language that allow them to familiarize themselves and self-service if need be next time they actually use the website feature on hand.

### 5.6.2 Assisted service options

*Email*

| What is it | General benefits | General challenges |
|---|---|---|
| Channel to exchange digital messages from one internet-enabled device to another via an email infrastructure | Fast, no user charges, low cost, personalization possible, archivable and trackable, branding opportunity | Netiquette standards for communication, responsiveness to customer queries |

Its ubiquity is amazing: With 2.5 billion email worldwide users and daily email traffic amounting to 204 billion globally, it is still by far the most popular internet-based communications channel in the world.[23] A significant portion of the customer service communication in the business world is conducted between people who are not present in the same geographic area and not connected in real time. Email overcomes these issues of logistics and asynchronization.

For the airline industry, email is one of the core channels for assisted customer service offered to web travelers today. All airlines offer it and web travelers have a strong preference for it besides phone and chat communication. Emails can be archived, they are trackable through message logs and their content is searchable. It therefore creates a useful mechanism for managing customer service requests.

When contacted by web travelers, carriers either respond (at least those who do respond) through a combination of so-called auto email responders and CSRs or through CSRs alone. Immediacy in responses to customer queries in today's 24/7 internet world has become the expected standard. Auto email responders are robot-like devices that, upon receiving an email from a customer, automatically send back an email within one to two hours and starting with a generic salutation like "Dear Customer" or "Dear Passenger." They not only acknowledge the receipt of the customer email but also provide for information on next steps including when and how the customer's issue would be handled. In a second step, an airline CSR then follows up with the customer through a personalized email.

An email response, be it automated and/or managed by a CSR, reflects on an airline's approach to web customer service in many ways. The speed by which a company reverts back to the web traveler, the degree of personalization via customer salutation and email sign offs, the branding of the airline in the email, and the handling of possible further queries by the customer are all a reflection of the airline's web customer service quality.

Airlines engaging in email communication need not only be concerned with their responsiveness to customers but also with the "netiquette" applied to this medium. As a general rule, communicating business issues by email should be no different from using other means of communication. A certain degree of formality is always required. Displaying the airline name as the sender and using an appropriate subject header should avoid the email being handled by the web traveler's email inbox as spam. Proper email letterheads and signatures, the recognition of a web traveler's name and title, and the actual message (including a reference ID for possible future correspondence) need to be managed in accordance with certain business communication standards.

Airlines also use the email channel to perform pre-emptive customer service activities. This is beneficial when an airline wants to alert web travelers about a situation before it turns into service issues. A notification regarding a cancelled flight and the web traveler's re-accommodation on another flight is an example. Pre-emptive service is applied by carriers to convey an apology for "after-the-fact" situations when a disservice occurred. Examples might be a malfunctioning inflight entertainment system or a delayed flight due to an overbooking. Reaching out to web travelers via email and apologizing for the inconvenience caused (and even possibly offering a token of reconciliation in the form of bonus miles or price discount on the next ticket purchase) can go a long way to differentiate an airline from competitors that might be silent in such circumstances.

Better than contacting web travelers in situations where most of them expect to receive an apology is to reach out so that this comes as a complete surprise. The author himself experienced this once with Delta (this is not a brand endorsement here since there are enough examples when their service was not so impressive) when put in a middle seat although his preference is an aisle. Two days after the flight, the author received an apology email from Delta stating that they know about the aisle seat preference because of the customer profile but unfortunately could not accommodate this and therefore issued a bonus of 500 miles. There had never been any comment made by the author to Delta, yet the airline came forward.

## Chat

| What is it | General benefits | General challenges |
|---|---|---|
| A way of exchanging text messages in the same chat room in real time | No long-distance charges, agent can handle multiple session and troubleshoot any issue | Can take longer than comparable phone conversation, more than two to three chat sessions simultaneously appear difficult |

This customer service channel lacks the personality of a phone-based conversation. However, it does have several attractive attributes. There are no long-distance phone charges for web travelers. The CSR can handle multiple sessions thereby reducing average service costs. It is possible to answer questions and troubleshoot any issues that an airline customer may have immediately. Also, online purchases can be completed that otherwise are often abandoned. Moreover, up-/cross-sell pitches are possible. On the down side, chat sessions can take longer than comparable phone conversations and the number of simultaneous sessions a CSR can effectively engage in does not seem to exceed more than two.

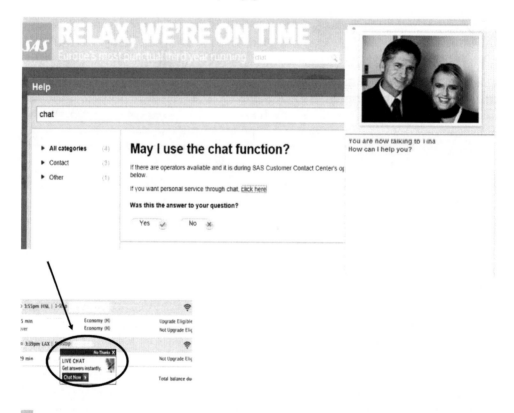

**Figure 5.13** *Examples of reactive and pro-active chat support*

*Source:* flysas.com (2015)[24] with kind permission of SAS Airlines

*Source:* US airline website (2013)[25]

One typically distinguishes between reactive and pro-active chat. The former is initiated by the web traveler on the airline website in need of support. SAS uses this type of chat on flysas.com and accompanies it with a human touch element by introducing the customer service representative "Tina" (Figure 5.13). On the other hand, pro-active chat is activated based on an airline's pre-defined business rules such as the FFP status of traveler, time spent without activity on purchase page, or type of airline ticket sought. It appears in the form of a pop-up box that floats on an existing page. The web traveler can escape the pop-up box by closing it or enter the chat by clicking on an activation button. Some US carriers offer pro-active chat to selected web travelers when they are on a flight selection or payment page of the website where live support from a customer service representative may help secure the purchase.

We can obtain a glimpse of how chat could evolve further when taking a closer look at Virgin America's inflight entertainment (IFE) platform called RED. In October 2012, Virgin America announced the launch of a "Chatter" feature on RED that would allow a real-time chat between the airline's CSRs on the ground and web travelers while inflight, using the in-seat screen of the IFE system for communication. For example, a web traveler concerned about a flight delay and possible misconnection could receive up-to-date information from Virgin America's CSR on how the company intend to handle the situation.[26] This could include providing for assistance on arrival if it is clear that the connecting flight will be missed.

*Click-to-call (CTC)*

| What is it | General benefits | General challenges |
|---|---|---|
| Targeted and personalized phone assistance on particular web pages | Improvement of sales conversion and reduction of site abandonment | Requires investment in new technology, integration of third party technology |

Click-to-call (CTC) lets web travelers engage in a telephone conversation with an airline CSR directly from their website. It should be more accurately labeled as request-to-call because the web traveler provides their phone number in a web dialog box and requests a phone call from the carrier. A more advanced form of CTC involves a button embedded on the airline's website that when clicked connects the customer with a CSR.

Unlike through traditional phone support, with CTC services, the airline has much better control over when and where web travelers can migrate from the website to the phone service channel. It can track each of the customer's online activities. Often, the abandonment of a website by web travelers occurs on payment pages where critical data including those for credit cards have to be entered. The former Continental Airlines decided to deploy click-to-talk technology on their purchase completion page if a customer typed a credit card number incorrectly. Also, when a customer attempted to leave the site at the point of purchase, a prompt would ask them if they would like a customer service representative to phone them. When customers decided to use the

CTC option, Continental found that 35% of the calls resulted in sales. Also, 22% of these callers said that they would have abandoned the site without the option.[27]

The latest form of CTC is video chat whereby a customer clicks on a button and then connects to a CSR who appears on the customer's web page via video and converses with them. Some travel suppliers have introduced video chat. For example, Starwood Hotel launched it in 2011 for sales and customer service purposes and claims that it has become the channel with the highest customer satisfaction.[28] It remains to be seen if an adoption of this form of assisted service in the airline industry occurs. Seeing the other person must really involve a compelling benefit for the web traveler, otherwise the addition of a visual element in a chat would not make much sense. If it helps build additional rapport and loyalty, maybe an airline could consider offering video chat between its top frequent flyers including corporate travelers and a selected team of CSRs that would provide customer service.

*Virtual hold / Scheduled call-back*

| What is it | General benefits | General challenges |
| --- | --- | --- |
| Virtual queuing, a call-back capability for customers waiting to speak to an agent | Minimizes a web traveler's waiting time, the number one complaint with callers | Investment in and integration in new technology |

Virtual hold or call-back is a CSR-assisted feature whereby web travelers who have decided to use an airline's phone service and are put on hold can hang up the phone and are called back as soon as a CSR becomes available. With this concept, also referred to as "virtual queuing," customers have the option to engage in other activities while they still keep their place in the calling queue. Southwest Airlines launched this feature in June 2009 and following this implementation, 40% of all on-hold callers opted for the callback.[29]

*Phone*

| What is it | General benefits | General challenges |
| --- | --- | --- |
| Telecommunications device for two or more users and one of the oldest forms of customer service channels | Like no other channel (except for in-person), it provides for live, real-time, and one-on-one communication, one of the most effective ways of achieving customer satisfaction | High cost, can be time consuming, interrupts a web user's browser session, limits data tracking as entries rely on CSR |

The airline industry was an early adopter of telephony technology in the late 1920s/ early 1930. Traveling by air heralded a new, faster transport era that required high-speed communication. Hence, the telephone was quickly embraced as a key customer service channel.

From an airline perspective, there are some downsides with this channel. The phone requires live CSRs and only one web traveler can be served at a time. This makes it by far the most expensive customer service channel. Also, although often recorded for training purposes, phone conversations are typically not systematically mined for data. Thus any relevant tracking relies on data entries by the CSR and much of the content of phone sessions is lost.

For a web traveler, calling a carrier can be time consuming, disruptive to website browsing sessions, and it costs money. Many airlines levy a telephone fee on callers and even in the US market (the land where the world's first nationwide toll free numbers were introduced in the 1980s), the days of free customer service calls offered by airlines might be numbered. This follows the announcement by ULCC Spirit to terminate its 1-800 toll free number and charge customers instead.[30] However, the phone is still the most preferred service channel because it delivers the most personal communication and results in high satisfaction rates.

All airlines offer customer service to web travelers by phone. Some do so on a 24/7 basis (at least in key markets) via complementary call centers located in different time zones. Some airlines even provide for a dedicated web support line that exclusively deals with issues relating to web bookings and technical website problems (see Air France in Figure 5.14). However, this type of phone support for web travelers is typically only available in a few locations such as in the airline's home market.

**Figure 5.14** *Dedicated phone assistance for web traveler on airfrance.com*

*Source:* airfrance.com (2014)[31] with permission from Air France

The evolution of the phone channel is not over. Some observers forecast the incorporation of emotion detection technology in call centers. An airline would "know" how a customer feels based on how loud they are talking and what the tone, pitch, and speed are when engaging in a conversation with the call center's interactive voice recognition (IVR) system. If a caller sounds vocally upset while on hold, they could receive a higher priority in the queue and connect to a CSR faster.[32] In 2012, Samsung introduced an emotion-sensing smart phone that infers a user's state of mind from how the phone is used. Depending on how much the phone shakes, how often mistakes are backspaced, and how many special symbols are used, the phone could predict with a 67.5% accuracy rate if the user was angry, happy, surprised, etc.[33] One has to see if and when such developments may find their way into the area of customer service at an airline. Airlines should be on the lookout because these applications could help differentiate the brand from that of competitors because they offer a more positive user experience.

On a more humble, less futuristic level, airlines have already integrated "smart" applications in their telephone channel. Take for example the introduction of "virtual hold/scheduled call-back" and "click-to-call" we have discussed earlier. Several airlines have launched these as new customer service options in recent years. The advent of the mobile smart phone is another important development in the evolution of telephony and its impact on customer service offered by airlines to web travelers is highly significant. We discuss mobiles in a later section.

*Avatar/Virtual agent*

| What is it | General benefits | General challenges |
|---|---|---|
| Virtual assistant representing a human being | Cost saving and personalized while still interacting with customer in "humanized" way | Limited know-how and language skills, lack of "attractive" avatar looks |

The term "avatar" is derived from the Indian language of Sanskrit. It refers to the embodiment of a deity on earth. Using this definition as an analogy, an avatar in cyberspace refers to a computer representation of a person. Avatars, also referred to as virtual agents or artificial intelligent agents, were first introduced in the mid-1980s as part of computer games that were launched at the time and used as the computer game players' visual on-screen in-game personas. They can take the form of a three-dimensional model or a two-dimensional icon. Companies outside the travel sector have introduced avatars on their website as virtual assistants. One popular example is "Anna" on www.ikea.com, the Swedish furniture manufacturer's website.

The airline industry's first website avatar was launched by Alaska Airlines in February 2008. At her fifth anniversary on alaskaair.com in February 2013, "Jenn" had been accumulating 43,800 hours of work, the equivalent of 22 years for a full-time employee with three weeks of vacation per year.[34] To obtain some idea of Jenn's customer service activities, between February 2008 and December 2012 she engaged in 11.5 million chat sessions involving 25.1 million questions.[35] Naturally, the question arises as to how many of these interactions were successfully handled in the sense that web travelers' questions were provided with an appropriate answer. TAM from Brazil, which introduced its website avatar "Julia" in June of 2013 (she was built by the same company Next IT as Alaska Airlines' "Jenn"), provides some insight. In the first two weeks of operation, Julia managed almost 72,000 sessions and replied to customer queries with a 82% success rate.[36] Other airline websites where avatars have begun to appear in recent years include "Eva" on the Swedish website of SAS, "Alex" on united.com, and the avatar on Virgin Australia's website.

All these avatars are powered by natural language processing (NLP) or structured language processing (SLP). Via digital conversations, web travelers are guided around the airline website and offered specific options and well-defined paths to an outcome. For an interaction sample, it is worth checking out the elaborate conversation between Jenn and Snyder Brett, a blogger on the Crankyflier website in February 2008.[37]

**Figure 5.15** Virtual assistant "Jenn" on alaskaair.com

*Source:* alaskaair.com (2014)[38] with kind permission of Alaska Airlines

Avatars are considered an effective way for a company to save cost while still engaging with consumers in a "humanized" way through naturalistic facial and body expressions. Research has shown that in situations where technology exhibits human-like behaviors including language production, taking turn in conversations and even using psychosocial phenomena such as flattery and politeness, web users tend to respond as they would to people.[39] Let us recall that one key inhibitor for online shopping is the internet's impersonal nature, specifically the absence of pleasurable experiences, social interaction, and personal consultation with face-to-face communication by a company representative. If avatars provide for an enhanced personification of technology, avatar-mediated interaction then should lead to more satisfied shoppers that perceive a product more positively and thus are more satisfied with a retailer.[40]

In this respect, we should mention the impact of an avatar's design. An attractive-looking avatar apparently has more persuasive powers on moderately involved shoppers due to its likeability while so-called expert avatars are more persuasive with highly involved shoppers because of their credibility. Judging from the current avatar design as applied by airlines, they all have opted for female, attractive-looking avatars at this stage. However, other designs could be introduced, even allowing web users to personalize avatars with faces and voices of their own choice.[41]

The presence of avatars will grow as they are "field proven." One estimates states that customer self-service search activities in 2015 would involve virtual agents for at least 1,500 large enterprises.[42] With continuous improvements of their capabilities to personify technology and make it more human, they will be able to address an ever-growing spectrum of customer service issues. These include the handling of purchase-related activities such as searching for low fares, processing credit card payments, and completing seat assignments. They will also have the potential to save an airline money in the live CSR area. All this could make an investment in avatar technology for customer service purposes important. In the area of customer-assisted service, avatars may turn out to be the next best thing besides real human airline CSRs and could lift the travel experience to a new level.

## Co-browsing

| What is it | General benefits | General challenges |
|---|---|---|
| Simultaneous navigation of two or more people accessing the same web pages | Contextualized and personalized customer service as the airline CSR sees what the web traveler sees | Privacy concerns of users investment in and integration of new technology |

Co-browsing is the simultaneous navigation of two or more people on the internet accessing the same website pages. Initially, co-browsing was achieved by communicating to the different online users the pages being accessed through traditional means such as the telephone. Today, software applications can automatically synchronize the browsers of different users.

As web travelers may encounter issues, such as trying to obtain clarification on some fare rules or being stuck in the payment process, an airline CSR could be contacted. They would then, through co-browsing, see what the customer sees on their website and would be able to assist with resolutions such as guiding a web traveler to specific pages and information that would help close the issue at hand. Customer interest in this technology exists. It is estimated that 15% of online shoppers would use it in the future as it provides for immediate and personal help.[43]

Security concerns of online shoppers about a CSR learning personal information when co-browsing can be addressed by sharing information on the security features of co-browsing. For example, a CSR could point out that they are not able to see personal information. Key about co-browsing is to offer it at the point of issue. To do so, a carrier would need to be aware of the possibility that other web service tools such as FAQ or chat would be more appropriate for an issue resolution. Otherwise, co-browsing could turn out to be time-consuming and lengthen the interaction time between the web traveler and the airline.

*Intelligent personal assistant (IPA)*

| *What is it* | *General benefits* | *General challenges* |
| --- | --- | --- |
| A software agent that takes user input such as voice commands to provide for information, to complete tasks, and to make recommendations. | Easily accessible at any point of time, user can speak to IPA naturally, IPA learns user preferences over time, and can interact with smart device application without user intervention | Might not recognize the queries if the user cannot hit the right voice modulation; also the user has to provide for specific keywords to make the right use of the IPA since providing a wrong keyword hinders its functionality. |

The rising popularity of intelligent personal assistants (IPAs) indicates that online users value applications that help them organize their lives better. Mainstream examples of IPAs include Google Now, Siri by Apple, Cortana by Microsoft, and "M" by Facebook (although theirs is a hybrid of artificial intelligence and Facebook employees dubbed "M Trainers"). Other IPAs for mobile apps that have found recognition include 24me, Quip, and Speaktoit. IPAs let people make calls, send texts and search the web, all while remembering everything from their favorite preferences, history, and dislikes.

Airlines have begun to integrate IPAs as part of their customer service offerings. Take for instance Google Now. It works with many airlines, ranging from Aeroflot to United Airlines, and a key application is itinerary and travel notifications. Information is organized into so-called "cards" that provide all the information that a web traveler might need for trip. Some of the travel cards Google Now offers include airports, boarding pass, currency, flights, translation, and weather. Web travelers benefit by receiving information before they even ask about flight details, directions to the airport with live traffic updates, reminders to leave, and local weather information.

Microsoft has even developed an IPA specifically for China Eastern Airlines called XiaoIce, It was launched in 2014 and can be used on social media sites such as Sina Weibo. It learns not only from past interactions with a web traveler but also from those around the country in China. Because of this insight, it can conduct life-like conversations with a web traveler.

How does XiaoIce specifically work? Prior to boarding, it provides passengers with updates on flight information, boarding notifications, and the option to pre-order meals and drinks. If the airplane is wi-fi equipped, a passenger can use XiaIce on their tablet or laptop (under civil aviation regulations in China, the use of mobile phones in-flight even in airplane mode with cellular services is not allowed) and socialize with other passengers, contact the crew, or send post-arrival pick-up reminders to people on the ground. In order to initiate a chat with XiaoIce, passengers have to type #XiaoIceFliesWithMe#, the flight number and the seat number.

IPAs are here to stay. Their supportive role and predictive power can only grow as their capabilities to perform beyond what coders have explicitly programmed them to do will grow. Accordingly, they will be able to use a web traveler's personal preferences and a near-infinite web of connections to answer almost any query and perform almost any function. For example, when asking a current IPA to book a plane trip, a web user is directed to a number of travel websites but flight options are not offered. Also, securing a particular seat is not feasible. However, in the future, complicated commands, say, "Give me the lowest fare from Los Angeles to Paris next week Wednesday with a return flight on Saturday" may very likely produce an answer like "Air France 65 fits your schedule and aisle seat 32C is available according to your preferences," then the IPA buys the ticket with the web traveler's credit card. With IPAs becoming more and more a mainstream affair, web travelers are not only likely to change their personal lifestyle, but also change the way they interact with airlines for customer service purposes.

*Mail*

| What is it | General benefits | General challenges |
|---|---|---|
| System for carrying written documents and tangible objects via an intermediary | Tangibility, good for customer service situations where invoicing/billing is involved and where original receipts and documents are required | Slowness, logistical handling of larger mailings, delivery can be unreliable, expensive |

Mail, or post, is the method that can be used for the transmission of documents and tangible objects. Written and printed documents, and also small packages, are sent by web travelers to airline customer service departments. Mail is one of the oldest channels of customer service offered by airlines to the traveling public. It has been used by customers since the early days of commercial aviation.

Traditional mail is still popular with the older generation of travelers but even younger web travelers occasionally use it because they have no choice: Some airline's policies need physical evidence. For example, customer requests for post-flight FFP mileage accreditation require the boarding pass and/or the original passenger ticket receipt to be sent in. Also, when a customer's luggage has been lost or damaged, many airlines only reimburse the customer's expenses for any replacement once they have received original receipts. Of course, there are also those web travelers who write a mail letter of complaint or compliment because they intend to be thoughtful and deliberate about their communication. If addressed directly to a particular person, especially a senior manager, this type of communication can attract more attention in a world otherwise inundated with email and social media communication.

*Field (ATO/CTO/sales representative/)*

| What is it | General benefits | General challenges |
|---|---|---|
| An in-person, face-to-face contact for customer service purposes, one of the oldest forms of customer service | Of all customer service channels, most personal, one-to-one interaction | Expensive resource, limited multi-tasking, availability limited to standard working hours, data tracking of interaction relies on entries by representative |

What would the role be for an airline field person in web customer service? Ticketing is a likely answer. Some airlines allow customers to reserve a ticket online (typically for a 24 to 48 hour period) and then to pay for it in person by cash or check at the airline's downtown CTO or ATO. This option is suitable for web travelers who do not have a credit card or other online forms of payment. Even if they do, their credit card might have transaction limits which requires them to pay for the ticket by other means. Airlines offering this kind of "quasi" online purchase typically levy a fee to account for the ticket issuance cost (see Figure 5.16 of Air Mauritius offering this service with a 72-hour window at three different ticket issuance locations).

### 5.6.3 Mobile customer service

With the widespread adoption of mobile devices by consumers, companies need to accommodate this platform into their web customer service activities. A total of 78% of customers indicate that they use mobile applications (or "apps") for a service purpose.[45] Moreover, 72% of customers would use mobile apps in place of traditional customer service channels (e.g. calling customer care) if the same services and assistance were available.[46] Apparently, customers are ready.

In light of this development and faced with growing demand from its customers, the airline industry has embraced mobile. Today many airlines feature mobile offerings in the form of websites optimized for a mobile environment and downloadable mobile apps. Before elaborating on them in greater detail, let us focus first on messaging services

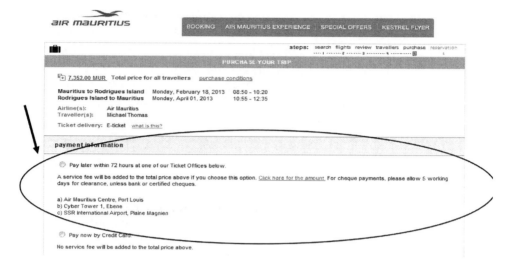

**Figure 5.16** *"Pay Later" option on airmauritius.com*

*Source:* airmauritius.com (2014)[44] with kind permission of Air Mauritius

such as SMS (short messaging service) and MMS (multi-media messaging service), the earliest forms of mobile engagement by airlines.

*Short message service (SMS)*

| What is it | General benefits | General challenges |
|---|---|---|
| Text messaging service for the exchange of short text between mobile or fixed phone devices | Low cost, practical for pro-active notification about "last minute" alerts and updates | Message delivery can be unreliable and untimely, higher security vulnerabilities |

Short message service (SMS) is a text messaging service component of phone, web, or mobile communication systems. It uses standardized communications protocols that allow the exchange of short text messages between fixed lines or mobile phone devices. SMS is the most widely used data application in the world, with 3.5 billion active users, or 78% of all mobile phone subscribers.[47] In the United States, for example, the average mobile subscriber sends or receives 357 text messages per month, compared to placing or receiving 204 monthly phone calls.[48]

Airlines worldwide have also adopted SMS in the last six to seven years as part of their pre-emptive customer service approach and to reach out to web travelers pro-actively. This is because many carriers have realized the prevalence of travelers' mobile phone usage and their need for instant information, especially when it comes to flight schedule information. For example, sending an alert on a flight cancellation with less than 24 hours' via email is not effective as it could be missed by the traveler.

Therefore, SMS technology is viewed as a better way of instantly notifying customers of any flight changes on their smart phones, offering an apology and even informing them of alternate travel.

However, no technology is foolproof and SMS messaging does have its challenges. Frequently cited concern is that a sender of an SMS message cannot determine if a message has been delivered in a timely manner. SMS traffic is generally treated as lower priority communications traffic. Therefore, the delivery of SMS text may be delayed and then would be beyond its relevance. Worse, it may not be delivered at all.

Nevertheless, many web travelers opt for an SMS notification to be informed by a carrier of any possible flight changes. In order to take advantage of this service, they have to register their mobile phone number on the airline's website. Figure 5.17 illustrates on aa.com the different types of SMS services available to web travelers and how they work.

*Customer service via airline mobile sites and mobile applications*

Many airlines have embarked on a drive to launch a mobile platform and leveraging consumer mobile technology is a top priority in airlines' IT investment

**Figure 5.17** *Text messaging services on aa.com*

*Source:* aa.com (2014)[49] with permission from American Airlines

activities: 66% are now investing or planning to invest by 2016 in this area.[50] The initial focus on mobile has been on rolling out features that enable customers to manage standard transactions of a travel journey such as flight search, check-in, booking, and boarding. Priorities appear to be shifting toward traditional customer service topics including complaint handling, re-bookings, and missing bags. For example, 57% of all airlines plan to introduce a customer complaint feature by 2016 (Figure 5.18).

Overall the airline industry has been swift to recognize the significance of mobile commerce. However, the question remains as to whether launching a subset of customer service features already existing in other channels is good enough for the mobile channel. More specifically (and we have posed this question before): Is an airline really taking advantage of the mobile platforms' unique and genuine strengths when it simply uses it to do things that can be done already through other channels such as checking an FAQ section or calling a CSR on the phone? Copying and pasting from one channel to another also has a history in the airline industry. The way the mobile channel has evolved so far—being a mini-version of an existing full HTML site—is rather reminiscent of these early days of e-commerce when website content was copied from printed brochures.

In order to truly take advantage of today's mobile marketplace, airlines need to do more than merely adding more customer service features to their mobile

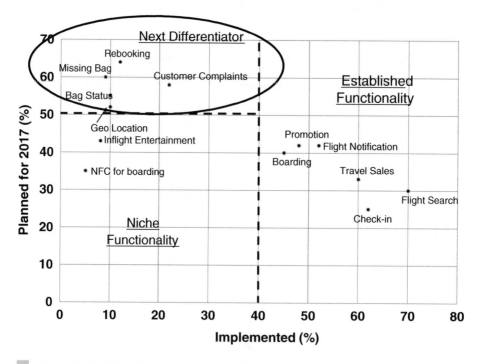

**Figure 5.18** *Airline adoption of mobile services by 2016*

Source: SITA (2013)[51]

platforms. They need to transform each and every mobile interaction into a personalized and satisfying customer experience. To do that, they must engage in a uniquely mobile conversation. A first step in this direction would be to acknowledge that people have a different, that is, closer and more emotional, connection, with their mobile devices, than with PCs or other technology. Mobile devices like smart phones are the first wearable computers and the interaction with them is expected to be impromptu, quick, and easy. Mobile web customers are literally on the go and they are moving around. Hence, the interaction with them for customer service purposes should be much more conversational and dynamic than with other channels.

A deeper and more personalized engagement via mobile technology is feasible and there are already multiple technology providers that offer interesting products. For instance, let us imagine a menu for contact options on a mobile platform that is clear, quick, and intuitive and almost performs like a "visual IVR." Figure 5.19 illustrates how this could look like for our fictitious airline OrangeJet that we have already met in Chapter 3.

The menu offers a spectrum of assisted service options including various ways to start a phone conversation. A mobile web traveler could select "schedule a call back" or "receive a call from a local agent when available." This approach, if implemented on a large scale, would certainly challenge today's airline call center operations. The technology and staff resourcing and scheduling of these are mostly geared toward routing and queuing incoming high-volume phone calls as efficiently

**Figure 5.19** *How customer service via smartphones should be…*

as possible as opposed to conducting outbound phone calls involving de-centralized CSR set ups.

Other options this mobile platform may offers include "start a chat" and "send an email." In all these instances, when the web traveler wants live CSR assistance from a mobile device, their overall travel history, traveler status, geographic location, and recent navigation on the mobile device's app would be known to the airline. The mobile device would therefore also serve as a form of identification. When using the airline's mobile app, all the information about the web traveler would be transparent and available to the airline contact center. Accordingly, the web traveler would be routed to the best-suited CSR based on a business logic that puts all the information known about them in an appropriate context. By the time a connection between the airline and the web traveler would be established, the web traveler would be fully identified. This is because to the so-called five "Ws" (who, what, where, when, why) would be made known before the engagement with the CSR. In terms of privacy concerns, people who would otherwise be nervous about being tracked and monitored when online in general, actually would *expect* a company to know what a person is doing online when they are using the company app.

The above information is a good illustration of how seamless and smart the customer service interaction could be:

- Information would be transferred over from one channel to the other without a delay or other problem.
- The most suitable CSR to assist the web traveler would be located as opposed to involving multiple CSRs and disconnection.
- Personalization would be possible because the CSR has prior knowledge of the web traveler's history and preferences.

The example is also important because it shows how close an airline may come to deliver customer service on a 1:1 basis. This concept has been applied for a while now in sales and marketing but is still elusive in customer service (it probably existed to some degree in the 1950s, before the era of mass transportation).

Airlines should strive to move toward the end of the mobile service spectrum that allows for unprecedented operational efficiency and personalization of customer service and also enables the maximization of the mobile channel's inherent characteristics. In a mobile context, the interaction with "always-on" customers is even more dynamic.

Airlines customer service departments need to embark on a migration from the more traditional phone and email culture to a mobile culture. This requires a new competency that currently does not exist at most carriers. They have to train their staff to handle relevant mobile devices and apps as well as to apply new soft communication skills. In conjunction with the advent of social media, airline service organizations face real difficulties in embracing this fundamental business transformation because mobile customer service solutions are now a necessity.

### 5.6.4 Social customer care

| What is it | General benefits | General challenges |
| --- | --- | --- |
| Interactive web platforms owned and/or operated by companies and also used for customer service among peers and between companies and peers | Medium allows informal and quick communication with mass audience | Monitoring social media and managing their ever-growing presence, measuring social media noise, proper resource support, public nature of communication |

With Facebook counting close to 1.5 billion active monthly users and Twitter boasting over 300 million users, it is no surprise that consumers have come to expect companies to engage in social media as part of their customer support. For example, in the United States almost 70% of consumers use social media for customer service[52] and 33% even prefer to contact companies through social media rather than by phone.[53]

The volume of social media interaction between consumers and companies is growing every year. For some companies, it might already be larger than the interaction via telephone. This is a significant development that all airlines should address by integrating social media in their overall management of web customer service. Organizational set-ups and staffing, technology infrastructure and tools, quality assurance, new metrics for measuring the interaction such as listening, identifying web traveler sentiments and social media influencers, are just a few areas that must be considered.

Unlike any other service tool, communication through social media is typically a public affair. It is not only that two parties are involved—in our case a web traveler and an airline—but the whole world is watching. Anyone with a Twitter account can follow tweets or, if they have internet access, can see the posting on blogs. Also, social media are typically in almost real time.

From an airline perspective, this brings both benefits and challenges. It is a valuable way to feel the pulse of the market and to learn of general customer concerns and address them immediately. At the same time, large amount of data can be collected for all kinds of data-mining purposes. However, airlines face numerous challenges when it comes to social media in a customer service context. Some crucial questions that require attention include:

- What third party sites should we monitor and how do we monitor them?
- Should we launch our own blog site?
- What resources do we need to manage our presence?
- What should the corporate communications policy for social media be?
- How do we measure success?
- What organization should be put in place to manage this?

Ignoring these questions would seriously hinder the delivery of a competitive social customer service.

One key requirement for web travelers seeking help through social media is speed. A situation where an airline is not responding quickly enough can lead to a viral outcry of global proportions. The majority of consumers expect companies to respond to queries within minutes or hours (Figure 5.20). Most companies including many airlines are not able to handle social customer service queries in such short timeframes. This may create a disappointment gap between users' anticipation and a company's ability to deliver.

To make things even more challenging, people expect a 24/7 social customer service by companies: 57% expect the *same* response time at night and on weekends as during normal business hours.[54] The implications for a company brand perceived to be a slow responder are serious. In the US market, 33% of social media users would recommend a brand that offered a quick but ineffective response.[56] It seems that it is better to be fast than effective when it comes to the world of social customer service. This may be a rather scary picture but it appears to be valid at least in a US context. It certainly raises some organizational questions. How much should one scale up to manage these expectations? What would be an appropriate structural set-up? It is easy to see how quickly an airline can be overwhelmed by social media in the customer service area. We will come back to these questions when discussing specific social media types such as blogs, forums, and networks.

Social customer care is not only about speed, although web travelers certainly have been conditioned to expect immediate feedback from companies. It is also about the social aspect. Knowing that fellow consumers can provide comfort if people come forward to express their empathy or to offer their own advice about what to do (this is called "crowd servicing") cannot be underestimated in its importance. It could also draw public attention to an issue and force a company to act. Companies generally respond to limit the brand damage inflicted on them by negative publicity.

An example of this is the classic case of the "United breaks guitars" incident. It occurred in 2008 and involved United Airlines that had mishandled a Canadian rock band's music instruments and actually destroyed their guitars during a baggage transfer in Chicago on their flight from Halifax to Omaha. Having tried unsuccessfully for nine

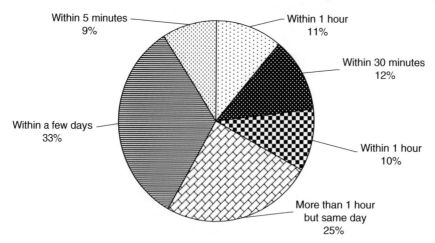

**Figure 5.20** *Consumers anticipate quick response times when using social media for customer service*

*Source:* Baer (2012)[55]

months to resolve the issue with United's service department, the group finally produced a five-minute music video called "United breaks guitars" and released it on YouTube. Within one week, it garnered a record of 1.5 million views and received worldwide TV and radio news coverage.[57] United's stock price fell during this incident by 10%, costing $180 million in stock value, although some people claim that there was no direct correlation. United eventually agreed to settle the issue with the customer.

Another more recent case happened in 2013 and involved a Twitter user and British Airways. Frustrated with the airline's slow customer service regarding the status of a lost bag, the individual decided to purchase a sponsored ad on Twitter for $1,000 and complained about the carrier. The tweet "Don't fly @ British Airways. Their customer service is horrendous." was initially aimed at the airline's 300,000 followers. However, it was quickly picked on the internet and by news media around the world. British Airways publicly apologized for the disservice and promised to deliver the missing bag.[58]

Both examples make clear why some web travelers might also use social media. They do not flock to social media as their first option but often as the last resort because airlines managed the customer service issue through other channels poorly or not at all. Considering the global proportions of social media, they are perfect from a web traveler's perspective for creating awareness and forcing a resolution.

Given that this is so, we need to raise the question that if a web traveler's last option is to escalate the issue and go "public" on social media networks, why other service tools such as self-service options, email, or the phone failed in the first place. It is impressive to see that some airlines allocate significant resources to social media and no one doubts that such resources are necessary if social media are to be managed effectively. However, to be a successful player in cyberspace means an airline's management of other service tools must not be cannibalized at the expense of social media. They should focus on getting the basics of the existing self-service and assisted tools right before committing to a larger-scale involvement in social media.

These other service tools including FAQs, email, and phones are also crucial because social media, due to their public nature and technical features, have limited potential for resolving unique service issues of an individual web traveler. Twitter caps out at 140 characters, so how much can one really dive into details? Therefore, the transition to other channels must be encouraged. The Twitter website of Southwest, for example, makes it clear that it would not address specific customer service issues on the site.[59] Offering the traveling public a service tool in isolation and disconnected from other service tools is dangerous. This issue highlights the need for an all-encompassing perspective on service options if an airline wants to succeed in managing web customer service.

Let us now turn to the most common social media used to deal with customer service issues. They include blogs, web forums, and social networks which are further discussed below and have been used for some time in the airline industry.

Social media are used by web travelers both for self-service and assisted service. In the self-service case, web travelers access social media sites of their choice and are looking for information that can shed light on their issue and help resolve it. They may monitor communications in travel forums, check out commentaries on travel blogs, and review posts of friends on social network sites. They absorb the information and then embark on self-servicing. There is no interaction taking place with other parties as they only browse through selected social media sites and then leave them.

However, in terms of assisted service, web travelers may reach out to social media in order to be helped by someone. If they do, help must arrive quickly and must be with a full appreciation of the fact that the world is watching. Possible websites for contact could be airline-owned and -operated blog sites "Nuts about Southwest," Southwest corporate blog, or an airline's microblog such as Twitter are examples. Another possibility is a travel forum such as Flyertalk.com. With social media, any service issue arising is put in the open. This creates an opportunity for other people, be it web travelers or people from other walks of life, to contribute. Such "crowd servicing," where the web traveler seeks the so-called "wisdom of the masses" makes social media a unique channel since no other service tool allows for comparable participation.

*Blogs used for web customer service*

Airlines may engage in blogging for customer service reasons through three type of blogs. One is through a blog website that is owned and maintained by the company. An example is JetBlue's blog "BlueTales" (Figure 5.21). JetBlue makes

**Figure 5.21** *JetBlue blog "BlueTales"*

*Source:* blogjetblue.com (2013),[61] with kind permission of JetBlue

**KLM** Passengers travelling FROM AMSTERDAM ONLY: Rebooked but can't check-in online? Proceed directly through customs and gate with old ticket.

about 6 hours ago via web

**KLM** All passengers will be rebooked automatically. Chk your flight details in Manage My Booking on www.klm.com. More info http://bit.ly/aBSVOx

about 7 hours ago via web

**KLM** Do not go to the airport. First contact the local service centres and keep looking at http://bit.ly/8YIW8B for the latest flight information.

about 12 hours ago via web

**Figure 5.22** *KLM Twitter customer advisories during the Icelandic volcano eruption in 2010*

*Source:* Nigam (2010)[62]

comprehensive use of its company blog for customer service purposes and provides specific advice on how problems customers might experience can be addressed. More airlines now have a similar blog presence but the overall number doing so is still small. Launching and, more importantly, maintaining such a digital product also for a customer service purpose is not cheap. Southwest Airlines has over 30 employees that contribute to its blog "Nuts About Southwest."[60] It takes resources, often full-time, and know-how to do so, something many airlines do not have currently have. Without a solid business case, it should not be attempted.

Besides their own corporate blog, many airlines deal also with customer service using third party blogging platforms. One of these platforms is the micro-blog of which Twitter is the primary showcase. It was introduced to airline web customer service through an event in 2010 that in a way can be considered a social media epiphany moment that sealed the union between Twitter and airlines. Specifically, we are referring to the eruption of Icelandic volcano Eyjafjallajökull in April 2010 that led to a nine-day shutdown of controlled airspace in most European countries.

The usage of Twitter was so widespread because its benefit as a vehicle for customer servicing and providing up-to-date information to a mass audience became instantly clear. Several airlines including Lufthansa and KLM introduced the #ashcloud on Twitter, and provided for a constant stream of updates (Figure 5.22). Other airlines such as Air Baltic and British Airways followed suit and in just seven days a total of over 55,000 mentions of the hashtag were recorded.

Airlines that currently do not partake in micro-blogs or do so but with a strong marketing and sales focus should take notice that this tool can be of valuable assistance in the communication of relevant information by customer service during major disruptions in an airline's operations.

Today, for airlines, the share of tweets related to customer service is high and can account for more than 70%.[63, 64] With close to two million followers each on their Twitter website, KLM, JetBlue and Southwest are the largest players on Twitter in the airline industry. KLM is very committed to dealing with customer service issues via Twitter. With a 24/7 staff of over 130 people, it manages around 35,000 traveler questions via social media every week. Approximately 25% of these are on Twitter.[65] JetBlue has more of a sales and marketing focus than Southwest with this medium but both carriers inform travelers constantly about what is happening and are responsive to customer queries and complaints.

In order to obtain an idea of airlines' performance in this area, it is common to look at two metrics. One is about responsiveness, the other is about speed. Figure 5.23 shows the world's Top 10 airlines in terms of how many tweets they responded to. This is an important aspect in determining an airline's performance because it indicates how much a web traveler can count on social care support by a carrier. American Airlines is the top airline with over 9,000 questions answered. Besides KLM on the second spot with more than 6,600 answers, Air Asia is also a strong performer with over 4,300 questions handled.

**Figure 5.23** *Top 10 airline performance in social customer care (Twitter, first quarter 2014)*

*Source:* Ross (2014)[66]

If we narrow the focus on European carriers only, KLM by far more responsive than its rivals. For example in 2013, KLM responded to 93% of all tweets received while other major airlines including Air France, Lufthansa, and easyJet replied to less than 25%.[67]

The other key metric in social customer care deals with speed. We recall from our earlier discussion how much consumers value a quick reply to their query. Figure 5.24 gives an indication how fast airlines respond. In the sample, the large majority (80%) of American Airlines replies are turned around within 15 minutes while over 50% of Air Asia's responses are handled within 24 hours. Apparently, the performance by carriers varies greatly.

In essence, to perform competitively in social customer care requires an airline's strong commitment. Only then is it possible to provide for precise and fast service information and doing so on a consistent basis with a global audience.

KLM took this commitment to a new, more transparent, level in November 2013. The carrier, already known for its leadership role in social media, decided to begin displaying its social media team's live response time to customer queries from Twitter, Facebook, and its customer support page on klm.com (Figure 5.25). KLM embarked on this step in order to manage expectations of web travelers and offer real-time insight into their performance.

Interestingly, as a growing number of airlines establish or expand dedicated social care teams, some other carriers have decided to do the opposite. A case in point is ULCC Spirit Airlines that put its twitter responses into "autopilot." Any web traveler contacting the airline on Twitter receives a so-called robo tweet. This is an automatically generated response with relevant information to the question asked (Figure 5.26). Spirit justifies this approach as part of its ultra-low cost business model that cannot support live

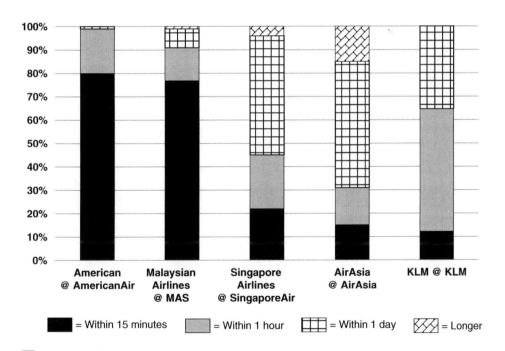

**Figure 5.24** *Response times by selected carriers on Twitter*

*Source:* Purnell (2014)[68]

**Facebook**

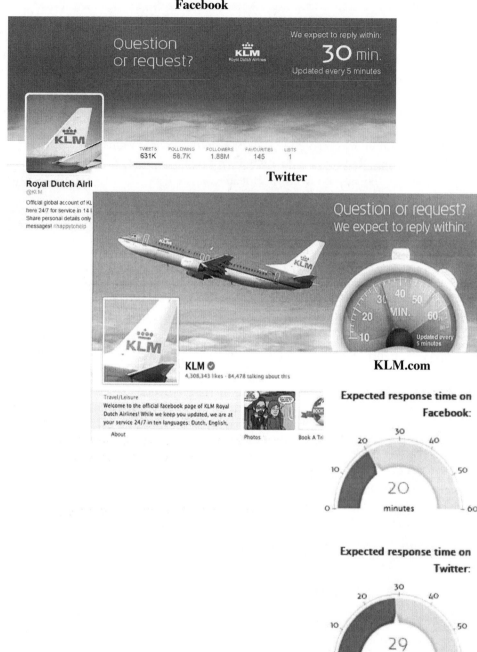

*Figure 5.25* KLM's transparency on social customer care

*Source:* klm.com (2015),[71] Twitter (2015),[72] Facebook (2015)[73] with kind permission of KLM

**George** @grichie96                                     22 Jul
@d_brink you know anything about spirit airlines? cause I'm checking a bag
and have a carry-on. this would be my personal item

**Spirit Autopilot** ⊘                          🐦 Follow
@SpiritAirlines

@grichie96 @d_brink  AutoReply//TJ893_[Bags]: Buy
bags early and online to save bit.ly/1o2wd2r
pic.twitter.com/5wAqdW6Po2

12:57 PM - 22 Jul 2014

**Figure 5.26**  *Spirit Airlines robo tweet*

*Source:* Rabinowitz (2014)[74] with kind permission of Spirit Airlines

customer service. The accuracy and speed of the airline's robo tweets are said to be reasonable.[69] However, it remains to be seen if robo tweets will catch on with other airlines. It may make sense considering that a personal response to thousands of tweets in real-time is a challenge. Some carriers including American Airlines are suspected of using robo tweets although the company denies this.[70] A possible explanation for this stand is that the airline does not want to be perceived as anti-social in its use of social media.

Besides an airline's own corporate blog or company blog operated on third party platforms, there is another blog category used for customer service. It is not owned or maintained by an airline but by a third party. A good example is 15-year-old www.flyertalk.com. It has half a million registered members and is considered one of the world's largest site blogs (and web forums) for air travelers. Web savvy airlines regularly monitor the postings on such websites in order to keep track of customer service issues.

### Web forums

An internet forum is an online discussion website allowing users to post messages and comments on other messages. Sometimes referred to as "slow motion" chat rooms— this is because the interaction between the users is not synchronous—forums perform functions very similar to traditional bulletin boards. A sense of virtual community often develops around forums that have regular users. For airline web customer service, web forums, like blogs, serve as venues for crowd service. They allow a web traveler to receive help from other fellow travelers regarding customer service issues, or obtain information and guidance without having to contact the carrier.

This "customer-helps-customer" scenario has become possible because of the introduction of social media and carriers pay increasing attention to this type of assistance in addition to the self-help by web travelers. Some have set up corporate forums where customers can interact with other customers if they need help. Outside the airline industry, good examples are the comprehensive community discussion boards on ebay or the general help forum on Amazon. Selected travel suppliers have also introduced web forums. Carnival Cruise Lines is amongst them (Figure 5.27).

As in the case with third party blogs, airlines should follow the activities on selected key third party forums to get an idea of what is happening in the marketplace regarding customer service. Equally important, however, is the fact that crowd service can contribute to cost savings for other more traditional forms of assisted customer service including phone and email.

### Social networks

In recent years, airlines worldwide have begun to integrate various social networks in their business processes. Sales and marketing are the primary drivers for this development but web customer service has also emerged as an area in its own right as well. Similar to blogging platforms, social networks have the advantage of reaching a large audience quickly.

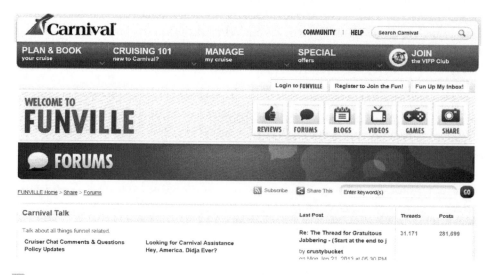

**Figure 5.27** *The travel forum on Carnival*

*Source:* carnival.com (2014),[75] with kind permission of Carnival Cruise Lines

Facebook is the premier social network used by airlines for web customer service. Most airlines use Facebook as a one-way posting platform. Specific information provided to web travelers includes:

- general service advisories
- a carrier's contact details including phone numbers and email addresses
- links to the company website's help section or other social media platforms such as Twitter where assistance is provided.

Some airlines also engage with individual web travelers on their specific customer service issues but this is rare. Instead, web travelers are encouraged to contact the airline through other venues including email and direct messaging on Twitter. An occasion when other airlines may override their policies not to engage one-on-one via social networks is in the event of emergencies. One example is the previously mentioned Icelandic volcano eruption in spring 2010. For many of the affected carriers, for instance, their phone lines quickly maxed out because of the increased call volume. SAS used its Facebook page to deal with customer service issues and addressed every single wall post with a team of three to five people. Virgin Atlantic linked its website to its Facebook fan page. This was where travelers discussed, commented, and shared tips of how to deal with the situation. An important lesson for airlines from this incident was that they should use social networks to broadcast general customer service messages and also participate in specific customer conversations.

It is worth noting that KLM as one of the few carriers in industry has already been applying this policy for some time now. They not only do this on the major global platforms such as Facebook and LinkedIn but also on regional social networks including VKontakte (a social network for Russian-speaking communities) and Weibo (a Chinese hybrid between Facebook and Twitter).

In this respect, one should mention that KLM's experience with social customer care on LinkedIn (offered since July 2014) for its currently 350,000 followers on this platform has surfaced several issues. Among them has been the realization that web travelers reaching out for support through LinkedIn are quite different from those the carrier deals with on Facebook or Twitter. Specifically, customers are much more knowledgeable, use a more professional tone of voice, ask more complex questions, and have overall higher expectations. Furthermore, as far as the abilities of the LinkedIn platform is concerned, KLM felt that more feature improvements for a mobile environment and for taking conversations private would be critical to make social customer care on this social network more effective.[76] Carriers that may consider offering individual web customer service on LinkedIn should carefully assess the KLM observations and what they mean for their social customer care operations.

## 5.7 EMERGING WEB SERVICE CHANNELS

Looking at how the service channel landscape might evolve, it is probable that the fragmentation is very likely to be a permanent feature. Web travelers have become too accustomed to engage with a broad spectrum of assisted and self-service options and they will always want this kind of flexibility. As far as emerging web service channels are concerned, there are some interesting possibilities that have received attention in the media as "next frontiers." We briefly introduce them below.

- *Customer Service Subscription.* An airline could devise a customer care program providing unlimited access to its live CSRs in return for an annual fee. This would be analogous to Apple's current service program. This is offered to customers who wish to have access to live support for products beyond the standard warranty period: for a fee of $169, for instance, a customer who bought an iMac can purchase a three-year support plan.[77]
- *Social media travel ambassadors.* Microsoft, in order to save costs in its own customer support area, has established the Microsoft Community Contributor (MCC) program. In this program, customer self-help is promoted through customers who provide for input to online communities and assist other customers in resolving their issues. In return for devoting their time and energy, these contributors are rewarded. They could qualify to be "official" MCC, a title that becomes part of their profile when interacting with other customers. Perhaps some airlines will want to work with web travelers who want to be seen as experts and gurus in their field and are interested in assisting other customers in online communities. Those who are superstars and contribute high quality and quantity could be rewarded with a special title like "travel ambassador" and/or other non-monetary benefits.
- *Video Chat.* Amazon launched video chat in fall 2013 to provide live support for its Fire Tablet. Upon clicking on a "May Day" button on Amazon.com, a customer is connected to a tech advisor within 15 seconds. Video chat has several benefits including humanizing the internet experience and the fact that a customer does not have to "leave" the website. Furthermore, one-way views (the customer only sees the agent) are possible and video chat is also said to increase resolution rates during the first-call. This is because comprehension for people is faster when visual elements are added to a conversation.

  As part of their customer phone support, numerous airlines already offer Skype calling. It allows customers to contact a carrier for free on an internet-based device from anywhere in the world. Perhaps some airlines will decide to expand on this service and also include Skype's video chat.
- *Social media for business.* Corporate tools that allow social interaction between company employees could also be used for customer service purposes. Although corporate social media are generally only accessible on the company's intranet, airlines may want to look into ways of being allowed to engage with these platforms. Similar to what some airlines already do today for the general public, the idea would be to have access to corporate traveler generated content regarding customer service issues.

  Furthermore, imaginable are airline Twitter accounts, for example, that could be set up for individual corporate clients. Other areas where social media for business could come into play are trip life cycle services. These would be uniquely tailored around specific corporate clients who receive assistance through pro-active social media postings when something goes wrong. Additionally feasible is the deployment of rating platforms where airlines would make themselves open to user-generated reviews by corporate web travelers who would access the platforms through trusted passwords.

- *Multimodal service channel.* This involves the combined use of two or more service channels at the same time. In our discussion on the Click-to-Call service option, we have already mentioned the emergence of video chat. Other hybrids could surface and make inroads in customer service for web travelers. For example, it is feasible that a multimodal channel involving a CSR who walks a web traveler through a dynamically generated FAQ section on a mobile device could be established. Considering the multitude of service options, a convergence among some of them should not come as a surprise.
- *Mediated customer service.* With mediated customer service, web travelers involve a third party service provider that resolves their issue, mostly post flight complaints, for them. The idea of such as service is to spare a web traveler the pain and time to resolve the complaints on their own and outsource it for settlement to a specialist. An example of this type of service is offered by Los Angeles-based company "Service". On its website (www.getservice.com), the company currently handles more than 100 requests a day for the US and UK with the lion's share being airline related complaints (delayed/canceled flights, lost bags). "Service" intends to charge either customers or the companies a fee. In the latter case, the argument is that they save a call to the call center and avoid tying up expensive resources while preventing poor brand impressions from Twitter rants and 1-star ratings on TripAdvisor.[78]

## 5.8 WEB CUSTOMER SERVICE: WHO IS ORGANIZATIONALLY RESPONSIBLE FOR MANAGING IT?

Organizationally, an airline's web customer service is generally concerned with the three areas of customer contact operations, web product development, and web product support (Figure 5.28). This is managed through internal resources, external third parties or a mix hereof.

### 5.8.1 Inhouse web customer service

Many airlines handle web traveler queries related to general travel issues and specific passenger name records (PNRs) through their call centers and CTOs/ATOs. This is because the handling of these current issues is the same for the non-web traveler. Incoming web travelers' phone calls are either distributed among the general call center CSR population or directed to a dedicated web support desk that is part of the call center. At smaller airlines, it is not unusual to see that call centers handle email queries as well. This is done either via multi-tasking CSRs during phone call downtimes or dedicated back office staff.

Larger airlines often operate a customer relations department assigned to manage email along with traditional mail. Recognizing that web travelers can also face technical issues such as website usability problems, some airlines have decided to set up a

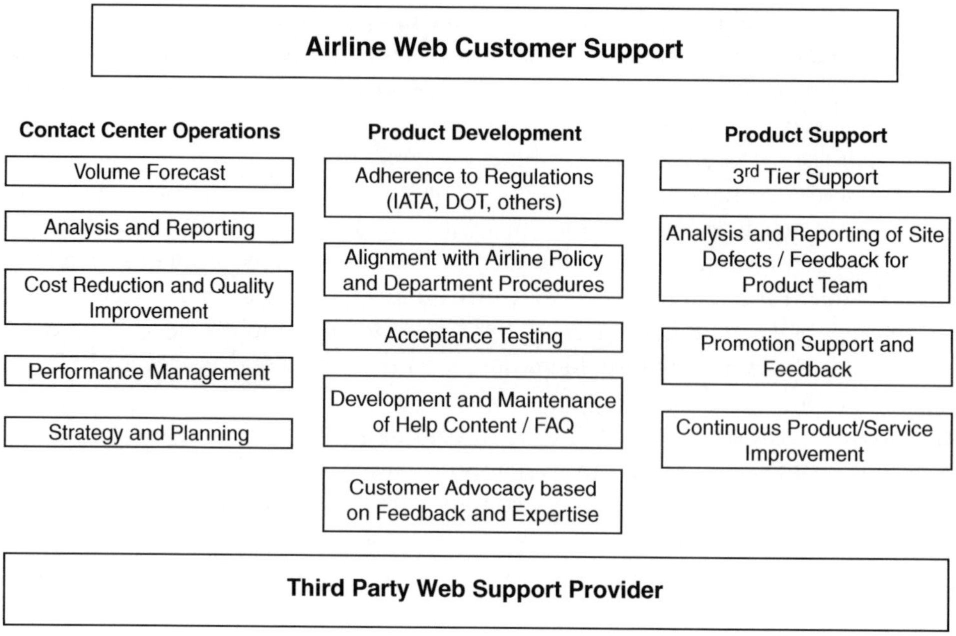

```
┌──────────────────────────────────────────────────────────────────┐
│                   Airline Web Customer Support                      │
└──────────────────────────────────────────────────────────────────┘
```

**Contact Center Operations**          **Product Development**          **Product Support**

| Volume Forecast |

| Analysis and Reporting |

| Cost Reduction and Quality Improvement |

| Performance Management |

| Strategy and Planning |

| Adherence to Regulations (IATA, DOT, others) |

| Alignment with Airline Policy and Department Procedures |

| Acceptance Testing |

| Development and Maintenance of Help Content / FAQ |

| Customer Advocacy based on Feedback and Expertise |

| 3rd Tier Support |

| Analysis and Reporting of Site Defects / Feedback for Product Team |

| Promotion Support and Feedback |

| Continuous Product/Service Improvement |

```
┌──────────────────────────────────────────────────────────────────┐
│                  Third Party Web Support Provider                   │
└──────────────────────────────────────────────────────────────────┘
```

**Figure 5.28** *Organizing airline web customer service support*

dedicated support desk. It offers web travelers unique contact information such as a special phone number or dedicated Twitter account and is staffed with CSRs versed in resolving these types of issues. In cases where a carrier manages web customer service through a dedicated department, rather than relying on the general set-up for assisted customer service, it might have its own support staff. At one point in its early e-commerce days, United Airlines used such a set-up. It had a group of six CSRs led by a senior manager that operated the web customer service for phone and email queries in conjunction with a third party. Other forms of assisted web customer service such as chat, co-browsing, and click-to-call are also often managed via an airline's call center. This is done either through multi-tasking or single-tasking CSRs.

The nature of self-service channels such as FAQs, search, and product demos precludes any interaction between a CSR and a web traveler. Therefore, an airline's call center (or other service department with direct customer contact) is out of the picture in terms of organizational responsibility. Assuming that an airline operates a website with self-service options in the first place (there are still plenty of carriers with a very limited presence in this area), they are usually managed by a department with responsibility for e-commerce. This is because such a department is responsible for the development and management of the website including self-service features.

The organizational responsibility of social media is often with an airline's PR/ Marketing Department. This has historical reasons as social media have started out with a heavy PR and marketing focus. Only in more recent years have airlines embraced the service aspect of social media as well. The question here is: How suitable is PR/Marketing to manage social media web customer service? The answer often is "not very" since this is not their core competency. A few progressive carriers have recognized this and begun to establish dedicated CSR teams in their customer relations departments that do nothing else except managing social customer issues that come to the airline via blogs and social networks. We have already mentioned KLM and its 130+ strong social customer care team. Others have adopted some form of interim measure and have passed social customer care issues from PR/Marketing on to departments traditionally involved in customer service while others have yet to decide how to accommodate web customer service via social media.

Besides the organizational dispersion of web customer service, there is also a geographic aspect that should be mentioned. Imagine an airline that operates international flights and has local offices in selected locations. These offices also fulfill web customer service functions and they are often the first point of live CSR contact for web travelers who use phone or email. Typically, local CSRs are (or should be) trained to manage standard web queries and provide for assistance on the spot. If the resolution of the web traveler issue needs to be forwarded to a subject matter expert for their input or to receive special approval from a higher-up manager at the head office, a "hot" communication link between the local office and head office should be available to address the pending issue swiftly.

Some airlines, especially in Europe and North America, have moved part of their domestic call centers to other countries or opened additional call centers in other countries to support their domestic and global customer service operations. Referred to as offshoring (not to be confused with outsourcing which we will address in the next section under "Third party web customer service"), airlines use this approach to take advantage of lower cost structures in foreign locations. Lufthansa, for example, operates call centers in eight countries including Turkey. These offshore offices must be also able to deal with web travelers' queries with the same efficiency and effectiveness as a carrier's domestic call center operation.

Finally, it is important to raise the issue of the growing mobility of today's workforce as a result of the explosion of mobile devices and mobile applications. It is quite possible that airline customer assistance itself will go mobile and leaves the four physical walls of the contact center behind. Staff armed with mobile devices connected to cloud-based applications could be a reality soon. After all, we already have virtual call centers with some airline CSRs working from home.

The above discussion largely addresses the aspect of customer contact operations. However, web customer service also plays a crucial role in web product development and web product support.

For the former area, involvement in prototype testing before a product launch, assistance in the development of help content such as a website's FAQ section, and also the observance of relevant regulations by industry bodies like IATA, are some of the activities. For web product support, web customer service can also be heavily involved. For e-commerce leading airlines, it is not unusual to have in place a comprehensive tracking system for problems web travelers experience and happen to share with the airline. Ongoing malfunctions are reported to respective product owners and monitored for remedy. Web customer service is frequently a key liaison to third party web support providers and shares up-to-date information on service relevant issues. Also, keeping web customer service in the loop for promotions support and feedback is important. All too often, airlines' marketing and sales people unleash special promotions to the marketplace without pre-alerting customer service. The consequence: sudden spikes in customer contact volumes that the support staff might be ill prepared for. Equally bad is the scenario whereby web customer service is not even made aware of certain marketing campaigns and therefore cannot address customer queries that might arise. It is a good policy to include web customer service in the run-up and preparations of an airline promotion so that an optimal support is offered on the frontline.

### 5.8.2 Third party web customer service

In combination with their own resources, some airlines work with third parties to deliver web customer service. The key external players in this situation are business process outsourcing (BPO) partners, ancillary travel providers, and general sales agents. Let us discuss each of them in greater detail.

*Business process outsourcing partners*

As in the case with offshoring, outsourcing also involves the expatriation of business activities such as customer support operations to other countries outside the company home base. The big difference, however, is that outsourcing involves a third party company. European carriers actually started the BPO trend in the 1980s and India was one of the first countries to offer front and back office support at a significantly lower cost to Western firms including airlines. With ever-growing communications infrastructure bandwidth, reliability, and affordability due to the internet and improving telecommunications, other countries have joined India. It has become a common practice, especially for global airlines, to outsource some of their call center activities to certain countries such as Australia, Ireland, Mexico, Poland, the Philippines, and South Africa.[79] However, in recent years, due to poor service performance and new cost competitive labor agreements in home markets, several airlines have insourced part of their call center operations again and brought them back home. Examples include Delta Airlines and US Airways. These carriers closed their call center operations in 2011 in South Africa and the Philippines, respectively.[80]

Airlines are also often drawn to outsourcing because they have a need for increased operational flexibility. For example, working with an outside company that operates a large staff on a 24/7 basis and can handle multiple languages allows an airline to tap into this resource without having to increase its own customer service staff or build additional infrastructure. Outsourcing can also be a beneficial arrangement during times of sporadic, seasonal increases in customer contact volumes, and it can be useful when specialist skill sets such as technical support is not available inhouse. Despite the fact that some carriers repatriate a portion of their customer service, it is likely that outsourcing remains a popular option with many airlines, especially legacy carriers as part of their ongoing efforts to reduce costs.

*Ancillary travel providers*

Besides dealing with an airline's core product, web customer service can also play a role with ancillary travel products offered on a carrier's website. This is of particular importance when an airline has acquired a so-called white label website that sells hotel rooms, car rentals, and tour packages. Expedia has been operating its white label product called "WWTE" for years and any airline adopting this product under its own brand usually also subscribes to Expedia's web customer support as part of the deal. This means that when a web traveler navigates on a web page dealing with ancillary products and they happen to encounter a problem, reaching out for phone or email assistance actually means contacting the Expedia support staff. The web traveler does not know this since the Expedia customer service representatives do not identify themselves: They pick up the phone and respond to an email in the name of the airline.

If an airline offers customer support for ancillary travel through a third party web under the airline's name, it is crucial to ensure that the third party's customer support does not compromise the airline's image. For instance, let us assume that a web traveler is on an airline web site's tour package section (and the carrier uses Expedia's WWTE product) and happens to seek assistance by phone to obtain clarity on the airline's ticket rules. The Expedia CSR may not know the relevant details and therefore has to involve someone from the airline. For a web traveler, this situation could be quite confusing and annoying because from their perspective, they are dealing with the airline already. Ideally, there would be a three-way call, with the airline CSR or a "hot transfer" to an airline CSR who could then address the fare rule question. For an airline and its white label partner to manage this kind of seamlessness in customer handling requires close coordination of each party's back/front office web customer service operations. It is difficult to achieve this without dedicated web customer service resources and leadership on the airline side.

The handling of ancillary travel support is different when another company and its respective products or services are not white labeled but marketed under its own brand. For hotel and car bookings, for example, web travelers are presented with distinctively branded companies and separate contact information. However, since these ancillary traveler partners' information is featured on the airline's website, web travelers may still contact the airline with service issues related to these ancillary products. In this case, a carrier can clearly refer the web traveler back to the travel partner. Whatever the agreement is between the airline and its ancillary travel partners, it needs to be clear to all players what the policies and processes involved are to avoid creating problems for the web traveler. It is also here where a dedicated web customer service leader can play a role in coordinating support policies with the processes of ancillary travel partners.

*General sales agent*

A general sales agent (GSA) represents an airline in a country or region where the carrier does not operate a flight but still wishes to maintain a presence for marketing, sales, and customer service reasons. Airlines also use GSAs in locations where they fly to but do not want to operate their own offices and staff due to cost reasons. GSAs perform various customer service functions as part of their contractual agreement and there has been some dissent between them and airlines as to how to account for the handling of web travelers. Historically, in the country or region where it represents a carrier, GSAs have typically earned a sales commission on tickets sold through them (they might also receive compensation for phone calls and emails handled, depending on the contract with the airline).

Since the early days of airline e-commerce, airlines gradually expanded their website presence beyond their home market borders and introduced local websites to cater to local web travelers. This also occurred in GSA markets. Understandably, with airlines treating websites as part of their direct sales channel, they have been reluctant to reward web ticket sales that occur on their own website in a GSA-managed country/region. One type of arrangement often seen today is the exclusion of customer service for web travelers. In this case, GSAs refer the web traveler to a designated airline contact (often a phone number or email address) for further assistance. In those instances where a mutual understanding for web customer service is reached between the airline and the GSA, financial compensation is paid to the GSA albeit on a lower level.

## 5.9 ANALYTICS AND MEASUREMENT OF WEB CUSTOMER SERVICE

The airline industry over the years has perfected the measurement of voice communication and the collection/analysis of call center data. Examples of common metrics used include the number of phone calls received, the number of calls abandoned, the wait time before a customer speaks to a call center CSR, and the length of the call. These performance metrics focus on productivity and efficiency. They do not measure satisfaction of customers. This is largely a reflection of the airline industry's dominating view where call centers/customer relation departments are often seen as cost centers and not as areas for delivering a superior customer experience.

If the cost focus is so important, one question is whether airlines measure the cost of web-based service channels. A number of metrics that capture activities for self-service, chat, social media, and mobile exist and could be applied (Table 5.3).

They allow an airline to monitor and understand how these channels perform. However, it seems that companies do not look much beyond the phone channel when it comes to measuring customer service cost (Table 5.4). For example, for smart phone service applications and web-based self-service options, the share of companies *not* applying any measurement is 87% and 70%, respectively.

These figures are not airline industry specific. However, they provide some indication of an overall, rather concerning, situation that may apply to airlines to a degree. Information on the cost of service channels and the time spent to complete service transactions through them is crucial for a company. An airline with this information is better positioned to allocate web service resources properly and prioritize investments in web-based customer service channels.

**Table 5.3** *Activity-based metrics of web customer service channels*

| Data source | Typical activity data captured |
| --- | --- |
| Phone | Number of calls, quality of phone service measured in wait-time before speaking to a live agent/customer call abandon rate/length of phone conversation, content of phone conversation. |
| Email communication | Number of emails, subject, response time, number of email follow-ups. |
| FAQ | Transaction logs (number of hits, topics searched, time spent, site clickstream). |
| Site map | Transaction logs (number of hits, pages/documents viewed, site clickstream). |
| Chat | Transaction logs (topics discussed, page location for chat intervention, length of chat, issue closure). |
| Search | Transaction logs (number of hits, keywords/sentences entered, clickstream and linking to other site areas). |
| Social media | Number of followers/fans/ tweets (or visitors in case of corporate blog), topics discussed, number of blog postings, number of positive/negative reviews, opinion leaders/ critical customers and their attitude vs company. |
| Product demo | Transaction logs (number of hits, clickstream). |
| Avatar | Topics queried, page intervention, length of conversation, clickstream. |

**Table 5.4** *Measuring cost and time on non-phone service transactions*

| Service option | Share of companies not measuring cost and time |
| --- | --- |
| Smart Phone Applications | 87% |
| Social Media | 76% |
| SMS | 73% |
| Website Self-Service | 70% |
| IVR | 70% |
| Chat | 69% |
| Email | 58% |

*Source:* Dimension Data (2014)[81]

Another question an airline should address relates to the type of web customer service measurement. Should an airline purely focus on metrics that measure activities like the number of times a web service channel is used by customers? Or should metrics be also considered that measure outcomes? The overall trend in customer service points to a change in perspective. For many companies, non-operational targets such as customer satisfaction have become a top priority in recent years. At the same time, other standard activity metrics including "first call resolution" and "agent call handling capacity" play lesser important roles.[82] It is a good policy for an airline to adopt outcome-oriented measurements in web customer service. Excelling in the area of customer satisfaction, for example, enables a carrier to differentiate itself better from competitors.

For an airline that wants to adopt customer satisfaction goals, a number of crucial steps need to be taken. Above all, a carrier needs to start collecting customer feedback at all points of interaction with a web traveler. This will have to be the new norm rather than the exception. Only with this approach can a carrier gain better insights on how satisfied its customers are. Pro-active invitations to solicit input are important. These could include participation in a phone survey to rate the performance of a call center agent. Also included could be website feedback tools to assess customer experience with web content and functionality. In the area of social media, *listening* to what web travelers have to say about the airline, detecting positive and negative attitudes, and identifying opinion leaders are some examples of new metrics that would need to be established.

It will undoubtedly be challenging to adopt a new measurement perspective and mix the standard operational metrics with the new "soft" outcome-based metrics. However, this balance is essential if an airline wants to move to a more holistic view and comprehend the full and real performance of its web customer service.

## 5.10 THE TIERED MULTI-CHANNEL APPROACH

A broad offering of service channels with a variety of CSR-assisted services and self-services is crucial. It allows an airline to satisfy web travelers' demand for more choices and it helps reduce customer service costs. When managing a portfolio with numerous service channels, an airline should not offer them indiscriminately to web travelers. For example, some carriers feature high-cost service options like phone support on a website homepage and even use trigger words ("Feel free to call") that encourage customers to call. At the same time, customer self-service features are not fully developed or not even available.

E-Commerce-leading carriers take a conscious approach on how to present their service options to users. They apply a "tiered" web customer service system that prioritizes self-service over assisted customer service (Figure 5.29). According to this concept, a web traveler requiring assistance is encouraged to use an airline's self-service options first. These include a website search function, a FAQ section, or others and they are part of the first tier. If any of these options cannot deliver a resolution because the issue is too difficult or complex, the next step is to offer assisted service options. In this second tier, we find low-cost options such as email, chat, and social media to address any web customer service issues. Only if these do not work either, should a transition to live one-to-one customer support via phone or in person be offered. This is the third tier.

We do not want to create the impression that an airline can force a web traveler to follow this path. It is possible that some people may not be comfortable or familiar with certain self-service options and therefore prefer assistance from a CSR as their first and only option. Nevertheless, carriers that are successful in applying the tiered system use a combination of tactics that "sell" self-service to web travelers. Generally, this involves promotional announcements via CSRs and marketing communications as well as offering incentives such as bonus miles or fee savings. Importantly, clever

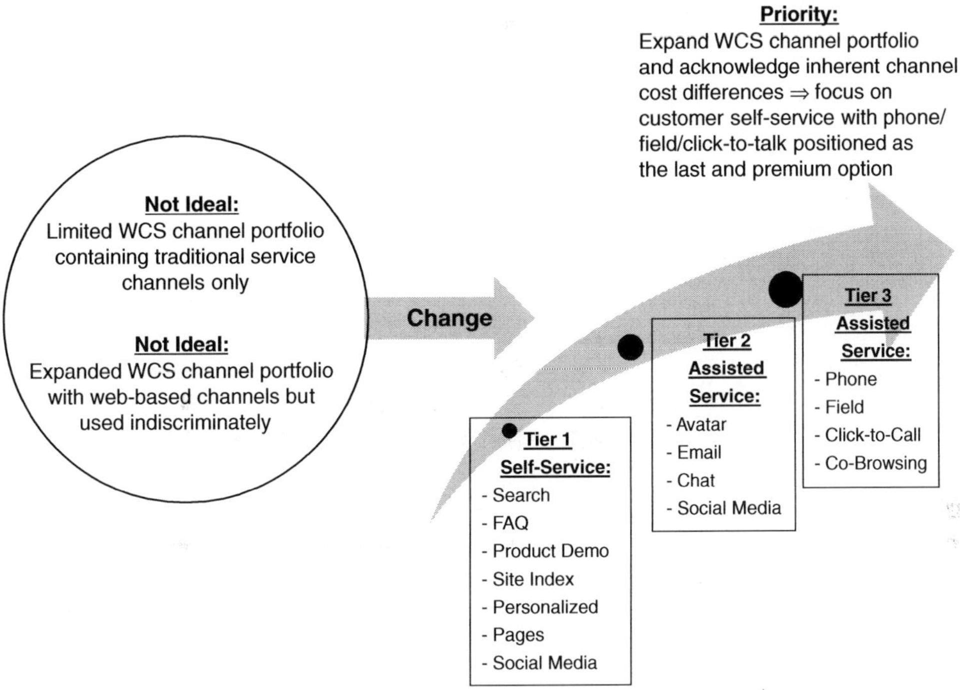

**Priority:**
Expand WCS channel portfolio
and acknowledge inherent channel
cost differences ⇒ focus on
customer self-service with phone/
field/click-to-talk positioned as
the last and premium option

**Not Ideal:**
Limited WCS channel portfolio
containing traditional service
channels only

**Change**

**Not Ideal:**
Expanded WCS channel portfolio
with web-based channels but
used indiscriminately

● **Tier 1**
**Self-Service:**
- Search
- FAQ
- Product Demo
- Site Index
- Personalized
- Pages
- Social Media

**Tier 2**
**Assisted**
**Service:**
- Avatar
- Email
- Chat
- Social Media

● **Tier 3**
**Assisted**
**Service:**
- Phone
- Field
- Click-to-Call
- Co-Browsing

*Figure 5.29* The "tiered" approach to web customer service

*Table 5.5* Common airline tactics to "sell" self-service

| Tactic for increased adoption of self-service tools | Commentary |
|---|---|
| Promotion of self-service via CSRs | ■ Automated call center, CTO, ATO greetings, and IVR system could feature messages about what self-service functions are available on the website<br>■ Conversational scripts between call center CSR and web travelers could include tips for web travelers how to do certain self-services<br>■ Emails and letters sent to web travelers could include specific tag lines and/or specific URLs highlighting self-service<br>■ Inflight announcements introducing the website and self-service options<br>■ Social media interactions should include reference to a specific URL for further self-service |
| Offering incentives for self-service use | ■ Provide bonus miles and fee reductions/waivers to web travelers who self-service (e.g. for self-handled ticket refunds, the ticket exchange/cancellation would be lower or eliminated)<br>■ Surcharge when using CSR assistance (telephone fee, ticket purchase fee) |
| Website design pronouncing self-service | ■ When web travelers uses the "Support," "Contact," or "Help" link, they should land on a customer service page that prominently displays self-service tools and not just shows a phone/fax number and email address<br>■ Consistent display of direct link to self-service tools on product description pages and purchase pages where web travelers frequently encounter issues |

**Figure 5.30** *Designed for self-service: Help pages of British Airways*

*Source:* ba.com (2014)[83] with kind permission of British Airways

website design measures to create certain navigational paths and thereby steer web travelers to particular self-help sections on a website are an integral part of this.

Table 5.5 shares more details for each of these tactics often seen in the market-place. It is not an accident that some websites, especially those of LCCs, usually do not feature customer service phone numbers. If available at all, they are buried deep in a website and not easy to find. This is because these airlines strongly push customer self-service ahead of customer-assisted options.

Figure 5.30 shows the help/contact web pages of ba.com. They are designed to support the tiered approach the carrier applies to web customer service.

## 5.11 THE IMPORTANCE OF SEAMLESS WEB CUSTOMER SERVICE

Web travelers frequently switch between different service channels when seeking assistance. This is not necessarily their choice because many attempt to resolve their issue with self-service first. However, when this fails to produce a solution, web travelers generally transition to assisted customer service.

Unfortunately, switching from one service channel to another is often not a smooth process. The usual experience is that a web traveler who attempts to resolve an issue in one channel but has to use another instead cannot transfer information and context. Web travelers therefore have to "share the same story" multiple times because the different service channels are not connected with each other. Figure 5.31 shows how fractured the transition from one channel to another can be. By the time a web traveler speaks to a live CSR, the agent has no idea about the web

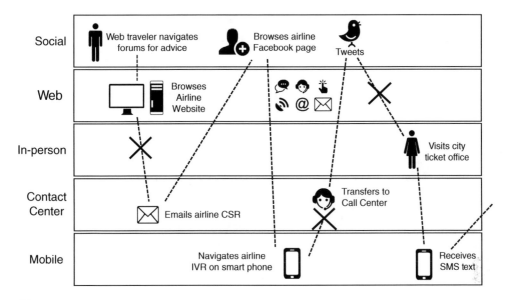

**Figure 5.31** *Transitions between customer service channels are often fractured*

traveler's prior attempts to address an issue via self-help or other assisted service options. This dis-connection does not only translate into a bad experience for the web traveler but also means an inefficient and unproductive use of corporate resources.

If online customers have one item on their wish list in terms of multi–channel interaction, it is that they do not want to be asked twice and re-share, re-enter, or re-submit information already provided. Some 44% of customers suggest that multi–channel conversations can be best improved by providing better CSR service. Specifically, the moment a conversation between the CSR and the customer is initiated, the agent should have been already provided with the customer's information through different service channels.[84] In reality, however, only a few companies are prepared to handle multi–channel conversations. Based on a 16-country cross-industry survey by Alcatel/Genesys, the share is estimated to be less than 10%.[85]

Moreover, the appetite for investments in multi–channel integration is not very strong. This is because implementing a framework for an integrated multi–channel web customer service system is a challenge. It requires the individual service channels to be viewed as part of a service channel portfolio and apply a coherent, all–encompassing perspective when managing it. Leading e-commerce airlines understand this. For them, the quality of web customer service performance is not tied to individual service channels but to a service channel portfolio as a whole. As web travelers move between various service channels offered by an airline, they expect an integrated experience across various touch points. This is because, from their perspective, they are interacting with the same one company.

For a web traveler to experience a seamless transition between different service channels, an airline needs to pay attention to several key aspects:

- The language, tone of voice, and information presented must be consistent no matter what service option is selected by the web traveler.
- Web travelers should be able to address and resolve their issues with any service option.
- There must be a clear and logical display of service options allowing for an intuitive transition path between the different alternatives.
- Iterations on the same topic across multiple service options are managed as a single thread.
- Self-service-to-live support transitions involves the passing of relevant information generated during self-service to a CSR.

An example of a seamless transition happened recently to the author on the ba.com website. It involved a transition from an initial assisted service to self-service. Specifically, the intention was to send an email to British Airway with a query about the carrier's policy for taking pets aboard an aircraft. Upon submitting the email, a popup window appeared and stated that the email had not been sent off yet. It went on to say that the question could be possibly answered by the website's FAQ section displayed in the same popup window (Figure 5.32).

Upon checking the FAQ section, the author could indeed find the appropriate answer. This made an email submission redundant and therefore saved the

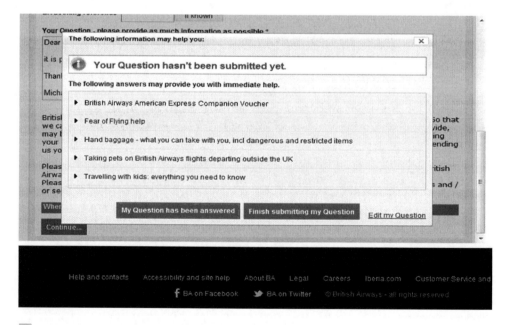

*Figure 5.32* British Airways' email handling on ba.com

*Source:* ba.com (2014)[86] with kind permission of British Airways

involvement of a CSR. BA managed this transition seamlessly by capturing key words from the author's written email content and generated an intelligent transition to a self-service channel. The customer experience was positive and British Airways did not have to involve a live CSR to handle the question.

There are several key challenges in delivering an integrated multi-channel web customer service approach. The next section sheds light on these and how an airline could tackle them.

## 5.12 DEVELOPING INTEGRATED MULTI-CHANNEL CAPABILITY

### 5.12.1 Challenge 1: Organizational set-up for multi-channel web customer service

The roadblock for many airlines in delivering an integrated experience to their customers is their organizational set-up. Usually, it is not configured to effectively handle the new, fragmented world of customer service where web travelers often engage multiple channels to resolve an issue. Departments frequently operate in disconnected silos and manage their respective service channels only.

For example, the head of an airline e-commerce department is usually responsible for managing self-assisted options such as FAQ and site search. However, the responsibility for web customer service offered via other channels lies elsewhere. An airline's call center typically deals with web travelers through the traditional phone channel and possibly email. PR/Marketing has become involved in customer service because of their responsibility to handle social media—unless an airline decides to use a separate group to handle this area.

This situation becomes even more complex (and messy) when taking into consideration that some airlines:

- operate an FFP department with its own set of dedicated service channels
- have outsourced/offshored customer service
- use GSAs for customer service in some countries
- rely on local staff in international locations to manage customer service outside the carrier's home market.

In essence, the touchpoints used by web travelers for customer service are not owned by a single organizational entity. The result of all of this organizational and also geographical dispersion of customer service? Web travelers are bounced between queues and systems and often receive conflicting information. This requires them to make repeat contacts and to provide the same information many times over. Airlines that lack integrated departments and systems cannot respond to web travelers in a timely, accurate manner. This in turn causes customer frustration and alienation.

*A possible solution*

In order to counter the disparate management of web customer service and offer consistency in content and experience to web travelers, an airline needs to adopt more effective organizational structures and processes. Above all, an airline should recognize that managing an ever-growing portfolio of customer service channels translates into a larger scope of roles and responsibilities. These include:

- The adoption of new skills and technology.
- The re-allocation of existing resources and/or the acquisition of additional resources including the entering of new partnerships with outside suppliers.
- The re-alignment of customer service processes (internally for the interaction with other departments and externally with web travelers).
- The development of goals and performance metrics.

Failure to keep pace with this development means losing an important part of the airline's competitiveness in the marketplace.

There are three organizational alternatives that an airline may consider for supporting integrated multi-channel customer service (Figure 5.33). In Alternative 1, there is some degree of coordination among the different corporate stakeholders responsible for customer service. This minimum set-up does not eliminate a silo mentality. However, the customer service delivery is at least more consistent across different customer touch points.

With Alternative 2, there is an overarching, company-wide, single-view perspective on customer service. One company executive with staff is in charge of web customer service

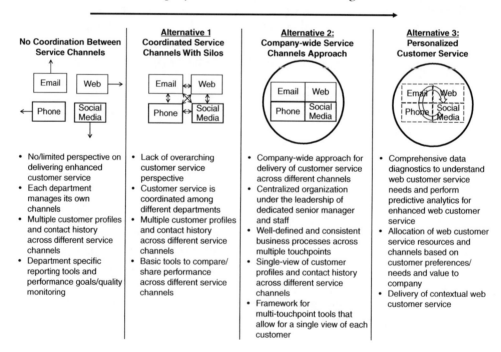

**Figure 5.33** *The evolution to an optimal multi-channel organization*

Source: Based on Capgemini (2012)[87]

that is managed as a portfolio across different service channels. The executive reports to a senior officer in the airline and has hands-on authority. This includes the power to:

- change rules and processes related to web traveler facing interactions
- recruit and dismiss web customer service staff
- be instrumentally involved in the selection, implementation, and maintenance of new customer service channels
- develop web customer service goals and policies
- develop a set of performance metrics in order to monitor the customer service performance
- plan and organize adequate customer support for special website campaigns and new web product launches, often with the assistance of other departments like marketing/PR, sales, FFP, and IT
- keep other internal stakeholders up to date about ongoing and emerging customer service issues.

This second alternative can evolve further. In Alternative 3, the airline not only optimizes the operations for web customer service across different service channels but also delivers a personalized and contextualized web customer service. This is based on the web traveler needs and preferences and their value to the carrier. This alternative only works if two critical conditions are met. First, the airline must use technology that bundles information from multiple sources and generates a 360-degree insight into web travelers. This information must be accessible to CSRs in the company. Second, there must be collaboration among the internal and external parties involved in web customer service. Collaboration specifically means to connect:

- a web traveler with another web traveler
- a web traveler with a CSR
- a CSR with a CSR
- a CSR with a back office subject matter expert.

The interaction among all parties needs to be encouraged and their interaction needs to be captured. By breaking down traditional walls and relaxing structures that typically divide these parties, a new, knowledge-sharing environment is established. It allows an airline to build up more know-how, achieve faster closure on customer service issues and create more satisfied web travelers.

### 5.12.2 Challenge 2: Optimizing relationship processes between airline and web traveler

Optimizing the interaction processes between the airline and web travelers is another important step toward building a successful multi-channel customer service operation. An airline should focus on a few key areas to achieve this. These include a

Voice-of-the Customer program, the quality and management of the CSR work-force, and the re-engineering of business processes. Each area is addressed in more detail below.

### Voice-of-the-Customer program (VOC)

It is important for an airline to understand a web traveler's service channel prefer-ences and service needs. In order to achieve this, leading e-commerce airlines deploy so-called voice-of-the-customer (VoC) programs. Voice of the customer is consid-ered as the wants and needs of a customer expressed in their language. By listening and using what a web traveler is saying, an airline can address specific shortcomings. It can also improve on its web customer service and deliver a better experience.

In the past, when airlines wanted to gather feedback from a larger number of travelers, they typically conducted customer surveys. This method was sporadic in nature, time consuming, not very targeted, and often generated a low response rate (around 10% based on some estimates).[88] A VoC program, however, works more rapidly and engages multiple touch points. Moreover, it is more relevant to the target audience and it yields a higher customer response rate. Alitalia, for example, reported a 65% response rate when it adopted its VoC platform solution from a technology supplier.[89] The key is to view a VoC program at an airline not merely as an initiative to conduct sporadic surveys but to collect feedback on a consistent basis from all channels. Doing so accounts for a web traveler's entire spectrum of interactions with an airline. This in turn enables an airline to establish a wider insight of what web travelers think, feel, and opine.

There should be no illusions about the challenges in managing a VoC program. The acquisition of a VoC technology platform is only the first step. When consider-ing an implementation, it is beneficial to remember a few key aspects. One is that listening to customers is hard work. Another one is that a carrier might already be doing it to some extent without knowing it. This means that opportunities are missed to deliver a better web customer service.

Stakeholders at an airline who do the "listening" are not the only frontline CSRs. They also involve senior managers, relationship champions, and analysts. Feedback received from web travelers comes from many different venues. These range from panel discussions and focus groups to special feedback pages and popups presented on an airline website. Email follow-ups sent to web travelers after a trip, postings by web travelers on relevant blogs, or web travelers' ratings on third party websites are other possibilities for capturing marketplace feedback. It is common to categorize feedback based on whether or not it is solicited (is the web traveler invited to share their input or do they volunteer information?) and structured (is the feedback pro-vided in a free-flow format or does it follow a pre-described format?) (Figure 5.34).

Collecting feedback across multiple channels is one step for an effective VoC. Additionally, an airline needs to be concerned about centralizing/organizing feedback data in a single repository and analyzing the data before embarking on corrective action. Closing the loop is a crucial step of a successful VoC program.

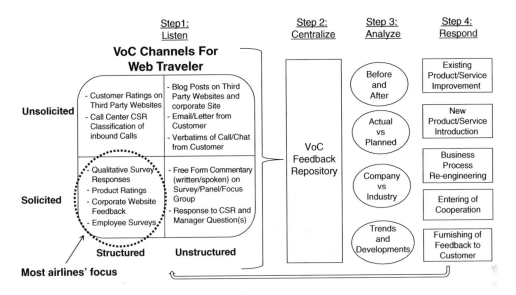

**Figure 5.34** *Voice of Customer (VoC) program: Conceptual overview*

*Source:* Based on Peaslee (2015)[90]

What makes a VoC program so powerful is the fact that it is a unifying mechanism for web customer service issues coming to the airline through multiple service channels. This in turns allows an airline to have a more holistic view of web traveler feedback and be able to respond to web travelers more consistently. Unifying the behind-the-scenes operations with a VoC program helps an airline deliver a more unified experience to web travelers on the frontline. JetBlue recognized the importance of a VoC already several years ago. It was awarded the prestigious Voice of the Customer Award by Forrester Research in 2011 for excelling, analyzing, and acting on customer feedback.

JetBlue's Director for Customer Experience viewed the company's VOC program as a measure to bring "humanity back to travel through listening to customers and acting upon their feedback."[91]

### Quality and management of CSR workforce

Boasting a competent and well-trained workforce that is motivated and collaborative has a direct impact on web customer service performance. About 63% of customers state that they would become disloyal because of a bad experience with contact center agents.[92]

### CSR RECRUITMENT AND RETENTION

An airline concerned with its competitiveness in the area of web customer service pays attention to the "people factor." A main source of concern is the high CSR attrition rate. For inbound call centers, this averages annually 30% and more.[93] This means that the lifespan of a CSR is about one year. This is not an indication of a stable workforce. Top reasons why CSRs quit and look for other opportunities include not being the right fit for the job, lack of fair pay and benefits, and problems with the teamleader/supervisor.[94]

In addition, there are new generations filling the work ranks. Millennials and soon Generation Z have different perceptions and expectations when compared with older peers. They are technically savvy, more self-sufficient, and look for immediate feedback from supervisors on their performance. They also expect to be engaged and have a "work to learn" philosophy. This is different from previous generations' "work to live" perspective.[95]

In order to counter a high turnover among customer-facing employees—attrition rates of 20% and less are considered desirable[96]—an airline may use some measures. For hiring and training, there must be clarity and documentation on skills, competencies, and capabilities that are required to deliver superior web customer service via the various service channels. With this approach, the chances of a mismatch between a recruit's ideas and an airline's expectations are kept small.

However, this is often easier said than done, especially when it comes to the new customer service channels. For example, what kind of communication skills are required for an airline CSR to handle chat or social media? Airlines may take some clues in this area from KLM, one of the leading airlines in social customer care. The company's staff employed in this area receives five weeks of training. Besides commercial awareness, particular attention is paid to engaging with the right tone of voice in order to deliver an on-KLM brand image.

Attractive compensation, benefits, and opportunities to acquire new skills and move up in the company are crucial as well. Furthermore, working off-site from home appears to be appealing to many CSRs. Studies have shown that performance levels can improve and a growing number of airlines including Alaska Airlines and JetBlue offer this arrangement to their call center CSRs.[97]

## CSR EMPOWERMENT

Typically, CSRs are quite limited in their access to cross-channel customer information and can see only a subset of the total customer picture. Separating the web customer service channels from each other means that a CSR does not have a full 360 degree view of the web travelers' relationship and interactions. Furthermore, less empowerment adversely impacts CSRs' task satisfaction.[98]

Linking stand-alone communication channels enable CSRs to be newly empowered. They are able to conduct a more focused conversation and facilitate a better channel switch because of improved information access. It is crucial to establish specific performance goals and metrics for CSRs. This should be combined with a program to do quality monitoring of web customer service performance and to provide for rewards that reflect the achievement of customer service objectives.

CSR TASK MANAGEMENT

Improving web customer service from an organizational structure and process point of view must also touch on the issue of single-channel/single-tasking versus multi-channel/multi-tasking. Many airline's web customer service CSRs handle multiple service channels during a typical workday, notably phone and email. Occasionally chat is also in the mix as a third channel.

Is multi-tasking, so often praised as the ultimate sign of corporate efficiency, the way to go for web customer service? Maybe not. The fact is that not all CSRs at the same time have great phone skills, can type fast, express themselves eloquently, and manage chat conversations well. Most are well versed in one channel and it may be therefore better to deploy single channel CSRs for work and cost efficiency reasons.

KLM follows this approach. Their social customer care team with around 130 people solely handles customer service issues worldwide in the social media sphere. The company's service channels such as phone and email are handled by other groups. Another carrier that applies a policy of single channel/single tasking for social customer service is American Airlines. They employ a team of 15 people who exclusively focus on customer issues handled via Twitter.

"Super CSRs" that can do it all (and should receive higher pay) are rare today because of the ever more fragmented landscape of web customer service channels. If they exist, an airline should deploy them for handling overflow situations or where service issues for specific premium corporate customers need attention.

There is one more issue to raise in connection with multi-tasking. If many of a carrier's CSRs are involved in multi-tasking, it is advisable to examine how many of these tasks could actually be handled by web travelers themselves. If some of these tasks are simple enough for self-service, an airline could free up CSR resources. This point is of particular importance to smaller carriers. They do not have large staff and therefore need to be very mindful where and how employees in customer service are utilized. In general, interaction with a live CSR should be reserved for more complex service situations and for sales tasks including up- and cross-sell scenarios that often require suggestive and persuasive language.

*Re-engineering the business process*

One of the principal reasons why multi-channel customer service management is challenging is because of the various company stakeholders involved in web customer service. They apply their respective rules for resolving customer issues. This is an outgrowth of the organizational dispersion of web customer service responsibility and the result of different technology applications used. In order to change this situation, an airline needs to consider a few action items.

First, it needs to eliminate conflicting, department/service channel-specific knowledge bases that are the sources for different answers to the same question.

There should be only a *single knowledge base* which is constantly fed and updated for accuracy and relevancy. Inputs for this knowledge base come from internal sources such as live CSRs, back office representatives that are subject matter experts as well as outsiders. These include vendors and participants in social media including forums and blogs. This approach highlights the importance of a collaborative approach. Importantly, performance management is extended from the frontline to the back office and even to outside the office. By using a single knowledge base, an airline can give web travelers highly consistent customer service information.

Second, all interactions between a web traveler and an airline need to be captured and reported, no matter what service channel is used. This enables an airline to gain a granular view and know-how about what is happening in each of the individual service channels. Additionally, it allows an airline to establish customer service performance goals, conduct quality monitoring, and execute a variety of relevant analyses. These cover internal trends and developments and comparisons against industry standards/best practices.

It cannot be emphasized enough that better reporting and analytics are crucial in gauging the overall performance in web customer service and optimizing each interaction's process flow. As we have stated before, a careful balance between activity-based and outcome-based metrics is important. This means further that an airline can develop a good understanding of the cost of its web customer service and also determine the success (or failure) of a web traveler's journey when engaging with web customer services.

Third, in order to generate a single view of the web traveler, there must be a platform that brings together the various interactions of a web traveler. If a transition to a live CSR is necessary, they know the full history of the web traveler. This information makes the interaction between the web traveler and CSR more effective because it is shorter, more personalized and contextualized (Figure 5.35).

### 5.12.3 Challenge 3: Multi-channel technology and infrastructure

Existing legacy applications and systems at airlines are riddled with the difficulty of tracking the diversity of a web traveler's interactions related to customer service. Their activities are not consistently captured across self-service and assisted channels because of the presence of single-channel legacy applications. Changing this technology in order to introduce a more flexible multi-channel approach is an evolutionary process. The new technology and infrastructure should accomplish the following:

- Standardize the customer service interactions across all the different channels.
- Empower the CSRs with contextual customer, product, and service information.
- Allow CSRs to easily collaborate with other CSRs and subject matter experts inside and outside the company to quickly resolve web traveler queries.
- Provide managers with the right analytics and reporting tools to track outcomes that have a business impact.[99]

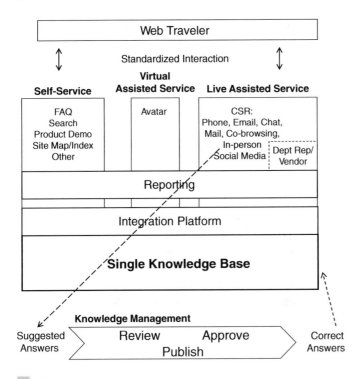

**Figure 5.35** *Putting it all together…*

At the core of the multi–channel technology set-up is a knowledge base that we have mentioned earlier. It houses all relevant information about the relationship with web travelers. An application platform governs the in- and outflow of data and provides for a unified interface to access the knowledge base. Different channel applications including phone, email, chat, self-service, avatars, and others reside on the outside of the system with a layer of enabling technologies such as switches, automatic call distributors (ACDs), and other network resources connecting them to the platform (Figure 5.36).

The technology and infrastructure that unifies multiple customer service channels and allows for an inter-channel management is neither cheap nor easy. A number of companies have expressed their concern over high cost and complexity of implementation.[100] The integration perhaps could be painful in the short term with few tangible "first" or "second" year benefits. Fortunately, single vendor solutions for different service channels are becoming more common as a result of merger/acquisitions and partnerships in the vendor landscape. Additionally, a growing number of customer service technology providers have matured in recent years and folded technology for new channels such as social media and mobile into their offerings portfolio. Airlines that today deal with a multitude of vendors (one for avatar technology, another one for chat services, and so on) benefit from this development. Disparate and often eclectic mixes of custom-built and standard off-the-shelf technologies can now be replaced by an integrated suite with standard products

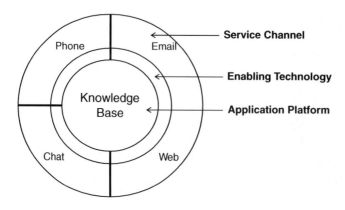

**Figure 5.36** *The multi-level technology in multi-channel customer service*

*Source:* Jupiter (1999)[101]

consolidated with fewer vendors. In the future, many integration pain points will be relieved and less resources will be needed to handle an implementation.

Technology provider Kana is a company that announced in spring 2013 the launch of one of the first multi-channel customer service suites. Called "Kana Enterprise," this single platform uses "both agent-based and customer self-service scenarios mixed with technology and capabilities that allow seamless customer service across the contact center, web, mobile, and social spheres."[102] One European airline, although not identified in the press release at the time, was said to be one of the early adopters.[103] Another technology provider offering multi-channel service solutions is Genesys. Its Customer Engagement Platform uses a so-called "Genesys Conversation Manager" to connect the frontline with the back office, manage in-/outbound, voice/non-voice communication, and self-/assisted service. They are unified to enable a continuous and seamless interaction across multiple channels.

Investing in new customer service technology and solidifying the technology solutions and related vendor base is one thing, the standardization of the underlying infrastructure is another. We need to remember that airlines, since the inception of the industry's first call centers in the 1970s, have been mostly concerned with managing voice transmission. This is not a surprise considering that the phone has been (and still is) a highly popular channel for live CSR support.

The protocol used for sending voice calls over traditional copper wires is called TDM (Time Division Multiplexing). The technology deployed to queue and route incoming phone calls is referred to as ACD (Automated Call Distributor). This analog TDM/ACD standard had been used throughout the 1990s until an internet protocol (IP)–based approach started to emerge. Among other things, it allows airlines to use VoIP (Voice over the internet protocol). VoIP or broadband phone service is a digital voice application. A web traveler and airline CSR can use it to conduct a computer-to-computer or computer-to-phone conversation over an existing internet connection. Customers appreciate VoIP because of the absence of any long distance phone charges, the availability of low-cost unlimited calling plans, and the abundance of enhanced and useful telephony features associated with VoIP technology. Companies value VoIP's lower costs when compared with traditional telecom operations, improved call quality, and increased employee productivity. Swiss International Air Lines introduced it in 2007 for its call center operation.[104]

The advent of new customer service channels in the form of email, chat, social media, and others has made clear that voice-only technology applications were no longer sufficient. It is estimated that only 25% of today's customer service communication is handled in voice-only form.[105] Therefore, an airline not looking for technology solutions to accommodate non-voice channels and manage them coherently is not able to compete effectively. Many carriers still operate the TDM/ACD standard or a hybrid version with some IP-based application. For them, it is crucial to address how and when to upgrade their current systems.

Enter SIP (Session Internet Protocol), a new protocol to control and direct communication including voice, data, and video that emerged in the 2010s. SIP treats all forms of communication as software and transmits it over the internet. Besides the ability to support multiple channels, SIP generates other compelling advantages over previous standards. They include infrastructure savings, increased staff efficiencies, faster upgrades, and last but not least, a better customer service experience.[106, 107] SIP has contributed greatly to minimize the complexity of dealing with multi-channel communication on one software platform. It is a good policy for an airline to explore how SIP can be leveraged for technology that supports web customer service.

Lastly, the discussion on multi-channel infrastructure and technology needs to touch on cloud services. Migrating to the cloud entails several benefits including cost reductions, increased scalability, and overall easier management of IT infrastructure. Forrester Research predicts that approximately 70% of companies either are using or are interested in a cloud service such as SaaS for managing business processes including CRM.[108]

## NOTES

1 Jupiter Research (2007) "Unified customer service exploring ROI and drivers of investment," research report.

2 Forrester Research (2011) "Customer experience online survey," North American Technographics, Q4 2011.

3 Genesys (2015) "How SIP DeLIVERS YOUR NEXT GENERATION SERVICE PLatform," www.genesyslab.com/news-and-events/webinars-index.aspx?ht= (accessed April 6, 2015).

4 Moxiesoft and Forrester Research (2013) "The secret sauce of customer service channel preference," www.youtube.com/watch?v=ZLjb4A25X0s (accessed May 32013).

5 Ibid.

6 Boies, J. (2013) "Expert advice on the future of customer service," http://blogs.salesforce.com/company/2013/06/future-of-customer-service.html (accessed April 6, 2015).

7 Clarkson, D. (2009) "It's time to give virtual agents another look," www.webspeaking.nl/images/ Forr_time_to_give_virtual_agents_another.pdf (accessed April 6, 2015).

8 Gartner (2012) "Gartner Says organizations that integrate communities into customer support can realize cost reductions of up to 50 percent," www.gartner.com/newsroom/id/1929014 (accessed April 6, 2015).

9 Ibid.

10 FutureTravelExperience.com (2015) "New technology, 'competition' and the '3Us' – aiming for the optimal customer experience," www.futuretravelexperience.com/2015/02/aiming-for-the-optimal-customer-experience/ (accessed April 6, 2015).

11 British Airways (2013) "British Airways," www.britishairways.com/travel/home/public/en_us (accessed September 23, 2013).

12 Swiss International Air Lines (2014) "Swissair," www.swissair.com/index_en.html (accessed January 23, 2014).

13 Japan Airlines (2014) "Japan Airlines," www.jal.com/ (accessed January 28, 2014).

14 JetBlue (2014) "JetBlue," www.jetblue.com/ (accessed January 28, 2014).

15 Wikipedia (2015) "Yahoo!" http://en.wikipedia.org/wiki/Yahoo! (accessed April 6, 2015).

16 Lufthansa (2014) "Your personal homepage," www.lufthansa.com/de/en/your-personal-homepage (accessed July 2, 2013).

17 Southwest Airlines (2014) "How to," www.southwest.com/ (accessed February 6, 2014).

18 Qantas (2015) "Online tutorials," www.qantas.com.au/travel/airlines/online-tutorials/global/en (accessed April 6, 2015).

19 Forrester Research (2008) "Best and worst of phone self-service design," www.forrester.com/Best +And+Worst+Of+Phone+SelfService+Design+2008/fulltext/-/E-res45238 (accessed as part of a subscription on April 4, 2013).

20 Jet Airways (2014) "Jet Airways," www.jetairways.com/ (accessed March 15, 2014).

21 Youtube (2015) "Youtube," www.youtube.com/watch?v=Y1_jRcfI5q0 (accessed April 6, 2015).

22 PR Newswire (2012) "Dimension data announces results of 2012 global contact center benchmarking report," www.prnewswire.com/news-releases/dimension-data-announces-results-of-2012-global-contact-center-benchmarking-report-176583731.html (accessed April 6, 2015).

23 The Radicati Group (2014) "Email statistics report, 2014–2018," www.radicati.com/wp/wp-content/uploads/2014/01/Email-Statistics-Report-2014-2018-Executive-Summary.pdf (accessed March 24, 2015).

24 SAS (2012) "SAS," www.flysas.com/ (accessed March 12, 2012).

25 This service was offered by a US carrier in 2013 that did want to be identified (website accessed in March 14, 2013).

26 Kollau, R. (2012) "Virgin America goes social and personal with new IFE system," www.airlinetrends.com/2012/10/17/virgin-america-chatter-social-personal-ife-system/ (accessed April 6, 2015).

27 eStara (2006) "Continental Airlines: A travel and hospitality case study," http://stage.estara.com/ resourcecenter/pdfs/continental_cs.pdf (accessed April 6, 2015).

28 Perez, J. (2011) "Top 6 companies using video for customer service, sales, & loyalty," www.customerserviceinthecloud.com/2011/08/16/top-6-companies-using-video-for-customer-service-sales-loyalty/ (accessed April 6, 2015).

29  Virtual Hold Technology (2009) "Southwest airlines hangs up on hold time," www.virtualhold.com/pressReleases/2009/06June09/060209_SWAhangsuponHoldtime.html (accessed April 6, 2015).

30  Fox News (2013) "Spirit Airlines switches to non-toll free customer help numbers," www.foxnews.com/travel/2013/05/08/spirit-airlines-switches-to-non-toll-free-customer-help-numbers/ (accessed April 6, 2015)

31  Air France (2014) "Nous contacter," www.airfrance.fr/FR/fr/local/transverse/footer/nous-contacter.htm (accessed February 23, 2014).

32  Fonolo.com (2012) "Top 10 call center trends for 2012," http://fonolo.com/blog/2012/03top-10-call-center-trends-for-2012/ (accessed April 6, 2015).

33  Anthony, S. (2012) "Samsung develops emotion-sensing smartphone," www.extremetech.com/computing/112603-samsung-creates-emotion-sensing-smartphone (accessed April 6, 2015).

34  Next IT (2012) "Next IT culture," http://blog.nextit.com/next-it-culture (accessed April 6, 2015).

35  Ibid.

36  CAPA Newsletter, "TAM Airlines virtual assistant registers 71,878 interactions with 82% response success rate," July 4, 2014.

37  Snyder, B. (2008) "Across the aisle from Alaska's hot virtual assistant," http://crankyflier.com/2008/02/08/alaska-horizon-virtual-assistant-jenn/ (accessed April 6, 2015).

38  Alaska Air (2014) "Ask Jenn," www.alaskaair.com/ (accessed March 13, 2014).

39  Gebhardt, G. (2006) "Creating a market orientation: A longitudinal, multifirm, grounded analysis of cultural transformation," *Journal of Marketing*, 70(4).

40  Ibid.

41  The Telegraph (2013) "Meet Zoe, the virtual assistant of the future," www.telegraph.co.uk/technology/technology-video/9938726/Meet-Zoe-the-virtual-assistant-of-the-future.html (accessed April 6, 2015).

42  VirtuOz and Moxie Webinar (2012) "The next evolution of customer service," www.slideshare.net/MoxieSoftware/the-next-evolution-of-customer-service" (accessed July 5, 2014).

43  Clarkson, D. (2011) "Co-browsing: A technology worth considering," http://blogs.forrester.com/diane_clarkson/11-03-03-co_browsing_a_technology_worth_considering (accessed April 6, 2015).

44  Air Mauritius (2014) "Air Mauritius," www.airmauritius.com/ (accessed July 23, 2014).

45  Call Center Times (2013) "Survey findings: Mobile apps for customer service," www.callcentertimes.com/Home/tabid/37/ctl/NewsArticle/mid/395/CategoryID/1/NewsID/338/Default.aspx (accessed April 6, 2015).

46  ClickFox (2011) "Survey findings: mobile apps for customer service," http://web.clickfox.com/rs/clickfox/images/cf-survey-results-mobile-apps.pdf?mkt_tok=3RkMMJWWfF9wsRoku6jPZKXonjHpfsXw7eslXrHr08Yy0EZ5VunJEUWy2YYJTNQhcOuuEwcWGog8wwBRGeuTc5g%3D (accessed April 6, 2015).

47  Wikipedia (2015) "Short message service," http://en.wikipedia.org/wiki/Short_Message_Service (accessed April 6, 2015).

48  EZ Texting (2015) "What are the uses of SMS Marketing?" www.eztexting.com/uses-of-text-messaging.html (accessed April 6, 2015).

49  American Airlines (2014) "Get flight info on the fly," www.aa.com/homePage.do (accessed April 2, 2014).

50  Wikipedia, "Short message service."

51  SITA (2013) "2013 SITA airline IT trends survey," www.sita.aero/surveys-reports/industry-surveys-reports/airline-it-trends-survey-2013 (accessed March 4, 2015).

52  J.D. Power (2013) "Poor social media practices can negatively impact a businesses' bottom line and brand image," www.jdpower.com/press-releases/2013-social-media-benchmark-study (accessed April 6, 2015).

53  Nielsen (2012) "State of the media: The social media report 2012," www.nielsen.com/content/dam/corporate/us/en/reports-downloads/2012-Reports/The-Social-Media-Report-2012.pdf (accessed April 6, 2015)

54  Ibid.

55  Baer, J. (2012) "Are consumer expectations for social customer service realistic?" http://socialhabit.com/uncategorized/customer-service-expectations/ (accessed April 6, 2015).

56  Benmark, G. and Singer, D. (2012) "Turn customer care into 'social care' to break away from the competition," http://blogs.hbr.org/cs/2012/12/turn_customer_care_into_social.html (accessed April 6, 2015).

57  Wikipedia (2015) "United breaks guitars," http://en.wikipedia.org/wiki/United_Breaks_Guitars (accessed April 6, 2015).

58  Fox News (2013) "British Airways apologizes to man who bought promoted tweet to complain about service," www.foxnews.com/travel/2013/09/04/british-airways-apologizes-to-man-who-bought-promoted-tweet-to-complain-about/ (accessed April 6, 2015).

59  Wakefield, K. (2012) "Southwest Airlines is flying high on Twitter," http://contently.com/blog/2012/07/20/southwest-airlines-is-flying-high-on-twitter/ (accessed April 6, 2015).

60  Drell, L. (2011) "How airlines have taken flight with social media (INFOGRAPHIC)" http://mashable.com/2011/09/16/airlines-social-media-infographic/ (accessed April 6, 2015).

61  JetBlue (2013) "Blue tales," http://blog.jetblue.com/ (accessed June 9, 2013).

62  Nigam, S. (2010) "How social media helped travelers during the iceland volcano eruption," http://mashable.com/2010/04/22/social-media-iceland-volcano/ (accessed April 6, 2015).

63  Franguel, S. (2012) "Twitter in 140 characters. That's it, that's all!," www.espressocommunication.com/en/communication-en/6060/twitter-in-140-characters-thats-it-thats-all (accessed April 6, 2015).

64  Drell (2011), How airlines have taken flight with social media".

65  Davis, B. (2014) "How KLM nails social customer care," https://econsultancy.com/blog/64779-how-klm-nails-social-customer-care/ (accessed April 6, 2015).

66  Ross, P. (2014) "Socially devoted preview: Top 10 airlines on Twitter," www.socialbakers.com/blog/2155-socially-devoted-preview-top-10-airlines-on-twitter (accessed April 6, 2015).

67  Bleenman, B. (2013) "Example of proactive use of social media: KLM," https://bleenman.wordpress.com/2013/03/20/examples-of-proactive-use-of-social-media/ (accessed April 6, 2015).

68  Purnell, N. (2014) "Airlines Take to Twitter to inform customers, world," www.wsj.com/articles/airlines-take-to-twitter-to-keep-world-informed-1406125253 (accessed April 6, 2015).

69  Rabinowitz, J. (2014) "Spirit Airlines puts Twitter on autopilot," www.forbes.com/sites/jasonrabinowitz/2014/07/22/spirit-airlines-puts-twitter-on-autopilot/ (accessed April 6, 2015).

70  Schiff, A. (2013) "Let's clear the air," www.dmnews.com/lets-clear-the-air/article/316875/ (accessed April 6, 2015).

71  KLM (2015) "KLM," www.klm.com/ (accessed April 1, 2015).

72  Twitter (2015) "KLM: Royal Dutch Airlines," https://twitter.com/klm (accessed April 6, 2015).

73  Facebook (2015) "KLM," www.facebook.com/KLM (accessed April 6, 2015).

74  Rabinowitz, "Spirit Airlines puts Twitter ON AUTOPILOT."

75  Carnival (2014) "Forums," www.carnival.com/ (accessed March 13, 2014).

76  Vogel-Meijer, K. (2015) "What KLM Royal Dutch Airlines has learned from one year of social service on LinkedIn", http://linkedintobusiness.com/What-KLM-Royal-Dutch-Airlines-has-learned-from-one-year-of-social-service-on-LinkedIn/ (accesed November 20, 2015).

77  Apple (2015) "AppleCare products," www.apple.com/support/products/ (accessed April 6, 2015).

78  Moore, M. (2016) "US Start-up seeks to ease pain of complaining", Financial Times, January 2/3, 2016.

79  Outsourcing Call Center Services (2009) "American Airlines call center comes to India," http://callcenter-outsourcing.blogspot.com/2009/10/american-airlines-call-center-comes-to.html (accessed April 6, 2015).

80  Global Delivery Report (2011) "Airlines bringing call centers back onshore," http://globaldeliveryreport.com/airlines-bringing-call-centers-back-onshore (accessed April 6, 2015).

81  Dimension Data (2014) "2013/14 global contact centre benchmarking summary report," www.dimensiondata.com/Global/Downloadable%20Documents/2013_14_benchmarking%20summary%20report.pdf (accessed April 6, 2014).

82  Ibid.

83  British Airways, "British Airways."

84  Alcatel/Genesys survey (2009) "The cost of poor customer service: The economic impact of the customer experience and engagement," www.slideshare.net/fred.zimny/the-cost-of-poor-customer-service-the-economic-impact-of-customer-experience-in-the-us (accessed April 9, 2014).

85  Ibid.

86  British Airways, "British Airways."

87  Capgemini (2012) "Optimizing multi-channel customer service to support customer centricity," www.pl.capgemini.com/resource-file-access/resource/pdf/optimizing_multi-channel_customer_service_to_support_customer_centricity_0.pdf (accessed April 6, 2015).

88  Klie, L. (2012) "Listening to the voice of the customer," www.destinationcrm.com/Articles/Editorial/Magazine-Features/Listening-to-the-Voice-of-the-Customer-83180.aspx (accessed April 6, 2015).

89  Ibid.

90  Peaslee, J. (2015) "Best practices of Voice of the Customer (VoC) programs," www.thriveanalytics.com/blog/?p=34 (accessed April 6, 2015)

91  Allegiance (2011) "Allegiance customer JetBlue Airways receives Forrester 2011 Voice of the Customer Award," www.allegiance.com/press-releases/guy-kawasaki-jeremiah-owyang-and-voice-of-customer-experts-highlight-day-two-of-allegiance-engage-summit (accessed April 6, 2015).

92  Anton, J. (2004) "Combining service quality with Profitability," www.asponline.com/egain_anton.pdf (accessed April 6, 2015).

93  Filwood, David (2014) "Why do your call center agents quit?" www.linkedin.com/pulse/20140518182546-3995896-why-do-your-call-center-agents-quit (accessed November 3, 2014).

94  Ibid.

95  Buchanan, Barbara (2014) "Manage customer experience expectations by lowering employee turnover," www.callcentertimes.com/Home/tabid/37/ctl/NewsArticle/mid/395/CategoryID/1/NewsID/864/Default.aspx (accessed November 3, 2014).

96  Legett, K. (2006) "Contact center agent turnover is a fact of life that must be tracked and managed," http://blogs.forrester.com/kate_legett/13-05-06-contact_center_agent_turnover_is_a_fact_of_life_that_must_tracked_and_managed (accessed April 6, 2015)

97  Bloom, N. (2015) "Does working from home work? Evidence from a Chinese experiment," www.stanford.edu/~nbloom/WFH.pdf (accessed April 6, 2015).

98  Georgia State University (2015) "Browse research and scholarship," http://digitalarchive.gsu.edu (accessed April 6, 2015).

99  Forrester Research (2012) "The next generation contact center," www.aspect.com/globalassets/aspect-ngcc-forrester-wp.pdf (accessed February 25, 2014).

100 Ibid.

101 Jupiter Strategic Planning Services (1999) *Site Operation Strategies*, Customer Service, Volume 7.

102 Tierney, J. (2013) "KANA launches omni-channel customer service suite," http://loyalty360.org/resources/article/kana-launches-omni-channel-customer-service-suite (accessed April 6, 2015).

103 Ibid.

104 Colt (2011) "Swiss International Airlines (SWISS) case study," www.colt.net/se/en/about-us/our-customers/swiss-airlines-case-study-en.htm (accessed April 6, 2015).

105 Genesys, "How SIP delivers your next generation service platform."

106 Spoken Communications (2012) "SIP vs TDM for the Contact Center," http://blog.spoken.com/2012/02/sip-vs-tdm-for-dummies.html (accessed April 6, 2015).

107 Genesys, "How SIP delivers your next generation service platform."

108 Forrester Research (2014) "Navigate the future of customer service." https://solutions.forrester.com/future-customer-service (accessed January 3, 2015).

# Chapter 6

# The airline e-commerce organization

*The secret of all victory lies in the organization of the non-obvious.*

Marcus Aurelius, Roman emperor

## 6.1 INTRODUCTION

An efficient and effective organization is a critical success factor in any airline. Selecting, setting up, and maintaining the right organizational structure to manage e-commerce initiatives is not easy. A key reason is that e-commerce is a unique crossover between technology and commerce that has not existed before, certainly not in traditional corporate hierarchies. Competition for e-commerce talent and changing business practices as a result of pressures from customers and the company's partners and vendors add to the challenge.

Airlines looking for ways to realize the full benefits of e-commerce need to address several important questions:

1. What is the right organizational structure for managing the e-commerce activities at an airline?
2. What are the challenges an airline faces when integrating e-commerce in its existing business?
3. Who is the ideal person to lead an airline's e-commerce efforts?
4. What are the organizational characteristics of an airline that is a leader in e-commerce?
5. To whom should an airline's e-commerce organization report?
6. How will e-commerce change organizational structures at an airline in the future?

The airline industry has been at organizational crossroads before. Going back to the 1960s, airlines just started to realize the growing organizational importance of the information technology revolution. Initially, computers had not been identified as a separate organizational entity. At some airlines including BOAC, one of British Airways' predecessors, it had been part of "Management Services."[1] However, within a few years, computers spread widely and were introduced on a larger scale within airlines. Computers were now pervasive in all departments, from commercial areas such as reservations to operational entities including flight routing and aircraft load control.[2] In the 1970s, a new distinctive group was born: The information technology department.

Fast forward into the digital era with the omnipresent internet, airline organizations have undergone similar changes. Again, pervasive PC/internet technology and applications are impacting all organizational areas as happened with the IT revolution before. This development contained the nucleus for a new organizational area that later emerged as the e-commerce department. Noteworthy is that the adoption of new technology today is largely consumer led—hence the label "consumerization" of IT—and not by companies. In the 1960s and 1970s, it was the other way around. The emergence of e-commerce can be considered as one of the most significant impacts on an airline's organizational structures in the last 30 years and the foreseeable future.

## 6.2 THE RIGHT AIRLINE E-COMMERCE ORGANIZATION: DOES IT EXIST?

Depending on a variety of company internal factors and the external environment, the "right organization" should be understood as an entity that:

- maximizes the transformation of its resources into a higher value such as increasing an airline's e-commerce profits and reducing its distribution costs
- has the optimal size and quality in terms of resources
- makes optimal use of the resources by way of efficient and effective processes.

An airline that exhibits these organizational characteristics operates a best-in class e-commerce business and can be considered a leader. Laggards are airlines that feature none or only a fraction of these characteristics. There is no such thing as *one* right organizational structure for airline e-commerce. Different set-ups work at different times and for different airlines.

When elaborating on the evolution of e-commerce organizations at airlines, we need to keep in mind a historical perspective. So far, four major change periods—with a fifth in the wings—have impacted airlines in the way they organize their online business:

1. *1996–2000.* Airlines' launch of informational websites and their transformation to transactional platforms for ticket sales.
2. *2000–2004.* Selling air travel online goes mainstream with more carriers; expansion of e-commerce activities outside home markets; website redesigns for digital brand refresh.
3. *2004–2007/8.* Websites evolve into online travel gateways with new shopping tools for award travel, self-service, and cross-ancillary travel offerings added.
4. *2007/8–2013.* Airlines establish and expand web presence on mobile platforms and social media; emergence of fare merchandising.
5. *2014–present.* Customer centric applications enabling personalized travel experiences and driven by big data and e-tracking technology, is starting to emerge as a new area of competency and differentiation.

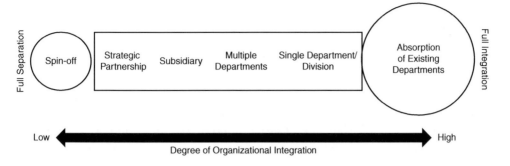

**Figure 6.1** *The spectrum of airline e-commerce organization set-ups*

Figure 6.1 illustrates the spectrum of organizational set-up scenarios that have come into play since airline e-commerce emerged in the late 1990s. On one extreme end of the organizational spectrum, we find the spin-off where e-commerce is a completely independent entity that is fully separated from the airline. The other end of the organizational structure spectrum involves a full absorption of the existing business structure into e-commerce. In between, airlines organize e-commerce via some type of inhouse entity such as a single department or spread across multiple departments/divisions.

When reviewing the last 15+ years, the overall trend in organizational structures has been a shift toward internalizing e-commerce. Airlines that often started out organizing e-commerce through an external partnership eventually "brought it home." Take for example Australian airline Qantas. In 2000, it entered the world of cyberspace through a strategic alliance with Telstra, a telecommunications company, to establish Qantas Ventures. Combining its airline industry expertise with that of a technology company allowed Qantas to operate this new entity that was now charged with developing an e-commerce strategy and spearheading various web activities.[3] Similarly, Lufthansa Airlines announced in 1999 a new subsidiary called "Lufthansa E-commerce GMBH" that would handle the company's internet sales activities,[4] while Air Canada established in 2001 a subsidiary called Destina that took care of the airline's e-commerce initiatives.[5]

Initial set-ups such as these reflected the realization among established airlines at the time that their existing organizational structures were not able to handle e-commerce successfully. Factors including big company size, lack of e-commerce know-how and savviness, and an uncompetitive compensation/unappealing working culture were not conducive to engaging with the fast medium of e-commerce. We need to remember that these were the heydays of the dotcom boom with e-commerce start-ups literally working out of a garage, shaking the foundations of existing companies, and challenging their ways of doing business. Common traits of these players included the offering of employee ownership in the company, a "work and play" office environment, and an emphasis on fast-to-market web product and service launches.

The (re-) discovery of "small is beautiful" led established airlines to the adoption of organizational concepts generally only found in small start-up firms known for their nimbleness and entrepreneurial spirit. Some airlines even eyed an eventual spin-off of their e-commerce subsidiary in order to cash in on the proceeds from an IPO (United Airlines had such an intention—see more details below in "Snapshot: organizing e-commerce at United Airlines") but the collapse of the dotcom bubble in 2000/2001 terminated those plans. Over the span of a few years, traditional airlines including Qantas and Lufthansa built up their e-commerce know-how and more parts of their organizations became involved in online activities. As a result, those e-commerce entities that initially had been set up outside the airline were eventually folded into the company's existing organization. E-Commerce either became a new business unit or was integrated into several traditional departments.

Other airlines, notably the early LCCs that had already existed before e-commerce entered its commercial phase in the 1990s, moved fast beyond just integrating e-commerce into their existing organizational structures. They actually absorbed e-commerce and traditional departments were completely subjected to it. LCCs have always known the benefits of interacting directly with customers and bypassing middlemen. This was first achieved through their telephone operations/call centers and later through e-commerce. With little sales and distribution legacy in the traditional offline world, they were quickly able to make e-commerce the new core of their business model and line up all departments behind it. Without such an approach, LCCs such as Ryanair and JetBlue would not have been able to grow their online revenue as fast as they did. In their case, unlike traditional legacy carriers, e-commerce is not perceived as a channel but as a medium that crosses over all functional areas in a company. A "digital divide" in these companies whereby some departments are heavily engaged with e-commerce while other departments pursue business in traditional ways is minimal, if it even exists.

Two examples illustrate this shift to the extreme right-hand side of the organizational structure spectrum. LCC UK-based easyJet worked at first with the outside company Tableau to manage www.easyjet.com when it launched in 1997. In 2002, easyJet brought its web business inhouse as soon as the website started generating significant revenue. It has stayed there ever since and it has completely penetrated the whole company from an organizational structure point of view.

Another airline that has fully absorbed e-commerce in its organization is Aer Lingus. In their case, it is even more remarkable considering their large footprint in the offline world with close to 80 years of corporate history. The fact that they managed to grow their online revenue contribution from less from 2% in 2001 to almost 50% in 2003[6] and today generate almost 80% of their revenue online is only possible because they completely altered the then existing organization to support e-commerce.

It is clear that the way airlines organize their e-commerce activities is not written in stone. On the contrary. There is constant movement on the organizational structure spectrum and the "perfect" organization today could be obsolete and overdue for change tomorrow. In order to develop a better grasp of what makes an airline e-commerce organization successful, we need to pay closer attention to some factors that play an important role. The following section addresses this.

## SNAPSHOT: ORGANIZING E-COMMERCE AT UNITED AIRLINES

United Airlines' organizational journey shows how a company moved through various structural set-ups over time. It came full circle in how it manages its e-commerce business. "Born" in the company's IT division and then managed by the Distribution Planning Department in the late 1990s, e-commerce was subsequently separated from the airline to become a subsidiary called UnitedVentures (UV). It was 100% owned by United Loyalty Services or ULS, which in turn was part of UAL, Inc., United Airlines' holding company.

UV was intentionally moved off site to be outside the sphere of United Airlines' head office near Chicago O'Hare Airport. Its offices were set up closer to Chicago downtown in order to more easily attract e-commerce talent from the city. UV employees also received special ownership shares that could be sold at a future date and the "work and play" aspect was accounted for with the company's pool billiard/dart boardroom.

From the beginning, the importance of co-locating business and technology on the same floor was recognized. This ensured that no departmental silos and attitudes of "us" versus "them" could evolve and fast decision-making could be maintained. The original intention to spin off this subsidiary as part of an IPO was abandoned with the stock market crash in 2000/2001. Despite this, several key objectives of this subsidiary were nonetheless achieved. These included:

■ The combination of inhouse, airline-industry-experienced employees and e-commerce industry talents under one roof.
■ The operation of a start-up-styled entity with a non-hierarchical working culture and attractive compensation.
■ The management of its own operational budget outside the airline.
■ The introduction of more efficient decision-making processes resulting in vastly shortened time-to-market launches for new website products launches.

Within two years after inception, the subsidiary generated close to 20% of United Airline's revenue online. This was a good start but also necessary due to mounting competitive pressure. Other major airlines including Southwest Airlines and American Airlines were already ahead because of their earlier e-commerce start. Furthermore, technology companies such as Microsoft decided to enter the travel space with the first online travel agency Expedia. United thus needed a radical solution if it wanted to be part of this new disruptive way of doing business. UV received more than one visit from UA's CEO and other senior officers who wanted to understand why certain decisions that took traditional airline departments five months were taken by UV in a small fraction of that time.

The e-commerce organization maintained its subsidiary status for several years before being dissolved and integrated into the airline in 2005/2006. Then, two entities were responsible for managing www.united.com: the Information Services Division, responsible for the area of e-commerce technology, and the Marketing Division, handling all business aspects. Both entities were combined with their respective counterparts as a result of the United Airlines-Continental merger in 2011.

## 6.3 THE ROLE OF RESOURCES, VALUES, AND PROCESSES IN AN AIRLINE ORGANIZATION

Regardless of what organizational structure an airlines chooses, there are certain pivotal ingredients that determine the capabilities of a company. There are three that constitute the organizational framework of a capable company. They are:[7]

- resources
- values
- processes.

For an airline to have a better understanding of what it takes to establish an effective e-commerce organization structure, it needs to take a look at each of these three factors in more detail.

### 6.3.1 Resources

In essence, resources include people working for the airline, office space, equipment, technology, brands, information, and cash. Furthermore, relationships with suppliers, distributors, and customers of the airline, and even the working culture are also part of the resources.[8] Hiring quality staff that have experience and skills relevant not only to the airline industry but also to e-commerce translates into a significant competitive edge for an airline.

Management often equates resources with the capabilities of an organization. This is wrong. Actually, two different airline e-commerce organizations may be equipped with an identical set of resources in terms of quality and quantity, yet their performance may be very different. This is due to the fact that an organization's values and processes are also important in determining its capability to perform.[9]

## 6.3.2 Values

The values of an organization are the criteria by which decisions about priorities are made.[10] Values include corporate goals and prioritization decisions about them are taken at every level in the company. It could be that senior management decides to expand into the corporate travel market with a new B2B web product or that front-line sales managers advocate the promotion of exclusive website fares in a particular market. It is important that these decisions are consistent with the company's overall strategic direction and that they are tied into the e-commerce organization's goals. These need to be clear, consistent and broadly understood[11] in the airline. Determining an airline's e-commerce values is an important part of a strategy process.

## 6.3.3 Processes

Processes are patterns of activities that enable an organization to transform inputs from its resources into products and services of greater worth in line with previously established values.[12] These activities include interaction, communication, decision-making, and coordination. Like any company aiming at running a capable organization, an airline e-commerce organization must establish the principles of its processes. These can be either formal since they have been well defined and explicitly documented or informal because they result from a certain way of working that has evolved over time.

As a company grows, it tends to adopt more formal processes because there are more resources and values with higher stakes to manage. Ironically, however, exactly this development can have a stifling effect on an organization's decision speed and innovativeness. This realization also dawned on the traditional network carriers when they were looking for ways to organize e-commerce when it first emerged in the 1990s. As we know from our above discussion, this led to efforts to set up entities outside existing airline organizations.

## 6.4 TYPES OF ORGANIZATIONAL STRUCTURE: WHO IS IN CHARGE?

Table 6.1 shows seven alternative structures for organizing e-commerce. They include:

- adhoc set-up
- steering committee
- IT department
- multiple department
- independent
- dedicated department
- absorption solution.

The listing sequence is not entirely accidental and reflects to a degree of how organizational structures for e-commerce evolved in the airline industry up to today.

**Table 6.1** *Airline organizational set-ups for e-commerce*

| Set-up | | Pros / Cons |
|---|---|---|
| **No One: Adhoc** | ⊕ | ■ Could have temporary justification when dealing with e-commerce products in early stages of life cycle |
| | ⊖ | ■ No logic/priority in decision-making<br>■ Fragmentary and inconsistent web presence |
| **Steering Committee** | ⊕ | ■ Could have temporary justification when dealing with e-commerce products and trying to figure out next moves |
| | ⊖ | ■ Meets only sporadically<br>■ Agreement typically only on lowest common denominator<br>■ Department interests take priority |
| **IT Department** | ⊕ | ■ Generally strong focus on edgy innovative technology |
| | ⊖ | ■ Perspective too narrow<br>■ Prevents cross-functional approach |
| **Multiple Departments** | ⊕ | ■ Each functional area in company has a role and responsibility to manage e-commerce |
| | ⊖ | ■ Risk of fragmentation as overarching e-commerce perspective is missing<br>■ Tendency to focus on offline business hence depriving e-commerce of resources and focus |
| **Independent e-Commerce** | ⊕ | ■ Faster, more nimble and entrepreneurial<br>■ Stand-alone budget and separate profit/loss |
| | ⊖ | ■ Brand inconsistency<br>■ Friction of e-commerce vs overall corporate goals<br>■ "Us versus them" employee mentality |
| **Dedicated e-Commerce** | ⊕ | ■ Full-time resources and budget<br>■ High degree of consistency in e-commerce planning, decision-making, and management |
| | ⊖ | ■ Silo mentality<br>■ Friction of e-commerce vs overall corporate goals |
| **Absorption** | ⊕ | ■ Full realization of e-commerce benefits including direct-to-consumer relationship, lower cost, new pricing & revenue models |
| | ⊖ | ■ Partially shut off from offline opportunities |

*Source:* Author based on Chaffey (2009)[13]

### 6.4.1 Adhoc set-up

The adhoc set-up was the starting point for most carriers, at least for those "born" in the mid-1990s and earlier. Airlines entering the marketplace later automatically incorporated e-commerce in some formal shape and form into their structures. The adhoc approach to e-commerce is largely a bygone.

If encountered today, it should be temporary and within the strict confines of a new e-commerce product that a carrier is experimenting with and trying to figure out how to move forward. For example, dealing on an adhoc basis with wearable computing and virtual reality applications in the early stages of their life cycles make sense—as long as a framework emerges of how to organizationally accommodate these new applications.

### 6.4.2 Steering committee

The same applies to the steering committee. It is a rare species to find these days and no airline should manage e-commerce this way on a long-term basis. The biggest downside to this approach is that e-commerce is generally subjected to particular departmental interests that are concerned with other priorities. Steering committees have their value and can play a role for a short period during an experimentation phase. In such a situation, a stakeholder from the carrier's e-commerce department should ideally lead the committee or at least have a key role.

### 6.4.3 IT department

The IT department was often the first organizational unit put in charge officially and formally to manage e-commerce. Senior management at the time viewed e-commerce mostly as an IT area that should be handled by corresponding specialists. Technology is a core competency of a typical airline IT department but the know-how and expertise for sales, marketing, and customer service reside in other airline departments.

Having IT exclusively run e-commerce translates into too narrow a perspective and should be avoided. One possibility where IT may be still in charge involves a situation where the head of the IT department is also the leader of the e-commerce department at the same time. Air Canada and Aer Lingus feature such co-heads and it may make sense if the company's focus is on edgy innovative technology.

### 6.4.4 Multiple departments

The multiple department set-up is more an exception than the rule. In this case, e-commerce is an "add-on" to each of a carrier's traditional departments. At first glance, it may make sense to organizationally distribute e-commerce in an airline this way because it helps permeate the subject throughout an organization. Each department has roles and responsibilities to support e-commerce. However, departments in this scenario are often concerned with managing the offline business and e-commerce therefore could be short-changed. Additionally, there is frequently a lack of e-commerce subject matter expertise with traditional stakeholders. This further debilitates the carrier's activities to be more competitive in cyberspace.

### 6.4.5 Independent

As an organizational form, the independent entity was to some extent an anomaly because some airlines had been driven by the desire to sell off their e-commerce subsidiary through an IPO. Furthermore, the days of a carrier looking to jumpstart their e-commerce basics by establishing a new subsidiary with a technology partner are gone.

Nonetheless, it is possible that this organizational model may have relevance for some airlines today. This is the case for carriers that want to formally venture into a specific area of e-commerce that is better managed outside the existing organization. Faster decision-making processes, a more entrepreneurial way of running the business, and a separate budget are major reasons. An increasingly important area where some airlines could consider the independent entity is the management and marketing of digital data. We have already mentioned Qantas' new data subsidiary Red Planet. Other leading e-commerce carriers may follow Qantas' lead with such a set-up. It is feasible that Red Planet may eventually be integrated into Qantas but for now, this subsidiary runs its own course. Maintaining a close relationship with the parent company is important for several reasons. Minimization of brand inconsistencies, alignment of business operations toward overall corporate goals, and avoidance of unnecessary friction as a result of an "us versus them" mentality among them.

### 6.4.6 Dedicated e-commerce

An airline looking to build a significant contribution of e-commerce to its business needs to organize its online activities in a way that is systematic, consistent, and cross-departmental. This is possible through the establishment of a dedicated e-commerce department with full-time resources, a sufficient budget, and strong senior leadership. Bridging traditional and new ways of doing things is often a key theme for an airline's dedicated e-commerce department.

Legacy carriers that have gone mainstream with e-commerce, and produce a significant share of their revenue online, fall into this category. The e-commerce leaders among them have not only stepped up to providing for more/better resources to manage the online business but have also appointed top e-commerce executives. An example is Delta Airlines generating over 50% of its revenue via Delta.com in the US domestic market[14] with the company's most senior e-commerce leader assuming a vice president position. The portfolio of this position was expanded to also include Delta's marketing in March 2012.[15]

A dedicated e-commerce department is an indication that the online business has become part of the overall company structure and the interdepartmental processes. However, the very existence of an e-commerce department does not necessarily translate into a full alignment between dotcom goals and the interest of other stake-holders from IT, traditional marketing, and sales. In other words, despite a dedicated e-commerce department, a carrier may still perform below par in cyberspace.

### 6.4.7 Full absorption

Interweaving all aspects of the business with e-commerce and transcending a channel-based perspective is the main approach of the full absorption organizational model. With the notable exception of Aer Lingus, no legacy carrier has matured this far yet—and might never do. This is because there will always be some element of history that has to be accounted for in their business operations. This is also the reason why legacy carriers often exhibit a "channel" perspective ("traditional channel-versus-the-web") when it comes to cyberspace. LCCs such as easyJet and JetBlue are different. For them, e-commerce is part of their corporate DNA and a significant part of their business revolves around it. One area where this might be a bit of a handicap for LCCs is the corporate travel market. This segment is still largely han-dled in traditional ways via intermediaries such as GDSs and offline travel agencies. Any LCC targeting this business would need to make some adjustments to their current organizational model for more effective management.

### 6.5 THE DEDICATED E-COMMERCE ORGANIZATION: A CLOSER LOOK

It appears that legacy companies organize their e-commerce activities for the most part via some centralized entity—42% of the companies in a study indicate this approach as their modus operandi.[16] Since this organizational entity is quite popular, we should elaborate on it in greater detail and see if it carries any merit for an airline.

This organizational model is essentially an indication that e-commerce has an established role at the carrier. There is a high degree of interfacing between the entity responsible for managing e-commerce and other departments/geographic areas in the airline. The traditional core departments at the airline have fully accepted e-commerce as an integral part of the overall company structure and the interdepart-mental processes between them and the e-commerce stakeholders are also well coordinated and established. This means that there is little separation between dif-ferent departments' interests as they relate to e-commerce and the dotcom goals are aligned between IT, marketing, sales, other traditional departments, and e-commerce.

The dedicated e-commerce organization may take on three scenarios:

■ *It is the major if not the sole decision maker for e-commerce activities.* However, it collaborates closely with other functional departments. Airlines with a single brand and associated dotcom strategy fall into this category.
■ *It is a consultant.* It advises and helps execute some or all of the e-commerce initiatives of stakeholders in the company that are the decision makers. These

stakeholders could be functional departments such as marketing or even other divisions including FFP and cargo. Carriers operating multiple digital brands, for example, Lufthansa with www.lufthansa.com and its FFP www.milesandmore.com and Air China with www.airchina.com and its cargo subsidiary's www.airchinacargo.com, pursue this approach.

■ *It operates as a hybrid.* The e-commerce department and other functional departments/divisions alternate as decision makers, depending on the e-commerce activity at stake. For example, the e-commerce department may be the driver for the airline's mobile activities while only assisting in managing social media because the airline's marketing or PR departments are responsible for this area.

In any of these organizational scenarios, the dedicated department is at the center of an airline's e-commerce activities. This means even when stakeholders from functional departments or divisions *manage* their own e-commerce activities, they should be still *governed* by the e-commerce entity.[17]

This governance means having an organizational unit in place where e-commerce products and services are conceptualized and e-commerce activities are coordinated for the entire company. In this case, the airline establishes an organizational e-commerce hub that enables the creation of company-wide cost/benefit e-commerce benchmarks as well as standardized measurements and methodologies. Furthermore, via this hub, an airline stands a better chance of managing its e-commerce initiatives across different company areas in a consistent and systematic way. These areas could be different functional disciplines, divisional departments, and even geographic zones.

This e-commerce hub serves several distinct purposes:

■ *Managing online sales, marketing, and customer service.* This covers mid-term to long-term strategic activities. Examples are the establishment of e-commerce goals or the structuring of online pricing, as well as day-to-day management activities such as website performance tracking and measurement.

■ *Promoting internal education and training.* The focus is on the facilitation of internal learning and skill upgrading in order to grow digital literacy among the company's staff. Frequent updates on the latest e-commerce trends and developments and the transfer of knowledge between the company's online and offline areas are part of this activity.

■ *Handling e-commerce vendors.* Included are the sourcing of vendors through request for proposals (RFPs) for e-commerce specialty services and their ongoing management.

■ *Incubating innovations.* The centralization of strategic e-commerce activities for the short-, medium-, or long-term development of new web products and services among different organizational entities center for e-commerce planning and e-roadmaps.

■ *Ensuring consistent decisions about hard- and software applications.* Reducing the duplication of efforts in the company by centralizing decision-making processes for hard and software applications.

Several years ago, Dutch carrier KLM, in response to its board's strategic target to significantly grow online sales, decided to organize e-commerce through such a set-up. By 2008, this hub had evolved to be the e-commerce R&D centers for the entire Air France–KLM group, one of the biggest of its kind among European airlines.[18]

## 6.6 INSIDE THE E-COMMERCE BOX: KEY ROLES AND AREAS FOR A SUCCESSFUL ORGANIZATION

Organizing e-commerce means rethinking traditional roles and even creating new ones in an airline's organization. Figure 6.2 shows four organizational levels including leadership, management, line, and third parties each supporting airline e-commerce through various roles and in many different areas.

People have different views what the roles and areas supporting e-commerce entail. Tables 6.2 and 6.3 provide some general guidelines in this regard. An airline should define as much as possible the various e-commerce roles and areas to ensure clarity in terms of organizational responsibility and authority.

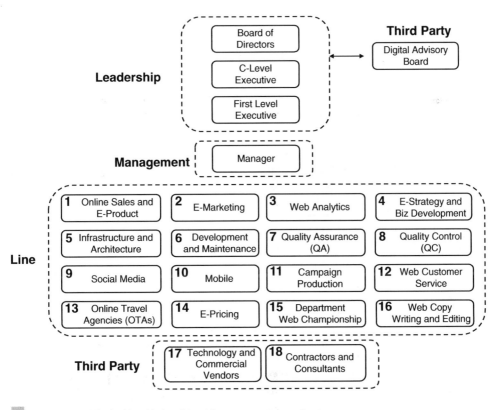

**Figure 6.2** *The building blocks of the airline e-commerce organization*

An important issue is how to arrange these e-commerce blocks in order to create a successful e-commerce organization at an airline. What needs to be looked at specifically is the organizational combination of the "e" and "commerce" or—put differently—the technology and business. The next section addresses this in greater detail.

**Table 6.2** *Levels of involvement and leadership for an airline e-commerce organization*

| Organizational level | Typical responsibilities |
|---|---|
| Board Director[19] | • Ensures that the management team is examining the threats and opportunities digital presents and devoting appropriate resources to digital initiatives<br>• Helps the board and CEO frame the strategic and organizational issues by asking detailed questions about the opportunities and risks, the company's digital capabilities and whether the organization is being as aggressive as it should be in this area |
| C-Level Executive (Chief Executive Officer, Chief Commercial Officer, Chief Operating Officer, Chief Information Officer)* | • Assumes role to champion companywide the benefits and advantages of e-commerce<br>• Leads major e-commerce initiatives including website technology and business overhauls, and re-organizations<br>• Tries not to meddle with mid-level management in tactical decisions |
| First Level Executive (Executive Vice President, Senior Vice President) | • Approves budget and overall website strategy<br>• Reviews high-level website performance metrics<br>• Approves major website changes and modifications<br>• Resolves conflicts regarding tactical decisions that might not be resolved on lower level*** |
| Manager | • Manages resources that do the actual work (website performance analyses, business planning, e-marketing, online sales, web customer service, user research)<br>• Develops and manages the airline's e-commerce budget<br>• Supervises implementation activities<br>• Drives website strategy<br>• Coordinates with other department heads to set priorities and allocate resources<br>• Monitors and judges the effectiveness of tactical decisions[20] |
| Digital Advisory Board | • Advising and informing board and C-level executive of leading-edge online trends and developments<br>• Facilitation of strategic innovation and digital road mapping |

*There has been a flood of C-level titles in companies over the last decade and while "Chief Creative Officer," "Chief Talent Officer," or even "Chief Apology Officer" (Southwest Airlines created this title back in 2007) sounds impressive, one needs to be careful not to over interpret their corporate rank and put them on the same organizational level as a CEO or Chief Financial Officer. A Chief Talent Officer is simply a fancy title for the most senior person in charge of HR at a company while the Chief Apology Officer heads the customer complaints department and Chief Happiness Officer at McDonalds is nobody else than the company's clown mascot Ronald McDonald. In other words, not every "Chief" is indeed a chief.[21]

**Table 6.3** *Key roles in the airline e-commerce organization*

1. *Online Sales/E-Product Management*

*Typical responsibilities*: Manages online sales for leisure/VFR/corporate segments in carrier's domestic and international markets. Contributes sales relevant information; makes recommendations to strategic online sales plans and reviews and forecasts budget requirements. Identifies online sales system improvements. Recommends new online product opportunities, surveys web traveler needs and tracks competitors. Partners with ancillary travel providers for generating incremental revenue streams from cross-sales. Works closely with IT and booking engine provider/payment service provider for digital platform improvements. Collaboration with company stakeholders including online marketing and web customer service to ensure optimal use of airline's digital properties for increasing online sales generation and brand equity with web travelers. Regularly reports to top management on sales performance.

2. *E-Marketing*

*Typical responsibilities*: Plans and executes all web, search marketing (SEO/SEM), marketing database, email, affiliate, social media, and display advertising campaigns; may also design, build and maintain airline's social media presence. Measures and reports performance of all digital marketing campaigns and assesses against digital benchmarks. Identifies trends and insights for opportunities to increase online sales/strengthen digital brand. Tasks includes coordination with digital media agencies for the development of e-marketing calendar and the management of e-online campaigns, and the optimization of media spending. Collaborates with other vendors including domain name registrars, web designers, e-market researchers, affiliates, and e-tagging taxonomy specialists for e-tagging. Leads establishment of website style guide and associated corporate standards for carrier's digital brand.

3. *Web Analytics*

*Typical responsibilities*: Develops/maintains efficient reporting process on performance of airline's digital properties, online marketing programs, and user interface design elements. This includes reports on graphics placement, content, click-through, conversion, entry and exit pages, time spent per visit, email, affiliate portals, and competitive tracking. Collaborates with numerous stakeholders including from IT, marketing, sales, and service for the development/implementation of analytics, digital property tagging, and testing for actionable insight. Ad-hoc analyses are also performed to guide decision making.

4. *E-Strategy & Business Development*

*Typical responsibilities*: Maintains and plans airline's overall goals, strategies, and policies regarding e-commerce. Develops and manages organizational changes needed to meet goals, identifies potential business partners and negotiates agreements. Establishes e-roadmap and future scenarios based on emerging business and technology trends. Conducts strategic analysis of airline's internal strengths/weaknesses and external threats/opportunities as they relate to cyberspace. May coordinate and negotiate with various departments including product development, marketing and/or sales group for the formulation of an e-commerce strategy.

5. *Infrastructure & Architecture*

*Typical responsibilities*: Develops/maintains website network and hosting of production, staging, and development servers, manages airline digital platforms, hardware and software for overall site structure, design navigation systems, and interactive applications, manages security protocols.

6. *Development & Maintenance*

*Typical responsibilities*: Software development and programming for front/back-end applications of airline digital properties, often aided by contractors, and in coordination with technology vendors. Maintenance of site content and application using HTML, CSS, Photoshop, Javascript, Flash, and other programs. Site maintenance is accomplished with content owner representatives from various departments and might also involve third parties such as copy writers and language translators.

**485**

7. *Quality Assurance (QA)*

*Typical responsibilities*: Usability testing of site and applications for performance optimization so that new web products and services fulfill quality requirements for the airline and affiliated websites. Involves all stages of a testing cycle, devising end-to-end test scripts with user scenarios, test goals and expected performance outcomes, conducting various testing techniques including unit, integration, systems, user acceptance, and stress testing, reporting actual vs expected test results, and re-testing once corrective action has been taken.

8. *Quality Control (QC)*

*Typical responsibilities*: Leads and coordinates the airline's overall efforts to maintain the quality and performance of website content and functionalities. With human assistance and robotic tools, regular monitoring of website performance metrics and reporting on findings of any errors or deviations to standard processes enhanced by the random selection of website content and functionalities for quality spot checks. Detects malfunction as a result of hosting, website performance or even security issues. Reviews website content for accuracy. Escalates of any corrective issues with relevant internal and/or external stakeholder for resolution.

9. *Social Media*

*Typical responsibilities*: Brand/reputation management of airline presence on wide spectrum of social media websites including airline blog, third party platforms, and gaming sites. This is based on previously determined posting types, posting frequency, and web traveler engagement goals. Relationship management with social media influencers may also be included. Social customer service and social purchase transactions may be handled by separate dedicated team in social media group or by different departments altogether.

10. *Mobile*

*Typical responsibilities*: Spearheads and develops business use cases for new mobile technologies. Establishes, implements, and measures the effectiveness of initiatives that drive awareness and adoption for airline's mobile products/services. Ensures that the right voice and high-quality content are optimized in mobile channels (mobile web, apps, SMS) for marketing, service, and commerce. Establishes mobile advertising partnerships and leverage marketing channels such as search, affiliate, social media, and existing media relationships to drive customer acquisition.

11. *Campaign Production for Sales & Marketing*

*Typical responsibilities*: Supports the airline's online sales and marketing efforts through the development of promotional content for product, sales and marketing webpages and microsites, both for the airline website and partner sites. Other areas of activities include the production of email campaigns and online sweepstakes. All campaign production efforts require the close coordination with the sales, marketing, and other departments as well as outside third parties.

12. *Web Customer Service (WCS)*

*Typical responsibilities*: Handles web traveler support including travel PNR issues and technical problems that web travelers might experience when interacting with the airline digital properties for shopping and self-servicing. WCS coordinates, and if necessary, escalates any specific support activity with other business departments within airline and/or outside third parties.

13. *Online Travel Agencies (OTAs)*

*Typical responsibilities*: Manages OTAs such as Opodo, Expedia, Priceline, and others relevant for an airline's online sales and marketing. This typically covers contract negotiations for the setting of revenue targets, commission payments to OTA, joint marketing programs and activities, web pricing policies, and performance reporting needs.

*Table 6.3* continued

14. *E-Pricing*

*Typical responsibilities*: Manages pricing and inventory controls for the full suite of airline fare products. Provides pricing and operational support to overall airline online sales strategy. Applies quantitative techniques and systems to drive yield optimization. Increases operational efficiencies, and unlocks new online revenue opportunities. Evaluates profitability and conducts cost/benefit analysis of web exclusive fares, advertising promotions and business partnerships. Delivers analysis and recommendations on inventory allocation, pricing, and systems improvements to management team.

15. *Department Web Championship (DWC)*

*Typical responsibilities*: A department web champion represents a department in the airline and interacts with the e-commerce organization to provide for informational content used for consumer-facing web pages and interactive applications. Being a subject matter expert in a particular functional area, a web champion may also serve as an internal consultant advising and assisting the e-commerce department with managing a particular web issue.

A web champion comes from divisional areas such as Legal, Frequent Flyer Program, Airport Operations, Inflight, PR, Training, and Cargo. A web champion may also be a local employee who represents an international station and serves as a liaison between the airline's head office and local office in e-commerce matters; review of web content translations and input for localized content are common activities.

16. *Copywriting & Editing*

*Typical responsibilities*: Works closely with all company website content owners to create, write, edit, manage, and art-direct website content in applicable languages. This is done in accordance with the airline's website style guide that requires the information on the company's products and services expressed in certain ways. Regular quality checks on the accuracy of website content and follow-up with content owners is required to ensure the adherence to the company's communication standards. Copywriting/editing involves writing copy for direct online marketing campaigns including banner placements, email newsletters, search marketing text, and sweepstakes.

17. *Technology and Commercial Vendors*

*Typical responsibilities*: Vendors are sourced to fulfill specialty skill needs for the development, implementation and maintenance of web technology and business services. Typical technology vendors include site portal developers and internet booking engine providers while digital media agencies, content vendors and translation companies represent the commercial side of vendors.

18. *Contractors and Consultants*

*Typical responsibilities*: Mostly because of insufficient airline inhouse e-commerce expertise and resources, third parties such as contractors and consultants are recruited to provide temporarily or longer term for a wide spectrum of know-how or manpower assistance needed for developing and managing business and technology initiatives.

## 6.7 TOWARD AN IDEAL AIRLINE E-COMMERCE ORGANIZATION

There are fundamentally two approaches to managing e-commerce (Figure 6.3):

- coordinated but separate business and technology/IT departments
- integrated business-technology departments.

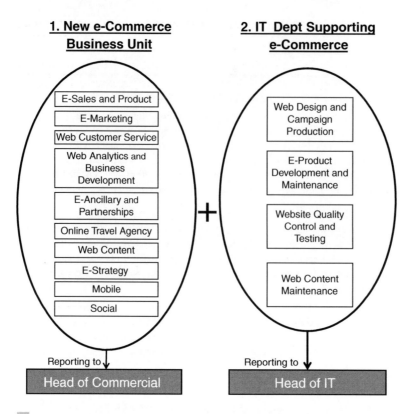

**Figure 6.3a** *Combining "e" and "commerce" into an effective organization: Separated–associated approach*

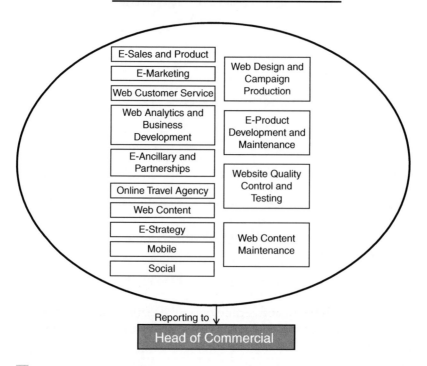

**Figure 6.3b** *Combining "e" and "commerce" into an effective organization: Integrated approach*

In the first scenario, business and technology are both dedicated to support e-commerce but they actually report to different department/division heads in the airline. In this case, business reports to Commercial (Sales/Marketing) and technology to IT. The alignment of e-commerce goals and activities may be a challenge because ownership and responsibility are dispersed among different commercial and technology stakeholders. For e-commerce to be successful with this set up, communication between the department leaderships has to be intensive and frequent. Different reporting relationships do not mean that co-location is not possible. On the contrary, airlines with this e-commerce set-up often accommodate IT and commercial staff in the same office location to improve productivity.

In the second scenario, e-commerce operates as a single unit with a direct reporting line to senior management. This may be a high-ranking person such as a senior vice president. With the integrated approach, business and technology often co-locate and share the same floor in an office building. The advantages of the integrated approach are compelling. There is a better alignment of e-commerce department goals and activities and also faster and more informal communication. All this leads to increased productivity of an airline's e-commerce activities.

In either case, the resources used are *dedicated* to e-commerce and not *shared* with other areas in the airline for offline purposes. This is one key reason that separates a leading e-commerce airline carrier from an e-commerce laggard. Another reason that we have already mentioned is the quality of staffing. Recruiting e-commerce talent that brings digital experience and value to these respective e-commerce units is important if one wants to be among e-commerce leading airlines. Furthermore, drawing on strong commercial and technology support from senior management and pursuing clear goals such as growing online sales and reducing distribution costs are other crucial characteristics of high performing e-commerce organizations.

## 6.8 WHAT IS GOING ON AT AIRLINES?

Airline organizational charts related to e-commerce are typically not disclosed to the public. Some fragmented pieces of information are occasionally available. In order to get some sense of how some airlines organize their e-commerce activities, we have reviewed the social media network linkedin.com as an insightful starting point.

### 6.8.1 Airline e-commerce job titles and responsibilities

A person's job title, accompanied by a brief description, is a good indication of corporate rank and responsibility. Let us start first with the top e-commerce executives at airlines before we elaborate on middle and lower level management. Table 6.4 shows the most senior person in charge of e-commerce at selected airlines.

In acknowledgment of e-commerce's growing importance to their business, some airlines have begun to create top management positions within their corporate hierarchy. Among the legacy carriers, Air Canada was a strong supporter of e-commerce

**Table 6.4** *Selected airline e-commerce titles and responsibilities (2014)*

| Airline | Title of Senior e-Commerce Head | e-Commerce responsibilities | Commentaries |
|---|---|---|---|
| Air Canada | Senior VP e-Commerce + Chief Information Officer | Overseeing company's e-commerce and IT activities | Combination of roles occurred in 2003, reporting to CEO, supported by VP e-Commerce |
| Air France/ KLM | Senior VP e-Commerce | Strategies and policies for e-sales and e-service, acquisitions, social media, and mobile | Created as VP e-Commerce + Distribution at KLM in 2006, upgraded to SVP e-Commerce in 2008 covering both KLM and Air France |
| Aer Lingus | Director IT Enterprise + Network Distribution (combo occurred in Jan 2013, Director Eco since May 2010) | Development/management of software applications and technologies including those supporting AerLingus.com and mobile commerce, CRS–GDS distribution, Call Center, Ancillary Sales, Inflight | Evolved from Director e-Commerce in 2010 to Director Network Distribution, combination of commercial with Director IT Enterprise occurred in 2013 to have single reporting line |
| Alaska Airlines | VP Customer Innovation | Manage cross-functional team that drives customer-facing innovation across e-Commerce, mobile and airport experience | Role was created in Spring 2013 with three direct reports (Managing Director e-Commerce and Distribution, MD Airline Operations Applications, MD Customer Support Systems supporting all customer-facing technology). VP Customer Innovation reports to Chief Financial Officer |
| Delta Airlines | VP e-Commerce | Development/management of delta.com on all digital platforms including website, mobile, kiosk, inflight, and emerging platforms | Reporting to Senior VP Marketing, position was created in 2010 as VP e-Commerce, combined with Marketing in 2012 (this arrangement was apparently dissolved again in 2014). Key person supporting VP is Managing Director e-Commerce |
| Emirates | VP e-Commerce and Mobile | Directly responsible for driving all commercial aspects of the Emirates Airline website and mobile site(s) to maximize online revenue. The remit of the role includes product development, operational stability, all systems related enhancements and sales development | None |

**Table 6.4** *continued*

| Airline | Title of Senior e-Commerce Head | e-Commerce responsibilities | Commentaries |
|---|---|---|---|
| JetBlue | VP Customer Connections, Marketing-Digital, Loyalty, and CSR | Overseeing digital commerce, loyalty marketing (CRM), and Corporate Social Responsibility (CSR) for JetBlue with main responsibility to deepen the relationship with JetBlue customers via smart marketing | Reporting to SVP Marketing and Commercial Strategy |
| LAN Chile | Senior Manager (note: The original Spanish title is "gerente senior") | e-Commerce strategy, e-sales/e-marketing, operations, user experience, branding | None |
| Lufthansa | VP Global Leisure Sales + Online | Global e-Commerce + mobile services | Reporting to SVP Distribution, Product, Marketing, key person supporting VP is Managing Director E-commerce |
| Virgin Australia | Head of e-Commerce | Definition and leading of e-commerce growth strategy, championship of new technologies, e-sales, customer service, database marketing, partnerships | Reporting to Director Sales and Marketing |
| Ryanair | Director Commercial Revenue | Responsibility for the Commercial Revenue and Ancillary Partner portfolio at Ryanair. Managing the Ancillary function at Ryanair to maximize the potential of the biggest travel website in Europe | None |

early on and it established a "SVP e-Commerce" position back in 2003.[22] To find the head of an airline's e-commerce portfolio on such a high senior level was (and still is) unique. Other examples of this set-up include KLM/Air France—it established the "Senior Vice President e-Commerce" position in 2008—and Emirates with a vice president position.

Depending on a company's size and corporate culture, other common titles used are "Director" (Aer Lingus and Air China) or just "Head" (Virgin Atlantic and Virgin Australia). Job titles of e-commerce heads at LCCs are often different. Due to the fact that the large majority of their revenue is generated online and e-commerce has absorbed their organizational structure, they typically do not see a need to specifically label e-commerce in order to separate it from other areas in the company. JetBlue's features the title of "VP Customer Connections, Marketing-Digital, Loyalty, and Corporate Social Responsibility." Ryanair bestows the title of "Director Commercial Revenue" on its top e-commerce executive whose main focus is largely on developing the ancillary revenue potential for ryanair.com. Wizz simply has a "Head of Sales, Marketing, and Communications" responsible for the airline's e-commerce activities.[23]

However, besides the job title, it is crucial to know how many organizational levels exist between the top e-commerce person and the airline senior management C-suite. The e-commerce top manager at Aer Lingus, although "only" carrying the title of a director but reporting directly to a company key person such as the chief financial officer or chief information officer is in a position that may involve more responsibility and decision-making authority than a vice president e-commerce at another airline who is two or three organizational levels away from the executive C-suite.

### 6.8.2 E-Commerce roles: Converging and growing

Some carriers' e-commerce heads hold concurrently two titles. One company applying this dual role concept is Air Canada. When it created the "SVP E-Commerce" position in 2003, it was assumed by the company's chief information officer who has led both areas with a single reporting line to the Air Canada's CEO ever since. Similarly, Aer Lingus' top e-commerce person also holds two titles at the same time: Director of network distribution (this includes among other areas aerlingus.com) and director of IT enterprise applications. This set-up has existed since January 2013[24] and could have been—although a speculative assumption by the author—due to a recommendation by Mr. Montie Brewer. He is the former CEO of Air Canada who was hugely instrumental in guiding Air Canada's e-commerce strategy, and is now a member of Aer Lingus' board of directors.

An airline that manages IT and e-commerce as distinct areas yet puts them under the merged leadership of a single top executive is a good indication that this airline has made technology innovation a crucial part in its e-commerce strategy. Both Air Canada and Aer Lingus are known to be leaders in e-commerce, so their current set-up appears more than justified. The focus on technology innovation in e-commerce is similarly strong at Alaska Airlines, another successful e-commerce pioneer in the airline industry. Although they do not have a single e-commerce person concurrently holding two organizational titles, they decided to create in Spring 2013 a VP position for customer innovations[25] who has three direct reports. These are managing directors each responsible for a unique area including e-sales and distribution, airport operations applications, and customer facing technology.[26] Airlines that value technology innovation highly in e-commerce should look at the symbiotic relationship Air Canada, Aer Lingus, and Alaska Airlines have created organizationally between e-commerce and technology to see if they could benefit from adopting a similar arrangement.

Another important development is the growing portfolio responsibility of top e-commerce executives. They used to be exclusively concerned with e-commerce but more and more airlines accommodate traditional commercial areas under their leadership. Lufthansa Airlines is one example with its "VP Global Leisure Sales + Online." Delta Airlines is another whose head of e-commerce had joined the company in 2010 initially as a VP e-commerce. In 2012, he also became responsible for the marketing portfolio and now carries the title "VP Marketing and Digital Commerce"[27] (this arrangement was apparently dissolved when the VP left Delta for a job at Apple in 2014). It is likely that we will see more of this convergence of roles and responsibilities at other airlines in the future. This is because traditional commercial areas such as sales, marketing, and customer service are becoming increasingly digitized. The door is thus opened to more organizational consolidation and re-orientation toward cyberspace. This should help break down still existing barriers between the two areas and lead ultimately to a more successfully run airline.

### 6.8.3 Mobile, social media, and personalization in airline organizations?

How do mobile, social media, and personalization fit in the organization? When looking at some e-commerce titles, it is noteworthy that some airlines explicitly call out specific digital areas managed by their e-commerce head. An example is the area of mobile e-commerce. The top e-commerce manager at Emirates carries the title "VP E-Commerce and Mobile."[28] Similarly, former USAirways' head of e-commerce was "VP E-Commerce, Mobile, and Distribution."[29] The fact that mobile is separately featured in a job title of a single person is a good indication that it is expected to fulfill similar if not the same sales and marketing objectives an airline pursues with its airline.com website. This answers the question often raised where mobile in an airline organization should report to. Even where "mobile" is not specifically featured in a job title, the tendency seems to be to put it under the same person heading the airline's overall e-commerce activities (see also another example in the snapshot "Lufthansa's Managing Director E-Commerce" on page 495-6).

The situation with social media appears different. There are essentially two approaches to how e-commerce leading airlines manage this area. One group assigns full-time resources to it. An example is KLM operating an organizational entity called social media hub. Staff, including the 130+ people who manage the carrier's global social customer care, are exclusively dedicated to social media. Another group of airlines pursues an "absorption" approach whereby the management of social media is integrated across multiple departments. JetBlue, for instance, has a customer commitment team of 25 people focusing on customer service tweets. At the same time, the airline's corporate communications department, marketing department, and even local customer service/airport staff also manage Twitter.[30]

Notably absent in either of these two organizational models is the area of sales. This is because the contribution of social media to online sales is relatively small when compared to other sources including website, mobile, and even call center. Given that this may also be so in the near future, a position bearing the title of "Social Sales Manager" or "Director—Social Sales" is not likely to appear in many airline organizations any time soon.

E-commerce leading airlines typically involve two types of managers for their handling of social media: The internal leader and the frontline manager. The internal leader is a social media strategist and common tasks include:

■ lobbying for support from senior executives
■ coordinating activities with other departments including legal, marketing, FFP, and corporate communication
■ educating other corporate departments
■ establishing social media goals and policies that support the airline's overall corporate strategy
■ securing and managing resources such as financial and manpower.

The job title for this role can be director or vice president. They are becoming increasingly common in industries such as telecommunications and banking but are still rare at airlines. KLM's social media hub is currently led by a person with a manager title while American Airlines has gone one step further and created a director position to oversee the carrier's social media strategy and communication. Focal points of this job portfolio are responsive customer service and proactive brand engagement and activation.[31]

The frontline manager is involved in the day-to-day management of social media. They:

■ oversee social media staff managing an airline's social customer care
■ are familiar with social media venues including blogs, forums, and networks
■ have in-depth knowledge of the carrier's products and services
■ have great editorial skills and find the right tone of voice for publishing social media content.

Common job titles of staff working on the social media frontline at an airline include social media specialist and social customer service experience manager. KLM makes a point by recruiting its social hub staff from a broad internal base including flight attendants who are highly familiar with direct customer interaction.[32]

For the newly emerging area of personalization, it is unclear yet how airlines are going to organize it. It may evolve as a stand-alone entity within airline organizations (the "personalization team") or be distributed throughout multiple departments. In either case, a carrier that has identified personalization as the next strategic breakout area would have little choice but to engage new and full-time resources for managing it. Where things are possibly heading, at least for larger and more e-commerce savvy airlines, is indicated by Lufthansa. In summer of 2014, they created the position of "VP Personalized Customer Experience" with a staff of 120 people. This portfolio is responsible for harnessing all customer data streams for the carrier and becoming a central hub for data analytics activities and the implementation of personalized products, services, and communication for all digital touchpoints with customers. The senior title of vice president and the full-time resources are all a clear indication of how committed the airline is to improve and personalize the travel experience in the next few years.

One thing is for sure: Designing, building and operating personalization features for thousands if not millions of web travelers globally, across all product lines and internet devices, is not a small undertaking for any airline. One should stay tuned for more announcements and organizational restructurings as they relate to personalization.

### 6.8.4 Organizing e-commerce on the frontline

An airline's e-commerce chief has mid- and high-level executives as their direct reports. For example, at a large carrier, a vice president is supported by someone carrying the title of managing director, senior director, or director. These executives function as the operational heads of the e-commerce department and they often liaise between the top e-commerce executive and the rest of the organization. Generally, they are more visible to the greater workforce than top management. They also spend most of their time developing and implementing strategic action plans needed to achieve the organizational goals set by top management.

The snapshot of Lufthansa's managing director activity profile (this person reports to the VP global leisure sales and online) shows how comprehensive the e-commerce responsibility at a major airline such as Lufthansa is.

---

## SNAPSHOT: LUFTHANSA'S MANAGING DIRECTOR E-COMMERCE

Responsible for online sales, website product development, content management and operations, online travel agency account management, mobile internet, tablet and mobile applications for more than 80 markets worldwide. Management of multi-tiered, international staff of 30 employees (project, marketing, and account managers) with four team managers. Revenue responsibility for €5 billion worldwide. Furthermore, the position:[33]

- oversees global e-commerce strategy and activities for www. lufthansa.com
- runs website development (new functionalities) and operations
- is responsible for mobile strategy and development of mobile services (for mobile internet, apps for tablet and smart phones, etc.)
- oversees mobile commerce push and promotions
- runs account management team for online travel agency sales worldwide
- manages international staff in 70 markets
- covers the managing director position of travel company XP Travel GmbH which runs a dynamic packaging website www.lufthansa-holidays.com

---

- responsible for search engine advertising, search engine optimization, meta-search and affiliate marketing programs
- manages web analytics, test and target (MVT) and session tracking team
- is in charge of UX design and digital costumer journey flows
- coordinates ancillary revenue partners, that is, insurance, hotel and car rentals for digital channels
- includes being a member of the supervisory board at ta.ts GmbH.

Below the organizational layer comprising the e-commerce executives at an airline, we find the frontline level of employees. They are responsible for the day-to-day management of e-commerce. Copy writers, web analysts, programmers, search engine specialists, Q&A testers, and social media customer service agents are just a few of the many jobs one can mention.

In order to obtain some impression of the scale and scope of interaction between e-commerce executives and other people in an airline organization, we take another look at Linkedin. Figure 6.4 shows details for JetBlue as an example with some of

**Figure 6.4** *A Linkedin.com perspective: JetBlue's head of e-commerce interaction with JetBlue employees*

Note: The positions displayed are one to two clicks away from JetBlue's top e-commerce executive (VP customer connections, marketing-digital, loyalty and CSR). The information is based on a profile page section called "people also viewed." The difference in font size reflects the rank in the corporate hierarchy: The smaller the font of a position, the lower the hierarchical position. Excluded were links to external people.[34]

these positions indicating traditional areas such as human resources and FFP marketing while others are purely e-commerce related.

## 6.9 FORMAL AIRLINE E-COMMERCE ORGANIZATION CHARTS

We can also obtain further insight into how airlines organize e-commerce by looking at some specific organizational charts (Figure 6.5). These charts are not evidence of a carrier's operational effectiveness and corporate culture in regards to e-commerce. However, they are insightful snapshots that provide an impression of what is going on with some airlines.

These airlines are considered leaders in e-commerce because their organizations share similar crucial traits including:

■ Smart governance:

- constant communication and interaction via regularly scheduled daily/ weekly meetings between IT and business leaders, supported by informal communication channels
- alignment between different departments' goals and activities, avoidance of vacuums among different stakeholders
- communication lines to senior management are open and good
- co-location of IT and business employees
- e-commerce group viewed as hub that not only drives its own initiatives but also advises, consults, and support other departments in their e-commerce efforts

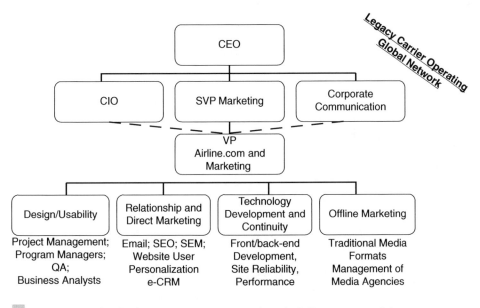

**Figure 6.5** *Selected airline e-commerce organization charts (excluding customer service)*

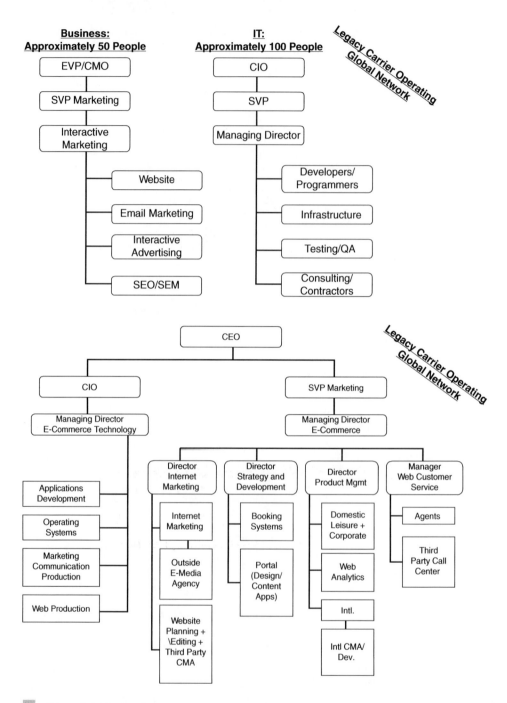

**Business:**
**Approximately 50 People**

- EVP/CMO
  - SVP Marketing
    - Interactive Marketing
      - Website
      - Email Marketing
      - Interactive Advertising
      - SEO/SEM

**IT:**
**Approximately 100 People**

- CIO
  - SVP
    - Managing Director
      - Developers/ Programmers
      - Infrastructure
      - Testing/QA
      - Consulting/ Contractors

*Legacy Carrier Operating Global Network*

- CEO
  - CIO
    - Managing Director E-Commerce Technology
      - Applications Development
      - Operating Systems
      - Marketing Communication Production
      - Web Production
  - SVP Marketing
    - Managing Director E-Commerce
      - Director Internet Marketing
        - Internet Marketing
        - Outside E-Media Agency
        - Website Planning + \Editing + Third Party CMA
      - Director Strategy and Development
        - Booking Systems
        - Portal (Design/ Content Apps)
      - Director Product Mgmt
        - Domestic Leisure + Corporate
        - Web Analytics
        - Intl.
        - Intl CMA/ Dev.
      - Manager Web Customer Service
        - Agents
        - Third Party Call Center

*Legacy Carrier Operating Global Network*

**Figure 6.5** *Continued*

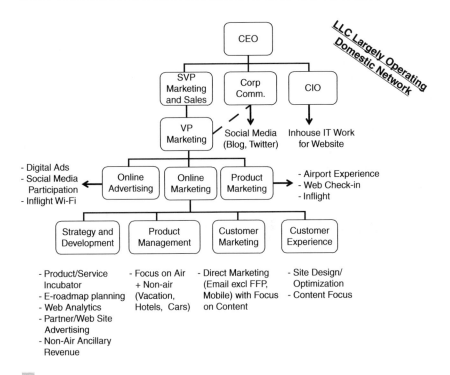

**Figure 6.5** *Continued*

■ Strong e-commerce focus:

— constantly searching for opportunities to "e-enable" transactions online while product/service development and refinement initiatives are always approached with the question "Can we do this online?"
— the website is the primary gateway for sales, marketing, and service
— the strong focus extends to employee communication and task-handling via the company's intranet
— provisioning of sufficient resources (financial, manpower) to execute e-commerce vision.

## 6.10 WHAT IS THE IDEAL DIGITAL LEADERSHIP AT AN AIRLINE?

An airline's growing engagement in e-commerce has implications for the type of talent and leadership needed. Starting at the very top of an airline, a CEO and board of directors do not need to be geeks but should be comfortable with technology and have a clear understanding of the digital landscape and the transition it goes through. This is not only an issue for the airline industry. Even a company such as Starbucks with 54 million Facebook fans globally and its handling of 3 million mobile payments per week has become, according to its CEO Howard Schulz, much more mindful of technology-driven changes in consumer behavior.[35]

A certain savviness when it comes to IT and its business application is helpful. This is especially the case considering that companies with higher IT spending and high IT savviness can achieve 20% higher margins than their competitors.[36] However, only nine companies of the Fortune 500 companies are regarded as being "highly digital" where a CEO and a board of directors have deep digital experience. Those companies, not surprisingly include Amazon, Apple, Microsoft, and Google that are all awash with digital talent.

A closer look at most major legacy airlines reveals that the "digitalness" among their leadership does exist but it is rather thinly sprinkled. This raises the issue whether e-commerce is successful because or despite of senior management experience in the digital area. Airline e-commerce undoubtedly advanced significantly in the early days because of LCC CEOs such as Michael O'Leary (Ryanair), Stelios Haji-Ioannou (easyJet), Herb Kellegher (Southwest), and David Neeleman (JetBlue). They saw ahead of others the internet's potential to build a direct relationship with customers and therefore pushed it forward. Since then, airline e-commerce has gone more mainstream and has become institutionalized. It can run its own course to some extent even though it is not necessarily on the top of the agenda of an airline leader. However, having a digitally savvy leadership benefits the quality of e-commerce strategies and an above-the-average cyberspace competitiveness.

Let us look at some specific cases. For example, there is American Airlines' Thomas Horton who left the company in 2002 to join AT&T as CFO and vice chairman, then returned to American Airlines in 2006 and became CEO and chairman in 2011 until 2014. While in this position, he was also serving on the board of Qualcomm, a leading innovator in wireless technologies and data solutions. Other airline CEOs whose careers comprise significant hands-on digital experience include South African Airways (SAA) CEO Nico Bezuidenhout, who headed the team responsible for South African Airways' foray into e-commerce before and was also responsible for the carrier's LCC subsidiary Mango in 2006 for six years.[37] There is also Willie Walsh, who was instrumental as Aer Lingus' CEO between 2001 and 2004 in reconfiguring Aer Lingus as a LCC and adopting an e-commerce-based business model. Today he is the CEO of the International Airline Group IAG, the parent company of British Airways and Iberia. Other notable leaders under whose support e-commerce expanded with several competitive e-products/services include Cai Jianjiang (chairman of Air China), Tewolde Gebremariam (CEO of Ethiopian Airlines), Temel Kotil (CEO of Turkish Airlines), and Akbar Al Baker (group CEO of Qatar Airways). In a remarkably brief timeframe of a few years, these carriers have all managed to excel in areas such as globalization, mobile commerce, and social media, thus boosting their cyberspace presence ahead of other competitors.

As far as airline boards are concerned, LCCs seem to have assembled more talent that matches their online-focused business models. Take for example John Browett, who was appointed to the board of easyJet in 2007 and who previously served as senior vice president of retail at Apple. He also held a number of executive director positions at UK mass retailer Tesco where he was responsible for running Tesco.com.[38] Likewise, Aer Lingus features several top-level stakeholders including Montie

Brewer, who was appointed to the company's board in 2010. As the former president and CEO of Air Canada, he was the chief architect of the company's online strategy and is a recognized industry innovator in airline pricing and online sales and distribution strategies. He is also serves in board functions with the low cost travel group Allegiant Travel Company and Thayer Venture, a company that creates and develops technology companies for the hospitality industry.[39] Occasionally, one may also witness a situation whereby an LCC executive joins the board of a technology company. An example of this is Kevin Krone, Southwest senior VP and chief marketing officer. In September 2015, he became a board member of Silicon Valley start-up Uplift, an operator of online payment marketing platform.

Another option to tap into e-commerce know-how and advice is through external digital advisory boards (DABs). Thomas Cook took advantage of this external organizational unit to obtain additional guidance for its e-commerce strategy. Under the leadership of the then group CEO Harriet Green, the company instituted in 2013 a team of a dozen e-commerce experts to advise the company on leading-edge digital trends and provide for input in digital strategy matters.[40]

Looking outside the immediate setting of airlines, we find some interesting showcases of digital leadership at the top. Both Fedex and Expedia are good illustrations. Of the 12 FedEx board members, for example, three have a wide-ranging background in the digital world. They include the former president and CEO of Netscape Communications Corporation (a provider of software, services, and website resources to internet users), the chairman of CDW LLC (a provider of technology products and services), and the former chairman, president, and CEO of ITT Corporation (a diversified high-technology engineering and manufacturing company).[41]

Expedia's board of directors features comprehensive expertise from digital media and technology companies. It includes the former non–executive chairman of Amadeus (an IT solutions provider for the travel industry), the chairman of Liberty Media (a mass media company with a heavy presence in cyberspace), and the chairman of FICO (an IT provider of analytics and predictive decision design tools; the chairman also currently serves or has served on other digital company boards including LinkedIn and Netflix).[42] The senior management group at Expedia, referred to as the "Travel Leadership Team," also has a comprehensive understanding of the digital landscape due to its vast experience, ranging from previous work at Microsoft Corporation to various travel start-up companies, Hotwire.com being one of them.[43]

What should an airline do that lacks such digital expertise? As far as a board of directors is concerned, a good starting point is to recruit at least one digital director but ideally two or more to the board. Their insight and experience can strengthen an airline's digitalness. Furthermore, an airline CEO and members of the most senior executive team should look for opportunities to be placed on company boards where exposure to digital business issues is guaranteed. This could include technology companies and travel industry-related companies. "Learning on the job" helps enhance critical knowledge of the digital landscape relevant to the travel space.

For example, as a result of buying a 19% stake in JetBlue in 2009, Lufthansa was entitled to nominate members to the JetBlue board of directors. CEO of LCC German Wings (a subsidiary of Lufthansa) and the Lufthansa management board member responsible for sales, revenue management, and international operations assumed these board seats. It is likely that they have learned and continue collecting insight from one of the airline industry's leaders in online travel that may be of value to their own e-commerce business operations.

## 6.11 THE LEADER OF AIRLINE E-COMMERCE

After our discussion on the ideal leadership at the very top of an airline, let us focus now on the head of an airline's e-commerce business. What kind of digital leader is required to be in a senior position such as VP e-commerce or managing director e-commerce?

A key aspect to remember is that e-commerce is a medium that is in a constant state of flux. Some new "hot technology" comes along all the time. This in turn triggers plenty of integration challenges for an airline. It is therefore advisable to put emphasis in the search for the ideal candidate on individuals that have a proven track record of performing well in conditions of uncertainty. At the same time, taking into account the multiple disciplines e-commerce involves, an experienced consensus builder is required who can diplomatically bridge between the different players and align them for e-commerce. Before embarking on a search to recruit from a talent pool of possible candidates, an airline should check on a few realities to make this process more efficient and effective.

### 6.11.1 Significance of e-commerce for the airline

A clear articulation of what e-commerce means for the airline is key. LCCs/ULCCs such as Ryanair or Spirit Airlines are known to heavily focus on generating ancillary revenue and bringing more of a general retailer's perspective to managing their websites. Their drive for talent and leadership is different from that of a global legacy carrier such as Lufthansa that leans more toward a marketing-based approach in its e-commerce activities. If there is a common thread between these two different types of airlines from an organizational perspective, it is that both look for plenty of functional experts.

The situation is different for an airline where e-commerce still plays a relatively minor role. Assuming that they target e-commerce for growth, they would require a person that leads the build up of this new business area across the airline. The end result may well be a capable e-commerce unit staffed by multiple experts who focus on managing the carrier's online activities.

In all this discussion, not to be neglected is an understanding of how e-commerce impacts employees internally, their interaction with it, and how productivity can be improved. With a better understanding of where an airline currently stands and what it plans to achieve with e-commerce, one could determine the type of expertise needed to add the most value.

### 6.11.2 Understanding the talent trade-off

Demand for talent with an in-depth understanding of technology and business has risen in recent years. However, the supply of qualified candidates in general is still small. This is because e-commerce for the most part is still a relatively new field.[44]

Airlines may need to compromise some of their conventional benchmarks when looking for their candidate. The recruiting process therefore should address what the possible trade-offs are the airline is willing to consider. Among the questions to explore are:

- Is it more important to recruit a person who can manage contemporary "hot" technology or someone with a broad and seasoned understanding of e-commerce?
- Is airline industry experience required or could a person be considered with background from other travel related companies or even non-travel industries that work with e-commerce business models?
- Considering that there are significant differences in how e-commerce is used globally, how crucial is it to hire an individual who understands the diverse international picture when developing and executing e-commerce initiatives in multiple markets?
- With big data becoming an integral part of today's e-commerce activities, how important are analytical skills?
- Is traditional experience that can bridge digital divides critical or is a "digital native" with no prior professional experience in the offline world sufficient?
- Should the candidate have prior leadership experience in the role as a senior manager?

One overarching question deals with whether or not the airline should appoint an internal person or someone from the outside. When choosing an individual from inside the company, it should be someone who has earned the trust and respect of other company veterans. At the same time, this individual should have the ability to pursue a new e-commerce vision and to attract and work with a new breed of managers and vendors who are critical in developing airline e-commerce. Unfortunately, it is not that uncommon to encounter situations where the less ideal person is promoted. This is because of company politics where competence is frequently trumped by loyalty. If an outsider was selected for the e-commerce leadership position, one cannot underestimate the effort that goes into the internal relationship building with key stakeholders including employees and departments. Furthermore, the cultivation of partnerships and distribution relationships, the assessment of employees, and the creation of consensus among the different stakeholders may be more of a challenge than for someone who comes from inside the company.

One comment on the issue of prior airline industry experience. Many top e-commerce executives come from within the airline industry and rise through the ranks at a single or multiple airlines. However, it seems that the number of top e-commerce managers who have built up their e-commerce expertise and honed their online skills in the general retail industry is growing. Taking into account that ancillary revenue has become more important to many carriers, this development is not too surprising. For example, Delta's former top e-commerce executive spent eight years with US retailer Target and managed Target.com, technology services, and distribution before joining Delta.[45] Similarly, Jetblue's VP e-commerce comes from 1-800-Flowers.com where he was responsible for the company's digital marketing activities for eight years.[46]

Regardless if an outsider or someone from within is selected, the chosen individual should be a "tempered radical." This is someone who is able and willing to initiate the changes in increments from the inside or rock the boat without falling out of it.[47] Whatever the answer to each of the above questions is, it allows an airline to focus its search on those candidates who are most in line with the immediate and long-term corporate goals and strategies of the company.

### 6.11.3 Setting the e-commerce leader up for success

The e-commerce leader should have a direct reporting relationship to senior management such as the CEO, president or SVP. It is important for the leader's position that they not only assume the responsibility of steering the airline's e-commerce course but are also provided with sufficient authority to manage. For instance, this means the power to do employee reviews, and with high-level management support, the leader would have the authority to:

- reward successes in the form of job promotion and salary raises
- punish failures including re-assigning or dismissing employees
- direct planning and implementation efforts
- centralize overall the e-commerce initiatives regardless of traditional business unit ownership.

There is often a mismatch between an e-commerce leader's responsibility and authority with too much of the former and too little of the latter. A perfect example is the airline industry's growing adoption of unbundled or à la carte business models. The initiatives to generate new ancillary revenue streams typically originate with departments outside e-commerce with little thought of what the actual implications are when going online. Yet the e-commerce leader/department bears the responsibility for selling, marketing, and servicing these new website features on the airline digital properties. By the same token, even when a match between responsibility and authority exists, one has to be realistic how successful an e-commerce leader can really be. In light of some of the industry's inherent weaknesses of legacy technology such as the 1960-based CRS platforms that have severe limits, what can a leader really accomplish in terms of implementing a merchandizing strategy at a carrier?

### 6.12 CHALLENGES IN THE AIRLINE E-COMMERCE ORGANIZATION

Deciding on the right e-commerce organization and leader is one step, integrating the appropriate structures into an airline and managing them is another. Essentially, the extent of the challenges depends greatly on the legacy of an airline's business

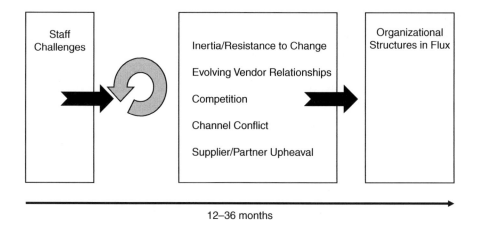

**Figure 6.6** *Challenges for airline e-commerce organizations*

model. The more footprint in the traditional world, the greater the challenges to adjust and adapt. Figure 6.6 illustrates several key challenges from an organizational point of view.

### 6.12.1 Staffing challenges

E-Commerce has changed the nature of work within an airline and several issues require attention.

*The rise of the Chief Marketing Technologist (CMT)*

In tomorrow's airline e-commerce organization, a number of roles that currently do not exist or are in an infant stage, are likely to be increasingly important for a company's competitiveness.

A good example is the role of Chief Marketing Technologist (CMT). In Chapter 3 we have already alluded to the need of airlines to respond organizationally to the growing technology-ization of marketing. Essentially, a CMT, sometimes also labeled as Marketing Business Information Officer, Marketing Technology Manager and Director of Marketing Technology, is responsible for supporting both the front-end and back-end technologies that power an airline's marketing activities. Specifically, a CMT aligns marketing technology with a carrier's business goals. In this capacity, a CMT serves as a technology advisor to a Chief Marketing Officer and other marketing leaders. As an airlines embarks on determining its cyberspace strategy, the CMT determines what technology portfolio could enable it. Furthermore, the CMT also liaises with the company's IT that is typically concerned with the marketing technology's cost efficiency and security. Lastly, a CMT is a key stakeholder in the vetting and selection of technology vendors. Let us not forget that it is not unusual, certainly not for larger carriers, that they use a myriad of marketing technology providers including those for multi-channel marketing automation, media optimization, tracking and analytics. In this regard, the importance of a CMT cannot be emphasized enough in integrating and building marketing technology platforms that constitute a cohesive portfolio. This minimizes if not eliminates the all so typical situation at many airlines where customer data are managed through multiple disconnected platforms.

Some observers consider CMTs as unicorns because it is a challenge to find individuals who are proficient in both technology and marketing. They are rare and likely to be found in technology start-ups and digital media agencies that have sometimes (informal) training programs. If an airline cannot attract an individual from these sources, it could look within its own IT department. There, skilled people may exist who understand the technology and marketing sides, have the ability to explain one side to the other, and are excited to have a front-office impact. One thing seems sure: an airline can poorly afford to move forward in e-commerce without accommodating such a role in its ranks sooner than later.

### Dedicated versus shared staff

The decision of employing dedicated versus shared staff is one of them. Sharing resources looks appealing because it is cost effective but one needs to be careful. A number of studies[48, 49] confirm that laggard companies often manage e-commerce in a shared service fashion. The consequence is that people's effectiveness declines as they are dealing with too many tasks at the same time. It is not only that they may have too many online tasks but it could also be that they are going back and forth between the online and offline world.

E-Commerce is multi-faceted and big business. It should be pursued with dedicated full-time resources. With the deployment of dedicated e-commerce resources being only the first step, the next one should address the strengths of the e-commerce team involved. An airline typically faces a double challenge. On the one hand, it has to train inhouse staff to acquire internet know-how critical for managing the transformation to an e-commerce savvy airline. On the other hand, it has to compete in the marketplace for outside e-commerce talent because it does not exist internally. The latter can be difficult for an airline as the competition for e-commerce talent is fierce and companies outside the airline industry sector generally offer more attractive remuneration and/or more desirable working environments.

### Hiring e-commerce talent

Senior management and the human resource department at an airline need to be careful not to make mistakes often seen with e-commerce laggards. They tend to promote from within and little attention is paid to someone's know-how and experience in e-commerce. "Learning on the job" is really not optimal if the goal is to seriously build up a company's e-commerce business. Senior managers involved in appointing an employee to a key e-commerce position should know that the lack of relevant experience, strength, and knowledge to manage a technology-business crossover area can backfire very quickly and cause the e-commerce performance at an airline to be weak.

Leading e-commerce airlines typically apply an exhaustive screening process. This is sometimes done with the help of a headhunter in order to source and select candidates with the right background. An e-commerce organization is only as good as the weakest link in its staff chain. If this means looking outside the airline industry and offering remuneration above the airline's average pay scale in order to hire a suitable candidate, then an airline should seriously consider this.

One of the areas where future staffing will be key is digital data management. Larger carriers are likely to attract talent in this area because, among other things, they have large resources to afford premium compensation. They also offer great opportunities for career advancement. For small- and medium size airlines, the attraction of digital data savvy talent is going to be a big challenge. Without it, they will face increasing difficulty in being an effective player in cyberspace and the digital divide between them and larger airlines is likely to widen.

On a related note, at Google, hiring talent is considered one of the most important things to do and interviewing is something literally everybody is involved with. This is very different from the 20th-century approach where hiring is done in a hierarchical fashion and a recruiting manager decides who gets the job. Google has established a trusted-interviewer program with an elite team of people who excel at interviewing and like to do it. Among other things, participating in this program also means receiving a higher score in performance reviews. In other words, not interviewing in the company is actually seen as a punishment.[50]

*Retaining e-commerce staff*

Training and recruiting staff for today's and tomorrow's e-commerce challenge is crucial. However, retaining staff mid- to long-term is also a key issue. With the marketplace being highly competitive for e-commerce talent, airlines need to be pro-active in providing for a meaningful environment in which e-commerce positions are designed and offer career opportunities. Airline e-commerce organizations with poor prospects for career advancement, limited decision authority, traditional, hierarchical structures, and low senior management support will not be an attractive place to stay longer term.

We need to remember that the digital era is increasingly populated by the millennial generation. By 2025, around 75% of the available workforce is estimated to come from this group.[51] They have different perceptions and expectations than those of older generations. For example, they are quite flexible and adaptive to new environments and they are at ease with technology (especially mobile technology and thus could be more open to working from home or non-office environment). Moreover, they are generally more self-sufficient, expect an open and cooperative workplace and want their bosses to be trustworthy, approachable, and respectful. A traditional top-down managerial style is certain to clash.[52]

### 6.12.2 Other challenges for an airline e-commerce organization channel: dis- and re-intermediation

Legacy business models and the deep history in offline selling via third party intermediaries are key reasons why some airlines have not been able to adopt e-commerce with greater success. The organizational structures supporting the traditional sales activities at these carriers had been growing into sizeable and powerful entities over the years, hence any adjustment to them is a challenge. From their perspective, the internet spelled erosion in corporate power and channel conflict because the established offline sales and distribution system were no longer as important. This in turn gave rise to confusion and even fear of how to manage this new situation. It is in this context where some of the seeds of a digital divide in airlines are found.

Questions such as "How much channel displacement?" and "Over what time-frame?" are delicate because the answers to them obviously have consequences to whatever the existing organizational structure is. This was true then (and probably still is for some traditional carriers) when it came to managing the business transformation from an offline-based sales and distribution system to an airline website. Today, this still applies, considering the discussions within airlines regarding the shift of e-commerce from the website to mobile platforms and the impact of social media and big data.

*Contribution of e-commerce*

The recognition of e-commerce as a source of contribution and value to the business is still mixed with some airlines. Although an airline's digital properties have emerged to become crucial venues to manage sales, marketing, and customer service, a number of carriers do not recognize e-commerce in its own right: that is treated as a distinct profit center. Instead, they see e-commerce as one of many pieces in the sales/marketing/customer service puzzle. With e-commerce permeating all aspects of an airline's business, this may be the natural default. However, from the perspective of justifying current and future investments in e-commerce as well as acknowledging e-commerce's strategic importance, a different vantage point is necessary.

*Competition*

Pressure to adopt new organizational structures does not only come from established competitors such as other traditional airlines that are gearing up for a larger role for e-commerce or from LCCs that have integrated e-commerce well into their organizations. Companies that have joined the online travel space in various shapes and forms include marketing and technology-savvy companies such as Amazon, Apple, Facebook, and Google. Their smart and nimble way of doing business continues exerting pressure on airlines to review and adjust their organizational structures to be better. This pressure can only grow as more companies of this cyberspace caliber enter the race. Amazon, just having launched its hotel booking platform in spring 2015, is a more recent example.

*Evolving vendor relationships*

Internet vendor relationships remain in a state of flux for airlines. Completely new skills are needed to manage a web presence and existing vendors in some cases do not have what it takes. An airline thus deals with a host of new specialty internet service firms and dependency on them is higher than on traditional partners due to the growing complexity of e-commerce coupled with a lack of sufficient inhouse expertise and/or resources.

## 6.13 THE FUTURE OF AIRLINE E-COMMERCE ORGANIZATIONS

E-commerce organizations are likely to need more and better resources. Adequate staffing levels, employees with relevant e-commerce skills, and sufficient financial funding for areas such as IT, marketing, sales, and service will be important ingredients for successfully managing the ever-growing complexity of an airline's web presence. Already today, many airlines are challenged with integrating the new demands and requirements of social media and mobile applications into their organizational structures. Without the right resource support, this situation will only worsen.

Also, as emphasized at the beginning of this chapter, a "one-size-fits-all" organization does not exist and re-organizations as well experimentations among airlines with new structural set-ups are likely to continue. A centralized approach with an e-commerce hub appears to be effective—at least for now—in developing online standards and methodologies, building skill sets and know-how, and providing for focus. Nevertheless, this should not preclude an airline from trying out other organizational variations that may be more suitable tomorrow. It is essential not to cast current organizational structures in stone and to remember that agility and speed are key traits of leading e-commerce carriers. In this regard, four organizational issues are discussed below that could become more relevant when moving forward:

- the rise of workplace diversity
- the emergence of hyperarchies
- the role of tiger teams
- the value of the synchronized organization.

### 6.13.1 The rise of workplace diversity

Airline e-commerce organizations are likely to face a rise in workplace diversity. Where is this development coming from? First, in today's age of technology ubiquity and the internet always on and accessible from anywhere anyhow, work is less and less defined by a physical place but rather by something that people do. The future airline e-commerce organization will thus be much more "offsite" than today due to the growing number of alternatives available for employees to do their work from other locations. This means working from home, public sites, and even co-working space where a person works in an office with other people usually not employed by the same organization. Based on one estimate, corporate employees account for 15% of the total co-working space population in the world.[53]

These offsite trends are driven by several factors:

- Companies' interest in reducing their cost from owning/renting office assets.
- Growing regulatory requirements. Take for example the United States's Telework Enhancement Act of 2010, which mandates all federal agencies to establish teleworking policies and procedures for employees.
- Employees having higher demand for more flexible work policies.
- Telecommuting becoming more popular and in the United States, for example, it has been growing from home and public sites between 2010 and 2012 from 18% and 5% to 27% and 12%, respectively.[54] JetBlue is active in this area and currently has around 1,800 home-based call center agents in Salt Lake City while the majority of its new call center in Orlando, Florida, also work from home.[55]
- The rise of mobile computing via devices including smart phones, tablets, and soon wearable computers that employees can use to manage their work, undoubtedly also contributes to the future airline e-commerce organization becoming more offsite. In 2015, approximately 55% of airline personnel used a smart phone for work tasks while the share related to tablets was 20%. This is set to increase, especially for tablets due to their larger screen size. Smart phones will still be the dominant mobile device of employees by 2018 (their share is 73%) but tablets are predicted to almost double to 39%.[56]

In order to obtain a better idea in what specific company areas airline employees use tablets, let us take a closer look at Figure 6.7. Aircraft maintenance is the principal area where over 50% of staff used tablets in 2015. This is followed by the usage of tablets in the aircraft cabin with around 30%. Over the next years, customer-facing areas are expected to attract the highest investment with tablets. For instance, by 2018, the deployment of tablets in the aircraft will increase to almost 70%.

Besides minimizing paperwork, primary use of tablets is to obtain key information about travelers and thereby improve, even personalize, the service for them. JetBlue, for instance, issued over 3,500 mini iPads for its flight staff to not only handle Apple Pay inflight payments but also use them to locate frequent fliers or those passengers celebrating their birthday. Another example of this type of tablet application is Dutch LCC Transavia. In spring 2015, they announced the introduction of "Connected Crew." In conjunction with an air-fi box installed on all the carrier's aircraft, this tablet-based solution enables the cabin crew to manage on-board sales, obtain detailed insight on passengers, and provide access to relevant manuals and forms that are stored on the tablet. Connected Crew allows passengers to use their own personal devices and interact with the crew such as when ordering beverages.[57]

On the ground, check-in/bag-drop areas, lounges, and boarding will also see an increased use of tablets by airline staff. Around 50% of airlines plan to have agents equipped with tablets to assist travelers.

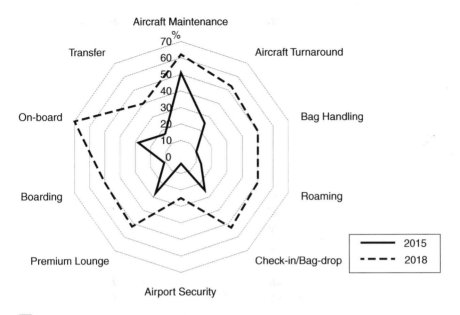

**Figure 6.7** *The growing use of tablets by customer-facing airline staff*

*Source:* SITA (2015)[58]

Another reason why workplace diversity is growing is because of changing demographics at work. Employees from Generations Y (the Millennials) and Z are now filling the ranks at workplaces and they have different perceptions and expectations when compared with older peers about how things should be managed. They are technically savvy, more self-sufficient, look for immediate feedback from supervisors on their performance, and expect to be engaged. They furthermore fuel largely the BYOD (Bring your own device) trend. This means they purchase their own computer devices for work-related activities and install "renegade" unsupported work-related software on their devices.[59] Future airline organizations will come under increasing pressure to manage this new proliferation of hard- and software and find a middle ground between accommodating this trend and enforcing certain corporate policy standards at the same time.

### 6.13.2 The emergence of hyperarchies and the end of hierarchies

When reviewing formal airline e-commerce organization charts, we know that they are an abstraction of organizational set-ups airlines have chosen for themselves at a particular point in time. These charts are hierarchical and the question is whether the interaction between the different areas and people is as formal and orderly as hierarchies typically imply if not even dictate. The answer is increasingly no. This is because companies have been moving away (the airline industry is not unique in this) from centralized, monolithic organizational models to more distributed, more modular network-type organizational structures for some time.

In his book *Company Men*, Anthony Sampson already observed in the early 1990s that computers would destroy bureaucracy. Moreover, computers would not only change the way of doing business in existing companies but also create a new type of company, run by "irreverent youngsters with no respect for structures or loyalties and who thrive on apparent anarchy or near chaos."[60] Steve Jobs, when founding Apple, is on record for having said that he wanted his company to model a "liberated" company.

Airlines applying old organizational designs that rely on a top-down centralized hierarchy are in an increasingly difficult position to cope with the new business age and dynamics that we witness today. At the core of the digital era are speed and adoption. This is where the old designs fail since they work with multiple layers in hierarchical pyramids that slow things down. A new structure that captures well what is going on is the so-called hyperarchy. A hyperarchy is characterized by stripped away formality and procedures, unprecedented information transparency, high-speed communication and decision-making, and networks that are constantly forming and dispersing relationships. Gone are the days when power and rich information are asymmetrically concentrated at the top of companies and an organization had only a few connections with the external environment.

Hyperarchies are said to challenge hierarchies, whether of logic or power, with the possibility (or threat) of multi-random access from anywhere (in- and outside the company) and information symmetry.[61] The growing importance of social media and mobile applications for customers and employees alike will only add further pressure on hierarchies to adopt a more hyperarchical approach toward organizing e-commerce and airlines are not exempted from this. This decentralized, flatter structure certainly looks more chaotic (Figure 6.8) but one should not be mistaken: It is a more self-sufficient environment where many more people have access.

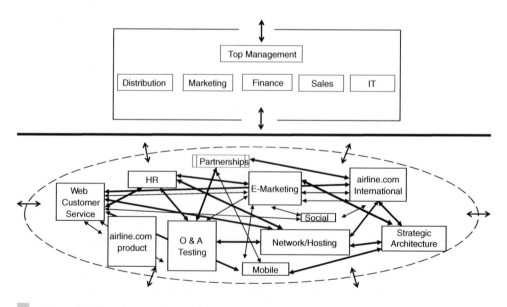

**Figure 6.8** *Hierarchy versus hyperarchy*

The collective and rapid learning and pursuit of solutions with hyperarchies is much better supported. The proportion of senior executives in relation to other employees is much smaller when compared with traditional hierarchies. Additionally, the accountability of the individual is high since the possibility of hiding in a hierarchical structure is limited. At the same time, it is typically backed by leadership and management principles that thrive on less rules and standardizations, wider spread of strategic thinking among employees, and more individual/risk taking decisions.[62]

A hyperarchy distributed network organization stands a better chance of spotting new opportunities for a company and manage more effectively any transformation required.

### 6.13.3 Tiger teams: Nucleus for network-based hyperarchies?

In essence, a team is a group of individuals with complementary skills who work together to achieve a common goal. Each team member has different capabilities, yet they collaborate to perform tasks. Many organizations are now using teams more frequently to accomplish work because they seem to be capable of performing at a level higher than individual employees. Additionally, teams tend to be more successful when tasks require speed, innovation, integration of functions, and a complex and rapidly changing environment.

A team can feature a team leader, who is sometimes called a project manager, a program manager, or task force leader. This person manages the team by acting as a facilitator and catalyst. They may also engage in work to help accomplish the team's goals. Some teams do not have leaders, but are self-managed instead. Members of self-managed teams hold each other accountable for the team's goals and manage one another without the presence of a specific leader.[63]

Tiger teams started out in the military and the field of computer security. They are specially assembled groups who were traditionally tasked with testing the effectiveness of an organization's ability to protect assets by attempting to circumvent, defeat or otherwise thwart the organization's internal and external security.[64] In recent years, the tiger team concept has spilled over into the business world. Tiger teams are used to tackle complex problems a company faces in a very tight timeframe and implement an effective solution at multi-dimensional levels including process, technical, and human.

A tiger team has an intensive focus. All of its members and not just the leader are extremely action oriented, and they are expected to think outside the box and even to break the rules in problem analysis and decision-making. The team members come from multiple disciplines and are chosen for mainly three reasons: Their talent as subject matter experts, their soft skills to handle high-performance meetings and consensus building, and their ability to arrive at solutions fast.

An airline looking into the deployment of tiger teams as an integral part of its approach to organize e-commerce in the future could do an experiment first in order to find out the pluses and minuses of this organizational concept. An example could be a mobile application on a tablet such as the iPad that the airline wants to launch rapidly as part of its mobile offerings. A cross-functional team could be assembled that is organized around the customer interaction touchpoint, in this case the tablet.

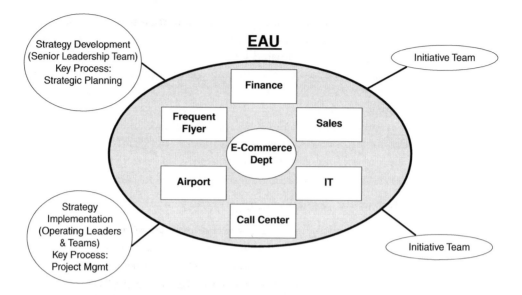

**Figure 6.9** *The tiger team operating as an e-commerce acceleration unit (EAU)*

Figure 6.9 shows a tiger team in the form of an e-commerce acceleration unit (EAU) made up of representatives from seven different departments. It interacts with representatives from other groups including those who have actually initiated the project and those in charge of strategic planning and implementation.

If enough pros from such as an experiment outweigh the cons, an airline could consider ramping up the scale and use multiple teams simultaneously and/or constitute the tiger team concept as a permanent feature in the organization. For an airline that intends to be on top of seizing new opportunities in the marketplace, either scenario is quite conceivable. The larger question is whether the tiger team concept could actually lay the foundation for a more network-based, hyperarchical organization.

An illustrative example of a company using a cross-functional team to embark on an enterprise-wide transformation initiative is Emirates. In October 2015, Emirates Group (this comprises Emirates Airlines and dnata, a supplier of various flight related services) announced the creation of an Enterprise Change Management team. Its task: to help lay the foundation for driving cross functional change throughout the entire organization and achieving the goal to provide customer-centric, personalized offerings on an unprecedented scale. New technologies and ideas including big data, predictive analytics, artificial intelligence, machine learning, robotics, crowd sourcing and collaboration would be all areas the company would consider to achieve its goal and become a leader in the industry. At the time of the announcement, Emirates was engaged in a global search for a candidate to lead this team.[65]

Considering that tiger teams have typically a narrow mission, they are small in size, they dissolve when the mission is accomplished, and their members are appointed/directed by other members of the hierarchy, the answer would have to be no. However, we would have one big EAU or the closest thing to a network-based hyperarchy characterized by speed, focus, and nimbleness if the following conditions existed to manage the airline's e-commerce activities:

- A tiger team that comprises a significant number, say more than 50%, of the organization's employees.
- A tiger team that does not expire but exists as an integral part of the organization.
- A tiger team whose members interact with each other without directions from the hierarchy and form/dissolve relationships as needed.

### 6.13.4 The synchronized airline e-commerce organization: Organizing from the outside in

We have already alluded to the organizational and technological silos that often exist at airlines. Resulting from different product/service lines, geographies, organizational entities, business processes, and IT systems, we find well-defined walls that separate customer-facing channels from each other. The phone is generally handled by the call center, emails are the domain of the customer relations and frequent flyer departments, the e-commerce department manages the airline's website, social media often fall into the Marketing/PR department, and face-to-face encounters with customer service representatives (CSRs) occur at an airline's city ticket/airport ticket office (CTO/ATO).

From the perspective of a web traveler, however, the interaction with an airline is not channel based but experience centered. It is actually not uncommon for an individual web traveler to use multiple channels, often even for the same one transaction. An organizational structure that is channel based diminishes a company's ability to interact with a web traveler on a consistent and seamless basis across different touchpoints. The area of customer service is particularly known for its fragmentation and we have discussed this already at length in the web customer service chapter.

The question is whether an airline structure that is organized around functional areas could be more effective in delivering a unified customer experience to web travelers. The answer may lie in the adoption of a synchronized airline e-commerce organization. In this set-up, the customer interaction between the airline and web traveler is decoupled from the channel. Communication and transaction handling underlie the areas of marketing, sales, and customer service where the airline and web traveler interact with each other. If these three areas are structured in a more channel agnostic way and decoupled from particular channels, the web travelers could experience more consistency in their communication and transaction handling with the airline. This would be made possible by deploying an IT infrastructure and business processes that disperse product/service and web traveler data to all stakeholders in the airline and not just to a few isolated units. Furthermore, the various customer interaction channels would be supported by different disciplines such as marketing, sales, service, and IT on a shared basis. They in turn are maintained by a corporate, comprising areas such as HR, purchasing, R&D, and finance (Figure 6.10). Even in this synchronized organization, the deployment of tiger teams is feasible.

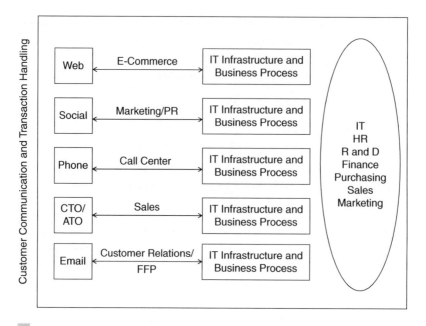

**Figure 6.10a** *From the uncoordinated organization…*

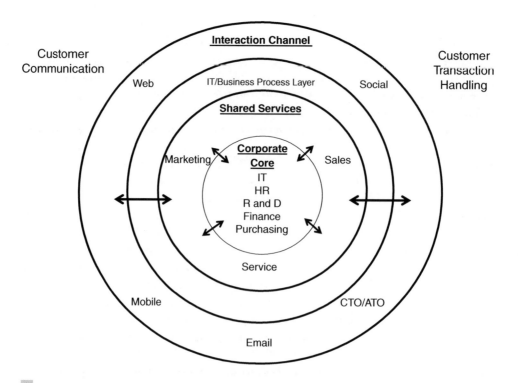

**Figure 6.10b** *…to the synchronized organization*

Lastly, it is important to recognize that the combined effect of an increased workplace diversity, emergence of hyperarchies, more team-oriented collaboration among employees, and the "outside in" perspective for working processes will also alter the design of the future office environment. We have already seen a glimpse of this when we discussed earlier in the chapter how United Airlines had intentionally incorporated a different office layout and design for its new e-commerce entity in 1998 in order to capture the increased efficiency and effectiveness of a dotcom start-up environment.

More airline e-commerce organizations could find themselves in companies with environmentally friendly new office designs featuring wide open office space to encourage collaboration, mobile working stations, and different office set-ups for work versus play. The large majority of airlines will not have the luxury to build a new corporate head office from scratch—unlike companies such as Facebook and Apple that incorporate all the relevant features in their new state-of-the-art headquarters. A less expensive alternative would be what the global design firm Gensler describes as the "hacking of buildings," which involves the alteration of existing office buildings[66] for the new office environment of the 21st century.[67]

### 6.13.5 The beginning of the end of airline e-commerce organizations?

In closing, whatever people and organizational entity are involved in e-commerce at an airline, they will continuously change and not stand still. This is the result of e-commerce's ongoing evolution in terms of touch point expansion with web travelers, proliferation of new internet connected devices, and demands by web travelers and next generation employees. It is very likely that it will take most airlines, certainly the legacy carriers, beyond the year 2020 until they have fully integrated e-commerce in their organizations and feature an e-commerce culture. This integration could take an extreme form in the sense that it is fully embedded in the airline's organization and as such ceases to exist as a separate organizational entity.

This brings us back to the absorption scenario described earlier whereby e-commerce is present across all areas of the organization. The corporate e-commerce literacy in this situation is high and all areas of the airline are e-commerce savvy. This is because e-commerce skills and talent are organizationally distributed as opposed to siloed in a particular area. LCCs to some extent are already at this stage while legacy airlines have still some way to go to organize e-commerce now and moving forward.

## NOTES

1  Lynch, J. (1984) *Airline Organizations in the 1980s*. New York, NY: St Martin's Press, p. 8.
2  Ibid.
3  Coleman, Z. and Morgan, G. (2000) "Qantas, Telstra enter online alliance set to generate $580 million in revenue," www.wsj.com/articles/SB965894480234686470 (accessed March 28, 2015).

4  Lufthansa (1999) "Lufthansa investor info including traffic figures December 1999," http://investor-relations.lufthansagroup.com/fileadmin/downloads/en/financial-reports/traffic-figures/Lufthansa/1999/LH-Investor-Info-1999-12-e.pdf (accessed March 28, 2015).

5  Flyertalk Forum (2001) "Media advisory – Air Canada News conference today on Destina.ca," www.flyertalk.com/forum/air-canada-aeroplan/17156-destina-ca.html (accessed September 3, 2013).

6  Coleman, Maurice (2005) "reGaining control of distribution and costs," Aer Lingus Presentation, EyeForTravel, Travel Distribution Summit USA, Chicago.

7  Christensen, C.M. (1997) "Managing disruptive technological change," in *The Investor's Dilemma: When New Technologies Cause Great Firms To Fail*. Boston, MA: Harvard Business Press, pp. 186–189.

8  Ibid.

9  Ibid.

10  Ibid.

11  Ibid.

12  Ibid.

13  Chaffey, D. (2009) *E-business and E-commerce Management: Strategy, Implementation and Practice*. Harlow, UK: FT Prentice Hall, p. 444.

14  ATPCO Conference (2005) Conversation with Delta Distribution Manager at conference in Miami in Spring 2013.

15  LinkedIn (2015) "Delta VP of ecommerce and marketing profile," www.linkedin.com (accessed March 28, 2015)

16  Johnson, C. et al. (2011) "eBusiness teams reorganize…again," www.forrester.com/eBusiness+Teams+Reorganize++Again/fulltext/-/E-res60918 (accessed August 3, 2014).

17  Bodine, K. (2006) "The people who make great web sites," www.forrester.com/home/ (accessed March 3, 2013).

18  Millman, G. (2008) "KLM's IT makeover," www.accenture.com/SiteCollectionDocuments/PDF/OutlookPDF_CaseStudy_02.pdf (accessed April 8, 2015).

19  Spencer, S. (2013) "The evolving role of the chief sales officer in an e-commerce era," www.spencerstuart.com/research-and-insight/the-evolving-role-of-the-chief-sales-officer-in-an-e-commerce-era (accessed May 23, 2014).

20  Johnson et al. "eBusiness teams reorganize…again."

21  Lutz, J. (2007) "Nicht jeder Chief ist ein Häuptling," www.handelsblatt.com/unternehmen/management/inflationaere-titelvergabe-nicht-jeder-chief-ist-ein-haeuptling/2896008.html (accessed March 28, 2015).

22  Fournel, L. (2013) "Putting IT at the center of customer experience," www.straighttalkonline.com/cio-articles/putting-it-center-customer-experience (accessed March 28, 2015).

23  Korn/Ferry International (2013) "Head of marketing, sales and communications," www.ekornferry.com/library/Process.asp?P=OpportunityandS=FL749 (accessed March 28, 2015).

24  LinkedIn.com (2015) "Ronan Fitzpatrick: Director of IT Enterprise Applications at Aer Lingus," www.linkedin.com/pub/ronan-fitzpatrick/8/99b/821 (accessed March 28, 2015).

25  PR Newswire (2013) "Alaska Airlines creates customer innovation department to make flying easier," www.prnewswire.com/news-releases/alaska-airlines-creates-customer-innovation-department-to-make-flying-easier-203408481.html (accessed March 28, 2015).

26  Customers.com (2012) "Managing customer innovation at Alaska Airlines," www.customers.com/articles/managing-customer-innovation-alaska-airlines/ (accessed March 2013).

27  LinkedIn.com (2015) "Bob Kupbens: VP, online retail," www.linkedin.com/in/bobkupbens (accessed March 28, 2015).

28  LinkedIn.com (2015) "Bob Kabli: Vice President E-Commerce and Mobile (Commercial) at Emirates Airline," www.linkedin.com/pub/bob-kabli/7/456/b67 (accessed March 28, 2015).

29  PR Newswire (2013) "US Airways names John Gustafson vice-president ecommerce, mobile, and distribution," www.prnewswire.com/news-releases/us-airways-names-john-gustafson-vice-president-ecommerce-mobile-and-distribution-187772781.html (accessed November 2, 2014).

30  Kolowich, L. (2014) "Delighting people in 140 characters: An inside look at JetBlue's customer service success," http://blog.hubspot.com/marketing/jetblue-customer-service-twitter (accessed May 3, 2015).

31  Social Chorus (2013) "Interview with industry leaders: Interview with Jonathan Pierce, Director Social Media Strategy American Airlines," www.socialchorus.com/interviews-with-industry-leaders-jonathan-pierce-director-of-social-media-american-airlines/ (accessed May 12, 2015).

32  Socialbakers (2013) "How KLM achieves such stellar success on social media," www.socialbakers.com/blog/1873-how-klm-achieves-such-stellar-success-on-social-media (accessed May 13, 2015).

33  LinkedIn.com (2013) "Marcus Casey: Vice President Personalized Customer Experience at Lufthansa," www.linkedin.com/in/marcuscasey (accessed September 9, 2013).

34  Linkedin.com (2015) "LinkedIn," www.linkedin.com/ (accessed March 31, 2015).

35  Weill, P. and Ross, J.W. (2009) *IT Savvy: What Top Executives Must Know to Go From Pain to Gain*, Boston, MA: Harvard Business Press.

36  Haggerty, N. (2012) "On becoming an IT savvy CEO," http://iveybusinessjournal.com/topics/leadership/on-becoming-an-it-savvy-ceo#.UjSfus3D85s (accessed March 28, 2015)

37  Sabela, Z. (2013) "Mango CEO takes over the reins at SAA," www.destinyconnect.com/2013/02/12/mango-ceo-takes-over-the-reins-at-saa-2013-02-12/ (accessed March 28, 2015).

38  EasyJet PLC (2013) "Board of directors: John Browett," http://corporate.easyjet.com/about-easyjet/our-management/board-of-directors.aspx?sc_lang=en (accessed March 28, 2015).

39  Bloomberg Business (2015) "Executive profile: Montie R. Brewer," http://investing.businessweek.com/research/stocks/people/person.asp?personId=8054908andticker=ALGTandpreviousCapId=3040180andpreviousTitle=AER%20LINGUS%20GROUP%20PLC (accessed March 28, 2015).

40  ThomasCook.com (2013) "Thomas Cook Group PLC digital advisory board," www.thomascook.com/press-centre/digital-advisory-board-1-march-2013/ (accessed March 28, 2015).

41  FedEx (2013) "Corporate governance: board of directors," http://archive.today/pXP67 (accessed March 28, 2015).

42  Expedia, Inc. (2015) "Executive leadership," www.expediainc.com/directors.cfm (accessed March 28, 2015).

43  Ibid.

44  Brown, A. and Helms, F. (2013) "The evolving role of the chief sales officer in an e-commerce era," www.spencerstuart.com/research-and-insight/the-evolving-role-of-the-chief-sales-officer-in-an-e-commerce-era (accessed March 28, 2015).

45  LinkedIn.com, "Bob Kupbens: VP, online retail."

46  LinkedIn.com (2015) "Michael S. Stromer: VP Digital and Loyalty Marketing, JetBlue Airways," www.linkedin.com/in/michaelstromer (accessed March 28, 2015).

47  Harvard Business Review (2002) "Turning an industry inside out: A conversation with Robert Redford," https://hbr.org/2002/05/turning-an-industry-inside-out-a-conversation-with-robert-redford (accessed November 4, 2014).

48 Johnson, C. (2008) "Taking the pulse of ebusiness organizations," www.forrester.com/Taking+Th e+Pulse+Of+eBusiness+Organizations/fullt ext/-/E-RES47594 (accessed July 23, 2012).

49 Mulpuru, S. et al. (2007) "Dissecting high performing ebusiness organizations," www.forrester. com/Dissecting+HighPerforming+eBusiness+Organizations/fulltext/-/E-res43684 (accessed October 30, 2014).

50 Schmidt, E. (2014) *How Google Works*. New York: Hachette Book Group, pp. 115–118.

51 Halverson, C. (2013) "Understanding "Gen Y's" workplace expectations," http://wheniwork. com/understanding-gen-ys-workplace-expectations/ (accessed March 28, 2015)

52 Ibid.

53 Belissent, J. (2013) "Forrester: CIOs need to support the workplace of the future now," www. computerweekly.com/news/2240185321/Forrester-CIOs-need-to-support-the-workplaces-of-the-future-Now (accessed March 28, 2015).

54 Ibid.

55 Amachchi, N. (2013) "JetBlue launches Orlando call center for bilingual support," www. nearshoreamericas.com/jetblue-launches-call-center-orlando-support-latam-operation/ (accessed March 28, 2015).

56 SITA (2015) "2015 SITA Airline IT trends survey," www.sita.aero/globalassets/docs/surveys--reports/airline-it-trends-survey-2015.pdf (accessed June 30, 2015).

57 Future Travel Experience (2015) "Transavia plans roll-out of tablets to empower crew," www. futuretravelexperience.com/2015/03/transavia-plans-roll-out-of-tablets-to-empower-cabin-crew/ (accessed April 3, 2015).

58 SITA (2015) "2015 SITA Airline IT trends survey."

59 Belissent, "Forrester: CIOs need to support the workplace of the future now."

60 Sampson, A. (1995) *Company Men: The Rise and Fall of Corporate Life*, New York: Simon and Schuster, pp. 89–91.

61 Evans, P.B. and Wurster, T.S. (1997) *Strategy and the New Economics of Information*, Boston, MA: Harvard Business Review.

62 Werner, C. (1998) *Unternehmenskultur und betriebliche Strukturen. Darstellung der Gestaltungsmöglichkeiten und Anwendung der Analyse auf die Lean Production*, Lohmar, Germany: Broschiert, pp. 31–33.

63 Simmering, M. (2006) "Management levels," www.referenceforbusiness.com/management/Log-Mar/Management-Levels.html (accessed March 28, 2015).

64 Mackin, D. (2011) "TEAMING: Tiger teams – the new frontier of teaming," http:// newdirectionsconsulting.com/leadership-engagement/tiger-teams-the-new-frontier-of-teaming-2/ (accessed March 28, 2015).

65 Future Travel Experience (2015) "Emirates transformation initiative to explore big data, predictive analytics, artificial intelligence, machine learning and robotics," http://www.futuretravelexperience. com/2015/10/emirates-group-announces-major-transformation-initiative/?utm_source=Futu re+Travel+Experience+Newsletter&utm_campaign=e365475556-fte_otg_nl_221015&utm_ medium=email&utm_term=0_c306aa3edf-e365475556-89609589 (accessed December 13, 2015).

66 Lagorio-Chafkin, C. and Cutrone, C. (2013) "World's coolest offices of the future," www.inc. com/worlds-coolest-offices/future-offices.html (accessed March 28, 2015).

67 Cruz, J. (2014) "'Hacked' offices: The future of workplace design?" www.archdaily.com/466904/ saving-north-america-s-office-spaces-by-hacking-them/ (accessed March 28, 2015).

# Chapter 7

# Airline e-commerce
# strategy

If you fail to plan, you plan to fail.

Benjamin Franklin

## 7.1 AIRLINE E-COMMERCE STRATEGY: DEFINITION
## AND NECESSITY

Strategy is about how an organization will move forward. It essentially involves an analysis of a situation to determine what is going on and what needs to be done. For an airline, it means to:

- assess its position on e-commerce in relation to internal needs, processes, and resources and to factors in the external environment
- establish a mission and goals for airline e-commerce
- apply organizational support through people and processes
- implement changes including those related to processes and behaviors.

Is strategy for airline e-commerce necessary? The answer is yes because it enables a pro-active and conscious engagement with a carrier's internal and external environment. E-Commerce strategy can support the overall strategic direction of the airline in areas such as financial, marketing, and customer satisfaction. However, it is important to realize that e-commerce strategy itself also influences airline strategy. Therefore, it is both a supporter and a shaper of an airline's strategic agenda. This two-sided aspect of e-commerce becomes clear when looking at the following aspects:[1]

1. *Airline e-commerce technology decisions are often strategic in nature.* Management frequently faces decisions that span long timeframes and involve large portions of an airline's resources. For example, an airline's acquisition of a new internet booking engine platform usually means a commitment of between five and ten years to the technology (and technology provider) involved. During this timeframe, an airline spends money on the platform for one-time developments, upgrades, monthly maintenance, and booking engine fees. In total, this can exceed several million dollars. Additionally, once a technology solution is implemented, it can

bind resources for several years and be difficult to change. Worse, if not living up to its original promise and improving an airline's performance, it can be a significant constraint on the company's e-commerce activities. In essence, the significance of e-commerce technology decisions cannot be underestimated.

2.  *E-Commerce directly affects an airline's competitive position.* E-Commerce alters the base of competition for an airline. This is because it provides for benefits such as lowering cost and dealing with customers directly. Defining an airline's engagement with e-commerce from a commercial and technological perspective through a strategy process is therefore significant to the company's success in the marketplace.

3.  *E-Commerce competes for resources within the airline.* Due to its multi-disciplinary nature, airline e-commerce has an impact across different departments. The ongoing investment in e-commerce technology and the management of e-commerce areas such as in marketing, sales, and customer service all demand the allotment of corporate resources. Doing so means that other areas in the airline might be precluded from receiving certain resources. Therefore, using a long-term resource allocation method in order to identify and support an optimal mix of proposed activities across the company is important. The lack of such an integrative view could debilitate an airline in pursuing a balanced progress and minimizing risks for the company.

4.  *Structures, resources, and processes for supporting e-commerce are costly.* Implementing disruptive technology and engaging in a new way of doing business means that organizational structures, processes, and resources in an airline need some degree of adjustment. This is not cheap. In addition, there are opportunity costs and external effects associated with this which in turn could limit or enhance an airline's ability to execute other critical tasks.

5.  *Information technology systems for managing e-commerce are costly.* The digitization of an airline's value chain requires the deployment and management of information technology systems. These play a particularly crucial role for an airline's big data activities. Without them, a carrier cannot capture and quantify activities, behaviors, or whatever phenomena are associated with web travelers. In big data parlance, this so-called "datafication" involves gathering, processing, transferring, and analyzing data – all key for a carrier's personalization activities. An airline therefore needs to introduce information technology through internal developments and acquisitions from third parties. This is a strategic issue because of its long-term nature and has significant cost implications.

6.  *Integration among diverse organizational units is often required.* The various airline departments need to be primed for support, otherwise e-commerce is less likely to be successful. Effective coordination among sales, marketing, customer service, IT, and other departments is important. The reason is the natural tendency for any organizational unit in a company to focus only on their immediate environment and goals. The appreciation and understanding of other stakeholders is therefore limited. This tendency is often exacerbated due to the fact there is a difference in worldview and corporate language between departments. An "us versus them" situation can be often observed when stakeholders from commercial departments meet IT representatives.

Furthermore, non-technology managers frequently do not understand the underlying technology driving e-commerce. They may not feel comfortable with the uncertainty arising from unanticipated problems created by the technological functions. To overcome all these differences and manage them successfully in the long term, a formal integrative approach is required that fosters a more common understanding and narrows the gaps.

Is the strategy process for e-commerce different from that for other areas in the airline? It depends. On the one hand, dealing with the e-commerce does not change the fundamentals of managing its strategy process. An airline still has to review multiple factors in the internal and external environment. This is necessary in order to assess their impact on the business, to formulate objectives of what to achieve, and to pursue certain ways of how to achieve them. In other words, the e-commerce strategy process still moves in the same direction or moves by the same degree as strategy processes for areas outside e-commerce.

However, the caveat is that with time and space collapsed in cyberspace, the e-commerce strategy process recycles at a higher velocity. It also involves the handling of much more information. If one adds to these factors the inherent characteristics of e-commerce such as its 24/7/365 ubiquity, unprecedented consumer empowerment, and the ongoing proliferation of new technology devices, some people might argue that the e-commerce strategy process is different. When compared with the strategy process in other corporate areas, e-commerce may be different in *kind*.[2]

When an airline engages in e-commerce strategy, it has to be prepared for a very dynamic, if not hyperactive, process that is much more consumer driven than that is observed for an airline's non-e-commerce areas. The e-commerce strategy process requires a new, higher level of improvisation. This aspect is typically absent in the business strategy models that have their roots in the Industrial Age. In those instances, the environment was much more supplier driven and involved relatively predictable market conditions. This has all changed with today's internet-based societies and the significant role that e-commerce plays.

## 7.2 THE STRATEGY PROCESS IN AIRLINE E-COMMERCE: GETTING STARTED

Today, many airlines have in place a more or less structured process to deal with e-commerce strategy. This has not always been the case. E-Commerce strategy, like e-commerce itself, had to evolve and it took time to become more sophisticated and competent. In essence, we can distinguish between four strategy levels related to e-commerce: Experimentation, absorption, integration, and transformation.

There is an evolutionary aspect to these e-commerce strategy levels. However, it does not mean that a carrier follows a step-by-step process from the experimentation level to the transformation level. On the contrary. LCCs including Ryanair and Jet-Blue leapfrogged intermediate levels and adopted e-commerce strategy as their overall corporate strategy. Only this explains why within a few years they managed to generate

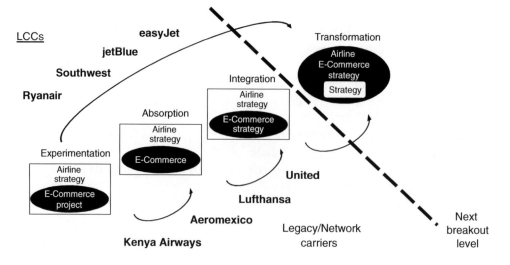

**Figure 7.1** *The four levels of airline e-commerce strategy*

almost all of their revenue online from their own digital properties. This is an accomplishment that legacy carriers still have not achieved after two decades of e-commerce. Arguably, however, this might not be their ultimate focus in the first place (Figure 7.1).

### 7.2.1 The four levels of airline e-commerce strategy

*Experimentation level*

Experimentation is the level where every airline's e-commerce journey begins. Today, it is rare to find an airline that only deals with e-commerce on an experimentation basis. However, they do exist. They are in markets where the overall customer readiness for online shopping is still at an infant stage due to a variety of factors including lack of online forms of payment, poor IT infrastructure, and strong traditional shopping culture. In this case, the experimentation with e-commerce at an airline is largely a reflection of what is going on in the marketplace. Not surprisingly, as a result, e-commerce does not play a formal role at a carrier and there is no e-commerce strategy.

E-Commerce on this level exists in the form of isolated website product development initiatives. These initiatives often have the character of experiments and are undertaken by single departments or individuals. There is no connection to the corporate strategy of the airline. The initiatives might not even be officially known to senior managers or they are tolerated only by superiors in the absence of better alternatives. The payoffs from these web product site initiatives and their impact on other departments are unclear. At most, they serve the interest of a few employees and may be relevant for a narrow customer segment base. The levers for these isolated e-commerce initiatives are diverted budgets for purchasing basic e-commerce products and services.

*Absorption level*

On this level, the emerging importance of e-commerce at the airline is acknowl-edged by senior leaders who lend their support for dedicated resources in terms of manpower and funds. A basic web presence exists in the form of an official retail website presence with standard features for informational content, internet booking engine, and web customer service.

The IT department is often in charge of driving e-commerce. The scope of e-commerce in this airline is small since other commercial departments are only peripherally involved. E-Commerce in areas such as marketing, sales, and customer service is not leveraged to the extent it could be. If, however, a dedicated e-commerce person or group exists, they frequently do not have much organiza-tional power and many times lack quality in terms of e-commerce experience and skills. The e-commerce activities found throughout different areas in the airline are very likely uncoordinated with each other, inconsistent, and do not amount to a well-thought-out strategy. Overall, despite senior management support, e-commerce is not viewed as a key area.

*Integration level*

On this level, a carrier has an e-commerce strategy and it supports the carrier's overall corporate strategy. E-Commerce is well dispersed throughout the company across dif-ferent areas including IT, marketing, sales, and customer service. Through dedicated e-commerce resources, e-commerce is managed with clear leadership and an exclusive budget. Senior managers responsible for e-commerce pro-actively partake in a process-driven approach for the formulation and implementation of an e-commerce strategy. Specific e-commerce targets in marketing, sales, and customer service are established, closely monitored, and regularly communicated to key stakeholders including senior management. Web product development initiatives are conducted cross-functionally with stakeholders from various disciplines and involve comprehensive financial mod-eling analyses to ensure that the airline's overall business strategy is indeed supported. The involved staff has the right skillset to manage e-commerce. Moreover, a number of comprehensive airline–vendor relationships are in place to manage e-commerce.

An airline on this level boasts a significant online revenue penetration (a minimum of 25–30%). It handles a large amount of customer issues via self-servicing tools and is also relatively savvy in the use of digital media. Many legacy airlines are found in this category. For them, e-commerce has become a mainstream business. This is the result of the air-line's decision to utilize e-commerce for the company's larger ambitions including rev-enue enhancement, cost reduction, and strengthening of brand and customer loyalty.

*Transformation level*

E-Commerce strategy on a transformation level is similar to what we have just discussed for the integration level—and much more. On the transformation level, e-commerce has become *the* driver of an airline's business. The strategy for airline e-commerce is the corporate strategy for the carrier. LCCs fall into this group as a result of their radical adoption and use of e-commerce as the core of their business starting in the mid- to late 1990s.

An airline in this category is relentless in its focus to adopt and use e-commerce in everything it does. Any interaction with the marketplace is always first approached from the angle "Can we do this online?" The quality of people including vendors managing the airline's e-commerce activities is high. Senior management's commitment to e-commerce is strong, comprehensive, and, one might even say, demanding. This last point is important to highlight because e-commerce is not just seen to support existing ways of doing business and making them more efficient and effective. E-Commerce is expected to generate new revenue streams and to create new business models. Furthermore, e-commerce is also expected to improve customer service and customer satisfaction. Figure 7.1 identifies this level as the "next breakout level." This is because on this level, a carrier breaks away from other competitors and differentiates itself in the marketplace.

In the early days of e-commerce, this breakout was achieved by launching a booking engine on a website. Airlines that did this differentiated themselves from those competitors that only offered a content website with marketing information. At that time, the overriding question for airlines was "if" to do airline e-commerce. This has changed and today's focus is on "how" to do airline e-commerce. It is likely that the next breakout could take place in the context of personalization. This should not be surprising. Some of the key enablers including a well-advanced IT infrastructure, big data technology applications, and legal/regulatory factors are already in place to support it.

Furthermore, leading online retailers like Amazon have successfully applied personalization concepts for some time and consumers are ready for it. Despite the fact that airlines overall have significantly advanced in e-commerce in recent years, their presence in cyberspace is largely commoditized. A high degree of similarity in technology platforms, website features, online marketing tactics, and web customer service handling are the principal reasons for this. Therefore, the ability to use information about travelers and provide for individually tailored offerings will be a pivotal driver for an airline to establish a unique market position.

An airline that strives for this kind of transformation can only succeed if it is ready. Our following strategy discussion shares more insight into what needs to be undertaken and what needs to be in place in order to be ready. As part of this discussion, we also introduce an assessment tool called "DAS" or Digital Airline Score that helps evaluate an airline's overall degree of readiness.

## 7.3 THE QUIET BEGINNING OF AIRLINE E-COMMERCE STRATEGY

Airline e-commerce strategy generally deals with several immediate questions:

- What mission and goals should be established for airline e-commerce?
- What core competencies are critical to manage it?
- How should one manage airline e-commerce?

There is no doubt that these questions must be addressed as part of a solid strategy process. However, before one can even formulate key questions, something else may have already happened.

The beginnings of a strategy process are often inconspicuous but it could look like this. Someone at an airline has heard, seen, or experienced something that is outside the normal course of business. With this realization, memos are written, meetings arranged and/or telephone calls conducted in order to share this information. Looking back to the mid-1990s, this is what likely happened at many airlines following the appearance of the first shopping websites with retailers such as Amazon, and even travel industry players including Alaska Airlines, British Midland, and Expedia. Fast forwarding to current events, one of the "hot" topics today is personalization of the online customer experience.

Whatever the subject, the attention of an airline is now focused on the following question: What is going on and what does this mean for us? The conversations following are rather informal. People educate and explain to each other this "new thing" and put it into the perspective of to the existing way of running the business operations. If a wide enough range of different departments participate, from sales and marketing to IT and finance, a fairly rounded picture and common understanding of the situation could emerge. In other words, the "new thing" is becoming somewhat more internalized. It might be that even new corporate vocabulary surfaces to describe it (Figure 7.2).

The common understanding among the diverse stakeholders partaking in these discussions can lead to conclusions on further activities. "What if" questions like "what if we launched exclusive e-fares on our website?" or "what if our competitors implemented an airline website personalization application?" are often posed in this situation and help clarify the decisions on the next steps. Aborting further actions and discarding the "new thing" as irrelevant to the airline is one possible outcome. Another possibility is the decision to delay and revisit the issue later. Another possibility still is the kick-off of a strategy process for airline e-commerce. All of this—realizing, internalizing, concluding, and acting—is an ongoing cycle that really never stops.

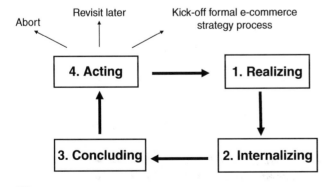

**Figure 7.2** *Starting the airline e-commerce strategy process*

**Figure 7.3** *Drivers of airline e-commerce strategy*

*Source:* Based on Hambrick and Frederikson (2001)[3]

## 7.4 DRIVERS OF AIRLINE E-COMMERCE STRATEGY

There is not one single ideal approach to manage strategy for airline e-commerce. Too many factors vary from airline to airline and have their unique bearing. These factors include the size of the business operations, the managerial style, and management priorities. Nevertheless, there are several elements that drive an airline's e-commerce strategy and apply irrespective of these variations.

Figure 7.3 is an abstract illustration of these elements. This picture looks rather clean and organized. The reality is different. There are lots of back and forths occurring between all strategy drivers until some understanding emerges on how to move forward.

It is important to emphasize that these drivers *guide* a strategy but they are not the strategy by themselves. There is often confusion about this. For instance, offering the best fares online is equated by some people with a low fare strategy. Likewise, the aim to adopt new e-commerce innovations ahead of competitors is considered a first-mover strategy. And to hire e-commerce specialists is viewed as a human-resource strategy. These examples are not strategies but ambitions at best. Unfortunately, "strategy" has become an omnipresent label to describe everything and nothing. Strategy is not about stand-alone goal-setting or environmental analyses. It is a "package" that encompasses multiple elements such as analyses, policy setting, and implementation actions. Only when these components are dealt with coherently, should we refer to strategy. In our following discussion, we elaborate on strategy elements that an airline should consider when addressing e-commerce strategy.

## 7.5 THE AIRLINE E-COMMERCE MISSION STATEMENT

Defining a mission is at the heart of the e-commerce strategy process. Here, a carrier states a perspective on the relevance and benefits of e-commerce, ideally for both the airline and the web traveler. A mission statement is not required by an outside body but it helps accomplish several things. These include:

**Table 7.1** *Example of airline e-commerce mission statement*

'Make orangejet.com the Best Place to Plan, Purchase, and Manage Travel on OrangeJet'

| Best for Airline | Best for Customer |
|---|---|
| ■ Distribution Savings | ■ Available 24/7, 365 Days |
| ■ Increased Revenue | ■ Low Fares, guaranteed |
| ■ Ancillary Revenue | ■ Self-servicing |
| ■ Self-service Cost Savings | ■ Bonus Miles |
| ■ Increased Engagement with Customer | ■ Localized Website in different Countries |
| | ■ Special Features |

- the embodiment of the airline's decision makers regarding e-commerce
- the description of the airline's web products and services
- the identification of the customer needs the airline intends to satisfy
- the implication of the image the airline seeks in the marketplace.

How could a mission statement for airline e-commerce look? In reference to our previously mentioned fictitious airline OrangeJet, it could be as bold as "Make orangejet.com the best place to plan, purchase, and manage travel on OrangeJet". In addition, some pointers on why e-commerce is beneficial for both the airline and customers may be used to further underline the statement's message (Table 7.1). When defining its e-commerce vision, an airline must address one overarching question: Is e-commerce a medium to complement the existing business activities or to replace them? The answer varies and is different for an LCC and a legacy carrier. LCCs have only a small presence in the offline world and this question therefore bears little relevance for them. However, legacy carriers still do and depending on what they intend to accomplish with e-commerce, the answer is different. Considering the growing internet adoption rates among consumers worldwide and the compelling value proposition of e-commerce, many traditional airlines today view e-commerce more as a way to replace existing business activities.

## 7.6 THE IDENTIFICATION AND SETTING OF E-COMMERCE GOALS

The e-commerce goal-setting process should establish a balanced goal portfolio. Rather than solely working with goals for marketing, sales and distribution, leading e-commerce airlines formulate goals for a wider range of areas. These include a mix of operational goals related to the e-commerce infrastructure, web customer service/satisfaction, and legal/regulatory. Furthermore, human resource or "people goals" are also of importance. The sales and distribution and marketing goals should address specific e-commerce assets a carrier might have. One commonly (at least nowadays) includes a company's main domestic website, its international websites, mobile properties, social media platforms, and others (tomorrow, popular assets could also cover IoT, wearable computing, and virtual reality). At the same time, both operational and people goals cut across different assets and apply to all of them (Figure 7.4).

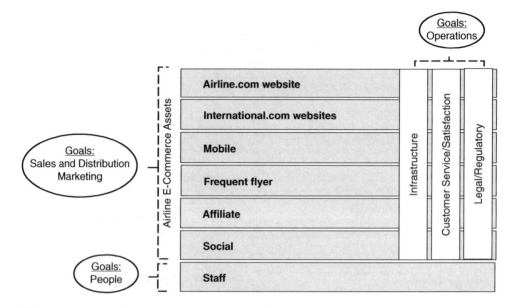

**Figure 7.4** *Example of an airline e-commerce goal portfolio*

The broad framework within which specific goals are suited for each area is shown below:

- *Sales and distribution.* To increase the airline's revenue through electronic channels while improving the overall cost of sale efficiency.
- *Marketing.* To increase the customer awareness for the airline's digital brand and support the business activities on the airline's digital properties and for the company both within and beyond cyberspace.
- *Customer service and satisfaction.* To deliver exceptional web customer service and be recognized by web travelers and the industry as a leader.
- *Infrastructure.* To implement and maintain a technology platform that is cost efficient, reliable, and scalable to the airline's growth needs.
- *Staff.* To attract external e-commerce talent, develop/retain employees, and be a place that people enjoy working.
- *Legal/Regulatory.* To be in compliance with government web rules and regulations and operate a safe and secure website.

The airline's financial and marketing e-commerce goals are achieved by meeting or exceeding the goals assigned to each of the airline e-commerce properties. Specific market segments such as leisure or corporate are generally rolled up under an individual e-commerce property. Infrastructure, customer satisfaction, and legal/regulatory goals cross all airline e-commerce properties and therefore would not be set individually.

Table 7.2 provides for a sampling of goals commonly applied for an airline's e-commerce activities.

**Table 7.2** *Selected airline e-commerce goals and metrics*

| Area for e-commerce goal | Example of e-commerce goal and metric |
|---|---|
| E-sales and distribution | ■ Financial<br>   – Revenue from online ticket sales<br>   – Customer acquisition cost<br>   – Number of unique visitors<br>   – Look-to-book ratio |
| E-marketing | ■ Brand awareness<br>   – Number of website page views<br>   – Website stickiness<br>■ Support of offline marketing<br>   – Acquisition rate of new customers<br>   – Conversion rate of visitors to buyers |
| Web customer service and satisfaction | ■ Service levels<br>   – Number of emails responded to within 1 hour<br>   – xx% of tweets handled within xx minutes<br>■ Customer ready product<br>   – Conduct user acceptance testing on all new web applications prior to launch<br>■ Industry recognition<br>   – Awards for online service innovation and excellence |
| IT infrastructure | ■ Quality of service<br>   – Platform availability (xx% 24/7/365)<br>   – System response time (xx seconds + network latency)<br>■ Process improvement<br>   – Content and functionality release to production without failure<br>■ Operational costs<br>   – Meet budgeted operational systems costs<br>■ Technical innovation<br>   – Win award for innovation<br>   – Speaking engagement at leading technology events |
| E-organization staff | ■ Attraction<br>   – Time to fill vacancies<br>■ Development<br>   – Number of vacancies filled internally<br>■ Retention<br>   – Maintain undesired turnover to less than xx% |
| Legal/regulatory | ■ Compliance with mandatory federal/state law<br>   – disclosure of digital data privacy practices<br>   – transparency in online fare advertising<br>   – web accessibility for disabled online users<br>■ Protection of intellectual property<br>   – Keep IP rights in website "terms of use" section updated<br>   – Counter third party violations of airline IP rights through court system/WIPO/ICANN resolution processes |

When devising airline e-commerce goals, it is important that they are suited to the broad aims of the airline's e-commerce mission statement. Furthermore, they need to be motivating and realistic: High enough to present a challenge but not too high to cause frustrations for those who own them.

## 7.7 STRATEGIC ANALYSIS

### 7.7.1 Macro external environment

The macro-external environment is the wider environment of an airline. It addresses "big picture" topics that also affect airline e-commerce. Included are factors of political, legal/regulatory, economic, social, and technological significance. The following section covers these factors in more detail.

*Political factors*

Political factors play a role as a result of interaction between governments, business lobbies, consumer groups, and public opinion/attitude. They drive the enactment of laws and establishment of regulatory frameworks that also impact airline e-commerce. Political factors manifest themselves in many ways. They include:

- *Legislation such as in the area of digital data privacy.* The goal is to protect consumers against invasions/abuses of their personal data by government agencies and businesses. Providing companies with guidance for compliance with data privacy legislation as it relates to new emerging internet platforms such as wearable computing and virtual reality is also part of this.
- *Setting up of bodies governing the internet.* An example is ICANN that regulates the worldwide domain name system.
- *Promotion of public safety and welfare.* One example is net neutrality. According to this concept, all internet traffic is to be treated equally and not to be discriminated against/charged differently because of content, user, platform, and other aspects.

*Legal/Regulatory factors*

For the most part, the focus of airlines with regards to legal/regulatory factors is on managing risks, specifically the minimization of them. Issues at stake include:

- damage to airline brand name and reputation
- penalties and fines
- litigation for potential and incurred losses.

Because of this, an airline should engage in compliance efforts as mandated by federal and state laws in different countries. One of the areas to pay close attention to is data privacy. Personal data of consumers are an important subject in privacy matters. The reason is that personal data can be used for different purposes such as commercial and security/law enforcement. Examples are the personalization of online offerings by airlines and the digital profiling of travelers to detect terrorists and criminals. It is therefore no understatement that personal data in today's internet-based society is the digital currency and of utmost importance for business and governments alike.

The airline industry has had its own fair share of data privacy controversies. JetBlue made the headlines in 2003 because it had shared information on 5 million travelers with a contractor for the Department of Defense without seeking permission or alerting its customers. In a more recent case, Delta Air Lines was sued by the State of California claiming that the company had violated California's internet privacy law because its mobile device "Fly Delta App" application's lack of a clearly posted privacy policy.

It is critical that a carrier undertakes specific measures to develop and maintain a solid data privacy program for web travelers. Several legislative developments that are certain to impact airlines' data privacy programs are listed in Table 7.3.

Another area where airline e-commerce is impacted by legal/regulatory factors deals with requirements for transparency in price advertising. As we discussed in Chapter 4 on e-sales and distribution, it is today commonly required by law to include mandatory charges in any advertising and specify a single price as opposed to breaking them out separately. Importantly, legislation in the United States and EU appears to be focusing more now on the practice of merchandising and pricing fare products on an à la carte basis. This is the result of the overall industry trend going toward segregating products and introducing new ancillary product and services.

An area where legal/regulatory factors also apply deals with website accessibility. In the Unites States for example, airlines have to be compliant with US DOT regulations that prohibit the discrimination of web users because of disabilities. Accordingly, by December 12, 2015 (this has been extended to June 30, 2016), all web pages that provide for core travel services and information (e.g. booking engine, frequent flyer account) need to be upgraded.

Besides compliance with federal and state laws, protection of intellectual property (IP) rights is also of concern to carriers in cyberspace. Airlines often address this area via a "terms of use" section on their websites. There, a carrier details the extent of its IP rights that generally include patents, trademark rights, database rights, and copyright. Furthermore, it has become common to also include under IP rights software code that enables innovative business processes. Famous cases where this applies includes Amazon's "1-click" shopping method that was patented in 2002 and Priceline's "Name your price" e-commerce system from 1998. In both cases, patented technology is used to enable new ways of shopping. An airline using these types of applications needs to pay royalties to the patent owners or may be sued.

Trademark law from the offline world extends to e-commerce. An airline that sees its trademark infringed upon can therefore use existing rules and regulations to protect its brand name. Trademark infringements are frequently observed in the domain name space and can be resolved via the special ICANN dispute resolution process or in court.

**Table 7.3** *Legislative data privacy initiatives*

| Legislative driver | Effective | What it is |
| --- | --- | --- |
| EU Data Protection Regulation | Est. 2016 | The current legislation draft aims at a reform of EU Directive 95/46/EC to account for changes in technology and globalization. With focus on building consumer trust in online environment, key pursuits are individuals' security and safety by making data sharing simpler, more transparent, and optional. Two major points: Data breaches must be reported within 24 hours and "the right to be forgotten." |
| "Do Not Track" law in US | January 1, 2014 | Absent a federal law on this topic, California as the first state adopting "Do Not Track" legislation could pave the way for other US states to follow. Requirement of website operators to let website users know how the site responds to so-called "Do Not Track" mechanisms, which are typically small pieces of code—similar to cookies—that signal to websites or mobile applications that the user does not want the website operator to track his or her visit to the site, including through analytics tools, advertising networks, and other types of data collection and tracking practices. |
| | | The law applies to all companies that collect tracking information from California residents, and accordingly applies to companies that do business in California and track California residents, even if the company does not have a physical presence in California. |
| Russia personal data storage law | Planned for September, 2016 | Russia's lower house of parliament has passed a law obligating companies doing business in the country to store data on Russian users within Russia itself. Companies ignoring this rule face having their access blocked inside the country. |
| | | Some analysts fear that Russia may be seeking to create a closed and censored version of the internet within its borders and that this could set a precedent for other countries to follow suit. The law still has to be passed by the upper house of parliament and signed by Putin himself. If this occurs, it would take effect in September 2016. |
| US Senator Rockefeller's inquiry into US carriers data mgmt practices | Not known | Legislative initiative to gain better insight into airlines' current personal data collection and data use practices. Specifically, US carriers have to supply feedback on data retention periods, data collection mechanisms, possibilities for customers to have data access, and whether they share or sell passenger data to third parties. |

Copyright enters the picture because airlines view their websites as property of the company. Information posted on the website, its design, and software code used are typically copyrighted. Databases like an airline's FFP database may also be copyrighted unless a separate database right applies. We recall from our discussion on airline website screenscraping by meta-search engines how controversial the area of copyright can be. An airline needs to constantly monitor the legal landscape in order to ensure that the company and any users of its digital properties are in compliance with the latest IP laws.

*Economic factors*

In prosperous times, people have more disposable income and companies have more budget. Demand for air travel is said to be a multiple of GDP growth and rates of 1.5 to 2 times GDP growth are common.[4] GDP growth in most Western countries is anemic but other parts of the world notably, Asia and Africa, performs much better. At the same time, economic growth of a country is known to be linked to its level of digitization. The more consumers, business, and governments have adopted digital applications and information/communications technology, the higher also the economic benefits and the GDP per capita.

Understanding these economic conditions is part of planning for airline e-commerce. This is because it provides for some insight on the propensity of consumers in a country to not only buy travel products but also purchase *online* travel products. The outlook for travel demand is generally good. In 2014, global travel generated $1.2 trillion in revenue and it is still rising. The emergence of new travel source markets such as Brazil, China, and India also contribute to this. The online travel market benefits from this development as well. It is expected to rise to over $523 billion by 2016.

Globalization is an important aspect in today's economy. It is driven by international trade and investments and supported by information technology. Airlines participate in globalization through e-commerce. Among other things, they can increase their market reach which may also help shield them from economic downturns in particular countries.

*Social factors*

It is beneficial for airlines to understand the numerous factors that affect internet adoption. One of these factors is internet access—without it, airline e-commerce is severely hampered. Internet access varies globally. For example, in North America, the share of households connected to the internet is almost 88%; in Asia and Africa, it is 35% and 27%, respectively.[5] Even within one country, the adoption rates can vary substantially depending on user demographics. It is also important for an airline to have insight into users' technographics. Depending on what internet access devices people use, where and how long they use them, an airline's website design and online marketing communication should be adjusted accordingly.

Social factors have also to do with societal values and attitudes. On the one hand, people see technology as something beneficial that improves the quality of life. In this regard, the consumerization of IT should be mentioned. It describes the impact on companies including airlines of consumer-led technology introductions. An example is the rapid adoption of smart phones that started in the consumer space rather than with the corporate sector. A similar trend can be now observed in regards to wearable computing and virtual reality applications. Airline e-commerce in this kind of environment has an opportunity to prosper.

On the other hand, concerns over e-commerce have also emerged. One noteworthy area is data privacy. Massive, arguably excessive, data collections for commercial and security/law enforcement purposes, data privacy breaches and abuses, and covert government surveillance programs, are key reasons for people's growing concern. As a result of this development, airlines have become more transparent and disclose information of their data management practices in website privacy policies. At the same time, they are increasingly subject to various data protection laws.

Other social factors affecting airline e-commerce include society's growing environmental awareness and social causes around the world. Airlines have responded to this by accommodating special features on their websites. These include the possibility for web travelers to buy carbon emission offsets or donate money to charities when purchasing a ticket online. Furthermore, carriers often feature website information on their activities in the area of social/corporate responsibilities.

*Technological factors*

Improvements in technology and new innovations typically affect every industry. It is a big challenge for an airline to be able to assess what internet-based technology may provide for a competitive edge. However, several trends and developments should be mentioned whose impact on airline e-commerce is likely to increase even more in the future.

One is the rapid growth of mobile devices. As stated in previous discussions, there are two billion people who have a smartphone and this number is expected to double by 2020. The number of tablet users exceeds one billion and the forecast is one and a half billion by the end of the decade. Computing tied to a desktop will soon be an exception. In order for an airline's e-commerce position to remain competitive, this overall consumer shift to mobiles needs to be addressed. This ranges from optimizing all web traveler-facing interactions in sales, marketing, and customer service to adjusting back office operations that can support mobile platforms. The same approach applies to other emerging platforms such as wearable computing and virtual reality if and when these enter the mainstream and become mass adopted.

Other key areas where technological factors come into play are e-marketing and e-sales and distribution. The merchandising and personalization of products, fares, and services for airlines is possible and will become more pervasive because of a combination of new technological applications. This includes the application of technology for large-scale collecting/tracking of web traveler data, the adoption of XML communication standards in e-sales and distribution as part of the airline industry's NDC initiative, and the ongoing enhancements of airline's revenue management technology.

### 7.7.2 Micro internal environment

The micro-environment analysis involves factors that are of immediate concern to a carrier's e-commerce activities. Examples of factors that are relevant for monitoring and assessing for their impact on airline e-commerce include web travelers, activities by actual and emerging competitors, and the sales and distribution landscape.

An analysis of the micro-environment is essential in order to gauge the overall dynamics of the online travel market. Throughout previous chapters, we have touched on several key trends and developments in this regard. They are not further elaborated on here. However, as a refresher, a list of several micro-external environmental trends and developments are listed below:

- Web travelers

  - The rise of the millennial travelers who are predicted to account for the largest share of online travel demand and also reach their peak in spending power and travel activities over the next 10 to 15 years.
  - How web travelers travel is changing. As a result of the growing sharing economy, corresponding travel products and experiences are becoming more popular. Examples include the use of private accommodations and ground transportation as provided by companies such as AirBnB and Uber.
  - The blurring lines between business and leisure trips ("bleisure trips," "bizcation").
  - The rise of the "silent" do-it-yourself traveler.

- Sales and distribution

  - Enabled by big data and new technology applications/standards, improvement of airline personalization capabilities. This leads to incremental sales and strengthened 1:1 relationships with travelers.
  - The e-marketing-ization of e-sales and distribution.
  - Airlines' growth in direct sales and direct connect relationships to lower distribution costs.
  - Airline pressure on GDSs and travel agency community to upgrade their infrastructure to enable widespread ancillary sales.
  - Domination of global OTA market by Expedia and Priceline.

- Competitors

  - Increased handling of web traveler within airline alliance ecosystem such as OneWorld and Star Alliance.
  - Disruption of online travel marketplace by powerful technology and marketing players such as Apple, Amazon, Facebook, and Google.

### 7.7.3 Internal environment

The analysis of a carrier's internal environment assesses the company's e-commerce strengths and weaknesses. This is done by reviewing key areas that determine an airline's e-commerce competency. They include the company's organization, resources, schedule, portfolio, value chain management, technology, and governance (Figure 7.5).

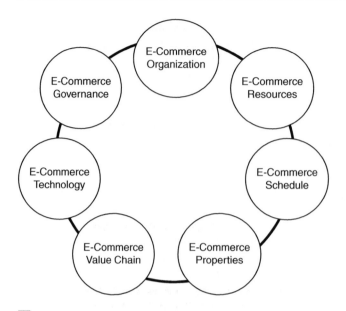

**Figure 7.5** *The seven key competencies of airline e-commerce*

In Table 7.4, we show for each of these seven areas key questions that are meant to trigger a critical assessment of the current state of e-commerce at an airline. The actual list of questions is generally very exhaustive and we show only a few samples. These questions are related to certain benchmarks such as web traveler expectations, key competitors, best industry practices, legal/regulatory requirements, and company internal ambitions. Completing this step provides insight into how wide the gaps are versus the carrier's benchmarks. Narrowing or completely closing these gaps constitutes an important piece of an airline's e-commerce strategy agenda.

## 7.8 SUPPORTING ORGANIZATIONAL ARRANGEMENTS

Culture, people, and processes are another strategy driver. Airlines have different arrangements in place and their impact on how strategy is handled should not be underestimated. Strategy guru Henry Mintzberg has identified several organizational styles and how they influence a company's strategy.[6] According to his analysis, the extreme ends of the organizational style spectrum are classical administration and entrepreneurial approach. In between are hybrids such as adhocracy and professional approach. We briefly discuss these in an airline e-commerce context below.

### 7.8.1 Management styles for airline e-commerce

*Classical administration*

This organizational style is found with airlines that are highly mature and several decades old. They often have a history of government ownership and may still be

**Table 7.4** *Assessing the airline's core competencies*

| Core competency | Sample questions for assessments |
|---|---|
| Organization | ▪ Do we have the right organizational structure?<br>▪ Are roles, responsibilities, and reporting relationships optimal? |
| Resources | ▪ Size of e-budget sufficient?<br>▪ Quantity and quality of manpower?<br>▪ IT systems competitive to support our web presence?<br>▪ Are partners and suppliers for product and services cost competitive and deliver top quality? |
| Schedule | ▪ What is the timing, speed and sequencing of our e-commerce initiatives?<br>▪ Do we have the right priorities? |
| Properties | ▪ What is our spectrum of e-commerce properties?<br>▪ Are our features competitive?<br>▪ Do we pursue a first-mover status in feature adoption?<br>▪ How localized vs globalized are our features?<br>▪ What is the degree of personalization?<br>▪ Are our websites accessible for disabled web travelers? |
| Value Chain | ▪ What are our differentiators in e-marketing, e-sales and web service?<br>  – E-marketing<br>    • Compelling website design?<br>    • Frequency of customer communication across a wide range of digital media formats?<br>  – E-sales<br>    • Lowest fares?<br>    • Spectrum of up/cross sell ancillaries and forms of payment?<br>  – Web customer service<br>    • Wide range of service channels including social care?<br>    • How fast do we reply to queries?<br>    • Are the different service channels integrated with each other? |
| Technology | ▪ What generation of IBE technology do we feature?<br>▪ Do web pages download fast enough?<br>▪ Are our e-commerce properties reliable and available?<br>▪ Should we deploy cloud computing and if yes for what areas? |
| Governance | ▪ What are our performance metrics, do we measure enough and the right things?<br>▪ Is our process for updating regular website content efficient?<br>▪ Do we have an effective process to handle website malfunctions including security breaches?<br>▪ How do we evaluate and prioritize e-commerce initiatives?<br>▪ Can we optimize our RFP processes for selecting vendors?<br>▪ Is our web data privacy policy transparent to travelers, compliant with legal requirements, and providing the right protection? |

fully or partially government controlled. They conduct strategy in a centralized, highly formalized, if not bureaucratic, way and depend on standardization of work processes for coordination. Airline e-commerce strategy is managed by specialists who may be part of corporate strategy and functional strategy. Danger: Paralysis by analysis with much time spent on assessments and over-evaluating pros and cons of various scenarios. Legacy/flag carriers often fall into this group.

### Diversified approach

This is a version of the classical approach. The airline has several (semi-) autonomous divisions including passenger, cargo, and vacations that manage e-commerce related strategy within their respective entities.

### Professional approach

This organizational style is closely related to classical administration. The professional approach to strategy is also highly centralized. The difference is that outside experts are also involved. They organize and carry out strategy-related work as autonomous and independent specialists. Supporting them and exercising the ultimate control in the airline are senior managers. Standardization of processes are emphasized in this environment.

### Adhocracy approach

Organized to carry out expert work in highly dynamic settings, experts work in project teams and matrix form. Coordination of strategic issues is addressed by mutual adjustment and flexibility. This approach is very much a trait of start-ups and e-commerce offshoots of traditional airlines where much value is placed on speed and informality.

### Entrepreneurial approach

With this approach, airline e-commerce strategy is managed in a more informal and unstructured way. It could very likely be controlled by just one senior manager. This might even be the CEO who, by direct supervision, engages in the strategic management process and sets goals and controls performances for e-commerce matters in the airline.

The entrepreneurial approach is often found in the start-up phase of an airline where strong leaders, often with aggressive style, are hands-on involved in many aspects of running the airline. Michael O'Leary of Ryanair and Stelios Haji-Ioannou of easyJet are such examples. To their credit, they saw early on and ahead of other rivals, the potential of using an airline website as a new low-cost direct sales channel. Accordingly, they spearheaded the rapid integration of e-commerce in their companies. The downside to this managerial approach is "extinction by instinct." This is because very little formality and structure is applied in deciding how to move forward. Acts of judgment based on gut feeling could work for some time initially.

However, this approach can cause more headaches as an airline grows and transitions to becoming a more mature carrier.

It is possible that unofficial pockets of this entrepreneurial approach are found in larger traditional airlines. This applies often in situations when there is a large geographic distance between a frontline manager and the airline's head office. The author remembers several country managers at United Airlines who had engaged in "undercover e-commerce" activities by diverting portions of local marketing budgets to fund the launch of a website for their markets.

These were noteworthy efforts to advance the e-commerce agenda locally. However, they were not sustainable in light of the company's need to have a more globally unified web brand in the marketplace. Ultimately, these renegade websites were folded although—in coordination with the same local stakeholders—some parts of them were repurposed for the "official" websites that were eventually released.

## 7.9 BUILDING AN AIRLINE E-COMMERCE STRATEGY

### 7.9.1 First step: Setting priorities

Today, there are fundamentally three potential directions which an airline can focus on for the growth of its e-commerce business. They include transaction and distribution focus, investment focus, and e-customer relationship management (e-CRM)/ personalization focus (Figure 7.6). Depending on what an airline decides to pursue, its e-commerce strategy is colored accordingly. Although divergent, they are not mutually exclusive. An airline, while focusing on one direction, could also engage in the other directions, albeit with a lower priority and less resources.

In the early days of e-commerce, airlines' strategies for cyberspace were mostly about growing online revenue through channel shift and lowering distribution costs. A few carriers in the build-up toward the dotcom boom expanded this sales and distribution focus to an investment focus. The idea was to build equity stakes and enter joint ventures with other travel related e-commerce companies. This allowed an airline to broaden its sales and distribution network, to acquire access to proprietary technology/ intellectual know-how, or to look for an investment opportunity that would generate a rich return on investment upon divesture. One prominent example at the time was Delta's equity investment in Pricline.com, the United Airlines-Buy.com joint venture, to create Buytravel.com, and the launch of Orbitz and Zuji by airline consortia.

The transaction and distribution focus among airlines is still strong. Evidence of this is the continuously growing range of web products available on the digital properties of airlines. In the past, airlines were only concerned with offering a seat inventory of their own flights. Today, featured are flights of codeshare/alliance partners and a wide array of up- and cross-sell products including à la carte fares, travel insurance, and hotel/car bookings. The investment focus is not common these days (it is for OTAs and to some extent for GDS, however, as we remember from Chapter 4 on e-sales and distribution), although they do exist. For instance, Ryanair announced in 2014 that it is considering a number of acquisitions in the technology and retail

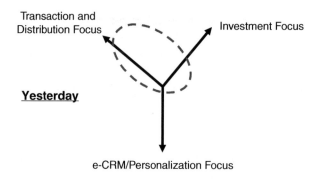

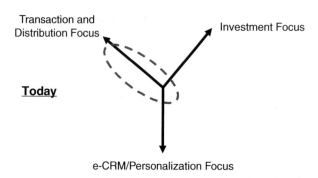

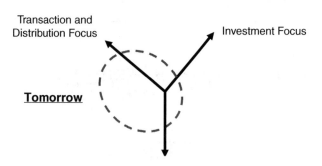

**Figure 7.6** *The shifting focus of airline e-commerce strategies*

sectors. Targeted are deals over the next ten years that could support the carrier's efforts to improve "the product, the distribution, and the service."[7]

One area that appears to increasingly occupy the space of airline e-commerce strategy is e-CRM. The topic is not new and airlines have been utilizing a variety of technology applications to manage their interactions with travelers in sales, marketing, and service. However, what is new is the data-driven approach to understanding customers' needs and behaviors and applying this insight to deliver individualized offers. From this, airlines hope to realize increased loyalty and new incremental revenue streams.

Therefore, unlike in the past when cost reduction was a key driver behind e-commerce strategies, today it looks as if more airlines are building new online capabilities. Another way to phrase this change in strategy focus is by saying that airlines in the past spent money on e-commerce to save money while today they spend money to make money. The key buzzword in this regard is personalization. The number of airlines currently focusing on building this area as part of their e-commerce strategy is small and only 28% offer a targeted experience on their website (for smart phones, the share is 13%). However, it is anticipated that this share will grow to 44% (and 52% for smart phones) by 2017.[8]

### 7.9.2 Next steps: Determining the cornerstones of strategy

Once the overall focus is identified, the airline can embark on the next steps for concrete action. Specifically five areas should be looked at:

1. What is the business model?
2. What are the segments to focus on?
3. What are the mechanisms to generate these revenue streams?
4. What are the differentiators used to uniquely position the airline?
5. What is the timeframe and prioritization for implementation?

Figure 7.7 is an illustration of the five areas with selected key questions to take into consideration.

Let us assume the case of an airline that decides to transform its existing e-commerce strategy and to break out in the marketplace by offering personalization features on its website. Our discussion below shows how the five cornerstone areas could apply to the airline's decision.

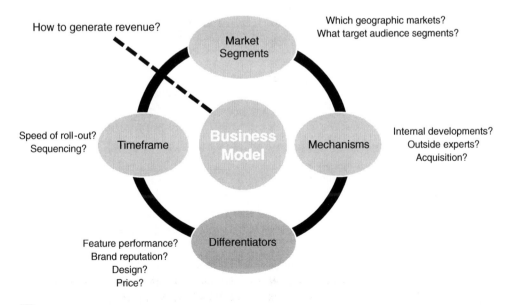

**Figure 7.7** Cornerstones of strategy

Source: Based on Hambrick and Frederickson (2001)[9]

*Business model*

The business model has to show how the airline intends to secure revenue streams from personalization. It is crucial that the carrier develops a clear idea of its unique selling position (USP) in terms of:

- the marketing of tailored offerings that is more efficient than that provided by competitors
- the customer experience that is more attractive than a traveler would encounter with other airlines.

If what the carrier offers is difficult to match by other airlines and the targeted web travelers view the personalization offers as superior, then a basis is established for an enduring business model that can generate revenue streams for some time to come.

*Market segments*

The carrier has to decide in what geographic markets to offer personalization features on local websites. Domestic versus international markets, regional versus global markets, key markets vs secondary markets, or possibly something else, are part of the considerations. An airline needs to be as specific as possible because this decision sets the stage for subsequent actions.

Segmentation also must be addressed in terms of target audience. One possibility is to offer personalization to all those web travelers who are registered users. This means that personalization is enabled by any web traveler via their authentication when they log in on the airline's website. Another possibility is that a carrier decides to make personalization only available to certain premium customer segments such as corporate travelers or top tier members in the airline's FFP.

*Mechanisms*

Mechanisms indicate by which means a carrier intends to achieve its stated intention. For personalization features, a carrier has essentially three options: Build, buy, or rent.

By using the "build" option, the feature is developed from scratch and exclusively used by the airline. The build option could mean a purely internal development effort by the airline or a cooperation between the airline and a technology provider. Large carriers with strong inhouse IT know–how and large IT/non–IT resources are occasionally engaged in this.

The build option has recently taken an interesting twist through so–called "hack-athons." Essentially, a hackathon (also referred to as code or hackfest) is a collaborative event where a large number of computer programmers work in an extreme manner during a short timeframe on a project. Some airlines have adopted this concept and develop e-commerce applications through hackathons for specific areas.

For example, American Airlines conducted a special hackathon flight in summer 2014 between New York and San Francisco. Computer programmers that had been working for 30 days prior to the flight on the project—American was looking for wearable computing applications that could be used inflight—demonstrated their work during the six-hour flight.[10] Companies sponsoring a hackathon usually keep the work results of the participants. Some cynics might say that this approach is an inexpensive way to manage technology projects. Nevertheless, the tapping into e-commerce talent outside conventional corporate structures can also help an airline incorporate innovative technology solutions quickly.

With the "buy" option, an airline buys a standard "off-the-shelf" product from a technology provider. Within limits, some degree of customization to the carrier's needs is generally feasible. This is what the large majority of airlines do. In the case of personalization, this means to partner with a booking engine platform/web portal providers and others that can implement a number of personalization features.

The "rent" option allows an airline to acquire a white label product for a limited time and offer it to web travelers under its own brand. Some airlines have chosen this route. Website features commonly made available on an airline website via a rented platform include cross-sell products such as hotels, cars, and even tour packages. For example, some airlines work with Expedia and use its WWTE (World-wide Travel Exchange) private label program. White label provider Barilliance is an example of a company that also offers e-commerce personalization suites.

One question that often surfaces when involving third parties is why an airline has to work with vendors in the first place. Is it not better to do this inhouse themselves, save money and build up new know-how? A review of inhousing versus hiring third party is always beneficial and should be conducted by a carrier. This process helps identify the pros and cons of each alternative. Many airlines have found that it is more efficient to outsource value-creating activities. Most carriers do not have large and advanced enough internal resources to perform well in multiple core compe-tency areas. The development and implementation of personalization features falls into a non-core category and an airline is better off with outside resources. The airline's focus should be on developing a good understanding what specific products are necessary, sourcing the best vendor, and turning the relationship into a partner-ship in the long run.

*Differentiators*

With differentiators, an airline distinguishes itself from competitors. An airline could decide to rely largely on the power of its brand name that may stand for excellent service, low fares, or innovative marketing. It is essential that a carrier early on sharp-ens a few brand attributes rather than trying to be unique across a wide range of areas.

Personalization can be a powerful differentiator for an airline's presence in cyber-space. Not many carriers currently have the digital-databased ability to match fare, product, and service offerings to a web traveler's individual profile. Therefore, being an early adopter of this feature can translate into a competitive advantage for an air-line. By the same token it is prudent to also reflect on how an airline could sustain its superiority in this field. As personalization undoubtedly is becoming a more common feature, an airline needs to ensure that its 1:1 offerings are more compelling than those of competitors. Because of this reason, it is crucial to identify the core areas where personalization is managed. These include:

- personalized products, fares, and services
- personalized communication
- personalized relationship management
- web traveler data management and analysis
- new governance frameworks to manage personalization.

Depending on how well (or not) an airline manages these areas, the quality of its personalization program will be influenced accordingly. This in turn has a significant impact on how an airline's personalization is perceived by web travelers in relation to those of other carriers.

*Staging*

Staging addresses the speed and sequencing of strategic initiatives. A decision is driven by several factors including resource availability. If funds and manpower are limited, the speed by which personalization features are to be offered in the marketplace could be hampered. Another important determinant in staging deals with the urgency to be among early movers. An early mover approach could help strengthen the airline's reputation and offer opportunities for premium pricing.

Sequencing is best handled through a gradual approach. Best practices for the launch of new digital features show time and again that a step-by-step roll-out is safer. By entering the area of personalization gradually, for example, a carrier stands a better chance of optimizing and fine-tuning the new feature as it's application scale widens. This approach also allows for the project to gain momentum over time. Many airlines consider their home market as the natural starting point before expanding into other regions.

## 7. 10 IMPLEMENTING STRATEGY

### 7.10.1 Fundamental aspects

The area of e-commerce strategy implementation is concerned with putting into practice the conclusions or agreements that have emerged from the strategy analysis and composition. As easy and straightforward the implementation of strategy might look to some observers—after all, most companies spend an exorbitant amount of time on analyzing and formulating their strategy—it is not. The corporate sector's record when it comes to implementing strategies is rather poor. Over 60% of companies admit to struggling with strategy implementation and only about 56% of strategies are actually successfully rolled out.[11]

What are the reasons for this weak performance? The most common are:[12]

- Senior managers from the C-level suite are missing in action—only 50% of companies appear to receive attention from their top managers during this part of the strategy process.
- Too many C-level managers micro-manage as opposed to staying focused on the big themes such as providing corporate leadership, deciding on the selection and prioritization of strategic initiatives, and providing for resource allocation.
- Many companies lack the skills or fail to deploy the manpower needed for strategy implementation.

In order to avoid a similar fate, an airline should develop an implementation plan that identifies specific action items for the three areas of ownership, mode of interaction, and resource allocation (Figure 7.8).

There must be clarity of who assumes ownership of a specific strategic initiative. This could be a person who has both the responsibility and the accountability to manage the implementation. The timeline involved ranges from the conceptual idea stage to prototype development and testing and the ultimate marketplace launch. Lack of ownership can cause major problems including delays and budget overruns.

Being an owner is not a small task. A series of qualitative and quantitative analyses need to be completed in order to obtain detailed insight of what resources are needed to pull off the initiative, how much time is needed and what it costs. Considering the scale of a project, it should come as no surprise that the owner occasionally may comprise a group of people. For our personalization initiative, there are project managers for five competence areas who work under a program lead. This person in turn interacts directly with a C-suite manager (Figure 7.9).

Owners do not work in a vacuum. They frequently bring other stakeholders onboard. These could be internal specialists from the IT and finance departments. Furthermore, there are vendors and subject matter experts (SMEs) who contribute

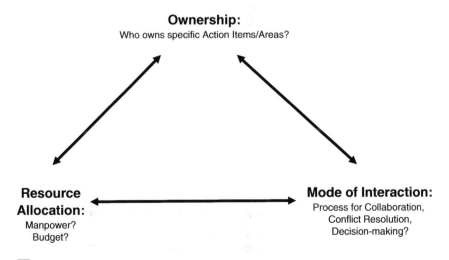

**Ownership:**
Who owns specific Action Items/Areas?

**Resource Allocation:**
Manpower?
Budget?

**Mode of Interaction:**
Process for Collaboration,
Conflict Resolution,
Decision-making?

**Figure 7.8** *Critical areas for successful strategy implementation*

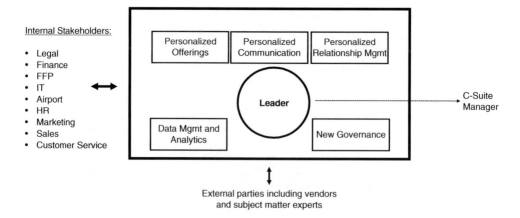

**Internal Stakeholders:**

- Legal
- Finance
- FFP
- IT
- Airport
- HR
- Marketing
- Sales
- Customer Service

Personalized Offerings

Personalized Communication

Personalized Relationship Mgmt

Leader

Data Mgmt and Analytics

New Governance

C-Suite Manager

External parties including vendors and subject matter experts

**Figure 7.9** *Crucial parties in strategy implementation*

with their input. Not inviting relevant parties and pursuing a silo approach translates into ineffective implementation riddled with delays and cost overruns.

The mode of interaction among the different internal and external stakeholders is of great significance. It not only addresses what specific action items are undertaken but also deals with communication among the different players in the strategy implementation. Decision-making processes and how to manage conflict/roadblocks are some of the examples.

One comment on speed. With activities in cyberspace being time compressed, it is hardly surprising that there is a premium on speed of strategy implementation. If the delivery cycle from initial assessment to launch is to be reduced, an airline needs to focus on streamlining steps notorious for causing delays. This is accomplished by addressing the following issues:

■ *Speed in decision-making.* Key is to improve the interface between the various stakeholders with particular emphasis on endowing the initiative lead and the various project managers with both power and credibility to enforce strict time-box discipline.

■ *Speed in project management.* Collaboration between airline and technology vendor/other third parties is improved vastly by co-location (various stakeholders are on the same premise/same room), dedicated resources, and regular checkpoint meetings.

■ *Speed in roll-out.* As opposed to pursuing a 100% perfect solution, an airline should pursue a 90% perfect solution and pilot the prototype before upscaling it to 100%. This approach saves both time and cost.

Lastly, resource allocation in terms of funds and manpower (both quality and quantity) is a key aspect in strategy implantation as well. The issue of resource is already identified as part of the initial strategy assessment. However, it also assumes an important role at the outset of the implementation plan.

**Table 7.5** *IT spending as a percentage of revenue*

| Year | Airline Industry (1) | Cross-Industry (2) |
|------|----------------------|--------------------|
| 2014 | 2.2% | 5.1% |
| 2013 | 2.1% | 5.0% |
| 2012 | 2.1% | 5.0% |
| 2011 | 2.3% | 3.6% |

*Source:* SITA(2014),[13] Krigsman (2014)[14]

When looking at "IT spending as a % of total revenue," a popular metric to gauge the resource situation of a company, the airline industry does not look too impressive. Between 2011 and 2014, it hovered around 2%. When compared with average cross-industry figures ranging between 3.6% in 2011 and 5.1% in 2014, it looks like airlines on average are underspending in the IT area (Table 7.5). Taking into account that many airline e-commerce initiatives are funded from IT budgets, it seems that the industry's IT spending would need to increase if carriers aim at strengthening their e-commerce capabilities via personalization features.

The right approach to resource management is to mix strong internal talents at the airline with adequate capabilities offered by various vendors. Internal resources could contribute through:

- technological developments by the company's IT department
- expertise, know-how, idea inputs from functional areas like marketing, sales, customer service, FFP, airport, and legal
- involvement in prototype testing.

At the same time, external parties including subject matter experts, customer focus groups, and vendors are also likely to play a role in the development, implementation, and maintenance of new web products such as personalization features. The decision to engage third parties makes sense in situations where additional manpower is required for a temporary period and/or when expertise is needed that goes beyond an airline's core competency. Typical examples of the latter deal with topics like web product development and change management.

### 7.10.2 The people factor and change management

Strategy implementation involves changes of processes and behaviors. This brings us to an important aspect in strategy implementation. Human beings are creatures of habit and change is not necessarily welcome by everybody. The standard "one-third" rule says that one-third of employees readily embrace, another one-third are hesitant first but come around, while the remaining one-third will never change.

Figure 7.10 shows a common transition curve with the reaction by staff from the time when change is first proposed.

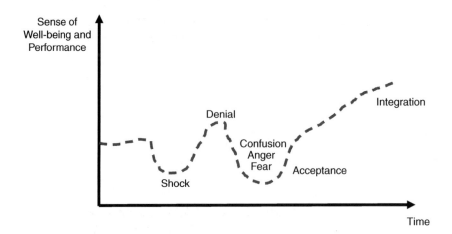

**Figure 7.10** *Transition curve*

*Source:* Bocij et al. (2003)[15]

It is essential that senior managers continuously engage with all employees throughout the entire strategy implementation process from beginning to end—and beyond—in order to win their commitment. In this regard, an airline's senior management needs to pay attention to the following topics:

■ *Preparation.* Senior leaders express their willingness to transform. This must be demonstrated by providing additional resources and redefining existing resources, by forming a new strategy, and by establishing new processes and values. At the same time, communication with key stakeholders should be pro-active, consistent, and constant. Common venues for communication include regular staff meetings, special meetings, workshops, and presentations. They are used to explain the necessary changes and share information on how to deal with them. Some airlines even conduct off-site e-commerce workshops (sometimes also referred to as "e-boot camps"). These are typically one to two days long and involve employees from a wide cross-section of the company. It is not unusual for senior management including the CEO or president to attend this type of meeting as well and to spell out their e-commerce vision.

■ *Leadership.* Senior managers outline the vision on the changes and what the consequences are for employees, customers, and business partners. It is key to be open to people's concern as to how the change could impact them. This is part of a collaborative and consultative approach to leadership. By addressing these concerns, senior leaders should be able to alleviate possible resistance to the proposed change. Realistically, however, there will always a group that is looking for more persuasion or continues living in denial. This should be respected provided that this group's view does not become obstructive in pursuing the airline's new business interest.

■ *Change.* Continued communication during the change period is crucial to win people over and gain support. Rallying and unifying is not an easy task considering the many organizational and technological silos that exist at most airlines. Nevertheless, it needs to be done and done frequently. Many airlines suffer from a "launch and leave syndrome" where senior management disappears after a successful product launch. This is detrimental and undermines the credibility of the strategic initiative. Communication and involvement by senior management needs to continue beyond the implementation phase.

## 7.11 ADVANCING AIRLINE E-COMMERCE AND CREATING A COMPETITIVE PRESENCE IN CYBERSPACE

Our discussion in previous chapters has shown that today's marketplace for airlines has been transformed forever by e-commerce. From the first few airline tickets sold in December 1995 by Alaska Airlines and the former British Midland via their newly launched websites, global online travel has grown to generate half a trillion dollars in annual revenue. More and more travelers use internet-based products and services to manage various aspects of their travel life cycle.

At a growing number of carriers, leaders are taking decisions through e-commerce strategies on how to promote and structure their presence in cyberspace. These decisions have significant impacts. Airlines that have achieved an advanced e-commerce stage, defined as the widespread adoption and competitive use of the internet and digital applications to market and sell products, deliver customer service, and share/exchange information, realize important benefits. These include improved economic performance and stronger brand attraction. This is the result of two aspects:

- The focus on a "direct-to-consumer" approach. It offers the best value only directly, it drives loyalty and it supports new pricing and revenue models. It also means that the consumer comes to the airline first.
- The taking of control of their destiny by re-engineering business processes related to sales, marketing, and customer service and by having transactions done cost efficiently, electronically, and simply.

Airlines in an advanced e-commerce stage are best suited to manage the next frontiers in cyberspace. One of these frontiers is the personalization of online offerings to individual travelers. Airlines in less developed e-commerce stages are going to fall proportionally behind their leading rivals.

An airline's level of development in e-commerce is often associated with how much revenue it generates online. The higher a carrier's online revenue as a share of total revenue, the arguably more advanced the company is in its e-commerce capabilities. However, this outcome-based focus is quantity driven and says very little about the quality that a carrier applies to e-commerce.

A case in point is LCC Ryanair. The airline produces somewhere between 95% and 98% of its annual revenue via ryanair.com, one of the highest online revenue shares of any carrier in the world. Does this make Ryanair the most advanced airline in cyberspace? When taking into account, for example, that prior to the airline's website redesign in 2013, it took an online booker on average 17 mouse clicks to purchase a ticket on the carrier's website (the standard for efficient website navigation is about five clicks), the answer has to be no. Similarly, until summer 2015, Ryanair did not have a presence on Facebook or feature a mobile website.

The carrier undoubtedly has a justification for this late-mover approach; after all, it is among the most profitable airlines in the world. However, it can be argued that other airlines—take 95-year-old KLM as an example—offering a wide range of these types of web products for several years now and providing better online experiences to travelers are actually more advanced in cyberspace even though they produce less revenue online.

Travelers today look much beyond the basic task of being able to buy a ticket online and getting low prices. They seek out those airline digital brands that offer superior quality, trust, service, and innovation. An airline's performance in these areas largely determines its digital competitiveness and ultimately its success in the online marketplace.

Two key factors determine how advanced an airline is in cyberspace: Adoption and use of e-commerce. Examples of these factors include user-friendly digital properties—websites that are fast, intuitive, and click-efficient in site navigation, rich in features, and also optimized for mobile commerce. Other examples include superior digital data privacy practices, a wide range of digital media use for online advertising and promotion, competitive e-sales and distribution policies, and top-quality web customer service via superior self-/assisted service tools and quick responsiveness to customer queries. A carrier aiming at success in cyberspace needs to manage these multiple factors—not only well, but also concurrently.

Moving to an advanced e-commerce stage does not happen by accident. Senior airline managers have a crucial stake in this process. In their approach, they need to shift their attention to airline e-commerce adoption and use. Specifically, this means de-emphasising single popular metrics such as an airline's online revenue share. Instead, they should focus on capturing and systematically tracking the company's e-commerce activities in a wide range of areas. This approach implies that e-commerce is a prioritized topic on an airline's corporate strategy agenda and that it is recognized as a key driver in the company's future.

## 7.12 MEASURING THE STATE OF AIRLINE E-COMMERCE: THE DIGITAL AIRLINE SCORE (DAS)

An airline's adoption and use of e-commerce can be measured across seven attributes. Four of these attributes are fundamental, or the essential minimum, for operating an airline digital brand. They include digital performance, digital presence, digital brand appearance and protection, and digital data privacy. Furthermore, three attributes are differentiators that airlines usually apply in their e-commerce value chain to distinguish themselves from competitors. These attributes are online advertising and promotion, e-sales and distribution, and web customer service (Figure 7.11).

The impact of these attributes can be measured through proxy indicators (Table 7.6) that apply a rating scale. For each proxy indicator of the four fundamental

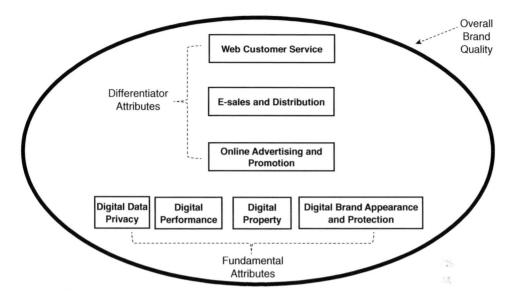

**Figure 7.11** *Attributes to determine the adoption and use of airline e-commerce*

attributes, the scale ranges from 1 (Poor) and 2 (Fair) to 3 (Good), and 4 (Excellent). For each proxy indicator of the three differentiator attributes, the scale is doubled (2 = Poor, 4 = Fair, 6 = Good, 8 = Excellent) in recognition of their relatively higher importance.

The proxy indicators and the rating scale allow for determining a score called digital airline score (DAS). The total maximum score a carrier could earn is a DAS of 160 (64 for the fundamental attributes + 96 for the differentiator attributes) while the total minimum is a DAS of 40 (16 for the fundamental attributes + 24 for the differentiator attributes).

The DAS is a useful tool for several reasons:

■ It allows a better understanding of an airline's level of e-commerce adoption and use relative to rivals.
■ It provides for enhanced insight into the extent of improvement required by an airline to move to an advanced e-commerce stage.
■ It can be used for a change readiness assessment that evaluates a carrier's ability to adopt and implement an e-commerce breakout strategy.

One important aspect needs to be highlighted. A carrier's "digitalness" does not exist in a vacuum and is not the only aspect that drives a traveller to engage online with an airline. A traveller's brand affinity to a carrier is also key because of the company's reputation. This recognizes the fact that an individual's overall impression of and experience with an airline exerts some influence. If, for instance, an airline is held in low esteem by a customer because of past poor service or because of the company's poor reputation in the marketplace, it might not matter if an airline

**Table 7.6a** *Components of the Digital Airline Score (DAS): Fundamental E-commerce Attributes*

| Attribute | Proxy Indicator | Rating Scale: 1- Poor | 2-Fair | 3-Good | 4-Excellent |
|---|---|---|---|---|---|
| **Digital Data Privacy** | Timeliness | No time stamp, broken links, outdated privacy contact information | → | | Time stamp of recent updates, current with latest country specific privacy laws, industry regulation, best practices, current contact information |
| | Transparency | No link posting to privacy section, limited if any information of airline's data privacy practices | → | | Disclosure and clear language on data practices including data collection sources and purpose, data retention periods, third party sharing and protection standards |
| | Customer Control | No customer control over personal data collected by airline | → | | Customer has a say in data sharing/selling by airline, has access to their data profile to view/change, opt-in option if in agreement to be tracked |
| | Query Responsiveness | No reply to email customer query on data privacy matters | → | | Email response by designated privacy contact with clear information relevant to the initial query |
| **Digital Performance** | Desktop Site Download Speed | > 10 sec | → | | < 4 sec |
| | Mobile Site Download Speed | > 6 sec | → | | < 2 sec |
| | Desktop Site Uptime | < 98% | → | | 100% |
| | Mobile Site Uptime | < 98% | → | | 100% |
| **Digital Properties and Features** | Platform Range | Desktop only | → | | Multiple platforms incl. desktop, mobile, inflight airport kiosk, wearable, virtual |
| | Website Types | Retail site only | → | | Site family incl. blog, all major social sites, subsidiary sites, other special target group sites |
| | Website Features | Industry standard offerings for content, booking, and service. | → | | Cutting edge features, early adopter |
| | Globalization | One site fits all markets | → | | Localized web presence for content, booking, service and site design |
| **Digital Brand Appearance and Protection** | Website Content Quality | Stale content and poor editing | → | | Updated multiple times per week, professionally web edited, correct language translations |
| | Website Design Quality | Dated digital look and feel factors, non-responsive to different digital platforms, poor click efficiency, not accessible for disabled users | → | | Modern, superior look and feel, platform responsive, all major tasks can be accomplished within 5 clicks, site accessibility for disabled under WCAG, AA |
| | Domain Name Portfolio | No usage of .com for airline brand, no country specific domains, no brand protection via other domains (cc domains, misspellings, etc) | → | | Site uses .com, domains for major sub-brands (FFP, cargo, etc), internationalized/local domains and domains protecting against brand infringement |
| | Legal Notice/Terms of Use | No disclaimer to serve as liability limitation and no protection of airline intellectual property (IP) | → | | Separate site section with specific information on liability limitation and IP protection |

**Table 7.6b** *Components of the Digital Airline Score (DAS): Differentiator E-commerce Attributes*

| Attribute | Proxy Indicator | Rating Scale: 1- Poor | 2-Fair 3-Good | 4-Excellent |
|---|---|---|---|---|
| **Web Customer Service** | Service Options | Standard assisted-customer service including phone and email only | → | Mix of assisted customer service including advanced options (social care, avatars) and range of self-service (FAQ, search, site map, product demos, intelligent personal assistants) |
| | Service Efficiency | Indiscriminate offering of high and low cost service options | → | Presentation/priority of low-cost self service options over high-cost assisted service options |
| | Service Channel Integration | Different service options are disconnected and provide for fragmented customer experience | → | Different service options are integrated with each other and offer seamless transition among them |
| | Service Responsiveness | Below-the-average turn around time in responding to customer queries | → | Above the average response time (email: 2-4 days, chat 1-2 mins, social care within 1 hour) |
| **E-sales and Distribution** | Channel Pricing | No differentiation between offline and online channels for pricing | → | Lowest fares on airline web site only |
| | Ancillaries | No offering of ancillaries | → | Full spectrum of up-/cross sell products including bundled and à la carte options |
| | Range of E-sales and Distribution | Focus on direct online sales channels and leisure/VFR segments only | → | Direct sales online channels + cooperation with multiple third parties including OTA, metasearch, corporate segments |
| | Direct Connect | No direct connect relationship with travel agency/corporate client | → | Multiple direct connect partners in the travel agency and corporate sector |
| **Online Advertising and Promotion** | Range of Digital Media Formats | Promotional display ads on own web site and email newsletter | → | Comprehensive media mix with email, display, search (SEM, SEO), augmented reality, advertaming, various social including use of social media influencers |
| | Communications Frequency | Sporadic communication across digital formats | → | Media calendar drives regular communication for key formats (search: all year, email :3-4 x//month, social 5-10 posts/week), programmatic banner advertising |
| | Optimization for Digital Platform | Communication configured for desktop platform only | → | Optimization of all communication for desktop + mobile platforms |
| | Communication Message | Focus on broad push-sales promotions only | → | Mix of sales and brand messages, broad and individualized communication, interactive communication inviting customer to participate |

otherwise excels in e-commerce. The reverse can apply; because of an airline's over-all high-brand quality, a traveller might overlook some weaknesses in the carrier's cyberspace presence and still engage online with the company's digital properties.

### 7.12.1 The level of airline e-commerce advancement: An initial assessment, applying DAS

During spring 2015, a sample of 35 carriers from varying geographies and market positions was used for their DAS. In assessing the level of e-commerce advancement for these carriers, four distinct groups emerged (Figure 7.12).

*The constrained e-commerce carrier (DAS: 40–79)*

Airlines in this category have not begun to engage with e-commerce on a larger scale. Adoption and use are limited and below par. Lack of customer readiness may be one of the external reasons, although several internal aspects including lack of overall corporate vision for e-commerce, small talent base, and insufficient resources often play a role as well. Carriers included in this group are TAME of Ecuador, TAAG Angola, Air Greenland, and Philippine Airlines (PAL). Except for their digital performance in terms of website speed and website up-time availability, these four airlines otherwise only earned low scores for both the fundamental and the differen-tiator e-commerce attributes. TAME achieved the lowest score with a DAS of 66 while PAL finishes toward the higher end with a DAS of 73.

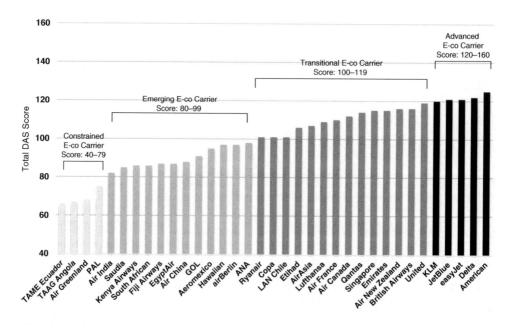

**Figure 7.12** *The level of airline e-commerce advancement (spring 2015)*

*The emerging e-commerce carrier (DAS: 80–99)*

These airlines have made significant progress in adopting e-commerce. However, its adoption and use are still sub-optimal due to number of internal factors. They may include insufficient resources, limited senior management support, and weak governance/organizational structures. Air India is at the low end of this range with a DAS of 82 while All Nippon Airways (ANA) is the highest performer in this group with a score of 99.

*The transitional e-commerce carrier (DAS: 100–119)*

Transitional e-commerce carriers have a solid and experienced handle on e-commerce. Its adoption and use are above average competitively and constantly expanding. E-Commerce plays a significant role in all aspects of these airlines' business. A crossover to an advanced level in the near future is likely for the top performers including United Airlines, British Airways, Air New Zealand, Emirates, Singapore Airlines, and Qantas.

*The advanced e-commerce carrier (DAS: 120–160)*

Airlines in this group are most mature in their digitalness. They are in the forefront of deploying new digital applications and related managerial practices. They are also highly sophisticated in the use of e-commerce. Their talent base is strong and e-commerce is a key priority for corporate strategy. Advanced e-commerce carriers are most prepared to embark on a breakout strategy. For example, the implementation of personalization is a next logical step in these carriers' e-commerce activities.

A total of five airlines in the sample are in an advanced stage of e-commerce. Contrary to popular perception that e-commerce is mostly a domain of LCCs, this group includes several legacy airlines. American Airlines actually achieved the highest score with 125 followed by Delta Airlines with 122. Next easyJet and JetBlue are in a tie with 121 while KLM earned a score of 120. The score range among these carriers is narrow and each of them could own the top spot depending on what they do next.

### 7.12.2 Improving the level of e-commerce use and adoption

Airlines seeking to advance their e-commerce adoption and use need to have a good understanding of where their digital strengths and weaknesses are. In terms of DAS, this means taking a closer look at the company's performance in the fundamental and differentiator areas of e-commerce.

Figure 7.13 provides insight into how the sampled carriers scored in this regard. It is evident that there is room for improvement for all carriers. The question is what needs to be done and how it should be done. Depending on how advanced a carrier is in e-commerce, decision makers at airlines should focus on a few key imperatives.

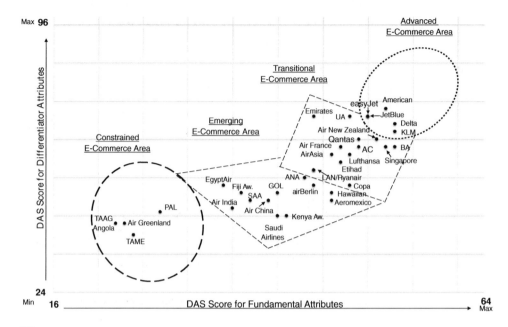

**Figure 7.13** *A closer look at DAS: Fundamental versus differentiator factors*

*Elevation of e-commerce on the corporate agenda*

This is first and foremost an action item for carriers that are e-commerce constrained. They have significant deficiencies across all relevant areas and the development of an overall framework for e-commerce is essential. In our sample, affected carriers include TAME of Ecuador, TAAG Angola, Air Greenland, and PAL. For the fundamental e-commerce factors, they scored a low DAS between 23 and 28 (the maximum is 64). In terms of differentiator factors, they ranged between 39 and 45 (the maximum is 96).

In order to become more effective e-commerce players, each of them has to elevate e-commerce on the corporate agenda. Importantly, both the involvement and the oversight of the senior management are critical. If leaders at these airlines do not take ownership of e-commerce, it will continue being managed as a by-product with non-aligned stakeholders who pursue their own e-commerce agenda for the company. Leaders at these airlines have to view e-commerce as an opportunity that creates benefits for both company and customers alike.

There are several immediate action items that constrained e-commerce carriers must tackle. Besides providing additional funds and recruiting e-commerce know-how, an improvement of the current web presence is important. This specifically means overhauling the current website design, repurposing existing website content, and introducing industry standard website features. Furthermore, a mobile platform is a "must-have" in today's marketplace but is typically either missing or sub-standard with carriers in this category.

Launching/upgrading this area would be desirable as soon as possible. Changes like these are instantly visible to customers, who will have a better online experience when using the carrier's digital properties. Only when a carrier has successfully addressed these fundamental issues should an orientation toward the differentiator factors in sales, marketing, and customer service be considered.

*Introducing better governance and organizational structures*

A sub-optimal e-commerce performance is often a reflection of poor organizational processes and structures. This is particularly an issue at emerging e-commerce carriers. As a result, a number of crucial e-commerce factors that should receive utmost attention are improperly managed, possibly neglected, or do not even register on the corporate e-commerce agenda. For example, carriers that have progressed in e-commerce but otherwise do not regularly monitor their website speed or account for the internet access device type online bookers use, do not handle the basics of today's e-commerce requirement effectively. The same can be said for an airline that does not offer a localized website presence in different markets or up-to-date booking engine features.

In the fundamental e-commerce category, Air India earned one of the lowest scores with a DAS of 36. One of the reasons is its slow website. Based on different tests conducted, it took almost 12 seconds to complete page loading, although EgyptAir with 16 seconds and Fiji Airways with 18 seconds were the poorest performers in the entire sample. The benchmark for superior performance is less than four seconds for desktops and less than two seconds for mobiles.

Other reasons include a non–optimized website design for smart phones and tablets and the carrier's highly fragmented e-commerce presence in markets outside India. For example, on airindia.com, a link to only two websites outside India is featured (United States and UK) although the carrier operates flights to many countries. At the same time, Air India managers in some countries such as Germany and Italy have launched local website versions that are differently branded and apparently have no connection to the airline's official website.

In the differentiator e-commerce category, Saudi Airlines achieved one of the lowest scores with a DAS of 44, due to its weak performance in online promotion and advertising, e-sales and distribution, and web customer service. Among the specific reasons leading to the carrier's low score are:

- Except for the company's website in Saudi Arabia, all other 21 country websites do not promote a single fare special. A dedicated fare special page shown on each website is either blank or not accessible.
- The carrier on average does only two posts per week on Facebook (the ideal range is 5–10, JetBlue manages 14 as the leader).
- There appears to be only limited, if any, sponsored search engine marketing for key search terms. For example, generic searches including "Flight to Jeddah" and "Fares to Riyadh" return Emirates, Etihad, and Lufthansa on Google's first result page (over 90% of Google search traffic comes from page one—if a brand is not visible there, it does not exist for a web user).

Furthermore, other key reasons why Saudia and carriers including Aeromexico, EgyptAir, and Kenya Airways earned low scores in online promotion and advertising, e-sales and distribution, and web customer service are:

- The airlines do not apply programmatic display advertising. This form of advertising is more efficient than traditional online advertising because it is less expensive and more targeted to an individual user. Advanced e-commerce carriers apply it on a larger scale.
- There is no direct participation with major meta-search engines such as Kayak.
- The carriers' digital brands are poorly protected due to a lack of relevant domain name registrations—for example, country specific domains, internationalized domains where the airline brand is featured in language-specific script such as Chinese, and corporate hate domains (usually operated by a consumer with a complaint or a disgruntled ex-employee). Furthermore, the websites' legal notice/terms of use sections are often inadequate in terms of spelling out intellectual property rights and protecting the airline brand against digital content inaccuracies.
- There are no or only very limited online cross-sell/up-sell ancillary products offered.
- Twitter and email queries are not returned at all or with severe delays by the carriers' customer relations/customer service department.

Carriers from the emerging e-commerce group to close the gap on these essential weaknesses will need to organize e-commerce better. The assessment and implementation involved in this process takes time (6–12 months). Effective collaboration among stakeholders at the airline and outside companies and efficient decision-making processes are examples of what needs to be achieved. Furthermore, recruitment of e-commerce talent, clear organizational roles and responsibilities (no mismatch between authority and responsibilities), and senior level leadership are also important. Advanced e-commerce airlines such as KLM and JetBlue and the top performers in transitional e-commerce including Air New Zealand have all of this in place, otherwise their ability to deliver quality offerings in cyberspace would not be as high as it currently is.

*Adopting an ecosystem perspective on e-commerce is vital to success in cyberspace*

This requires an airline to engage in multiple e-commerce areas at the same time—only feasible if a carrier acknowledges the convergence among and between fundamental and differentiator e-commerce factors.

For example, advanced e-commerce airlines do not view mobile platforms in isolation from desktops or wearables. There is no discernible disconnect between the "e" and "commerce." IT, e-marketing, e-sales and distribution, and web customer service are viewed as part of the same equation. Advanced e-commerce carriers manage the different "e" and "commerce" components so that they compliment and reinforce in each other. They also ask "How can we do this online?" and "What is the impact on other components and stakeholders?" Travelers benefit from this holistic approach in the form of better e-commerce products and a more integrated and consistent online experience.

Less advanced e-commerce carriers often struggle with transcending siloes and approaching e-commerce as a coherent ecosystem. This is particularly the case when dealing with the differentiator factors applicable to e-sales and distribution, online advertising and promotion, and web customer service. They are arguably more challenging to manage than fundamental e-commerce aspects such as a website's speed and uptime reliability.

Copa Airlines, Aeromexico, and Hawaiian are examples of this situation and to a lesser extent also airBerlin and Kenya Airways. These carriers perform relatively well in the fundamental e-commerce category. However, their performance in the differentiator category could improve. Here, the airlines' scores are comparatively lower, which indicates performance gaps especially in the online advertising and promotion as well as the e-sales and advertising areas.

Common issues are:

- *Lack of optimization in marketing communication for mobile devices.* For instance, when using a smart phone, links from the airlines' sponsored search engine keywords, email newsletters, and Facebook postings generally direct a website user to the airline's desktop site as opposed to a mobile site. In today's e-commerce environment where mobiles are so widespread, a mobile user should be presented with a correspondingly optimized page. Leading e-commerce carriers recognize this issue and configure all their marketing communication with travelers accordingly.
- *Limited ancillary activities.* Advanced companies offer ancillaries and produce substantial incremental revenue streams from them. Examples for 2014 are easyJet with 19%, JetBlue (12%), American (8%), Delta (7%), and KLM (6%). In comparison, Copa and Aeromexico generated an estimated 3% while airBerlin and Kenya Airways produced 0.7% and 0%, respectively. Managing ancillaries is not an easy task. It requires a higher level of e-commerce know-how and a coordination of stakeholders from multiple departments and outside third parties.
- *Some inconsistency in online pricing.* The good news is that all airlines in the sample appeared to recognize their websites' lower cost of sale in comparison with that of their call centers. Accordingly, fares offered on the carriers' websites are consistently lower and offline bookers are subject to a surcharge. This policy certainly helps increase the "stickiness" of airline websites and migrate bookers from an airline's offline channels.

The situation is different for some airlines when it comes to fare products distributed via online travel agencies (OTAs). Here, the lowest fares were available on OTA websites like Expedia. The difference to a carrier's website fare ranged from small to, sometimes, large. OTAs are valuable to airlines not only because of their role as online sales partners with a large market presence but also because they drive significant traffic to airline websites (the quasi-search engine functions of OTAs).

However, even though there can be strategic reasons for doing so, an airline needs to exercise care in offering consistently lower fares via third party channels as this undermines efforts to capture more customers (and their data) directly.

### Stimulating e-commerce demand

Web users can be encouraged to do more business online provided airlines manage their e-commerce adoption and use it well. Airlines doing so are more likely to attract web users and generate demand for their online offerings. The top performers with American, Delta, easyJet, JetBlue, and KLM have learned to raise online demand and do an exceptional job in this area. However, despite their superior performance, there are some areas where even these carriers were sub-optimal. These areas include digital data privacy, web customer service, and website accessibility. Across all airlines of the sample, these are the categories with the lowest scores.

## DIGITAL DATA PRIVACY

All carriers' website privacy policies were thoroughly examined against the so-called FIPs (Fair Information Practices). These are internationally recognized practices that address the privacy of information about individuals. Within the context of FIPs, airlines' data privacy practices were assessed based on the privacy policies posted on their websites. In addition, the responsiveness of airlines to a data privacy query sent via email was also captured. The maximum score for this fundamental e-commerce category is a DAS of 16.

One aspect of the FIPs deals with the timeliness of privacy policies. Considering the numerous changes occurring in the data privacy field, it is of some concern that the majority of carriers do not display a timestamp when their website privacy policies were drawn up or last amended. The perception a data–privacy–minded traveler may have from this lack of information is that the airline is not necessarily on top of this subject—or worse—that it might change its privacy policy at any time without notification. Air New Zealand is pro-active in this area and a good example that could be followed by more carriers. The airline not only has a privacy policy section titled "Changes to This Privacy Policy" but also clearly states that it would specify the dates of any updates.

As far as the FIP area of data management transparency is concerned, no airline in the sample performed well. The language used in the website privacy policies is often convoluted, if not too legalese, and difficult to understand for an average reader. Furthermore, while information on data collection sources and purposes are relatively clear with many airlines (American Airlines is good example), meaningful insight into data storage locations is very limited. Most carriers share no information at all or vaguely refer to "other countries." JetBlue was the only carrier explicitly stating that any data collected would be processed and stored in the United States. The picture is similar for information on data retention periods. Where an airline even mentioned this issue, it often stated that data would be kept "as long as necessary."

The other area of FIPs examined for all carriers dealt with traveler control of their data. On a positive note, most carriers grant access to the data they hold so that travelers could review and/or correct them. The few exceptions to this policy included EgyptAir, Fiji Airways, Saudi Airlines, and South African. Noteworthy is that some airlines actually levy a fee for this service. LCCs like Ryanair can be "excused" for this in light of their business model to monetize services offered. However, it was some surprise to see that other airlines like Emirates and Etihad were among them. If there was a choice between no access and access for a fee, certainly the latter is preferable. Nevertheless, a fee-based approach suggests an anti-consumer policy in terms of data privacy management.

Data sharing by airlines with third parties is a common practice. It is generally done for the fulfillment of online commercial services and for law enforcement/national security reasons. However, travelers often have only little if any idea who these third parties are. Both easyJet and JetBlue are exceptions in sharing a concrete list; most carriers simply refer to "external service providers" and "legal authorities." This is not necessarily an approach for building trust with online users.

Airlines allow travelers to indicate if they consent to receiving marketing, sales, and flight operational information either from the airline itself or from its partners. This is an important piece of protection and control over the travelers' data. Many carriers in the sample appear to pursue an opt-out policy whereby travelers receive communication by default. This translates to a lower degree of protection for travelers but still furnishes them with some control. In this instance, travelers have to be pro-active in notifying the carrier to indicate that they do not want to receive certain types of communication. Opt-in/Opt-out selections are also relevant for travelers in the context of website tracking technologies, particularly cookie applications that are used by airlines. Most airlines apply these and in all instances, the default setting is for "opt-in." This means that a traveler is assumed to agree to being tracked. If a web user prefers not being tracked, it is generally not easy to opt out. Many airlines share no information at all on how to do this while some provide for links to generic third party sites like allaboutcookies.org. Only a small number of airlines including American, Aeromexico, and easyJet feature specific opt-out choices.

The final area assessed for digital data privacy dealt with the responsiveness of carriers to privacy policy queries. With a few exceptions, the responsiveness of airlines to privacy policy queries was poor. In three cases (Air India, Air China, Egyptair), the email sent to their dedicated privacy contact bounced due to broken links. Ryanair sends customers on a perpetual cycle as their auto-reply directs customers back to the original contact form where the same query has to be filled out again.

A total of eight airlines did not respond at all and this group includes high-profile names such as Air Canada, American, JetBlue, and Saudi Airlines. Others responded with an auto-reply stating that it would take them a few days to return an answer—in Fiji Airways' case, this period would be 21 days—a lifetime in cyberspace while Air France said that their reply would be delayed due to a strike. This is still preferable to what All Nippon Airways does: They request data queries to be sent via traditional mail to their office in Japan—where a customer service fee is payable.

Those who did respond often provided generic information as opposed to answering the specific privacy questions asked. Referring to the airline's privacy policy is a common tactic. In Delta's case, it took two follow-up emails to finally obtain a more concrete reply; easyJet performed relatively well—following up on their initial auto-reply within seven days, they provided detailed information; GOL replied within two days and answered the questions raised.

In summary, for airlines' performance in the area of data privacy, British Airways was the best performer with a DAS of 12, followed by American and Singapore Airlines with 11 each. Air New Zealand, Delta, JetBlue, easyJet, and United each scored 10. All remaining carriers scored below 10. In essence, this is an indication that data privacy practices and related customer service support for customer queries leave much room for improvement in terms of their data management from a web user perspective.

In practice and over and above any legal duties, these issues may seem small; but they do hint at professionalism and a level of sincerity in terms of taking e-commerce seriously.

## WEB CUSTOMER SERVICE

After digital privacy, web customer service is the second weakest area for all carriers in the sample. The analysis has revealed significant gaps in carriers' capabilities. In essence, this shows what is already a known fact for airlines in the offline world: The delivery of good customer service is not easy but those that excel at it truly differentiate themselves from rivals.

Out of the total possible score of 32 for web customer service, the highest score earned by any carrier was a DAS of 22 by British Airways. Next were Lufthansa and easyJet that scored 20 each. Every other carrier otherwise achieved a score somewhere between 8, the lowest possible score—all four constrained e-commerce carriers fall into this—and 18.

The large majority of airlines offer a less than sufficient range of online service options. Particularly, self-service tools such as FAQ, site search, and edgy options such as virtual assistants were often missing. Interestingly, even when self-service tools are available, most carriers do not appear to take advantage of their relatively lower costs (self-service costs $0.10 or less per customer contact while phone support ranges between $6 and $12). This often shows itself on websites where both self-service and assisted service options are somewhat randomly presented.

Advanced e-commerce carriers, however, offer a wide range of different service options. They do this because they know that travelers often bounce back and forth between numerous channels in order to resolve their issue. Also, they know that customers from different age groups have different preferences when it comes to certain service options. Offering a wide range thus allows an airline to fulfill the needs of a larger audience.

At the same time, e-commerce savvy airlines are also cost conscious when it comes to web customer service. They prioritize low-cost self-service options over higher, customer-assisted, service cost options. For example, instead of featuring a toll-free phone number on the homepage, these carriers encourage web travelers to use self-service options first before escalating to email, chat, or phone. This approach is supported by clever web design and "penalties" in the form of surcharges that are occasionally levied on travelers if they engage a customer service representative.

Another aspect looked for in scoring web customer service was the degree of integration among the different service options. Customers dislike nothing more than disconnected service channels that not only make the transition between them a challenge but also require them to share their service issue multiple times over. For instance, by the time a web traveler contacts an airline via phone, the customer service representative very likely has no idea that the traveler might have already tried to self-help on the carrier's website or received assistance via social media from other customers. Making transitions among different service channels more seamless and carrying over content from one service channel to another provide an improved customer experience and makes better use of corporate resources. With the exception of British Airways, no airline in the sample performed well.

A lack of responsiveness to customer service queries contributed to low ratings in this category. For instance, the quality of social customer care varied significantly. A total of eight carriers did not reply at all (e.g. Aeromexico, Air Asia, Fiji Airways, and Singapore Airlines). Some airlines took hours (Air China with 14 hours) while others came back in less than 10 minutes (e.g. JetBlue, KLM, and Lufthansa) to reply to a Twitter question.

In the area of email communication, the performance was poor for most airlines. For example, JetBlue and KLM did not reply while easyJet responded within seven days. Lack of communication and lack of consistency in communication across different service channels within a single carrier appears to be a big issue.

## WEBSITE ACCESSIBILITY

Website accessibility for the disabled is becoming a legal necessity as well as a valued customer service. As we have stated before in Chapter 3, together with their families, approximately 2 billion people are directly affected by disability, representing almost a third of the world's population. This issue is expected to become even more prominent with ageing societies in key travel markets.

Several airlines have made some modifications to their websites in this regard (Air India, ANA, British Airways, Delta Airlines, easyJet, and Qantas). However, none of the 35 carriers' websites in the sample is fully accessible for users with disabilities according to the Worldwide Web Consortium (W3C) and its web content accessibility guidelines (WCAG)/level AA. Any airline websites (at least those of carriers serving the United States) that were not upgraded to this standard with effect from December 2015 are in violation of the US DOT regulations mandating compliance. The consequences may include financial penalties, temporary website shutdowns, and negative PR.

In summary, if the issues described in these three areas are not addressed and managed more effectively in the near future, they may depress potential online demand by travellers. They certainly present an opportunity for an airline to stand out from others if they perform well.

## 7.13 IN CONCLUSION: THERE IS PLENTY OF ROOM FOR IMPROVEMENT IN AN UNDERPERFORMING FIELD

The art and science of airline e-commerce is steadily evolving. There are, as always, some standouts at each end of the spectrum and all can learn from their peers.

Yet there is no one way to success in this area, just as there are many different goals that airlines establish (or not) to achieve what they wish to achieve through the e-commerce medium. But it is evident that most carriers are still not well positioned to compete effectively in cyberspace, nor to reap the rewards available.

Although judgments on airline effectiveness must necessarily be subjective, a tool such as DAS allows an insight into the gaps in an airline's adoption and use of e-commerce. The statistics and thoughts shared in our discussion may serve as a wake-up call.

Companies that fall into the constrained or emerging categories are well advised at least to initiate an analysis of their situation, to look at market best practice, and to determine what is going on and what needs to be done. This is the underpinning for a sound strategy for airline e-commerce.

Even where airlines have scored well with DAS and are categorized as advanced or about to be advanced and are doing a lot of things better than the rest, the question is for how long. There can be no room for complacency in this fast-moving territory. Today's empowered consumers are frequently much more proficient—and demanding—in cyberspace than airlines. It is vital for airlines to adopt a mentality that recognizes the opportunities—and potential threats—in dealing with consumers in cyberspace. The best e-commerce airline practitioners will always be in catch-up mode as the periods of relative market stability shrink constantly. Thus a true break-out strategy, for example via personalization, may always remain elusive for even the best of airlines.

Nevertheless, the key is to be best prepared for the transitions ahead. Improving its digitalness is a corporate imperative for any airline, while regularly conducting internal audits to assess its core competencies in the area.

A DAS-based approach should be conducted at least once a year along the lines set out in the above discussion and offer one way to evaluate an airline's position and those of its competitors. As necessary, strategic directions for e-commerce can then be constantly adjusted. No one will "get it right," but an important start is at least to recognize fully the importance of this activity and to put in place the necessary structures to apply best practice—and even eventually to create it. With this approach, an airline is best positioned to move from a current status quo to a possible breakout area ahead of competitors.

---

## NOTES

1 Goodman, R. and Lawless, M. (1994) *Technology and Strategy: Conceptual Models and Diagnostics*, Oxford: Oxford University Press.

2 Hofrichter, D. *Strategies to Survive the Invasion of E-people*, Handbook of Business Strategy, pp. 41–46.

3 Hambrick, D. and Frederikson, J. (2001) "Are you sure you have a strategy?" http://turbo.kean. edu/~jmcgill/havestrategy.pdf (accessed April 7, 2015).

4 BCG (2006) "Understanding the demand for air travel: How to compete more effectively," www. bcg.com/documents/file14820.pdf (accessed April 7, 2015).

5 InternetWorldStats.com (2014) "Internet usage statistics: The internet big picture," www. internetworldstats.com/stats.htm (accessed April 7, 2015).

6 Mintzberg, H. (1989) *Mintzberg on Management*, New York: Free Press.

7 Lundgren, K. (2014) "Ryanair considering acquisitions in technology and retail," http://skift. com/2014/09/16/ryanair-considering-acquisitions-in-technology-and-retail/ (accessed April 7, 2015).

8 SITA (2014) "2014 SITA Airline IT Trends Survey."

9 Hambrick and Frederikson, "Are you sure you have a strategy?"

10 Clay, K. (2014) "American airlines and wearable world complete first ever in-flight wearable technology hackathon," http://wearableworldnews.com/2014/07/14/american-airlines-wearable-world-hackathon-avegant-nod-pebble/ (accessed April 7, 2015).

11 The Economist (2013) "Why good strategies fail: Lessons for the C-suite," www.pmi.org/~/media/PDF/Publications/WhyGoodStrategiesFail_Report_EIU_PMI.ashx (accessed April 7, 2015).

12 Ibid.

13 SITA (2014) "2014 SITA Airline IT Trends."

14 Krigsman, M. (2014) "IT spend is growing, but CIOs 'just don't get it'," www.zdnet.com/article/it-spend-is-growing-but-cios-just-dont-get-it/ (accessed April 7, 2015).

15 Bocij, P., Greasley, A., and Hickie, S. (2003) *Business Information Systems: Technology, Development and Management*, 2nd ed., Harlow, UK: Financial Times Prentice Hall.

# Index

Locators in *italics* refer to figures and illustrations and those in **bold** to tables, numbers are filed as spelled out.